INTERNATIONAL RELATIONS AND THE ARCTIC

International Relations and the Arctic

Understanding Policy and Governance

EDITED BY

Robert W. Murray and Anita Dey Nuttall

CAMBRIA
PRESS

Amherst, New York

Copyright 2014 Cambria Press

Requests for permission should be directed to:
permissions@cambriapress.com, or mailed to:
Cambria Press
University Corporate Centre, 100 Corporate Parkway, Suite 128
Amherst, New York 14226, U.S.A.

Library of Congress Cataloging-in-Publication Data

International relations and the Arctic : understanding policy and
governance / edited by Robert W. Murray & Anita Dey Nuttall.

pages cm
Includes bibliographical references and index.

ISBN 978-1-60497-876-6 (alk. paper)

1. Geopolitics--Arctic regions. 2. Political geography--Arctic regions. 3.
Arctic regions--Foreign relations. 4. Arctic regions--Strategic aspects. 5.
Arctic regions--International status. I. Murray, Robert W., 1983- , author,
ditor of compilation. II. Dey Nuttall, Anita, author, editor of compilation.

G593.I67 2014
341.4'5091632--dc23
2014000175

Cover photograph: Nuuk Fjord, Greenland by Rohan Nuttall

TABLE OF CONTENTS

LIST OF FIGURES

ACKNOWLEDGMENTS

What began as a casual conversation between two colleagues at the University of Alberta in the fall of 2010 has finally ended up as a collection of thoughtful, insightful and well-crafted essays of which we are extremely proud. There is no denying that interest in the Arctic has intensified in recent years for scholars, policy-makers and casual observers, and this book illustrates how the political variables at play are at the forefront of discussion and debate about the future of the region, its peoples and environments.

A project of this magnitude could never have been achieved without a large team of people all believing in the importance of making a significant scholarly contribution to Arctic political discourse. We owe a profound word of thanks to the world-class group of contributors who donated their time and brilliant scholarship to this project. Without them, this book would never have come to life. The team at Cambria Press, especially Paul Richardson, Toni Tan and Michelle Wright, have been so helpful in both the manuscript editing and preparation processes, but also as fierce supporters of this project from start to finish. Together, we are indebted to the Canadian Circumpolar Institute, the University of Alberta, OCSTA and the Frontier Centre for Public Policy for their encouragement and support as we worked through the various stages of the project. We would like to acknowledge Mark Nuttall for his generous time in sharing his broad knowledge, expertise and advice on Arctic issues, and we are especially grateful to the anonymous reviewers who made careful and considered comments on individual chapters as well as the volume in its entirety. We owe thanks to Justin Bedi and Jennifer Makar for their assistance in reading through the final manuscript.

On a more personal level, we are both eternally grateful to our families, friends and colleagues that stood with us through the various stages of this project and supported, without hesitation, what we were aiming to do.

Robert W. Murray and Anita Dey Nuttall

International Relations and the Arctic

UNDERSTANDING POLICY AND GOVERNANCE IN THE ARCTIC

Robert W. Murray and Anita Dey Nuttall

From the outset, the academic field of study that became known as international relations (IR) was preoccupied with the study of inter-state relationships in the international system. Conflict, power, security, and the perception of and the prospects for peace have been constant themes in how scholars come to understand the international realm, as well as the various actors and trends involved in global complexity. Typical studies of international security and conflict have focused on two world wars, the Cold War and nuclear deterrence, civil conflicts, prospects for humanitarian intervention, gender and neocolonial issues, and, more recently, the effects of modern globalization processes. All of these matters are important in their own right, but there remains one prominent element of the contemporary international security environment that continually goes unnoticed, and that is the Arctic.

Discussion on the changing Arctic environment, as well as on the impacts of such change on the cultures and livelihoods of indigenous and local communities, plays out against the backdrop of the shifting views on the concept of sovereignty in international relations and international law, and it generates both concern and interest over the future of the region and its peoples. Questions about the defense of state territorial rights over the Arctic, the impact of changing maritime borders, climate change and protection of vulnerable ecosystems, safeguarding of future livelihoods of local inhabitants, and enforcing regulations of ice-free waterways and sea routes, to name a few, deepen the complexities of interstate relations and bilateral or multilateral agreements of the Arctic states. As contested territorial claims in the Arctic remain, and as non-polar countries look increasingly to the circumpolar North and imagine it to be a region that will provide global resources for the future, the potential stresses these developments place on international security cannot be ignored.

LOOKING NORTH

The proliferation of interest in the circumpolar region has been an exceptionally noteworthy trend in state and institutional policy making since the end of the Cold War. There are a variety of factors that have led to such intense interest on the part of states and the organizations they comprise. Mark Nuttall summarized some of the reasons for intense Arctic interest in recent decades:

> Previously, it could be argued, the Arctic had, since the end of World War II, been divided between the Western Arctic and the Soviet Arctic, with the two regions becoming strategically important in a military sense. From the late 1980s and early 1990s, however, awareness of the effects of contaminants, transboundary pollutants and climate change played its part in new

circumpolar initiatives to assess, understand and call for the development of policy strategies to deal with significant environmental issues that affect the region but are global in origins or impact. Initiatives such as the Arctic Environmental Protection Strategy (AEPS) and, since 1996, the Arctic Council have aimed to ensure that Arctic issues remain high on the domestic and international agendas of the eight Arctic states (Canada, the United States, Denmark/Greenland, Iceland, Norway, Sweden, Finland and Russia), as well a handful of non-Arctic states.[1]

Despite the overt policy strategies being developed by numerous states, the reactions of existing international organizations, as well as the concerns of indigenous peoples within Arctic nations and the formation of new entities designed to specifically address issues in the Arctic, international security scholars have paid relatively little attention to the region in a way that has advanced theory in the study of international relations.

There are many reasons why this could be the case, though no singular explanation is entirely adequate. The field of security studies has grown well beyond the traditional focus on interstate relations and war and now involves many more actors, trends, and theoretical elements that in some ways results in a situation where the importance of state-based conflict has become conveniently ignored or overlooked. There is also a marked increase in the distance between international relations or security research and policy, thus in many ways begging whether IR scholarship is even capable of engaging in matters of Arctic security because of its growing abstractness. Whatever the reason, states have certainly shown their interests in looking north, and it is time international security scholarship followed suit. This volume is an effort to examine the theoretical, policy, and strategic trends of actors in the Arctic region through an IR perspective. However, the uniqueness of this volume lies not simply in understanding the Arctic from the disciplinary perspective of IR, but more importantly we want this compilation of chapters to throw light on how the Arctic as an area of study contributes to the development of the IR discipline. In addition to IR specialists and political scientists, we consciously chose international expertise on Arctic security and sovereignty from different disciplinary backgrounds, such as anthropology, geography, law, and history. Hence this volume is distinctive in that it provides coverage of Arctic issues by scholars from those disciplines whose work converges on areas traditionally seen as the intellectual domain of IR. We believe that the contributors to this book bring critical perspectives to our focus on the confluence of politics, society, and environment to inform a better and comprehensive understanding of contemporary Arctic issues.

EXAMINING THE THEORIES AND POLICIES OF CIRCUMPOLAR POLITICS

This ambitious project aims to bring together some of the most important voices in the study of the Arctic to demonstrate the region's vital importance in discussions of international relations and security. While it is difficult to encompass the vast array of explanations and issues currently facing the Arctic, this volume is divided into three sections that all seek to influence how observers can contemplate the political landscape of the circumpolar region.

Section 1: Arctic Sovereignty in Theory

Before exploring the responses and strategies of individual states or institutions in the Arctic, it is essential to place debates about the security and behavioral dynamics of circumpolar relations in context. To do so, this section focuses on four of the most relevant and popular approaches to foreign policy analysis that apply to the Arctic. This is not to dismiss theoretical camps not included here but rather to emphasize the four schools of thought currently dominating explanations of Arctic sovereignty and security.

The first approach presented, which likely comes as little surprise because of its prominent place in international security debates, is realism. In a time when realist thinking finds itself constantly under attack and, according to many critical theorists, in serious decline, Robert Murray asserted that there is no better explanatory model for contemporary Arctic relations than realism. To make his case, Murray presented the subvariants of realist theory and remarked that, while realists themselves may not be entirely united in their analyses of current world events, the "three S's"—statism, survival, and self-help—are all alive and well in the strategies being employed by states in the High North. To ground his theoretical analysis of realism empirically, Murray focused on two states in particular, namely Canada and Russia, whose Arctic strategies both employ heavily militaristic and survivalist elements. Murray contended that, far from being a theory of the past, the field and its onlookers must revisit the traditional works of realism to comprehend effectively just how various actors are approaching the Arctic region.

In response to Murray's claims, Tom Keating dissected the liberal-internationalist aspects of Arctic affairs and offered an intriguing argument that states have actually sacrificed their independence and have instead chosen to embed themselves into institutions designed to mitigate conflict and hard power solutions. To do so, Keating provided a useful explanation of liberal international theory and its foundations in idealistic thinkers such as Locke and Kant. These foundational precepts, Keating claimed, have led to a regime where states seek to cooperate through systems of law, governance, and organization that would prevent the pessimistically realist prediction of conflict in the Arctic. Keating's empirical demonstration for liberal ideology in the Arctic highlights the role of treaties and agreements that allow the Arctic to be managed and conflicts resolved, rather than states allowing their competing claims to escalate unnecessarily into real conflict.

Rather than presenting the case for Arctic sovereignty and strategy as a black-and-white argument, Matthew Weinert intervened in the theoretical debate by presenting a case for a hybrid approach, encapsulated through the English School of IR theory. Weinert's chapter presents the reader with a comprehensive explanation of the English School's tenets and shows quite compellingly that states and their leaders rarely (if ever) make decisions in world affairs using a singular lens of international theory. The beauty of the English School, according to Weinert, is that it allows decision makers to employ multiple frameworks in one coherent way of thinking, premised primarily on the function of international society. Weinert highlighted the complexity of defining sovereignty and the importance of secondary institutions in helping states to navigate their competing claims over the Arctic. At the core of the English School contribution to thinking about the Arctic, as explained very clearly by Weinert, is the concept of legitimacy. Realists see a claim as legitimate if State A can outgun State B; liberal internationalists see legitimacy as preference or institutionally driven; the English School, however, reminds people that legitimacy and how they address claims change over time with the values of a given international society. Historical context, then, is a core element in how one comprehends actors' strategies toward a given problem.

In a demonstration of one of the most contemporary outlooks in international relations, the next chapter introduces the perspective of green theory and ecological discourse on Arctic relations. Guy-Serge Côté and Matthew Paterson argued convincingly that the Arctic has become an ideal demonstration of postsovereign politics. This contention is predicated on the notion that, without a single site of authority to dictate or settle conflictual claims, the transnational nature of emerging institutions, practices, and networks all serve to bring traditional ways of thinking about sovereignty, like those presented by Murray, Keating, and Weinert, into question. Further, Côté and Paterson went on to introduce a new way of thinking about green theory and its understanding of sovereignty, noting that the Arctic poses both challenges and opportunities for ecopolitical progress in the High North. The emphasis on ecological and environmental aspects of the Arctic debate in both theory and policy plays a major role in how and why attention is being paid to the circumpolar region and should not be omitted from any conceptualization of the Arctic's strategic significance.

Section 2: Arctic Sovereignty in Practice

Turning from international theory to application, the second section of the volume is dedicated to a consideration of how individual Arctic states are themselves dedicating national resources to their northern regions and how they are expressing their claims to Arctic territories and articulating identities as circumpolar nations. All five Arctic littoral states (Canada, Norway, Denmark/Greenland, the United States of America, and Russia), for instance, have made claims that, if accepted under the United Nations Convention on the Law of the Sea (UNCLOS), they would extend their ocean boundaries—but some of these partly overlap with those of another country, and although press coverage of this suggests that overlapping claims could lead to tension between states, Arctic countries themselves insist that pragmatic and negotiated settlement is the more likely outcome rather than entrenchment or the enactment of a new "Great Game." Beyond these specific territorial and boundary issues, all eight Arctic nations have engaged in a process of establishing their credentials as the major players in Arctic geopolitics, with some taking more of a lead than others. It is important to bear in mind the lessons learned from section 1 in reading the contributions in both sections 2 and 3, given that they serve as a roadmap for how national leaders and organizations have positioned themselves in relation to domestic and international Arctic issues.

It is well documented that over the last decade, all eight Arctic states have begun to reassert their claims in the North and have developed strategies (and in some cases implemented policies) consistent with their desires to maintain a border in the Arctic, but they also have begun to map out strategies for governance, sustainable development, and environmental management. Canada, the United States, Russia, Norway, Denmark, Sweden, Finland, and Iceland each have unique approaches to their northern borders and to nurturing their own identities as Arctic states, though all have made one point very clear—the Arctic is a region of intense interest in modern international relations and, as such, non-Arctic states should recognize the sovereignty of northern nations. The contributors in section 2 of this volume present and analyze the various policies and strategies of the eight Arctic states.

The section begins with Rob Huebert's presentation of Canada's Arctic policy. Canadian foreign policy is rarely expressed in terms of nationalism and sovereignty claims, but Huebert contended the last two decades of Arctic policy in Canada have seen a distinct change and the growth of a renewed domestic political interest in the nation's northern affairs. Arctic sovereignty and security have been enduring elements of Canada's foreign and defense policy, and Huebert argued that Canadian claims in the Arctic are intrinsically tied to the nation's modern identity and, as such, Canada is now taking its approach to the Arctic more seriously than perhaps it has done in recent years. Such approaches are often performative in the form of military exercises and symbolic acts that make statements about sovereignty, but they are increasingly expressed in the form of federal government commitment to the economic development of the North. Canada held the first chairmanship of the Arctic Council when the forum was established in 1996, and in May 2013 it assumed the role for the second time. Unlike its first chairmanship period, when it could be argued the Arctic was not in such sharp international focus as it is now, Canada's second period coincides with a time of reappraisal of the role of the Arctic Council and with the future of Arctic governance.

To many, the United States would appear not to have any sort of major interest in the Arctic beyond its Alaskan borders. Traditionally, the Americans have been content to do as they please within their boundaries and, though they may not entirely agree with the claims of others, have respected them for the most part. Phil Steinberg presented a case that would bring traditional interpretations of American Arctic policy into question. Although the United States may not see the Arctic as an area that might in itself present a pressing security threat, Steinberg argued that the region has become an increased concern for American policy makers as a result of their questions about regional stability. Steinberg stated very clearly, "The United States looks warily at the region as a site of potentially dangerous institutional experimentation that, if adopted, could have global ramifications that would challenge some of the fundamental legal principles and norms that underpin U.S. hegemony." Such a realization may seriously influence how other states pursue their interests in the region moving forward.

Of course, in any discussion about American interests and global politics in the North, one must also include the policies and interests of the Russians. Some commentators have suggested that Russia has emerged as the most aggressive Arctic state in recent years, evident in a northern military presence and explicit and unequivocal claims to parts of the Arctic Ocean. Russia has asserted its identity as a northern state, has demonstrated its intention to defend its territorial claims, and has hinted at extending them if it so desires. Gleb Yarovoy traced Russia's Arctic policies and made a case for how and why the Russian government has made a notable shift in its Arctic strategy since 2008. Announcements of new military brigades in the North, the launch of new submarine classes, and advancements in missile technology all speak to how many feel, or worry, the Russians intend to stake their claims. Yarovoy is sure to remind readers as well that, regardless of the situation, the power and influence of the Russian president is a key element in how Russia will pursue or defend its claims in the Arctic.

Some of the smaller Arctic states have also begun to reform their strategies toward the North, out of either necessity or opportunity. Geir Hønneland effectively showed how Norway's Arctic policies have altered dramatically since the end of the Cold War. Norway's involvement in NATO was certainly an important one during a time when tension characterized relations between the Western Arctic and the

Soviet Arctic, and since the fall of the Soviet Union, Hønneland argued, Norway has welcomed prospects for cooperation in the region and has done much to advance efforts in this direction. The era of cooperation with Russia throughout the 1990s, followed by the emergence of the High North as a Norwegian national priority (especially within the context of the creation of the Barents Arctic region as a political and cultural project), has shown Norway's recognition of the Arctic to be vital to its national interests. Moving forward, it is clear Norway has placed cooperation with Russia and the maintenance of good relations with the Russians as a high priority for seemingly obvious reasons.

Recent developments in the political, economic, and cultural spheres in Greenland and the Faroe Islands, as well as growing concern over the scale and impact of climate change and the large-scale development of extractive industries, have contributed to international attention being focused increasingly on these Danish self-governing territories in the northern North Atlantic. Indeed, Greenland is often positioned by scientists, policy makers, and the media at the epicenter of climate change. The tangible aspects of global warming are evident in thinning sea ice and the melting of glaciers, and many of Greenland's coastal communities are facing significant challenges to local economies and everyday life, but climate change brings opportunities as well as threats, particularly in the form of oil, gas, and mining development. Mark Nuttall evaluated the Kingdom of Denmark's Arctic strategy, released in 2011, as a document that both addresses these issues and makes a statement about the kingdom's position as an Arctic state with claims for a significant role in international diplomacy. Greenland has been central to Denmark's historical and contemporary status as an Arctic nation, but greater autonomy in the form of Self Rule raises significant questions about the future of Danish practices and performances of power, security, and sovereignty in the Arctic and North Atlantic. For example, Greenland is undergoing a process of state formation and has assumed importance in discussions of global energy security, with the Self Rule government courting multinational corporations and foreign investors interested in hydrocarbons and minerals. Yet, precisely at the time when Greenland and the Faroe Islands appear to be more confident in asserting greater autonomy within the Kingdom of Denmark, with occasional political gestures anticipating eventual political independence and the complete severing of ties to Copenhagen, the strategy reinforces the importance of maintaining strong relations among the three constituent parts of the Danish Realm. As Nuttall argued, the Arctic strategy emphasizes the distinctive nature of the kingdom's boundaries while recognizing the political and cultural diversity apparent within them.

Through its involvement in the affairs of the European Union, Swedish Arctic policy has evolved gradually throughout the last twenty years. In May 2013, Sweden ended its chairmanship of the Arctic Council, which also marked the end of a period in the council's history in which all member states had held the position. Yet Sweden has been perhaps one of the most reluctant of all Arctic states to consider itself as such. As Carina Keskitalo argued in her chapter, although Sweden's inclusion in the Arctic Council has been based on recognition of the country as an Arctic state, "Sweden has often been seen as a laggard in Arctic policy. It has only recently formulated an Arctic policy, which it made public in May 2011 when taking over the rotating chairmanship of the council. However, that Sweden has not traditionally defined itself or its domestic areas as Arctic to any particular extent is hardly surprising, given that it has no climatically Arctic areas or Arctic coastline (only climatically sub-Arctic areas, which are located in the northernmost parts of the country)." The absence of an Arctic policy prior to 2011 may not in itself be sufficient to accuse Sweden of tardiness in positioning itself in circumpolar affairs—after all, the Kingdom of Denmark released its Arctic strategy later the same year after it had relinquished the chairmanship of the Arctic Council—yet, Keskitalo did point to the intriguing fact that the creation of the Arctic Council has no direct impact on Swedish domestic or foreign policy. Nor does the involvement of Swedish Saami in circumpolar politics and movements for the recognition of indigenous rights and self-determination seem to have contributed to the shaping of a

Swedish position on the Arctic. Rather, Keskitalo argued that Sweden's role in Arctic cooperation must be understood with reference to its involvement in Nordic, rather than circumpolar, cooperation, and its recent statements on Arctic policy have been influenced more by the emerging interests in the Arctic expressed by the European Union.

The emergence of the Arctic as an international political region since the late 1980s owes much to Finnish initiatives on environmental cooperation and efforts to focus the European gaze on the Nordic regions and on northwest Russia. Lassi Heininen explored Finland's identity and political prominence as both a northern European country and an Arctic nation, manifest in its Northern Dimension policy and Arctic strategy. Following World War II, Finnish foreign policy—often framed by a concern for security and the maintenance of independence—was deeply influenced by relations (and trade) with the Soviet Union. With the collapse of the Soviet Union in 1991, Finland's international relations were characterized by a deeper movement into Europe by way of its Northern Dimension initiative. Heininen considered the significance of this initiative, explored Finland's Arctic strategy (which was first adopted in 2010), and provided analysis of how these declarations assert and position Finland as an Arctic as well as (northern) European state. Through its strategy on the Arctic, Finland articulates a position that provides strong support for international cooperation on a range of Arctic issues and emphasizes the importance of security and stability based on international treaties, a position that Heininen argued is entirely consistent with Finland's long-term national interests.

One of the intriguing aspects of the nurturing of a political identity as an Arctic state is that this particular expression of northernness is not always commensurate with a country's geographical extent. The diversity of scientific definitions of the Arctic notwithstanding, most of the states of the circumpolar North do not lie entirely within the Arctic. Although Canada's Northern Strategy makes an unequivocal claim that with "40% of our landmass in the territories, 162,000 kilometres of Arctic coastline and 25% of the global Arctic—Canada is undeniably an Arctic nation,"[2] most Canadians would be hard pressed to argue that Toronto or Montreal are Arctic cities, no matter how far below freezing the temperature plummets in winter. Yet, whereas Canada is quintessentially a northern nation, there are specific attributes and supposed qualities of the "Arctic" that mark it off from the "North" (although the two terms are often used interchangeably). Similarly, Denmark, as Nuttall showed in his chapter, would cease to be an Arctic state should Greenland become independent.

Iceland is the one Arctic state that describes itself as situated entirely within the Arctic, thus making a distinctive claim among all circumpolar nations (it has also recently argued that it is an Arctic coastal state). Alyson Bailes and Margrét Cela discussed why and how this is so in the final chapter of this section of the book. Iceland is perhaps more dependent on Arctic resources than most other Arctic states, and the economic crash of 2008 was a brutal reminder of its precarious position at the northern edge of the North Atlantic. Although determined partly to fish its way out of its economic crisis (the mackerel fishing boom is one example), Iceland has begun to take advantage of its strategic location by providing harbor facilities to northern shipping, while companies are benefiting from oil and minerals exploration by providing air transport or logistics. Other economic advantages are seen as arising from expertise in construction and technology. Bailes and Cela argued that the Icelandic position is a pragmatic one in terms of being strategic in order to take advantage of the economic possibilities emerging in a region undergoing transformation, but they pointed to the contested issues arising (for example, over rights to fisheries) that define some international relations in terms of possible conflict, such as between Iceland and Norway and Iceland and the European Union, rather than cooperation. Iceland is also particularly supportive of the Arctic Council while encouraging of non-Arctic states and institutions being involved in Arctic issues.

Section 3: Shared Sovereignty and Global Security Interests
As international interest in the Arctic grows, a number of non-Arctic states, institutions, and organizations are laying claim to a right to be involved in discussions over the governance of the region and have sought observer status in the Arctic Council. The third section of this book focuses on the role of non-state actors and intergovernmental institutions in addressing international challenges arising from Arctic sovereignty issues, as well as the increasing interests of non-Arctic states in the circumpolar North. It examines how states accommodate their obligations to protect and uphold the principles of international law and at the same time safeguard their individual national interests.

Although three Arctic Council member states are part of the European Union (Denmark, Finland, and Sweden) and seven other EU member countries have observer status (the United Kingdom, Germany, France, Italy, the Netherlands, Poland, and Spain), the EU as an institution has expressed its interest in the Arctic in recent years. Clive Archer traced this interest, asking why the EU has become involved in Arctic issues, examined concepts of sovereignty in the EU and the Arctic as the background to the EU's Arctic policy, and considered the evolution of current EU involvement in the region. While Finland's Northern Dimension initiative meant the EU's gaze was directed somewhat northwards, Archer argued that this came to rest mainly on aspects of relations between Russia and the Baltic states. In 2007, however, the European Commission's integrated maritime strategy referred to the Arctic Ocean in the context of global warming, as did the High Representative and Commission policy paper on climate change and international security, which recommended an EU Arctic policy. After a European Parliament debate on the subject, the commission issued a communication on the EU and the Arctic region at the end of 2008, and in December 2009 the council agreed a conclusion on the Arctic issue. The commission and the EU's High Representative for Foreign Affairs issued a joint communication on the EU and the Arctic region in June 2012. The EU has also applied for observer status in the Arctic Council, although continued opposition from member countries such as Canada and Norway (mainly because of the EU's position of the importation of sealskins) is likely to mean discussions and negotiations will be protracted.

In the context of an intergovernmental body such as the United Nations (UN), Andy Knight explored the question of what kind of governance structure is needed to address evolving Arctic security and sovereignty issues in the face of climate change. He argued that the foundation for that governance structure can be found in the UN. While conflict management, conflict mitigation, and conflict prevention are central to the UN's essential mandate, Knight's chapter emphasizes that the UN is a global organization that is about more than conflict management. The multilateral governance arrangement of the UN system is also equipped to address complex global issues that individual states within the Arctic region may not be able to deal with adequately on their own. Knight also argued that as more is understood about how global warming and climate change are affecting the Arctic region, it becomes important to consider the possibility that other institutions of governance besides those in the UN system may be needed to address adequately evolving Arctic issues. Knight reminded readers that there is need for the UN governance structure to adjust in order to address the impacts and effects of global warming and climate change on the Arctic. He however deemed that the one contribution the UN system can make in informing the policy makers of Arctic states is in the many lessons that have been learned through debates and discussions in various UN bodies about the potential dangers and negative effects of unregulated exploration and exploitation of that very fragile area. Although Knight stated that the UN system is only one of many actors that play a role in the governance of the globe, he added further that the combination of multilateral and plurilateral governance arrangements in the Arctic is a reminder of the limitations of the UN system. As a multilateral organization designed by states to carry out the wishes of states collectively, the UN has particular instruments, Knight informed, that are at times unable to function in the way they were intended, and therefore he reckoned that the work of governance is a process that is continually evolving. Knight believes that addressing pressing issues of the Arctic should conceivably be a shared responsibility between a regional forum such as the Arctic Council and a global governance body such as the UN system.

Timo Koivurova and Piotr Graczyk provided a comprehensive analysis of the changing nature of the Arctic Council (AC). As they showed, the Arctic institutional framework involves both legal and political arrangements—with the 1982 UNCLOS and the AC as its anchors—and is affected by state sovereignty and jurisdiction, although the Arctic Council does not deal with matters of security. Yet this could change as issues of security, safety, and emergency responses (as a result of oil and gas development) or search and rescue (because of increased marine shipping) challenge governance and management in the region. The central question is how to adapt existing regional governance structure to improve its ability to deal with new phenomena occurring in the Arctic. Koivurova and Graczyk considered whether the Arctic Council is likely to retain its current role as the predominant forum where a wide range of Arctic issues is considered and debated, thereby contributing to enhancing regional stability. They discussed the role of the AC in regional security and sovereignty discourses, even though military-related issues are explicitly excluded from its mandate and more controversial issues are implicitly banned from its agenda. The chapter identifies the main challenges to the council's position that could diminish its role in the midst of pressures to address issues related to traditional security and stronger and more exclusive multilateral options to govern the region, as well as what means could be devised to overcome them.

Betsy Baker placed the melting Arctic's shifting geophysical and biological barriers, and geopolitical barriers, as the backdrop to discuss the need for international law to adapt in finding practical solutions for the region. Baker considered why concepts of sovereignty in international law must evolve to reflect new ways of managing resources and sharing jurisdiction. Emphasizing that notions of sovereignty and terri-

torial integrity can no longer be regarded as separate, but that international law must acknowledge the connectedness of shared environmental systems and shared circumpolar indigenous rights, Baker specifically addressed three strands of international law—territorial boundaries, environment, and human rights. She took the example of the
UNCLOS, a key instrument of international law recognized by all Arctic
states, as containing the beginnings of the notion of shared sovereignty.
Baker also observed that traditional international law has learned to
recognize this in developing the two newer strands of international environmental law and indigenous rights law. Baker stressed the interaction between national legislation and international treaty obligations as
vital in not only addressing current challenges in the Arctic, but also
providing the space for creative use of existing international norms in
articulating national interests there. However, she gave precedence to
international law for Arctic states to protect a changing environment
and to promote human health, prosperity, and engagement in political
processes.

Whereas Arctic states nurture and assert Arctic identities, outline
Arctic strategies, and implement policies dealing with their northern
reaches, Jessica Shadian reminded readers that, in the last few decades,
the Arctic as a specific region within the global political landscape has
also acquired its own distinct political identity as defined and articulated by northern indigenous peoples. The politicization of indigenous
issues is closely linked to issues of management and governance of
resources, particularly in relation to indigenous rights, and Shadian's
chapter takes a normative approach to explore what existing indigenous
governance arrangements can contribute to broader debates over Arctic
governance. She began with a consideration of the nature and practice of
co-management and then explored the Alaska Eskimo Whaling Commission (AEWC) as a case study and possible starting point for debates about
governing newly emerging resource management issues in the Arctic.
Taking particular interest in the governance framework of the AEWC,
Shadian asked if it might be applicable for the current governance discus-

sions regarding Arctic offshore oil and gas development. The chapter reflects on how a postsovereign resource management approach could contribute to the broader theoretical debates concerning who owns the Arctic and who decides about resource management. Importantly, it offers one possible way to envision the future of a strengthened Arctic Council engaging with a world where states are not the only actors with legitimate claims to participate in the governance of the Arctic.

Such actors are also non-Arctic states and, by way of illustration, Klaus Dodds wrote about the United Kingdom's Arctic interests, which have intensified over the last ten years or so. Dodds showed that the United Kingdom's focus has moved from hard security concerns during the Cold War to multidimensional ones with energy, climate change, shipping, scientific research, and governance coming to dominate political discussion. Contemporary U.K. interest in the Arctic now involves a more diverse set of stakeholders in the wake of widespread acceptance within scientific and policy-orientated communities that the Arctic is becoming more accessible and, in the process, is undergoing a profound state-change. Noting that the northern boundaries of the United Kingdom could qualify it as a sub-Arctic neighbor to the Arctic states, Dodds pointed to three key trajectories of U.K. interests, those of science/environment, military, and energy. In briefly assessing the possible development of a U.K. Arctic strategy, Dodds observed that the United Kingdom has to balance the need to prioritize Arctic interests and maintain political attention at ministerial levels with that of allaying possible concern by Arctic states that a U.K. Arctic strategy might suggest a more forceful pursuit of its interests in fields such as energy, fishing, and shipping.

A new wave of interest from non-Arctic states in the Arctic also comes from the Asian continent. Nong Hong and Anita Dey Nuttall described in their chapter how the changing geopolitical realities in the Arctic as a result of climate change opening possibilities for access to potential Arctic resources have broadened the international focus on the Arctic to include more geographically distant countries such as China, Japan,

South Korea, and India. Their chapter examines the nature of the interests and motivations of these states in claiming and legitimizing their
involvement and maintaining a presence in the region. They identify
participation in Arctic governance affairs, access to potential resources,
shipping opportunities, and cooperation in polar research as areas where
these states demonstrate their strongest interests. Nong and Dey Nuttall
emphasized that transregional implications of a melting Arctic demands
that the basis of a partnership between Arctic and non-Arctic states must
lie in recognizing and respecting each other's rights under international
law. The political guarantee for such cooperation requires mutual understanding and trust.

Enhanced cooperation in scientific research between Arctic and non-
Arctic states is regarded as important in viewing transregional issues
from a wider perspective and facilitating the settlement of the Arctic's
environmental, jurisdictional, and resource issues. In this context the
final chapter takes the example of the Antarctic Treaty of 1959 as having
relevance to the politics of Arctic affairs. Although many do not see
the relevance of this treaty to Arctic issues because of the fundamental
environmental and political differences between the two polar regions,
Dey Nuttall argued that the focus needs to be less on the contrasts in
the historical, geopolitical, and social bases between the two. Rather, she
pointed to how the political rationality shown by the original Antarctic
Treaty parties that was espoused in the universal principles of peace,
cooperation, and reciprocity of the treaty has thus far successfully
guided national activity and accommodated political interests of multiple
nations in the southern continent. She also reminded readers of the
collective and long-term association of non-Arctic states with Antarctica
and its governance and that the perspectives and experience they bring
from their involvement there and the positions they hold in international
Antarctic affairs need to be contemplated and considered in the context
of the growing global interest in Arctic governance issues.

By combining elements of theory, national policy, and global governance issues, this volume is an important contribution to how international relations scholars, especially those interested in security and foreign policy analysis, can examine the politics of the Arctic region. In a broad sense, the volume presents varying theoretical perspectives on just how one is to begin to comprehend recent trends in the circumpolar region and how events may unfold in the near and distant future. Whether through analyses grounded in realist, liberal, English School, or green theories, the scholars included in this collection all make one point abundantly clear—that politics in the Arctic are deserving of far greater attention from international relations scholars and that the Arctic region is likely to continue as an arena of power politics as states attempt to make their claims and negotiate their interests through international institutions.

There is no doubt that the scholarly interest in the Arctic region has grown immensely in recent years, and understandably so. The High North has truly embodied what international politics is all about—power, development, environmentalism, cooperation, conflict, and uncertainty about the future. To date, international relations and security literature has only touched the surface of Arctic affairs. The hope is that a comprehensive volume such as this can serve as a flashpoint for debates to continue and grow. Whether one is interested in the theoretical implications of state, institutional, or human behavior, the case studies of how individual states are approaching the Arctic, or the effects of institutions on northern affairs, this volume serves as a starting point for how international relations can learn from, and contribute to, understanding Arctic politics.

NOTES

1. Mark Nuttall, "Introduction: Politics, Science and Environment in the Polar Regions," *The Polar Journal* 2, no. 1 (June 2012): 1.
2. http://www.northernstrategy.gc.ca/sov/index-eng.asp.

PART I

ARCTIC SOVEREIGNTY IN THEORY

CHAPTER 1

WESTPHALIAN SOVEREIGNTY AND REALISM IN CONTEMPORARY INTERNATIONAL SECURITY

Robert W. Murray

INTRODUCTION

In the age of human rights, environmentalism, NGOs, and global civil society, it is sometimes easy to overlook or forget the foundations of international relations theory. From its outset, the field that became known as international relations (IR) sought to explain and understand the causes and outcomes of conflict and, in many cases, how nation-states could avoid such conflictual behavior in the future. It is no coincidence that the first scholarly endeavors under the auspices of international relations came about in the wake of World War I in the British university system. Since its inception, the academic study of politics between states has evolved and, arguably, progressed. Debates about the nature of conflict in the post–World War I era tended to focus on states as the primary actors in the international system and were divided along two lines, realism and idealism. The initial theoretical explanations of international politics led, over time, to a variety of new and original reactions, and taken together, these competing lenses have provided a varied and often incoherent view of politics in the global realm. In many respects, the approaches to examining the *international* have changed, but never are the foundational elements of the study far from memory.

Among the cornerstones of international relations study, even to this day, is the importance of realism. Realist theories tend to argue in favor of a worldview that explains interstate behavior as inherently uncooperative, distrustful, uncertain, and tense. The primary actors in the international system, namely states, are utility maximizers whose underlying motivation is survival and who make foreign policy decisions based on rational calculations about both other states and the constraints of the anarchic structure of the system. Realists tend to place emphasis on the study of hard, military power and its role in achieving beneficial outcomes when used to influence or coerce the actions of other states. Some of the most important features of the realist international system that maintains a semblance of balance and stability among states are the rights of independence and non-intervention guaranteed by the Westphalian conception of sovereignty. Under the Peace of Westphalia in 1648, the modern state system came into existence with the explicit understanding that states were able to conduct themselves internally free from outside interference and from the prospect of their sovereignty being violated except in extreme cases.[1]

With the fall of the Soviet Union in 1991 and the rise of critical philosophical arguments about the nature of global politics, realist ideas of state primacy, security, and sovereignty have been challenged and considered by some to be outdated. Despite these recent criticisms, there is little doubt among theorists and policy makers that realism remains the most useful explanatory model to understand the behavior of states in contemporary international politics, especially in terms of security dynamics. Nowhere is the continued relevance of realism as an explanatory model clearer than in the Arctic region.

As sovereignty over Arctic territories is being consolidated and settled by the eight Arctic states (some of whose claims overlap with one another) and as submissions are made to the UN commission on the limits of continental shelf claims, it is essential to examine how Arctic states define their security and self-interest and the consequences of such assumptions. Often framed as an issue of human or economic development rather than a security-focused problem because of it being frozen over, this area has continually been used as a military test ground by various states, as demonstrated in the various chapters in this volume, and such behavior is unlikely to cease anytime soon. Understanding why states are so willing to demonstrate their keen interest by displaying hard power capabilities is difficult, if not impossible, when relying upon liberal or critical approaches to international relations alone. By exploring realist theory from its foundational principles to its conceptions of security and sovereignty, this chapter will argue that while issues of economic development, the environment, and social norms play a role in why certain states make claims regarding Arctic sovereignty, it is ultimately realist assumptions about the nature of international politics that better explain the current foreign policy dynamics of interstate assertions about the Arctic and prospects for future outcomes.

THE POSTULATES OF REALISM

As Arctic states frame foreign policy strategies, it can be argued that realist theory is quite capable of providing explanatory power as to why the area has become so important in the contemporary international political environment. What must be first noted about any discussion of realism is that there is no singular theory of realism per se—as the field of international relations has developed over time, the umbrella concept of *realism* actually represents a number of different conceptions of how to interpret interstate behavior. That said, at the core of the realist school of thought are concepts such as self-interest, security and power maximization, and the vital importance of hard, or military, power. According to Stephen Krasner,

> The *explanatory variable* for realism is the distribution of power among states. The basic claim of realism is that given a particular distribution of power among states it is possible to explain both the characteristics of the system and the behaviour of individual states...Realism makes no effort to probe the domestic determinants of foreign policy; what counts is state power and external constraints.[2]

The essential characteristic, then, in comprehending the realist approach to international politics and security is the anarchic nature of the international system, which compels states to engage in self-help behavior.[3] According to Robert Art and Robert Jervis, when using realist theories to explain international politics, one must focus on the behavior of states in an anarchic environment, where no authority exists above the domestic level. "States can make commitments and treaties, but no sovereign power ensures compliance and punished deviation. This—the absence of a supreme power—is what is meant by the anarchic environment of international politics."[4] The centrality of states and the lack of a governing power above states are at the core of realist theories.

What is meant by the term *international system*? As noted by Art and Jervis, the system of states is an environment in which states interact without the existence of an overarching authority to compel them toward certain kinds of ethical or morally righteous behavior. This is why the character of the system is described as anarchic. According to Kenneth Waltz, one of the most prominent realist scholars of the modern era, the anarchic nature of the international system is the defining characteristic that explains interstate behavior at the international level.

In describing what anarchy means for the international system, Waltz argued,

> In anarchy there is no automatic harmony...A state will use force to attain its goals if, after assessing the prospects for success, it values those goals more than it values the pleasures of peace. Because each state is the final judge of its own cause, any state may at any time use force to implement its policies. Because any state may at any time use force, all states must constantly be ready either to counter force with force or to pay the cost of weakness. The requirements of state action are, in this view, imposed by the circumstances in which all states exist.[5]

With an understanding of the anarchic nature of the international system in place, one can then examine how realism explains the motivations, fears, and strategies of states by recognizing the various interpretations that influence the theoretical tradition. To comprehend realist theory better, it is important to divide the tradition into three distinct sub-classifications—classical, structural realism, and neoclassical realism.

CLASSICAL REALISM

Realist explanations of international politics remain among the most predominant theories in IR to this day, but they are constantly being refuted from all sides of the theoretical spectrum.[6] In 1939, E. H. Carr described an environment of international politics that was anarchic and competitive, and he spent considerable effort in warning against the pitfalls of utopian thought in international policy making. His major work, *The Twenty Years' Crisis*, tells a story of international amorality in the vein of Machiavelli and Hobbes, a lack of common interests among states and the dismal probability for interstate cooperation. Carr argued, "In the international order, the role of power is greater and that of morality less...When self-sacrifice is attributed to a state, the chances are greater that this alleged self-sacrifice will turn out on inspection to be a forced submission to a stronger power."[7] This work set the stage for a series of early realists, such as Arnold Wolfers and Walter Lippmann, to build a foundation for realism in IR theory.

Of course, many of Carr's predictions and warnings came to the forefront of international study when World War II broke out in September 1939. Some of the problems that early realists saw in the Treaty of Versailles, such as the treatment of lesser powers and state self-interest during the negotiations at the Paris Peace Conference, only added to the growing popularity of realist theory. In the wake of World War II, Hans Morgenthau published his famous classical realist manifesto, *Politics Among Nations*, in 1948. This book, combined with those that came before, told a very specific version of international political history and articulated similar prospects for future relations as described by Carr —first, that states are the primary actors in an anarchic international system; second, that self-interest is the motivating principle for state action; third, that the trends of self-interest and quest for power are historically universal and have always been the motivations for human action; and finally, that states only cooperate with one another if it is within their interests to do so, because they have no social nature. This point is emphasized by Morgenthau when he asserted, "The essence of international politics is identical with its domestic counterpart. Both domestic and international politics are a struggle for power, modified only by the different conditions under which this struggle takes place in the domestic and in the international spheres."[8]

Though classical realist theory differs from structural realism in its articulation of how the international system is to be understood, they both highlight the lack of authority in the international realm above the state level, the centrality of the state in international politics, and the self-interested nature of state behavior.[9] For its version of the international system, classical realism looks to two primary sources: the first are philosophical texts that describe humans as naturally self-interested, as well as those thinkers who theorize about man's actions or motives in the state of nature[10]; the second is human history, which classical realists believe tells a story of perpetual self-interest tracing back to Thucydides's *History of the Peloponnesian War.*[11] Morgenthau argued that

> the world, imperfect as it is from the rational point of view, is the result of forces inherent in human nature. To improve the world one must work with those forces, not against them. This being inherently a world of opposing interests and of conflict among them, moral principles can never be fully realized but must at best be approximated through the ever temporary balancing of interests and the ever precarious settlement of conflicts. This school, then, sees in a system of checks and balances a universal principle for all pluralist societies. It appeals to historical precedent rather than to abstract principles and aims at the realization of the lesser evil rather than of the absolute good.[12]

Classical realism, then, sees the international system as a realm in which states attempt to maximize their power and where there are no universal moral principles to guide state action.

STRUCTURAL REALISM

The structural variant of realism differs from its classical counterpart because of its preference for systemic theorizing, as compared to the classical emphasis on how philosophical traditions of human nature and desire for power condition states. John Mearsheimer effectively summarized the structural realist thesis by providing five bedrock assumptions:

> The first assumption is that the international system is anarchic...The second assumption is that great powers inherently possess some offensive military capability, which gives them the wherewithal to hurt and possibly destroy each other...The third assumption is that states can never be certain about other states' intentions...The fourth assumption is that survival is the primary goal of great powers...The fifth assumption is that great powers are rational actors.[13]

From these basic assumptions, Mearsheimer claimed that three broad patterns of interstate behavior can be deduced: "fear, self-help, and power maximization."[14]

In an effort to refine the original realist postulates articulated by such scholars as Morgenthau, Kenneth Waltz sought to promote a different understanding of the international system that was not contingent upon philosophical debates over human nature. In his 1979 *Theory of International Politics*, Waltz used a combination of political, economic, and mathematical theory to create an understanding of the international system that differs greatly from that conceived of by classical realists, liberals, and critical scholars alike because of its rational choice foundations, its emphasis on testable theoretical hypothesis in the Lakatosian tradition, and its fairly narrow scope of explanatory power.[15] Waltz argued in this work that states are the primary actors in the system, that the system is defined by economic and mathematical game theory rules based on anarchy, and that any effort to discuss domestic, economic, or individual features of the world are reductionist in nature, meaning they provide no useful insight into how or why states act. He claimed that "reductionist theories explain international outcomes through elements and combinations of elements located at national or subnational levels. That internal forces produce external outcomes is the claim of such theories."[16] Waltz's disagreement with reductionism and preference for systems-level theory in the economics tradition virtually discounts all theories that focus their analysis on anything but the systemic level.

NEOCLASSICAL REALISM

In an effort to overcome the criticisms and shortcomings experienced by structural realism at the end of the Cold War, a new variant of realism has emerged, which is known as neoclassical realism. According to Gideon Rose, this new stream of realist thought explicitly incorporates both external and internal variables, updating and systematizing certain insights drawn from classical realist thought. Its adherents argue that the scope and ambition of a country's foreign policy is driven first and foremost by its place in the international system and specifically by its relative material power capabilities. This is why they are realist. They argue further, however, that the impact of such power capabilities on foreign policy is indirect and complex, because systemic pressures must be translated through intervening variables at the unit level. This is why they are neoclassical.[17]

Among the many reasons this school of thought has become quite popular among former classical and structural realists in the wake of the Cold War is its aversion to trying to find a universal theory of international politics. Rather than making arguments about ahistoricism and the eternal explanatory power of realists' postulates, as some like Waltz have been prone to do, neoclassical realists take a more nuanced approach to theory and its uses in explaining foreign policy behaviors of states.

There is, of course, a legitimate charge to be made at neoclassical realism that it is simply an effort to back away from positivist methodological and causal assumptions, which have traditionally been at the center of realism's supposed explanatory power. Instead of seeing self-help or power maximization tendencies as eternal and unchanging, neoclassical realists prefer to see state pursuits of their interests (and thus explaining such strategy) as contingent on historical circumstance. William Wohlforth argued that neoclassical realism begs the question, "which realist school (if any) is most useful for analysing issues of foreign policy at a given time and place?"[18] What is essential to note is that neoclassical realism is heavily concerned with the relation of theory to useful foreign policy analysis, and the interpretation that strategic outcomes and variables need to be grounded in specific historical contexts has, according to some, led to the belief that this is an approach to realism that resembles constructivist thought. This notion is supported by Rose:

Neoclassical realists occupy a middle ground between pure structural theorists and constructivists. The former implicitly accept a clear and direct link between systemic constraints and unit-level behavior; the latter deny that any objective systemic constraints exist at all, arguing instead that international reality is socially constructed and that "anarchy is what states make of it." Neoclassical realists assume that there is indeed something like an objective reality of relative power, which will, for example, have dramatic effects on the outcomes of state interactions. They do not assume, however, that states necessarily apprehend that reality accurately on a day-to-day basis.[19]

Regardless of which variant of realism one chooses to examine, the basic arguments that stem from realist theory—namely those focusing on security, power, and pursuits of self-interest in an anarchic structure—all remain heavily prevalent in the contemporary international security environment. What becomes essential for the purposes of this study is to demonstrate how theory relates to practice and how these tenets influence or help explain state foreign policy strategy. The next section is dedicated to highlighting the crucial ideas of security and sovereignty and how the realist explanation of self-interested actors in an anarchic arena describes how states are approaching the Arctic region.

SOVEREIGNTY AND AUTONOMY IN A REALIST SYSTEM

At the heart of realist analyses of interstate behavior is the concept of self-interest. According to realist scholars, the anarchic structure of the international system naturally leads to states making rational calculations about how best to survive in an environment without an overarching authority to protect them. As E. H. Carr made clear in the wake of World War I, "We must therefore reject as inadequate and misleading the attempt to base international morality on an alleged harmony of interests which identifies the interest of the whole community of nations with the interest of each individual member of it."[20] Among the main obstacles to a harmony of interests, which would lead to a more hospitable and cooperative political environment at the international level, is the constant distrust among self-interested actors. As Waltz contended, "If harmony is to exist in anarchy, not only must I be perfectly rational but I must be able to assume that everyone else is too."[21] Without such assurances of perfect rationality among states, distrust and competition are what dominate state psyche.

Though it may be a central tenet of the umbrella of realism that states are concerned with their survival in an anarchic system, there are different ways to interpret how states go about achieving such security within various realist sub-schools. In an effort to explain why states chase security differently, or at times not at all, Waltz noted,

> Beyond the survival motive, the aims of states may be endlessly varied; they may range from the ambition to conquer the world to the desire merely to be left alone. Survival is a prerequisite to achieving any goals that states may have...The survival motive is taken as a ground of action in a world where the security of states is not assured, rather than as a realistic description of the impulse that lies behind every act of state.[22]

In order to survive, realists claim states must retain their independence from other states. Independence in the Westphalian state system is marked by the external and internal recognition of a state as sovereign. As such, sovereignty plays a key role in states' perceptions of their own security. At the outset of any discussion surrounding state independence, it must be immediately qualified that there is no one way of defining what is meant by the term *sovereignty*. According to Krasner, there are a number of different ways to conceptualize sovereignty, but perhaps the largest mistake students of international relations make is to see the idea of sovereignty as accepted or fluid.[23] He argued,

> Altering the domestic political structures of other states, violating their Westphalian sovereignty, has always been an option for rulers just as invasion has been an option, but much more has

been written about war. And even less is understood about the conditions under which alternatives to conventional notions of sovereignty are viable.[24]

A common misconception is that realists see sovereignty as somehow "absolute" or inviolable. Of course, some ideas of sovereignty have been presented by critics as fixed, strong, and related to power.[25] Although these interpretations are important to comprehend realist ideas of sovereignty and its relationship to security, even the more staunch realists tend to be more pragmatic about the nature of sovereignty. For instance, Waltz himself discussed this point:

> To say that states are sovereign is not to say that they can do as they please, that they are free of others' influence, that they are able to get what they want...To say that a state is sovereign means that it decides for itself how it will cope with its internal and external problems, including whether or not to seek assistance from others and in doing so to limit its freedom by making commitments to them. States develop their own strategies, chart their own courses, make their own decisions about how to meet whatever needs they experience and whatever desires they develop.[26]

One finds especially in humanitarian intervention or human security literature debates about the meaning of sovereignty. Those in favor of non-intervention and what is sometimes referred to as Westphalian sovereignty are normally framed as operating in opposition to those favoring a more conditional conception of sovereignty, which denotes sovereignty as a responsibility rather than a legal right. The "absolutist" school is derived from the works of nineteenth-century German thinkers who presented sovereignty as an excuse for states to pursue material power aggressively.[27] Though this inaccurate idea of absolute sovereignty has little historical grounding, the more traditional or Westphalian understanding of sovereignty remains highly relevant in realist theories of autonomy and independence. Realists do not see states as being free from external interference, because this would outright reject

the history of the state system all together. Rather, in order to comprehend the realist thesis regarding sovereign autonomy, states are said
to enjoy the right of non-interference. Of course, this right has been
violated both in times of war and by other forms of intervention, but such
breaches are not done out of legal, normative, or moral purposes. Rather,
the right and practice of sovereign independence is typically violated
when other states rationally calculate they can overpower another state
in order to achieve their goals and pursue their interests. Aidan Hehir
noted,

> The significant aspect of juridical sovereignty is the fact that it
> derives from a recognition by the international community of
> a state's right to exist and thus the prohibition on *unsolicited*
> external interference. This at least imbues the state with an inter-
> national identity which brings with it the right, though not the
> guarantee, of inviolability.[28]

States, according to both historical convention and international law,
are said to enjoy the right of independence and non-intervention, which
realists see as the imperative method through which states avert conflict.
It is through distrustful and uncertain instances of interaction that states
normally enter into conflict, whether political or military, with each
other, and so by creating and maintaining a system that seeks to protect
states' rights as autonomous, states have consciously created a system
of reluctant, though passive, interaction that mitigates the effects of
anarchy.

   Though sovereignty may not be as absolute as some might suggest,
the vital idea to note is the connection between sovereignty and security in a realist world. Because states function in an anarchic system,
they can never be sure about the intentions of other states, especially
when it comes to the use of violence. Because of inherent distrust among
self-interested actors, the retention of independence and an aversion to
high levels of cooperation are two means by which states can maintain
their survival in a system in which other states will take advantage of

their lack of capabilities. Waltz noted the connection between sovereign autonomy and anarchy: "What each state does for itself is much like what all of the others are doing. They are denied the advantages that a full division of labor, political as well as economic, would provide... Rather than increased well-being, their reward is in the maintenance of their autonomy."[29] Retaining a semblance of autonomy in a system of like-minded, self-interested actors all trying to secure themselves and paying close attention to the relative gains of others is at the epicenter of realism's theory of security.

With an understanding of realist ideas of interstate autonomy, self-interest, and distrust in an anarchic arena, it becomes necessary to describe how theory is put into foreign policy practice by states on a daily basis. Perhaps no current case study better exemplifies the continued explanatory power and relevance of realism as the Arctic region, as a result of the constant use of military posturing and tactics by some states, as well as the inherent distrust that exists among states regarding the intentions of others over the region.

THE ARCTIC REGION AND REALISM IN PRACTICE

In order for a theory to have relevance at any time, it must be able to both inform policy and explain daily outcomes; otherwise, it simply highlights particular problems or issues, sometimes without empirical verification, and provides no novel suggestion for improvement, change, or forecasting ability. In the realist sense, the basic commonalities among all realist theories according to Tim Dunne and Brian Schmidt, the "three S's"—statism, survival, and self-help[30]—are mostly accepted, but these tend not to explain how states implement realist concerns or assumptions in daily foreign policy strategies. In order to comprehend the use of realism in understanding foreign policy better, one must first underscore the importance of national security.

For realism, if survival is the primary goal of all states, the policy best suited to protect a state's self-interest is national security. Schmidt argued, "The most important duty of the statesperson and the chief objective of foreign policy is to ensure the survival of the state. For realists, the fundamental national interest of all states *is* national security."[31] Naturally, there is no singular or straightforward interpretation of national security that drives all leaders in their foreign policy decisions. Perhaps the most succinct idea of how to articulate national security can be found in the works of Eric Nordlinger: "National security refers to the preservation of the country's highest values as these are purposefully threatened from abroad, primarily by other states, but by other external actors as well."[32] When formulating or implementing foreign policy, states must constantly be aware of the capabilities of other states and also determine, in a strategic calculation sense, the goals of other states. This, in some cases, leads to tension and even war, which are both central parts of realist thought.

It is impossible for states to be evaluated or explained on an individual basis—national security calculations, and strategic concerns, are all contingent upon perceptions of other units because of the interactive nature of international relations. Dan Madar contended, "Because behaviour in the international system is interactive[,] states respond to one another in a continually reciprocal process."[33] This system of extensive interaction, which is inherently distrustful, can sometimes compel states to use conflictual foreign policy strategy to achieve their goals, which has, in the past, led to the outbreak of both major and cold wars. Such policy decisions, however, must be considered very carefully because of the potential for miscalculation and the possibility that war or conflict may affect the initiating state's position in the system. According to Dale Copeland, "Hard-line strategies and crisis initiation, however, pose risks of their own: they can lead to an action-reaction spiral that brings on major war through inadvertent means. Thus the rational security-seeking state must constantly grapple with profound least-of-many-evils choices."[34] It is in the anarchic climate, with profound foreign policy decisions to make, that states pursue their interests. By examining the approaches of the eight Arctic states, most notably Russia and Canada, toward the circumpolar region, one can better appreciate how the "three S's" remain highly important from both offensive and defensive perspectives.

Though it may be difficult to conceive of a state using the Arctic as grounds for a major war, the Russian approach to the region has been of extreme importance in describing the explanatory power of realism. Since the end of the Cold War, Russia has been heavily concerned with its decline as a great power in both hard and soft power terms and has been seeking to make gains to return itself to power prominence. Gleb Yarovoy's chapter in this volume supports this view, as Yarovoy argued that Russia's dependence on the Arctic for its economic security sets the region as a high priority in its defense and foreign policies. With the post–Cold War system's most stable character attributable to American hegemony, Russia has placed high priority on soft power gains, but it also has not forgotten or ignored its military capabilities either. One of the areas that Russia has been paying very close attention to in its foreign policy strategy is the Arctic region, but why this is the case is certainly up for debate.

Idealistic thinkers tend to believe Russia is more interested in global integration than it is in national security. Caitlin Antrim, for instance, argued,

> The increased accessibility of the Arctic, with its energy and mineral resources, new fisheries, shortened sea routes and shipping along the rivers between the Arctic coast and the Eurasian heartland, is both enabling and propelling Russia to become a major maritime state. As the Arctic becomes increasingly accessible, Russia will no longer be susceptible to geographic isolation or encirclement. At the same time, these changes will lead Russia to become more closely integrated into global commercial and financial networks, to welcome foreign business partners, and to participate in international agreements and organizations that

harmonize international shipping, safety, security, and environmental regulations.[35]

Russia's integration into the global economy is certainly a likely consequence of its Arctic extension, but such perspectives fail to account for the true nature of what Russia's interests are.

In many ways, Russia is operating according to the offensive realist thesis with its recent actions in the High North.[36] Offensive realism claims that "the ultimate goal of the great powers...is to gain hegemony, because that is the best guarantor of survival."[37] Global hegemony, in almost any form, is a virtual impossibility, and therefore offensive realists argue that great powers hope to become a regional hegemon. Imperative to note, however, is that "states that gain regional hegemony have a further aim: they seek to prevent great powers in other geographical regions from duplicating their feat. Regional hegemons do not want peer competitors."[38] When discussing regional hegemons in the modern international system, one can point to the role of Brazil in South America, South Africa and Nigeria in Africa, Iran and Israel in the Middle East, and the United States in North America. Russia retains its role as hegemon in Eastern Europe and arguably is becoming the hegemon in the Arctic region precisely because the developmental, environmental, and scientific aspects of Arctic debates overlook or omit the increasing security and military dynamics.

Since 2005, Russia has used the circumpolar region as a means of demonstrating its continued status as a great power, particularly in the hard, military sense. Examples such as planting a Russian Federation flag on the seabed beneath the North Pole, test-firing long-range missiles, resuming bomber overflights, and sailing two nuclear subs through the region and then proceeding down the eastern seaboards of both Canada and the United States obviously bring the liberal or idealist perspective into serious question. According to the findings of the Carnegie Endowment Arctic Climate Change and Security Policy Conference,

Russia's activities could be disruptive to the region if its recent focus on politics and territorial claims retains priority over increased attention to science and international cooperation. The driving factors may be Russian prestige, identity, and image, which converge on borders and territorial claims. For Russia, sovereignty in the Arctic is a "hard" security issue. Russian military interests center on the Kola Peninsula, home to the Russian nuclear submarine fleet, and on rebuilding the Northern fleet.[39]

Russia's offensive posturing clearly signifies two things: First, the Arctic region falls directly within Russia's national security calculations and it requires at least part of the region to maintain its security interests. Second, offensive posturing is an obvious demonstration that Russia is seeking to be the regional hegemon in the Arctic, especially in a time when the United States has virtually no hope of being able to extend itself in the region after its prolonged military campaigns in Afghanistan, in Iraq, and more recently in Libya. By defining the Arctic as both essential to its survival and as a possible area of power maximization, Russian foreign policy in the Arctic can be seen as very much in line with the offensive realist thesis.

Russia is not alone in employing more offensive strategies toward Arctic pursuits. Offensive realist behavior is heavily dependent upon a state having the capabilities to extend its sphere of influence and to project that influence into a region such as the High North. As such, offensive posturing is far more a tool of great powers than it is of lesser powers in the international system. This certainly helps to explain why states such as the United States, China, India, and Great Britain, along with Russia, would pursue their Arctic interests quite differently than middle or minor powers. China, for instance, has aggressively begun to make its Arctic interests known by its voyages through the region, by its quest for observer status at the Arctic Council, and in the massive influx of resources into Arctic technology. As Hong and Dey Nuttall argued in this volume, India is following suit, and while neither China nor India have sovereignty or territorial concerns associated with the Arctic, their posturing is evidently out of pure economic self-interest, though both states have made it known they would seek to protect those interests by military means if necessary.

Middle and minor powers have no choice but to adopt different strategies than great powers, primarily because they lack the capabilities to enforce their claims on their own. Often, these states are keen to embed themselves in international institutions as a way of overcoming their lack of independent capabilities and instead gaining the advantage of numbers and alliances with larger powers through collective security and trade agreements. This has traditionally helped to explain the propensity of states so willingly entering into organizations such as the United Nations, NATO, and in the circumpolar case, the Arctic Council.

The majority of Arctic states are not great powers. Russia and the United States are notable exceptions, but the others would be classified as either middle or minor powers when assessing their national capabilities. Therefore, it becomes important to ponder how states such as Denmark, Norway, Sweden, or Iceland would have any hope of protecting their interests if Russia or America employed offensive strategies aimed at challenging Arctic claims of lesser states. To better comprehend the approach of these other states, one can find logic in the school of defensive realism.

Lesser powers approach the Arctic quite differently than great powers but continue to speak to the power of realist ideas in foreign policy creation. Among the best examples of middle-power strategy toward the Arctic is Canada. Rather than overt offensive posturing, Canada's approach to asserting its Arctic sovereignty falls more into a defensive realist posture than it does offensive.[40] Schmidt effectively summarized the defensive realist position:

> The international system, according to defensive realists, only provides incentives for moderate behaviour, and expansionistic

> policies to achieve security are generally not required because the international system is basically benign. In order for a state to ensure its own survival in the self-help, anarchical environment therefore, a prudent foreign policy is one that seeks only an appropriate, rather than a preponderant amount of power.[41]

Though most scholars would not see Canada as being capable of attaining a preponderance of power, even on a regional scale because of its historically middle-power status, the defensive strategy of Canadian Arctic policy indicates a more nuanced approach to securing its Arctic sovereignty, though it is still framed as a national security issue. One of the key features that compels a defensive realist analysis of Canada's Arctic strategy is its limited capabilities. As a middle power, Canada is militarily incapable of extending its sphere of influence or aggressively pursuing its claims in the Arctic if tensions ever lead to physical confrontation. It is irrational for Canada to use an offensive strategy in its sovereign claims, and thus it has elected to pursue a defensive strategy aimed at protecting its claims through military means that strengthen domestic security without acquiring means for offensive posturing.

Since his election in 2006, Prime Minister Stephen Harper has made the Arctic a preeminent aspect of his foreign policy. In his chapter later in the volume, Rob Huebert highlighted the historical policy progression of Arctic affairs in Canadian defense and foreign policies, and the geopolitical drivers behind an increased level of attention. While framing it as an indispensable geographical area for Canada's development and identity, Harper's government has been equally vocal about the circumpolar region being a matter of Canada's national security and has approved the spending of new military and coast guard resources aimed at protecting Canada's sovereign claims from more aggressive states. At no time was this more obvious than after the Danish navy placed a national flag on Hans Island, a piece of contested territory in the High North. In response to this, and other offensive actions by Russia in particular, the Canadian government issued its *Statement on Canada's Arctic Foreign Policy* in 2010, which states,

Three priority areas that Canada will pursue in the Arctic are: seeking to resolve boundary issues; securing international recognition for the full extent of our extended continental shelf wherein we can exercise our sovereign rights over the resources of the seabed and subsoil; and addressing Arctic governance and related emerging issues, such as public safety.[42]

Included in Canada's efforts to protect its sovereignty in the Arctic is a clear defensive strategy, articulated most clearly in 2008 with the Canada First Defence Strategy, which includes provisions for the use of the Canadian Forces to establish, protect, and defend national security interests if threatened. Further, the Canada First Defence Strategy is entirely predicated on the idea of defending sovereign territory and national security and not on extending its claims at the risk of enemy engagement. Therefore, Canada has not embarked upon offensive strategic behavior in the Arctic and maintains a more defensive posture than anything else. Interesting to note, however, is that while the Canadian government has made the Arctic a priority for social, environmental, cultural, and political reasons, the interest of national security is receiving far more attention and funds than any other priority area.

Perhaps no better example of Canada's defensive posturing can be found than in its reactions to recent Russian aggression. Beyond its claims to areas of the High North, Russia has announced its intention to permanently station an army brigade in the North, its release of the new Borei-class nuclear submarines, and its testing of new intercontinental ballistic missiles, all aimed at demonstrating its serious intentions to protect Russian sovereignty.[43] Even more noteworthy is the fact that Russian defense minister Anatoly Serdykov made these announcements on July 1, 2011, Canada's national independence day. It is no coincidence that the Russians are offensively posturing in the Arctic against Canada, given that Canada represents the largest territorial rival in the race for the North, though Russia also knows all too well that Canada is unable to assert itself. In response, Canada has shown virtually no military response to counter Russian aggression but instead has reasserted its desire to strengthen domestic security measures against potential enemy hostility.

Throughout this volume, contributors highlight the fact that Arctic states such as Norway, Sweden, and Denmark have dedicated considerable national resources to bolstering their military and technological capabilities focused on Arctic interests. As middle or minor powers, these states have little choice but to increase their domestic capabilities, particularly as the Russians appear more and more aggressive in their rhetoric and action. Further, it is really the less powerful Arctic states emphasizing the work of the Arctic Council and the United Nations based on their collective need for diplomacy and multilateralism, without which they would be incapable of asserting their interests unilaterally. Lesser powers are still driven by self-interest and concerns relating to national security, but they are forced to employ strategies consistent with their ranking in the international system. In all, the behavior of great powers and lesser powers toward the Arctic region are effectively explained by realism's various sub-schools of thought.

CONCLUSION

This chapter has attempted to demonstrate the continued explanatory power of realism in broad outcomes in the international system, but in particular, in how states are approaching the issue of Arctic sovereignty and security. Regardless of which state or interstate organization has any Arctic interests whatsoever, the notions of national security and Westphalian sovereignty are vital components in any strategic calculation. Whether one is looking at great powers, middle powers, or smaller states with virtually no capabilities in the hard, military sense, the issue of sphere of influence cannot be detached from assessing or explaining how states have been pursuing, and will continue to pursue, circumpolar interests.

The contributors to this volume in sections 2 and 3 focus on national or institutional policies and strategies, but it is vital for readers to remind themselves of the theoretical and ideological undertones inherent in the writings of these chapters. Themes such as self-interest, national security, and alliance formation are all prevalent throughout the volume, and one must continue to bear in mind *why* these strategies and attitudes would prevail.

Realism, as an umbrella term, remains the most important and effective theory in the field of international relations for both explaining the motivations behind state behavior and forecasting potential outcomes in the future. It is evident that there are a multiplicity of issue areas included in the debate over Arctic sovereignty, which include more social, environmental, human, and political concerns. Though all are worthy of consideration, no matter compels state action more than maintaining national security in an anarchic international system. It is truly not difficult to see evidence of this type of thinking in state foreign policy based on the many hard-power-based stances being demonstrated by Arctic-interested states.

Like most other theories of international relations, realism has its flaws, its critics, and its limits. Despite accusations to the contrary, realism has never purported to be an all-encompassing method of describing interstate behavior in all circumstances. Wohlforth supported this argument by claiming that "realism is not now and never has been a monolithic and universal 'theory of international politics.' It has always been diverse, even its grandest theories contingent in scope if not name."[44] Under the broad descriptor of *realism* exist many subtheories, all aiming to explain different instances of interstate behavior, conflict, and reluctant cooperation. Though not perfect, the realist school of thought and its "three S's"—statism, survival, and self-help—cannot be excluded from any solid comprehension of the race for the High North.

NOTES

1. It is noted here that Krasner's idea of Westphalian sovereignty would take exception to this definition. See Stephen Krasner, *Sovereignty: Organized Hypocrisy* (Princeton: Princeton University Press, 1999).
2. Stephen Krasner, "The Accomplishments of International Political Economy," in *International Theory: Positivism and Beyond*, ed. Steve Smith, Ken Booth, and Marysia Zalewski (Cambridge: Cambridge University Press, 1996), 115.
3. See ibid., 114–115.
4. Robert Art and Robert Jervis, "Anarchy and Its Consequences," in *International Politics: Enduring Concepts and Contemporary Issues* (New York: Pearson Education, 2007), 2.
5. Kenneth Waltz, *Man, the State and War* (New York: Columbia University Press, 1959), 160.
6. Martha Finnemore, *National Interests in International Society* (Ithaca, NY: Cornell University Press, 1996), 1.
7. E. H. Carr, *The Twenty Years' Crisis* (New York: Palgrave Macmillan, 2001), 151.
8. Hans Morgenthau, *Politics Among Nations* (New York: McGraw-Hill, 2006), 37.
9. William Wohlforth, "Realism," in *The Oxford Handbook of International Relations*, ed. Christian Reus-Smit and Duncan Snidal (Oxford: Oxford University Press, 2008), 135.
10. For instance, see the works of Thomas Hobbes and Jean-Jacques Rousseau.
11. For instance, see the works of Thucydides and Niccolo Machiavelli.
12. Morgenthau, *Politics Among Nations*, 3.
13. John Mearsheimer, *The Tragedy of Great Power Politics* (New York: W. W. Norton & Company, 2001), 30–31.
14. Ibid., 32.
15. For more on why Waltz sees Lakatos as being relevant to IR, see Kenneth Waltz, "Foreword: Thoughts about Assaying Theories," in *Progress in International Relations Theory*, ed. Colin Elman and Miriam Fendius Elman (Cambridge, MA: MIT Press, 2003), vii–xii.
16. Kenneth Waltz, *Theory of International Politics* (New York: McGraw-Hill, 1979), 60.

17. Gideon Rose, "Neoclassical Realism and Theories of Foreign Policy," *World Politics* 51, no. 1 (1998): 146.
18. William Wohlforth, "Realism and Foreign Policy," in *Foreign Policy: Theories, Actors, Cases*, ed. Steve Smith, Amelia Hadfield, and Tim Dunne (Oxford: Oxford University Press, 2008), 35.
19. Rose, "Neoclassical Realism," 152.
20. Carr, *Twenty Years' Crisis*, 57.
21. Waltz, *Man, the State and War*, 169.
22. Waltz, *Theory of International Politics*, 91.
23. See Krasner, *Sovereignty*.
24. Stephen Krasner, "Problematic Sovereignty," in *Problematic Sovereignty*, ed. Stephen Krasner (New York: Columbia University Press, 2001), 20.
25. See for instance Jon Holbrook's discussion of sovereignty in "Humanitarian Intervention and the Recasting of International Law," in *Rethinking Human Rights*, ed. David Chandler (Houndmills, UK: Palgrave Macmillan, 2002), 136–156.
26. Waltz, *Theory of International Politics*, 96.
27. See Alex Bellamy, *The Responsibility to Protect* (Cambridge: Polity Press, 2009), 12–13. For more on the question and nature of Westphalian sovereignty, see P. A. Hayman and John Williams, "Westphalian Sovereignty: Rights, Intervention, Meaning and Context," *Global Society* 20, no. 4 (October 2006): 521–541.
28. Aidan Hehir, *Humanitarian Intervention after Kosovo: Iraq, Darfur and the Record of Global Civil Society* (Houndmills, UK: Palgrave Macmillan, 2008), 25.
29. Waltz, *Theory of International Politics*, 107.
30. Tim Dunne and Brian Schmidt, "Realism," in *The Globalization of World Politics*, ed. John Baylis, Steve Smith, and Patricia Owens (Oxford: Oxford University Press, 2005), 172.
31. Brian Schmidt, "The Primacy of National Security," in *Foreign Policy: Theories, Actors, Cases*, ed. Steve Smith, Amelia Hadfield, and Tim Dunne (Oxford: Oxford University Press, 2008), 159.
32. Eric Nordlinger, *Isolationism Reconfigured* (Princeton: Princeton University Press, 1995), 10.
33. Daniel Madar, "Fate, Will and Forecasting," *International Journal* 62 (Spring 2007): 281.
34. Dale Copeland, *The Origins of Major War* (Ithaca, NY: Cornell University Press, 2000), 36.

35. Caitlin Antrim, "The New Maritime Arctic: Geopolitics and the Russian Arctic in the 21st Century," *Russia in Global Affairs*, October 15, 2010, http://eng.globalaffairs.ru/number/The-New-Maritime-Arctic-15000.

36. For the definitive work on offensive realism, see Mearsheimer, *Tragedy of Great Power Politics*.

37. John Mearsheimer, "Structural Realism," in *International Relations Theories: Discipline and Diversity*, ed. Tim Dunne, Milja Kurki, and Steve Smith (Oxford: Oxford University Press, 2007), 83.

38. Ibid.

39. Kenneth Yalowitz, James Collins, and Ross Virginia, *Arctic Climate Change and Security Policy Conference: Final Report and Findings* (Washington, DC: Carnegie Endowment for International Peace, 2008), 15.

40. For the definitive work on defensive realist thought, see Waltz, *Theory of International Politics*.

41. Schmidt, "Primacy of National Security," 160.

42. Ministry of Foreign Affairs and International Trade, *Statement on Canada's Arctic Foreign Policy*, last modified June 3, 2013, http://www.international. gc.ca/arctic-arctique/arctic_policy-canada-politique_arctique.aspx?lang= eng.

43. Vladimir Radyuhin, "Russia Sets Up Arctic Forces," *Hindu*, July 1, 2011.

44. Wohlforth, "Realism," 145.

CHAPTER 2

INTERNATIONAL INSTITUTIONS AND STATE SOVEREIGNTY

FROZEN IN TIME OR WARMING TO CHANGE

Tom Keating

INTRODUCTION

Liberal approaches to international relations emphasize the possibility and desirability of cooperation among states to facilitate a more prosperous and peaceful global order. These liberal approaches rest on both empirical and theoretical claims. The empirical claims look to the increased prevalence of democratic governments, cross-border economic transactions, and intergovernmental organizations. The theoretical claims draw from liberal philosophers who highlight the central place of individuals and a belief in the good life in the realm of politics. Some contemporary liberal approaches to international relations adopt realist assumptions on the nature of anarchy, the central role of states, and their pursuit of self-interest and identify patterns of cooperation that may result in what has been labeled neoliberal institutionalism. Although many of these liberal approaches have embedded within them

normative assumptions of a more peaceful and more prosperous community of nations and people, they have often been criticized for their
failure to account for the realities of interstate relations in the importance of power, the privileged position of sovereign states pursuing
national interests rooted in security considerations, the shallowness and
limited efficacy of international law, and the persistence of empirical
conditions of poverty and conflict. These criticisms point to the concentration of economic and political power, the prevalence of sovereign
states enmeshed in self-interested practices that bring them into competition and conflict with one another, and serious and ongoing problems
that beset the global community and seem to refute claims of progress
toward a more peaceful and prosperous planet. Such observations are
also evident in many of the debates surrounding the future of the international relations of the Arctic region. The increased attention to the
potential for competitive resource acquisition in the Arctic has concomi-
tantly encouraged an emphasis on power politics as states in the region
scramble to assert jurisdictional claims while enhancing their coercive
capabilities with which to enforce these claims.

Alongside and in contrast to these realist indicators, however, a
number of more cooperative measures can be seen, measures that speak
to the relevance of liberal institutionalist approaches focused as they
are on multilateral diplomacy, international law, institutions, and the
more human-centric aspects of security and development. The Arctic,
like many other regions of the globe, has witnessed a number of these
measures and has also been subject to increased regulation through
diplomacy, international institutions, and international law as a variety
of individuals and groups (including governments) with interests in the
region that encompass commercial, environmental, and social affairs
seek to manage political and environmental change without recourse to
force or its threatened use. Realist critiques rest on the assumption that
international law and institutions represent a "false promise" in that as
issues become more important or contested, the room for and relevance

of these institutions and liberal approaches diminishes.[1] Such a position
may underestimate the degree to which global politics have shifted.

> The world is full of international institutions. How much and
> how adequately these institutions of international governance
> tame anarchy is open to question, but the world is witnessing
> an increase in supranational governance, created by states and
> in which states increasingly live. Understanding and explaining
> international politics (and even many areas of national politics)
> increasingly requires incorporating the role of international insti-
> tutions.[2]

Whereas interstate conflicts tend to demarcate politics at the global
level for many observers, interactions across national borders have never
been more widely or thoroughly regulated as they are at the start of
the twenty-first century. These regulations continue to proliferate into
more areas of political, economic, and social life, often spilling over into
the domestic affairs of sovereign states. As a result one would be hard-
pressed to describe the contemporary international system as anarchic
or sovereign states as able to escape from the regulating effects of institutions and law. Instead these states are embedded in layers of regulations that enmesh them in a variety of institutional commitments while
international laws increasingly define their rights and responsibilities.
Although it is true that such commitments are often difficult to enforce,
when states are adamant about breaching them, they are more often
respected than violated, with compliance resulting from a combination
of self-interest and respect for the legitimacy of international agreements among other factors.[3] To a degree this has always been true, but
the scope and effects of these institutional and legal practices are more
pervasive and influential in the contemporary period than in the past.
They encompass more areas of economic, environmental, and political
practice and intrude more directly into areas previously considered the
domestic affairs of sovereign states. In this chapter I explore some of
these liberal approaches to international relations and the central place
of international institutions and international law that are a part of such

views. This chapter also briefly considers their special relevance to many of the issues that surround relations in the Arctic region and how institutions and law hold the potential to temper interstate conflict in the region.

LIBERALISM AND INTERNATIONAL RELATIONS

Liberal approaches to international relations find their inspiration from different sources. Michael Doyle provided a useful summary of these sources and identified three primary ones: the individual rights ideas of John Locke; the commercial relations themes that are prominent in the writings of Adam Smith; and the seventeenth-century writings of Immanuel Kant on the sources of perpetual peace. According to Doyle, "Despite their many differences, Liberals, it is said, protect human rights, support international cooperation, profess international law, and support international norms."[4] Among the first liberals, Locke viewed government's role as rather minimal. "Government for Locke meant the making of laws (to protect civil liberties and property), the execution of those laws, and the defense of the commonwealth against foreign threats."[5] Individuals looked to governments to serve and protect their liberties and property. They also invested the state with the "federative power" to oversee foreign relations and protect those same liberties and property from foreign threats. Locke recognized that the international realm was not governed by the same degree of protection as that afforded to domestic society, but drawing on the analogy with the domestic realm he saw the value in trying to replicate law and institutions as a way of dealing with the inconveniences that would occur in the international arena.[6] Kant emphasized four characteristics for maintaining peaceful relations among states: republican states, free trade, universal hospitality, and the rule of law.[7] Since then liberals have returned to one or more of these characteristics in identifying and advancing practices that serve a peaceful and prosperous international order. The origins of liberal views on international relations are derived from concerns about the occurrence of conflict and the desirability of peaceful relations among states. Operating from different assumptions, liberal writers have emphasized different paths—liberating individuals and enabling them to control policy or engage in unfettered trade or adopt cosmopolitan identities have all been cited by liberals as potential paths to peace and prosperity. These normative concerns have been influential in different historical periods and in the origins of the modern study of international relations after World War I.[8]

Despite these normative origins, recent work of liberal international theorists draws from empirical data and calls attention to the changes that have occurred in international relations over time. Fundamentally liberals take the position that the past is not doomed to be repeated and that states and peoples can and do change and will likely continue to do so. In adopting this non-cyclical view of history, liberals distinguish themselves from many realists, who take the position that international relations are, have been, and always will be in a recurring pattern of interstate conflict as states pursue power in a competitive anarchic international system. Instead, liberals have identified a number of areas where international relations have changed, noting especially the growth of international institutions, international law, economic transactions, and democratic states.

Some liberal writers look upon the late twentieth century as a time of change and development of an international order increasingly populated by liberal values and practices.[9] Liberals have had second thoughts about whether such practices have transformed international politics, but they do cite a noteworthy shift in many practices.[10] Bruce Russett, in a survey of liberal views, called attention to the significant transformations that have taken place in three of these arenas—democratic governance, international trade, and intergovernmental organizations.[11] Russett noted that there has been a proliferation in each of these areas in the twentieth century and particularly since the 1990s. He argued that these developments distinguish the contemporary period from previous

eras in international politics and help to account for the decline in violent
conflict between sovereign states in the late twentieth century even
as the number of sovereign states has increased. Russett pointed out
how each of these developments has helped to shape international relations in a manner that reduces the likelihood that states will resort to
force in resolving differences. Democratic governments, for instance,
are considered to be more likely to refrain from using violent force
to resolve disputes with other democratic governments, though they
often use it against non-liberal regimes. Increased international trade,
economic interdependence, and resulting processes of globalization are
argued to increase the material incentives for cooperation. International
institutions, for their part, provide a number of functions that mitigate
conflict, offering mediation, shaping and reinforcing norms and narra-
tives of cooperation, and reducing uncertainties and transaction costs by
providing information and a forum for iterative exchanges among states.

The advancement of these liberal practices has not been a linear one,
nor is their permanence by any means guaranteed. John Ikenberry,
drawing from historical practices, argued that there have been different
phases in the liberal world order over the last century, suggesting that
the process of cooperation, though progressive, is by no means linear or
even certain given that it has been subjected to conditions that have both
facilitated and impeded the development of a liberal order.[12] Ikenberry
identified five dimensions of liberal international orders, including their
scope, the degree of sovereign independence, the degree of sovereign
equality, the role of the rule of law, and the extent of the policy domain
in which they operated. Based on these dimensions, he noted three
relatively distinctive phases of liberal order in the twentieth century.
The first he dated to the Wilsonian initiative at the end of World War
I that privileged self-determination as the basis for state sovereignty
and a more peaceful international order. A second phase entered after
World War II based on economic liberalism and international institutions, though in this instance the scope of the liberal order is not
universal but limited by the ideological divisions between East and West.

A third phase demarcates the post–Cold War period since the 1990s when liberal ideas and practices have been advanced in a much more comprehensive and assertive manner. The effort to distinguish these phases of liberalism is useful in demonstrating the rich variety of liberal approaches to international relations and how this variety has played out in historical developments. Foremost among these developments are the themes Russett discussed—democratic governments, economic and other forms of interdependence, and the extent of institutionalization at the international level.

Liberal scholars in noting these developments have called attention to the greater institutionalization of sources of authority created by states but also superseding them. David Lake, for example, described the characteristics of these authorities and the manner in which governance has developed to manage interstate relations cooperatively. The characteristics highlighted by Lake are "zones of peace and commerce among states subject to a common authority; binding rules and compliance from duty or obligation; coercion used legitimately to create order and discipline wayward states; authorities, including states, limiting their power to preserve their legitimacy; social actors defending private and supranational authorities from state encroachment."[13] The proliferation of institutions in the Arctic region demonstrates the relevance of such characteristics as many states bordering the region have sought to initiate and sustain cooperative practices. Initially encouraged by the shift in the foreign policy of the Soviet Union under Gorbachev, a number of institutions were developed in the 1990s, including the International Arctic Science Committee (1990), the Arctic Environmental Protection Strategy (1991), the subregional Council of the Baltic Sea States (1992) and the Barents-Euro Arctic Region (1993), and the Arctic Council (1996). These institutions were designed to facilitate cooperation and complementary practices in a wide variety of areas, encouraging a zone of peace and cooperation alongside the development of common rules governing economic and other activity. In introducing the role of nonstate actors, Lake provided a reminder of the increased prevalence and prominence of such actors in international relations. Craig Murphy has also discussed how private actors have played an influential role in the development of international institutions since the mid-nineteenth century.[14] Their return to prominence in the contemporary period can be seen in these Arctic institutions because scientists and environmentalists, among others in these different countries, were among the first and strongest proponents of more institutionalized cooperation.[15] This experience reinforces liberal views on the importance of such actors both within states and beyond states in a variety of transnational exchanges.

These views also highlight trends within international relations countering the common assumption that conflict among states is rife and that there are few alternatives to a constant preparation for such conflict and a balance of power to prevent the outbreak of war. For liberals, states are not motivated purely or even primarily by security considerations but, in response to demands from a variety of domestic interests, pursue material and non-material interests (economic, social, and cultural), as well as security, and often forego the accumulation of hard-power assets in order to achieve these non-security objectives. States are extensively engaged in cooperative behavior with other states in the pursuit of these interests and willingly cede sovereign authority to international law and organizations in their efforts to secure these interests. Cooperation is not impeded by conditions of anarchy, though it takes different forms usually involving contracts (treaties) between states. The history of maritime relations has been extensively populated by such arrangements, as have commercial and environmental relations, all very relevant for the sorts of activities prevalent in the Arctic region. Liberals' support for a more cooperative approach to global relations is also based on the recognition of the important role that international institutions and international law play in managing and regulating interstate relations. The proliferation of these institutions at the regional and global levels is an indication of the extent to which states have turned to such mechanisms to conduct their relations. This is another side to the history of global politics than the one commonly highlighted in the media and in many historical accounts, a side that is marked by a vast array of international agreements, extensive cooperative behavior, and a network of laws and institutions that connect governments and private actors in a multiplicity of different arenas.

A second group of scholars working more from a theoretical position than an empirical one has also challenged arguments on the persistence of conflict and the inherent limits to cooperation among states. Neoliberal institutionalists adopt a different approach in developing their ideas on institutional cooperation among sovereign states, one that draws directly and explicitly from realist assumptions of interstate relations in an anarchic international system. Foremost among these scholars has been Robert Keohane, whose work *After Hegemony* stands as the centerpiece for such theorizing.[16] Keohane adopted core realist assumptions that identify states as the principal actors in an anarchic international system pursuing self-interests. Drawing from public choice and game theory, Keohane argued that cooperation among these states is possible and often likely. Neoliberal institutionalists do not argue that cooperation is automatic, that it will persist, or that it will progress into all areas. They argue, however, that it can and does occur, that it is rooted in self-interest, that it occurs at times because of a stable hegemon, but that it can also occur *after hegemony*, when there is not a dominant power to absorb the costs and distribute the benefits. Part of this explanation lies in the role that international institutions play in facilitating and reinforcing cooperation, in part by assuming some of the roles that hegemons serve, such as providing information and assistance as well as removing uncertainty around future interactions. Neoliberal institutionalism emphasizes the relevance of a rules-based international order and argues that these rules can be informal, such as accepted customary practice, or rooted in more formal treaty-based institutions.[17] These regimes have been defined as "sets of implicit or explicit principles, norms, rules, and decision-making procedures around which actors' expectations converge in a given area of international relations."[18] For neoliberal institutionalists, international institutions help to remove the uncertainty and lack of information that plagues the classical prisoner's dilemma game, often used by structural realists to symbolize interstate relations under conditions of anarchy. The classical prisoner's dilemma game locks the participants into non-cooperative solutions because of the lack of trust, information, and communication. Institutions, it is said, help to overcome each of these. They also provide some guarantees of future interactions that render past behaviors important in shaping future relations. "The point to be made, however, is that relative gains notwithstanding, there is a great deal of institutionalized cooperation and much of it having quite differential payoffs. The international hierarchy of power and wealth has changed over the last half-century, and those shifts have occurred in part because of, and certainly in the context of, the workings of international institutions."[19]

Institutionalized cooperation in the Arctic was delayed by Cold War politics but has developed since the 1990s, most notably with the establishment of the Arctic Council in 1996 following on a Canadian initiative. The United States' approach to the Arctic Council is an interesting illustration of how institutions can help shape a state's practice given that initially the U.S. government delayed giving support for the council and sought successfully to limit its role in security matters. Subsequently the United States has seen greater value in working with the council and "began contributing actively to programmes under it, and has assumed leading roles in many Council activities."[20] Indeed, somewhat ironically, in 2010 it was U.S. Secretary of State Hillary Clinton who lectured Canadians on the importance of inclusive multilateralism and institutional cooperation in the Arctic region.[21]

LAW, INSTITUTIONS, AND INTERNATIONAL GOVERNANCE

The role of law and institutions and the very idea of governance at the global level present a challenge for observers of international politics, yet the reality is that international law and institutions are an integral

part of contemporary international politics and provide a key component of governance at the regional and global levels. "While it may
be difficult analytically to assess the impact of institutions, it remains
striking that states use institutions to arrive at outcomes they want."[22]
Global governance is both evident and significant in many areas of international politics at present, the Arctic among them.[23] There are thousands of agreements that regulate how states interact with each other.
Within the liberal internationalist perspective, sovereignty continues to
play a central role, but sovereignty and sovereignty claims need to be
understood in this context of an array of institutions and law that effectively serve to limit the autonomy of states while investing them with
a wide variety of both rights and responsibilities. "Perhaps the most
important development is that institutions have become more intrusive
and constraining over time. To deal with the challenges that have led
them to construct international institutions in the first place, states have
demanded and accepted unprecedented intrusiveness in their domestic
affairs."[24]

The expansion of international law has been one of the more remarkable developments of the late twentieth and early twenty-first centuries.
The proliferation of treaties and conventions in such areas as trade,
human rights, and the environment has been unprecedented, as has the
growth in transnational legal activity by citizens and private commercial interests. International law has developed to the point where it
touches on many aspects of life in all states. Indeed international law is
no longer restricted to states and now intrudes into areas of domestic
economic, political, and social life, often in ways unanticipated by local
authorities and unknown by local citizens. "The areas of heretofore
domestic law into which such treaties have ventured are many. Human
rights, trade, environmental protection, labour standards, crime, migration, taxation—these are only the most obvious examples. Such inward
looking treaties have inevitably influenced domestic legal developments,
whether by prompting the adoption of new legislation or by other,
more subtle means."[25] There has also been a proliferation in the groups,

practices, and forums in which international law is designed, administered, and enforced. Anne-Marie Slaughter discussed this more globalized approach to justice in an essay entitled "Judicial Globalization."[26]
Slaughter took note of the extensive amount of cross-border interaction that surrounds legal affairs in the contemporary global order. "Judicial globalization...describes a much more diverse and messy process of
judicial interaction across, above, and below borders, exchanging ideas
and cooperating in cases involving national as much as international
law."[27] She went on to argue that this increasingly intermeshed globe
"requires recognition of participation in a common judicial enterprise,
independent of the content and constraints of specific national and international legal systems."[28] This reflects an active attempt on the part of
some actors, including many at the governmental and nongovernmental
levels, to foster a more interconnected community of legal experts and
legal practice.

The proliferation of international law and institutions has raised a
number of issues, four of which will be discussed here. The first that
has been raised by critical observers from both the left and right of the
political spectrum is that international law is constraining the autonomy
of sovereign states and national governments. There is considerable
evidence that international law and institutions have sought to impose
constraints on the domestic practices of states and in a particularly intrusive way, especially in the economic realm. The pervasiveness of international law has reached the point where it has become a major political issue even within the more powerful states in the society of states,
as evident in the extensive debates in the United States and the reaction of what Peter Spiro has referred to as the "new sovereigntists" who
argued for American exceptionalism on the grounds that international
treaties were undermining the authority of the U.S. Constitution and
that the latter must prevail. These "new sovereigntists" were evidence
of the changed circumstances in which the United States and other
states found themselves at the turn of the millennium as international
law, including those involving human rights, challenges the authority

of national constitutions. This is not a completely unforeseen development. Lester Pearson, former Canadian foreign and prime minister, once acknowledged the likely need for national sovereignty to yield to international-level authority if peace and order were to prevail. "We may find it desirable to make adjustments in respect of some aspects of legal sovereignty in return for larger advantages. Such concessions do not, however, worry me. If we are to remove the recurring anarchy of war, all states will have to abandon some of the attitudes of sovereignty in the interest of larger associations of nations."[29] It is important to recognize the development of international law in the economic area and the extent to which such law has supported the global economy, where private investors can move their money around the globe from their home computers, consumer products can be found worldwide, and economic decisions made in one corner of the globe reverberate in factories and homes on the other side of the world, affecting jobs, incomes, the local environment, and individual lives. Whether one considers this global economy good or bad, it is clear that a considerable body of international law has helped to create it. Stephen Clarkson and Stepan Wood have raised concerns over the increased scope and efficacy of international law in this area. "The steady accumulation of intergovernmental agreements and organizations has constituted a complex but substantial world order, which we can best conceptualize as comprising an emerging global constitution."[30] Many of the arguments and debates around constitutionalism refer to developments in the global economic order and the increased intrusiveness and effectiveness of global and regional economic institutions that promote norms and rules, impose obligations on governments, define rights of private actors, and establish processes and adjudication measures that supersede the authority of national governments.

The alleged autonomy of these institutions has given rise to considerable anxiety on the part of both proponents of and opponents to the form of global governance that these institutions represent. The argument is that some institutions have a degree of independence from national governments and from the pressures of various global social movements and are thus isolated from political influences, much like a domestic constitution acts as an independent source of power from domestic politics. The argument for a form of constitutionalism rests on the assumption that these institutions and the international legal regime they represent carry influence over national governments. Proponents who favor such a regime see it as a way of ensuring that no state has the ability to undermine the principles and rules governing international commerce. They maintain that for this liberal trading order to work, politics should not interfere with the application of rules. Constitutionalism represents a way of doing this. Opponents of the policies and practices of these institutions take a more negative view of constitutionalism and see it as a way of isolating the institution from political pressures. In their view, these arrangements protect the institution's ideological agenda from political pressures that might seek to reform it. The institutions and the rules they uphold thus act as an effective barrier to domestic or transnational pressures for a change in policy.

The constitutionalist reading of international institutions presents both a normative and an empirical problem. On the empirical side the problem is that politics can permeate existing institutions, if and when the political pressure is sufficient. One sees this, for example, in the World Trade Organization (WTO), where negotiations have been disrupted by the numerous street demonstrations that have constrained negotiators, but more importantly by the political pressure arising from national governments such as Brazil, India, and China, which are resisting the pressures for pursuing negotiations designed primarily to serve the economic interests of the more powerful members of the global economy. The normative problem concerns the value of isolating such policies from political debate and discourse. Not only are such efforts likely to be ineffective for the reason just stated, but also the attempt to do so is likely to generate more opposition and conflict.

Nowhere have these concessions of sovereignty been more pervasive than in Europe through the gradual evolution of the European Union (EU). The EU exemplifies the "constitutional pluralism" that has resulted as national sovereignty, national institutions, and national law have yielded to their "international" counterparts.

Despite the considerable attention that has been given to constitutionalism, there are some who maintain that this is an inappropriate label for what exists at present in most areas of international law and most regions of the world. Although the EU might be the most exaggerated form of such a transformation, observers have mixed feelings as to whether something similar is emerging in other regional and global economic institutions or in other policy arenas. For example, European-wide environmental laws could end up setting the regulatory environment that some Arctic states operate under, but it would not provide an encompassing framework for all contiguous states in the region because the United States, Russia, and Canada continue to rely largely on domestic law. Existing international law that supersedes domestic law has tended to be most well developed in the commercial arena and least well developed in environmental and human security arenas, leaving these Arctic areas outside of such a robust international legal framework.

A second issue of note is what Christian Reus-Smit has referred to as the "cosmopolitanisation" of international law: "A distinctive feature of the contemporary legal order is the progressive 'cosmopolitanisation' of international law, the movement away from a legal system in which states are the sole legal subjects, and the domestic is tightly quarantined from the international, toward a transnational legal order that grants legal rights and agency to individuals and erodes the traditional boundary between inside and outside."[31] The transformation of the international legal order into "cosmopolitanisation" is an important story in its own right. Its importance is even greater, however, as one considers how this order now impinges directly on national governments and their citizens around the world and the effect this has on the accountability of and democratic controls over law, governance, and international order. The extension of international law to cover individuals, primarily evident in the area of human rights and human security, brings international law into direct competition with national authorities, sometimes in ways that challenge and potentially subvert these authorities.[32] Recent debates in the United States, some extending from treatment of detainees at Guantánamo, illustrate both the issues involved and the repercussions of such debates for general views about the applicability of international law and the responsibility of states to adhere to it.[33] The International Criminal Court has established the capacity of international law to provide redress for individual victims of war crimes and crimes against humanity regardless of where they reside. These developments in international law, though the result of state practice, nevertheless serve to legitimate human rights and thus at the same time serve to constrain states. The effect in the Arctic may very well be to provide some measure of protection for indigenous communities in the region.

A third issue that has been identified in the progression of international law and institutions is the growing influence of corporate interests at the expense of more democratic controls. The influence of corporate interests in global economic institutions governing trade and investment has been widely acknowledged.[34] Claire Cutler has called attention to the increased presence and influence of corporations in the process of globalization, governance, and areas of international law. For her, this raises a series of important questions that are not easily addressed by traditional approaches to international law and governance.

> The enhanced power of private capital is rendered "invisible" by liberal theories of international law and organization. This portends a legitimacy crisis that is empirical, theoretical and normative. From an empirical point of view, the law governing international legal personality tells us very little about the nature of the corporate world, the authority wielded by corporations, or

their complex relationships with states, both national and foreign. Theoretically, international law is unable to theorize about its "subject" in any but the most formalistic and artificial ways. The corporation is under-theorized, while the state is over-theorized. Finally, and probably most importantly, the normative implications of the problem of the "subject" are obscured by the same moves suppressing the corporate subject. The problem of corporate accountability is concealed by avoiding the question of "who or what produces law?," "what are the political conditions for legitimate agency in the creation and enforcement of law?," and "who legitimately determines outcomes in the global political economy?"[35]

This emergent network of global governance suggests a move to a more institutionalized approach to international politics and a more intrusive international regulatory regime in which the establishment and enforcement of these rules would be carried out by international institutions. The issue of who controls these institutions thus takes on greater significance as the institutions themselves have become more important. If international law alongside regional and international institutions are to acquire the authority and capacity to regulate international relations effectively, then they will need to gain greater legitimacy. Legitimacy in international relations is always problematic given the diversity of views and the autonomy of many of the principal agents. There is also an ongoing discussion of the nature of legitimacy, whether it is derived from principles (legal or moral) or political practice. One common source of legitimacy is a consensus among these principal agents as demonstrated by such things as votes in international institutions or signings and ratifications of international agreements. Yet in certain areas, the push for common international standards and new legal norms has often anticipated rather than followed a consensus among member governments. As a result, as Louis Pauly wrote, the authority of international institutions "can be fundamentally compromised, that is, the sense of political legitimacy underpinning the organization can be seriously eroded, if the organization is required to impose on the weak a consensus among the strong that turns out to be illusory. Perceptions of fairness in the process of norm creation and even more so in the process of rule enforcement, are essential."[36] There is a need for a more inclusive and transparent process for rule making and, for many, a process that involves non-state actors as well, to reinforce the legitimacy of international law and institutions. As a result of international law's intrusion into domestic space and the efforts to establish a common rule of law for diverse societies throughout the globe, there has been much discussion of the legitimacy of such efforts. "Legitimacy refers to the normative belief by an actor that a rule or institution ought to be obeyed. It is a subjective quality, relational between actor and institution, and defined by the actor's perception of the institution. The actor's perception may come from the substance of the rule or from the procedure or source by which it was constituted."[37] Legitimacy may result either from the rule itself or from the way in which the rule was established. The legitimacy of the rule of law has been questioned on both accounts, yet Oonagh Fitzgerald argued that international law's legitimacy has been derived from a mix of factors. At its most practical level, legitimacy is acquired through the consent of the member states that subscribe to it. Votes at international conferences, signatures on treaties, and ratifications deposited with regional and international institutions all signal acceptance on the part of national governments, which in turn legitimizes the legal norms involved. Overriding these specific measures is the acceptance by states of the general principle *pacta sunt servanda* that tends to act as a constitutive rule enabling the more practical measures of signature and ratification.

In addition, Fitzgerald noted that a further source of legitimacy is an evolving conception of state sovereignty "along with the development of a new kind of international law that qualifies state sovereignty and starts to recognize the individual."[38] Alongside a view that renders international institutions fully compatible with sovereignty is an increased concern for the need to take into account individual citizens and communities as part of the emergent institutional framework at the regional and international levels. The Arctic Council is a reflection of how some of these concerns have played out to date in the Arctic because it includes provisions for the recognition and participation of indigenous communities. There are also provisions for a number of nongovernmental organizations and agencies to have observer status. The implication here is that a transformation is underway in which the more absolutist views of sovereignty have yielded to more qualified ones that serve to limit a state's authority within its own jurisdiction. This in turn provides an opening for more intrusive conditions being applied to national governments through international law and for this law to incorporate a variety of private interests.

The issue of legitimacy has become most pronounced as international law has crossed into the domestic practices of states throughout the globe and as it is pushed on other states through inducements or by coercion. Whereas these concerns point to an important consideration, they do perhaps underestimate the degree to which the situation has changed over time. The state-dominated world of the mid-twentieth century no longer exists. As Claire Cutler wrote, "The actors, structures, and processes identified and theorized as determinative by the dominant approaches to the study of international law and organization have ceased to be of singular importance. Westphalian-inspired notions of state-centricity, positivist's international law, and 'public' definitions of authority are incapable of capturing the significance of non-state actors, like transnational corporations and individuals, informal normative structures, and private economic power in the global political economy."[39] The proliferation and concomitant influence of various non-state actors in the design and implementation of international law has altered not only the process of law making in a profound manner but also its substantive content, as the law has come to reflect the concerns of these non-state participants. The change has not gone far enough for some, who argue that the institutions overseeing the process must be subjected to greater democratic control. Yet this is not always feasible. "It is neither practical nor strategic for a nation such as Canada to go to international meetings with a hundred disparate voices representing its many selves: the nation's position would be too incoherent to have any influence. On the other hand, people's identities often cross international boundaries so it is possible that diverse Canadian voices might help to represent people around the world who are not well represented by their own state."[40] The development of law and institutions in the Arctic presents an interesting illustration of this process in practice.

Legitimacy is not only to be derived from popular participation and the increased inclusion of civil society organizations. It will also require the support of national governments affected by these regulations and governed by these institutions. At this level the record in the Arctic has perhaps not been quite as effective, given that a growing number of states' parties request access to policy deliberations affecting the region, in part by seeking status on the Arctic Council. China, South Korea, Japan, India, and Italy were added to the council's observers group in 2013 while the EU waits in the wings. Efficiency and inclusivity are not easily reconciled, and an expanded membership will render diplomacy more complicated and may render rule making more difficult. Yet representational issues may prove crucial in legitimating an effective legal regime for the region. "The difficulty in finding solutions to the representation challenge indicates the complexity of managing the development of international and domestic law in the postmodern world...Just as domestic notions of constitutionalism and democracy evolves to meet the changing values of a nation, so too the institutions and instruments of international governance may need to evolve to address changing global values."[41]

INSTITUTIONS, LAW, AND THE ARCTIC

The connections between international institutions and international law, and the manner in which both intersect with state sovereignty, is perhaps nowhere better exemplified than they are in the Arctic region. Much of the current activity around delineation of legal jurisdictional claims derived from extensions of the sovereignty invoked territorial boundaries has been conducted largely within the framework of international law and institutions, specifically the Law of the Sea treaty (LOS), as many of the chapters that follow discuss. In addition, each of the major states in the region has made a concerted effort to pursue multilateral understandings concerning not only environmental issues but also resource management and dispute settlement procedures as well. Diplomatic contacts within the region are extensively institutionalized in a variety of settings, many with a particular regional focus. There is even a rather extensive network of nongovernmental entities, many of these transnational, that are also active in the area. So as with many areas of contemporary international relations, it would seem that the primary framework within which Arctic states are operating is not one of unmitigated anarchy but one that is significantly defined by international law and institutions.

The third United Nations Conference on the Law of the Sea (1973–1982) stands as one of the most extensive institutionally based exercises in creating international law that the international society has ever experienced. The process demonstrated some of the best and worst aspects of multilateral diplomacy conducted in the UN. It was a process that was regularly and repeatedly infected by the domestic politics of member governments, by unilateral displays of disregard for this lawmaking process, by the assertion of power politics at numerous stages of the process, and most importantly, by the blatant pursuit of national interest, particularly evident among coastal states. As such it provided many instances and illustrations of the limits and inefficiencies of international institutions and the suspect heredity of much of what passes for international law. At the same time, however, the institution provided real opportunities for member governments and coalitions of states to bring forward ideas and policy recommendations that would have been exceedingly difficult outside of the framework provided by the institution. Of Canada, for example, Barry Buzan concluded, "Although the Canadian case at UNCLOS offers no certainties and seems to depend on a number of factors being favorably disposed, the suggestion is that a well mobilized and resourceful middle power has a reasonable chance of making a disproportionate impact on a selected multilateral negotiation."[42] Additionally, the process demonstrated the manner in which private commercial interests were able to intervene at different levels in an effort to shape the outcome of the negotiations. The final agreement, now ratified by more than 160 states (though not yet by the United States, a handful of landlocked states, and a number of states from the Middle East), represents an attempt on the part of states to regulate their use of common ocean space and to define the rights and responsibilities of coastal states. The final document makes clear that states were concerned first and foremost with their national interests, for example in the efforts of coastal states to gain legal recognition for their "right" to exploit offshore resources. The treaty, like many international agreements, reflects a large measure of customary practice that states have adopted in their relations with one another for matters of convenience and mutual interests, such as maritime transportation and environmental management, as well as territorial recognitions. It also, however, includes some innovative areas such as management of migratory transboundary fish stocks. The Arctic region stands as another area where the treaty has sought to define both how and on what grounds the ocean is to be distributed and managed. To date it is evident that states in the region have displayed a concerted effort to reinforce and sustain this legal framework. With the exception of the United States, where congressional politics continues to prevent the administration from gaining Senate approval of the treaty, other states in the region have worked within treaty provisions in mapping and submitting continental shelf claims. They have also given formal acknowledgment of the continued relevance of the LOS through the 2008 Ilulissat Declaration.[43]

It is worth noting that the refusal of the United States to ratify the treaty is difficult to account for in terms of American national interests. Instead it reflects a combination of private commercial interests worried about losing access to deep seabed resources and an ideological predisposition that reverberates in the U.S. Congress against the very principle of international agreements and sees the UN and other international agreements as part of some malevolent global conspiracy to usurp American sovereignty. (Oddly this group probably sees international law and international organizations as more powerful than even the most idealistic of world federalists would ever imagine.) Thus far this has been enough to forestall U.S. Senate approval despite the fact a variety of U.S. presidents, including the UN-skeptic George W. Bush, have advocated ratification. Formal ratification aside, the United States has regularly invoked the treaty in stating its position on maritime issues, including those under discussion in the Arctic, and has been compliant with treaty provisions.

There are any numbers of indications that states within the region are pursuing their interests within the framework established by international law and governed to a considerable extent by international institutions. Diplomacy—bilateral and multilateral—and international legal norms are more the order of the day than are displays of hard power and assertions of demands based on such. It would seem that states in the region continue to see much value in the legitimacy and efficacy of international law for protecting their interests. Among the indicators are such developments as the boundary delimitation between Russia and Norway,[44] the determination of continental shelf extension,[45] and scientific research and environmental management.[46] States in the region have repeatedly stressed both in words and action their interest in working collaboratively and within the rules and regulations established by existing or developing international law. Although one could dismiss these as mere posturing, the realities on the ground suggest far more by way of collaboration and cooperation than they do of conflict. None of this is to suggest that cooperation is inevitable. As many liberal theorists have noted, cooperation is by no means a foreordained possibility in relations among sovereign states. It is, however, a possibility, and historical practices both in general and in the Arctic specifically point to the increased frequency and wider legitimacy and efficacy of cooperative approaches to managing competing states' interests in potential areas of conflict.

CONCLUSION

This review has identified the growing prevalence and influence of international institutions and international law as well as providing an indication of some of the explanations for these developments. Both historical practice and theoretical insights demonstrate the possibility and likelihood that states can and do cooperate in managing and resolving competing interests. Practice also suggests that institutions and law work alongside or in place of power in determining the outcome of differences among states. It is clear that these developments have not replaced states and the prominent role they continue to play in international relations, the formation of international institutions, and the application of international law. It is equally clear that states have been displaced as the sole (if they ever were) or always the most influential actors and that neither are states the unconstrained absolute sovereigns that some realist accounts would suggest nor do they operate in an anarchic system. Instead the international system contains layers of institutions and legal regimes that confine and confound states. As a result there is little question that anarchy no longer serves as an adequate descriptor of the contemporary international system. Not surprisingly, it is also an inappropriate perspective for viewing and interpreting interstate politics at play in the Arctic region. Instead it is necessary to recognize that many of the issues confronting these states and many of the competing interests challenging them in the years ahead fall within existing and developing international law and are as likely to be resolved through cooperation and managed by agreements and institutions as they are to be resolved by power and force.

NOTES

1. John Mearsheimer, "The False Promise of International Institutions," *International Security* 19, no. 3 (Winter 1994–1995): 5–49.
2. Arthur A. Stein, "Neoliberal Institutionalism," in *The Oxford Handbook of International Relations*, ed. Christian Reus-Smit and Duncan Snidal (Oxford: Oxford University Press, 2008), 217.
3. Abram Chayes and Antonia Chandler Chayes, *The New Sovereignty: Compliance with International Regulatory Agreements* (Cambridge, MA: Harvard University Press, 1995).
4. Michael Doyle, *Ways of War and Peace* (New York: W. W. Norton, 1997), 213.
5. Ibid., 216.
6. See the discussion in ibid., 219–226.
7. Immanuel Kant, *Perpetual Peace* (New York: Columbia University Press, 1939).
8. A brief, though unsympathetic, survey with a focus on liberal views on war is Michael Howard, *War and the Liberal Conscience* (New York: Columbia University Press, 2008).
9. Francis Fukuyama, *The End of History and the Last Man* (New York: Free Press, 1992); also see Michael Mandelbaum, *The Ideas that Conquered the World: Peace, Democracy, and Free Markets in the Twentieth Century* (New York: Public Affairs, 2002).
10. Michael Ignatieff, reacting to developments in Syria and the lack of an international response, lamented the passing of this liberal age; see his "How Syria Divided the World," *New York Review of Books*, July 11, 2012, http://www.nybooks.com/blogs/nyrblog/2012/jul/11/syria-proxy-war-russia-china/; and less pessimistically see G. John Ikenberry, "The Future of the Liberal World Order," *Foreign Affairs*, May/June 2011.
11. Bruce Russett, "Liberalism," in *International Relations Theories: Discipline and Diversity*, 3rd ed., ed. Tim Dunne, Milja Kurki, and Steve Smith (Oxford: Oxford University Press, 2013).
12. G. John Ikenberry, "Liberal Internationalism 3.0: America and the Dilemmas of Liberal World Order," *Perspectives on Politics* 7, no. 1 (2009): 71–87.
13. David Lake, "Rightful Rules: Authority, Order and the Foundations of Global Governance," *International Studies Quarterly* 54 (2010): 587–613.

14. Craig Murphy, *International Institutions and Industrial Change* (New York: Polity Press, 1994).
15. Olav Schram Stokke and Geir Hønneland, *International Cooperation and Arctic Governance: Regime Effectiveness and Northern Region Building* (London: Taylor & Francis, 2006).
16. Robert O. Keohane, *After Hegemony: Cooperation and Discord in the World Political Economy* (Princeton: Princeton University Press, 1984); also see Kenneth Oye, ed., *Cooperation Under Anarchy* (Princeton: Princeton University Press, 1986).
17. Robert O. Keohane, "International Institutions: Two Approaches," *International Studies Quarterly* 32, no. 4 (1988): 379–396.
18. Stephen D. Krasner, ed., *International Regimes* (Ithaca, NY: Cornell University Press, 1983), 2.
19. Stein, "Neoliberal Institutionalism," 210.
20. Stokke and Hønneland, *International Cooperation and Arctic Governance.*
21. "Clinton Criticizes Canada over Arctic Talks," BBC World News, March 30, 2010, http://news.bbc.co.uk/2/hi/8594291.stm.
22. Stein, 2010, 212.
23. Oran Young, *Governance in World Affairs* (Cornell, NY: Cornell University Press, 1999).
24. Stein, 2010, 216.
25. Gib Van Eert, "What Is Reception Law?" in *The Globalized Rule of Law*, ed. Oonagh E. Fitzgerald (Toronto: Irwin Law, 2006), 88.
26. Anne-Marie Slaughter, "Judicial Globalization," *Virginia Journal of International Law* 40 (1999–2000) 1103–1124.
27. Ibid., 1104.
28. Ibid., 1124.
29. Lester Pearson, *Words and Occasions* (Toronto: University of Toronto Press, 1970), 34.
30. Stephen Clarkson and Stepan Wood, "Canada's External Constitution and Its Democratic Deficit," in *The Globalized Rule of Law*, ed. Oonagh E. Fitzgerald (Toronto: Irwin Law, 2006), 97.
31. Christian Reus-Smit, ed., *The Politics of International Law* (Cambridge: Cambridge University Press, 2004), 7.
32. See, for example, Amy Gurowitz, "International Law, Politics, and Migrant Rights," in Reus-Smit, *Politics of International Law.*
33. See among others Philippe Sands, *Lawless World* (London: Penguin Books, 2006).

34. See, for example, Deborah D. Avant, Martha Finnemore, and Susan K. Sell, eds., *Who Governs the Globe?* (Cambridge: Cambridge University Press, 2010).
35. Claire Cutler, "Critical Reflections on the Westphalian Assumptions of International Law and Organization: A Crisis of Legitimacy," *Review of International Studies* 27 (2001): 148–149.
36. Louis Pauly, "Good Governance and Bad Policy: The Perils of International Organizational Overextension," *Review of International Political Economy* 6, no. 4 (1999): 404.
37. Ian Hurd, "Legitimacy and Authority in International Politics," *International Organization* 53 (1999): 381.
38. Oonagh Fitzgerald, "Question of Legitimacy in the Interplay between Domestic and International Law," in *The Globalized Rule of Law*, ed. Oonagh Fitzgerald (Toronto: Irwin Law, 2006), 149.
39. Cutler, "Critical Reflections," 133.
40. Fitzgerald, "Question of Legitimacy," 135.
41. Ibid., 135–136.
42. Barry Buzan, "Canada and the Law of the Sea," *Ocean Development & International Law* 11, nos. 3–4 (1982): 176.
43. The Ilulissat Declaration, May 28, 2008, http://www.oceanlaw.org/downloads/arctic/Ilulissat_Declaration.pdf.
44. Tore Henriksen and Geir Ulfstein, "Maritime Delimitation in the Arctic: The Barents Sea Treaty," *Ocean Development & International Law* 42, nos. 1–2 (2011): 1–21.
45. Elizabeth Riddell-Dixon, "Canada and Arctic Politics: The Continental Shelf Extension," *Ocean Development & International Law* 39 (2008): 343–359.
46. Ian G. Brosnan, Thomas M. Leschine, and Edward L. Miles, "Cooperation or Conflict in a Changing Arctic?" *Ocean Development & International Law* 42, nos. 1–2 (2011): 173–210.

CHAPTER 3

SOVEREIGNTY AS AN INSTITUTION OF INTERNATIONAL SOCIETY

Matthew S. Weinert

INTRODUCTION

Melting polar ice could result in the eventual opening of the previously impassable Northwest Passage between Europe and Asia.[1] Greater accessibility to and likely passage through the region pose opportunities for international cooperation involving resource acquisition and distribution. But new opportunities, more ominously, could also expose fault lines along which conflicts might be waged. With multiple claims to sovereignty exercised in the region—Canada, Denmark/Greenland, Finland, Iceland, Norway, Sweden, Russia, and the United States possess territory north of the Arctic Circle—and some states legally challenging the claims of others,[2] competition no doubt will come to characterize interstate relations in the Arctic region.

But competition, both in terms of how one understands it and how it may be manifested, is open to interpretation. First, one may think of competition in a visceral sense—that is, in terms of rivalries, alliances, violence, and possibly war. The international relations theoretical tradition of realism would thus read Russia's flag-planting on the deep sea bed beneath the North Pole in 2007;[3] Canada's sea, land, and air force operations in 2009;[4] Canadian-Danish joint military exercises in 2010;[5] and American naval planning[6] as posturing, indicative of overlapping and thus conflicting claims to propriety that might ultimately be resolved through some recourse to violence.

Second, given the interest in exploiting the vast natural resources thought to exist in the Arctic region, one may construe competition in a market sense—as, perhaps, a push by multinational corporations (e.g., Shell, BP) to secure exploration and resource-extraction contracts from proximate/bordering states to access oil, gas, and mineral deposits. Competition may spur development of innovative techniques and technologies related to resource extraction, which would stimulate the global economy by reducing gas and oil prices, providing new jobs, and increasing state (and corporate) revenue.

Third, one may think of competition in legal terms—as illustrated, for example, by the decision among Russia, Canada, and Denmark "to file claims to the United Nations asserting their respective rights to the Lomonosov Ridge, an underwater mountain range" that some suggest could contain massive oil reserves and mineral deposits.[7] Russia submitted its case to the UN Commission on the Limits of the Continental Shelf in December 2001, asserting that the ridge is an extension of the Siberian continental shelf. But the commission requested scientific and geological surveys, which has prompted Russia, Canada, and Denmark (via Greenland) to initiate discrete studies to map the Arctic sea floor and ascertain whether or not the ridge protrudes from one of their particular landmasses. Legal and scientific communities thus offer a different interpretation of the 2007 flag-planting incident: far from being an assertive or aggressive move, it rather underscored the extent to which Russia is staking its position on science and the law. Flag-planting was "just a photo-op part of what was in fact a well-organized scientific expedition aimed at proving the geological continuity of the Lomonosov Ridge with Eurasia."[8] Failure of any state to provide defini-tive scientific proof of the status of the ridge might compel states, in the interests of economic development and resource exploration and extrac-tion, to conclude an arrangement similar to the 2011 maritime delimita-tion treaty between Russia and Norway, which resolved their forty-year dispute by dividing nearly in half the contested territory.[9]

Finally, one may think of competition in terms of gains (and, concomi-tantly, losses). Structural realists maintain that cooperation between states is limited because they are chiefly concerned with relative gains. Thus in this view, cooperation between littoral states in the Arctic will be stymied precisely because states may perceive others to gain more in, say, the finite goods of territory and natural resources. Yet competition may implicate the opposite. (Neo)liberals aver that state desire to gain, no matter the distribution of such gains, motivates cooperative endeavors. Competitive instincts are, in this view, sublimated within or mitigated by institutions, whether in the form of bureaucratic organizations or constellations of rules, norms, and principles that clarify boundaries of acceptable, socially agreed upon behavior. The consequent reduction in uncertainty as a function of increased transparency ensures cooperation.

There are undoubtedly other ways one may construe competition; but the aim in this chapter is not to provide an exhaustive account. Different theoretical traditions in international relations underscore different forms of competition. Realism emphasizes the more visceral forms competition may take; liberal traditions study the ways competing claims and conflicts are alleviated or resolved within ideational, market, institutional, and legal contexts; and constructivism focuses on the constraining and constitutive role of shared norms, ideas, principles, and rules in the conduct of international relations.

In this chapter, I retreat from consideration of real or imagined forms of competition in the Arctic region and instead reflect more broadly on the meaning of the term *competition*, as well as the distinct ways in which competitive behaviors are channeled through, enacted within, and resolved within the international society of states. Put differently, I do not treat with any specificity (potential) competition in the Arctic theater but consider the general phenomenon of competition through the lens of the English School tradition of international relations and what it might teach us about competition in the Arctic. The English School's conceptual triad of international system, international society, and world society, not to mention international order and world order, captures in varying degrees the multiple kinds of (competing) theoretical insights offered by other theories of international relations. English School theory treats international relations as a distinct kind of sociological enterprise and makes claims about the type, depth, and extent of social elements that bind all members through rules, institutions, and the like.

A majority of contemporary English School theorists have focused on international society as a *via media* between the extremes of an instrumental international system and a complex, cosmopolitan-based world society. An international system is said to exist when two or more states have sufficient contact between, and impact on, one another such that they behave "as parts of a whole."[10] Viewed through the prism of the international system or what Martin Wight called the realist, Hobbesian, or Machiavellian tradition,[11] sovereignty is defined largely in permissive terms. Restrictions on the actions of a sovereign state stem primarily from a state's capabilities to effectuate its will or from the (presumably rational) calculations of elites rather than from any agreements among sovereign states or sense of community. Security in the international system tradition is very much a matter of self-help given that competition results from sovereign wills continually confronting each other as something alien and potentially subversive.

By world society, Hedley Bull meant "not merely [as] a degree of interaction linking all parts of the human community to one another, but a sense of common interest and common values, on the basis of which common rules and institutions may be built."[12] Within the world society framework, or what Wight labeled the revolutionist or Kantian tradition, sovereignty is framed by cosmopolitan concerns and thick conceptions of shared norms.[13] Sovereignty is thus defined more restrictively, perhaps even—in a contemporary idiom—as responsibility to self and, importantly, to others. Though the emphasis is squarely placed on the vast arena of potential cooperation, it is worth noting that competition may result from violations of a common interest, value, or institution, differing normative interpretations, or clashes between levels of responsibility.

Situated between the international system and world society, the English School locates international society, which Bull maintained exists "when a group of states, conscious of certain common interests and common values...conceive themselves to be bound by a common set of rules in their relations with one another, and share in the working of common institutions."[14] Chiefly, the international society approach recognizes that "the ethics underpinning the actions of states can move beyond simple notions of the 'national interest' towards more cosmopolitan bases for action."[15] The extent to which such actions move toward cosmopolitanism is the subject of the pluralist-solidarist debate, which I later discuss. Suffice to note that within the contours of this debate, it may be hypothesized that sovereignty, as the chief condition for membership in the society of states, saddles the causal burden of states' inability or unwillingness to move beyond narrowly construed national interests.

Matthew Paterson's criticism of Bull expresses well the essence of such an encumbrance. Bull, Paterson maintained, ignores sovereignty's negative structural presence and effects precisely because Bull located the sources of conflict in human disagreement (and presumably plurality) rather than in the states system.[16] This may be technically true: states are but legal fictions (to use Bentham's term) that, notwithstanding the legal personality attributed to states, serve as convenient shorthand for the decisions made by individual leaders or, as in the case of parliaments, collectively, within them. Yet for Paterson, this understanding minimizes the import of the legal fiction: for sovereign statehood amplifies human disagreements because it gives institutional form and gravitas to disagreements in ways that politicize and enlarge disputes on the international level.[17]

However, one may read Bull more sympathetically. Within and through the states system, Bull wrote,

> a greater sense of human solidarity in relation to environmental threats may emerge...[since] the states system provides the present structure of the political organization of mankind, and the sense of common interests and values that underlines it —meagre though it is and inadequate as it is likely to prove in relation to long-term challenges to world order—is the principal expression of human unity or solidarity that exists at the present time, and such hope as we may entertain for the emergence of a more cohesive world society are bound up with its preservation and development.[18]

Bull sketched what one might call a realistic or pluralistic cosmopolitanism by highlighting the possibility of human solidarity within the sovereign states system, rather than hinging solidarity on an imagined or ideal world in which one hopes to live; it is in this states system, no matter how flawed it may be, that one must search for solutions.[19] Chris Brown furthered the argument: "states are local agents of the common good,"[20] and sovereignty very well might be the crucible on which a brave new world is constructed.

The larger point appears a quintessentially English School one: international relations is a social domain in which common rules and institutions, and "imperatives of morality and law," guide or constrain interstate activity.[21] Robert Jackson analogized the English School to a conversation characterized by

> a variety of theoretical inquiries which conceive of international relations as a world not merely of power or prudence or wealth or capability or domination but also one of recognition, association, membership, equality, equity, legitimate interests, rights, reciprocity, customs and conventions, agreements and disagreements, disputes, offenses, injuries, damages, reparations, and the rest: the normative vocabulary of human conduct.[22]

If Brown underlined the primacy of the sovereign state as a form of human organization that captures particular loyalties, identities, and a shared sense of a common good, then Jackson highlighted the importance of other kinds of principles and practices that underpin sociality, express sovereign claims, and situate sovereignty (and its varied meanings) within a complex of rules, norms, values, and institutions that modify understandings and practices of sovereignty itself. Paterson phrased the point differently. If one construes sovereignty as "a bundle of rights and responsibilities, which can be traded off against each other," then sovereignty "becomes positively important as the mode of authority through which states can be expected to keep bargains and implement agreements."[23] But this is also Bull's, albeit muddled, argument: world order challenges (e.g., terrorism, environmental degradation, and the like) "can strengthen sovereignty rather than erode it."[24] Sovereignty may magnify disagreement; yet so too may it amplify agreement.

For if we understand international relations as a society "with rules, norms, [and] mutual recognition playing important parts in shaping the interaction between states and constituting their relation to each other, there is no reason in principle to assume that they will not be able to develop new rules, norms," and institutions to deal with such challenges.[25] In this regard, the international society concept, even if it is at its core state-centric, necessarily blurs at one end into world society if one locates the sources of some challenges to the state system, contributors to transnational problems, and purveyors of solutions in non-state actors—a point to which I return later.

To give my exploration a context, the next section briefly summarizes the state of sovereignty studies writ large. Even if centrally disconnected from English School theory, the overview serves to highlight two features of sovereignty studies: first, divisions within sovereignty theory, and second, the fact that meanings and practices of sovereignty are shaped within particular sociohistorical contexts. I identify three dominant strands of sovereignty theory and argue that the third, which ties normative understandings and practices of sovereignty to legitimacy, fits comfortably within the English School, even if its proponents have not offered a systematic account of sovereignty.[26] I then set up particular claims with regard to sovereignty, security, and the Arctic specifically, and sovereignty and institutions in English School theory more generally.

SOVEREIGNTY: THE GLOBALIZATION PERSPECTIVE

In many instances, globalization is presented as a challenge to the states system.[27] Globalization, with its attendant cross-border processes (e.g., of economic and political liberalization), proliferations, and migrations (e.g., of capital, crime, disease, information, people, pollution, technologies, weapons), has spawned a veritable industry of sovereignty studies. Yet despite what James Caporaso called a "lively research program," those who study sovereignty "speak past one another." Intellectual understanding, he contended, "is impeded by the lack of clarity and agreement on basic concepts."[28] A brief survey of the literature, which I divide roughly into three categories, confirms his diagnosis.

One subset of sovereignty literature reflects on a narrowly framed query of whether the dispersion of functional responsibilities to non-state actors and certain material and ideational migrations challenges the ontological certitude of sovereignty.[29] Arguing that sovereignty declines or collapses under the weight of globalizing processes and functional dispersion, these scholars not only reiterate a debate that began in the late nineteenth century and has periodically resurfaced given changing global realities,[30] but, further, *imply* the very thing they critique: sovereignty as an irreducible, indivisible, immutable, reified, essentialized "chunk."[31] In other words, sovereignty appears in F. N. Hinsley's terms as "supreme authority in political community,"[32] with the emphasis on *supreme*. Either authority is complete or, if parceled out, dispersed, or curtailed by exogenous agents or forces, it is compromised.

Others challenge this line of argument by tying sovereignty to structures of command, control, and elite preferences, which underscores sovereignty's immutability or, at the very least, its resilience. This view has a distinctive pedigree. Bodin's absolute monarch[33] and Hobbes's Leviathan[34] reappear theoretically as Weber's monopoly of the legitimate use of force.[35] Meyer and Jellinek's nineteenth-century theory of sovereignty qua *Kompetenzkompetenz*, meaning state competence to self-determine and self-restrict the scope of its competence,[36] translates into structural realism's iteration of sovereignty as a state's freedom to "decide for itself how it will cope with its internal and external problems."[37] The formulation ultimately favors the rational calculations of state elites, which it shares with the neoliberal conception of sovereignty.[38] In this view, state participation in globalizing processes, whether manifested in the dispersion of functions or the liberalization of state policy, does not undermine, but rather is an expression of, sovereignty.

Even if both approaches somewhat exaggerate their respective claims, both offer fundamental contributions to an understanding of sovereignty. The former alerts one to the variability over time of sovereignty's content, which equates with functions ascribed to the sovereign; the latter locates sovereignty's durability in structures of command, control, and decision making. However, by tethering sovereignty so intimately with material structures and factors, both in the end minimize the shaping and constraining effects of norms on sovereignty.

Thus, a third subset of sovereignty literature poses more complex sovereignty architectures. This body of scholarship articulates sovereignty in normative terms that involve some degree of endogenous (domestic) and exogenous (international) socialization.[39] Sovereignty appears as a contingent practice, process, and "thing" or social property constituted and regulated in part by norms and rules to which states must adhere if they are to be perceived as members of the international community in "good standing."[40] According to Cohen, because "it is the rules of international law that tell us in what sovereignty consists,"[41] one might construe sovereignty as a persistent yet evolving institution subject to an ongoing process of rule and norm construction and modification that affects international relations through its regulative and governance functions.

This formulation avoids the pitfalls of the other two approaches in two important ways. First, it treats sovereignty not as an impenetrable structure of command and control driven by elite, rational calculations of material and ideational interests despite or in spite of international norms or citizen preferences.[42] Rather, by connecting sovereignty to processes of socialization and rule construction buttressed by perceptions of legitimacy, this literature opens sovereignty theory to considerations of external influences such as normative advances in international relations and historical (that is, actual policy) emendations of sovereignty rules such as the extension of religious liberty to individuals (as granted by the 1648 Peace of Westphalia); international abolition of slave trading and slavery—a process begun at the 1815 Congress of Vienna; codification of the laws of war; the ban on the production, use, sale, and stockpiling of anti-personnel landmines as formulated in the 1997 Ottawa Convention; proliferation of human rights law and norms; development of individual criminal responsibility in international law; numerous environmental protections, and the like. Two salient points follow. Each of these developments owes in significant measure to non-state agents, which strongly suggests that sovereignty is modified by multiple actors. Hence scholars must eschew the singular agent orientation of most sovereignty definitions, which in turn indicates that one must more critically conceive of authority (if indeed sovereignty is a significant statement about authority) and of the purposes for which authority is instituted. Likewise, most importantly, scholarship must take into account that the "thing" (sovereignty) that constitutes the state likewise modifies it and its behavior, forcing one to retreat from the position that sovereignty is a "hard," invariable fact of international political and social life—a point that directly relates to English School ideas of international and world societies, which capture variations in the depth of normative and institutional commitments.

Second, the legitimacy-oriented literature sidelines the "globalization debate." Importantly, it adopts the idea that sovereignty morphs over time but ties this metamorphosis to conceptions of legitimate authority, processes of socialization, and normative structures. Socialization affects state identity and behavior by providing a context within which states negotiate the contours of what it means to be sovereign. In the case of the Arctic, one might find that this means the great powers (Russia and the United States) will not wage war (as the United States has explicitly stated); that disputes are to be resolved through peaceful, perhaps legal, means; and that cooperation, whether in terms of joint military expeditions or in terms of resource extraction, must prevail in harsh environments if their instrumental value is to be realized. States exist not in social vacuums but in contexts animated by competing interests and values, cooperation and dialogue, exchange and interpretation. Sometimes these dialogic and interpretive networks yield convergences of interests and values (especially during and after crises or, as seen in the Arctic, in the accessibility of a previously inaccessible region), which provide fertile ground upon which to construct sociopolitical orders and explore new ideas about the just content of such orders. These, in turn, constrain sovereignty practices and alter sovereignty's meaning, whether expressed in softer terms as general and non-binding behavioral prescriptions and proscriptions or as more precise, binding directives.

As indicated, the basic premises of this third branch of sovereignty literature may be comfortably subsumed under the rubric of the English School approach to international relations, to which I now turn.

SOVEREIGNTY: THE ENGLISH SCHOOL'S INSTITUTIONAL PERSPECTIVE

Even if sovereignty displays remarkable staying power, its character and normative understandings change. Thus, English School theorists find it helpful to think of sovereignty and the state as institutions—that is, as a congeries of rules and norms—not as inveterate, immutable realities. The prominence of institutions in English School theory owes to at least three reasons, according to Barry Buzan. First, institutions help theorists flesh out "the substantive content of international society." Second, institutions capture what English School "writers mean by order." Third, conceptually, "the particular understanding of institutions in [English School] thinking is one of the main things that differentiates it from the mainstream, rationalist, neoliberal institutionalist, study of international regimes."[43]

Hedley Bull identified five primary institutions of international society: the balance of power, international law, diplomacy, war, and the great powers.[44] Institutions, he maintained, are fairly "persistent" sets of "connected rules prescribing behavioral roles, constraining activity, and shaping expectations."[45] While many English School writers construe sovereignty as an institution of international society—and a salient one at that[46]—Bull noticeably omitted it from his account. The issue may seem largely academic, yet something important might be gleaned from the omission. Bull's *The Anarchical Society* sought to provide an accounting (however incomplete) of the institutions that contribute to the creation and maintenance of order. Such institutions are properly understood as institutions of coexistence; that is, they are regulative or governance institutions. Yet sovereignty, for Bull, is fundamental in a foundational or constitutive sense; it is thus a primary institution or, put differently, an institution or rule of recognition the function of which is to constitute a particular kind of society (as distinct from "a universal empire, a cosmopolitan community of individual human beings, or a Hobbesian state of nature of state of war") based on distinct kinds of agents.[47] Sovereignty in this reasoning enables because it signifies reciprocal recognition; hence, it is the condition for agency in a state-based international society. Consequently, sovereignty is also permissive because it cloaks a particular kind of actor—the state—with a legitimate and recognized claim to agency that is in turn subject to rules and institutions that govern coexistence, and thus to varying degrees of restrictions on internal and, more importantly, external behavior.[48]

Sovereignty may be foundational in both enabling and permissive senses, but it does not perform the quotidian work required to create and maintain (international) order. Other primary and secondary institutions assume those burdens in ways that ultimately mediate and modify sovereignty. On this point Buzan helped clarify.[49] He defined primary institutions as "durable and recognized patterns of shared practices rooted in values commonly by the members of interstate societies, and embodying a mix of norms, rules, and principles." These may be subdivided into two categories: master and derivative.[50] Master institutions such as sovereignty, diplomacy, or great power management contain or generate others. Whereas master institutions "stand alone," derivative institutions stem from master institutions (e.g., non-intervention stems from sovereignty, bi- or multilateralism arise from diplomacy). Secondary institutions in turn work to effectuate the objectives of master and derivative primary institutions. Examples include well-known intergovernmental organizations such as the United Nations and the North Atlantic Treaty Organization, and lesser-known ones such as the International Seabed Authority, as well as treaty-based regimes revolving, say, around human rights or arms control. Summarily, whereas sovereignty is foundational in a deep constitutive sense, and thus central to the enterprise of studying international society, the job of creating and maintaining order within this society hinges precisely on the development and deployment of other master, derivative, and secondary institutions.

Yet one is left with a nagging question: given that other theoretical traditions invoke the concept of institutions, how specifically does the English School enhance one's understanding? Buzan responded to that question by underscoring the English School preference for excavating the "shared culture elements that precede rational cooperation"; in other words, the English School understanding of institutions rests more on "fundamental and durable practices that are more evolved than designed."[51] Institutions, as sedimentations of normative commitments, knowledges, and practices, do not simply mirror state preferences but crucially constitute, shape, and constrain such preferences by embedding states in dense networks that exert cognitive and behavioral effects. An English School approach then pitches these frameworks in terms of order.

By international order, Bull meant "a pattern or disposition of international activity that sustains those goals of the society of states that are elementary, primary or universal."[52] Such goals include "the preservation of the system and society of states itself"; the maintenance of "the independence or external sovereignty of individual states"; "the goal of peace," meaning "the absence of war among member states...as the normal condition of their relationship, to be breached only in special circumstances and according to principles that are generally accepted"; and "the common goals of all social life," including "limitation of violence resulting in death or bodily harm, the keeping of promises, and the stabilization of possession by rules of property."[53] World order, alternatively, is defined with reference to sustaining "the elementary or primary goals of social life among [hu]mankind as a whole."[54] If any tensions exist between international and world order, they might be obliquely referenced by the pluralist-solidarist debate.[55] Whereas pluralism reflects the position that states do not often agree on principles or institutions beyond the primary goals of international order, solidarism refers to states' ability to cooperate with respect to and agree on a broad range of issues, norms, and values, and, importantly, enforce their agreements.[56]

I reference the debate to raise the issue that there is room in the English School framework to discuss the nature of sovereignty as an institution (the depth and extent of its insularity, self-referentiality, and social moorings) and to acknowledge that sovereignty becomes the locus of changing meanings and practices. But change may be effectuated not only by solidarist aspirations but also, importantly, by pluralist commitments. For instance, a pluralist commitment to preserve the society of states (by limiting great power conflict, maintaining territorial borders, settling disputes peacefully) may exert enormous pressure on states' competing claims, as in the Arctic, thereby gently pushing them to resolve their differences in less viscerally conflicting ways. To wit, instead of resorting to unilateral displays of military might and trumping a militarily weaker Norway, Moscow concluded a treaty to divide in half long-disputed, potentially oil-rich Arctic waters with Oslo.

But another issue is at stake, and here I wish to return to a point made earlier: that the international society approach, even if it is at its core state-centric, blurs at one end into world society if one construes non-state actors as challengers to the state, contributors to transnational problems, and potential sources of solutions to such problems. (One might think of transnational corporations eager to obtain access and resource-extraction contracts from states as gently pushing governments to minimize or even eschew competition manifested as force in the Arctic region.) Theoretically, world society's situation by Bull in a chapter entitled "The Decline of the States System?" gives the unfortunate perception that world society opposes and even replaces a state-based international society. Such a reading equates world society with Martin Wight's "revolutionary" or Kantian tradition of international relations.[57] In this reading, cosmopolitans will transform the society of states by means of ideological homogeneity, erection of a world empire, or the construction of cosmopolitan networks of individuals and their agencies that produce "a world society of individuals which overrides nations or states."[58]

Yet such an oppositional view of international and world societies, which "has become rooted in English School thought,...serves to cut off the possibility of positive interaction between them."[59] This contravenes earlier notions (by Bull, Wight, and Butterfield among others) that stressed in particular overlap between the societies.[60] World society, Bull wrote, "stands to the totality of global social interaction [just] as...international society stands to the concept of the international system."[61] World society, moreover, is constituted by a "world political system," meaning a "worldwide network of interaction" among states and non-state actors;[62] it "in no way implies the demise of the states-system" because, historically, "the states system has always operated within a wider system of political interaction."[63] Yet the oppositional view prevailed, perhaps because concepts without distinctiveness lack analytic utility. Hence solidarism has come to be identified with world society as a statement about or a vision of the normative transformation of existing international society in light of cosmopolitan concerns, while pluralism remains wed to international society as a statement about the ethical value of diversity.[64]

Christian Reus-Smit impugned the corner into which the polarization of pluralism/solidarism and international society/world society has forced the English School. Arguing that this polarization has limited "the English School's capacity to respond to" the challenge of the September 11 attacks, Reus-Smit placed blame on the

> pluralist insistence on developing a theory of international society as a relatively discrete social realm, with relative autonomy from the actors, structures, and processes of surrounding world society. Their goal is to develop a political and ethical theory "of international relations understood as a 'society' with its own distinctive

standards of conduct." Because of this, pluralists go to some length to deny that world society is encroaching on the society of states. In Jackson's words, "world society is...a client of the society of states rather than the reverse." This claim rests on the concomitant idea that non-state actors do not fundamentally alter the basic principles and dynamics of the society of sovereign states. Here, the question is almost always posed in terms of whether non-state actors are displacing the primacy of sovereign states, with pluralists supposedly winning the broader argument by claiming that this is not the case.[65]

The effects are damning: by eschewing recognition of "the continuous interplay of elements of realism, rationalism, and revolutionism,"[66] divisively formulated concepts decrease the likelihood that the English School will be perceived as a viable theory to understand international relations.

The lines of division need not be drawn so resolutely, however. Solidarism, in Bull's sense, very much exists in international society, and the point can be made with reference to security and sovereignty, to which I now turn.

SECURITY AND SOVEREIGNTY: CLARIFYING THE RELATIONSHIP

The intimacy that characterizes the relationship between security and sovereignty cannot be overstated within the English School's international society tradition. I refer not only to the security and independence of the state, but also to the security of the international society of states itself. Barak Mendelsohn maintained that although Bull did not commit himself to a ranking of the goals, he strongly implied that "the preservation of the system overrides the other goals and even justifies violation of the principle of sovereignty."[67] In Bull's view, "peace has been viewed by international society as a goal subordinate to that of the preservation of the states system itself...and as subordinate also to the preservation of the sovereignty or independence of individual states."[68] But the reading does not diminish peace as an objective; it simply entails that peace narrowly defined as the absence of war is secondary to enforcement action against recalcitrant states. The preservation of the society of states, and of its individual entities, demands as much.

Contemporary international legal architecture underscores the point. Article 2(4) of the *Charter of the United Nations* outlaws the threat or use of force against the territorial integrity or political independence of another state. Yet the charter nevertheless recognizes the distinct role of force in international relations: first, by granting the UN Security Council, the primary responsibility of which is the maintenance of international peace and security, the authority to sanction the use of force, and second, per Article 51, by recognizing and affirming states' rights, whether individually or collectively, to self-defense in the event an armed attack occurs. The Geneva Conventions layer onto the charter framework limitations on permissible activities on the battlefield, at sea, in the air, and against civilians.

The point is not to provide an exhaustive accounting of restrictions on the sovereign in the arena of security. Certainly the administrations of George W. Bush and Tony Blair made everyone aware that states can, and do, push the boundaries of the permissible and authorize conduct—conduct that has previously been recognized in both domestic and international law as illegal—when the security of the state is threatened or perceived as being threatened. Rather, the point is to emphasize the fact that even on that most hallowed of terrain, that of the security and sanctity of the state, institutions of various sorts carry normative weight, even if that normative weight is only rhetorically expressed, as happened in the case of the United States and its 2003 invasion of Iraq. But even in such cases, rhetoric, especially when it reflects prevailing world public and political opinion, feeds back into strengthening normative commitments and institutions, which in turn shape the way people think about and act under the banner of sovereignty. Sovereignty is not, even as a constitutive principle, "static...but is subject to constant development."[69]

CONCLUSION: SOVEREIGNTY, THE ENGLISH SCHOOL, AND THE ARCTIC

Given that subsequent chapters address a range of issues pertaining to the Arctic, including territorial claims, secondary institutions (the UN, the Arctic Council), potential military engagement, and the like, I refrain from engaging any of those matters with any specificity. Here I wish to return to the idea of competition as articulated in the introductory section of this chapter.

Different theoretical traditions offer distinct explanations as to why competition emerges and offer in varying degrees predictions as to how competition might evolve. This chapter sought to highlight an English School approach to competition and sovereignty. By understanding sovereignty as a congeries of regulative and governance rules and norms —that is, as an institution, the legitimacy of which hinges on rule and norm adherence—we come to appreciate that the "thing" (sovereignty) that constitutes the state likewise modifies it. This in turn, as iterated earlier, forces one to retreat from the position that sovereignty is a "hard," invariable fact of international political and social life.

The case of the Arctic offers fertile ground on which to think about sovereignty as an institution. Competition, no matter how it may manifest, reveals that the international society sovereignty has constituted increasingly appears as the master sovereignty serves.[70] Thus, for instance, territorial and resource-based competition may result, as international society and world society perspectives might predict, in increased reliance on law. In this scenario, the sheer likelihood of massive oil and gas reserves, not to mention other potentially lucrative finds, may compel the resource-extractive industry to push states to settle territorial claims in courts (the International Court of Justice being primary here) or in organizational venues such as the UN Commission on the Limits of the Continental Shelf (which is already entertaining claims to the Lomonosov Ridge), the Arctic Council ("a high level intergovernmental forum to provide a means for promoting cooperation, coordination and interaction among the Arctic States"),[71] or even the International Seabed Authority.

In the event geologists and scientists cannot definitively settle claims related to the Lomonosov Ridge, competition may result in the creation of new organizational arrangements or in new practices and norms to govern the way states coordinate their activities and interests. To that end, states might construct a regime to handle resource distribution issues. A world society frame might even envision an architectural replication of the Antarctica Treaty System that revives the Roman legal concept of *res communis*, or communal property, to restrain sovereign prerogative and elevate normative and practical commitments to the Arctic as a common heritage of humankind. Yet the Arctic differs substantially from Antarctica given the presence of multiple littoral states with unresolved territorial claims. Hence some might expect competition to assume a different, more visceral form, whether as minor skirmishes or outright military confrontation. Even if competition were to manifest as violence, an English School perspective would highlight the degree to which actions undertaken in the name of sovereignty (over territory and thus over resources) are constrained by the laws of war and rules of engagement. All of the scenarios point to an appreciation that although sovereignty may be a stable, constitutive institution, it is not stagnant, inveterate, or ahistorical. By conceiving of sovereignty as an institution that is mediated by other institutions of and in international society, English School theory underscores sovereignty's durability and variability of meaning and practice over time in ways that serve a greater good of order.

NOTES

1. National Snow and Ice Data Center (NSIDC), http://nsidc.org/asina/2 010/081710.html.
2. Russia, Canada, and Denmark plan "to file claims to the United Nations asserting their respective rights to the Lomonosov Ridge, an underwater mountain range" believed to contain massive oil reserves and mineral deposits. Nataliya Vasilyeva, "Putin Doesn't See War over Resources in the Arctic," *The Star*, September 23, 2010, http://www.vcstar.com/news/ 2010/sep/23/putin-doesnt-see-war-over-resources-in-the/.
3. Doug Struck, "Russia's Deep-Sea-Flag-Planting at North Pole Strikes a Chill in Canada," *The Washington Post*, August 7, 2007, http://www. washingtonpost.com/wp-dyn/content/article/2007/08/06/AR200708060 1369.html.
4. Lee Carter, "Canada in Arctic Show of Strength," BBC News, August 16, 2009, http://news.bbc.co.uk/2/hi/8204531.stm.
5. "Arctic War Games: Canada, Denmark Team up for Military Exercise," Global Research: Centre for Research on Globalization, March 23, 2010, http://www.globalresearch.ca/index.php?context=va&aid=18287.
6. U.S. Department of the Navy, "Strategic Objectives for the U.S. Navy in the Arctic Region," Memorandum for Distribution, 5000/Ser. N00/10063, May 21, 2010, p. 6, http://greenfleet.dodlive.mil/files/2010/09/US-Navy-Arctic-Strategic-Objectives-21-May-2010.pdf.
7. Vasilyeva, "Putin."
8. Nigel Hannaford, "The Russians—and Everyone Else—in Canada's Arctic," *C2C: Canada's Journal of Ideas*, June 22, 2009, http://c2cjournal.ca/2009/ 06/the-russians-and-everyone-else-in-canadas-arctic/.
9. Stimson.Org, "Evolution of Arctic Territorial Claims and Agreements: A Timeline (1903–Present)," April 15, 2013, http://www.stimson.org/ infographics/evolution-of-arctic-territorial-claims-and-agreements-a-timeline-1903-present/.
10. Hedley Bull, *The Anarchical Society: A Study of Order in World Politics* (New York: Columbia University Press, 1995), 9.
11. Martin Wight, *International Theory: The Three Traditions* (New York: Holmes & Meier, 1992), 15.
12. Bull, *Anarchical Society*, 269.

13. Barry Buzan argued that people need to move beyond identifying world society and, related, solidarism, nearly exclusively with human rights and examine other thick conceptions of shared norms such as those related to the world economy. See Barry Buzan, "International Political Economy and Globalization," in *International Society and Its Critics*, ed. Alex J. Bellamy (New York: Oxford University Press, 2005), 115–134.

14. Bull, *Anarchical Society*, 13.

15. Matthew Paterson, "Global Environmental Governance," in *International Society and Its Critics*, ed. Alex J. Bellamy (New York: Oxford University Press, 2005), 163.

16. Bull, *Anarchical Society*, 283.

17. Paterson, "Global Environmental Governance," 164.

18. Bull, *Anarchical Society*, 284.

19. Ibid., 285.

20. Chris Brown, "World Society and the English School: An 'International Society' Perspective on World Society," *European Journal of International Relations* 7, no. 4 (2001): 428.

21. Bull, *Anarchical Society*, 25.

22. Robert Jackson, "Pluralism in International Political Theory," *Review of International Studies* 18, no. 3 (1992): 271.

23. Paterson, "Global Environmental Governance," 177n9.

24. Ibid. The footnote also contains relevant citations.

25. Ibid., 167.

26. On this point, see Edward Keene, *Beyond the Anarchical Society: Grotius, Colonialism and Order in World Politics* (Cambridge: Cambridge University Press, 2002), in particular 29–39.

27. Barak Mendelsohn, "Sovereignty under Attack: The International Society Meets the Al Qaeda Network," *Review of International Studies* 21 (2005): 50. See also Robert Jackson, *Sovereignty: Evolution of an Idea* (Malden, MA: Polity, 2007), ch. 6 for a critique of that view.

28. James Caporaso, "Changes in the Westphalian Order: Territory, Public Authority, and Sovereignty," *International Studies Review* 2, no. 2 (2000): 3.

29. See Jens Bartelson, *A Genealogy of Sovereignty* (Cambridge: Cambridge University Press, 1995); Thomas Biersteker and Cynthia Weber, "The Social Construction of Sovereignty," in *State Sovereignty as Social Construct*, eds. Thomas Biersteker and Cynthia Weber (Cambridge: Cambridge University Press, 1996), 1–21; David Elkins, *Beyond Sovereignty: Territory and Political Economy in the Twenty-First Century* (Toronto:

University of Toronto Press, 1995); Michael Fowler and Julie Bunck, *Law, Power, and the Sovereign State: The Evolution and Application of the Concept of Sovereignty* (University Park: Pennsylvania State University Press, 1995); Jean-Marie Guehenno, *The End of the Nation-State*, trans. Victoria Elliot (Minneapolis: University of Minnesota Press, 1995); Susan Hainsworth, "Sovereignty, Economic Integration, and the World Trade Organization," *Osgoode Hall Law Journal* 33, no. 3 (1995): 583–622; Ruth Lapidoth, "Sovereignty in Transition," *Journal of International Affairs* 45, no. 2 (1992): 325–346; Nicholas Onuf, "Sovereignty: Outline of a Conceptual History," *Alternatives* 16 (1991): 425–446; Nicholas Onuf, *The Republican Legacy in International Thought* (Cambridge: Cambridge University Press, 1998); James Rosenau, *Along the Domestic-Foreign Frontier: Exploring Governance in a Turbulent World* (Cambridge: Cambridge University Press, 1997); Susan Strange, "Wake up, Krasner! The World Has Changed," *Review of International Political Economy* 1 (1994): 209–219; and Susan Strange, *The Retreat of the State: The Diffusion of Power in the World Economy* (Cambridge: Cambridge University Press, 1996).

30. See, chronologically, Sir Henry Maine, *International Law: A Series of Lectures Delivered Before the University of Cambridge* (1887; repr., Cambridge, MA: Harvard University Press, 1915); James Garner, "Limitations on National Sovereignty in International Relations," *American Political Science Review* 19, no. 1 (1925): 709–744; Karl Loewenstein, "Sovereignty and International Co-operation," *American Journal of International Law* 48, no. 2 (1954): 222–244; and Brian Schmidt, *The Political Discourse of Anarchy: A Disciplinary History of International Relations* (Albany: State University of New York Press, 1998).

31. Fowler and Bunck, *Law, Power, and the Sovereign State.*

32. F. N. Hinsley, *Sovereignty* (Cambridge: Cambridge University Press, 1986), 1.

33. Jean Bodin, *Six Books of the Commonwealth*, ed. and trans. M. J. Tooley (1576; repr., New York: MacMillan Company, 1955). For a non-absolutist interpretation of Bodinian sovereignty, see Preston King, *The Ideology of Order: A Comparative Analysis of Jean Bodin and Thomas Hobbes* (New York: George Allen & Unwin, 1974).

34. Thomas Hobbes, *Leviathan*, ed. Edwin Curley (1668; repr., Indianapolis: Hackett Publishing Company (1994).

35. Max Weber, "Politics as a Vocation," in *From Max Weber: Essays in Sociology*, ed. H. H. Gerth and C. Wright Mills (New York: Oxford University

Press, 1946), 77–128. Weber appropriated material power's shadow in the false sense that it is sovereignty and the state's substance.

36. As discussed in Hymen Ezra Cohen, *Recent Theories of Sovereignty* (Chicago: University of Chicago Press, 1937).

37. Kenneth Waltz, *Theory of International Politics* (New York: McGraw Hill, 1979), 96. Cf. Janice Thomson and Stephen Krasner, "Global Transactions and the Consolidation of Sovereignty," in *Global Changes and Theoretical Challenges*, ed. Ernst Czempiel and James Rosenau (Lexington, MA: Lexington Books, 1989), 195–219.

38. See Stephen Krasner, *Sovereignty: Organized Hypocrisy* (Princeton: Princeton University Press, 1999); from a similar neoliberal perspective, see Robert Keohane, "Hobbes's Dilemma and Institutional Change in World Politics: Sovereignty in International Society," in *Whose World Order? Uneven Globalization and the End of the Cold War*, ed. Hans-Henrik Holm and Georg Sorensen (Boulder, CO: Westview Press, 1995); and from a postmodern view, Cynthia Weber, *Simulating Sovereignty: Intervention, the State and Symbolic Exchange* (Cambridge: Cambridge University Press, 1995).

39. See, for example, Mlada Bukovansky, *Legitimacy and Power Politics: The American and French Revolutions in International Political Culture* (Princeton: Princeton University Press, 2002); J. Samuel Barkin, "The Evolution and the Constitution of Sovereignty and the Emergence of Human Rights Norms," *Millennium: Journal of International Studies* 27, no. 2 (1998): 229–252; J. Samuel Barkin and Bruce Cronin, "The State and the Nation: Changing Norms and the Rules of Sovereignty in International Relations," *International Organization* 48, no. 1 (1994): 107–130; Abram Chayes and Antonia Handler Chayes, *The New Sovereignty: Compliance with International Regulatory Agreements* (Cambridge, MA: Harvard University Press, 1995); Jean Cohen, "Whose Sovereignty? Empire versus International Law," *Ethics & International Affairs* 18, no. 3 (2004): 1–24; Gregory Fox, "New Approaches to International Human Rights: The Sovereign State Revisited," in *State Sovereignty: Change and Persistence in International Relations*, ed. Sohail H. Hashmi (University Park: Pennsylvania State University Press, 1997), 105–130; Ian Hurd; "Legitimacy and Authority in International Politics," *International Organization* 53, no. 2 (1999): 379–408; International Commission on Intervention and State Sovereignty, *The Responsibility to Protect* (Ottawa: International Development Research Centre, 2001); Daniel Philpott, *Revolutions in Sovereignty: How Ideas Shaped Modern International Relations* (Prince-

ton: Princeton University Press, 2001); Christian Reus-Smit, *The Moral Purpose of the State: Culture, Social Identity, and Institutional Rationality in International Relations* (Princeton: Princeton University Press, 1999); and Matthew S. Weinert, *Democratic Sovereignty: Authority, State and Legitimacy in a Globalizing World* (London: University College of London Press, 2006).

40. See Chayes and Chayes, *New Sovereignty.*
41. Cohen, "Whose Sovereignty?," 15.
42. See, generally, Krasner, *Sovereignty.*
43. Barry Buzan, *From International to World Society? English School Theory and the Social Structure of Globalisation* (Cambridge: Cambridge University Press, 2004), 161.
44. See Bull, *Anarchical Society,* part 2.
45. See Keohane, "Hobbes's Dilemma," 167.
46. See Buzan, *From International to World Society?,* 187.
47. My account derives from Bull's treatment of rules, *Anarchical Society,* 64–68. The quotation appears on 65.
48. Stephen Krasner recognized this, though as he argued such mediations may be inconsistent and hypocritical (*Sovereignty*).
49. Buzan, *From International to World Society?,* 181–182.
50. I would argue, however, that great power management in the sense of powerful, or capabilities-rich, states managing international relations in concert presupposes a particular kind of actor: the sovereign state. This reasoning would indicate that great power management is a derivative institution. One might also claim that great power management derives from or is a consequence of diplomacy.
51. Buzan, *From International to World Society?,* 167; see also 161–162.
52. Bull, *Anarchical Society,* 16.
53. Ibid., 16–18.
54. Ibid., 19.
55. Buzan has unpacked the pluralist and solidarist concepts and generated a spectrum of descriptors of various types of international society that range from an *asocial* international society (which of course begs the question as to why something labeled asocial is a kind of society), to *power political, coexistence, cooperative, convergence,* and, finally, to the most solidarist type, a *confederative* international society. *From International to World Society?,* 159–160.
56. On the pluralist-solidarist debate, see Hedley Bull, "The Grotian Conception of International Society," in *Diplomatic Investigations: Essays in*

the Theory of International Relations, ed. Herbert Butterfield and Martin Wight (Cambridge, MA: Harvard University Press, 1966), 51–73; Buzan, From International to World Society?, 45–62; and Andrew Linklater and Hidemi Suganami, The English School of International Relations: A Contemporary Reassessment (Cambridge: Cambridge University Press, 2006), 59–68.

57. Wight, International Theory, 8.
58. Ibid., 40–48.
59. Buzan, From International to World Society?, 29.
60. See John Williams, "Pluralism, Solidarism, and the Emergence of World Society in English School Theory," International Relations 19, no. 1 (2005): 21.
61. Bull, Anarchical Society, 269.
62. Ibid., 266.
63. Ibid., 271.
64. See Williams, "Pluralism, Solidarism."
65. Christian Reus-Smit, "The Constructivist Challenge after September 11," in International Society and Its Critics, ed. Alex J. Bellamy (New York: Oxford University Press, 2005), 90–91 (quoting Jackson).
66. See Matthew S. Weinert, "Reframing the Pluralist-Solidarist Debate," Millennium: Journal of International Studies 40 (2011): 40.
67. Barak Mendelsohn, "Sovereignty under Attack: The International Society Meets the Al Qaeda Network," Review of International Studies 21 (2005): 49.
68. Bull, Anarchical Society, 17.
69. Ibid., 66.
70. For a version of this argument, see Bruce Cronin, Institutions for the Common Good: International Protection Regimes in International Society (Cambridge: Cambridge University Press, 2003).
71. http://arctic-council.org/article/about

Chapter 4

Ecological Sovereignty and Arctic Politics

Guy-Serge Côté and Matthew Paterson

Introduction

The question of sovereignty is of particular interest in the context of political ecology. The resurgence of sovereignty discourse in the Arctic helps reflect on ecological questions about sovereignty itself. It does so in two principal ways. First, the condition enabling the possibility of this sovereignty discourse is precisely a series of ecological changes associated with climate change, principally the rapid retreat of sea ice,[1] and the way this is seemingly allowing a new scramble for resources in the oceans and on the seabed as well as new questions about the status of the Northwest Passage. It also suggests that the attempts to reimpose or extend sovereign control may well hinder attempts to manage the

Arctic sustainably, given that such management requires dealing with the complex ecological conditions in the region.

The second way is that the Arctic can be seen as a site where long-established and well-understood processes of state building are being reproduced. Without extending the analogy too far, many of the processes outlined by Charles Tilly in his classic essay "War Making and State Making as Organized Crime" can be seen in contemporary Arctic politics.[2] For Tilly, central to the consolidation of state power is the intertwining of processes of resource extraction (by state elites from those they dominate, in return for claims to protect those people) and processes of legitimation of that increased concentration of power.[3] Whether or not this argument is accepted, Arctic sovereignty is not an established "fact" but rather a set of claims currently being asserted. So exploring the processes of claims here is important to understanding the contemporary conditions under which the construction of sovereignty works.

More recently, there has been some reconsideration within green theory of whether sovereignty is necessarily anti-ecological. There are two types of critical reconstruction here. The first type is an argument that states are more flexible or perhaps contradictory in their ecological potential. In particular states are believed to be a political form that holds certain sorts of coordination functions within societies that could be used for ecological goals. Their capacities for taxation, redistribution, and economic management more generally are one element here, an argument closely associated with the notion of ecological modernization.[4] There is also an argument that precisely their sovereign capacities render the management of collective action problems more tractable, given that sovereignty creates the potential for the sorts of confidence and trust that collective action requires.[5]

The second type is more a claim that sovereignty is an emptier signifier than that implied by the account in most green discourse, which in fact shares much with realism in international relations (i.e., that sovereignty is a claim to exclusive jurisdiction and cannot be interpreted any other way). Litfin and Eckersley contained the principal arguments here, suggesting that in practice sovereignty is a "bundle of rights and responsibilities" whose contents shift over time.[6] Drawing closely on Wendt's constructivist notion of "cultures of anarchy" (1999), Eckersley attempted to chart the shift in sovereignty norms regarding environmental questions from one of "international anarchy" to one of "environmental multilateralism," where sovereignty refers less to the rights of states to non-interference and increasingly to a set of responsibilities in relation to other states regarding mutual environmental impacts.[7]

There are two principal reasons why the question of sovereignty in the Arctic is currently of interest. The first is that there is an ongoing development of interesting, essentially postsovereign, modes of governance in the Arctic region. These have existed for a while (since 1977 in the case of the Inuit Circumpolar Council, for example), but in the last twenty years they have become progressively denser in the way they govern various aspects of life in the Arctic, as well as increasingly interconnected between them. There is a range of governing institutions; they frequently involve the indigenous peoples in the region, who are themselves organized transnationally. The second reason, however, goes in an opposite direction and lies in the resurgence of a sovereignty discourse based on the ownership of a territory and the marginalization of what Kuehls called the "not state politics."[8] This sovereignty discourse is contested, implicitly or explicitly, both by other states contesting specific sovereignty claims (the Hans Island dispute between Canada and Denmark is perhaps the most obvious) and by states from outside the region wishing to regard the Arctic as effectively *terra nullius* and thus subject to normal Law of the Sea norms.

The Arctic represents a laboratory for postsovereign politics, which can be defined as governing institutions, practices, and networks that are being developed transnationally, without a single site of authority. The notion of postsovereign politics entails a deterritorialization of politics. This is the idea that we aim to develop in this chapter.

These contexts immediately raise an ecological question about sovereignty. How does sovereignty jeopardize ecological cooperation in the Arctic? This chapter will try to answer this question by showing how sovereignty may constitute an obstacle for green theorists. The reasons are twofold: First, by imposing artificial boundaries, sovereignty creates an inside space—i.e., an "inside" of the state political space and an "outside" of the state space. Therefore, as argued by Deleuze and Guattari through the words of Kuehls,[9] it is very difficult for the state to take account of non-state political activities. For example, the constantly shifting nature of conditions in the region—the seasonal and other shifts in sea ice, the transitory nature of passage, and so on—means that stable control by a single state, in the classic Weberian model, is difficult to achieve, if not by definition an impossibility. So the Arctic can be seen as a useful case in which ecological conditions shape governance patterns, acting to limit the possibility of the imposition of sovereignty. Secondly, sovereignty constitutes an obstacle to the political formation of a non-human and human collective in the Arctic, which the postsovereign governance arrangements may be seen to be attempting to pursue. Sovereignty imposes a boundary or limit, focusing on human relationships to each other and to broader ecological contexts, thus allowing little space for the development of a new collective that would include association of human and non-human entities.

THE GREEN CRITIQUE OF SOVEREIGNTY

Ecological traditions of thought have long been critical of sovereignty. There are a number of elements in this critical stance. First, state sovereignty is understood in ecological debates to entail a concentration of power that renders dealing with ecological problems increasingly difficult compared to more dispersed systems of power. There are two aspects to this problem, one to do with spatiality, one to do with authority.

Regarding the former, Dryzek used a range of ecological literature to show how centralized decision-making systems, such as those of sovereign states, create feedback loops between ecological processes and the social decision-making systems that are too complex and long.[10] This creates inadequate social feedback mechanisms and prevents societies from responding adequately to ecological disruptions as they appear. Decentralized systems would be much more responsive to and thus able to deal effectively with these problems because they shorten the feedback loops. Dryzek's argument is represented in the decentralizing impulse of most green theory and green movements, most famously perhaps in the classic manifesto of the German Green Party issued in 1983.[11]

But the concentration of power is also a question of authority systems. Internally, sovereignty entails the creation of authority structure and the progressive creation of a large bureaucratic decision-making structure that, though it enables at times representative systems to emerge, nevertheless makes decision making dominated by a technocratic elite.[12] Externally, the construction of sovereignty simultaneously creates a radically simplified international structure of inside and outside.[13] Here sovereigns are only to be accountable internally, if they are accountable at all. This is the classic problem of sovereignty in international relations as seen by realists, which in ecological terms means that states have no incentives to respond to claims that they damage others ecologically, and if anything they have positive incentives to externalize the ecological costs of their activities in order to bolster domestic legitimacy.[14]

There is also an ecopolitical discourse about sovereignty that situates the emergence of state sovereignty in relation to the broader emergence of capitalism and modernity. State sovereignty as an institution co-evolved with a range of other modern institutions that mutually reinforced each other. Two are regarded as particularly important. One is that of capitalism—the social relations organized around the commodification of land and labor and the pursuit of limitless accumulation, which emerged first in England in the sixteenth century and have become progressively globalized. This claim, usually made most forcefully by eco-Marxist writers,[15] concerns the way that the combination of wage labor relations and competitive markets creates a dynamic of techno-logical innovation, enhanced labor productivity (and exploitation), and growth imperatives that set in train a radical and constant increase in the throughput of resources. These capitalist dynamics generate both scarcity in particular resources and, increasingly importantly, the systematic production of a range of pollutants that by the second half of the twentieth century had rendered contemporary societies completely unsustainable. The sovereign state is usually regarded as fundamental to this process, being the condition of possibility of capitalist development, given that it sets different capitals, labor forces, and resource sources in competition with each other, as well as providing the necessary support for capital in the form of the basic legal infrastructure (private property rights, enforcement of contracts) and a range of public goods infrastruc-tures (transport, communications, education, defense).

Another character of the sovereign state is the scientific revolution and the sort of conceptual/ontological shift this brings about. Moder-nity is here conceptualized as entailing reducing the world to a series of mutually constitutive dualisms, of nature/culture, man/woman, rational/irrational, and so on. As a form of knowledge, ecologists frequently critique modern science for being reductionist, for reducing the world to its constituent objects, thus neglecting the interconnections between object that constitute ecological systems, and for being instrumentalist—developing knowledge about nature purely in order to better exploit it.[16] These mentalities reduce ecosystems to objects to be exploited, which legitimizes that exploitation but also impedes the observation of the sorts of systemic interconnections that characterize environmental problems.

This is the critique of modernist dualism extended by Bruno Latour[17] in Politics of Nature. Latour entertained the idea that the concep-tion of modernist dualisms derived from Plato's myth of the cave.

According to Plato, the social is trapped in the cave with no access to nature. The philosopher or the scientist is the only one able to escape the cave and bridge the social and nature. Latour tried to show that this modernist conception of dualism constitutes a great challenge to democracy because of the power and the authority invested in the philosopher/scientist. The modern conception of political ecology is also trapped in that conception of dualism. Modern political ecology, for Latour, consists in the effort to reconstruct political life without relying on the nature-society dualism and by extension relying on a single site of politics represented by the institution of sovereignty:

> Political ecology can no longer be fairly described as what caused concerns about nature to break into political consciousness. This would be an error of perspective with incalculable consequences, for it would reverse the direction of history and would leave nature, a body invented to render politics impotent, at the very heart of the movement that is proposing to digest it. It seems much more fruitful to consider the recent emergence of political ecology as what has put an end, on the contrary, to the domination of the ancient infernal pairing of nature and politics, in order to substitute for it, through countless innovations, many of which remain to be introduced, the public life of a single collective.[18]

The sovereign state is the political expression of this dualistic ontology, organized around a strict separation between inside and outside, with the ecological consequences just outlined. Ecologists thus argue for various reconfigurations of political space, from bioregionalism (which argues for the realigning of political borders with ecological systems)[19] to networked or "rhizomatic" political forms.[20] Latour insisted here on taking seriously that this sort of political reconstruction entails more than just humans—it involves reconstructed relations involving combinations of human and non-human agents, without lumping the latter into some catchall category of "Nature." We return to this sort of argument later.

These various ecopolitical arguments all combine in green discourse to suggest a series of processes by which the construction and institution of state sovereignty is intimately tied to the production of environmental degradation. State elites pursue the enhanced extraction of resources in order to enhance military advantage, to consolidate their power both domestically against a range of challenges and against international competitors. States also foster capitalist social relations and techno-scientific development that generate both systemic pressures (in the case of capitalist social relations) and technical capabilities to further enhance resource extraction. The process of economic growth that is the primary driver of environmental degradation has as one of its conditions of possibility the concentration of power represented by state sovereignty. At the same time, sovereignty entails relations of responsibility that hamper efforts to deal with collective action problems and that create incentives to shift the costs of environmental degradation outside a state's borders.

GREENING SOVEREIGNTY?

As Mick Smith ably contended, these arguments within green debates about sovereignty rarely deal with one of the core aspects of sovereignty that ecological critiques raise—that the pursuit of sovereignty and thus statehood by elites is always about the enhanced capacity to control and exploit natural resources.[21] More specifically, Smith showed how the idea of sovereignty is not what "green state" theorists such as Eckersley argue, and at the core of the idea of sovereignty is the notion of a single site at which the "exceptions" to normal political can be made. Smith drew on Agamben as a source for such a claim.[22] Conceived this way, sovereignty operates as a key anchoring institution in modern politics that confers on some the ability to decide that the normal political rules do not apply. Furthermore, there is no external ground on which one can appeal the decision to invoke the exception—the sovereign moment of deciding the exception is an act of pure force, an act to eliminate politics per se. As Smith showed, "greening" sovereignty, though it may be able to provide various ameliorating techniques, cannot get around the core problem of sovereignty, which is the ability of sovereign elites to suspend politics. And given that dealing with ecological problems, as suggested later, requires *more* politics not less—in the sense of more deliberation, participation, even open struggle—leaving open possibilities for shutting such key political processes down must be resisted.

This argument is reinforced by the consideration of Derrida's notion of coup de force.[23] In this, Derrida showed that not only does the operation of sovereignty always contain the possibility of the suspension of the law and of normal politics, but by the very establishment of state sovereignty, something that is ongoing is always an act of violence—a coup de force—by putting an end to any public consultations or public participations or negotiations. "The law is always an authorized force, a force which justifies itself or which is justified in its application, even if this justification might be judged unjust from another perspective or in another situation."[24]

Bruno Latour defined politics as a process of assemblage, as a *progressive composition of the common world*,[25] a new collective that includes human and non-human entities. The claim to sovereignty thus involves a coup de force, a moment where politics is eclipsed. Sovereign claims therefore attempt to shut out politics. Politics, or perhaps more precisely "the political"—in the attempt to render into English the French meaning of le politique, which conceptually does not really exist in English—is understood here in a classical sense as the space of public deliberation and agonistic disagreement, a perspective on the meaning of politics perhaps most associated with Hannah Arendt and recently revived in particular by Chantal Mouffe and reconceptualized by Latour in the ecological contexts as suggested earlier.[26] The political is essential to the process of creating a new collective and to protect this process from a coup de force, which would suspend the negotiations around the assemblage of the new collective.

In normative terms, what is pretty much universally agreed upon in green discourse is that in fact what is needed is more politics, not less. Much of the debate in green theory, including by those authors associated with a green reconstruction of sovereignty (notably Eckersley), is couched in terms of the need for further development of deliberative institutions, even those that go beyond state borders.[27] But from this point of view, what such arguments miss is how sovereign claims effectively shut out the space for deliberation.

Andrew Barry extended this type of analysis by showing how it works in relation to the classical account of politics given earlier.[28] Barry outlined how two aspects of the meaning of politics intertwine in this sort of way. He used "the political" to refer to the space of deliberation in public space, whereas "politics" is used in the more common English sense of being about the pursuit of power.[29] Claims to sovereignty can be clearly understood as such processes. But at the same time such attempts in the end produce their own repoliticizations, as the attempt to enclose a process, often through rendering it technical, produce what Barry, following Callon, called overflowings.[30] Barry's analysis focuses on the attempt to deal with vehicle emissions through a variety of pollution-control technologies, and the overflowings consist commonly in the inability of specific technologies to resolve the problems societies expect of them or in the collapse of authority of the agencies managing them (either state agencies or the mechanics monitoring and ensuring their implementation). In the Arctic sovereignty case, these depoliticizing strategies would be more through reference to international legal convention—historically existent claims and the practices that sustain them. But they are constantly repoliticized in this case because of the ambiguities of legal norms and the facts on which claims rely, and more importantly for this argument given that the basis on which claims are being made are constantly disrupted by the changing ecological conditions themselves.

In the case of the debate around state sovereignty in the Arctic, this coup de force is happening at two levels. First, sovereignty puts an end to the political debate around reassembling a collective based on association of human and non-human entities as described by Bruno Latour. Secondly, the coup de force of sovereignty contributes in making the state's vertical authority inefficient to capture the politics outside its territorial boundaries. It creates an "inside" and an "outside" where the outside in often marginalized politically.

In Derrida's account, the coup de force involved in state making is always aporetic. This is both in the sense that it can never itself provide the normative ground for state power in the way that those engaging in the coup want, and in the sense that the establishment of state power is never as total as its designers desire. It has a series of internal tensions that create ongoing problems for those trying to stabilize it as an authority structure. Michel Callon referred more generally to such processes as ones of framing—attempts to create a way of organizing social relations that are total, internally coherent, and self-reproducing. For Callon, as for Derrida or Kuehls, however, such framing is always associated with processes of overflowing—elements within the way the social is put together that have their own trajectories, which undermine the totality. Framing never thus succeeds. Sovereignty is a special case of framing that has its own overflowings, notably ecological ones.

POSTSOVEREIGN ECOLOGICAL POLITICS IN THE ARCTIC

The extension of state sovereignty in the Arctic is ecologically problematic for a number of reasons. The Arctic Council and the Inuit Circumpolar Council are arguably the best-known governance institutions in the Arctic. But according to the Arctic Governance Project, there are seventy-seven governance arrangements in the Arctic. Of these, fourteen are what they term "innovative governance projects"—i.e., ones that put together a range of different types of actors and thus represent complications for the idea that governance in the region operates purely via the interaction of sovereign actors.[31] Some of these deal with a specific area (the Svalbard Treaty for example); others with specific aspects of life in the Arctic (the regime for Northern fur seals); some deal with both (the Bering Sea pollack agreement).

Our point is that many of these initiatives, in varying ways, involve attempts to respond to the complex ecological conditions of life specific to the Arctic and to the inability of sovereignty to address such conditions adequately.[32] Following Kuehls's critique of sovereignty, such arrangements are rhizomatic[33]—they operate horizontally, attempting to deliberate and coordinate activities among non-sovereign actors. This reflects Kuehls's account of ecological politics closely.

Kuehls's argument that one should see ecopolitics as "rhizomatic" is a normative argument not only that people "need" to pursue postsovereign political forms but that such political forms already exist, though they are obscured by the obsession with sovereignty. He argued that political scientists should not limit themselves to the confines of state sovereignty in identifying sites of politics. Ecological politics constitute a perfect example of politics not being restricted to the vertical-form authority of the sovereign states. As the popular saying goes, "pollution knows no borders," and its politics to an extent follow this logic.

According to Kuehls,

> Deleuze and Guattari's attempt to extricate thought from the state model maps political landscape differently. Their map is not centered around a sovereign authority. It does not represent a territory shaped by a sovereign presence. Such a territory is, in the minds of Deleuze and Guattari, arboreal—treelike. It has roots that sink deep into the ground, fixing a particular place. It has a single trunk that branches out, sending aspects of itself away from the center while always remaining connected to unifying trunk, that in turn is firmly rooted in one place. The map that Deleuze and Guattari construct is far more rhizomatic than arboreal.[34]

The trajectories of air pollution, the impacts of climate change, transboundary water pollution, and so forth all illustrate this rhizomatic character of ecopolitics in general. In the Arctic, the flows of fish, seals, bear, or caribou, as well as ice, ocean currents, or toxic chemicals, are all emblematic of this sort of organization of space. The forms of governance alluded to earlier extend this rhizomatic logic to the governance of these various flows. As Kuehls put it,

> Where state thought traces territories around a sovereign point of view, rhizomatic thoughts, not-state thoughts, draw their maps "with a more multiple, lateral, and, circular ramifications." Rhizomatic thoughts are not centered around a specific point of view, but follow flows and think territories in different ways.[35]

States have difficulties capturing the movement of bodies in space, such as the ecological flows already mentioned, because of this restricted conception of sovereignty based on territory. They try to control movements and flows that are central to ecological challenges. Animals, pollutants, or impacts of climate change are nomadic; they do not recognize borders. This is why it is so difficult for the state to deal with ecopolitics. It attempts to enclose such flows within its territorialized account of politics, but transboundary flows are never adequately captured by the state's territorial logic. How can one stop a fish from swimming in Arctic seas across state borders? The same can be said for transboundary air pollution, caribou, human inhabitants, polar bears, or the sources or impacts of climate change.

THE ARCTIC AS A HUMAN/NON-HUMAN COLLECTIVE

But is this rhizomatic focus enough as a way to understand ecological politics in the Arctic? Arguably, such an account of politics risks reducing these flows of specific organisms, or of nutrients, water, and so on, to a functionalist sort of politics that is organized technocratically. This is not perhaps what Kuehls or Deleuze and Guattari intended, but in the existing arrangements in the Arctic, this technocratic focus is readily identifiable. It is Latour who provided a specific sort of normative argument for how such arrangements might become both properly political and properly ecological.

For Latour, the very dichotomy between nature and society limits the conceptual imaginary that might enable one to think about such arrangements, but also, more practically, the knowledge about the various processes by which humans and non-humans combine to produce the various ecopolitical problems that exist. Central here is that the "Society-Nature" dualism maps strongly onto a "Subject-Object" dualism, which is the focus of much green critique—treating "nature" as solely an object for human use.[36] Latour's contribution is to suggest that one abandons the totalizing term "Nature" in favor of more complex and particularistic associations between humans and non-humans. Latour defined an association in these words:

> Extends and modifies the meaning of the words social and society, words that are always prisoner of the division between the world of the objects and that of subjects; instead of making the distinction between subjects and objects, we shall speak of association between humans and non-humans.[37]

It is political ecology's main task to reassemble the new collective and to create associations between humans and non-humans. Its objective, according to Latour, is to shed some light on these associations.

The particularity of the governance arrangements in the Arctic alluded to earlier meets some of these conditions. But the non-humans (pollack, polar bears, fur seals, ice) are conceived of as objects, not participants, in a complex ecological process. The task for Latour is to transform them into a new collective in which the relation between humans and non-humans is one of association rather than appropriation.

For Latour, associations between human and non-human entities should be the cornerstone of a new understanding of political ecology and of the development of a new collective formed by the movement of these associations. The key word in the last sentence is *movement*. Latour critiqued sociologies that take for granted the constitution of a group or of society. He blamed sociologists for creating walls and artificial boundaries around politics. The process of association is a never-ending movement because the combinations are infinite.

The choice is clear:

> [E]ither we follow social theorists and begin our travel by setting up at the start which kind of groups and level of analysis we will focus on, or we follow the actor's own ways and begin our travels by the traces left behind by their activity of forming and dismantling groups.[38]

Furthermore, according to Latour, one should learn that there are many types of social aggregates "and that no established component can be used as an incontrovertible starting point."[39]

In the context of the Arctic, there are many examples of association of human and non-human entities: humans and ice, humans and fish, humans and caribou, humans and climate change, or humans and oil, to name but a few. The enforcement of sovereignty in the Arctic changes the dynamic of this associative process. The Arctic ecosystem is at risk of being separated in five, between Canada, Norway, the United States, Denmark, and Russia. State borders alter the associative process in the Arctic by imposing five different structures of authority on one ecosystem. The inhabitants of the Arctic region are thus constrained in their abilities to make decisions about their ecosystems, even if those decisions will only have a very local impact.

Thus, although there are many human/non-human associations in the Arctic, the collective that this entails does not have a collective *political* life. There is, for example, no deliberation around the impacts of climate change on the collective. Can people live with impacts of climate change? Can they live with the ice melting? What about the association between humans and seals, if the seals have to go farther to give birth to their pups? What will be the association between humans and polar bears? And what about humans having to live with transboundary mercury? These questions are not being addressed by the Arctic collective but by five state capitals that have different answers to these questions.

Nevertheless, despite this ongoing problem of sovereign control, it is possible to see many such associations not based on sovereignty. One well-known example is that of the Saami and in particular their relation to reindeer.

The 70,100,000 Saami people share the Sápmi territory, which, in the language of state sovereignty, is divided between four countries: Norway, Sweden, Finland, and Russia. Across these borders, the Saami people share culture, lifestyle, and language. Many rely on hunting, fishing, gathering, and trapping as the basis of their livelihood. They have developed a traditional knowledge of the far north, which has been transmitted across many generations.[40]

Reindeer are of great importance to the Saami. Historically the Saami were partly nomadic, following the herds of reindeer during the season. Reindeer herding still plays a major role in Saami culture and lifestyle. The Saami and the reindeer formed a strong association that is a cornerstone of their lifestyle and of the collective developing over generations by the Saami people and other non-human entities. Their association with snow and ice is also very important, evident in a rich linguistic terminology. The association between Saami and the reindeer has been problematic for the four states claiming sovereign control over the same area. Their practices exist in tension with the concept and practice of state sovereignty based on territory. The Saami peoples challenge the conception of sovereignty based on territory. This can be illustrated by their request for more autonomy, which would enable them to protect their culture and language but also their herding practices. Self-determination and autonomy in this context is to be understood as outside the realm of the traditional state and as the creation of a political space that goes beyond the state territory.

The Saami are also facing another threat, namely that their homeland is being redefined. Their reindeer pasture reduction is due to a transformation of pastures into agricultural land (as well as conservation areas in many parts of northern Fennoscandia). Two visions, two approaches regarding the development of the territory are in confrontation: pastoralism versus agriculture. In Latour's terms, the imposition of state sovereignty entails a curtailing of politics; the state's coup de force in facilitating the imposition of agriculture short-circuits the association between Saami people and reindeer. Or to use the language of Deleuze and Guattari, the Saami people are victims of a hostile takeover of non-state space.

James Anaya, UN Special Rapporteur on the Rights of Indigenous Peoples, has noted in his January 2001 report that the Saami peoples are politically organized around the *siida*, which plays an important role in land distribution.

> Within the *siida*, members had individual rights to resources but helped each other with the management of reindeer herds, hunting and fishing. On the basis of these structures, the [Saami] developed sophisticated systems for land distribution, inheritance and dispute resolution among *siida*. Although historical developments have weakened the [Saami] people's traditional patterns of association, the *siida* system continues to be an important part of [Saami] society.[41]

According to Anaya, the states' borders cut through the cultural and linguistic communities but also through the reindeer herding practices. The Saami peoples are seeing their traditional land distribution system cut by vertical and somewhat artificial state borders. They also have to share their land with Norwegian, Swedish, and Finnish farmers.

However, Norway, Sweden, and Finland (and less so Russia) are making efforts to capture this non-state politics by negotiating with the Saami a cross-border Nordic Saami Convention that would grant self-determination to the Saami people, which would allow them to protect their culture and language but also, among other things, to preserve their traditional association with the reindeer. This self-determination does not constitute a separation with the state though.[42] On this subject matter, the Office of the High Commissioner of Human Rights has mandated James Anaya to report on the situation of human rights and fundamental freedoms of indigenous people. An advanced copy of a special report on the Saami people is currently available. In it, James Anaya noted,

> Throughout the world few examples exist thus far of specific, formal arrangements to advance the self-determination of one indigenous people across the borders of several states. Still, the move toward such arrangements is part of developments over the last several decades that challenge the assumption that national borders are the sole marker of political organization and authority. As noted, the [Saami] people have made significant efforts to advance their collective self-determination through the development of cross-border institutions and initiatives, and have taken noteworthy steps in this regard; but ongoing barriers persist.[43]

The Saami argue for a structure of government in which they will able to exercise their capabilities of self-government and hopefully exercise their rights to create their collective, which would include non-human entities, such as the reindeer, the impacts of climate change, and pastures.

Self-determination is explicitly a tool to protect Saami culture and the traditional knowledge they have acquired over many generations. This traditional knowledge is directly linked to non-human entities surrounding them: plants, pastures, reindeer, ice, snow, and so forth. This is valuable knowledge for reassembling their collective; indeed, in

Latour's terms it is an integral part of the collective itself, given that one important part of the assembling of the collective is the knowledge of the various entities that compose it.

In order to situate where the proposed Nordic Saami Convention stands, imagine two lines: one on the vertical representing what Deleuze and Guattari described as the arboreal type of politics, based on the vertical structure of state authority; and the second one on the horizontal representing rhizomatic politics or the non-state politics. The meeting point of those two lines constitutes the meeting point of state politics and non-state politics. It is the intersection of a definition of a vertical state authority based on geography and the claim advanced by Saami for recognition of their self-determination.

Ecopolitics is located at the junction of the two lines. Political ecology as defined by Latour constitutes the bridge between state sovereignty and non-state politics. The deterritorialized ecopolitics is the cornerstone of self-determination. It is recognition of the legitimacy of humans and non-humans to create their own association based on an ongoing effort to reassemble a collective.

However, the negotiations between the sovereign state and the applicants for self-determination are not a simple process. It is not a negotiation where the parties are equal. The authority of the state is strong, and it uses the coup de force against anything that would threaten its sovereignty. The non-state politics are in the not-so-comfortable seat of those demanding spaces beyond sovereignty control. The territory is a state possession. The coup de force allows the state to develop its territory the way it chooses: extraction of natural resources, exploitation of oil and gas, fishing, agriculture, and so on.

The negotiation process, the power exercised by all parties around the negotiations, constitutes what Latour called political ecology, the reassembling of a collective. The process regarding the Nordic Saami Convention is what can be defined as political ecology because there is willingness by all parties to recognize the importance of the association of humans and non-humans, particularly the association between Saami people and reindeer.

CONCLUSION

The sort of reconstructed green theory of sovereignty offered here argues that claims to sovereignty in the Arctic should be understood as framing devices that have three principal sorts of ecopolitical consequences. First, they have definite anti-ecological effects. The contemporary claims to sovereignty, whether over contested places (Hans Island, etc.) or in newly opened-up commons (the Russians planting a flag on the ocean floor), are being driven largely by state concerns to secure access to resources for commercial development. Although this is in part just rent-seeking—one state seeking to maximize its control of a resource that would otherwise fall to another—it is also the possibility of the exploitation of the resource, with all the ecological consequences that follow. Historically, the imposition of sovereign control has been a precondition for the accelerated extraction of resources, from coal in England, to forests in Brazil, to oil in Saudi Arabia. There is no reason to believe that successful extension of sovereign control will be any different.

Second, such claims operate as a coup de force; that is, they close down many of the possibilities for deliberative co-management of the Arctic that are present in many existing governance arrangements in the region. This makes it harder to develop such arrangements that might help societies deal with ecological shocks as they emerge.

Third, such claims to sovereignty always have what Michel Callon called overflowings. In the Arctic, various actual and potential processes may undermine the successful claim to sovereignty. Oil rig or shipping disasters, straddling fish stocks, unintended effects of ice melting, shutting down of the Gulf Stream or Labrador current, temporary re-expansions of sea ice after development has already occurred in the region, and successful legal claims by indigenous groups are just a few such events or processes one might imagine could undermine such sovereign claims.

These overflowings draw attention to the ongoing conflictual dynamic between attempts at sovereign control over territory and the development of a range of innovative governance practices that emerge in the context of the complexity of socio-ecological processes. We have drawn in particular on Bruno Latour here to suggest ways that such co-management projects are the basis for thinking about ecological politics in the Arctic. Pursuing such schemes, however, needs to be understood not as a reconstructed or "shared" sovereignty, as implied in later chapters in this volume, but rather as an explicitly postsovereign form of politics, refusing the possibility of a "final" source of authority in favor of ongoing deliberative processes between varied actors, including imaginative ways of incorporating non-humans into the collective.

NOTES

1. According to the IPCC Fourth Assessment report, produced in 2007, sea ice in the Arctic had declined by around 2.7 percent per decade since 1978, for a total of around 8–9 percent. It projected summer sea ice was likely to have disappeared by 2100. Another way of seeing this data is that 1.5 million square kilometers (around the size of Alaska) has been lost from summer sea ice since 1978. New data emerged rapidly after the publication of that report, suggesting a much quicker rate of loss, particularly stimulated by the observation of a record loss of sea ice in the summer of 2007. See Josefino C. Comiso et al., "Accelerated Decline in the Arctic Sea Ice Cover," *Geophysical Research Letters* 35 (2008): 1–6; and IPCC, *Climate Change 2007: Synthesis Report* (Geneva: Intergovernmental Panel on Climate Change, 2007).

2. Charles Tilly, "War Making and State Making as Organized Crime," in *Bringing the State Back In*, ed. Peter Evans, Dietrich Rueschemeyer, and Theda Skocpol (Cambridge: Cambridge University Press, 1985), 169–191.

3. Ibid.

4. James Meadowcroft, "From the Welfare State to the Ecostate," in *The Global Ecological Crisis and the Nation-State*, ed. John Barry and Robyn Eckersley (Cambridge, MA: MIT Press, 2005), 3–24. On ecological modernization, see in particular Arthur Mol, "Ecological Modernisation and Institutional Reflexivity: Environmental Reform in the Late Modern Age," *Environmental Politics* 5, no. 2 (1996): 302–323.

5. Robert Goodin, *Green Political Theory* (Cambridge: Polity Press, 1992).

6. Karen Litfin, ed., *The Greening of Sovereignty* (Cambridge, MA: MIT Press, 1998), and Robyn Eckersley, *The Green State: Rethinking Democracy and Sovereignty* (Cambridge, MA: MIT Press, 2004).

7. Eckersley, *Green State*, and Alexander Wendt, *Social Theory of International Politics* (Cambridge: Cambridge University Press, 1999).

8. Thom Kuehls, *Beyond Sovereignty: The Space of Ecopolitics* (Minneapolis: University of Minnesota Press, 1996).

9. Ibid., quoting Gilles Deleuze and Félix Guattari, *Anti-Oedipus: Capitalism and Schizophrenia*.

10. John Dryzek, *Rational Ecology: Environment and Political Economy* (Oxford: Basil Blackwell, 1987).

11. Die Grünen, *The Programme of the German Green Party* (London: Heretic, 1983). On decentralization as a part of green ideology, see Matthew Paterson, "Green Theory," in *Theories of International Relations*, 4th ed., ed. Scott Burchill et al. (London: Palgrave Macmillan, 2009), 89–115.

12. Robert Paehlke and Douglas Torgerson, eds., *Managing Leviathan: Environmental Politics and the Administrative State*, 2nd ed. (Peterborough, ON: Broadview Press, 2005).

13. R. B. J. Walker, *Inside/Outside: International Relations as Political Theory* (Cambridge: Cambridge University Press, 1993).

14. Colin Hay, "Environmental Security and State Legitimacy," in *Is Capitalism Sustainable? Political Economy and the Politics of Ecology*, ed. Martin O'Connor (New York: Guilford Press, 1994), 78–102. A whole suite of international norms has of course emerged to attempt to temper this sovereignty norm, and whether such shifts undermine the fundamental logic of sovereignty here is a key question, which we address later.

15. See for example F. E. Trainer, *Abandon Affluence!* (London: Zed, 1985), or O'Connor, *Is Capitalism Sustainable?*

16. See for example Carolyn Merchant, *The Death of Nature: Women, Ecology and the Scientific Revolution* (San Francisco: Harper & Row, 1980), or Val Plumwood, *Feminism and the Mastery of Nature* (London: Routledge, 1993).

17. Bruno Latour, *Politics of Nature: How to Bring Science into Democracy* (Cambridge, MA: Harvard University Press, 2004).

18. Ibid., 31.

19. Usually these bioregions are defined by watersheds. See in particular Kirkpatrick Sale, *Human Scale* (San Francisco: W. H. Freeman, 1980).

20. Gilles Deleuze and Félix Guattari, *A Thousand Plateaus: Capitalism and Schizophrenia* (Minneapolis: University of Minnesota Press, 1987).

21. Mick Smith, "Against Ecological Sovereignty: Agamben, Politics, and Globalisation," *Environmental Politics* 18, no. 1 (2009): 99–116.

22. Giorgio Agamben, *Homo Sacer: Sovereign Power and Bare Life* (Stanford, CA: Stanford University Press, 1998).

23. Derrida. *Force de loi* (Paris: Galilée, 1994).

24. Ibid.

25. Latour, *Politics of Nature*, 247.

26. Hannah Arendt, *The Human Condition* (Chicago: University of Chicago Press, 1958), and Chantal Mouffe, *On the Political* (London: Routledge, 2005).

27. Eckersley, *Green State*. See also John Dryzek, "Transnational Democracy," *Journal of Political Philosophy* 7, no. 1 (1999): 30–51; and Dryzek, *Deliberative Global Politics: Discourse and Democracy in a Divided World* (Cambridge: Polity Press, 2006).

28. Andrew Barry, "The Anti-Political Economy," *Economy and Society* 31, no. 2 (2002): 268–284.

29. See Colin Hay, *Why We Hate Politics* (Cambridge: Polity Press, 2007), ch. 2 for an extended account of the different usages of the term *politics*. The notion of politics as about the pursuit of power is perhaps most famously associated with Max Weber. See Max Weber, "Politics as a Vocation," lecture at Munich University, 1919, http://anthropos-lab.net/wp/wp-content/uploads/2011/12/Weber-Politics-as-a-Vocation.pdf.

30. Barry, "The Anti-Political Economy," and Michel Callon, ed., *The Laws of the Markets* (Oxford: Blackwell, 1998).

31. See the Arctic Governance Project's website, http://www.arcticgovernance.org.

32. This is not to suggest that such arrangements succeed in creating "nonsovereign" spaces. Rather, they work in tension with attempts at sovereign control of territory in the region.

33. Kuehls, *Beyond Sovereign Territory*.

34. Ibid., 38.

35. Ibid., 39.

36. See for example Plumwood, *Feminism and the Mastery of Nature*.

37. Latour, *Politics of Nature*.

38. Bruno Latour, *Reassembling the Social: An Introduction to Actor-Network Theory* (Oxford: Oxford University Press, 2005), 29.

39. Ibid.

40. James Anaya, *Report of the Special Rapporteur on the Situation of the Human Rights and Fundamental Freedoms of Indigenous People*, advanced version, January 2011, http://www2.ohchr.org/english/issues/indigenous/rapporteur/.

41. Ibid., 4.

42. Ibid. See also John B. Henriksen, "The Continuous Process of Recognition and Implementation of the Saami People's Right to Self-Determination," *Cambridge Review of International Affairs* 21, no. 1 (2008): 27–40.

43. Anaya, *Report of the Special Rapporteur*, 10.

PART II

ARCTIC SOVEREIGNTY IN PRACTICE

CHAPTER 5

CANADIAN ARCTIC SECURITY

SHIFTING CHALLENGES

Rob Huebert

INTRODUCTION

Arctic sovereignty and security have been enduring elements of Canadian foreign and defense policy. Both in terms of actual security policy and in the imagination of Canadians and their leaders, the protection of the country's Arctic regions has remained one of the central challenges facing Canada. Although its actual importance has ebbed and surged over time, the Arctic has remained a key Canadian concern. One of the most intriguing aspects of the long-term nature of the challenges facing Canada concerns the nature of both the perception and response to what many believe threatens Canadian Arctic security.

This leads to the second element that must be considered in any evaluation of Canadian Arctic security. Canadian policy makers, the Canadian public, and Canadian researchers have tended to focus on sovereignty and security in the Arctic in a way that often intertwines and mixes the two terms in both policy and public discourse. This has created very interesting complexities around Canadian Arctic security issues. Important normative differences regarding the understanding and application of these two terms further influences this discussion. In international terms, the protection of sovereignty tends to mean to protect the *boundaries* of the state from foreign interference. Security tends to be associated with the means by which a state provides protection from foreign threat against the well-being of its citizens. Traditionally, this threat is understood in military terms, but in the modern context other types include environmental and health threats. Thus, to talk of the protection of Canadian Arctic sovereignty is to talk of the protection of Canada's northern boundaries. The protection of Canadian Arctic security means responding to foreign threats to the well-being of Canadians in the Arctic region. It is often difficult to determine if the Canadian commitment to the protection of Arctic sovereignty is about the protection of boundaries or of the people. Canadian leaders have conveniently used the terms synonymously.

THE EARLY YEARS: ARCTIC SOVEREIGNTY AND SECURITY BEFORE CANADA

Whereas the traditional view argues that the Arctic sovereignty and security challenges facing Canada did not begin to emerge until the Second World War, a closer examination demonstrates this is not the case. Rather issues relating to the protection and security of both the boundaries and the people of the region extend much further back into the historical record. It is ethnocentric to suggest that Arctic security in this region does not evolve as a topic until the arrival of the Europeans.[1] Some scholars believe that there may have been other northern indigenous populations such as the Dorset culture that were in fact displaced by the ancestors of the Inuit populations.[2] It can be speculated that there were significant security issues among the peoples of the region just as there were in other parts of the globe. The problem is that an understanding of this era in the context of security simply does not exist.

The first contact between Canadian Northern peoples and Europeans probably occurred with the arrival of the Vikings. Once again the historical record is fragmented.[3] An intriguing possibility shaping the Viking experience in the region concerns the impacts of climate change.[4] One of the greatest challenges to the Viking efforts to settle Greenland and Northern Canada was a substantial period of climatic cooling. Is this the first instance of environmental insecurity driving foreign actors from the region?

When subsequent European explorers and traders began to arrive in the Canadian northern regions, there are some limited records of both cooperation and violence.[5] There was a general disregard by the Europeans for any ownership rights by the Inuit in this region. Most Europeans saw this as an empty wasteland and not as someone's homeland.[6] Thus it is clear that the early history of the Canadian North provides some tantalizing, albeit incomplete, insights into larger security issues that retain their relevancy into the modern era. Undoubtedly future research will provide important contributions toward a better understanding of this period.

CONFEDERATION: THE AWAKENING OF CANADIAN ARCTIC SOVEREIGNTY AND SECURITY ISSUES

In the years following confederation in 1867, the Canadian claim over its Arctic region was slowly consolidated. Great Britain transferred ownership of the Arctic region in 1880. However, the transference was vague and incomplete. From that time and up to the 1930s, Canada engaged in a series of activities to consolidate its claim.[7] This included sitting on an international tribunal to determine the border between the Yukon, northern British Columbia, and Alaska; and extinguishing any existing or potential claim that Scandinavian countries may have had to the northern lands.

The process used to delimit the Alaska border was the first time that Canadian officials faced American interests in the Arctic. The need to determine a border was a direct result of the vagueness of the 1825 treaty between Russia and Great Britain. Following the sale of Alaska to the United States and with Canada achieving self-governing status, both in 1867, there was no pressing need to provide for more specific determination of the border.[8] This changed with the discovery of gold in the Klondike region in 1896. Canadian concerns were that the United States might apply their doctrine of Manifest Destiny to Canada's north. Canada moved to increase its domestic security of the Yukon region through the deployment of the Northwest Mounted Police, along with other steps to demonstrate its control of the region.[9]

Canada also moved to resolve the long-standing boundary dispute, agreeing to create an international tribunal to adjudicate the issue. Three members of the tribunal were appointed by the United States, and three members were appointed by the United Kingdom. The British made the decision to appoint one of the three from the United Kingdom and the other two from Canada. Ultimately, the one British member of the tribunal sided with the United States and not with the Canadian members. The net result was a growing Canadian nationalism and determination to achieve complete control over its foreign relations, including the protection of their northern region.[10]

In many ways this issue set the stage for the future. The control of the Canadian North became important because of resources (in this case gold). Canada also engaged in an international effort to resolve the core problem. Yet its ability to act on its own was limited by its status as a self-governing dominion. The fact that the British representative on the tribunal sided with the United States created strong nationalist feelings in Canada. The protection of Canadian Arctic territory became an important rallying point for Canadian nationalism.

WORLD CONFLICT IN THE CANADIAN NORTH: THE NEED FOR ARCTIC SECURITY

The outbreak of World War II brought the first modern conflict to the Canadian Arctic. Technological and geopolitical realities allowed the combatants to move farther north than had been the case in previous wars. Specifically the Germans recognized the need to have weather stations situated along the northern coast of Canada to allow for their meteorological services to be able to monitor weather for their U-boats.[11]

But a more direct threat developed in the Pacific theater from the Japanese. In 1942 the Japanese attacked several islands in the Aleutian chain. The purpose of these attacks and occupation of two islands— Kiska and Attu—were to divert American attention from their attack on Midway Island. In order to respond to this threat, the Americans decided to build a road that would connect Anchorage to the road systems of North America. The Alaska Highway was constructed in a very quick fashion and was a model of Canadian-American cooperation.[12] The United States provided most of the funding as well as the labor for its construction. As soon as it was completed, the Americans handed complete control of this section in Canada to Canadian officials.

The German weather stations and the Japanese Aleutian campaign were relatively small exercises in the overall scope of the war. However, they did point out several important issues. First, enemies of Canada and the United States were becoming aware of the strategic importance of the Arctic. Second, the cooperation between Canada and the United States was excellent—as it was in most elements during the war. Although there were some concerns expressed by the Canadian government, such as that the Americans may not want to leave Canadian territory voluntarily once they completed their task, there is no evidence to suggest the American intention was to stay. Third, despite the great challenges that existed in building the Alaska Highway, once the need was recognized, the Americans and Canadians put every effort into its construction to ensure its successful completion.

THE COLD WAR AND THE DEVELOPMENT OF THE MODERN CANADIAN ARCTIC SECURITY THREAT

The modern test for Canadian Arctic security came with the arrival of the Cold War. As it quickly became apparent that the former Allies of the war would soon become enemies, technological developments from the war placed the Canadian Arctic, and the entire Arctic region, at the center of the conflict. The growing hostilities between the Soviet Union and the Western powers became evident by the end of the 1940s. Canadian leaders shared the same suspicions of the USSR as all of the other Western leaders and began to fear the aggressive intent of the Soviets.[13] Compounding the challenge for Canada was the development of nuclear weapons and long-range missile technology. Once the Soviet Union had developed its own nuclear forces and then had learned to place the weapons on a rocket, geography positioned Canada between the Soviets and the Americans' strategic forces.[14] The shortest and most direct line of attack for both long-range bombers and missiles was over the Arctic region and therefore overhead of the Canadian North.[15]

In the initial phases of the conflict, Canadian officials recognized the need to cooperate with the United States to defend against a possible bomber strike by the Soviet Union. Given the vastness of the region, any effort by Canada to act on its own would be prohibitively expensive. In order to respond to the Soviet threat, Canada and the United States embarked on two major defense projects. They developed a string of radar sites that spanned the entire North American Arctic region. It began in the westernmost regions of Alaska, crossed Canada, and was extended into Greenland. Known as the Distant Early Warning Line (DEW Line), it was a major engineering achievement.[16] There was yet again concern among some Canadian officials that the Americans may not leave after the construction. But the Americans transferred to Canada full control of the system once it was completed.[17]

Following the outbreak of the Korean War, Canada quickly built up its air force.[18] But even with this expanded interceptor capability, Canadian officials soon recognized that the defense against Soviet bombers attacking over the Arctic region would require close cooperation with the Americans. This led to the second major Canadian project—the creation of a defense agreement to protect the aerospace regions of North America—NORAD (North American Air [and subsequently aerospace] Defense). Once again there was sensitivity in Canada about threats to Canadian sovereignty regarding American flights into Canadian airspace. In order to mitigate these concerns, Canada and the United States formed NORAD.[19] It provided for the joint monitoring of North American Arctic airspace and provides for a joint command structure. This arrangement is still in operation at the time of this publication.

As the Soviet nuclear delivery systems for their nuclear weapons evolved from bombers to missiles, the Canadian and American core mission in the Arctic changed from defense to deterrence. Missiles could not be shot down. The United States developed a series of systems to deter the Soviets from launching an attack in the first place instead of offering a defense against an attack. This was done by improving the existing surveillance systems, such as the DEW Line, and developing its own missiles that could be launched as soon as a warning of Soviet missile launch was received. The net result of such a launch would be the destruction of both the American and Soviet targets. Both states (and presumably their allies as well) would suffer total annihilation. It was hoped that the knowledge that the United States and its NATO allies would be both capable of and determined to commit mutual suicide would be sufficient to deter the Soviet leadership from ever launching in the first place.[20]

The Canadian Arctic was not going to be a battlefield for land forces. But it was to play the critical role in the maintenance of nuclear deterrence. If deterrence failed, the missiles would be launched over it. But the success of deterrence required that the Soviet Union completely understood and believed that it could not launch a successful surprise attack because of the surveillance capabilities deployed by the North American states in the Arctic.

Canada's role in the maintenance of nuclear deterrence was based on cooperation and as a junior partner with the United States over its northern territory. There were initial concerns by Canadian political elites and some members of the Canadian public that the United States would take advantage of its more powerful capabilities and attempt to retain some form of control over Canadian sovereign territory in the Arctic. But again this did not happen. Once the DEW Line was constructed—and periodically updated—and once NORAD was created, the United States did not attempt to seize or assert control of any part of the Canadian North and instead remains sensitive to Canadian concerns.

In the 1970s further technological developments in weapons added again to the importance of the Arctic. The United States and Soviet Union developed the means to place a small nuclear reactor to power their submarines. Submarines now did not have to surface to replenish their batteries. Nuclear power provided submarines with virtually unlimited power that could be used to produce oxygen and drinking water as well.[21] The duration of the submarine voyage underwater became determined only by the endurance capability of its crew. Prior to this development, no submarine could go under the ice cover of the Arctic Ocean for fear of running out of power by not being able to surface.

The Arctic became even more important when both sides gained the ability to place nuclear armed missiles in the submarines and launch them from beneath the surface (known as SSBN).[22] The development of the submarine-launched ballistic missile (SLBM) was profound. The Soviet Union now had the means of hiding its nuclear deterrence at sea by sailing directly into the ice-covered Arctic Ocean from its northern bases.[23] Whereas both sides had developed sophisticated surveillance means of locating the land-based strategic missiles of the other side, it was now very difficult to find all of the submarines of the other side. The submarines had a much higher probability of surviving a surprise attack by the opponent. This reinforced the notion that a surprise attack could not achieve success.

Because the geography of the Soviet Union meant that the most secure location to deploy its submarines was from the Kola Peninsula, American attack submarines were soon also entering the Arctic region. In this instance, the United States did not want or seek Canadian assistance. The complexity of operating submarines in the Arctic was difficult enough without having to deal with an ally. Canada considered purchasing nuclear-powered attack submarines twice, in the 1960s and again in the 1980s.[24] In both instances the purchase of the submarines was considered too expensive and never acted upon.

Despite the significance and importance of this under-ice theater of operation, Canadian officials were content to play almost no role. The costs of maintaining the weapons necessary for Canadian involvement simply seemed too high. In this regard, Canadian officials were willing to allow the Americans to take full responsibility for the security of the ice-covered Arctic Ocean.

The Canadian effort to maintain military control over its Arctic ended almost as soon as the Cold War ended. The navy ceased its northern deployments (NORPLOYs) in 1989. The air force reduced its northern sovereignty overflights of its Aurora long-range patrol aircraft from a high of twenty-two in 1987 to two by 1995. The only land force presence is the Canadian Rangers Units, a militia unit composed of local volunteers who are given a minimum of training, a red sweatshirt, a rifle, and some ammunition. Whereas the Canadian Forces have traditionally provided them with very little, the Rangers provide the forces with a wealth of information and capabilities. Equally important is that they have always provided the forces with a rich source of traditional knowledge. They know the land and how to survive on it. Thus they have proven to be a very important asset whenever the regular forces have wanted to operate in the North.

Throughout the Cold War when Canadian officials were convinced that a threat to the safety of Canadians existed, they were willing to take action that required considerable resources. They also demonstrated a willingness to work as closely as necessary with the Americans to provide for the common defense of North America, including its northern regions.

THE NORTHWEST PASSAGE AND THE DEVELOPMENT OF THE MODERN CANADIAN ARCTIC SOVEREIGNTY THREAT

Although Canadian officials preferred to ignore issues relating to security under the Arctic ice, they were not able to avoid issues on the surface. As discussed in previous sections, the United States had never attempted to use any of its cooperative military activity in the Arctic region to undermine Canadian Arctic sovereignty. However, the one area where this does not remain true is in regards to commercial maritime traffic through the Northwest Passage.

The international legal status of the Northwest Passage has been the major Arctic diplomatic dispute between Canada and the United States in the modern era.[25] The specifics of the dispute revolved around whether or not the Northwest Passage was a strait used for international navigation. Under international law, an international strait is determined by two criteria: geography and functionality. It needs to be a body of water that joins two international bodies of water. The Northwest Passage meets this criterion. In terms of functionality, an international strait needs to be used by international shippers. It is on this criterion that Canada and the United States disagree. Because the Northwest Passage has been icebound for most of the last 100 years, very few vessels have been able to transit the passage. Those that have almost always asked for Canadian permission. There have only been three voyages of two vessels that have not requested Canadian permission.

In 1969 and 1970, the USS *Manhattan*, an ice-strengthened tanker, sailed through the passage. Its mission was to determine the feasibility of transporting the recently discovered oil on the north slope of Alaska.[26] The Americans were trying to decide if it would be better to ship the oil by tanker through the Northwest Passage or if a pipeline should be built from the north of Alaska to the south of Alaska and then to ship the oil by tanker from the port of Valdez.[27] Ultimately the difficulty of the transit of the *Manhattan* convinced the Americans that the pipeline to Valdez was the better way to transform the oil. In 1985 the American icebreaker the *Polar Sea* also made a transit of the passage without asking permission.

The American position is that these three passages combined with the future expected voyages through the Northwest Passage means that the Northwest Passage is a strait used for international navigation. The primary ramifications of this are that under international law, international vessels have the right of transit passage. This means that the coastal state—Canada—cannot require that permission be requested before the voyage occurs. As long as the vessel follows international standards and international law, it can proceed.

The Canadian position is that because of the very low number of transits that have occurred without permission, and the very difficult ice conditions that have existed, Canada has historically demonstrated that the functionality criterion has not been met. Therefore, the passage is not a strait used for international navigation and is instead Canadian internal waters. This in turn means that any international vessel that intends to transit the passage is required to request permission from Canada before proceeding.[28]

The irony relating to security is that it would be in the United States' favor if the Northwest Passage was Canadian internal waters. This would allow Canada to completely control the passage of all vessels.[29] Specifically, it could stop vessels that were hostile to Canadian and American interests from entering these waters. Given the sensitivity the Americans now have for the protection of their borders, this would seem to be very enticing for them. The problem facing the Americans, however, is that should they be seen agreeing with the Canadian position, it would set a precedent regarding their position on international straits elsewhere. In particular, Iran, China, Indonesia, or any other coastal state that borders an international strait would argue that special circumstances allow them also to impose controls on free navigation through their straits. This is of course very dangerous to American and Canadian economic and security interests beyond the Arctic. So the issue is not about the Northwest Passage but is instead about an international precedent that the United States does not want to set.

The Americans have actually demonstrated considerable sensitivity to the Canadian position while being careful not to undermine their position internationally. Following the voyage of the *Polar Sea* in 1985, Canada and the United States entered into negotiations in an effort to resolve the issue of the status of the Northwest Passage. Largely because of the close relationship between President Ronald Reagan and Prime Minister Brian Mulroney, the two sides were able to reach an agreement regarding the transit of American icebreakers through the Northwest Passage. The Americans agreed to ask for consent (not permission), and Canada was expected to give it. The 1988 Arctic Waters Cooperation Agreement ensures that the political dispute over the passage of American icebreaker *Polar Sea* will not be repeated.[30] Under the terms of the agreement, both the Americans and Canadians can claim that their interests are protected. But more importantly, it eliminates an irritant in the Canadian-American relationship. This does not allow for a final resolution of the issue, but it does allow Canada and the United States to move on to more important issues.

CLIMATE CHANGE AND RESPONDING TO THE NEW CANADIAN
ARCTIC SECURITY THREAT

With the end of the Cold War, scientists were able to improve cooperation in looking at Arctic scientific issues. It had been assumed by most
scientists in Canada and abroad that the Arctic was a pristine environment. One set of researchers began to examine the impact of persistent
organic pollutants (POP) on Canada. They were initially baffled but soon
horrified to discover that the Arctic was more heavily contaminated than
southern latitudes in Canada.[31] It was discovered that trans-boundary
pollution was contaminating much of the Arctic region through a series
of complicated processes. This ultimately led Canada to champion the
creation of an international response directly in regard to persistent
organic pollutants, but more importantly it began to create a mindset
in Canada of the need to address environmental security in the Arctic
region.

When the Cold War came to an end in 1989, most observers believed
that the main security issues in the Arctic were resolved. With the
collapse of the Soviet Union, the strategic imperative to maintain
powerful military forces was removed. Furthermore, the economic
collapse of the Soviet Union also resulted in the virtual disappearance of
the Soviet navy and in particular their submarine forces. The submarines
were literally allowed to rot in harbor.[32] In time, the fear that there
could be substantial radioactive contamination from the submarines led
the United States and Norway, and eventually the entire G8, to provide
substantial resources to assist the new Russian regime in the dismantling
of the submarines and their nuclear reactors.[33]

Canada along with all the other NATO states, with the exception of
the United States, also stood down most of their military forces. For
example, the Canadian government canceled plans to purchase ten to
twelve nuclear-powered attack submarines (SSN) as well as a planned
large icebreaker at this time.[34]

Canada quickly shifted its attention from military security in the Arctic to a focus on improving international cooperation in the region. Prime Minister Mulroney suggested in 1989 the creation of an international body that would include all of the Arctic states to address issues relating to improvement of relations in the region.[35] However, the United States was somewhat reluctant to create new multilateral organizations at this point and preferred to deal with its Arctic neighbors on a bilateral basis.[36]

At the same time that Canada was recognizing the need to develop a far more robust response to the problem of environmental security, Finland was looking for a means of consolidating and improving relationships with the then Soviet Union. It launched what became known as the Finnish initiative to create the Arctic Environmental Protection Strategy (AEPS).[37] However, Canadian officials played a critical role in the successful creation and negotiation of this agreement. Building on an existing Canadian domestic policy known as the Arctic Environment Strategy (AES), the Finns internationalized what Canada had created internally.[38] The focus of this agreement was to create international Arctic cooperation to better understand the environmental threats to the Arctic region and then to respond to these threats. A secondary objective that was championed by Canada was the involvement of northern aboriginal peoples in the process.[39] In Canada's domestic policy, a critical component was the inclusion of Canadian Northern peoples in the decision-making process of addressing environmental issues. Canada argued that it was not only the smart thing to do, given that the Northern peoples had a vast repository of traditional knowledge about the environment, but it was also the right thing to do because this was their home.[40]

The United States was initially reluctant to accept the creation of a special status for indigenous peoples in an international agreement (ultimately to be known as permanent participants). However, the good personal relationship between President Bill Clinton and Prime Minister

Jean Chrétien eventually enabled the United States to accept this new designation. However, the Americans also demanded that the organization specifically not look at issues related to military security for this new body.[41]

The agreement to form AEPS then led to the creation of a series of working groups and task forces that then examined specific environmental issues in the North. Individually the output of the separate working groups was mixed, but overall the AEPS was a success. It provided the first means of cooperation in the Arctic and it discovered the severity of the environmental degradation of the North. It also provided an important means for including all of the northern aboriginal peoples in the process.

However, Canada never lost sight of its desire to create a high-level political forum that dealt with all international issues pertaining to the Arctic. Although it was the Conservatives under the leadership of Prime Minister Mulroney who first suggested the creation of such a body, it was the Liberal government of Jean Chrétien that continued to champion the idea. The Canadian efforts were ultimately successful, and agreement was reached by the eight Arctic state members of the AEPS to create a new body to be known as the Arctic Council.[42] Canadian officials had hoped that this council would not be simply a modification of the AEPS. They hoped that they would be able to create a high-level political forum to address all political issues concerning the North.[43]

Officially formed in September 1996, the new body continued the good work of the AEPS. It was the Arctic Council in partnership with other scientific organizations that began an extensive study of climate change and the Arctic region. With results coming out in 2004, the Arctic Climate Impact Assessment (ACIA) was a multiyear effort among all the major Arctic scientists.[44] The most profound finding of the study was that the permanent ice cap was melting. The study concluded that somewhere in the future the year-round ice (also known as multiyear ice) will melt in the summer months. The report predicted that this would likely occur somewhere toward the end of the current century.[45] In 2012 many scientists revised their estimations to project that the multiyear ice will completely melt in the summer months by 2020–2025![46]

Perhaps the most important political impact of this finding for issues regarding Canadian Arctic security and sovereignty has been the realization by both the Arctic and non-Arctic states that the Arctic Ocean is moving to become an ocean like any other ocean. This growing recognition of the transformation of the Arctic Ocean has created an eagerness on the part of the international community to take advantage of the melting ocean. While the division of the Arctic Ocean in regard to the mineral wealth on and under the seabed will be determined by the terms of the United Nations Convention on the Law of the Sea (UNCLOS, Article 76), many other issues remain uncertain.[47] It is possible that new fish stocks may either move into the waters or be discovered as the ice melts. Beyond the 200-mile exclusive economic zone (EEZ), which will remain under the sovereign control of the coastal state, international fishing fleets will have the right to exploit these new stocks, if they exist. There will certainly be issues regarding international navigation. Both Canada and Russia will find increasing interest in using these waterways as the ice melts for longer periods. Some studies have already been conducted by the Arctic Council to determine the impact of shipping once the sea ice melts.[48]

RESPONSE OF THE CANADIAN GOVERNMENT TO THE NEW THREATS AND CHALLENGES

The environmental security of the region will be fundamentally transformed as the ice melts. The impacts of a warming Arctic will substantially alter the traditional hunting lifestyle of the Inuit. There is already recognition that the changes occurring are affecting both fish and animal activity. This influences the ability of the Inuit to hunt. The thinning ice is also making transportation much more dangerous.[49]

The melting ice and growing interest of the world has compelled Canada to reexamine its view on strategic security issues. In 1999 the Canadian Forces began to seriously reconsider their role in the Arctic to address this decline.[50] Concerns of senior officers led to the creation of an interdepartmental (federal and territorial) security work group named the Arctic Security Intergovernmental Working Group (ASIWG) as well as an internal Department of National Defence review of its Arctic capabilities. After the terrorist attacks of September 11, 2001, the entire Canadian government began to take security issues much more seriously. In 2002, Canada resumed military training operations in the North. Initially limited affairs that took place on a small scale in August, they have now become an annual event and are continually evolving into more complex operations. Since that time, the Canadian Forces have continued to increase both the scope and frequency of these exercises in the northern region. Canada has also invited two of its northern neighbors, the United States and Denmark, to participate in some of its exercises since 2009.[51]

During the Paul Martin administration, Canadian political leaders began to share the view that Canadian Arctic security required improvement. Although too short-lived to act upon this realization, the Martin government either developed or was developing policies that highlighted the need for action. Upon the release of a set of policy papers on defense, diplomacy, development, and international trade, the need to provide for Arctic security received substantial attention in the defense and diplomacy papers. The document, focusing on the expected rise of activity in the North, stated, "The demands of sovereignty and security for the Government could become even more pressing as activity in the north continues to rise."[52] It then states that Canada will need to increase its ability to act in the North.

The Martin government also began developing a domestic policy statement on the North. This was an attempt to move away from the traditional approach of department-specific policy and was hoped to provide a government of Canada Arctic policy. Referred to as the Northern Strategy, it was to be built on seven pillars or subsections, one of which was "Reinforcing Sovereignty, National Security and Circumpolar Cooperation."[53] Despite the Martin government conducting numerous meetings, this document was not finalized before the government's defeat in the 2006 federal election.

Although the Martin government initiated a renewed thinking on traditional security in the Canadian Arctic, its efforts to implement these policies were interrupted by its fall from power and subsequent winter election campaign of 2005–2006. The leader of the Conservative Party, Stephen Harper, made the protection of Canadian Arctic security and sovereignty one of his main campaign platforms.[54] This was somewhat unusual in that Canadian political parties have seldom campaigned on this topic. Nevertheless, while campaigning in Winnipeg in December 2005, not only did Harper attack the Liberals for their lack of effort in this regard, but he also made several concrete promises, including a commitment to build armed icebreakers for the Canadian navy.

Harper won the election and formed a minority government. He remained committed to the issue of improving the protection of Canadian Arctic sovereignty and security. He has visited the North on official business every year—something no other prime minister has ever done. He has also used what many have viewed as a much more aggressive rhetoric to talk about Canadian Arctic sovereignty. In particular, he began to use the phrase "use it or lose it."[55] Although in recent years he has moved away from this terminology, his government has developed and begun to implement a robust and expensive program to improve the ability for Canada to operate in the Arctic. The emphasis has been on improving Canada's surveillance and enforcement capabilities.

DEVELOPMENT OF A NEW POLICY FRAMEWORK

The Harper government continued the development of new policy framework that had been initiated by the Martin government. Specifically it has released a similar set of documents that followed in the direction of both the international and domestic policies that have been in the works. The government of Canada introduced Canada's Northern Strategy in 2007 and followed it up with a written document in 2009 entitled *Canada's Northern Strategy: Our North, Our Heritage, Our Future.*[56] The strategy established four Canadian northern domestic priorities. They included exercising Arctic sovereignty, protecting the Arctic environment, promoting social and economic development in the region, and improving and devolving northern governance. Of the four, the first priority was the most important relative to Arctic sovereignty and security issues.

In the document, Canada reaffirmed that Canada's sovereignty over its Arctic lands and waters is long-standing, well established, and based on historical title, international law, and the presence of Inuit and other aboriginal peoples for thousands of years. Canada also recognized that the international community has become much more interested in the region. In response Canada is now taking steps to demonstrate its effective stewardship and international leadership to promote a stable, rule-based Arctic region where the rights of sovereign states are respected. The government has highlighted four major accomplishments and initiatives that it has pursued under this priority. These include a statement on Canada's Arctic foreign policy, Canada's effort to map its continental shelf in the Arctic region, new capital projects to build new enforcement and surveillance potential, and the expansion of Canadian Forces facilities and operations in the Arctic.[57]

The Department of Foreign Affairs released the *Statement on Canada's Arctic Foreign Policy: Exercising Sovereignty and Promotion Canada's Northern Strategy* in August 2010.[58] Released as a pamphlet, it explained how Canada plans to pursue its four main Arctic priorities. It also provided a list of the main international focus areas of Canadian northern strategy: engaging with neighbors to resolve boundary issues; securing international recognition for the full extent of Canada's Arctic continental shelf; addressing Arctic governance and related emerging issues such as public safety; creating the appropriate international conditions for sustainable development; seeking trade and investment opportunities that benefit northerners; encouraging a greater understanding of the human dimension of the Arctic; contributing to and supporting international efforts to address climate change and the Arctic; strengthening Arctic science and the legacy of the international polar year; engaging northerners on Canada's Arctic foreign policy; supporting indigenous permanent participant organizations at the Arctic Council; and providing Canadian youth with the opportunity to participate in the circumpolar dialogue.[59]

IMPLEMENTING THE NEW FRAMEWORK FOR CANADIAN ARCTIC SECURITY

The intention of the Harper government is to demonstrate that it is attempting to protect a broad understanding of Canadian Arctic security. There is no mention of a geopolitical threat, but there are talks of a changing geopolitical environment. The government has initiated some discussions regarding the Beaufort Sea boundary dispute. In the summer of 2010, Canadian and American officials met to begin to discuss this issue.[60] It is not known how well these negotiations have gone or if there is any clear agenda for movement. There has also been some media attention on a possible resolution of the dispute regarding Hans Island.[61] In November 2012, the Canadian and Danish governments announced that they had resolved differences in the Lincoln Sea, north of Ellesmere Island and Greenland.[62] However, the two countries still failed to resolve their long-standing differences regarding Hans Island.

At the same time, Canada has invested substantial resources in the science necessary to determine the coordinates of the Canadian extended continental shelf in the Arctic region. This will represent a very significant extension of Canada's northern territory. However, under the terms of UNCLOS, this extension will be restricted to the soil and subsoil of the extended continental shelf. Nevertheless, this represents important new potential in oil and gas holdings in the region. Canada, the United States, and Denmark have all cooperated in the scientific effort to measure the extended continental shelf in this region.[63] It is not known if Canada's submission will overlap with any of its Arctic neighbors. This will only be determined when Canada officially submits its coordinates sometime in 2013. It is possible that Canada has already resolved any differences with Russia, United States, and Denmark, but it is equally likely that there will be an overlap with one or more of these nations. All of these countries have committed to resolving any differences peacefully and in terms of the procedures outlined by international law.

Canada's commitment to security through international cooperation will be highlighted during the two years when Canada holds the chairmanship of the Arctic Council in 2013. This role comes as the Council is enjoying newfound respect and challenges.[64] The Arctic Council has been responsible for several important studies regarding the Arctic,[65] as well as for the creation of a search and rescue treaty in the Arctic.[66] But one of the ironies of its successes has been the growing interest it has created in the outside world. The European Union, China, and Japan are among a growing number of international actors that now want to join the body as a permanent observer. For a wide range of reasons, there has been considerable resistance in the council to these requests.[67]

The Harper government has been sending somewhat mixed messages regarding its intended use of the chair to further its stated policy regarding the chairmanship. Whereas several outside groups have been holding workshops and conferences about this issue, the government itself has been secretive with its own plans. The government announced that Minister of Health Leona Aglukkaq will act as the Senior Arctic Official for Canada and therefore will be chairing the council during Canada's term.[68] This has led to speculation that Canada will be focusing on community health and northern economic well-being during its term. The Harper government has been criticized for eliminating the position of circumpolar ambassador, a position created by the Chrétien government when it pushed for the creation of the Arctic Council. The appointment of a senior minister, however, suggests a renewed importance that is now being applied. It is too soon to know what this ultimately will mean.

Canada's efforts to increase its abilities to protect its northern territories are ongoing. The Harper government has announced a wide range of new initiatives to improve Canada's surveillance and enforcement capabilities. Among the many promises, the most important are (1) the construction of six to eight ice-capable and armed naval vessels known as the Arctic Offshore Patrol Ships (AOPS); (2) the construction of a large multipurpose icebreaker for the Canadian Coast Guard, with hints of the construction of a second vessel; (3) improving and expanding the training, numbers, and capability of the Canadian Rangers; (4) developing and improving Canada's surveillance capabilities in the Arctic; (5) increasing and expanding Canada's military exercises in its north; and (6) developing a High North resupply location for refueling of Canadian vessels. A seventh, more general element has been the Canadian commitment to improve the overall capabilities of the Canadian Air Force, including the ability to operate in the Arctic. The addition of the four CF-177 (Globemasters) was put in the context of improving Canadian ability to expand its strategic airlift worldwide. But efforts have already been made to ensure that these aircrafts can operate in the High North. The proposed purchase of the F-35 is also tied to maintaining Canadian abilities to operate fighter aircraft in its Arctic regions.[69]

In the face of the international economic crisis that began in 2008, the government has slowed the process in fulfilling some of these commitments, but as of 2012 the Harper government remains officially committed to each of these promises. The development of the AOPS and icebreaker has been delayed by the government's commitment to also develop a national shipbuilding strategy. Although it is impossible to officially confirm at this time, coast guard and navy officials have both commented on their ongoing efforts to develop these projects, and there is a guarded optimism that the governments will deliver. But at this point the actual construction has not yet begun on either project.

Improvements to the Rangers have also occurred. The Canadian Rangers in the North are an interesting hybrid of militia and Canadian Northern peoples.[70] There are Ranger units throughout Canada. These were created at the end of World War II to provide a greater surveillance capability by relying on local populations. The Ranger units in the Canadian Arctic, however, have become very well known for two attributes. First because they have proven to be very popular among the local populations, they include a large number of northern aboriginal peoples whose knowledge of the land is exceptional.[71] These Rangers provide the Canadian Forces with an ability to operate in the High North that would not otherwise exist. Second, because the Rangers have the ability to operate on the land and in areas that would be difficult for other Canadians, they have been very useful in spotting foreign incursions in Canada. There are indications that they have sighted a large number of foreign submarines in Canadian waters. But the actual number remains classified.

The Canadian Forces have provided the Rangers with a red sweatshirt, a very old rifle—an Enfield 303—and some limited training. The rifle dates back to the First World War, but ironically enough the Rangers have found that it operates better in the conditions of the High North than more modern rifles. The Canadian Forces have now increased the training and exercises of the Rangers. In each of Canada's Arctic exercises, the Rangers are always heavily involved. They remain a very important element in Canada's ability to operate in this region.

Canada has also been attempting to develop its own underwater surveillance capabilities—known as Northern Watch. Over the last few years, Canadian scientists associated with the Department of National Defence have been testing a system in the Canadian North. It is difficult to get details on this program, so it is equally challenging to know its current status.[72] If successful, it will give Canada the ability to listen for and detect submarines entering and leaving the Northwest Passage.

Canadian Arctic military exercises and operations were resumed in 2002 following their hiatus at the end of the Cold War. They continue to be expanded in scope and duration and are now being conducted during the winter months.[73] The proposed refueling site at Nanisivik is still in development. The scope of the project has been reduced and slowed partially because it is proving to be much more difficult to develop than was expected.[74]

Overall, these policy actions will significantly enhance Canada's ability to operate in the Arctic—as long as they are not canceled or substantially scaled back. If Canada does complete its commitments, it will have an enforcement and surveillance capability that has not existed before. Perhaps the most interesting element of this development is the fact that it is based on an anticipated need, not an actual need. In both the Northern Strategy and the *Statement on Canada's Arctic Foreign Policy*, the Harper government made it clear that it does not see an immediate military threat to the Canadian Arctic, but it does see a changing geopolitical environment.[75] It is not entirely clear what it means by this distinction. But an examination of the promised capital projects suggests that it does see a need for a much more robust ability to respond to the expected arrival of new international actors to the region.

Because the Canadian government is preparing in anticipation of growing international challenges, one of the critical debates now taking place is in regard to the nature of the threat to Canadian security. The debate has been substantial and wide-ranging. In the early twenty-first century, the concern was about growing international threats to

Canadian control of its Arctic resources and territories.[76] There was concern that the United States or some other states might attempt to take control of Canadian Arctic resources in its maritime zones. However, this concern receded as better understanding emerged regarding existing international law in the division and control of the Arctic resources.

There has also been concern about the growing Russian military strength in the Arctic. In 2007 the Russians resumed long-range bomber patrols up to Canadian airspace in the Arctic. These patrols continue currently. The Russians' rebuilding of their military capabilities including land and maritime forces has also created concerns in Canada.[77] There is debate as to whether the Russian efforts represent an attempt to become a more aggressive state in the region or they are merely refilling the void created when the Soviet troops in the region experienced total collapse.[78] The Russians are rebuilding their strategic deterrent with an emphasis on their submarine forces located in the North. What it ultimately means for Canada remains to be seen.

What is now confounding some observers is the entry of the Asian states into the Arctic region. China in particular has begun to dedicate very significant resources into Arctic scientific research.[79] The Chinese are also becoming increasingly interested in participating in the international governance regimes evolving in the Arctic. They have been successful in becoming an observer on the Arctic Council. In the long term, the resources they are now dedicating to strengthening their ability to operate in the polar regions demonstrate that China will increasingly be an important player in the region. Once again, what this means to the long-term security interests of Canada is still uncertain.[80]

CONCLUSION

Examining the development of Canadian Arctic security requirements provides a fascinating insight into the Canadian psyche. There is no question that the Canadian North plays a central role in Canadian political culture. The Canadian public and leaders understand this. But the extreme nature of both the climate and geography has meant that the actual abilities of outsiders to threaten or challenge Canadian control of this region have been relatively few. When these challenges have arisen, Canadian policy makers have shown an interesting ability to be innovative in responding to the specific need at the time. Within this context, Canada's willingness to work with the United States has been impressive despite the misgivings that some Canadians may have in this regard.

However, the fact that it has been so difficult for outsiders to come to the Canadian North has meant that Canadian policy makers often can talk big on the subject without having to take concrete actions. This is now changing. The impact of climate change and the concurrent interest of the outside world now present Canada with an uncertain future that it needs to prepare for. The question is what is the most effective manner by which it can do so? This is proving to be a very interesting exercise. In part it is because something changes in the Arctic on a constant basis. Policy makers are left with a moving target that is difficult to understand and prepare for. Ultimately it still leaves open the question as to what is truly Canadian Arctic security. The answer is that it is partly military, it is partly environmental, it is partly cultural, and it is partly unknown. Canada is in new territory as it attempts to adjust to this new reality and prepares for a new and expanded requirement of Canadian Arctic security.

NOTES

1. Chris Southcott, "History of Globalization in the Circumpolar World," in *Globalization and the Circumpolar North*, ed. Lassi Heininen and Chris Southcott (Fairbanks: University of Alaska Press, 2010): 29–30.
2. Shelagh Grant, *Polar Imperative: A History of Arctic Sovereignty in North America* (Vancouver: Douglas & McIntyre, 2010), 31–33.
3. See for example Frances Abele and Thierry Rodon, "Inuit Diplomacy and the Global ERA: The Strengths of Multilateral Internationalism," *International Journal* 13, no. 3 (2007): 45–47.
4. Antoon Kuijpers et al., "Climate Change and the Viking-Age Fjord Environment of the Eastern Settlement, South Greenland," *Geology of Greenland Survey Bulletin* 183 (1999): 61–67, http://geus.dk/publications/review-greenland-98/gsb183p61-67.pdf.
5. Frances Abele, "Northern Development: Past, Present and Future," in *Northern Exposure: Peoples, Powers and Prospects for Canada's North*, ed. Frances Abele, Thomas Courchene, Leslie Seidle, and France St-Hilaire (Ottawa: Institute for Research on Public Policy, 2009), 20–21.
6. Thomas Berger, *Northern Frontier/Northern Homeland: The Report of the Mackenzie Valley Inquiry* 1 (Ottawa: Department of Supply and Services, 1977).
7. Ken Coates, Whitney Lackenbauer, William Morrison, and Greg Poelzer, *Arctic Front: Defending Canada's Interests in the Far North* (Toronto: Thomas Allen, 2008), 9–53.
8. Grant, *Polar Imperative*, 115–134, 155–192.
9. See William Morrison, *Showing the Flag: The Mounted Police and Canadian Sovereignty in the North: 1894–1925* (Vancouver: University of British Columbia Press, 1985).
10. In recent years new studies have suggested that both the United States and Great Britain were more reasonable than had been suggested in the past. See David G. Haglund and Tudor Onea, "Victory without Triumph: Theodore Roosevelt, Honour, and the Alaska Panhandle Boundary Dispute," *Diplomacy & Statecraft* 19, no. 1 (2008): 20–41.
11. Wihelm Dege, *The Last German Arctic Weather Station of World War II*, trans. William Barr (Calgary: University of Calgary Press, 2004).

12. Ken Coates and W. R. Morrison, *The Alaska Highway in World War II: The American Army of Occupation in Canada's Northwest* (Norman: University of Oklahoma Press; Toronto: University of Toronto Press, 1992).

13. There is a large body of literature on this. One of the best studies is James Eayrs, In Defence of Canada—Peacemaking and Deterrence (Toronto: University of Toronto Press, 1972).

14. Bernard Brodie, *Strategy in the Missile Age* (Santa Monica, CA: Rand Corporation, 1959).

15. For excellent overviews see R. J Sutherland, "The Strategic Significance of the Canadian Arctic," in *The Arctic Frontier*, ed. R. St. J. Macdonald (Toronto: University of Toronto Press, 1966), 264; K. Eyre, "Forty Years of Defence Activity in the Canadian North, 1947–87," *Arctic* 40, no. 4 (1987): 292–299.

16. Canada, DEW System and Mid-Canada Line, in Canada, Documents on Canadian External Relations, vol. 19, 1953, ed. Donald Barry (Ottawa: Supply and Services Canada, 1991), 698 (February 10, 1953).

17. Alexander Herd, "A Practical Project: Canada, the United States, and the Construction of the Dew Line," in *Canadian Arctic Sovereignty and Security: Historical Perspectives, Calgary Papers in Military and Strategic Studies*, Occasional Paper no. 4, ed. Whitney Lackenbauer (Calgary: Centre for Military and Strategic Studies, 2011), 171–200.

18. Joseph Jockel, *No Boundaries Upstairs: Canada, the United States, and the Origins of North American Air Defence, 1945–1958* (Vancouver: University of British Columbia Press, 1987).

19. Ibid.

20. Lawrence Freedman, *The Evolution of Nuclear Strategy*, 3rd ed. (New York: Palgrave Macmillan, 2003), 117–130.

21. Jim Christley, *US Nuclear Submarines: The Fast Attack* (London: Osprey, 2007), 4–8.

22. Ronald O'Rourke, *Navy SSBN(X) Ballistic Missile Submarine Program: Background and the Issues for Congress*, Congressional Research Service 7-5700, May 3, 2010, 2–6.

23. Norman Polmar and Jurrien Noot, *Submarines of the Russian and Soviet Navies, 1718–1990* (Annapolis, MD: Naval Institute Press, 1991), 145–211.

24. Marc Milner, *Canada's Navy: the First Century* (Toronto: University of Toronto Press, 2010), 230–231, 291–292.

25. There is a large body of literature on this subject. By far the best legal examination of the issue is by Donat Pharand, *Canada's Arctic Waters in International Law* (Cambridge: Cambridge University, 1988), and his

more recent work "Arctic Waters and the Northwest Passage: A Final Revisit," *Ocean Development and International Law* 38, nos. 1–2 (2007): 3–69. For the politics of the issue, see Franklyn Griffiths, ed., *Politics of the Northwest Passage* (Kingston and Montreal: McGill-Queen's University Press, 1987); and his more recent work with Rob Huebert and Whitney Lackenbauer, *Canada and the Changing Arctic: Sovereignty, Security and Stewardship* (London, ON: Wilfrid Laurier Press, 2011).

26. Edgar Dosman, "The Northern Sovereignty Crisis 1968–70," in *The Arctic in Question*, ed. Edgar Dosman (Toronto: Oxford University Press, 1976), 33–62.

27. John Kirton and Don Munton, "Protecting the Canadian Arctic: The Manhattan Voyages, 1969–1970," in *Canadian Foreign Policy: Selected Cases*, ed. John Kirton and Don Munton (Toronto: Prentice-Hall, 1992), 206–221.

28. Whitney Lackenbauer, "From Polar Race to Polar Saga: An Integrated Strategy for Canada and the Circumpolar World," in Griffiths, Huebert, and Lackenbauer, *Canada and the Changing Arctic*, 118–145.

29. This idea was developed in detail by Franklyn Griffiths in "The Shipping News: Canada's Arctic Sovereignty Not on Thinning Ice," *International Journal* 58, no. 2 (2003): 257–282.

30. Rob Huebert, "Polar Vision or Tunnel Vision: The Making of Canadian Arctic Waters Policy," *Marine Policy* 19, no. 4 (July 1995): 343–364.

31. David Downie and Terry Fenge, eds., *Northern Lights against POPs: Combatting Toxic Threats in the Arctic* (Montreal and Kingston: McGill-Queen's University Press, 2003).

32. For a good (albeit critical) review of the Arctic Military Environmental Program (AMEC), which was the main means of responding to the rotting Soviet submarines until the G8 took over, see GAO, United States Government's Accountability Office, "Russian Nuclear Submarines: U.S. Participation in the Arctic Military Environmental Cooperation Program Need Better Justification," *Report to Congress* GAO-04-924, September 2004, http://www.gao.gov/assets/250/243985.pdf.

33. Canada, Foreign Affairs and International Trade Canada, *Dismantling of Nuclear Submarines*, January 11, 2011, http://www.international.gc.ca/gpp-ppm/nuclear_submarines-sousmarins_nucleaires.aspx?lang=eng.

34. Rob Huebert, "Renaissance in Canadian Arctic Security?" *Canadian Military Journal* 6, no. 4 (2005–2006): 17–29.

35. Arctic Council Panel, "To Establish an International Arctic Council: A Framework Report," *Northern Perspectives* 19, no. 2 (Summer 1991): 1–5.

36. Rob Huebert, "New Directions in Circumpolar Cooperation: Canada, the Arctic Environmental Protection Strategy and the Arctic Council," *Canadian Foreign Policy* 5, no. 2 (Winter 1998): 37–57.
37. *Arctic Environmental Protection Strategy—Declaration of the Protection of the Arctic Environment,* June 14, 1991, http://www.arctic-council.org/index.php/en/document-archive/category/4-founding-documents.pdf.
38. Esko Rajakoski, "Multilateral Cooperation to Protect the Arctic Environment: The Finnish Initiative," in *The Arctic: Choices for Peace and Security,* ed. Thomas R. Berger (Vancouver: Gordon Soules, 1989), 53–60.
39. Timo Koivurova and Leena Heinamaki, "The Participation of Indigenous Peoples in International Normmaking in the Arctic," *Polar Record* 42, no. 221 (2006): 101–109.
40. Timo Koivurova and David VanderZwaag, "The Arctic Council at 10 Years: Retrospect and Prospects." *UBC Law Review* 40, no. 1 (2007): 121–194.
41. Huebert, "New Directions in Circumpolar Cooperation," 42.
42. Evan T. Bloom, "Establishment of the Arctic Council," *American Journal of International Law* 93, no. 3 (July 1999): 712–722.
43. Department of Foreign Affairs and International Trade, "The Arctic Council: Objectives, Structures and Program Priorities," May 1995.
44. Arctic Climate Impact Assessment (ACIA), *Impacts of a Warming Arctic: ACIA Overview Report* (Cambridge: Cambridge University Press, 2004), http://amap.no/acia/.
45. Ibid., 82.
46. CBC News North, "Arctic Ice Could Vanish in 10 Years, Scientists Warn," August 13, 2012, http://www.cbc.ca/news/canada/north/story/2012/08/13/arctic-ice-melting-faster.html.
47. Oran R. Young, "Whither the Arctic? Conflict or Cooperation in the Circumpolar North," *Polar Record* 45 (2009): 73–82.
48. Arctic Council and PAME, *Arctic Marine Shipping Assessment (AMSA) Report,* 2009, http://www.pame.is/amsa-2009-report.
49. James Ford, "Dangerous Climate Change and the Importance of Adaptation for the Arctic's Inuit Population," *Environmental Research Letters* 4, no. 2 (2009): 1–10.
50. Huebert, "Renaissance in Canadian Arctic Security?"
51. Rob Huebert, Heather Exner-Pirot, Adam Lajeunese, and Jay Gulledge, *Climate Change and International Security: The Arctic as a Bellwether* (Washington, DC: Center for Climate and Energy Solutions, 2012), 1–58,

http://www.c2es.org/publications/climate-change-international-arctic-security.

52. Canada, Department of National Defence, *Canada's International Policy Statement: A Role of Pride and Influence in the World—Defence* (Ottawa: Department of National Defence, 2005), 17.

53. Canadian Arctic Resource Committee (CARC), *Northern Perspectives* 30, no. 1 (Winter 2006): 2, http://www.carc.org/pubs/v30no1/CARC_Northrn_Perspctves_Winter_2006.pdf.

54. CTV.ca, "Harper Pledges Larger Arctic Presence," December 22, 2005, http://www.ctv.ca/servlet/ArticleNews/story/CTVNews/20051222/harper_north051222/20051222?s_name=election2006.

55. CBC News, "Arctic of Strategic Importance to Canada: PM," August 19, 2009, http://www.cbc.ca/news/canada/story/2009/08/19/harper-nanook-arctic-north-sovereignty414.html.

56. Canada, Canada's Northern Strategy, "Achievements under Canada's Northern Strategy, 2007–2011," January 1, 2012, http://www.northernstrategy.gc.ca/cns/au-eng.asp.

57. Canada, Canada's Northern Strategy, "Exercising Our Arctic Sovereignty," August 15, 2012, http://www.northernstrategy.gc.ca/sov/index-eng.asp.

58. Department of Foreign Affairs and International Trade, *Statement on Canada's Arctic Foreign Policy: Exercising Sovereignty and Promoting Canada's Northern Strategy*, August 2012, http://www.international.gc.ca/arctic-arctique/arctic_policy-canada-politique_arctique.aspx?lang=eng.

59. Ibid., 6–7.

60. Embassy of the United States, Ottawa—Canada, "Podcast Transcript: Evan Bloom, Director, Office of Ocean and Polar Affairs, Department of State," July 21, 2010, http://canada.usembassy.gov/2010-podcasts.html.

61. John Ibbitson, "Dispute over Hans Island Nears Resolution: Now for the Beaufort Sea," *Globe and Mail*, January 26, 2011, http://www.theglobeandmail.com/news/politics/dispute-over-hans-island-nears-resolution-now-for-the-beaufort-sea/article563692/.

62. Kim Mackrael, "Canada, Denmark Closer to Settling Border Dispute," *Globe and Mail*, November 29, 2012, http://www.theglobeandmail.com/news/national/canada-denmark-closer-to-settling-border-dispute/article5831571/.

63. Natural Resources Canada, "Canada's Arctic Continental Shelf: Research under Ocean and Ice," May 18, 2010, http://publications.gc.ca/collections/collection_2010/nrcan/M34-4-9-2010-eng.pdf.

64. Koivurova and VanderZwaag, "The Arctic Council at 10 Years."

65. See Arctic Council and PAME, *Arctic Marine Shipping Assessment (AMSA) Report*; and Arctic Climate Impact Assessment, *Impacts of a Warming Arctic.*

66. Agreement on Cooperation on Aeronautical and Maritime Search and Rescue in the Arctic. August 18, 2011, http://www.ifrc.org/docs/idrl/N813EN.pdf.

67. Timo Koivurova, "Limits and Possibilities of the Arctic Council in a Rapidly Changing Scene of Arctic Governance," *Polar Record* 46 (2010): 146–156.

68. CBC News, "Health Minister Leona Aglukkaq to Chair Arctic Council," August 23, 2012, http://www.cbc.ca/news/politics/story/2012/08/23/pol-arctic-council-leona-aglukkaq-chair.html.

69. Huebert et al., *Climate Change and International Security*, 27–28.

70. Whitney Lackenbauer, "The Canadian Rangers: A Postmodern Militia That Works." *Canadian Military Journal* 6, no. 4 (2005–2006): 49–60.

71. Whitney Lackenbauer, "Canada's Northern Defenders: Aboriginal Peoples in the Canadian Rangers, 1947–2005," in *Aboriginal Peoples and the Canadian Military: Historical Perspectives*, ed. P. W. Lackenbauer and Craig Mantle (Kingston: CDA Press, 2007), 171–208.

72. Anna Paperny, "Ottawa Investing $10 Million in Arctic Surveillance," *Globe and Mail*, June 18, 2012, http://m.theglobeandmail.com/news/politics/ottawa-investing-10-million-in-arctic-surveillance/article4104646/?service=mobile.

73. National Defence and the Canadian Forces, *Backgrounder: The Canadian Forces in the North*, February 28, 2012, http://www.forces.gc.ca/en/news/article.page?doc=canadian-forces-northern-area/hnlhlxi9.

74. CBC News, "Arctic Naval Facility Downgrade due to High Cost, Says DND," May 27, 2012, http://www.cbc.ca/news/canada/north/story/2012/03/27/north-nanisivik-high-cost.html.

75. Department of Foreign Affairs and International Trade, *Statement on Canada's Arctic Foreign Policy*, 5.

76. One of the core themes of Franklyn Griffiths, Rob Huebert, and Whitney Lackenbauer, *Canada and the Changing Arctic: Sovereignty, Security and Stewardship* (London, ON: Wilfrid Laurier Press, 2011), is to examine these debates in detail.

77. Huebert et al., *Climate Change and International Security*, 31–31.

78. Whitney Lackenbauer, "Mirror Images? Canada, Russia, and the Circumpolar World," *International Journal* 65, no. 4 (2010): 879–897.

79. Linda Jakobson, "China Prepares for an Ice-Free Arctic," *SIPRI insights on Peace and Security* no. 2010/2 (March 2010), http://books.sipri.org/files/insight/SIPRIInsight1002.pdf.
80. For different perspectives on China's impact on Canada, see Frédéric Lasserre, "China and the Arctic: Threat or Cooperation Potential for Canada?" *China Papers* no. 11, Canadian International Council, June 2010, http://www.opencanada.org/wp-content/uploads/2011/05/China-and-the-Arctic-Frederic-Lasserre.pdf; and David Wright, *The Panda Bear Readies to Meet the Polar Bear: China and Canada's Arctic Sovereignty Challenge* (Calgary: Canadian Defence and Foreign Affairs Institute, March 2011), http://www.cdfai.org/PDF/The%20Panda%20Bear%20Readies%20to%20Meet%20the%20Polar%20Bear.pdf.

CHAPTER 6

U.S. ARCTIC POLICY

REPRODUCING HEGEMONY IN A MARITIME REGION

Philip E. Steinberg

INTRODUCTION

> The United States is an Arctic nation, with varied and compelling interests in that region.
>
> —United States Arctic Region Policy[1]

> As a nation, the United States views the Arctic with relatively minimal interest compared to every other Arctic nation...The United States is not focused on the Arctic, and, for the most part, other countries prefer it to be that way.
>
> —Commander James Kraska (U.S. Navy)[2]

These two quotations point to a seeming contradiction in U.S. Arctic policy. Put simply, is the United States concerned or not about its northern frontier? How can Commander Kraska assert that the United States "is not focused on the Arctic" when just three years earlier the U.S. government, in a national policy document drafted in part by that same Commander Kraska,[3] declared that the United States has "varied and compelling interests" there?

As this chapter[4] illustrates, the two quotations, while certainly reflecting different aspects of U.S. policy, are not as contradictory as they might seem. The United States has few concerns about the Arctic as a pressing security threat, notwithstanding fears raised in the popular press about a likely scramble for Arctic riches and ensuing resource wars. Furthermore, in contrast with most Arctic nations, the region plays little role in the country's national identity. Nor does the Arctic have a significant role as a driver of the nation's overall global policy positions.

However, the United States, as a leading global military and commercial power, is concerned about *stability*. From this perspective, the Arctic is viewed as a site of possible instability in the global political system. Climate change, increased resource demand, and technological advances are leading state and non-state Arctic players to experiment with governance in the region in ways that, in the eyes of the United States, might set disruptive precedent. Thus, the United States looks warily at the region as a site of potentially dangerous institutional experimentation that, if adopted, could have global ramifications that would challenge some of the fundamental legal principles and norms underpinning U.S. hegemony. This has led the United States to display the curious mix of disinterest and interest suggested in the two quotations that began this chapter: relative disinterest in the Arctic as a place in itself or as a focal point of U.S. global policy is coupled with a high level of interest in the Arctic as a region in which responses to emergent challenges and opportunities could potentially undermine the global political-economic system of which the United States is a world leader.

THE ARCTIC AS A MARITIME DOMAIN

The starting point for any analysis of U.S. Arctic Policy is the Arctic Region Policy Presidential Directive.[5] Officially known as *National Secu-*

rity Presidential Directive 66/Homeland Security Presidential Directive 25, and more often referred to as NSPD-66, this policy document was signed by President George W. Bush on January 9, 2009, after the November 2008 presidential election and just eleven days before Barack Obama was to assume office. Despite the timing, which might suggest political motivations to formalize policy prior to the change of government, interviews with several individuals involved in the drafting process suggest that the document was written with little partisan conflict. In any event, NSPD-66 has largely been adopted by the Obama administration.

The document's drafting was spurred by the realization that climate change, technological advances, and rising energy prices might in the near future lead to new economic opportunities and political challenges in the region. More directly, the impetus for the document—which superseded a 1994 classified policy that covered Antarctica as well as the Arctic —occurred in 2007 when Russia planted its flag on the seabed at the North Pole.[6] The Russian flag-planting, although not explicitly intended to claim the North Pole as Russian territory, elicited angry reactions from foreign ministries of other Arctic nations. For instance, Canada's foreign minister Peter MacKay paired a rejection of Russia's claim ("This isn't the 15th century. You can't go around the world and just plant flags and say, 'We're claiming this territory'") with an aggressive counter-claim ("The question of sovereignty of the Arctic is not a question. It's clear. It's our country. It's our property. It's our water...The Arctic is Canadian").[7] Sensing a potential battle for Arctic resources, the popular media spawned a range of books with titles such as *Arctic Gold Rush*,[8] Arctic Doom, Arctic Boom,[9] and *The Scramble for the Arctic: Ownership, Exploitation, and Conflict in the Far North*,[10] while a frequently cited *Foreign Affairs* article warned of an impending "Arctic meltdown."[11] In contrast, the United States' response to the flag-planting episode was simply dismissal: "It was an amazing technological feat, but nothing else," remarked one State Department official interviewed, and another U.S. government official noted, "From a governmental perspective we don't get exercised by flags being planted along the Lomonosov Ridge."

This reaction echoed the more general U.S. position that, even amid new economic opportunities and increased interest of states and other parties from within and beyond the region, the Arctic can be managed within existing national and international institutional, policy, and legal frameworks. It was in this context that NSPD-66 was issued, as a proactive restatement and elaboration of U.S. interest in the region, as well as serving as a framework for guiding future efforts there.[12]

Perhaps the foundational sentence in NSPD-66 can be found near the beginning of the main section on policy: "The Arctic region is primarily a maritime domain."[13] As such, and because "freedom of the seas is a top national priority,"[14] all responses to changes in the region must be guided by the overriding principle of guaranteeing these freedoms: principally the freedom of navigation and, secondarily, a more general principle mandating freedom of access to living and non-living resources. Because these principles are enshrined in the United Nations Convention on the Law of the Sea (UNCLOS),[15] which the United States has committed to following as customary law, the United States maintains that no additional broad-reaching international framework is necessary for Arctic governance. Indeed, the United States has consistently held that the Arctic is just like any other ocean, notwithstanding its often frozen state,[16] and in recent years it has expanded on this position to maintain that it therefore must be governed within the UNCLOS framework.[17]

Of course, these two sets of freedoms—freedom of navigation and freedom of access to living and non-living resources—are often in conflict with each other. Compromises made by the United States during the UNCLOS negotiations, particularly pertaining to the establishment of exclusive economic zones (EEZs), reveal that when necessary the United States has found it expedient to sacrifice some resource-extraction access in exchange for navigational rights.[18] Of more direct relevance here, however, is how the U.S. delegation reacted when faced with proposals in which *both* navigational access and resource-extraction access were being threatened, from either of two directions, *internationalization* or *territorialization*. On the one hand, the United States perceived that open access was being threatened by calls for intensified management of the sea by a self-funding international treaty organization. This concern was evidenced by the United States' reluctance to support global governance of the international seabed as the "common heritage of mankind" and, when it became clear that UNCLOS was to go into force, its insistence that the International Seabed Authority's powers be reduced through the 1994 Part XI Implementation Agreement.[19] Wariness about establishing an international institution that could override free access to the sea persists today in congressional refusal to accede to UNCLOS. Conversely, the U.S. position toward UNCLOS has also been guided by the parallel concern that open access would be threatened if increasing portions of ocean space were to be claimed as territory by coastal states. Indeed, initial U.S. support for the UNCLOS process in the 1950s was in large part precipitated by several states, particularly in Latin America, seeking to extend the breadth of the waters over which they claimed sovereign jurisdiction.

Most analysts, inside and outside of government, feel that UNCLOS successfully institutionalizes a middle ground that avoids the extremes of either internationalization or territorialization (although conservatives in the United States who oppose accession because it would require a surrender of sovereignty contend that there is still too much internationalization in the convention). However, these twin concerns continue to guide U.S. ocean policy, including in the Arctic, as U.S. officials, somewhat awkwardly, seek to protect the integrity of a convention that their legislature has refused to ratify. According to NSPD-66 as well as various statements and writings by individuals associated with its drafting and implementation,[20] cooperation with other nations in bilateral and multilateral fora, realization of economic opportunities, engagement with indigenous peoples, and protection of the environment should all be undertaken in the region, but always with the caution that such efforts must not endanger the fundamental maritime freedoms that are enshrined in UNCLOS.

DEFENDING AGAINST FURTHER TERRITORIALIZATION

The United States' vigilance against increased territorialization in Arctic waters is evidenced in the various protests it has made against straight baseline and historic waters claims that have been asserted by each of the four other Arctic coastal states—Canada, Denmark, Norway, and Russia.[21] Most recently, the State Department has filed a diplomatic note objecting to Canada's declaration that vessels entering its northern waters (whether internal waters, territorial waters, or EEZ) must notify Transport Canada through participation in the Northern Canada Vessel Traffic Services Zone Regulations (NORDREGs) scheme.[22] While the United States acknowledges that Article 234 of UNCLOS gives coastal states special rights to institute environmental protections in adjacent waters (including EEZ waters) that are ice-covered for most of the year, the diplomatic note asserts that it finds mandatory NORDREGs participation to be an excessive extension of Article 234. Following a series of legal reasons for its protest, as well as a restatement of the U.S. position that similar efforts at protecting environmentally sensitive Arctic waters could be achieved through strengthening the International Maritime Organization's code for ships operating in polar waters, the diplomatic note concludes with the following paragraph, which reveals an underlying objection:

> The United States noted with concern the references to "sovereignty" in the statements accompanying the regulations. The United States wishes to note that the NORDREGs do not, and cannot as a matter of law, increase the "sovereignty" of Canada over any territory or marine area.[23]

This policy opposing territorial control in Arctic waters is potentially problematic because the waters off the coast of Alaska are themselves resource-rich (especially in gas and oil) and, particularly at a time when energy security is also a national priority, the United States might be loath to sacrifice access to offshore oil and gas reserves in return for guaranteeing freedom of navigation. NSPD-66, however, takes pains to show that there is no contradiction between access to Arctic waters for navigation and access for resource extraction:

> The Secretaries of State, the Interior, Commerce, and Energy, in coordination with heads of other relevant executive departments and agencies, shall...continue to emphasize cooperative mechanisms with nations operating in the region to address shared concerns, recognizing that *most known Arctic oil and gas resources are located outside of United States jurisdiction.*[24]

By reminding readers that most oil and gas resources are located beyond United States sovereign control, NSPD-66 preemptively rebuts isolationists who, paralleling the charge that UNCLOS sacrifices U.S. sovereignty, might charge that the policy's emphasis on keeping the ocean accessible could diminish the United States' rights to engage in resource extraction.

The other issue area that might conceivably lead the United States to support a higher level of territorial control in the Arctic is that of border security. Although increased U.S. territorial control in the High North is not on anyone's agenda, Paul Cellucci, U.S. ambassador to Canada from 2000 through 2004, was an advocate of Canadian control of the Northwest Passage. Arguing from a post–September 11, 2001, security perspective, but in opposition to the official position of the U.S. government, which maintains that the Passage is an international strait, Cellucci suggested that U.S. security would be enhanced if Canadian control of the Passage were recognized. Cellucci's argument, which he continued to make until his death in 2013, was based on the calculation that would-be terrorists seeking a back door to North America would more likely be stopped in Canadian territory than in an international (and thus largely unpoliced) strait.[25]

However, Cellucci's proposal has received no traction in U.S. policy circles; for instance, a staffer with the U.S. Senate Foreign Relations Committee remarked in an interview that he had never heard that Arctic policy proposal. This suggests that just as keeping other nations from encroaching on U.S. mineral resources is not a driving force behind U.S. Arctic policy, neither is homeland security (which is not to be confused with the military objective of maintaining free transit through the Arctic for U.S. warships and submarines). As the historian Elizabeth Elliot-Meisel has noted, "The Passage is an issue of precedent and principle, not one of national security,"[26] with the concern here being specifically the precedent that recognition of the Passage as Canada's internal waters would have for other international straits in which free transit is guaranteed under UNCLOS. As NSPD-66 states in its paragraph reaffirming the position that the Northwest Passage and the Northern Sea Route are international straits, "Preserving the rights and duties relating to navigation and overflight in the Arctic region supports our ability to exercise these rights throughout the world, including through strategic straits."[27]

DEFENDING AGAINST FURTHER INTERNATIONALIZATION

Just as the United States—in its overall ocean governance strategy but also specifically in the Arctic—is wary of increased territorialization, it is also wary of increased governance by a controlling international authority. As section III.C of NSPD-66 reiterates, the central platform for Arctic governance should be UNCLOS, and the policy urges the Senate to accede to UNCLOS "promptly." Beyond that, the United States sees a role for the Arctic Council. However, paralleling its concerns about excessive territorialization through, for instance, expansive interpretations of UNCLOS Article 234, the United States is similarly wary of excessive internationalization through the Arctic Council exceeding its mandate.

In the first of three paragraphs in NSPD-66 that discuss the Arctic Council, the United States subtly puts the Arctic Council in its place:

> The United States participates in a variety of fora, international organizations, and bilateral contacts that promote United States interests in the Arctic. These include the Arctic Council, the International Maritime Organization (IMO), wildlife conservation and management agreements, and many other mechanisms.[28]

By including the Arctic Council among a host of other organizations, NSPD-66 effectively removes from consideration any possibility that the council's mandate might be expanded to provide an overall framework for Arctic governance. In case there is any ambiguity on this point, it is made explicit two paragraphs later:

> The geopolitical circumstances of the Arctic region differ sufficiently from those of the Antarctic region such that an "Arctic treaty" of broad scope—along the lines of the Antarctic Treaty—is not appropriate or necessary.[29]

Most intriguing, however, is the paragraph between these two, which, after extolling the contributions of the Arctic Council, states,

> It is the position of the United States that the Arctic Council should remain a high-level forum devoted to issues within its current mandate and not be transformed into a formal international organization, particularly one with assessed contributions. The United States is nevertheless open to updating the structure of the Council, including consolidation of, or making operational changes to, its subsidiary bodies, to the extent such changes can clearly improve the Council's work *and are consistent with the general mandate of the Council.*[30]

As a State Department official made clear in a 2010 interview, the "main point" of that section of NSPD-66 was that "we don't want [the Arctic Council] to become an international organization." As in the document itself, however, the State Department official was quick to note that the United States *was* open to expanding the Arctic Council's competencies. In this context, he mentioned the ongoing negotiation of a

Search and Rescue Agreement (which was to be the first binding agreement negotiated under Arctic Council auspices and which was subsequently agreed upon at the Nuuk ministerial meeting in 2011), the report on short-lived climate forcers (which is the first Arctic Council working group study containing specific policy recommendations for governments, rather than simply assessing a situation), and the growing U.S. openness toward the establishment of a permanent secretariat (which also was subsequently agreed to in Nuuk in 2011). Nonetheless, even when showing an openness to giving the Arctic Council new powers and responsibilities, the State Department (and the United States more generally) has been clear that the Arctic Council can only supplement, not supplant, UNCLOS as the foundation for governance in this maritime region.

A TALE OF FOUR CITIES: MONTEBELLO, ILULISSAT, CHELSEA, AND NUUK

In short, U.S. Arctic policy has sought to preserve the sanctity of UNCLOS while steering between the extremes of territorialization and internationalization. This can be illustrated further by tracing U.S. policy positions at four international meetings between 2007 and 2011.

First, at a meeting of the leaders of Canada, the United States, and Mexico in Montebello, Quebec, in 2007, President Bush proclaimed,

> There are differences [between the United States and Canada] on the Northwest Passage. We believe it's an international passageway. Having said that, the United States does not question Canadian sovereignty over its Arctic islands, and the United States supports Canadian investments that have been made to exercise its sovereignty.[31]

Here, President Bush was echoing the long-held U.S. position that the Arctic was not exceptional space. According to the norms of international law, land territory is part of the internal territory of one or another sovereign nation (in this case, Canada) and oceans are classified according to their function and relation to land as mandated by UNCLOS (in this case, the Northwest Passage falls under the regime for international straits, according to U.S. interpretation). Perhaps more remarkable than the fact that President Bush uttered these sentences is that in two separate interviews conducted in 2008—one at the U.S. Embassy in Ottawa and one at the Pentagon—I was presented with handouts of slides from PowerPoint presentations that reprinted the final sentence ("The United States does not question Canadian sovereignty over its Arctic islands, and the United States supports Canadian investments that have been made to exercise its sovereignty"). Clearly the United States was prepared to assure the world (and, in particular, Canada) that its opposition to Canada's claiming of the Northwest Passage as internal waters did not reflect a broader agenda of constructing the Arctic as an exceptional space, either under the control of the United States or the world community.

The United States made another attempt to avoid the twin dangers of territorialization and internationalization the next year, when it met with representatives from the four other coastal Arctic states in Ilulissat, Greenland. In the declaration that emerged from Ilulissat, the five states reaffirmed,

> [The UNCLOS] framework provides a solid foundation for responsible management by the five coastal States and other users of this Ocean through national implementation and application of relevant provisions. We therefore see no need to develop a new comprehensive international legal regime to govern the Arctic Ocean.[32]

Although the declaration also reaffirmed the five states' intention to be active members of the Arctic Council, other parties involved in the Arctic Council—most notably the three non-coastal Arctic states (Finland, Iceland, and Sweden) and the six indigenous peoples' organizations that have the status of permanent participants—expressed concern that the council was being abandoned for a more exclusive and state-centric forum that would fail to give voice to the breadth of actors in the Arctic arena. In effect, the excluded parties, and most explicitly the Inuit Circumpolar Council, were arguing that the Arctic had exceptional properties as a maritime region and that the interests of various parties could not simply be represented by coastal states.[33]

In 2010, the five coastal states (the Arctic 5, or the A5) met for a second time in Chelsea, Quebec, where Secretary of State Hillary Clinton famously criticized the five-nation forum for excluding indigenous peoples and representatives of the three non-coastal states.[34] In its support for the Arctic Council, the United States sought to negotiate a paradox in its position: although the United States was seeking to achieve stability in the Arctic by reaffirming that the Arctic was just like any other maritime region (and thus should not be the site of either exceptional territorialization or exceptional internationalization), stability is best achieved under conditions of inclusion. In the case of the Arctic, inclusion required giving some status to parties beyond those who would typically be given a voice under the norms of international law.

Asked about the apparent change in the U.S. position between Ilulissat and Chelsea, a State Department official explained in an interview,

> It would be a little bit of a misreading of the situation to say that we were enthusiastic about Ilulissat, because we were not. There was some reason to do Ilulissat, not the least of which was that it was coming on the heels of the Russian flag planting, when all the world's media were talking about an impending war in the Arctic because the Arctic countries were all racing to claim the shelf up there, and one of the purposes of Ilulissat was to show that that is not what was happening. The second purpose that you will see in the Ilulissat Declaration is to explain that the Law of the Sea already provides sort of a framework for the Arctic, [and so] there is no need for some sort of overarching Arctic treaty that is going to govern the Arctic like the Antarctic.

The State Department official revealed here that Ilulissat was designed to counter trends toward both territorialization and internationalization. Primarily, the appeal to UNCLOS as the guiding framework for Arctic governance, and indeed the Ilulissat meeting itself, was designed to contradict the impression that a territorialization process was occurring in the region. Presumably this was deemed necessary because, if left unchecked, the impression that there was an ongoing competition could lead politicians and the general public in each coastal state to pressure their government to intensify its own territorialization efforts, which could lead to the "land grab"—or "ice grab"—that all parties feared. Secondarily, however, Ilulissat was designed to stave off a backlash that could lead others to use the sense of an impending struggle for the Arctic to call for internationalization of the region.

The State Department official then went on to explain what happened at the 2010 Chelsea meeting:

> In terms of Chelsea, the last line of the Ilulissat Declaration makes it clear that the Arctic Council is the main place where we should be doing high-level diplomacy,[35] [but] the idea of doing a second meeting of the A5 started to imply that there was sort of an ongoing process...[Secretary Clinton's] overall remarks were talking about areas of cooperation, but again making the point that for diplomatic purposes, for high-level diplomatic purposes, for circum-Arctic issues, the Arctic Council should be the place where we are doing that. We already have this organization, we already have this forum where we have all the major stakeholders, or most of the major stakeholders, involved. One of the real concerns with the A5 format was that there is no voice for the indigenous people at the table.

This statement reveals that the ideal situation, from the U.S. perspective, is primary reliance on UNCLOS as the guiding framework for Arctic governance (with Arctic states controlling land territory as sovereign space, and with the regime for the ocean incorporating UNCLOS's compromise of coastal state jurisdiction with freedom for navigation) but with the Arctic Council existing as a parallel organization that contributes additional stability to the system by facilitating cooperation and by giving voice to stakeholders whose interests otherwise would not be heard.

This goal may well have been realized at the fourth Arctic meeting considered here, the 2011 Arctic Council ministerial meeting in Nuuk, Greenland. This meeting was unusual in that Secretary of State Clinton attended it personally, in contrast with most previous ministerials, at which the United States had sent a lower-ranked State Department official to lead the delegation. At this meeting, in addition to establishing a permanent secretariat for the Arctic Council, the parties established the Arctic Council's first binding agreement, on search and rescue operations.[36] In this document, the eight member nations established sectors wherein an individual nation would be responsible for search and rescue activities, and procedures were established for obtaining cooperation, including overflight rights, for such missions. The agreement explicitly states that its proposal to share and allocate resources is consistent with UNCLOS and that the delineation of search and rescue sectors has no bearing on sovereignty claims.

As the U.S. Navy's Commander Kraska, in particular, stated, however, this vision of the Arctic temporarily realized at Nuuk—that of a well-governed maritime space where the rule of law laid out in UNCLOS is enhanced with specific acts of issue-oriented intergovernmental cooperation facilitated by the Arctic Council—is not necessarily the vision of other Arctic states:

> All Arctic states would do well to mind their manners. Like vacationers who forget how to act when they're away from home, most Arctic nations have been prone to boorish behavior in the region, acting in ways that are popular at home but harmful to their own long-term interests in regional stability. Russia and Canada suspect each other's intentions. Norway and Denmark, like Russia and Canada, are too close to the problem to offer

responsible and detached multilateral leadership in the region. Only the United States can fill that role.[37]

Kraska thus found the answer to Arctic exceptionalism in American exceptionalism (with assistance from Finland, Iceland, and Sweden, who all "display a refreshing lack of Arctic emotionalism and are thus likely to be natural supporters of American leadership in Arctic governance").[38] Regardless of one's position regarding the inevitability of U.S. leadership (or the emotionalism of Norwegians), Kraska's central point is that it will require constant vigilance for the United States to pursue its goal of maintaining the Arctic as a maritime zone governed by UNCLOS with no other substantive framework that could set a precedent for other world regions. The United States' support of Ilulissat (even if lukewarm) and its subsequent renunciation of any attempt to repeat it at Chelsea suggest that maintaining this position will require delicate diplomatic maneuvers as the United States steers between the threats of territorialization and internationalization, either one of which could have significant ramifications for U.S. global strategy.

THE ARCTIC AS FOREIGN POLICY WEDGE

Because the United States' policy perspectives on the Arctic are so strongly shaped by the implications for U.S. global leadership, the Arctic frequently is treated less as a region in its own right than as a wedge for advocating one or another political future. For instance, in the 2012 Senate Foreign Relations Committee hearings on UNCLOS, fourteen of sixteen speakers who testified in favor of accession specifically mentioned the Arctic, using opportunities and challenges in the Arctic to support their argument.[39] Although UNCLOS was lauded as helpful for the extension of U.S. interests in the Arctic, the attention being given to the Arctic in the popular press was clearly seized by several of the speakers to bolster their arguments for formally adopting the UNCLOS regime.

This perspective, wherein the Arctic is not so much a region in its own right but an arena in which norms are set for other regions, was echoed by a State Department interviewee who noted that, in order to attract resources within the State Department, the Office of Polar Affairs rarely stresses how the Arctic is either a potential site of conflict or one of cooperation. Such a strategy would meet little success because, as the respondent noted, "the natural constituency on [Capitol] Hill [for Arctic issues] consists of a grand total of three members," the two senators and one representative from Alaska. Rather, he continued, the Office of Polar Affairs stresses that the Arctic is an arena in which the United States is engaged in two very important bilateral relationships (with Canada and Russia) and that a good Arctic policy will facilitate relations with these two countries in other, higher-profile arenas. Even NSPD-66, where one might expect U.S. Arctic priorities to be isolated from broader concerns, reproduces the discourse wherein the Arctic is valuable not simply as a space in itself but because of the example that it sets for other regions, as is illustrated by the previously quoted sentence: "Preserving the rights and duties relating to navigation and overflight in the Arctic region supports our ability to exercise these rights throughout the world, including through strategic straits."[40]

This construction of the Arctic as an *instrumental* space is further elaborated by the U.S. Navy's Commander Kraska:

> Maintaining operational air and sea access and the ability to operate unimpeded in the Arctic Ocean is a cornerstone of U.S. nuclear deterrence. Situated among the continents of North America, Europe, and Asia, and with access to the Pacific and Atlantic oceans, the geographic proximity of the Arctic Ocean makes it an especially attractive area for submarine patrols. Taking refuge near the ice, stationary submarines are virtually undetectable and therefore invulnerable to attack. Furthermore, the tyranny of vast distances and the presence of the hovering ice canopy make antisubmarine surveillance systems particularly inefficient.[41]

When he was leader of the Soviet Union, Mikhail Gorbachev also spoke of the Arctic as an ocean where the continents came together, but for Gorbachev the Arctic was a maritime region that joined peoples and interests across its various coastlines.[42] For Kraska, by contrast, the Arctic is a defensive perimeter. According to this vision, the United States is an "Arctic nation" simply because it has strategic interests there; the homeland that is to be protected by military presence in this Arctic fringe is implied as being far removed from the frigid Arctic theater of operations.

THE FORGOTTEN DIMENSION: ALASKA

Missing from this perspective is that the United States actually *is* an Arctic nation. This point is often lost on "detached" strategists who lack "Arctic emotionalism" when calculating the implication that certain policies will have for global principles such as the freedom of navigation, and it arguably is equally lost on U.S. environmentalists outside Alaska who idealize the country's northern periphery as an unspoiled frontier. Canadian commentators often argue that their nation's strategic interests in the North are best met through economic growth and social integration of the population there,[43] but acceptance of an equivalent argument linking Arctic security with national development would involve a significant leap for the U.S. public, although the promulgation of a more comprehensive National Security Strategy for the Arctic Region in 2013 may be an attempt to move Americans in this direction.[44] The lack of perceived connection between national security and Alaskan development issues, which in Canada are discursively linked through the concept of "sovereignty," was illustrated in 2010 in the small talk that transpired at the end of an interview in Washington, DC. After mentioning that I would be heading to Anchorage in a few days to conduct another round of interviews there, the respondent, an academic with strong links to government, wondered why I was making the long trek to Alaska if my interests were on sovereignty issues, given that these were all determined in Washington. I doubt that a similar conversation would have occurred in Ottawa if I had told a respondent there that I would soon be heading to Iqaluit to continue my research on Arctic sovereignty.

In part the inability (or unwillingness) of U.S. policy makers to link Arctic policy and the interests of protecting sovereignty with an Alaskan (and, in particular, northern and indigenous Alaskan) development agenda is due to distance and the marginal status of Alaska in the American economy and national imagination. But it is also due to the particular emphasis on natural resources (oil and gas, and its antithesis, wilderness preservation) in the Alaskan development trajectory. In effect, there are two different sets of "American Arctic interests," each of which rests on opposite sides of a binary division. On one side is "Alaska," which typically is understood as a body of land that is seen as either ripe for development or requiring environmental preservation. On the other side is "the Arctic," which is viewed as a water (or ice) environment that, because it lies outside state territory, exists merely to be crossed.[45] From a policy perspective, this is expressed in two largely autonomous imperatives: that of promoting or restricting (predominantly onshore) Alaskan oil and gas development versus that of protecting open access so as to reproduce global principles of maritime freedom. Outside of specific media-grabbing events such as the Russian flag-planting at the North Pole, the former receives much greater attention from the U.S. public and policy makers: "While national and homeland security are stated as primary concerns in US Arctic policy, it is clear that the prospect of economic opportunity, and especially energy development, is the strongest driver for the new attention that the region is receiving."[46] Even on the Senate Foreign Relations Committee, according to a staffer there, the Arctic issues that arise typically concern "Alaska and potential mineral exploitation on the continental shelf" and not the freedom of navigation and sovereignty concerns emphasized by the Departments of State and Defense. Presumably the sentence in NSPD-66 asserting that most oil and gas resources in the Arctic are outside U.S. control was written in this context, to ensure that the Arctic Region Policy, which largely concerns the United States' global posture, would not be misunderstood by readers whose inclinations would be to filter it through the much more prevalent discourse of Alaskan resource development.

A third reason for this disconnect between the "domestic" and "foreign" components of U.S. Arctic policy is that, despite (or perhaps because of) the decentralization of domestic government in the United States, foreign policy is cordoned off as an exclusively Washington-based affair. This point was emphasized in an interview with an Alaskan who had attended several meetings of the Arctic Council and other international pan-Arctic fora:

> At my very first meeting of the Arctic Council, I was shocked that there were no Alaskans. And there have been many other meetings where I was the only Alaskan at the table...[It is important] to bring Alaskan, I'm not even talking about indigenous, but Alaskan interests [to these meetings]. Because, I mean it's not a secret that people from the State Department, they don't know much about Alaska. And Alaska is, it's an overseas territory...
> Denmark [always] has a Greenlandic representative and a Faroe Islands representative at the table, and they have three flags. And I've been trying to see if there is support for having an Alaskan flag next to the U.S., which I think would be appropriate. Alaska is a special state...But the State Department is very sensitive. For example, on [circumpolar] maps, [the United States] is often indicated just by Alaska. You know, you have all of the countries and then Alaska. And every map from the State Department will cross out "Alaska" and put "U.S."...I do not think that there would be a real danger if Alaska was given a little bit of its own place.

These concerns, however, are not incorporated into NSPD-66, a document in which there is a notable disconnect between U.S. Arctic policy and related issues concerning Alaskan development, the integration of Alaska (and Alaska Natives) into U.S. society, and the special role of Alaska (and Alaska Natives) in providing the United States' Arctic footprint. Indeed, it is telling that the word *Alaska* appears nowhere in NSPD-66.

CONCLUSION: THINKING *WITH* THE ARCTIC OR THINKING *OF* THE ARCTIC?

By many measures, the Arctic is receiving increased attention in U.S. policy circles. Secretary of State Clinton's personal appearance at the 2010 Chelsea Arctic 5 meeting and the 2011 Nuuk Arctic Council ministerial, her own statements regarding the heightened importance of the Arctic in U.S. thinking,[47] the continual references to the Arctic at the 2012 Senate Foreign Relations Committee UNCLOS accession hearings, and of course the release of NSPD-66 in 2009 and the subsequent release of the National Security Strategy for the Arctic Region in 2013 all point to the Arctic rising on the U.S. policy agenda. At the same time, this transformation in U.S. attention is far from complete. Over the course of the 2008 and 2010 interviews, two individuals with close ties to the U.S. Arctic policy community independently offered their opinions that the main reason the United States and Canada had not settled their maritime boundary dispute in the Beaufort Sea was because the State Department had not seen fit to devote the technical resources to negotiating the issue. As another indicator, through the end of October 2013 the website of the State Department's Office of Polar Affairs consisted of just four woefully out-of-date pages, which may suggest that the Arctic remains low on the State Department's overall radar.[48]

Of greater concern, however, than whether the Arctic is receiving *enough* attention from U.S. policy makers is whether the individuals who are giving the Arctic attention are thinking *of* the Arctic or merely thinking *with* it. Is the Arctic being considered as a space in its own right, in which the United States has integrated interests ranging from Alaskan resource development to the rights of indigenous peoples to the stewardship of Alaska's environment, or is it simply a dynamic maritime zone that must be carefully watched lest it be the site of governance arrangements that, in trending too far toward either territorialization or internationalization, set dangerous precedent for other, more strategically central, world regions? This may well be the central question for U.S. Arctic policy in the coming decades.

NOTES

1. George W. Bush, *National Security Presidential Directive and Homeland Security Presidential Directive: Arctic Region Policy (NSPD-66 and HSPD-25)* (Washington, DC: The White House, 2009), http://www.fas.org/irp/offdocs/nspd/nspd-66.htm, para. II.A.

2. James Kraska, "The New Arctic Geography and U.S. Strategy," in *Arctic Security in an Age of Climate Change*, ed. James Kraska (Cambridge: Cambridge University Press, 2012), 256–257.

3. Commander Kraska served through 2008 as the Oceans Law and Policy Adviser for the U.S. Joint Chiefs of Staff, where he was active in drafting portions of the Arctic Region Policy (NSPD-66). See James Kraska, "Arctic Strategy and Military Security," in *Changes in the Arctic Environment and the Law of the Sea*, ed. Myron H. Nordquist, John N. Moore, and Tomas H. Heidar (Leiden, the Netherlands: Martinus Nijhof, 2010), 251–281; Kraska, "New Arctic Geography and U.S. Strategy."

4. Some of the data presented in this chapter is derived from forty-four interviews conducted in 2008 and 2010, primarily in Washington, DC, and Anchorage, with individuals who were involved with U.S. Arctic policy, either in its design, its implementation, or its effects. Respondents included retired and current staff of U.S. government agencies in Washington and in satellite locations in Alaska and overseas embassies, congressional staff, Alaska state government officials, and representatives of nongovernmental and quasi-governmental organizations advocating for industry, local government, the environment, scientific research, world peace, and indigenous peoples. These interviews were complemented by over 100 parallel interviews in Ottawa, Toronto, Iqaluit, Nuuk, Copenhagen, Oslo, Tromsø, Moscow, and St. Petersburg by various members of the research team: Mauro Caraccioli, Sandra Fabiano, Hannes Gerhardt, Elizabeth Nyman, Rob Shields, Jeremy Tasch, and Barret Weber, as well as myself. I am grateful for their assistance and collaboration, as well for support from the International Council for Canadian Studies, the U.S. National Science Foundation's Geography and Social Science and Arctic Social Science programs, and the European Commission's Marie Curie Incoming Faculty Fellowship program for funding research and writing of this chapter.

5. Bush, *NSPD-66*.

6. Kraska, "Arctic Strategy and Military Security," and Kraska, "New Arctic Geography and U.S. Strategy." This was confirmed in several interviews with State Department officials. As one official noted, the State Department paid much less attention to Russia's 2001 filing with the Commission on the Limits of the Continental Shelf than it did to the 2007 flag-planting incident, even though the former was of much greater legal significance.

7. CanWest Media, "Russians Plant Flag on North Pole Seabed," *Regina Leader-Post*, August 3, 2007, http://www.canada.com/reginaleaderpost/story.html?id=55f5b74e-3728-4245-97ed-f6713c3f1bb8&k=40585.

8. Roger Howard, *The Arctic Gold Rush: The New Race for Tomorrow's Natural Resources* (London: Continuum, 2009).

9. Barry S. Zellen, *Arctic Doom, Arctic Boom: The Geopolitics of Climate Change in the Arctic* (London: Praeger, 2009).

10. Richard Sale and Eugene Potapov, *The Scramble for the Arctic: Ownership, Exploitation, and Conflict in the Far North* (London: Francis Lincoln, 2010).

11. Scott G. Borgerson, "Arctic Meltdown: The Economic and Security Implications of Global Warming," *Foreign Affairs* 87, no. 2 (2008): 63–77.

12. Following Klaus Dodds, "Flag Planting and Finger Pointing: The Law of the Sea, the Arctic and the Political Geographies of the Outer Continental Shelf," *Political Geography* 29 (2010): 63–73, NSPD-66 may be seen as an effort by the U.S. government to make "legible" the Arctic, as well as U.S. Arctic policy.

13. Bush, *NSPD-66*, para. III.B.3.

14. Ibid., para. III.B.5.

15. United Nations, *The United Nations Convention on the Law of the Sea of 10 December 1982 (A/Conf.62/122)* (New York: United Nations, 1982), http://www.un.org/Depts/los/convention_agreements/texts/unclos/unclos_e.pdf.

16. Frances M. Auburn, "International Law and Sea-Ice Jurisdiction in the Arctic Ocean," *International and Comparative Law Quarterly* 22 (1973): 552–557.

17. John N. Moore, "The UNCLOS Negotiations on Ice-Covered Areas," in *Changes in the Arctic Environment and the Law of the Sea*, ed. Myron H. Nordquist, John N. Moore, and Tomas H. Heidar (Leiden, the Netherlands: Martinus Nijhof, 2010), 17–26.

18. Philip E. Steinberg, *The Social Construction of the Ocean* (Cambridge: Cambridge University Press, 2001).

19. United Nations, *Agreement for the Implementation of Part XI of the United Nations Convention on the Law of the Sea of 10 December 1982 (UNGA 48/263)* (New York: United Nations, 1994), http://www.un.org/Depts/los/convention_agreements/texts/unclos/closindxAgree.htm.

20. See for example John Bellinger, "Treaty on Ice," *The New York Times*, June 23, 2008, http://www.nytimes.com/2008/06/23/opinion/23bellinger.html; Kraska, "Arctic Strategy and Military Security"; Kraska, "New Arctic Geography and U.S. Strategy."

21. United States Department of Defense, *Maritime Claims Reference Manual (DOD 2005.1-M)* (Washington, DC: United States Department of Defense, 2005), http://www.jag.navy.mil/organization/documents/mcrm/MCRM. pdf; United States Department of State (Office of Oceans Affairs, Bureau of Oceans and International Environmental and Scientific Affairs), *Limits in the Seas: National Claims to Maritime Jurisdictions (No. 36, 8th revision)* (Washington, DC: United States Department of State, 2000), http://www.state.gov/documents/organization/61543.pdf.

22. Embassy of the United States of America in Canada, *Diplomatic Note no. 625, August 18, 2010*, http://www.state.gov/documents/organization/179287.pdf.

23. Ibid. See also Eric Benjaminson, "Letter from Eric Benjaminson (Minister-Counselor for Economic, Energy, and Environment Affairs, Embassy of the United States of America in Canada) to Robert Turner (Manager for Navigation Safety and Radiocommunications, Transport Canada)," March 19, 2010, http://www.state.gov/documents/organization/179286.pdf.

24. Bush, *NSPD-66*, para. III.G.4.g, emphasis added.

25. Water.ca, *The Water Chronicles: Special Feature: Northern Sovereignty*, September 17, 2007, http://www.water.ca/listenaod.asp?artid=227.

26. Elizabeth Elliot-Meisel, "Still Unresolved after Fifty Years: The Northwest Passage in Canadian-American Relations, 1946–1998," *American Review of Canadian Studies* 29 (1999): 419.

27. Bush, *NSPD-66*, para. III.B.5.

28. Ibid., para. III.C.1.

29. Ibid., III.C.3.

30. Ibid., para. III.C.2, emphasis added.

31. George W. Bush, *The President's News Conference with Prime Minister Stephen Harper of Canada and President Felipe de Jesus Calderon Hinojosa of Mexico in Montebello, Canada*, August 21, 2007, http://www.presidency.ucsb.edu/ws/index.php?pid=75725.

32. Arctic Ocean Conference, *The Ilulissat Declaration* (Ilulissat, Greenland: Arctic Ocean Conference, 2008), http://www.oceanlaw.org/downloads/arctic/Ilulissat_Declaration.pdf.

33. Inuit Circumpolar Council, *A Circumpolar Inuit Declaration on Sovereignty in the Arctic* (Tromsø, Norway: Inuit Circumpolar Council, 2009), http://inuitcircumpolar.com/section.php?ID=25&Lang=En&Nav=Section.

34. Rob Gillies, "Clinton Rebukes Canada on Arctic Meeting," *Associated Press*, March 29, 2010, http://www.msnbc.msn.com/id/36085624/ns/world_news-americas/t/clinton-rebukes-canada-arctic-meeting/#.UCbKC0TR6jc.

35. In fact, this is a highly interpretive reading of the Ilulissat Declaration. The final paragraph reads, in its entirety, "The Arctic Council and other international fora, including the Barents Euro-Arctic Council, have already taken important steps on specific issues, for example with regard to safety of navigation, search and rescue, environmental monitoring and disaster response and scientific cooperation, which are relevant also to the Arctic Ocean. The five coastal states of the Arctic Ocean will continue to contribute actively to the work of the Arctic Council and other relevant international fora." This would seem to fall well short of the State Department official's claim that the Ilulissat Declaration reaffirmed that "the Arctic Council is the main place where we should be doing high-level diplomacy."

36. Arctic Council, *Agreement on Cooperation on Aeronautical and Maritime Search and Rescue in the Arctic* (Tromsø, Norway: Arctic Council, 2011), http://www.arctic-council.org/index.php/en/about/documents/category/20-main-documents-from-nuuk?download=73:arctic-search-and-rescue-agreement-english.

37. James Kraska, "Northern Exposures," *American Interest*, Summer (May/June 2010): 67–68.

38. Ibid., 68.

39. United States Senate Foreign Relations Committee, *United Nations Convention on the Law of the Sea: 103-39*, last modified June 28, 2012, http://www.foreign.senate.gov/treaties/details/103-39. (This website contains transcripts of testimony and other documents associated with hearings held in 2012 by the United States Senate Foreign Relations Committee concerning access to the United Nations Convention on the Law of the Sea.) The two speakers who did not mention the Arctic were Admiral Locklear from the U.S. Navy, who spoke from his perspective in the U.S. Pacific Command, and Lowell McAdam from the telecommunications

firm Verizon, who spoke on how UNCLOS accession would facilitate protection of submarine cables, a topic that is not relevant to the Arctic because there are no cables there.

40. Bush, *NSPD-66*, para. III.B.5.

41. Kraska, "New Arctic Geography and U.S. Strategy," 254.

42. Mikhail Gorbachev, *Mikhail Gorbachev's Speech in Murmansk at the Ceremonial Meeting on the Occasion of the Presentation of the Order of Lenin and the Gold Star to the City of Murmansk*, October 1, 1987, http://teacherweb.com/FL/CypressBayHS/JJolley/Gorbachev_speech.pdf.

43. See, for instance, Michael Byers, *Who Owns the Arctic? Understanding Sovereignty Disputes in the North* (Vancouver: Douglas & McIntyre, 2010).

44. Kristofer Bergh, *The Arctic Policies of Canada and the United States: Domestic Motives and International Context (SIPRI Insights on Peace and Security, no. 2012/1)* (Solna, Sweden: Stockholm International Peace Research Institute, 2012); Barack Obama, *National Security Strategy for the Arctic Region* (Washington, DC: The White House, 2013), http://www.whitehouse.gov/sites/default/files/docs/nat_arctic_strategy.pdf.

45. Elsewhere, I discuss extensively the land-sea binary that underpins the dual U.S. views of the Arctic. See Steinberg, *The Social Construction of the Ocean*; Philip E. Steinberg, "Sovereignty, Territory, and the Mapping of Mobility: A View from the Outside," *Annals of the Association of American Geographers* 99 (2009): 467–495; Philip E. Steinberg, "Free Sea," in *Sovereignty, Spatiality, and Carl Schmitt: Geographies of the Nomos*, ed. Stephen Legg (London: Routledge, 2011), 268–275.

46. Bergh, *Arctic Policies of Canada and the United States*, 14.

47. See, for instance, Hillary R. Clinton, "Interview on CTV's *Power Play with Tom Clark*," March 29, 2010, http://www.state.gov/secretary/rm/2010/03/139207.htm.

48. The four pages consisted of a home page (http://www.state.gov/e/oes/ocns/opa/arc/index.htm) devoted entirely to fisheries issues and three linked pages: a page on search and rescue cooperation that appeared to have last been updated in January 2010, a page on the International Polar Year that was written prior to the commencement of the most recent IPY in March 2007, and a page on the Arctic Council that consisted solely of a reprint of a 1999 *American Journal of International Law* article authored by then State Department official Ashley Roach (who has since retired). It was only in the final months of 2013 that the Arctic section of the State Department's website finally received long-awaited revisions.

CHAPTER 7

RUSSIA'S ARCTIC POLICY

CONTINUITY AND CHANGES[1]

Gleb Yarovoy

INTRODUCTION

Russia's policy toward the Arctic region has deep roots in the time of
the Russian Empire. During the periods of tsarist rule, interest in the
Arctic was often inhibited by the constraints of geographical remote-
ness and the expense of defending sovereignty—the transfer of Alaska
to the United States in 1867 is perhaps the best example of the latter.
In early Soviet times the Arctic provoked the interest of Communist
leaders for political, economic, and propagandist reasons. In 1926, the
Presidium of the Central Executive Committee of the Union of Soviet
Socialist Republics (USSR) had adopted the resolution "On Declaration
of the USSR Territory, Lands and Islands Located in the Arctic Ocean"
and thereafter followed a process of intensive economic development of
Russia's vast northern territories.

For much of the twentieth century, Russia's Arctic was considered
an economic storehouse and was a region closed to outsiders, who

could only gain access with Russia's permission. During World War II, the Arctic assumed strategic significance as the only permanent link for lend-lease aid, and northern convoys plied northern sea routes to Murmansk and Arkhangelsk. Throughout the Cold War period, the Arctic became an arena of militarization and military tensions. Mikhail Gorbachev's coming to power, his "New Thinking" approach to foreign policy, and, significantly, his 1987 Murmansk speech resulted in a normalization of circumpolar international relations and further de-militarization of the Russian High North. The last decade of the twentieth century was a time of multilateral cooperation in the region, exemplified by initiatives such as the Barents Euro-Arctic Council (BEAC) and the Arctic Council (AC), and was characterized by the absence of any specific Russian domestic or foreign strategy toward the Arctic. Almost two decades after Russia's emergence as an independent state, there was almost no "Arctic" in Russian politics, and no special attention was paid to Arctic issues.

The situation, however, has changed dramatically since around 2007. In September 2008, President Dmitry Medvedev chaired the first meeting of the Russian Security Council since his inauguration. The strategic document "Basics of the State Policy of the Russian Federation in the Arctic for the Period until 2020 and for a Further Perspective"[2] was adopted during the meeting. This marked the beginning of a new era in Russian Arctic policy. This was followed in 2013 by the adoption of "The Strategy for the Development of the Arctic Zone of the Russian Federation and National Security Protection,"[3] which has somehow displayed the "idealism to realism" turn in Russia's Arctic strategy.[4] Evidently, Arctic issues are among the most topical questions on the political, economic, and societal agendas of the largest Arctic littoral state.[5]

In this chapter, I explore the continuities and changes, as well as perspectives, of Russia's Arctic policy by touching upon the history and development of its strategies in the Arctic. The main question to be put forward, even if it is not one that can immediately be answered, is which of the possible scenarios of Russian Arctic policy development would prevail and how can it be achieved? To place this in context, I begin with a history of Russia's Arctic and policy perspectives on the region before moving to a discussion of recent strategic and policy thinking.

A HISTORY OF THE RUSSIAN ARCTIC

There are several significant historical periods that have influenced, shaped, and characterized Russia's policies toward its Arctic regions. In the 1920s and beyond (certainly until the end of the Cold War), because Arctic sovereignty issues were not at that time high on the agenda of international relations, the USSR dedicated its efforts to the economic development of Arctic lands and waters in order to use them for strategic and military purposes. The most ambivalent and complex phase of Russian Arctic policy began in the late 1980s and early 1990s and is still continuing. During this period, national interests of the various Arctic states have often been challenged and influenced by the interplay of regional cooperation and the often divergent interests of a number of different actors in the Arctic.

The Imperial Arctic: In Search of the North East Passage

Russia's early interest in the Arctic was limited to expeditions that aimed to describe unknown territories and establish the extent of the borders of the Russian Empire, key examples of which include the 1648 Russian Arctic expedition of Semeon Dezhnev, who was the first to prove that Russia is divided from America by a strait; the famous expedition of Vitus Bering inspired personally by Peter the Great in 1724;[6] and the Russian Admiralty expedition that explored the huge area alongside the whole coastline of the Arctic Ocean from the White Sea to Alaska. Numerous geographic expeditions were led to develop trade relations with the Aleutians, which resulted in the establishment of the Russian-American Company (RAC) in 1799.[7] The RAC managed Alaska until the lands of Russian America were sold to the United States in 1867 according to the Treaty Concerning the Cession of the Russian Possessions in North America by His Majesty the Emperor of All the Russians to the United States of America.[8] The sale of Alaska is perhaps the best example of how the Arctic (or at least its American part) was not considered a strategic dimension of Russian politics.

The cherished dream of many generations of Arctic explorers was the "passage to India" or "North East Passage," now known as the Northern Sea Route. Russians—primarily Russian merchants—had long been interested in the Northern Sea Route, although Russian governments had not.[9] Yet after the beginning of Suez Canal operations in 1869, many European merchants and entrepreneurs lost interest in the North East Passage. However, the Arctic Ocean still attracted the attention of Russian trade and industry companies. In 1904 a commission on the Siberian sea route to the Far East was established under the jurisdiction of the Navigation Society.[10] The commission attracted voluntary donations to study the Northern Sea Route extensively and even published books to attract public attention.[11] Inside the Russian government, the scientist D. I. Mendeleev was one of the most active proponents of the study of the Arctic. He convinced the government to allocate substantial resources to the construction of the first Russian icebreaker, *Ermak*, in 1897–1899. Mendeleev was also instrumental in creating a strategy for the development of a unified Russian transport system, which included linking the Trans-Siberian Railroad and the Northern Sea Route to each other by the great Siberian rivers.[12]

The defeat suffered by Russia in the Russo-Japanese War of 1904–1905 provided the impetus for the Russian government to perform further studies of the Northern Sea Route's potential for the development of naval forces. V. Vize, a prominent Arctic researcher, cited Admiral V. P. Verkhovksy as saying after the Russo-Japanese War, "One can be 100% sure that after two years...Russian naval squadrons will navigate to Vladivostok via the Arctic Ocean every year."[13] Between 1910 and 1914, hydrographic and oceanographic research was carried out by the first scientific "icebreaker-type" vessels, *Taimyr* and *Vaigach*.[14] The results of their work were not considered exciting enough for the government to focus too much attention on the Arctic. Nonetheless, interest did begin to grow during World War I, but it was the Bolshevik government that intercepted the Arctic relay baton.

As a consequence of the imperial government's inconsistent Arctic policy, which resulted in insufficient attention and funding for the investigations of Arctic Ocean navigation routes, the entire voyage from Europe to the Pacific Ocean via the Northern Sea Route was completed only three times before the collapse of the Russian Empire and the creation of the Soviet Union. According to some commentators, "the Soviet government showed much more interest in the possession of the North and much more initiative in exploring it than the imperial government did."[15]

The Soviet Arctic: Economic Development and Military Use

In contrast to the fact that by the beginning of the twentieth century "scarcely any part of Russian history before Peter the Great has been adequately treated and properly understood by non-Russian historians,"[16] much attention had been paid to the development of the Arctic strategy of the Soviet Union in non-Russian academic literature since the 1920s.[17]

From a number of political, economic, propaganda, and military strategy perspectives, the Arctic (or the High North) was recognized early on as an important region by the Soviets. "Untraveled air routes and undeveloped resources in the Arctic are now being thought of as valuable for the future, even the near future," wrote D. H. Miller in 1925.[18] Legislative recognition of sovereign rights in the Arctic was made by the USSR between 1924 and 1926, almost simultaneously with Canada. The first legislative act defining the status of Russian lands and islands in the Arctic was a note by the Ministry of Foreign Affairs of the Russian Empire in September 1916. Vast areas along the northern coast of Siberia, as well as the Arctic islands located close to Russia's Euro-pean coast and those that were the continuation of the Siberian conti-nental plateau, were included as Russian possessions according to the document. The note's provisions were confirmed by the memorandum of the Peoples' Commissariat (Ministry) of Foreign Affairs of USSR in November 1924. The final legislative recognition of the Soviet Arctic possessions happened in 1926 by the adoption of the resolution of the USSR's Central Executive Committee Presidium "On the Announcement of the Lands and Islands Located in the Arctic Ocean the USSR's Terri-tories." The resolution underlined that Soviet sovereignty is to apply to "all lands and islands, both discovered and which may be discovered in the future."[19]

However, for unknown reasons (potentially rather understandable ones such as World War I and civil war in Russia), the Bolshevik govern-ment did not identify the potential of the Arctic immediately. It is not widely acknowledged that the first Arctic and polar initiatives of Soviet Russia came from a group of scientists who proposed the systematic exploration of the Russian Arctic in the late 1910s. It should be noted, though, that the "proletarian" government grabbed the idea much faster and with more interest than the "imperial" one. The private nature of Arctic exploration was kept a secret for many years. An official Soviet version states that Vladimir Lenin was personally interested in exploring the Russian North and even promoted the creation of the first Soviet program for northern exploration in spring 1918.[20]

One way or the other, on March 4, 1920, the Northern Scientific and Field Expedition (*Severnaya nauchno-promyslovaya ekspeditsiya*) was created by the Decree of the Highest Council of the National Economy. In 1925 the Northern Scientific and Field Expedition was reformed into the Research Institute of the North, then into the All-Union Arctic Institute, and finally as the Arctic and Antarctic Science and Research Institute,[21] which is still functioning in St. Petersburg. Today the institute coordi-nates and carries out (as it did during Soviet times) scientific research in the Russian Arctic and in Antarctica. In the early 1920s, the attempts to "conquer" the Northern Sea Route (NSR) resumed. In 1921 Lenin signed the decree for the establishment of the Floating Sea Research Institute, which began its work in the Arctic Ocean as well as along the Russian coastline from the Barents Sea to the Bering Strait. The new economic and, later, military aims and goals set by the government called for the development of an Arctic transportation system and the full-fledged use of the Northern Sea Route. To this end, the Main Administration of the Northern Sea Route (*Glavsevmorput*) was established in 1932. One of the main aims—sailing the NSR in one shipping season—was achieved the same year and repeated in subsequent years by the institute's research staff, such as O. Y. Shmidt, R. L. Samoilovich, V. Y. Vize, and others. Many of them were later repressed and executed (only to be vindicated in the late 1950s).[22] This did not impede Stalin in making the "conquest of the Arctic" an important idea behind societal mobilization and turning its particular events, such as the crash of *Chelyuskin*,[23] into a "national epic."[24]

In 1936 the Floating Sea Research Institute initiated a program of ice monitoring in order to forecast sailing conditions and provide information necessary for Arctic navigation—for the same reasons, an ice-air reconnaissance developed. In 1937 a high-latitude air expedition disembarked the first drifting station, "North Pole—1," which then helped to implement the trans-Arctic flight of V. Chkalov and M. Gromov. This fact not only declared the "victory of humankind over the Arctic" but also opened the shortest way from the USSR to the United States, the future ideological enemies and Cold War strategic competitors. It was during the high-latitude expeditions that one of the Lomonosov Ridge peaks was discovered. With this "finding," an "Age of Discovery" of the bottom of the world's oceans began.[25] It also paved the way to future Russian claims in the Arctic.

Such a rapid development of different activities in the Arctic was not possible without powerful icebreakers. The Soviet icebreaker fleet contained over forty vessels by 1940. Moreover, *Glavsevmorput* obtained "an exclusive responsibility for the development of all the territories above the 62nd parallel in the fields of transportation, industry, urban development, education and science etc." In 1937, at the height of Stalin's Great Purge, *Glavsevmorput* had a budget of about US$1 billion and employed about 40,000 workers.[26] The Northern Sea Route, together with the active economic and infrastructural development of the High North, became one of the bases of national security in the prewar period.[27] In 1940, one year after the double end-to-end voyage by the Northern Sea Route in one shipping season, Vize wrote that "although the end-to-end passages will doubtless have economic significance in the future, now they are important for us for security reasons...because it entirely runs in our soviet waters. Thus the closure of Suez or Panama Canals cannot prevent us to carry out the deployment of the warships from the Atlantic to Pacific or vice versa."[28] Smolka was also very perspicacious by predicting the significance of the Arctic region for military affairs during the then "hypothetical but not impossible" conflict between the USSR and Germany and Japan. As he put it, "The Soviet strategy of rapid developments in the Arctic has improved Russia's strategic position in comparison with what it was in 1905 and in 1914."[29]

Indeed, during World War II the Northern Sea Route had vital importance, first, as a route of international transportation of military cargo (lend-lease, Arctic convoys) and, second, as a route of domestic evacuation of industrial enterprises from the European part to the eastern part of the USSR, as well as arms and other goods delivery to the front line, carrying warships from the east to the west. During the war, the volume of goods transported through the Northern Sea Route increased tenfold.[30] The Arctic convoys were essential for the transportation of military and non-military goods provided in the framework of the lend-lease. Over a quarter of all lend-lease supplies to the USSR were conveyed through the Arctic.[31] This became possible because the command of Wehrmacht and Kriegsmarine recognized the Arctic Ocean as an important battlefield only in 1942, after the failure of *blitzkrieg*.[32] Thus, by the end of 1941, Arctic convoys delivered to the northern ports of the USSR (Murmansk, Arkhangelsk, Molotovsk) 699 aircraft, 466 tanks, 330 tankettes, and other military hardware and arms.[33] All in all, more than 800 ships in forty Arctic convoys arrived with goods for the Soviet army between 1941 and 1945. Arctic convoys, lend-lease, and the Arctic in general not only played an important military role in supplying the army with arms but also provided psychological support, meaning that the USSR did not fight alone but in alliance with Western democracies. The success of the Arctic convoys and other deliveries was in substantial measure achieved owing to the great work performed by the *Glavsevmorput* and the Arctic institute, whose staff supported and maintained the military and transportation operation in the Arctic seas.[34]

By the end of Stalin's rule, and as the Cold War heated up, USSR actions (as well as those of the United States) displayed the increasing importance of the Arctic as a theater of military operations for the deployment of strategic weapons systems, and the Arctic became increasingly militarized. Military bases were urgently created in Chukotka and Kamchatka. Soviet and American navy commands considered the Arctic as both a place to hide their own missile-launching submarines and to track down and destroy enemy submarines. Soviet planners designed huge submarines, which were able to carry a battalion of marines or a number of fighting vehicles. In the 1970s and early 1980s, Soviet strategic submarines broke surface on the North Pole pack ice, demonstrating the possibilities of missile launches.

Polar stations also had a "twofold purpose" (i.e., for military aims). One of their tasks was to assess the possibilities of creating the ice prestrike staging base for long-range bomber aircraft. This experience, however, was finally used only to take workers to the polar stations. Another task was to construct SODARS (sound detecting and ranging) for submarine orientation under the ice cap, ultimately achieved by Ukrainian engineers.[35] Similar activities were performed by U.S. researchers and the U.S. Navy. In some fields the Americans achieved even a greater success,[36] so the only "twofold purpose" where the USSR led was the creation of the Arctic Ocean's bottom relief chart.

The stage of active Arctic confrontation was over by the second half of the 1980s. The Murmansk speech given by Mikhail Gorbachev, the last secretary general of the Central Committee of the Soviet Communist Party and the only president of the USSR, is widely cited as characterizing the beginning of a new period of international Arctic cooperation. On October 1, 1987, he said, "The Soviet Union is in favour of a radical lowering of the level of military confrontation in the region. Let the North of the globe, the Arctic, become a zone of peace. Let the North Pole be a pole of peace. We suggest that all interested states start talks on the limitation and scaling down of military activity in the North as a whole."[37] This "new thinking" on Soviet foreign policy was partly a result of the influence of some *institutchiki*[38] over the political elite of the USSR.[39] In contrast, such initiatives as the North Calotte, a peaceable public movement of the Arctic regions of four states (Finland, Sweden, Norway, and the USSR) that aimed at multidimensional regional cooperation, had been in existence since its establishment in Kemi (Finland) in 1962. Its main activity consisted of triennial "Peace Days" held in one of the regions. From 1962 to 1987, ten international meetings were conducted.

Thus, events in the Soviet Arctic moved a long way from the first private initiatives of early researchers to the activities of full-fledged scientific exploration, economic development, and military engagement. Behind those sporadic heroic achievements, "minor" Arctic issues such as severe living and working conditions in the Arctic, environmental problems, biodiversity preservation, indigenous people's livelihoods, and other "low politics" and "soft security" concerns were moved aside. These challenges, however, alongside the more general problems of "normalization" and "demilitarization," became important items on the agenda of international cooperation in the Arctic at the end of the twentieth and the beginning of the twenty-first centuries. However, it must not be forgotten that the Arctic (nation) states' interests, expressed in terms of traditional military security, did not cease to exist. In recent years they have risen to the top of the international circumpolar agenda. Today's Arctic is a plexus of problematic issues, where the traditional techniques of defending national interests and sovereign rights meet the inevitability of mutually beneficial collaboration of Arctic states. The future of the circumpolar North depends on the strategies of the eight Arctic states, and Russia's Arctic policy is a significant factor in this.

THE MODERN ARCTIC: FROM THE "NEW THINKING" TO NATIONAL INTERESTS AND BACK?

In the early 1990s, after the end of the Cold War and the collapse of the Soviet Union, Russia had to organize relations with the world community and, as Germany did after World War II, it had to construct a new image of itself as a democratic and friendly country. And yet, as a successor of the USSR, Russia had (and still has) ambition to be a great world power. This dissonance partly explains the ambiguity and zigzags of Russian foreign policy from the very beginning until today.

In 1996, Yakov Plyais wrote about the complexity and confusion of Russian foreign policy in the first half of the 1990s. He defined five stages of Russian foreign policy, starting from the "romantic illusions," "infantile euphoria," and "excessive rest upon the West" of 1990–1992 to the "beginning of sobering" and "legitimization and adoption of the presidential foreign policy" of 1993–1996. Plyais also stated that Russian foreign policy faces grandiose problems and that there is substantial doubt if Russian foreign policy is in fact evolving at all.[40] In 2002, Andrey Melville claimed that Russia still "has to obtain its new 'Ego' in the rapidly changed environment, where democracy became the 'Zeitgeist.'"[41] He also noted that Russia's foreign policy is a projection and continuation of domestic politics and even of public opinion. But the situation changed considerably in the beginning of the twenty-first century, after Vladimir Putin's "enthronement": currently the *vox populi* mirrors the foreign policy, not the other way around. For the most part of modern Russian history, Arctic issues have been important concerns mostly for polar researchers and for the people who live in the High North, especially since the early 1990s, when the collapse of the Soviet Union resulted in economic and social disaster—in today's Russian Arctic, vast regions devastated by social, economic, and environmental problems are far too common.

No specific policy appeared even after the launch of the Northern Dimension initiative[42] of the European Union in the late 1990s. The only evidence of the existence of the "Russian Arctic" was the participation of Russia in the BEAC (which was established in 1993) and the Arctic Council (established in 1996). The Arctic became a focus of interest of the Russian political establishment only since around 2007, when it became clear that "the main competitive advantages of Russia in the foreseeable future are its natural resources, oil and gas ante omnia," and the "main security guarantor is nuclear weapons."[43]

Currently, I would argue, Russia depends on the Arctic in the sphere of economic security much more than any other Arctic state. The Russian economy has maintained its raw-material orientation. The general feeling is that for years to come it will not change considerably even in spite of the merely populist efforts (such as the notorious "Skolkovo" project or the talks over nanotechnology development) of ex-President Medvedev and the Kremlin administration. Participants in the "Russia-2020: Scenarios for the Future" project run by the Carnegie Endowment for International Peace have argued that the most realistic scenario for the development of the Russian economy for the next ten years is an "inertial" scenario,[44] or the "business-as-usual *dirigisté* course."[45] The central idea of any scenario is a share of the oil and gas component in the Russian GDP. Even in the most optimistic scenarios, this share is rather large. Thus, the long-term economic and social development of Russia (i.e., inertial scenario, energy raw materials develop-

ment scenario, and innovative development scenario), defined by the
Ministry of Economic Development and Trade of the Russian Federation, completely or partly rely upon the preservation of influence and
the development of the energy sector of the economy.[46]

The "Arctic macroregion" assumes a special role in the energy and
raw materials development scenario. This scenario may be considered
a rather optimistic one, given that the innovative development scenario
seems unrealistic even in the long term. The fundamental cause of this
is neither a lack of material or intellectual resources for the implementation of the innovative scenario nor a problem with human resources
(which is in fact an obvious impediment to any innovation in Russia).
The main obstacle to the implementation of the innovative scenario is
weakness of existing institutions, which are not ready at all and are not
suitable for the transition of the economy to a postindustrial level. This
concerns the current situation in democracy, civil society, governance,
corruption, and so on. At present, Russia maintains a position among
25 percent of the less developed countries in the world according to
the "quality of the state" index. "So far, no state succeeded to achieve
the postindustrial level of economic development, having such weak
institutions."[47] Hopes for a gradual improvement of the institutional
development appear to be elusive even after some new legislative acts
promoting political participation entered into force in 2012.[48] According
to V. Gel'man, Russian politics fell into the "institutional trap," and the
situation is worsening.[49] This is precisely why the energy and raw material scenario, which does not require an institutional breakthrough and
in which the Arctic becomes one of the priority regions, is expected to
be the most relevant for implementation. Yet this scenario would also
demand substantial efforts on the part of the Kremlin administration.
Therefore, "the state apparatus can neither avoid nor postpone the solution of the problems [of exploration of the Arctic resources] without
causing a serious damage to the national interests."[50]

The sovereignty issue is a dependent variable in Russia's current Arctic policy. The Kremlin's intention to maintain the role of a leading Arctic power rests against a need to find economically sound decisions of using Arctic resources, such as the extraction of hydrocarbons, a justification of the Arctic shelf delimitation claims (this "resources-based future" is considered to be a key to sustainable economic growth and maintenance of the economic sovereignty in the long-term perspective), and a full-fledged exploitation of the Northern Sea Route. Everything related to Arctic resources is the number one priority of the "Putinomics"[51] and, consequently, of the political stability discourse that was the main slogan of Putin's electoral campaign for the third presidential term.[52] Another side is military security issues, which are, if not a part of Putinomics, part of the "sovereign democracy" and a claim for stability. In this respect, it perhaps explains why such issues as the environment or indigenous peoples have become secondary issues.

Environmental Protection

Environmental protection and cooperation as a part of Russian Arctic strategy clearly refers to the Gorbachev speech of 1987, which led to various environmental initiatives, such as Finland's initiative on Arctic environmental protection cooperation in 1989. From 1989 to 1991, a number of technical and scientific reports were prepared under this initiative. Finally, this led to the development of the Arctic Environmental Protection Strategy (AEPS)[53] in 1991. Russian authorities seemed to consider Arctic environment issues as a matter of international cooperation rather than an internal problem that had to be solved. The Barents Euro-Arctic Region (BEAR) and the Arctic Council became the international fora to discuss Russia's Arctic environmental problems. In the framework of BEAR, a "Barents Environmental Hot Spot List" was approved in 2010 based on a report produced in 2003 by the Nordic Environment Finance Corporation (NEFCO) in collaboration with the Arctic Monitoring and Assessment Programme (AMAP). The list included forty-two "hot spots" of the Barents region, all of them situated in the Russian part of BEAR.[54] In 2013, the eight-step process of reduction of the "hot spots" will begin with the financial support of the Barents Hot Spots Facility, managed by NEFCO on behalf of the governments of Finland, Iceland, Norway, and Sweden.[55] The AC represents a loose platform for meeting the environmental and other related problems of the Arctic. Although criticized for being too state-centric and, consequently, unable to discuss "real" problems of the Arctic environment, it still promotes the engagement of the Russian government with the circumpolar discourse over the need to improve the environment protection system in the Arctic zone of Russia.[56]

In this respect, Vladimir Putin raised the issue of a "general cleaning in the Arctic" in 2010. The first move toward this was taken in mid-2011, when the Ministry of Natural Resources and Environment announced a tender for the "liquidation of the sources of negative impact" on the Franz Josef Land archipelago. One of the affiliated structures of the Ministry of Economic Development won the competition. The main aim of the program under preparation is to clean the archipelago completely by 2020. In September 2011, at the opening ceremony of the second International Arctic Forum in Arkhangelsk, Putin announced that the government allocated 2.3 billion rubles (approximately US$77 million) until 2015 for cleaning the archipelago of barrels with waste oil. The Wrangel Island and Russian villages on Spitsbergen are next in line, as well as the comprehensive analysis of the environment in another seven major Arctic zones. However, preservation of the environment competes with the other priorities of the "Basics of the State Policy of the Russian Federation," such as military presence.[57] It seems that environmental protection is considered to be a supportive factor for economic development, for example, in relation to the extraction of hydrocarbons and other natural resources, and will be implemented as long as it does not hinder military activities.[58] One of the latest, and rather illustrative, examples here is the arrest of the entire crew of the Greenpeace *Arctic Sunrise*, charged of piracy in blocking the Prirazlomnaya offshore oil platform. In spite of the rewording of the charges to "hooliganism,"[59] this seemed to be a clear signal for the environmentalists to stand back when it comes to the economic interests of Russia in the Arctic.

Indigenous Peoples Policy

According to expert opinion, "contemporary Russia represents a case of a less articulated and responsive policy toward its northern territories,"[60] where the indigenous population constitutes a significant part. Twenty-seven indigenous peoples, with the total number of about 200,000 persons, representing the carriers of ancient cultures and traditions, live in the High North of Russia.[61] Although the "improvement of the quality of life for indigenous peoples and their economic activities" is mentioned among the strategic priorities of the Basics, a special document called "Concept of Sustainable Development of Indigenous Small-Numbered Peoples of the North, Siberia and the Far East of the Russian Federation"[62] was adopted and released in February 2009. The document describes the measures undertaken by the federal and regional authorities during the fifteen years prior to the adoption of the Concept document, such as implementation of federal and regional target programs,[63] legislative recognition of the measures of state support (in the form of incentives, subsidies, and quotas on the use of biological resources), and active participation in the International Decade of the World's Indigenous People (1995–2004) and the Second International Decade of the World's Indigenous People (2005–2015). At the same time, the serious problems in economic and social development of the indigenous peoples (incongruity of traditional way of life and the current economic conditions, low level of competitive ability of the traditional economic activities, growth of diseases and pathologies, high infant mortality rate, alcoholism, etc.[64]) are also recognized. Thus, the Concept implementation should result in the creation of favorable conditions for the sustainable development of the indigenous peoples, meaning the improvement of their quality of life by reaching the average Russian level and the reduction of the mortality of infants by at least two times, compared with 2007, by 2025.

In April 2009, two months after the introduction of the Concept, the Sixth Congress of the Indigenous Peoples of the North, Siberia and Far East of the Russian Federation adopted the resolution addressing the list of unsolved problems of indigenous peoples and sustainable development. The list—prepared by the Russian Association of Indigenous Peoples of the North, Siberia and the Far East (RAIPON)—included such issues as the ineffective management of problems of sustainable development; the absence of effective mechanisms of involvement of indigenous peoples in the decision-making process; imperfect legislation, lack of norms to guarantee some specific rights in conformity with the Constitution of the Russian Federation; and impossibility of the implementation of the right to use lands and other natural resources to protect the traditional lifestyle of the indigenous peoples.[65]

However, lack of actions taken by the federal government following the adoption of the Concept, the incoherence of the state policy, and disregard of RAIPON's position and activities has concerned indigenous peoples' representatives greatly.[66] Years after the adoption of the Concept, the situation remains ambivalent. On the one hand, executive authorities introduced new documents emphasizing the importance of support for the indigenous people, organized numerous activities in the framework of the Second International Decade of the World's Indigenous People,[67] and transferred millions of rubles to the regional budgets for the support of indigenous peoples.[68] On the other hand, the indigenous peoples themselves consider the efforts of the authorities unsuccessful: "Concept of Sustainable Development—a very important document—has failed. The implementation measures for this Concept include only what the Ministry of regional development finds relevant; and even those measures, to my deep regret, are not met," first vice president of RAIPON Pavel Sulyandziga said to then prime minister Putin in July 2011.[69] RAIPON's position echoes in the Public Chamber of Russia[70] and in the Upper House (Council of Federation) of the Russian Parliament. In September 2011, Public Chamber chaired a roundtable, "The Legislation Development on the Rights of Indigenous Peoples of the North,

Siberia and the Far East: Issues and Horizons." The roundtable's conclusions were rather pessimistic: federal legislation on indigenous rights is regressing (they have to prove their nationality in the court to be able to hunt, fish, and receive a social pension), the federal government, while not developing proposals to the Forest Code, Land Code, and Water Code, does not support the legislative initiatives prepared by the Council of Federation. Furthermore, there is still no progress in legislation on health, education, and support of indigenous peoples' languages.[71] In April 2012, the Council of Federation discussed the Court of Auditors' report on the application of federal funds of indigenous people support in 2009 and 2010. The main conclusion of the report stated that the funds were used in an ineffective manner, that the substantial funds did not result in the noticeable improvement of indigenous peoples' lives (living standards are lower than average in the related regions; unemployment rate is 1.5–2 times higher than the national average), and that the core problem is that imperfect legislation still has to be improved.[72]

The situation with the policy on indigenous peoples became even more ambivalent with the attempt of the Russian Ministry of Justice, which has finally failed, to shut down RAIPON in 2012 and 2013. First vice president Rodion Sulyandziga explained, "There is an extensive rise in industrialization in the north, and the indigenous peoples are among the last barriers against the business and the state developing the resources."[73] In mid-March 2013, two weeks after permission was given for RAIPON to continue its activities, Vladimir Putin welcomed the participants of the Seventh Congress of the Indigenous Peoples of the North, Siberia and the Far East, organized by RAIPON, with the following statement: "I emphasize that the implementation of large-scale territorial development programs in Russia should be carried out in continuous dialogue with representatives of national communities and other public organizations, consideration of their position, opinions and interests."[74]

To this end, it remains to be seen how Moscow's policies on indigenous peoples will develop in the future. So far, the situation is rather similar to that of the protection of the environment. Where the interests of indigenous people would clash with the interests of big business, as well as with the national interests—the need to secure extraction and processing of natural resources, upon which the political and economic stability of the country is based—the decision is unlikely to be in favor of indigenous peoples, even if it would undermine Russia's image worldwide.

ECONOMIC POLICIES AND ACTIVITIES

So far, economic activities are determined by the attempts to keep the Northern Sea Route in service, exploration and exploitation of onshore and offshore oil and gas reservoirs, and the endeavors to gain "ownership" in the Arctic (claims over the Lomonosov and Mendeleev Ridges submitted to the United Nations Convention on the Law of the Sea, or UNCLOS, Commission) or to settle old boundary disputes (the Norway-Russia Barents Sea delimitation agreement).

The Northern Sea Route

The Northern Sea Route is of vital importance for Russia in both economic (it is actively used by Norilsk Nikel, Lukoil, Gazprom, Rosneft, Rosshelf, Novatek, and others) and social (supplying the northernmost settlements of Russia) senses. While the Arctic ice is melting,[75] the NSR becomes more accessible for navigation. Thus, in 2009 (and then in 2010), the German company Beluga Shipping GmbH together with the Russian Atomflot organized the voyages of several ice-class vessels from South Korea to Rotterdam.[76] In 2010, a number of transportations through the NSR to China were implemented, including the transportation of 72,000 tons of gas condensate by the *Baltica* tanker.[77] The 2011 sailing season was a record length, a month longer than the previous one. Eight times more oil was transported via the NSR in 2011 than in 2010.[78] Also that year, the speed record of sailing the NSR was broken twice. The Panamax-class oil tanker sailed from Murmansk through the North East

Passage in only eight days (the whole way from Murmansk to Thailand took less than a month, June 19–August 16, 2011[79]). One month later, the first supertanker ever to sail through the NSR—the Suezmax-class *Vladimir Tikhonov*, which transported 120,000 tons of gas condensate for Novatek—made the journey from Novaya Zemlya to the Bering Strait in less than eight days.[80] That year, Japan joined the "Arctic" states by sending the first vessel through the NSR; in summer 2012, China increased its Arctic presence by sending the icebreaker *Xue Long* (*Snow Dragon*) along the entire length of the NSR from the Bering Strait to the Barents Sea and back.[81]

Russia is trying to react to the internationalization of the NSR. In order to control the development of the NSR, the federal law on its regulation was drafted by Arthur Chilingarov in 2009.[82] This was not considered but, in October 2011, the subcommittee for northern affairs and indigenous peoples of the Council of Federation (the upper chamber of the Parliament) issued a positive "Opinion" on a similar draft law, which amended the existing legislation in order to promote state control of the NSR.[83] In November 2011, it successfully passed the first reading in the State Duma (the lower chamber of the Parliament).[84] However (and this is a truly "Russian style" of policy implementation, where financial allocations are made without a proper legislative financial framework), "in 2012–2014 over 21 billion rubles will be assigned for construction and modernization of maritime infrastructure in the Arctic," the then prime minister Putin said in November 2011.[85] In this light, some experts expect the potential volume of freight traffic in both eastern and western directions of the NSR to reach 35–40 million tons per year by 2020,[86] although many of them not only still seriously doubt the prospects of the NSR for shipping but also question the necessity for infrastructural development in the High North.[87]

While Russian experts discuss the need of the NSR development, the government continues to invest and slowly improve legislation. One cannot but agree with the fact that, if current trends—such as melting

Arctic ice, expected growth in commercial maritime traffic, piracy and political instability along the route through the Suez Canal—persist, then by the end of this decade the NSR could become a full-fledged transport corridor.[88] Europe (primarily Germany) and Asia (predominantly China) already have their eyes on the NSR. In these circumstances, it would have been imprudent for the Kremlin to give up on NSR development and use. Unless Arctic ice makes trans-Arctic passages difficult, Russia will be able to control the navigation along the NSR; its importance for both Russian oil and gas companies and their foreign partners will increase as a result of development of technologies for extracting hydrocarbons on the continental shelf. Transnational business has to invest in transport and security infrastructure of the NSR on par with the state.

TERRITORIAL CLAIMS AND DEALS

In the early twenty-first century, the Kremlin began to promote the idea of international legal confirmation of Russia's rights over specific parts of the Arctic shelf. In December 2001, Russia prepared an application to determine the outer boundary of the continental shelf of the Russian Federation within the framework of UNCLOS 1982[89] and submit it to the UN secretary general. According to experts, the potential area of an extended Russian continental shelf is about 1.2 million square kilometers; this may contain some 83 to 110 billion tons of hydrocarbons.[90] The UN Commission on the Limits of the Continental Shelf (CLCS) dismissed Russia's application because of a lack of geological evidence. In order to reapply Russia has to produce the necessary scientific data. After Russia applied to CLCS, other Arctic states—Canada, Denmark, the United States, and Norway—accelerated their efforts in claiming the continental shelf. Canada and Denmark ratified UNCLOS in 2003 and 2004 respectively, so they have to submit their respective applications no later than 2013 and 2014. But since the Lomonosov Ridge passes through Greenland to Canada's Ellesmere Island, the two countries joined their efforts in collecting the scientific data to substantiate the potential claim over that ridge.[91] Denmark continues to gather the data that are necessary to claim an extension of the continental shelf off Greenland by the Lomonosov Ridge, most notably in 2012 through the work of the LOMROG III project.[92] Thus, the potential applications from Russia, Denmark (Greenland), and Canada could overlap and intersect, which could result in growing political tensions between Arctic states.

As stated by Spielman, "if the Arctic countries, including Russia, wish to have their continental shelves set, then the five nations are left with two choices: sit down and work out boundary delimitations or amend UNCLOS."[93] Although the author did not find any of these scenarios likely to be realized, there is at least one example of implementing the "negotiations scenario" regarding the Arctic delimitation, in which Russia's interests are of direct concern.

In September 2010, Russia and Norway signed the Treaty on Maritime Delimitation and Cooperation in the Barents Sea and the Arctic Ocean. According to the treaty, the area, which had been disputed for some forty years,[94] was divided in two almost equal (in terms of territorial space) parts (see figure 1), thus demonstrating Moscow's willingness to resolve disputed issues on a legal basis.[95]

In Norway, the treaty has been ratified unanimously,[96] whereas in Russia strong debates on the document's negative consequences ended up with the treaty being ratified by the State Duma only because of the constitutional majority of the United Russia Party.[97] Both political and expert communities are split over the division of the disputed area.[98]

Officially in Moscow, the fact of equal delimitation is seen as being in accordance with Russian national interests. First, it is considered to be the basis for further cooperation with Norway. Second, it opens the door to a second Russian application to the CLCS. Third, it allows for the start of exploration for hydrocarbon resources in the former disputed area.

The main counter-argument for all pro-treaty statements holds that they are totally formal and are far from political reality. Although the Moscow-Oslo relations should improve, there are many cases that contradict this, such as, for example, the economic conflict over fisheries[99] and discussions over the "administrative sovereignty" of Norway at Svalbard.[100] Furthermore, should hydrocarbon extraction in the area be technically possible in the future, the financial aspects of offshore drilling will still be an insurmountable obstacle for such activities, as the cases of Shtockman and Prirazlomnoe show.[101]

Thus, the dilemma involving "good intentions" or the "diplomatic impotence" of the Russian authorities arises. There is clearly a strong argument behind both statements. I would argue that on the one hand Russian diplomacy in recent years shows its weakness and incoherency as being a part of a bad governance system. On the other hand, it is probably symptomatic of the appearance of the new system of international relations in the (European) Arctic that the Barents delimitation agreement was signed in Murmansk, where Mikhail Gorbachev delivered his speech in 1987. If this leads to the rise of an updated "new thinking" in the Arctic, similar to that of Gorbachev in the late 1980s, then the weakness of Russian diplomacy could turn into the recognition of its wisdom.[102] But a *conditio sine qua non* of the rise of a new system of cooperation in the Arctic is, evidently, the positions and strategies of all Arctic states. Otherwise, the unilateral initiatives or even bilateral agreements will be senseless.

MILITARY AND STRATEGIC DIMENSION

In respect to Russia's claims over the Arctic ridges, some Russian academics and officials are aware of a dangerous trend toward the "widening of the elements of supranationalism and exterritoriality, reduction of the sovereign rights of states in favor of international bodies and regulatory institutes while dealing with the exploitation of the Arctic resources."[103] This trend directly contradicts both the Kremlin's aspiration to exert control over all possible Arctic resources and Russian foreign policy, which is still being formulated in *Realpolitik* terms. This leads to attempts to "stake a claim" to the Arctic, which seem to be the essence of modern Russia's Arctic policy in general. In a way, it is much easier to control the Arctic than some regions and states that were under the control of the Soviet Union and that Russia had to "give up" in the 1990s and the following decade. Even taking into consideration a certain "renaissance" of the Russian positions in global politics, the number of states under Moscow's control has decreased significantly. In these circumstances the Arctic resembles one of the last outposts of Russian power and becomes essential to exert Russian influence in contemporary world politics. Thus, Russian presence in the Arctic is important for Moscow in every respect and its retreat from Arctic interests is unlikely. In other words, Russia's Arctic policy could be considered as a form of compensation for many foreign policy failures of the last decade and a half. Consequently, the military presence in the region is declared a guarantee of national security protection.

Although economic policy has to be "proactive," military security policy might well be "reactive," but some alarmist attitudes and appeals à la "let's defend our Arctic"[104] have resulted in some pretentious statements in Russia's Arctic strategy. Thus, it is declared, one of the basic objectives of the Arctic policy is to maintain "a favorable operative regime in the Arctic zone of the Russian Federation, including maintenance of a necessary fighting potential of groupings of general purpose armies (forces) of the Armed Forces of the Russian Federation, other armies, military formations and organs in this region."[105]

However, the ability of Russia to present a balanced response "to the real threats to the interest of Russia in the Arctic in light of the main geopolitical goals of the USA and NATO"[106] is rather limited. "Military infrastructure does not match any current, much less future needs."[107] All military forces are concentrated in the westernmost part, on the Kola Peninsula. There are no forces based in the Arctic part of Russia east of Severodvinsk. The Northern Fleet remains the only available Russian naval instrument deployed on the world's oceans in general. Russian military expenditure declined from $303 billion to $4 billion between 1989 and 2000. During the last few years, however, military expenditure increased consistently despite the world economic crisis. According to the Stockholm International Peace Research Institute, the military expenditure of the United States in 2010 was $698 billion (4.8 percent of GDP), whereas Russia's military expenditure is estimated at $58.7 billion (4 percent of GDP), which is still ten times less than the U.S. military budget.[108] The Russian budget of 2012 was even more military-oriented. The Russian media were rather sore[109] about the military expenditure increase by 1.5 percent of GDP to an unprecedented 5.5 percent. This brings the discussion back to the question about the long-term scenarios of Russian economic development. It appears that military security interests and expenditures would ban the innovative and all other positive scenarios of economic development but would not guarantee the effectiveness of the Russian Arctic military forces. Thus, the military budget is too large to let the country develop duly but too small to implement the military ambitions of the Kremlin.

CONCLUSION

Some experts consider two alternatives for the future development of circumpolar international relations. The first scenario supposes further militarization and show of muscle by the traditional and new Arctic actors, such as China, India, and Japan. The other one assumes that the disputes over the delimitation of the Arctic will cease in ten to fifteen years because of the activities of international institutions (e.g., UN, BEAC, AC) and bilateral diplomacy, so that mutually beneficial cooperation will bloom.[110] So far, the circumpolar macroregion remains the subject of the clash of different states' interests rather than cooperation,[111] although any type of military conflict between the littoral states is far from being possible.[112] Politicians are also often rather controversial in their assessments of Arctic cooperation.[113] Beyond all doubt, there is a crucial need for a more transparent, predictable, and consistent Arctic policy of all the circumpolar states insofar as global sustainable development, at least for the foreseeable future, depends on the Arctic. I would go as far as to argue that the Arctic needs a kind of updated form of Gorbachev's "New Thinking." The problem is that Russia considers itself as a loser of the Cold War (partly because of Gorbachev's policy), thus one has to speak about the wider Arctic "new thinking," namely desecuritization in the Arctic, which is actually not impossible.[114] In Russia, this idea has obtained a certain amount of support in academic circles; some scholars prescribe a "code of conduct" for the Arctic states,[115] and others propose the idea of an International Arctic Union and of Arctic solidarity, which is destined to replace the "anti-Russian" Atlantic solidarity.[116] Russia officially reacted to these initiatives by adopting the Arctic strategy and organizing Arctic economic fora,[117] different polar projects (such as "Arctic—the Territory of Discovery") and Arctic expeditions (such as Arctic 2007), thus attempting to underline Russia's ownership over the Arctic and not exhibiting any understanding of the necessity for "internationalization" and desecuritization of the Arctic.

When one considers all pros and cons, it becomes clear that (at least for Russia) the arguments about wide-ranging circumpolar cooperation weigh more than the will to exclusive ownership of the Arctic resources.[118] As with many other issues in modern Russia, the Arctic strategy and the perspectives of the Arctic policy seriously depend on the political will of the president. Former president Medvedev was about to become a new "Arctic Gorbachev" by signing the Barents Delimitation Treaty with Norway. President Putin has a far more *Realpolitik*-style vision of international relations, defending the idea of Russia as the leading Arctic power.

Should the leading position of Russia depend upon the technological, not military, development and the will to reach the consensus or at least mutually beneficial agreements in the context of complex interdependence, a new system of international relations in the Arctic could arise.

The Arctic dimension of Russia's policy, considering its strategic importance for the country, should be a part of a wide modernization process, which was announced by Medvedev.[119] This points to an internationalization, not a nationalization, of the Arctic. The focal point of internationalization is wide cooperation in the Arctic, involving not only Arctic states ("A8+" instead of the "A5" model) but also transnational actors—such as international organizations, both inter- and nongovernmental—international business, and subnational actors, most importantly the indigenous people, who should have their voice in Russia's Arctic decision making. For Russia, this would bring not only international investments and technology for both economic development and "general cleaning" of the High North. Internationalization of the Arctic can be an important impetus for institutional modernization, specifically in relation to Arctic policy to begin with. Europe has already witnessed the birth of the "New Thinking" policy in the High North once; is it a good time to recall a "New Arctic Thinking" in favor of Russia, of the Arctic region, and even of the whole globe?

Figure 1. The map of Delimitation Treaty of the Barents Sea 2010.

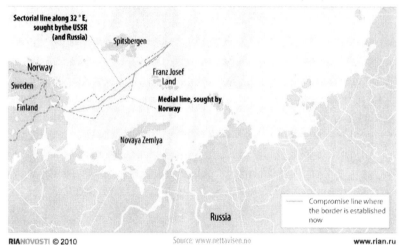

Russia, Norway divide disputed Barents Sea territory

Under the new agreement, the disputed territory of around 175,000 square kilometers will be divided into two equal parts

Source. http://en.rian.ru/infographics/20100916/160612791.html.

NOTES

1. The chapter was prepared as part of the activities in the framework of the Strategic Development Program of Petrozavodsk State University 2012–2014 (research subproject "North European Security in 21st Century"). I would like to express my great appreciation to Lassi Heininen from the University of Lapland and to the international team of the University of the Arctic's Thematic Network on Geopolitics and Security for inspiration and mutually beneficial activities.

2. "Basics of the State Policy of the Russian Federation in the Arctic for the Period until 2020 and for a Further Perspective" (Moscow; adopted September 18, 2008, promulgated March 30, 2009), published in *Rossiyskaya Gazeta*, http://www.scrf.gov.ru/documents/98.html. An English translation is available at http://arcticgovernance.custompublish. com/getfile.php/1042958.1529.avuqcurreq/Russian+Strategy.pdf.

3. Strategy for the Development of the Arctic Zone of the Russian Federation and National Security Protection for the Period up to 2020 (Moscow; adopted February 20, 2013), http://government.ru/news/432. An English translation is available at http://www.iecca.ru/en/legislation/strategies/item/99-the-development-strategy-of-the-arctic-zone-of-the-russian-federation.

4. See, e.g., Lassi Heininen, A. Sergunin, and G. Yarovoy, "New Russian Arctic Doctrine: From Idealism to Realism?" July 15, 2013, http://valdaiclub.com/russia_and_the_world/60220.html. In this context, "idealism" and "realism" refer to the change of perception of the distinct possibilities of Russia to realize the ambitious goal announced in the Basics 2008 (i.e., to remain the leading Arctic power).

5. By way of example, during two weeks in early autumn 2010 (from September 23 to October 3), Russia hosted two prominent international fora devoted to the Arctic. One was the Second Arctic Murmansk International Economic Forum, which was organized with the support of seven federal ministries and the Russian State Duma. The other, the International Arctic Forum in Russia, "The Arctic—Territory of Dialogue," organized by the Russian Geographical Society and held in Arkhangelsk, brought together more than 300 well-known scientists, experts, officials, and businesspeople from Russia as well as internationally and was opened with a welcome address by then president Medvedev and a

speech by then prime minister Vladimir Putin, who remarked, "It is very important to keep the Arctic as an area of peace and cooperation. The Arctic region should serve as a platform for...real partnership in economics, security, science and education, and protection of the cultural heritage of the North" ("Russia Considers Necessary to Keep the Arctic as a Zone of Peace and Cooperation—V. Putin," September 23, 2010, http://archive.government.ru/docs/12304/. This was followed up by the Third Arctic Murmansk International Economic Forum in September 2011 and the Second and Third International Forums, "The Arctic—Territory of Dialogue," in Arkhangelsk (September 2011, see http://ria.ru/trend/arctic_forum_13092010/) and Salekhard, with participation of the presidents of Russia, Finland, and Iceland (September 2013, see http://ria.ru/arctic_news/20130924/965430401.html). Participants placed special attention on the resources of the Arctic sea shelf, the Northern Sea Route, and the environmental aspects of economic development of the Arctic, which, according to Vladimir Putin, should become the keynote of human activities in the High North ("The Arctic Will Be Provided with Environmental Security," September 27, 2011, http://www.polit.ru/news/2011/09/27/arctica). See also Svetlana Borisovna Savel'eva and Anton Nikolaevich Savel'ev, "Spatial Reorientation of the National Interests of Russia" [Prostranstvennaya pereorientatsiya natsional'nyh interesov Rossii], *Vestnik MGTU* 13, no. 1 (2010): 73–76; Yury Georgievich Barsegov et al., *The Arctic: Russia's Interests and International Conditions of Their Realization* [Arktika: Interesy Rossii i mezhdunarodnye usloviya ih realizatsii] (Moscow: Nauka, 2002).

6. Vladimir Zenzinov, "The Soviet Arctic," *Russian Review* 3, no. 2 (1944): 66.

7. Nikolai Nikolaevich Bolkhovitinov, "The Sale of Alaska: Documents, Letters, Memoirs" [Prodazha Alyaski: Dokumenty, pis'ma, vospom-inaniya], *The USA—Economics, Politics, Ideology* [SSHA—Ekonomika, politika, ideologiya] 3 (1990): 47.

8. The full text of the treaty is available at http://avalon.law.yale.edu/19 th_century/treatywi.asp.

9. Vladimir Yul'evich Vize, *The Northern Sea Route* [Severnyi Morskoi Put'] (Moscow and Leningrad: Izdatel'stvo Glavsevmorputi, 1940), 24.

10. *Sudokhodnoe Obshchestvo.*

11. See, e.g., Leonid Lyudvigovich Breitfuss, *Siberian Sea Route to the Far East* [Morskoi sibirskii put' na Dal'nii Vostok] (St. Petersburg: Izdatel'stvo Sudokhodnogo Obshchestva, 1904).

12. Aleksandr Grigor'evich Granberg and Vsevolod Il'ich Peresypkin, eds., *Problems of the Northern Sea Route* [Problemy Severnogo Morskogo Puti] (Moscow: Nauka, 2006), 11.

13. Vize, *Northern Sea Route*, 43.

14. Al'bina Ivanovna Timoshenko, "Soviet Initiatives in the Arctic in 1920s (The Strategic Continuity Revisited)" [Sovetskie initsiativy v Arktike v 1920-e gg (K voprosu o strategicheskoi preemstvennosti)], *Humanitarian Sciences in Siberia* [Gumanitarnye nauki v Sibiri] 2 (2010): 49.

15. Zenzinov, "Soviet Arctic," 65.

16. Charles Raymond Beazley, "The Russian Expansion Towards Asia and the Arctic in the Middle Ages (to 1500)," *American Historical Review* 13, no. 4 (1908): 731.

17. See, e.g., David H. Miller, "Political Rights in the Arctic," *Foreign Affairs* 4, no. 1 (1925): 47–60; John Ball, "Soviet Work in the Arctic," *Geographical Journal* 81, no. 6 (1933): 532–535; "Soviet Work in the Arctic, 1938," *Polar Record* 3, no. 17 (1939): 13–14; "Soviet Work in the Arctic, 1939," *Polar Record* 3, no. 18 (1939): 106–107; Harry P. Smolka, "Soviet Strategy in the Arctic," *Foreign Affairs* 16, no. 2 (1938): 272–278; Timothy A. Taracouzio, *Soviets in the Arctic: An Historical, Economic and Political Study of the Soviet Advance into the Arctic* (New York: Macmillan, 1938); Zenzinov, "Soviet Arctic"; Clifford J. Webster, "The Economic Development of the Soviet Arctic and Sub-Arctic," *Slavonic and East European Review* 29, no. 72 (1950): 177–211; Michael Marsden, "Arctic Contrasts: Canada and Russia in the Far North," *International Journal* 14, no. 1 (1959): 33–41; Joseph S. Roucek, "The Geopolitics of the Arctic," *American Journal of Economics and Sociology* 42, no. 4 (1983): 463–471.

18. Miller, "Political Rights in the Arctic," 47.

19. Anatoliy Kolodkin and Sergei Glandin, "The Russian Flag on the North Pole," *International Affairs* 53, no. 6 (2007): 6–16.

20. Aleksey Fedorovich Treshnikov, "The Order of Lenin's Arctic and Antarctic Science and Research Institute Celebrates the 50th Anniversary" [Ordena Lenina Arkticheskomu i Antarkticheskomu Nauchno-Issledovatel'skomu Institutu—50 Let], *Problems of Arctic and Antarctic* [Problemy Arktiki I Antarktiki] 36–37 (1970): 5.

21. For more information about the history and the Soviet period of the functioning of the institute, see Treshnikov, "Order of Lenin's Arctic and Antarctic Science and Research Institute," and Vyacheslav Vasil'evich Frolov, "Studies of the Soviet Arctic at the Present Stage" [Issledovaniya Sovetskoi Arctiki na sovremennom etape], in *Problems of the Arctic*

[Problemy Arktiki] (Leningrad: Morskoi Transport, 1957), 5–18. For the modern history of the institute see Aleksandr Alekseevich Dmitriev and Vladimir Timofeevich Sokolov, *Chronology of the Main Events in the History of AASRI, Arctic and Antarctic in the XXth and the Beginning of the XXIst Century* [Khronologiya vazhneishikh sobytii v istorii AANII, Arktiki i Antarktiki v XX i nachale XXI veka] (St. Petersburg: AANII, 2010).

22. One of the greatest Soviet Arctic researchers, Rudolf (Ruvim) Samoylovich, was arrested in 1938, executed in 1939, and vindicated in 1957; a memorial museum was opened in 1981 in the house where Samoylovich was born. See Zinoviy Mikhailovich Kanevsky, *The Whole Life Is Expedition (Life and Work of R. L. Samoylovich)* [Vsya zhizn'— expeditsiya (Zhizn' i deyatel'nost' R. L. Samoylovicha)] (Moscow: Mysl', 1982).

23. Named after the Russian sailor and northern researcher, *Chelyuskin* was a Soviet steamship of the ice-breaking type built in Copenhagen in 1933. Its initial designation was to ply the mouth of River Lena to Vladivostok. During its first trip from Murmansk to Vladivostok, *Chelyuskin* was trapped in ice several times and was finally crushed near the Bering Strait on February 13, 1934.

24. Dmitry Trenin and Pavel Baev, *The Arctic: A View from Moscow* [Arktika: Vzglyad iz Moskvy] (Moscow: Carnegie Center, 2010), 21.

25. Nikolai Zaitsev, "The Battlefield Is Arctic" [Pole boya—Arktika], *North* [Sever] 5–6 (1996): 100.

26. Smolka, "Soviet Strategy in the Arctic," 273.

27. In complete secrecy, mostly for security reasons, the Soviet Union built new motorways and railroads (such as the Baikal-Amur Mainline) and expanded its industries concerned with the extraction of minerals (such as gold, copper, coal, iron, and nickel mines) in the High North.

28. Vize, *Northern Sea Route*, 65.

29. Smolka, "Soviet Strategy in the Arctic," 272.

30. Granberg and Peresypkin, *Problems of the North Sea Route*, 14.

31. Sergei Monin, "Routes of Lend-Lease" [Marshruty lend-liza], *Обозреватель-Observer* 6 (2010): 51.

32. Mikhail Nikolaevich Suprun, *The Arctic in the Strategy of World Powers during the Second World War* [Arktika v strategii mirovyh derzhav v gody Vtoroi mirivoi voiny], http://arcticwar.pomorsu.ru/sea/nc3/research/souprun.html.

33. Monin, "Routes of Lend-Lease," 56.

34. Treshnikov, "Order of Lenin's Arctic and Antarctic Science and Research Institute," 13.
35. Evgenii Zhirnov, "Cold War in the Arctic" [Holodnaya voina v Arktike], *Kommersant Vlast'* 46, no. 397 (November 21, 2000), http://www.kommersant.ru/doc/18022.
36. For some examples see Alfred S. McLaren, *Unknown Waters: A First-Hand Account of the Historic Under-Ice Survey of the Siberian Continental Shelf by USS Queenfish (SSN-651)* (Tuscaloosa: University of Alabama Press, 2008).
37. Mikhail Sergeevich Gorbachev, "Speech of Comrade Gorbachev M.S." [Rech' tovarishcha Gorbacheva M.S.], *Pravda* 275, no. 25262 (October 2, 1987). The English translation of a substantial part of the speech is available at http://teacherweb.com/FL/CypressBayHS/JJolley/Gorbachev_speech.pdf.
38. "Institutchiki" was named after "institut/institute"—a specialized division of the Soviet/Russian Academy of Science (e.g., Institute of the USA and Canada (ISK), Institute for World Economics and International Relations (IMEMO), and Institute of Oriental Studies)—meaning the high-ranked research staff of the institutes who had access to the Soviet political leaders. For example, the Institute of Oriental Studies and IMEMO were, at different times, headed by the future Russian Minister of Foreign Affairs, Evgeny Primakov.
39. Kimberly M. Zisk, "Soviet Academic Theories on International Conflict and Negotiation: A Research Note," *Journal of Conflict Resolution* 34, no. 4 (1990): 679–680.
40. Yakov Plyais, "The Evolution of the Foreign Policy of the New Russia" [Evolutsiya vneshnei politiki novoi Rossii], *Обозреватель—Observer* 5 (1996), http://www.rau.su/observer/N05_96/5_05.HTM.
41. Andrey Yur'evich Melville, "A Liberal Foreign Policy Alternative for Russia?" [Liberal'naya vneshnepoliticheskaya al'ternative dlya Rossii?], in *Foreign Policy and Security of the Modern Russia, 1991–2002* [Vneshnyaya politika i bezopasnost' sovremennoi Rossii, 1991–2002], ed. Tat'yana Alekseevna Shakleina (Moscow: ROSSPEN, 2002), 333.
42. See, e.g., Hanna Ojanen, ed., "The Northern Dimension: Fuel for the EU?" (Programme on the Northern Dimension of the CFSP) (Helsinki: UPI, 2001).
43. Trenin and Baev, *The Arctic: A View from Moscow.*
44. Natalia Zubarevich, "Social-Economic Development of Russian Regions by 2020" [Sotsial'no-ekonomicheskoe razvitie regionov Rossii k 2020

godu], http://russia-2020.org/ru/2010/08/23/soc-ec-development-of-rus-regions; and Natalia Zubarevich, "Regions and Cities in Russia: Scenarios-2020" [Regiony i goroda Rossii: Scenarii-2020], *Pro et Contra* 15, nos. 1–2 (2011): 64, http://carnegieendowment.org/files/ProetContra_51_57-71_all.pdf.

45. Vladimir Milov, "Russian Economy in Limbo," http://russia-2020.org/ru/2010/07/13/russian-economy-in-limbo.

46. Ministry of Economic Development and Trade of the Russian Federation, "Conceptual Foundations of Long-Term Socio-Economic Development of Russian Federation" [Kontseptsiya dolgosrochnogo soysial'no-economicheskogo razvitiya Rossiiskoi Federatsii] (Moscow, 2007), http://www.economy.gov.ru/minec/activity/sections/strategicplanning/concept/doc1185283411781.

47. Michail Dmitriev, "Russia-2020: Challenges to Long-Term Development" [Rossiya-2020: Dolgosrochnye vyzovy razvitiya], a public lecture delivered December 21, 2007, http://www.polit.ru/article/2007/12/21/dmitriev.

48. First of all, the backward turn to the elections of the heads of the regions and the facilitation of the registration process for political parties are considered.

49. Vladimir Gel'man, "Russia in Institutional Trap" [Rossiya v institutsional'noi lovushke], *Pro et Contra* 14, nos. 4–5 (2010): 23.

50. Barsegov et al., *The Arctic: Russia's Interests and International Conditions of Their Realization*, 11.

51. The term *Putinomics* appeared in Russian media in the beginning of the twenty-first century. It is now used worldwide to describe features of the Russian economy in both its functional and institutional dimensions. For the latest examples, see "Deconstructing Putinomics," http://en.rian.ru/analysis/20120201/171063368.html, and "Why Putinomics Isn't Worth Emulating," http://www.foreignpolicy.com/articles/2012/01/27/why_putinomics_isnt_worth_emulating.

52. Without going into detail, it is worth noting that the third presidential term for Putin does not contradict "the letter" of the Russian constitution but does contradict its "spirit," as well as demonstrating his attitude toward common democratic values.

53. The full text of the AEPS is available on the official site of the Arctic Council, at http://www.arctic-council.org/index.php/en/document-archive/category/4-founding-documents?download=53:aeps.

54. The BEAR includes thirteen regions from four countries—Finland, Norway, Russia, and Sweden. The list of the "hot spots" is available on the official website of the Barents Euro-Arctic Council at http://www.beac.st/Hot_Spots_Information_System.iw3.

55. Environmental Hot Spots in the Barents Region, http://www.nefco.org/en/financing/environmental_hot_spots_in_the_barents_region. See also NEFCO, *Updating of Environmental "Hot Spots" List in the Russian Part of the Barents Region: Proposal for Environmentally Sound Investment Projects* (Oslo: AMAP Secretariat, 2003), http://www.amap.no/documents/doc/updating-of-environmental-hot-spots-list-in-the-russian-part-ofank-the-barents-region/838.

56. Lassi Heininen, "Circumpolar International Relations and Cooperation," in *Globalization and the Circumpolar North*, ed. Lassi Heininen and Chris Southcott (Fairbanks: University of Alaska Press, 2010), 280–281.

57. Lassi Heininen, *Arctic Strategies and Policies: Inventory and Comparative Study* (Akureyri: University of Lapland Press/Stell, 2011), 50, http://www.nrf.is/images/stories/Hveragerdi/Arctic_strategies_6th_final.pdf.

58. One of the arguments in favor of such a statement may be delaying the process of Russia's joining the Espoo Convention (Espoo Convention 1991), ratified by all Nordic countries except Iceland. Russia's accession to the convention would create a kind of environmental impact assessment regime in the Arctic, which would also provide the possibility of the participation of the indigenous people. See Timo Koivurova, "The Regime of the Espoo Convention in the Arctic: Towards a Strategic Environmental Assessment Procedure," in *Arctic Governance*, Juridica Lapponica 29, ed. Timo Koivurova, Tanja Joona, and Reija Shnoro (Rovaniemi: Sevenprint, 2004), 61–87.

59. See, e.g., Trude Petterson, "Greenpeace: Situation More Unpredictable than Ever," *Barents Observer*, October 25, 2013, http://barentsobserver.com/en/arctic/2013/10/greenpeace-situation-more-unpredictable-ever-25-10.

60. Riabova, Larissa, "Community Viability and Well-Being in the Circumpolar North," in *Globalization and the Circumpolar North*, edited by Lassi Heininen and Chris Southcott (Fairbanks: University of Alaska Press, 2010), 132.

61. Savel'eva and Savel'ev, "Spatial Reorientation," 75.

62. "Concept of Sustainable Development of Indigenous Small-Numbered Peoples of the North, Siberia and the Far East of the Russian

Federation" (Moscow: adopted February 4, 2009), http://www.kamchatka. gov.ru/oiv_doc/2023/6461.doc.

63. Federal and regional target programs (FTPs and RTPs) are sets of research and development, production, socioeconomic, organizational, economic, and other measures to ensure the efficient solution of structural problems in public, economic, environmental, social, and cultural development of the Russian Federation. FTPs are one of the most important means of implementing the state structural policy. Although the FTPs appeared for the first time in the early 1990s, the actual implementation of the FTPs began in the following decade, when the inflow of the "oil money" increased. Since 2002, some forty-six FTPs were implemented, including the FTP "Economic and Social Development of the Indigenous Small-Numbered People of the North (until 2008)" with a total cost of 2,744 billion rubles (http://www.programs-gov.ru).

64. I would also mention suicide as one of the most important problems. As stated by Sulyandziga, first vice president of RAIPON, "According to statistics, 30% of mortality among the indigenous people are suicides" (See Sulyandziga's speech during the meeting with Prime Minister Putin on July 19, 2011, http://archive.government.ru/docs/15972/). For an in-depth analysis of the causes of indigenous peoples' problems, see, e.g., Aleksandr Ivanovich Pika and Bruce Grant, eds., *Neotraditionalism in the Russian North: Indigenous Peoples and the Legacy of Perestroika*, Circumpolar Research Series 6 (Edmonton: Canadian Circumpolar Institute; Seattle: University of Washington Press, 1999).

65. See "Resolution of the 6th Congress of the Indigenous Peoples of the North, Siberia and Far East of the Russian Federation" (Moscow: adopted April 24, 2009), http://www.indigenousportal.com/News/RESOLUTION-OF-THE-6TH-CONGRESS-OF-THE-INDIGENOUS-PEOPLES-OF-THE-NORTH-SIBERIA-FAR-EAST-OF-RUSSIA.html.

66. Olga Murashko, "Why Did the Important Events in the Indigenous Peoples' Lives Take Place in the Atmosphere of Alienation?" http://www.raipon.info/en/component/content/article/8-news/35-why-did-the-important-events-in-the-indigenous-peoples-life-take-place-in-the-atmosphere-of-alienation.html.

67. The list of activities includes thirty-seven items for the period 2011–2014, divided into four parts: (1) improvement of regulatory framework and development of effective economic mechanisms to maintain the traditional lifestyle of the indigenous peoples; (2) realization of activities in the sphere of health care and education of indigenous peoples; (3)

preservation and promotion of the cultural heritage and traditional culture of indigenous peoples; (4) carrying international, national, and interregional events (Decree of the Government No. 2455-p., Moscow; adopted December 28, 2010, published in *Rossiiskaya Gazeta*, January 11, 2011, http://www.rg.ru/2011/01/11/koren-narody-site-dok.html.

68. In 2011, the Ministry of Regional Development transferred 240 million rubles of state subsidies to the twenty-eight regional budgets in the framework of the Concept 2009 implementation (according to the Order of the Ministry of Regional Development No. 35, February 7, 2011, http://severcom.ru/officials/id326.html).

69. See Sulyandziga's speech during the meeting with Prime Minister Putin on July 19, 2011, at http://archive.government.ru/docs/15972/.

70. The Public Chamber of Russia (created in 2005) is an organization facilitating the interaction of citizens and public organizations (NGOs) with public and local authorities to take into account the needs and interests of Russian citizens and the protection of their rights and freedom. The Public Chamber supports the activities of NGOs, conducts the public expertise of the draft legislative acts, meets the high officials to discuss the societal problems, and supports the activities of regional Public Chambers.

71. See "The Legislation on the Indigenous Rights Was Discussed in Russian Public Chamber," at http://www.raipon.info/en/component/content/article/8-news/70-the-legislation-on-the-indigenous-rights-was-discussed-in-russian-public-chamber.html.

72. See "The Problem of Ineffective Use of Federal Funds of Indigenous Small-Numbered Peoples Support Was Discussed in the Council of Federation," at http://raipon.info/component/content/article/1-novosti/2913-2012-04-03-13-33-34.html.

73. Atle Staalesen, "Hard-Fought New Life for RAIPON," *Barents Observer*, March 15, 2013, http://barentsobserver.com/en/society/2013/03/hard-fought-new-life-raipon-15-03.

74. http://www.raipon.info/home/arhiv-sobytij/vii-sezd-kmnss-i-dv-rf.html.

75. See, e.g., Trude Pettersen, "Ice Extent in Barents Sea Less than Half of Average," *Barents Observer*, March 12, 2012, http://barentsobserver.com/en/topics/ice-extent-barents-sea-less-half-average; Trude Pettersen, "NASA: Thickest Parts of Arctic Ice Cap Melting Faster," *Barents Observer*, March 2, 2012, http://barentsobserver.com/en/topics/nasa-thickest-parts-arctic-ice-cap-melting-faster; Thomas Nilsen, "Kara Sea Is Ice-Free," *Barents Observer*, February 14, 2012, http://barentsobserver.com/en/news/

kara-sea-ice-free; Thomas Nilsen, "Alarm: Ice Free North Pole by 2015," *Barents Observer*, November 11, 2011, http://barentsobserver.com/en/news/alarm-ice-free-north-pole-2015.

76. "Beluga Shipping Conquers Northeast Passage," September 8, 2009, http://www.heavyliftpfi.com/news/beluga-shipping-conquers-northeast-passage.html.

77. Ivan Smirnov, "Arctic Transit," *ChinaPRO*, February 21, 2011, http://www.chinapro.ru/rubrics/2/5780/.

78. Thomas Nilsen, "Record Long Arctic Navigation Season," *Barents Observer*, November 18, 2011, http://barentsobserver.com/en/business/record-long-arctic-navigation-season.

79. Trude Pettersen, "Speed Record on Northern Sea Route," *Barents Observer*, August 17, 2011, http://barentsobserver.com/en/articles/speed-record-northern-sea-route.

80. Trude Pettersen, "Supertanker Sets Speed Record on Northern Sea Route," *Barents Observer*, September 1, 2011, http://barentsobserver.com/en/briefs/supertanker-sets-speed-record-northern-sea-route.

81. Thomas Nilsen, "Beijing Sends Icebreaker to Barents," *Barents Observer*, March 13, 2012, http://barentsobserver.com/en/arctic/beijing-sends-icebreaker-barents.

82. "Arthur Chilingarov Drafted a Bill on Northern Sea Route," February 12, 2009, http://www.kommersant.ru/Doc/1117721.

83. See Council of Federation, *Opinion on the Draft Federal Law No. 608695-5 "On Amendments to Some Legislative Acts of the Russian Federation Regarding State Regulation of Merchant Shipping in the Waters of the Northern Sea Route,"* October 28, 2012, http://severcom.ru/activity/section5/doc340.html.

84. See more information and the text of the draft at http://www.duma.gov.ru/systems/law/?number=608695-5&sort=date .

85. "Russian Prime Minister Vladimir Putin Chaired a Government Presidium Meeting," November 22, 2011, http://archive.premier.gov.ru/events/news/17172/.

86. "Reactivation of the Northern Sea Route as an Impetus to the Arctic Regions: The Report of the Advisory Board of the Administration of Arkhangelsk Region Meeting (26 November 2009)," http://www.dvinaland.ru/economy/priority/smp_doclad.html.

87. For argumentation on the statements, see, e.g., Alexei Polubota, "Great Non-Silk Road," *Svobodnaya Pressa*, April 1, 2012, http://svpressa.ru/society/article/53803.

88. See Margaret Blunden, "Geopolitics and the Northern Sea Route," *International Affairs* 88, no. 1 (2012): 115–129.

89. United Nations Convention on the Law of the Sea, signed December 10, 1982, http://www.un.org/Depts/los/convention_agreements/texts/unclos/UNCLOS-TOC.htm.

90. Valeriy Nikolaevich Konyshev and Aleksander Anatol'evich Sergunin, *The Arctic in International Politics: Cooperation or Competition?* [Arktika v mejdunarodnoi politike: Sotrudnichestvo ili sopernichestvo?] (Moscow: RISI, 2011), 44–45.

91. Several joint projects have been implemented since 2005: LORITA-1, LOMROG I and II, and others. For more information, see http://a76.dk/greenland_uk/north_uk/index.html.

92. See http://a76.dk/greenland_uk/north_uk/gr_n_expeditions_uk/lomrog_2012_uk/index.html.

93. Brian Spielman, "An Evaluation of Russia's Impending Claim for Continental Shelf Expansion: Why Rule 5 Will Shelve Russia's Submission," *Emory International Law Review* 23, no. 1 (2009): 348, http://www.law.emory.edu/fileadmin/journals/eilr/23/23.1/Spielman.pdf; Treaty between the Kingdom of Norway and the Russian Federation concerning Maritime Delimitation and Cooperation in the Barents Sea and the Arctic Ocean, September 15, 2010, http://www.regjeringen.no/upload/ud/vedlegg/folkerett/avtale_engelsk.pdf.

94. For more information on the history of the dispute, see Ingrid Kvalvik, "Assessing the Delimitation Negotiations between Norway and the Soviet Union/Russia," *Acta Borealia* 21, no. 1 (2004): 55–78.

95. Dmitry Trenin, "Perspectives of Russian Foreign Policy" [Vneshnepoliticheskie perspektivy Rossii], *Pro et Contra* 15, nos. 1–2 (2011): 105.

96. Thomas Nilsen, "Unanimously Approved," *Barents Observer*, February 8, 2011, http://barentsobserver.com/en/sections/briefs/unanimously-approved.

97. Atle Staalesen, "Border Treaty Will Affect Spitsbergen and Shtokman, Say Communists," *Barents Observer*, March 25, 2011, http://barentsobserver.com/en/sections/politics/border-treaty-will-affect-spitsbergen-and-shtokman-say-communists.

98. See, e.g., Tamara Shkel, "Divided Sea," *Rossiiskaya Gazeta* 5440, no. 64 (March 25, 2011), http://www.rg.ru/2011/03/25/norvegia-site.html; Pavel Gudev, "Treaty on Cession," *Odnako* 26 (August 2, 2011), http://www.odnako.org/magazine/material/show_12166; Aleksandr Oreshenkov, "The Arctic's Square of Possibilities" [Arkticheskii kvadrat vozmojnostei],

Russia in Global Affairs [Rossiya v global'noi politike] 6 (2010): 194–202, http://www.globalaffairs.ru/number/Arkticheskii-kvadrat-vozmozhnostei-15069.

99. See, e.g., Olga Samofalova, "Unprecedented Number of Arrests," *Vzglyad*, October 10, 2011, http://www.vz.ru/economy/2011/10/10/529145.html.

100. In Russian, the title *Spitsbergen* is used. For discussion on Russian-Norwegian disputes over Svalbard, see, e.g., Aleksei Fedorovich Federov and Sergei Alekseevich Kovalev, "Is Norway in Compliance with Svalbard Treaty Obligations of 1920?" [Soblyudaet li Norvegia dogovornye obyazatel'stva 1920 g. o Shiptsbergene?], *Fish Industry* [Rybnoe hozyaistvo] 5 (2006): 12–15; Oreshenkov, "Arctic's Square of Possibilities"; Aleksandr Oreshenkov, "The Norwegian Assault to the North-East: Dedicated to the Memory of A. Kvitsinsky" [Norvejskii natisk na severo-vostok: Pamyati Yu. A. Kvicinskogo posvyaschaetsya], *Representative Power—XXI Century* [Predstavitel'naya vlast'—XXI vek] 1 (2011): 26–29; Aleksandr Konstantinovich Portsel, "Spitsbergen, or Svalbard? Problems of Russia's Presence on the Archipelago in the XX–Early XXI Centuries" [Shpitsbergen ili Sval'bard? Problemy prisutstviya Rossii na arhipelage v XX–nachale XXI vekov], *Bulletin of the Murmansk State Technical University* [Vestnik Murmanskogo gosudarstvennogo tehnicheskogo universiteta] 13, no. 2 (2010): 261–264; "Russia and Norway Once Again Try to Solve the Problems of Fisheries around Svalbard," February 8, 2012, http://interfax.ru/politics/news.asp?id=22 9854; "Battle of the Svalbard," *Nezavisimaya Gazeta*, January 13, 2009, http://www.ng.ru/energy/2009-01-13/12_Shpicbergen.html; "Quiet War around Svalbard," *Nezavisimaya Gazeta*, November 10, 1999, http://www.ng.ru/world/1999-11-10/6_shpitsbergen.html. Russia is not the only country that contests the way Norway has used their "sovereign" right over Svalbard. See, e.g., Torbjørn Pedersen, "Denmark's Policies Toward the Svalbard Area," *Ocean Development & International Law* 40, no. 4 (2009): 319–332.

101. For an overview of the different issues of Russia's Arctic energy policy, see, e.g., G. Yarovoy, A. Sergunin, and L. Heininen, "Russia's Energy Strategies in the Arctic," *Valdai*, January 7, 2013, http://valdaiclub.com/economy/59747.html.

102. See Gleb Yarovoy, "Russia's Arctic—A Call for the New Arctic Thinking," *Baltic Rim Economies* 4 (2011), http://www.tse.fi/FI/yksikot/erillislaitokset/pei/Documents/BRE2011/BREArctic%2030.11.2011.pdf.

103. Konstantin Valentinovich Voronov, "The Arctic Horizons of Russia's Strategy: Current Dynamics" [Arkticheskie gorizonty strategii Rossii: Sovremennaya dinamika], *World Economy and International Relations* [Mirovaya ekonomika in mezhdunarodnye otnosheniya] 9 (2010): 59.

104. See, e.g., Vassiliy Ivanocich Sosnin, "The Arctic—A Complex Knot of Interstate Contradictions" [Arktika—Slozhnyi uzel mezhgosudarstven- nyh protivorechii], *Military Thought* [Voennaya Mysl'] 7 (2010): 3–9; Anatoly Dmitrievich Tsyganok, "Russian Confrontation in the Arctic: Will Russia Be Able to Defend the North?" [Rossiiskoe protivostoy- anie v Arktike: Smozhet li Rossiya otstoyat' Sever], *Bulletin of Analyt- ics* [Vestnik analitiki] 1 (2010): 83–89.

105. "Basics of the State Policy," part III, article 6b.

106. Barsegov et al., *The Arctic: Russia's Interests and International Condi- tions of Their Realization*, 60.

107. Valeriy Nikolaevich Konyshev and Aleksander Anatol'evich Ser- gunin, "National Interests of Russia in the Arctic: Myths and Reali- ties" [Nacional'nye intersy Rossii v Arktike: Mify i real'nost'], *Russia's Priorities* [Prioritety Rossii] 29 (2011): 9.

108. The fifteen countries with the highest military expenditure in 2010, http://www.sipri.org/research/armaments/milex/resultoutput/milex_1 5. According to the Centre for Analysis of World Arms Trade (CAWAT, Moscow), Russian military expenditure in 2010 was $41.61 billion, http://www.armstrade.org/includes/periodics/news/2011/0412/134578 39/detail.shtml.

109. "Kudrin Debar the Innovative Development Scenario the Right to Life," February 18, 2011, http://newsru.com/arch/finance/18feb2011/kudr. html; "Scenario Without the Right to Life," February 18, 2011, http:// www.finmarket.ru/z/nws/hotnews.asp?id=1939794; "Military-Police Budget," February 18, 2011, http://www.mk.ru/politics/army/article/20 11/02/18/566988-voennopolitseyskiy-byudzhet.html.

110. Voronov, "Arctic Horizons of Russia's Strategy," 64.

111. Valeriy Nikolaevich Konyshev and Aleksander Anatol'evich Ser- gunin, "Arctic on the Crossroads of the Geopolitical Interests" [Ark- tika na perekrest'e geopoliticheskih interesov], *World Economy and International Relations* [Mirovaya ekonomika in mezhdunarodnye otnosheniya] 9 (2010): 53.

112. Aleksandr Anatol'evich Khramchikhin, "Politico-Military Situation in the Arctic and Scenario of Possible Conflicts" [Voenno-politicheskaya situatsiya v Arktike I stsenarii vizmozhnyh confliktov], *Arctic and*

North [Arktika i Sever] 2 (2011): 14, http://narfu.ru/upload/iblock/7f9/grjopufvqlvzveqamx.pdf.

113. Sergey Lavrov, Russian Minister for Foreign Affairs: "All problems existed in the North...can be solved politically and legally; the hand-wringing over the potential war over the resources is provocation." ("Lavrov: Talks about the Possible War over the Arctic Resources Is Provocation," January 13, 2011, http://ria.ru/arctic_news/20110113/321042542.html.) Admiral James G. Stavridis, Supreme Allied Commander for Europe: "For now, the disputes in the north have been dealt with peacefully, but climate change could alter the equilibrium over the coming years in the race of temptation for exploitation of more readily accessible natural resources." ("Senior NATO Commander: Climate Change Could Lead to Arctic Conflict," *Guardian*, October 11, 2010, http://www.guardian.co.uk/environment/2010/oct/11/nato-conflict-arctic-resources). Jonas Gahr Støre, Norwegian Minister for Foreign Affairs: "If we put together resources, transport routes and people, then we have a mixture which is needed for a potential conflict" (Andrew Ward, "Battle Hots up for Arctic Resources," *The Financial Times*, July 4, 2011, http://www.inosmi.ru/arctica/20110705/171619818.html).

114. See Kristian Åtland, "Mikhail Gorbachev, the Murmansk Initiative, and the Desecuritization of Interstate Relations in the Arctic," *Cooperation and Conflict* 43, no. 3 (2008): 289–311.

115. Trenin and Baev, *The Arctic: A View from Moscow*, 10–11.

116. Yury Fedorovich Lukin, *The Great Redivision of the Arctic* [Velikii peredel Arktiki] (Arkhangelsk: Northern (Arctic) Federal University, 2010), 111–113.

117. *Arctic Murmansk International Economic Forum (http://murmansk.kp.ru/daily/theme/4891; International Arctic Forum in Russia, "The Arctic—Territory of Dialogue" (http://www.arctic.ru/forum).*

118. One of the main rationales under the internationalization of the "Russian" and even more so "potentially Russian" parts of the Arctic is the cost of the exploration and exploitation of the resources of the shelf, which require the investment of more than $2.5 trillion until 2050. See "How Much Does the Cold War in the Arctic Cost?" [Skol'ko stoit holodnaya voina v Arktike?] *Kommersant* 4, no. 4059 (January 14, 2009), http://www.kommersant.ru/doc/1102508.

119. In his article "Russia Forward!" he identified three main problems in Russia: centuries of economic backwardness, centuries of corruption,

and widespread paternalistic attitudes in society. To remedy this miserable and dangerous situation, he proposed five dimensions of modernization. All of them are limited to economic development, and the first priority is to become a leading country in production, transportation, and utilization of energy resources. However, political modernization, including foreign policy, was mentioned. "It is not nostalgia that should determine our foreign policy, but strategic long-term goal of modernizing Russia," he wrote. Dmitry Medvedev, "Russia Forward!," September 10, 2009, http://www.kremlin.ru/news/5413.

CHAPTER 8

NORWAY'S HIGH ARCTIC POLICY

Geir Hønneland

INTRODUCTION

Because Norway is located on the Arctic rim of the European mainland, Arctic affairs are an integral part of the country's foreign policy.
However, the strength of the Arctic component of Norwegian foreign
policy has varied over time, as has its profile and formal designation.
In general, the term *Arctic* is rarely used in Norwegian foreign policy
discourse. When it is used, it often refers to something farther off in
either time (like polar exploration and expeditions before World War
II) or space (outside Norway's immediate sphere of interest, such as the
North Pole area or the North American Arctic). "The North" (in Norwegian: *nord*) or "the northern regions" (in Norwegian: *nordområdene*) have
been the preferred terms for describing practical foreign politics in the
European Arctic. In practice, Norway's northern foreign policy is mainly
about relations with other states in the Barents Sea region, including the

Svalbard archipelago (see figure 2). Of particular importance are relations with Russia.

With the end of the Cold War, reference to "the North" in Norwegian foreign policy discourse almost disappeared because it smacked of Cold War tensions or even of Norway's earlier reputation as an expansionist polar nation. Norway was now building up a reputation as a "peace nation," heavily involved in mediating peace in various southern corners of the world. This did not mean that Norwegian foreign politics in the European Arctic no longer existed—only that the main focus was now on institutional cooperation with Russia, referred to as "strategies toward Russia," or "neighborhood policies." Around 2005, "the northern regions" (nordområdene, with "the High North" as the official English translation) were again explicitly defined as the number one priority of Norwegian foreign policy. Although this happened to coincide with the international buzz about a "rush for the Arctic," it can largely be explained, as will be shown later, by internal issues in Norwegian politics and in the country's relationship with Russia. Above all, this new northern policy has seen the disappearance of the division between foreign and internal politics. It encompasses both traditional security politics in the European Arctic and the "softer" institutional collaboration with Russia initiated in the 1990s, though many see Norway's "new" northern policies as mainly an instrument for further developing business and science in the country's northern regions.[1]

This chapter presents these three layers of Norwegian high Arctic policies.[2] It starts with the legacy from the Cold War, namely the European Arctic as a high-tension interface between East and West, and with the Kola Peninsula considered to be the most heavily militarized region on the globe. The final decades of the Cold War also saw fundamental changes in the law of the sea, which placed most of the Barents Sea under Norwegian and Soviet jurisdiction but also left several jurisdictional issues unsettled. As a result of the same legal developments, Norway and the Soviet Union entered into a formal partnership to manage the rich fish resources of the area, a rare example of East-West collaboration in the Arctic during the Cold War era. This partnership set the example for cooperation in several other areas after the Soviet Union fell apart, which is discussed in further detail in the next section. This is followed by examining the "new" Norwegian politics on the High North from around 2005, briefly presenting the major public documents and discussing the driving forces behind this new policy. The concluding section determines which conflicts remain in the region and which legacies—from the three different layers of Norwegian high Arctic policies—actually dominate. It further discusses briefly which interest groups are represented in the internal Norwegian debate on the High North.

THE COLD WAR LEGACY: SECURITY, JURISDICTION, AND FISHERIES MANAGEMENT

The Northern Fleet, established on the Kola Peninsula in 1933, remained the smallest of the four Soviet naval fleets until the 1950s, when a period of expansion set in. By then, the Soviet Union had entered the nuclear age: the country's first nuclear submarine was stationed on the Kola Peninsula in 1958, at Zapadnaya Litsa, close to the border with Norway. Six new naval bases for nuclear submarines were built, as well as several smaller bases for other vessels. By the late 1960s, the Northern Fleet ranked as the largest of the Soviet fleets.

In this situation, Norway chose the combined strategy of deterrence and reassurance.[3] Deterrence was secured through North Atlantic Treaty Organization (NATO) membership and by maintaining the Norwegian armed forces at a level deemed necessary to hold back a possible Soviet attack until assistance could arrive from other NATO countries. To ensure that the Soviets did not misinterpret activities on the Norwegian side as aggressive, Norway imposed a number of restrictions upon itself. Notably, other NATO countries were not allowed to participate in military exercises east of the 24th parallel, which runs slightly west of the middle of Norway's northernmost county, Finnmark. The border between Norway and the Soviet Union was peaceful but strictly guarded. There was no conflict, but there was also little interaction across that border.

Besides regular diplomatic contact, management of the abundant fish resources of the Barents Sea was an area of particular joint interest for Norway and the Soviet Union. From the late 1960s, the two countries had informally discussed the possibilities of bilateral management measures. A window of opportunity came with the drastic changes in the law of the sea that were implemented in the mid-1970s. The principle of 200-mile exclusive economic zones (EEZs) was adopted at the third UN Conference on the Law of the Sea (UNCLOS) in 1975. The right and responsibility to manage marine resources within 200 nautical miles offshore was thus transferred to the coastal states at this time. When Soviet Minister of Fisheries Aleksandr Ishkov visited Oslo in December 1974, the two countries agreed to establish a joint fisheries management arrangement for the Barents Sea.[4] The agreement established the Joint Norwegian-Soviet (now Norwegian-Russian) Fisheries Commission, to meet at least once every year, alternately on each party's territory. When the first session took place in January 1976, the parties had agreed to manage jointly the two most important fish stocks in the area, cod and haddock, sharing the quotas 50-50. In 1978, they agreed to treat capelin as a shared stock and split the quota 60-40 in Norway's favor.

During the 1980s, a specific quota exchange scheme developed, whereby the Soviet Union gave parts of its cod and haddock quotas in exchange for several other species found only in Norwegian waters. These species, especially blue whiting, were found in large quantities but were of scant commercial interest to Norwegian fishers. By contrast, in the Soviet planned economy, volume was more important than (export market) price, so the arrangement was indeed in the mutual interest of both parties.

All of this changed with the dissolution of the Soviet Union and the introduction of a market economy in Russia. Now cod and haddock, both high-price species on the global fish market, attracted the interest of not only Norwegian but also Russian fishers. Transfers of cod and haddock quota shares from Russia to Norway were reduced, and Russian fishing companies began to deliver their catches abroad, primarily in Norway. For the first time, Russian fishers had a real incentive for over-fishing their quotas, while Russian enforcement authorities lost control of Russian catches, given that quota control had traditionally been exercised at the point of delivery. Norwegian fishery authorities in 1992–1993 suspected that the Russian fleet was overfishing its quota and took steps to calculate total Russian catches, based on landings from Russian vessels in Norway and at-sea inspections by the Norwegian Coast Guard. Norway then claimed that Russia had overfished its quota by some 50 percent. The Russian side did not dispute this figure, and the two parties agreed to extend their fisheries collaboration to include enforcement as well.[5] This involved exchange of catch data, notably the transfer by Norwegian authorities to their Russian counterparts of data on Russian landings of fish in Norway. The successful establishment of enforcement collaboration was followed by extensive coordination of technical regulations and joint introduction of new measures throughout the 1990s.

Around the turn of the millennium, a new landing pattern emerged. Russian fishing vessels resumed the old Soviet practice of delivering their catches to transport ships at sea. Instead of going to Murmansk with the fish, however, these transport vessels now headed for other European countries: Denmark, the United Kingdom, the Netherlands, Spain, and Portugal. Norway again took the initiative to assess the possibility of overfishing but now encountered a less cooperative Russian stance. Thereupon Norway took unilateral measures to calculate overfishing in the Barents Sea and presented figures that indicated Russian overfishing began in 2002, rising to nearly 175 percent of the total Russian quota in 2005, gradually declining to zero in 2009.[6]

Both Norway and the Soviet Union established their EEZs in 1977 (see figure 3). However, the two states could not agree on the principle for drawing the delimitation line between their respective zones. The two had been negotiating the delimitation of the Barents Sea continental shelf since the early 1970s, and the division of the EEZs was brought into these discussions. The parties had agreed to use the 1958 Convention on the Continental Shelf as a basis for negotiations. According to this convention, continental shelves may be divided between states if so agreed. If agreement is not reached, the median line from the mainland border shall normally determine the delimitation line, but special circumstances may warrant adjustments. In the Barents Sea, Norway adhered to the median-line principle, whereas the Soviet Union claimed the sector-line principle, according to which the line of delimitation would run along the longitude line from the tip of the mainland border to the North Pole. The Soviets generally held out for the sector-line principle, having claimed sector-line limits to Soviet Arctic waters as early as 1926. Moreover, they argued that in the Barents Sea, special circumstances—notably the size of the Soviet population in the area and the strategic significance of this region—warranted deviation from the median line.[7]

In 1978, a temporary Grey Zone agreement was reached to avoid unregulated fishing in the disputed area.[8] This agreement required Norway and the Soviet Union to regulate and control their own fishers and third-country fishers licensed by either of them and to refrain from interfering with the activities of the other party's vessels or vessels licensed by them. The arrangement was explicitly temporary and subject to annual renewal. The Grey Zone functioned well for the purposes of fisheries management, but the prospects of underground hydrocarbon resources in the area pressed the parties to a final delimitation agreement, which was reached in spring 2010.[9] The agreement is a compromise, which splits the formerly disputed area in two equal parts.

Another area of contention is the Fisheries Protection Zone around Svalbard. Norway claims the right to establish an EEZ around the archipelago but has so far refrained from doing so because the other signatories to the 1920 Svalbard Treaty have signaled that they would not accept such a move.[10] The Svalbard Treaty gave Norway sovereignty over the archipelago, which had been a no man's land in the European Arctic. However, the treaty contains several limitations on Norway's right to exercise this jurisdiction. Most importantly, all signatory powers enjoy equal rights to let their citizens extract natural resources on Svalbard. Further, the archipelago is not to be used for military purposes, and there are restrictions on Norway's right to impose taxes on residents of Svalbard. The original signatories were Denmark, France, Italy, Japan, the Netherlands, Norway, Sweden, the United Kingdom, and the United States of America. The Soviet Union joined in 1935.

The signatories (other than Norway) hold that the non-discriminatory code of the Svalbard Treaty must apply also to the ocean area around the archipelago,[11] whereas Norway refers to the treaty text, which deals only with the land and territorial waters of Svalbard. The waters around Svalbard are important feeding grounds for juvenile cod, and the Fisheries Protection Zone, determined in 1977, represents a "middle course" aimed at securing the young fish from unregulated fishing. As follows, the zone is not recognized by any of the other states that have had quotas in the area since the introduction of the EEZs. To avoid provoking other states, Norway refrained for many years from penalizing violators in the Fisheries Protection Zone. Force was used for the first time in 1993, when Icelandic trawlers and Faroese vessels under flags of convenience—neither with a quota in the Barents Sea—started fishing there. The Norwegian Coast Guard fired warning shots at the ships, which then left the zone. The following year, an Icelandic fishing vessel was for the first time arrested for fishing in the Svalbard Zone without a quota.

The Soviet/Russian vessels have been fishing in the Svalbard Zone regularly since its establishment—indeed, they represent the main part of fishing operations in the area. They do not report their catches in the area to Norwegian authorities, and Russian captains consistently refuse to sign inspection forms presented by the Norwegian Coast Guard. On the other hand, the Russians have welcomed Norwegian inspectors on board, and the same inspection procedures have been pursued in the Svalbard Zone as in the Norwegian EEZ. A change in the Norwegian practice of lenient enforcement was first observed in relation to Russian fishers in 1998. The Norwegian Coast Guard decided to arrest a Russian vessel for fishing in an area that had been closed for juvenile-density reasons, but arrest procedures were interrupted before the vessel reached Norwegian harbor, as a result of diplomatic exchanges between the two countries. In 2001, the first arrest of a Russian vessel was carried through in the protection zone around Svalbard. Norway claimed that the vessel was guilty of serious environmental crimes, having violated several fishing regulations.

Official Russian reactions were fierce. Russian authorities claimed that Norway had illegally detained a Russian vessel in international waters. Moreover, they accused Norway of breaking a nearly twenty-five-year-old gentlemen's agreement between the two countries, whereby Russia accepted Norwegian monitoring of fishing operations in the Svalbard Zone (including physical inspections of Russian fishing vessels) as long as Norway did not behave as if it had formal sovereignty in the area. The next time Norway attempted to arrest a Russian vessel in the Svalbard Zone was in 2005—a second time for serious violations of fishing regulations, including overfishing. Again the arrest was not carried through, but the reason was different from the 1998 incident: the captain of the Russian fishing vessel simply escaped to a Russian harbor, taking along the Norwegian inspectors who were still on board. He was later sentenced in a Russian court, and official Russian reactions to the Norwegian move were much milder than in 2001. In 2009 and 2010, the Norwegian Coast Guard carried out a handful of arrests of Russian fishing vessels in the Fisheries Protection Zone without any formal reaction from the Russian authorities.

In 2009, the Commission on the Limits of the Continental Shelf approved the Norwegian submission, confirming the existence of a Norwegian shelf beyond 200 nautical miles in three places: the Western Nansen Basin north of Svalbard, in parts of the "Loophole" in the east, and the "Banana Hole" in the southwest (see figure 4).[12]

The Legacy of the 1990s: Institutional Collaboration with Russia

Norway's foreign policy in the European Arctic during the 1990s was mainly about bringing Russia to commit to collaborative networks. The idea of a "Barents region" was first aired by the Norwegian Minister of Foreign Affairs Thorvald Stoltenberg in April 1992. After consulting with Russia and the other Nordic states, the Barents Euro-Arctic Region (BEAR) was established by the Kirkenes Declaration of January 1993, whereby Norway, Sweden, Finland, and Russia pledged to work together at both the regional and national levels.[13] At the regional level, BEAR initially included the three northernmost counties of Norway, together with Norrbotten in Sweden, Lapland in Finland, and Murmansk and Arkhangelsk Oblasts and the Republic of Karelia in Russia (see figure 5). They were joined in 1997 by Nenets Autonomous Okrug, located within Arkhangelsk Oblast, which became a member in its own right, and later by Västerbotten (Sweden), Oulu and Kainuu (Finland), and the Republic of Komi (Russia). All these regional entities are represented on the Regional Council of BEAR, as are the indigenous peoples of the region.[14] The Barents Euro-Arctic Council (BEAC), on which Denmark, Iceland, and the European Commission sit in addition to the four core states, was created to promote and facilitate intergovernmental cooperation. The following countries have observer status: Canada, France, Germany, Italy, Japan, the Netherlands, Poland, the United Kingdom, and the United States of America.

The BEAR was designed to promote stability and prosperity in the area. Its purpose is enshrined in the concepts of normalization, stabilization, and regionalization. It works at reducing the military tension, allaying environmental threats, and narrowing the East-West gap in standards of living in the region. It is also involved in the regionalization process underway in Europe as well as in the Arctic, turning previously peripheral border areas into places where governments can meet in a transnational forum serving a range of interests. Areas of particular concern are environmental protection, regional infrastructure, economic cooperation, science and technology, culture, tourism, health care, and the indigenous peoples of region.

One of the most striking features of East-West relations of the European North since the end of the Cold War has been the massive flow of people across national borders, some of whom decide to settle for good in the new country. Annual crossings between Norway and Russia increased from 3,000-plus in the early 1990s to nearly 110,000 by the middle of the following decade.[15] East-West tourism is thriving; political and business delegations frequently visit partners on the other side of the border; students visit for longer or shorter periods; and finally, most of the towns on the Nordic side of the border are home to Russian communities of varying sizes. Many Russians have married Scandinavians and become eligible for permanent residence; other newcomers are the result of numerous exchange programs run by BEAR, obtaining temporary residence and work permits on account of their special qualifications.

As a political project, the BEAR has had its ups and downs.[16] While ambitions were high during the formative years, creating viable cross-border business partnerships in the Barents region proved more difficult than anticipated. Ostensible successes ended in failure. In some notorious cases, the Russians simply forced out their Western counterparts once the joint company started to make a profit. As a result, the BEAR downgraded large-scale business cooperation as a priority in the late 1990s, devoting its energies instead to small-scale business and people-to-people cooperation such as student exchanges, cultural projects, and other ventures bringing Russians and nationals of the Nordic countries together. The BEAR set up a Barents Health Programme in 1999, focusing primarily on new and resurgent communicable diseases such as HIV/AIDS and tuberculosis.[17] Both people-to-people cooperation and the Barents Health Programme are generally judged to be successful, and cooperation between small businesses has also been growing.

A Joint Norwegian-Soviet Commission on Environmental Protection was established in 1988.[18] The previous year, the Soviet leader Mikhail Gorbachev had given his famous "Murmansk speech," in which he urged the "civilization" of the militarized European Arctic in general and wider international cooperation on environmental protection in particular.[19] The Soviet Pechenganikel nickel smelter had already ravaged the countryside on the Kola Peninsula (with visible damage also on the Norwegian side); the Joint Norwegian-Soviet Commission on Environmental Protection made it a top priority during the first few years of its existence to modernize Pechenganikel and reduce sulfur dioxide (SO_2) emissions. By the early 1990s, nuclear safety had become the new priority. It was public knowledge that the Soviets had been dumping radioactive waste in the Barents and Kara Seas because they were overwhelmed by an ever-growing stockpile of spent nuclear fuel and radioactive waste on the Kola Peninsula. There was also mounting concern about safety at the Kola nuclear power plant, located in Polyarnye Zori in the southern parts of the Kola Peninsula. Norway launched a Plan of Action on nuclear safety in northwestern Russia in 1995,[20] and three years later a separate Joint Norwegian-Russian Commission on Nuclear Safety was established. Over the next ten years, Norway spent around US$150 million on nuclear safety projects on the Kola Peninsula. The Plan of Action aimed at protecting public health, the environment, and business from radioactive contamination and pollution from chemical weapons. It addressed four defined areas: safety measures at nuclear facilities; management, storage, and disposal of radioactive waste and spent nuclear fuel; research and monitoring of radioactive pollution; and arms-related environmental hazards. The immediate priority was to make the Kola nuclear power plant safe, to investigate and report on pollution in northern ocean areas, and to hasten the construction of storage and effluent treatment facilities for radioactive waste and spent nuclear fuel. Since the turn of the millennium, the emphasis has been on preparing the removal of nuclear waste from the Northern Fleet's old storage facility in Andreeva Bay in western Kola Peninsula, replacing the old radioisotope thermoelectric generators used in navigation buoys with environmentally friendly solar cells, and finally enabling the Russians to maintain progress in dismantling nuclear submarines at the naval shipyard of the Kola Peninsula.

Although nuclear safety absorbed most of the funding earmarked for the environment under the bilateral environmental agreement between Norway and Russia, the Joint Norwegian-Russian Commission on Environmental Protection was promoting institutional cooperation between the two countries in areas such as pollution control, biodiversity, and the protection of cultural heritage. *Institutional* cooperation became the hallmark of the commission around the mid-1990s. Not only emphasizing solutions to urgent environmental problems, the commission also tried to build a workable system of cooperation between Norwegian and Russian environmental institutions. Norway was eager to help Russia strengthen its environmental bureaucracy, not least regarding specialist competence. The single largest project was the Cleaner Production Programme, where engineers at Russian enterprises were trained in saving resources and reducing waste. Since 2002–2003, protecting the marine environment of the Barents Sea has been the main objective of the commission. Its initial main priority, the modernization of the Pechenganikel combine, has not materialized. Norway pledged NOK300 million (at the time equivalent to some US$50 million) in 1990, but after years of planning the project was shelved in 1997. It was revived on a smaller scale in 2001, when the Norwegian Minister of the Environment and the Russian Minister of Economy signed an agreement on a modernization project that would involve a 90 percent reduction in emissions of SO_2 and heavy metals. The owner of the now privatized smelter, Norilsk Nikel, had little incentive to invest more in improving environmental performance, and Russian environmental authorities lack the political power to force the company to do so. By 2010, it had become clear that nothing would come of this modernization initiative either.

Norwegian High North Policy since the Turn of the Century
The first years after the turn of the millennium saw little attention given to the North in Norwegian foreign policy discourse. The northern waters were still seen as mainly a scene for Cold War theater. Moreover, the previous decade's institutional collaboration with Russia showed signs of wear. The BEAR had not produced the results many had hoped for in large-scale business cooperation between East and West. Norway's Plan of Action for nuclear safety in northwestern Russia was heavily criticized by the Norwegian public for spending too much money too quickly, again with limited practical results. When the Conservative Minister of Foreign Affairs Jan Petersen appointed a committee in early 2003 to evaluate opportunities and challenges in the North, this received little media attention. For many, the act was little more than a sop to Cold War romantics in the armed forces and the right-wing political establishment, who regretted that Norway's foreign policy was now mainly directed southward—to mediation for peace and humanitarian aid in the Third World. The committee was headed by the director of the Norwegian Polar Institute, Olav Orheim, and had representatives from academia, the state bureaucracy, business, the environmental movement, and indigenous peoples. Its report, published in December 2003, called for clarification in Norway's relationship with Russia through one overarching agreement that would solve all outstanding issues between the two countries—notably the delimitation line between their EEZs and the status of the seas around Svalbard.[21] The committee also proposed removing the national tier of the BEAR collaboration, leaving only cooperation at the regional level, and instead strengthening bilateral collaboration with Russia and Norway's participation in the Arctic Council. It further recommended a steep increase in funding to develop north Norwegian science and businesses and suggested that money should

be taken from the Plan of Action for nuclear safety in northwestern Russia. In sum, then, the Orheim Committee proposed a change of course away from the 1990s' institutionalized partnerships with Russia, toward greater attention to circumpolar issues and the development of north Norwegian science, trade, and industry. The report was sharply criticized by political actors in Kirkenes, the town in Norway's northeastern corner that had become the Norwegian "Barents capital" since the early 1990s. They condemned the scientific emphasis of the Orheim report, obviously fearing that funding and the political capital would be transferred to Tromsø, home to the Norwegian Polar Institute and the world's northernmost university.

In April 2005, the Norwegian government responded to the Orheim report through a white paper on opportunities and challenges in the North, prepared by the Ministry of Foreign Affairs.[22] It did not follow up on the proposals of the Orheim Committee. There was no mention of abolishing the national tier of the BEAR, nor of downsizing assistance to nuclear safety in northwestern Russia. The white paper paid considerable attention to the challenges associated with the latter, as well as to jurisdictional issues in the Barents Sea. It briefly mentioned circumpolar collaboration and indigenous issues without indicating any change of course.

In the time between the appointment of the Orheim Committee and the publication of the government white paper, a change had taken place in Norwegian public discourse. If the North had been considered "backward" (linked to the Cold War and to Norway's "polar past") in early 2003, this was not the case two years later.[23] A mounting euphoria about new opportunities in the North had emerged, led by north Norwegian businesspeople, retired military personnel, and the leading north Norwegian newspaper, *Nordlys.* The newspaper regularly criticized the government for not recognizing the petroleum opportunities that were opening up in the Barents Sea, leaving the floor to political adversaries.

Even worse, Norway's traditional allies had already established ties with Russia in the North, leaving Norway on the sidelines. The Russian gas monopolist Gazprom had started development of the gigantic Shtokman gas and gas condensate field in the Barents Sea together with American oil companies, the argument went. This was not actually true, but the Russians had indeed opened up in 2003 for foreign participation in the Shtokman development. The upbeat atmosphere in Norway was reinforced by the dramatically increased traffic of Russian oil tankers along the Norwegian coastline from autumn 2002. Many seemed to believe that the Russians had already started drilling in the Barents Sea, and those advocating a heightened focus on the northern waters silently let the public believe so through hints and half-truths. In fact, the tankers were transporting oil from land-based fields farther east in Russia because of capacity problems in existing pipelines. Nevertheless, the North became a major issue in the campaign leading up to Norway's general elections in September 2005.

Whereas the northern waters had until then largely attracted the interest of right-wing politicians concerned with military security and economic interest (except the BEAR, which was the Labour Party's "baby"), now even the leader of the Socialist Left Party declared that Norway's most important foreign policy challenges were those in the North. The elections were won by a "Red-Green coalition" consisting of the Labour Party, the Socialist Left Party, and the Centre Party, and rising star Jonas Gahr Støre (the preferred assistant of erstwhile prime minister Gro Harlem Brundtland) became Minister of Foreign Affairs. He had studied the challenges associated with the Shtokman development at the Oslo think tank Econ, rode on a mounting wave of northern euphoria, and used his excellent rhetorical skills to declare himself Mr. North of Norwegian politics. When Gahr Støre took office, it had just become known that the two major Norwegian oil companies, Statoil and Hydro, were on Gazprom's shortlist for the Shtokman project (in addition to American Chevron, ConocoPhillips, and French Total). In what was arguably the most famous political speech in Norway since the turn of the millennium, Jonas Gahr Støre, speaking in Tromsø, convincingly declared the North the number one priority of Norwegian foreign policy.

In early autumn 2006, events took an unexpected turn. Gazprom suddenly declared that it would not have any foreign partners in the Shtokman development but would go it alone instead. When the Norwegian government announced its *Strategy on the High North* in December 2006, the Shtokman issue was downplayed.[24] Now the northern areas —or the High North, which became the official English translation of the Norwegian term *nordområdene*—are declared a "national priority." The strategy lists all thinkable challenges in the region, ranging from environmental protection and indigenous issues to the business opportunities associated with future offshore petroleum extraction in the Barents Sea. Nevertheless, it erases the dividing line between foreign and national policies and stresses the development of Norway's northern regions mainly in terms of science and business.

This was followed up in the strategy's "step two" in spring 2009, *New Building Blocks in the High North*, a purely domestic-policy document.[25] The main topic in step two of the strategy was the establishment of a new scientific center on climate change and the environment in Tromsø. Fram —The High North Research Centre for Climate and the Environment (the Fram Centre) was opened in 2010, with the Norwegian Polar Institute as its main constituent body.

The Shtokman issue took yet another new turn in the summer of 2007, when Total was invited back in, and soon thereafter StatoilHydro as well (the merged Statoil and Hydro, which has been operating under the name Statoil since 2009). Total and Statoil have no ownership of the resources, however; their role is limited to that of partners in the development project. A final decision on whether the Shtokman field is actually to be developed has been postponed several times, most recently in August 2012. Changes in the international gas market have served to heighten insecurities in this respect. In the Norwegian public debate, the 2010 delimitation line has largely ousted Shtokman as the big promise for the future. Although it will take some time for things to actually happen, there are expectations that the former disputed area contains extractable hydrocarbon resources. So far, results from the Norwegian shelf in the Barents Sea have been somewhat disappointing, although the Snøhvit (Snow White) field was opened in 2007, producing liquefied natural gas (LNG) for the European market. A promising oil field, Skrugard, was found in early 2011. Nevertheless, the resources on the Russian side of the border are arguably much larger than those on the Norwegian side, so Norwegians still place considerable hope on offshore petroleum collaboration in the Barents Sea. This has remained an important driving force in Norway's High North policy.

The Three Layers of Norway's High Arctic Policy
Since about 2005, Norway has had an explicit policy on the high Arctic, designated as the *Strategy on the High North*. The strategy contains elements from three layers of the country's northern policies:

- the High North as an arena for great-power politics (mainly a legacy from the Cold War),
- the High North as an arena for institutionalized collaboration with Russia (mainly a legacy from the 1990s),
- the High North as a national priority (since around 2005).

The relationship with Russia ranks above most other concerns in Norway's High North policy. During the Cold War, the Soviet Union represented the Russian bear, in whose company small-state Norway could never allow itself to feel secure. In the 1990s, Russia became the impoverished recipient of humanitarian aid from Norway. Now, after the turn of the millennium, the Russian bear has re-emerged with both financial and military clout. The internal debate in Norway toward the end of the first decade of the twenty-first century centered on the continuation of financial support to Russian institutions and civil society. Specifically, critics of continued Norwegian support argued that a country that could manage to re-arm itself should also be expected to take responsibility for its environment and health services. Moreover, Russia was assuming a new role as a potential market and business partner for Norway. Participation in the Shtokman development was arguably the main driving force behind Norway's "new" northern policies. Thus, it is shown that Russia played the main role in Norway's High North policies during the Cold War, in the 1990s, and after the turn of the millennium.

Actors concerned with Norway's security have found common ground with those mainly interested in investments and better possibilities for north Norwegian business. These actors focus on Norway's "near abroad" in the Barents Sea region, generally seeing presence in the North —whether in the form of naval vessels or increased population—as a good in itself. Regional politicians, media, and business representatives have found allies in national top politicians concerned about Statoil's access to new resources, preferably in the "near abroad" so that regional trade and industry can also achieve ripple effects. Although there is a cleavage between actors located close to the border with Russia, mainly in Kirkenes, and actors in the rest of northern Norway, mainly in the academic regional capital of Tromsø, the emphasis of both groups is on relations with Russia and on the High North as a "national project."

An interest group that in part competes with these groups (only to a limited extent, given that the common interest is also highly visible) consists of those arguing for a greater focus on circumpolar cooperation and indigenous issues. As noted, the 2003 Orheim Committee had proposed downplaying BEAR collaboration and nuclear safety projects in Russia (though it, too, favored strong emphasis on relations with Russia and considerable new investments in northern Norway) and was criticized for being mainly concerned about "counting polar bears and ice flakes, [and disregarding] those of us who live here [in the High North]."[26] The committee's report is often referred to—despite its explicit call for investments in northern Norway—as a document that shifts the focus of Norway's foreign policy to somewhere far away in the distance, if not on humanitarian action in the Third World, then on indigenous and environmental concerns somewhere in the far-off Arctic. It is seen as defending the narrow interests of researchers from the Norwegian Polar Institute, keen to participate in Arctic Council–initiated activities across the circumpolar North. The establishment of the Fram Centre in Tromsø in 2010 also led many to conclude that science was the winner in the "new" Norwegian politics of the High North. Whereas Russia (whether as regards delimitation line discussions, settlement of fish quotas, or the opening of the Shtokman field) was definitely a moving target, scientific infrastructure in the North was safely within the control of Norwegian central authorities.

Turning to the budget of the Norwegian Ministry of Foreign Affairs, however, one sees that the High North politics of the 1990s—institutional cooperation with Russia—still dominates.[27] Despite the gradual decline in financing for the Plan of Action for nuclear safety in northwestern Russia, the plan still constitutes the single largest budget post of the ministry's High North initiatives: some NOK100 million of a total of around NOK400 million in recent years. The BEAR collaboration has seen its budgets increase. Collaboration with Russia in a wide range of arenas still seems to be top priority in Norway's foreign policy. Furthermore, major jurisdictional achievements have been made in the Barents Sea in recent years: the settlement of the outer limits of the Norwegian continental shelf in 2009 and the delimitation line with Russia in 2010. This is seen as paving the way for further offshore petroleum development in the near future. Norwegian high Arctic policy is indeed still primarily focused on the "lower" Arctic of the near abroad.

Figure 2. The Barents Sea region.

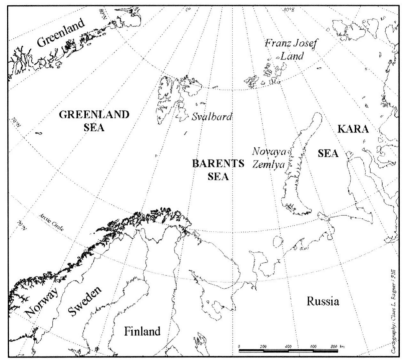

Source. Fridtjof Nansen Institute.

Figure 3. Jurisdiction of the Barents Sea.

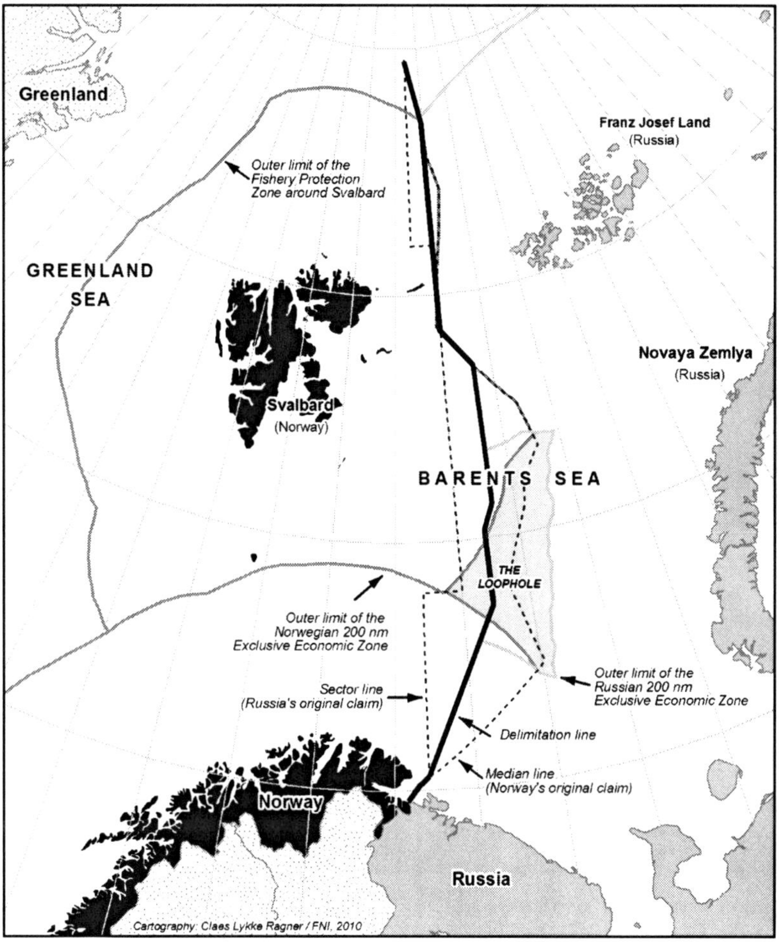

Source. Fridtjof Nansen Institute.

Figure 4. Barents Sea continental shelf.

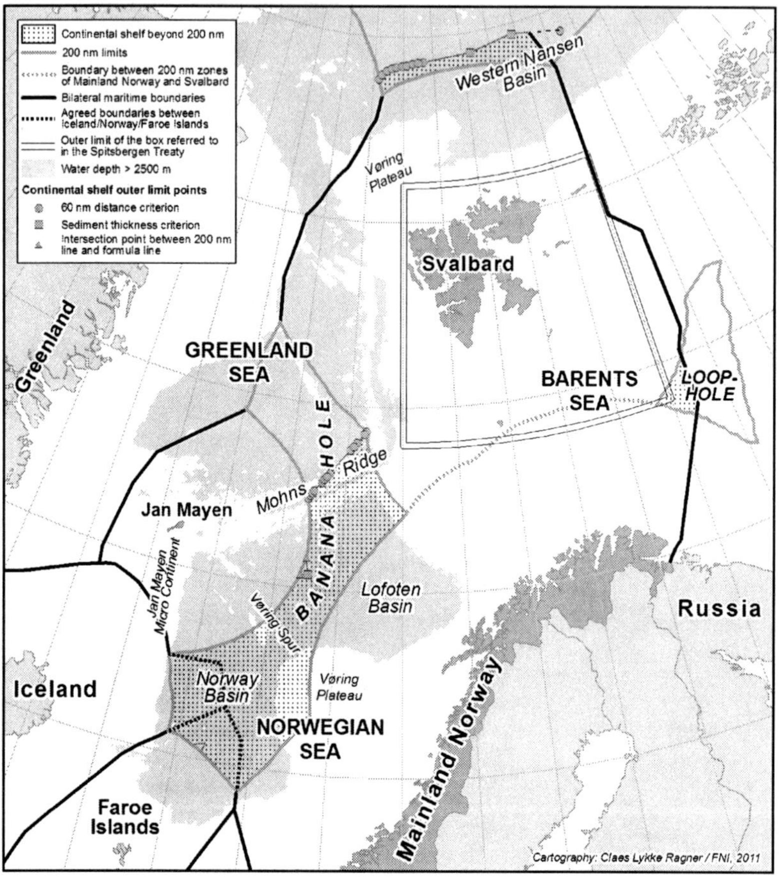

Source. Fridtjof Nansen Institute.

Figure 5. The Barents Euro-Arctic Region.

Source. Fridtjof Nansen Institute.

NOTES

1. For an overview of the Norwegian discourse on the international and domestic aspects of the country's Arctic policy, see Geir Hønneland and Lars Rowe, *Nordområdene—hva nå?* (Trondheim: Tapir Akademisk Forlag, 2010).
2. The chapter builds on several years of research on Norwegian High North politics, published by the author in a series of books in Norwegian; see Geir Hønneland, *Barentsbrytninger: Norsk nordområdepolitikk etter den kalde krigen* (Kristiansand: Høyskoleforlaget, 2005); Geir Hønneland and Leif Christian Jensen, *Den nye nordområdepolitikken* (Bergen: Fagbokforlaget, 2008); and Hønneland and Rowe, *Nordområdene—hva nå?* Cooperation between Norway and Russia on fisheries management and on environmental protection is discussed in Geir Hønneland, *Kvotekamp og kyststatssolidaritet: Norsk-russisk fiskeriforvaltning gjennom 30 år* (Bergen: Fagbokforlaget, 2006), and Geir Hønneland and Lars Rowe, *Fra svarte skyer til helleristninger: Norsk-russisk miljøvernsamarbeid gjennom 20 år* (Trondheim: Tapir Akademisk Forlag, 2008), respectively. The BEAR collaboration is discussed in Olav Schram Stokke and Geir Hønneland, *International Cooperation and Arctic Governance: Regime Effectiveness and Northern Region Building* (London and New York: Routledge, 2007). The section on the BEAR and bilateral environmental cooperation between Norway and Russia is a shortened version of Geir Hønneland, "East–West Collaboration in the European North," *International Journal* 65 (2010): 837–850. Reference to primary material in this chapter is generally limited to direct citations and the most central public documents.
3. See Knut Einar Eriksen and Helge Øystein Pharo, *Kald krig og internasjonalisering, 1949–1965*, vol. 5 of *Norsk utenrikspolitikks historie* (Oslo: Universitetsforlaget, 1997).
4. Ministry of Foreign Affairs, "Avtale mellom Regjeringen i Unionen av Sovjetiske Sosialistiske Republikker og Regjeringen i Kongeriket Norge om samarbeid innen fiskerinæringen," in *Overenskomster med fremmede stater* (Oslo: Ministry of Foreign Affairs, 1975), 546–549.
5. Ministry of Fisheries, *Supplement til protokoll for den 21. sesjon i Den blandede norsk-russiske fiskerikommisjon* (Oslo: Ministry of Fisheries, 1993).

6. Hønneland, *Kvotekamp og kyststatssolidaritet.* Ministry of Fisheries, *Protokoll for den 39. sesjon i Den blandete norsk-russiske fiskerikommisjon* (Oslo: Ministry of Fisheries, 2010).

7. See Ingrid Kvalvik, "Assessing the Delimitation Negotiations between Norway and the Soviet Union/Russia, *Acta Borealia* 21 (2004): 55–78.

8. Ministry of Foreign Affairs, "Avtale mellom Norge og Sovjetunionen om en midlertidig praktisk ordning for fisket i et tilstøtende område i Barentshavet med tilhørende protokoll og erklæring," in *Overenskomster med fremmede stater* (Oslo: Ministry of Foreign Affairs, 1978), 436.

9. Ministry of Foreign Affairs, "Treaty between Norway and the Russian Federation Concerning Maritime Delimitation and Cooperation in the Barents Sea and the Arctic Ocean," temporarily available at www.regjeringen.no/upload/UD/Vedlegg/Folkerett/avtale_engelsk.pdf.

10. For a thorough examination of the legal aspects of the Fisheries Protection Zone, see Geir Ulfstein, *The Svalbard Treaty: From Terra Nullius to Norwegian Sovereignty* (Oslo: Scandinavian University Press, 1995).

11. The strongest opposition to the Fisheries Protection Zone has come from the United Kingdom. The United States, Germany, and France have formally just reserved their position, which implies that they are still considering their views. Finland declared its support of the Fisheries Protection Zone in 1976 but has since not repeated it. Canada also expressed its support to the Norwegian position in a bilateral fisheries agreement in 1995, but this agreement has not entered into force. These other Western countries generally accept that the waters surrounding Svalbard are under Norwegian jurisdiction, but they claim that this jurisdiction must be carried out in accordance with the Svalbard Treaty. See Torbjørn Pedersen, "The Constrained Politics of the Svalbard Offshore Area," *Marine Policy* 32 (2008): 913–919; Torbjørn Pedersen, "Norway's Rule on Svalbard: Tightening the Grip on the Arctic Islands," *Polar Record* 45 (2009): 147–152; Torbjørn Pedersen, "Denmark's Policies toward the Svalbard Area," *Ocean Development and International Law* 40 (2009): 319–332; and Torbjørn Pedersen, "International Law and Politics in U.S. Policymaking: The United States and the Svalbard Dispute," *Ocean Development and International Law* 42 (2011): 120–135. Russia, in contrast, formally considers the waters around Svalbard to be high seas. See A. N. Vylegzhanin and V. K. Zilanov, *Spitsbergen: Legal Regime of Adjacent Marine Areas* (Utrecht: Eleven International Publishing, 2007). In practice, however, Russia has accepted Norwegian enforcement of fisheries regulations in the Svalbard Zone. See Geir Hønneland, "Compliance

in the Fishery Protection Zone around Svalbard," *Ocean Development and International Law* 29 (1998): 339–360; and Geir Hønneland, *Coercive and Discursive Compliance Mechanisms in the Management of Natural Resources: A Case Study from the Barents Sea Fisheries* (Dordrecht and Boston, MA: Springer, 2000).

12. For details, see Øystein Jensen, "Towards Setting the Outer Limits of the Continental Shelf in the Arctic: On the Norwegian Submission and Recommendations of the Commission," in *Law, Technology and Science for Oceans in Globalisation: IUU Fishing, Oil Pollution, Bioprospecting, Outer Continental Shelf,* ed. Davor Vidas (Leiden, the Netherlands, and Boston, MA: Martinus Nijhoff, 2010), 519–538.

13. See Barents Euro-Arctic Region, *The Kirkenes Declaration from the Conference of Foreign Ministers on Co-operation in the Barents Euro-Arctic Region* (Kirkenes, January 11, 1993).

14. The Saami are the only indigenous people found in all four countries in the region. On the Russian side, the Nenets in Nenets Autonomous Okrug and the Vesps in the Republic of Karelia also enjoy status as indigenous peoples.

15. Ministry of Foreign Affairs, *St.meld. nr. 15 (2008–2009) Interesser, ansvar og muligheter: Hovedlinjer in norsk utenrikspolitikk* (Oslo: Ministry of Foreign Affairs, 2009), 49.

16. A discussion of the BEAR cooperation at the time it was established is found in Olav Schram Stokke and Ola Tunander, *The Barents Region: Cooperation in Arctic Europe* (London and Thousand Oaks, CA: Sage, 1994). The achievements of the collaboration a decade later are discussed in Stokke and Hønneland, *International Cooperation and Arctic Governance.*

17. See Geir Hønneland and Lars Rowe, "Western vs. Post-Soviet Medicine: Fighting Tuberculosis and HIV/AIDS in North-West Russia and the Baltic States," *Journal of Communist Studies and Transition Politics* 21 (2005): 395–415.

18. Ministry of the Environment, *Overenskomst mellom Kongeriket Norges Regjering og Unionen av Sovjetiske Sosialistiske Republikkers Regjering om samarbeid på miljøvernområdet* (Oslo: Ministry of the Environment, January 15, 1988).

19. Gorbachev's Murmansk initiative is presented in Kristian Åtland, "Mikhail Gorbachev, the Murmansk Initiative, and the Desecuritization of Interstate Relations in the Arctic," *Cooperation and Conflict* 43 (2008): 289–311.

20. Ministry of Foreign Affairs, *Plan of Action for the Implementation of Report No. 34 (1993–94) to the Storting on Nuclear Activities and Chemical Weapons in Areas Adjacent to Our Northern Borders* (Oslo: Ministry of Foreign Affairs, 1995).

21. See Ekspertutvalg for nordområdene, *Mot nord!: Utfordringer og muligheter i nordområdene: ekspertutvalg for nordområdene nedsatt av regjeringen 3. mars 2003: Avgitt til Utenriksdepartementet 8. desember 2003, Norges offentlige utredninger; NOU 2003:32* (Oslo: Statens forvaltningstjeneste, Informasjonsforvaltning, 2003).

22. Ministry of Foreign Affairs, *St.meld. nr. 30 (2004–2005) Muligheter og utfordringer i nord* (Oslo: Ministry of Foreign Affairs, 2005).

23. A quantitative investigation of Norwegian newspapers during the first decade of the twenty-first century shows that usage of the word *nordområdene* (the High North) grew fivefold from 2003 to 2004. See Leif Christian Jensen and Geir Hønneland, "Framing the High North: Public Discourses in Norway after 2000," *Acta Borealia* 28 (2011): 41.

24. See Government of Norway and Ministry of Foreign Affairs, *Regjeringens nordområdestrategi* (Oslo: Government of Norway and Ministry of Foreign Affairs, 2006).

25. See Government of Norway, *Nye byggesteiner i nord: Neste trinn i Regjeringens nordområdestrategi* (Oslo: Government of Norway, 2009).

26. District Governor Helga Pedersen to *Nordlys*, December 9, 2003.

27. See annual budgets published on the Norwegian Ministry of Foreign Affairs website, www.mfa.no. The budget development is also discussed in Hønneland and Jensen, *Den nye nordområdepolitikken*, 39–43.

CHAPTER 9

TERRITORY, SECURITY, AND SOVEREIGNTY

THE KINGDOM OF DENMARK'S ARCTIC STRATEGY

Mark Nuttall

INTRODUCTION

Recent political, economic, and cultural developments in Greenland and the Faroe Islands, as well as growing concern over climate change and the large-scale development of extractive industries, raise questions concerning the future of Danish practices and performances of power, security, and sovereignty in the Arctic and North Atlantic. For example, Greenland is undergoing a process of state formation and has assumed international prominence in discussions of extractive industries and global energy security, with the Self Rule (*Selvstyre*) government courting multinational corporations and foreign investors interested in hydrocarbons and minerals. Yet, precisely at the time when Greenland and the Faroe Islands appear to be more confident in asserting greater autonomy within the Kingdom of Denmark, with occasional political gestures anticipating eventual political independence and the complete severing of ties to Copenhagen, Denmark has moved to declare and demonstrate its position as an Arctic state with claims for a significant role in international diplomacy. Most notably these declarations and articulations of Arctic political and cultural identity are evident in the Kingdom of Denmark's Arctic strategy, in Danish submissions to the United Nations Commission on the Limits of the Continental Shelf (CLCS), and in increased funding for Danish Arctic research. Given that Denmark is a member state of the Arctic Council, its participation in council meetings and activities includes Greenland and the Faroe Islands, and all three constituent parts of the kingdom sit at the table in partnership. The Danish chairmanship from 2009 to 2011 involved significant Greenlandic and Faroese contributions and placed priority on the peoples of the Arctic, the International Polar Year (IPY) legacy, climate change, biodiversity, megatrends in the Arctic, integrated resource management, operational cooperation, and the Arctic Council in a new geopolitical framework.

With reference to the Kingdom of Denmark's Arctic strategy, this chapter discusses emergent security and sovereignty issues that have both domestic and international significance. I comment on aspects of the strategy by way of illustrating Danish Arctic interests and, in particular, I consider security, surveillance, and the mapping of continental outer shelves. I then move on to explore the contemporary geopolitical situation of Greenland, which—ambitious for greater autonomy and, possibly, political and economic independence—is attracting interest from non-Arctic states such as China and South Korea, from the European Union, and from a number of multinational companies eager to explore for and exploit oil, gas, and minerals. Likewise, ambitions for independence in the Faroe Islands would be given a boost if oil is found in nearby waters.

For the purposes of this chapter, I discuss (albeit briefly) the place of Denmark, Greenland, and the Faroe Islands within global security concerns and current Danish territorial claims in the Arctic as well as refer to arguments between Denmark and Canada over Hans Island. My intention, however, is to show how the Kingdom of Denmark's Arctic strategy is an assertion of Arctic interests viewed from a domestic perspective, a mapping out of Danish Arctic space, and an indication of Denmark's future direction as an Arctic power in both a domestic political and an international geopolitical context. Significantly, the strategy makes it clear that it intends no change in the power-sharing that exists between Denmark, the Faroe Islands, and Greenland. Although the strategy hints at foreign policy in terms of relations with other Arctic states, it is also a statement about a strengthening of political, social, and cultural relations within the Danish Realm, which, simultaneously, emphasizes the nature of its boundaries as a distinctive Arctic region while recognizing the increasingly apparent political and cultural diversity within it.

THE KINGDOM OF DENMARK

The Kingdom of Denmark (*Kongeriget Danmark* in Danish) is a constitutional monarchy comprising the country of Denmark and two autonomous Danish North Atlantic territories, the Faroe Islands and Greenland. Because Greenland is geographically part of the North American continent, the Kingdom of Denmark is unique as a sovereign unitary state in the context of its membership of the Arctic Council in that it encompasses territory in both Europe and North America. The Danish Realm (*Rigsfælleskabet*) is the name often used to refer to the relations between the three constituent parts of the kingdom.[1] Given the increasing geopolitical and economic importance of the Arctic and northern North Atlantic for regional and global affairs, Greenland and the Faroe Islands have assumed prominence as significant places in discussions about international security and resource development in the contemporary global North. It is important to point out that this view is not just an international one but is a Danish domestic one too. In particular, Greenland has captured the Danish political imagination as well as the global imagination as a place that is both at the forefront of climate change, where the impacts of global warming are immediate and tangible, and undergoing a transformation into a potential supplier of oil and minerals (including rare earth minerals) for the global economy.[2] The impacts of climate change and extractive industries are contested issues stimulating heated public and political debate in Greenland, and they also precipitate discussion in Danish politics and media about Arctic sovereignty and security.

Both Greenland and the Faroe Islands enjoy far-reaching powers of self-government in terms of domestic affairs, whereas Denmark retains control over foreign affairs and defense for all parts of the Danish Realm. The Faroe Islands achieved Home Rule in 1948, while Greenland was granted a similar status in 1979, with a new political arrangement of Self Rule, or self-government, coming into effect in June 2009. All three constituent parts of the Danish Realm are often referred to as "countries," although it is more accurate politically and constitutionally to refer only to Denmark as a country and to Greenland and the Faroe Islands as self-governing territories (however, the Faroe Islands can be considered a stateless nation and, as I explain later, Greenlanders are also recognized as a nation). The Faroese and Greenlandic governments in Tórshavn and Nuuk have limited powers with respect to deciding on international arrangements and administrative agreements with foreign states and organizations that relate to Faroese and Greenlandic areas of responsibility. Neither territory is a member of the European Union (Greenland left the EU's predecessor, the European Economic Community, in 1985), although they have close ties with it (Greenland has Overseas Countries and Territories status); both Greenland and the Faroe Islands have been included by Denmark in recent years in aspects of international decision making; and both territories are individual members of certain international organizations (e.g., the Nordic Council) while they are recognized as members of the Arctic Council as constituent parts of Denmark.

AN ARCTIC STRATEGY FOR THE KINGDOM OF DENMARK

In January 2012, Klavs Holm was appointed Denmark's first permanent ambassador to the Arctic, a post established to serve the country's
regional interests in the Far North (Holm is also Denmark's Senior Arctic
Official (SAO) in the Arctic Council, representing Greenland and the
Faroe Islands as well as Denmark). One of Holm's tasks is to coordinate
the Kingdom of Denmark's ten-year strategy for the Arctic, which was
released in August 2011. Described as a roadmap for Denmark's engagement with the Arctic up to 2020, the strategy is a joint effort between
the governments of Denmark, Greenland, and the Faroe Islands, with an
emphasis on cooperation. But beyond its language of partnership and
cooperation on Arctic matters within the Danish Realm, a careful reading
of it suggests that the Arctic has now become a cornerstone of Danish
foreign affairs and foreign policy in a more solid way than in recent
years. As a precursor to the strategy, the Danish foreign ministry and
the Greenland Home Rule government had published a paper on Danish
and Greenlandic Arctic interests in May 2008,[3] but the Arctic strategy
sets out a more comprehensive set of priorities for all parts of the Danish
Realm.

As some commentators have pointed out, without its northern territories Denmark would be a small, rather nondescript northern European
country with little, if any, influence in the international community. Jon
Rahbek-Clemmensen has remarked that Danish presence in Greenland
is crucial for Denmark's wider foreign policy strategy, which rests on
both a European and an Atlantic pillar, although with Danish interests
in securing stronger relations with the United States beginning to over-
shadow Danish support of the EU in recent years. With nothing to gain
economically from Greenland, he argued that Denmark uses its Arctic
territory as a bargaining chip for political influence.[4] Thorkild Kjærgaard
from the University of Greenland has provided a historical argument
about Danish-U.S. relations for understanding that it is precisely because
of Greenland that Denmark has a seat at the table of international diplo-

macy.[5] Indeed, Greenland has been central to Danish foreign strategy since World War II, evident in the Danish Defence Agreement between Denmark and the United States of April 9, 1941, which was renewed on April 27, 1951. It is through Greenland, as an Arctic state, that Denmark is able to position itself as a key player in world affairs (hence the continued emphasis on the strategy on Arctic issues as being global issues). In particular, Danish relations with the United States must be understood in part through historical and current U.S. geopolitical interests in Greenland and how far Denmark is able to influence America's position on the Arctic. But Danish-U.S. relations must also be understood with reference to a shift in Denmark's overall foreign and security policy since the 1990s. Henriksen and Ringsmose have suggested that Denmark became a strategic actor in aligning itself closely with American foreign policy priorities with respect to Iraq and Afghanistan after 2003, thus reinforcing a "super-Atlanticism." Denmark's stance in supporting much of American policy—and indeed for its consistent support for the United States in NATO affairs—won the country admiration from the administration of George W. Bush, but most European states were frustrated by Denmark's reluctance to support a common European approach to aspects of American foreign policy.[6]

Although neither Denmark nor the Faroe Islands are geographically Arctic places, the introduction to the strategy makes an emphatic statement that "The Kingdom of Denmark is centrally located in the Arctic. The three parts of the Realm—Denmark, Greenland and the Faroe Islands—share a number of values and interests and all have a responsibility in and for the Arctic region. The Arctic makes up an essential part of the common cultural heritage, and is home to part of the Kingdom's population."[7] Similarly, in a separate strategic assessment initiative, the Faroese government argued that the Faroe Islands has a significant role as a key stakeholder in circumpolar cooperation and work is underway to enhance understanding of the strategic position of the country in relation to a changing Arctic. The strategic assessment produced a final report that was submitted to the Faroese prime minister, Kaj Leo Holm

Johannesen, in April 2013 and outlines how the Faroe Islands could contribute to and benefit from the changing circumstances and future opportunities arising from Arctic environmental, social, political, and economic transformations. Significantly, it situates the Faroe Islands as "a nation in the Arctic" and, pointing out its proximity to the Northern Sea Route, outlines recommendations for how it could develop as a northern maritime service center and educational hub, particularly for the northeast Atlantic.[8]

The *Kingdom of Denmark Strategy for the Arctic 2011–2020* engages at its outset with themes and storylines that have become familiar in recent years and that often frame much contemporary commentary and research on the Arctic. It emphasizes that the Arctic is a region that "is opening up," states that the vast changes taking place in the Arctic over the past ten years have become "significant global issues," and makes passing reference to international attention focusing increasingly on the Arctic. In this way, the strategy not only locates the Kingdom of Denmark centrally and firmly in the Arctic in both a geographical and rhetorical sense, it situates the kingdom within global discourses about pressing global concerns with an aim to secure a place for Denmark, Greenland, and the Faroe Islands to engage in international debate on the region and its future. As such it is a statement about a mapping of geographical space and territory and a marking out of a distinctive Arctic political identity.

The strategy identifies climate change as one of the most urgent concerns facing the Arctic, carefully pointing out that though there are considerable local, regional, and global challenges and pressures brought to bear by a changing Arctic climate, melting ice caps and shrinking sea ice also mean new opportunities for both Arctic residents and the global community rather than just bringing environmental catastrophe and dramatic ecosystem change. The strategy thus outlines a commitment to protect the Arctic environment, balance natural resource interests with international security issues, and improve maritime safety in the region. Yet it states that such a "strategy for the Arctic is first and foremost a strategy for a development that benefits the inhabitants of the Arctic." In particular, the strategy emphasizes Greenland's position as being of central importance, owing to its strategic location and potential mineral wealth both in its coastal waters and its hinterland, as well as its unique cultural and environmental heritage. Although dependency relations between Denmark and Greenland and between Denmark and the Faroe Islands are most strikingly evident in the form of an annual block grant both territories receive from Copenhagen (and, in the case of Greenland, imported Danish expertise in many areas), the Arctic strategy appears to support the idea that increased mineral activities in Greenland will benefit both Greenlanders and Danes because there will be a reduction in Greenland's block grant corresponding to the amount of revenues extractive industries will bring to Greenland's economy.

THE KINGDOM OF DENMARK AND SECURITY POLICY

One striking aspect of the Kingdom of Denmark's Arctic strategy is its approach to security policy as one of preventing conflict and militarization and supporting the idea of the Arctic as a region characterized by cooperation. The Arctic strategy points out that its impetus was the meeting of the five Arctic coastal states (Denmark, the United States, Canada, Russia, and Norway) in Ilulissat between May 27 and 29, 2008, following an invitation by the Danish Minister of Foreign Affairs Per Stig Møller and then premier of Greenland Hans Enoksen to discuss governance issues for the Arctic Ocean. That meeting was not without controversy. Sweden, Finland, and Iceland felt excluded and expressed concern that what became known as a gathering of the Arctic Five would undermine the Arctic Council but also place strain on relations within the Nordic Council. The six indigenous peoples' organizations that sit in the Arctic Council as permanent participants also objected to a meeting on the future of the Arctic Ocean that did not include them, a meeting they felt acted to marginalize them from discussions of environmental protection, governance, and sovereignty. Within a context of the re-imagining and representation of the Arctic Ocean as a place of geopolitical and economic importance, Dodds and Ingimundarson[9] have written about the significance of "coastal state" status. Examining the case of Iceland and its recent articulations of identity as not just an Arctic state but as an Arctic coastal state, they explore arguments for precisely why it has become politically expedient to be seen and recognized as an Arctic coastal state. Being a coastal state, they argued, has not only political resonance but also profound cultural meaning, and Iceland's claim to be an Arctic coastal state (and its hope to be recognized as one) is in part a reaction to the emergence of an apparently exclusive Arctic Five in the wake of the Ilulissat gathering.

Against the backdrop of a Greenlandic town located near an ice fjord that has become a global symbol of rapid climate change in the Arctic,[10] and as international concern was growing over climate change melting the perennial sea ice of the Arctic Ocean, supposedly leading to a future characterized by ice-free summers, the Arctic Five met to discuss this environmental transformation and the international attention that was beginning to focus on the possibility of new shipping lanes crossing the ocean and international companies moving in to the region to explore for oil and gas. The meeting resulted in the Ilulissat Declaration, by which the five Arctic Ocean coastal states recognized that dramatic changes were happening in the Arctic and affirmed their commitment to adhering to the United Nations Convention on the Law of the Sea (UNCLOS) as an extensive legal framework that applies to the Arctic Ocean. Through the declaration, the Arctic Five rejected calls for a specific comprehensive legal regime or treaty for the Arctic precisely because they argued that UNCLOS "provides a solid foundation for responsible management by the five coastal States and other users of this Ocean through national implementation and application of relevant provisions"[11] and for the management of overlapping claims. The Arctic Five also asserted a commitment to strengthen cooperation with one another and with other interested parties on the administration and governance of Arctic waters, on environmental protection, and in scientific data gathering.

The Ilulissat meeting was an intention on the part of Denmark and Greenland to promote cooperation among the Arctic Ocean coastal states because, as the declaration states, "[b]y virtue of their sovereignty, sovereign rights and jurisdiction in large areas of the Arctic Ocean the five coastal states are in a unique position to address these possibilities and challenges."[12] Although the declaration recognizes that climate change and the potential exploitation of natural resources will have impacts on local and indigenous communities, the emphatic message in the declaration is that issues of governance, security, and sovereignty are matters for states. In this respect, and despite concerns expressed by the Inuit Circumpolar Council–Greenland that indigenous peoples were being marginalized by their exclusion, the declaration is consistent with Greenland's position as a constituent part of a nation-state and also as a self-governing territory of that state that has been undergoing a process of nation-building and state formation of its own since Home Rule was introduced in 1979.[13] It is also tempting to view the Ilulissat Declaration as the closest Denmark has come to articulating a foreign policy position with regard to the Arctic, but it is above all significant as an example of how Denmark has pursued its interest in furthering cooperation in the region (albeit at the cost of excluding three other Arctic states from discussions in Ilulissat). But one aspect of it is often overlooked, and that is what both the meeting in Ilulissat and its outcome say about Danish access to American policy makers and Denmark's ability to influence U.S. policy on the Arctic. The United States is not a party to UNCLOS, and Henriksen and Ringsmose have argued that "the fact that Denmark succeeded in getting the Americans to support the so-called Ilulissat Declaration in 2008 was a major diplomatic achievement."[14]

The Kingdom of Denmark's Arctic strategy reiterates the importance of the Ilulissat Declaration for Denmark, Greenland, and the Faroe Islands. Thus, as I argued earlier, the strategy locates and positions the

Kingdom of Denmark as an Arctic state, but it also serves as a reminder that it is an Arctic Ocean coastal state. As such, it stakes a claim as a major global player in the international politics of the circumpolar North as a member of an exclusive group of Arctic coastal states. The strategy stresses the need for peaceful cooperation with an emphasis on UNCLOS but, while acknowledging UNCLOS as a solid foundation for how the Arctic Ocean coastal states can cooperate with one another on issues of Arctic development and governance, it also suggests some limits to it. "There may be a continuous need for more detailed regulating of certain sectors,"[15] it claims, and it provides as an example an agreement on search and rescue adopted at the Arctic Council Ministerial Meeting held in Nuuk in May 2011.

SURVEILLANCE AND PATROL

The Ilulissat Declaration makes it clear that the Arctic Five are opposed to internationalizing the Arctic and are committed to developing regimes to manage and govern increased economic activity in the region. Yet media and academic reports continue to express concern that renewed international tension over parts of the Arctic, together with increasing militarization, is likely to challenge such statements of cooperation. Robert Murray[16] wrote that, at a time when many international institutions and nongovernmental organizations are focused on human dimensions of global politics, the security environment in the Arctic is showing signs of being an area in which interstate tension and conflict may arise. Competing claims are being made over Arctic spaces and places, notably in the Arctic Ocean, throwing into relief contested perspectives on governance regimes as well as legal, normative, and sovereignty issues. Provocatively, Murray argued that there are indications that some Arctic states are willing to use militarism, evident in forms of military posturing, as a possible means of demonstrating their ownership over, as well as claims to, contested Arctic territory. For example, both Russia and Canada have increased their Arctic military presence and enact and perform military exercises as statements or expressions of their national interests in their far northern reaches. Denmark too has begun to consider the military aspects of the future of a region that will likely be characterized by ice-free seas, increased international shipping, and large-scale extractive industries. Writing on the prospects of military conflict in the Arctic, Jørgensen and Rahbek-Clemmensen argued,

> Even though NATO is not pursuing an offensive strategy in the Arctic, regional tensions could arise as a consequence of what could be called a security dilemma. As a point of departure, states are uncertain of each other's intentions and, as a rule, fear the worst. In a situation characterised by major insecurity, they will therefore attempt to guard against anticipated threats by increasing their military capacities. This could create a spiral in which each state rearms in reaction to the signals from its neighbour which, in the final analysis, could result in a conflict proper.[17]

Greenland has no military of its own, but there is a Danish military presence in the form of Arctic Command in Nuuk, which, until recently, was known as Greenland Command and was located at Grønnedal in southern Greenland. The Sirius Patrol in northeast Greenland is one of its units (Sirius originated as the Northeast Greenland Sledge Group, set up with assistance from the U.S. Coast Guard in 1942). These defense forces have traditionally been responsible for surveillance of Greenland's seas, lands, and air space; the maintenance of sovereignty; and, in the case of Greenland Command, fisheries inspection. The Danish Defence Commission has, in recent years, called for a greater military presence in the form of surveillance and naval patrol operations to protect territorial boundaries. During World War II, Greenland and the Faroe Islands were important strategically in terms of control over the northern North Atlantic, whereas Thule Air Base in northern Greenland became vital during the Cold War as an air and missile base. Taagholt and Hansen[18] argued that a shift in Danish security policy from hard to soft security in the 1970s, and particularly during the 1990s, also characterized events in Greenland. Hard security policy had been dominant for Greenland from the beginning of World War II until the end of the Cold War, during which period several American installations were built (including three air bases during World War II at Narsarsuaq in south Greenland, Søndre Strømfjord (Kangerlussuaq) on the west coast, Ikateq near Ammassalik on the east coast, and Thule Air Base, which was established in 1951 and entailed the forced relocation of the Inughuit to Qaanaaq some 140 kilometers north). During World War II, Greenland's strategic role was largely due to it being a vital link between North America and Europe, but during the Cold War this role was redefined as providing a strategic aerial base for the United States against the Soviet Union, and an agreement by Denmark to allow the United States to station nuclear missiles at Thule contradicted official Danish policy of allowing no nuclear weapons on Danish territory.[19] A transition to soft security came about as Greenland's significance to military strategy decreased. Until the 1990s, security policy for Greenland, beyond its geostrategic location, was concerned mainly with environmental protection, natural resources, and human concerns. As Taagholt and Hansen put it,

> In the environmental area, Greenland plays an important role partly because knowledge of meteorological conditions in Greenland have [sic] great practical importance for weather forecasting in Europe and partly because the Inland Ice contains frozen information about the environment and climatic conditions for thousands of years. With regard to resources, there is a possibility of utilizing strategic resources in Greenland and on the continental shelf. Information on these conditions can have decisive importance for setting up international rules on pollution and environmental protection. Research in Greenland therefore has a security policy dimension. Finally the human concerns—concerns for the survival of Greenland culture—play an important role in the consciousness of Greenland's people.[20]

Over a decade after Taagholt and Hansen's review, all of these remain significant for security policy in Greenland, yet these issues have become magnified and have increased in scope and intensity as scientific research has revealed the nature and pace of climate change, as Greenland is on the verge of a possible boom in megaprojects, and as rapid social and cultural changes affect Greenland's societal well-being and economic development.

In June 2009, eight parties in the Folketing signed an agreement on defense policy that recognizes Greenland's geostrategic position and the need to respond appropriately in terms of defense. One of the most significant changes is the creation of a single Danish Arctic Command and establishment of an Arctic Response Force. Denmark has also indicated its interest in using Thule Air Base for sovereignty and surveillance patrols by both the air force and the navy. In October 2012, Greenland Command was merged with the Island Command Forces (ISCOM-FAROES), the military unit based on the Faroe Islands, to form Arctic Command. From its base in Nuuk, Arctic Command continues to be responsible for fisheries protection and search and rescue (it acts as the maritime rescue coordination center for the Greenlandic search and rescue region)—as well as for surveillance, defense, and maintenance of territorial sovereignty—but it has a broad mandate to carry out quasi-civilian tasks in connection with maritime activities. These include anti-pollution and spill-recovery activities in the open ocean, providing ice-breaking support to local companies, carrying out hydrographic surveys, and monitoring commercial activities in Greenlandic waters. Related to these responsibilities and tasks, Arctic Command faces emerging challenges from increasing mining and resource exploration and development, new shipping routes, an increase in tourism (specifically in the form of greater numbers of cruise ships), and an expansion of scientific research. As a member of NATO, Denmark has also been involved in the formation of a Nordic alliance that includes fellow NATO member Norway, partners Finland and Sweden, and Greenland, the Faroe Islands, and the Åland Islands (Finland) for joint monitoring of Nordic marine areas, Nordic air space, and the Arctic.[21] Rahbek-Clemmensen argued that Denmark's "central policy-makers have already realized that their own military means will never be enough to hold on to Greenland,"[22] and the importance of such regional institutions and alliances may be critical if Denmark is to maintain a presence in Greenland and retain its status as an Arctic nation.

MAPPING AND DELIMITING THE KINGDOM OF DENMARK'S ARCTIC TERRITORY

With Greenland and the Faroe Islands together composing the Kingdom of Denmark's northern territorial extent, Danish geography expands beyond its part of the Jutland peninsula and an array of small Baltic islands into the vaster reaches of the North Atlantic and the Arctic. The Kingdom of Denmark thus shares a land (and maritime) border with Germany and maritime boundaries with Norway, Sweden, and the United Kingdom (in both the North Sea and northern North Atlantic), as well as with Iceland and Canada; and, depending on future decisions relating to continental shelf limits, an internationally recognized Danish maritime boundary may eventually extend from Greenland's northern coasts across the Arctic Ocean and over the North Pole to Russia. The maritime boundaries with Norway, Sweden, Germany, and the United Kingdom have all been determined in various agreements relating to the delimitation of the continental shelf between each country and Denmark (or, in the case of Denmark and Sweden, concerning the boundaries of the Øresund strait) and in agreements on fisheries limits. In the case of the Kingdom of Denmark's maritime boundary with Iceland, for example, an agreement was reached in November 1997 between the Danish government along with the Greenland Home Rule government and the government of the Republic of Iceland on the delimitation of the continental shelf and the fishery zone in the area between Greenland and Iceland. In May 1999, an agreement between the government of Denmark together with the Faroese Home Rule government and the government of the United Kingdom related to the maritime delimitation in the area between the Faroe Islands and the United Kingdom. These agreements are significant in the context of understanding Arctic claims and boundary disputes.

Under Article 76 of UNCLOS, a coastal state has the possibility to extend rights to its continental shelf beyond 200 nautical miles if, within ten years of ratifying the convention, it can submit scientific documentary evidence to the Commission on the Limits of the Continental Shelf (CLCS). The coastal state will then have the right to living and non-living resources on and under the seabed beyond 200 nautical miles. Denmark ratified UNCLOS on behalf of the kingdom on November 16, 2004 (the Danish Parliament had decided to ratify UNCLOS in April 2003, a decision later endorsed by the Faroese and Greenlandic Parliaments) and has until November 16, 2014, to make a submission to CLCS. The Danish Continental Shelf Project was launched following the Danish ratification to identify potential claim areas and to gather scientific data for the Kingdom of Denmark's submission.

Documentation for two claims near the Faroe Islands was submitted to CLCS in 2009. On June 14, 2012, Denmark and Greenland submitted documentation based on bathymetric and seismic data for an extended southern continental shelf beyond 200 nautical miles south of Greenland, thus making a claim for an area of some 115,000 square kilometers extending southwest into the Labrador Sea and east into the Irminger Sea.[23] The Labrador Sea areas are likely characterized by overlapping claims with Canada in its forthcoming submission, whereas Greenland's claim for part of the Irminger Sea overlap with Iceland's claims for its outer limits in its submission of April 29, 2009. These are likely to be resolved by consultation and bilateral agreement rather than resulting in hostility. Indeed, the Kingdom of Denmark's Arctic strategy emphasizes, "As highlighted in the Ilulissat Declaration, unresolved boundary issues in the Arctic will be resolved in accordance with international law."[24] It should perhaps also be remarked that both Denmark and Canada claim Hans Island, a tiny wedge of rock in the Nares Strait between Ellesmere Island and Greenland that has been the center of a growing dispute since

2004. Despite posturing by both sides, proposals are being entertained to divide the island through the middle, which would give Canada a second foreign land border.[25] It may be instructive to note that agreement over the delimitation of maritime borders between Denmark and other states, as mentioned already, came about with agreements following consultation; and, with reference to the Ilulissat Declaration, Danish commitment to peaceful negotiation outlined in the Arctic strategy could be considered to indicate a foreign policy position (with respect to Arctic claims) that is consistent with approaches taken to reach these earlier bilateral agreements in the Baltic, North Sea, and North Atlantic.

Currently, Danish research is continuing to survey, calculate, and map the properties of sub-surface areas in support of a formal claim to areas north and northeast of Greenland and extending to the North Pole. In particular, seismic and depth data are being gathered to prove that the Lomonosov Ridge, a submarine formation of continental crust stretching some 1,800 kilometers across the floor of the Arctic Ocean, is an extension of Greenland's land mass. In the areas northeast of Greenland, data are being gathered to determine whether the East Greenland Ridge can be considered a submarine elevation extending from Greenland according to Article 76 of UNCLOS. This area borders the exclusive economic zones (EEZs) of Greenland and the Norwegian territories of Svalbard and Jan Mayen. Such claims to territory—whether they extend southward or eastward and northeastward, or extend northward into and below the waters of the Arctic Ocean—are being based on bathymetric and oceanographic data that coastal states use to extend their claims to sovereign rights over outer continental shelf regions. Further research is being carried out with respect to maritime safety and marine exploration. The Kingdom of Denmark's Arctic strategy commits to the production of new nautical charts to avoid maritime accidents in Greenland but also to support oil and mineral exploration activities. Surveying of Greenlandic waters is to be done in close cooperation with other Arctic coastal states within the Arctic Hydrographic Commission.

Through scientific research expeditions and political expressions and statements of territorial extent, Denmark and Greenland are engaged in a process of mapping, surveying, and finger pointing on charts of the Arctic in the same way all other Arctic coastal states enact these processes, as performative gestures that help to provide the conditions for assertions and interventions of sovereignty.[26] The acquisition of scientific data as evidence for such claims also further backs up the Kingdom of Denmark's assertion of a political identity as an Arctic state —but one that, if its claims to the North Pole are backed up, would share maritime boundaries with five other polar neighbors (Norway, Sweden, Iceland, Canada, and Russia).

GREENLAND'S RESOURCES: AUTONOMY AND SECURITY

On June 21, 2009, Greenland achieved a greater degree of autonomy within the Kingdom of Denmark with the inauguration of the Act on Self-Government. This new political arrangement for Greenland ended a thirty-year period of Home Rule during which Greenlanders had been successful in taking control of a number of administrative areas previously overseen by the Danish state. In the ten years following the introduction of Home Rule in 1979, most institutions dealing with internal matters (e.g., education, the economy, health, domestic policy issues) had been devolved to the Greenlandic authorities. Home Rule set in motion a process whereby Greenlanders have been able to gain responsibility for many of the institutions of their own society and economy and to make decisions about the kind of future they want for Greenland. Under the present form of self-government, it is possible that Greenland could assume further responsibility for many other areas, including the justice system, police system, prison affairs, and the coast guard.

Greenland Home Rule has been held in high regard as a model for indigenous self-government,[27] yet a fundamental characteristic of it was a commitment to nation-building. The new arrangement of self-government instituted in 2009 marked a critical moment in Greenland's political development and in its relations with Denmark. Greater autonomy has strengthened and continued the Home Rule project, but nation-building has given way to political, economic, and cultural expressions and formulations of state-building. Indeed, the Kingdom of Denmark's Arctic strategy places considerable emphasis on the economic development of Greenland, and on the rights of Greenlanders to determine that development, thus seemingly prioritizing economic development over environmental protection.

Self-government does not in itself allow for an increase in Greenland's ability to influence, shape, or make foreign policy. However, it does point toward possibilities for how Greenland's international profile can be raised and how Greenland can have some influence over Danish foreign policy relating to Greenlandic affairs and other Arctic interests, which was a rather more informal arrangement under Home Rule. Significantly, the Self Rule statute recognizes Greenlanders as a nation under international law with an inherent right to independence if they choose it.[28] For some in Greenland, notably those politicians and business elites who wish to sever all ties to Denmark at some point in the not-too-distant future, self-government is one greater step toward eventual political and economic independence. Indeed, economic independence is a prerequisite for complete political autonomy. In 2012, a USA Club of Rome report predicted "a high likelihood that Greenland will become a new independent country within 5 or 10 years."[29] Even with the most optimistic of scenarios, such a statement may have little grounding in reality, however. Greenland will have to assume complete financial responsibility for the areas it may eventually take over from the Danish state. Yet the uncomfortable truth for those members of Greenland's political and business elite who are advocates of independence is that the Greenlandic economy remains dependent for almost 60 percent of its budget revenue on a 3.5 billion DKr annual block grant, which was frozen with the implementation of self-government, and other transfers it receives from Denmark, with the balance coming from local taxation. The most significant challenge to securing and sustaining greater self-government is overcoming this reliance on the Danish block grant (which some realists consider a form of artificial respiration) and replacing it with revenues generated from within Greenland and derived from new forms of economic development.

Greenlanders are a coastal people, and hunting (mainly of marine mammals such as seals and whales) and fishing have long sustained them (and have provided a cornerstone of trade and economy). Although these remain important economic and cultural activities particularly in the small, isolated settlements scattered around Greenland's coasts and continue to inform national debates about social and cultural identity, Greenlandic politicians have long considered that they cannot form the basis for the development of the national economy.[30] Politicians and business leaders argue that if Greenland wishes to improve living conditions and build its economy, it has no alternative but to exploit hydrocarbons and mine raw materials—the harvesting of renewable marine resources does not allow for the creation of a modern society free from dependency relations, but many believe the exploitation of oil, gas, and minerals would, and the development of extractive industries is now a stated aim of the Greenlandic government. This is affirmed by the Kingdom of Denmark's Arctic strategy as the way forward for the development of Greenland's economy and society. Greenlandic politicians widely agree that attracting foreign investment for the development of minerals and hydrocarbons—and turning Greenland into an oil-producing and mining nation and exporter of raw materials—is the key to economic and eventual independence, but many also acknowledge and publicly admit that one consequence is a trade-off between environmental protection and environmental disturbance.[31]

Much of the debate leading up to the referendum on self-government centered on Greenland's ownership of potentially lucrative sub-surface resources. This had been a controversial issue for Denmark in the discussions over Home Rule in the 1970s. This time around, the Danish-Greenlandic Self Rule Commission, which was established in 2004 to negotiate the terms of greater self-government, considered Greenland's claim to mineral rights, its ownership of subsoil resources, and its right to the revenues from non-renewable resource development. The commission concluded that minerals in Greenland's subsoil belong to Greenland and that the country had a right to their extraction. Under the self-government agreement, any income generated by sub-surface resource development will be administered by Greenland, with the level of the Danish block grant being reduced by an amount corresponding to 50 percent of the earnings from minerals and energy extraction once they exceed 75 million DKr. Future revenues from oil and mineral resources will then be divided between Greenland and Denmark, while the annual block grant would be reduced further and eventually phased out. Greenland took control over decision-making processes concerning sub-surface resources on January 1, 2010, thus paving the way for direct negotiation between the Greenlandic authorities and international companies interested in developing Greenland's resources.

The rapid developments taking place in the Arctic have highlighted the geopolitical importance of Greenland (international media reports also often place Greenland at the epicenter of global climate change) but have also focused international attention on its non-renewable resources and other commodities. The Club of Rome's report predicts that the Arctic will become the biggest supplier of the world's energy (particularly of oil, gas, and water), and what Greenland in its state-building process decides to do with its supposed treasure trove of hydrocarbons and minerals, including rare earth elements, as well as its tremendous source of freshwater locked in the inland ice and its outlet glaciers, is therefore significant for future developments in Arctic and global energy security. This new geostrategic position for Greenland in international affairs is recognized by the European Commission, and China, South Korea, and the United States are among the many nations interested in Greenland's emergence as a new resource frontier. A number of large-scale projects may be under way in the next few years. One of the first could be implemented by London Mining, a United Kingdom–based company, which was granted an exploitation license in October 2013 for a major iron ore mine northeast of Nuuk with Chinese financial backing. In summer 2012, the European Commission's vice president, Antonio Tajani, visited Nuuk as part of ongoing discussions with Greenland's government for an agreement on the development of natural resources, and much was made of his visit in European and Greenlandic media circles about the purpose of his trip being about "raw material diplomacy."[32] A few weeks later a South Korean delegation, which included the country's then-president Lee Myung-Bak, visited Greenland and negotiated agreements in cooperation on resources and geological research. Beyond European and Asian interests, the United States may well seek a more visible presence in Greenland and aim to develop cooperation in economic and resource development—energy demand in the United States and the decline in oil production from OPEC countries may mean American oil companies will express greater interest in Greenland in the coming years.

The strength of Danish-Greenlandic relations could be tried by potential uranium mining and the development of rare earth metals in south Greenland. Despite the existence of a Danish-Greenlandic agreement signed in 1988 that bans the mining of uranium and radioactive waste material, the Greenlandic government decided to relax its zero-tolerance uranium policy in 2010 based on scenarios that indicate Greenland could become a major uranium supplier. In October 2013, the Greenlandic Parliament voted by a narrow margin of 15–14 (with two votes not cast) to lift the zero-tolerance policy. Companies are beginning to explore the prospects for uranium mining and for rare earth metals that would involve the extraction of uranium and thorium as by-products, with the Australian-owned Greenland Minerals and Energy focusing on potential development at Kuannersuit (Kvanefjeld) near Narsaq in south Greenland. Kuannersuit is thus now being prioritized as a project that could supply as much as 20 percent of the global demand for rare earth metals. Domestically, uranium mining is a controversial issue,

with many people, environment groups, and emergent grassroots organizations in Greenland expressing concern over the potential environmental and social impacts and consequences (although there appears
to be some support for the mine in the town of Narsaq itself). As far
as relations between Greenland and Denmark are concerned, uranium
mining or even extracting uranium as an inevitable by-product of rare
earth metals production will probably test the 2009 Self Rule Act because
Copenhagen's position is that the exporting of Greenlandic uranium is
a matter for the Kingdom of Denmark to decide upon.

CONCLUSIONS

The Kingdom of Denmark's Arctic strategy is an important document
that sets out a number of Arctic interests, but it maps and defines a
distinct Danish Arctic space and the territorial extent of the kingdom
as an Arctic coastal state, as well as indicating future directions for
the kingdom as an Arctic power not just in the global North, but in
an international geopolitical context. Although it is a strategy, not an
explicit policy document, it does nonetheless intimate a policy approach
to relations and cooperation with other Arctic states, especially in terms
of sovereignty, Arctic territorial claims, and cooperation in research,
emphasizing the Ilulissat Declaration and UNCLOS as guiding principles
for negotiation. Above all, however, its purpose is to set out ways in
which the Kingdom of Denmark sees its future (and its future territorial
extent) as an Arctic state and how political, social, and cultural relations
within the Danish Realm are to be strengthened while recognizing the
political and cultural diversity within it, as well as acknowledging and
respecting Faroese and Greenlandic aspirations for greater autonomy.
It is a strategy worked out and endorsed by the three governments of
the Danish Realm, and it indicates ways forward for how Denmark can
retain a strategic presence and strategic mobility in the Arctic, not just in
a geographical sense but also within international institutions concerned
with the global North.

A number of current issues relating to sovereignty and international security have bearing on Denmark, Greenland, and the Faroe Islands in that they challenge the political, economic, social, and cultural relations of the Danish Realm as a commonwealth. Although unresolved boundary issues with other Arctic states are high on the agenda—and though the strategy commits to further research on climate change and the environment, and to working to introduce binding global rules and standards for navigation in the Arctic—internal political, economic, social, and cultural relations within the Danish Realm are as significant as international relations, transboundary environmental challenges, and international shipping transecting Arctic waters. Denmark will watch Greenland's rapidly evolving political landscape and its economic development closely. Without Greenland, Denmark will cease to be an Arctic state and, arguably, the Faroe Islands will also be diminished in terms of its claim to an Arctic identity—certainly, Denmark and the Faroe Islands would no longer sit as members of the Arctic Council in the case of an independent Greenland. Greater autonomy (and possible independence) is inextricably linked to the development of non-renewable resources in Greenland, and this brings resources and the environment into sharp focus as geostrategic issues. With the prospect of extractive industries forming the backbone of the Greenlandic economy, Greenland is being viewed as a resource frontier that will supply Europe, Asia, and North America with, among other things, oil, iron ore, rare earth minerals, water, and uranium.

The Kingdom of Denmark's Arctic strategy aims to strengthen relations within the Danish Realm, yet self-government in Greenland (and the current trajectory of economic development) means in reality a gradual loosening of political and economic ties between Denmark and Greenland. While there are concerns that Greenland could become dependent on powerful multinational corporations at precisely the moment Denmark's influence wanes, it has options to build strong economic links with North America and Europe. Greenland is looking to develop closer ties with the EU, which is one way in which it can raise a distinctive voice in foreign relations with European states without Denmark as an intermediary. One could even speculate that an independent Greenland could look away from Europe in favor of developing ties with North America instead, in which case it may benefit from the North American Free Trade Agreement (NAFTA). Yet retaining a close relationship with Denmark and the Faroe Islands may turn out to be the better approach, with a form of greater autonomy for Greenland (and the Faroe Islands) constituting an independence of sorts within the Kingdom of Denmark, which would leave the Danish Realm intact without breaking it up. Asian states too are likely to be influential trade and business partners, and it is worth noting that both Denmark and Greenland were supportive of China's application for observer status in the Arctic Council. Whatever Greenland's approach to international relations in the future, and it will certainly be the case that Greenlandic politicians will have more of a say over Danish foreign policy concerning Greenland, the development and control of natural resources as Greenland's key strategic assets may well become the dominant security issue for the Greenlandic government. Here, the Kingdom of Denmark's Arctic strategy comes into its own as a significant document, which maps out an approach to the Arctic that simultaneously asserts Denmark's claim to be an Arctic power that can also play a role in overseeing the security but not the disposition of those assets while acknowledging the rights of Greenlanders and Faroese as political agents who should determine their own futures.

NOTES

1. The total area of the Faroe Islands is approximately 1,400 square kilometers (540 square miles) with a 2010 population of almost 50,000 people. The Greenland population is 56,615 (January 2011 estimate), and the total area of the island is 2,166,086 square kilometers (836,300 square miles). The population of Denmark is around 5,574,000, and the country covers some 3,094 square kilometers (16,629 square miles). Greenland and the Faroe Islands have two elected members each in the Folketing, the Danish Parliament.

2. Mark Nuttall, "Imagining and Governing the Greenlandic Resource Frontier," *Polar Journal* 2, no. 1 (2012): 113–124; http://eu-arctic-forum. org/publications/opinions-publications/greenland-a-key-for-future-developments-in-the-arctic/attachment/greenland/.

3. Ministry of Foreign Affairs of Denmark and the Home Rule Government of Greenland, *Arktis i en brydningstid: Forslag til strategi for aktiviteter i det arktiske område.*

4. Jon Rahbek-Clemmensen, "Denmark in the Arctic," *Atlantisch Perspectief* 3 (2011): 9–14.

5. Thorkild Kjærgaard, "Den Amerikanske livline," *Weekendavisen*, April 20, 2012, 12–13.

6. Anders Henriksen and Jens Ringsmose, "What Did Denmark Gain? Iraq, Afghanistan and the Relationship with Washington," in *Danish Foreign Policy Yearbook 2012*, ed. Nanna Hvidt and Hans Mouritzen (Copenhagen: Danish Institute for International Studies, 2012), 157–181.

7. Denmark, Greenland, and the Faroe Islands, *Kingdom of Denmark Strategy for the Arctic 2011–2020* (Copenhagen: Ministry of Foreign Affairs; Nuuk: Department of Foreign Affairs; and Tóshavn: Ministry of Foreign Affairs, 2011), 7.

8. Prime Minister's Office, *The Faroe Islands: A Nation in the Arctic* (Tórshavn: The Prime Minister's Office/The Foreign Service, 2013).

9. Klaus Dodds and Valur Ingimundarson, "Territorial Nationalism and Arctic Geopolitics: Iceland as an Arctic Coastal State," *Polar Journal* 2, no. 1 (2012): 21–37.

10. Lill Rastad Bjørst, "Arktiske diskurser og klimaforandringer i Grønland: Fire (post)humanistiske klimastudier" (PhD thesis, University of Copenhagen, 2011).

11. Ilulissat Declaration, Arctic Ocean Conference, Ilulissat, Greenland, May 27–29, 2008, http://www.oceanlaw.org/downloads/arctic/Ilulissat_Declaration.pdf.

12. Ibid.

13. Mark Nuttall, "Greenland: Emergence of an Inuit Homeland," in *Polar Peoples: Self-Determination and Development*, ed. Minority Rights Group (London: Minority Rights Group, 1994), 1–28.

14. Henriksen and Ringsmose, "What Did Denmark Gain?"

15. Denmark, Greenland, and the Faroe Islands. *Kingdom of Denmark Strategy for the Arctic*, 14.

16. Robert Murray, "Arctic Politics in the Emerging Multipolar System: Challenges and Consequences," *Polar Journal* 2, no. 1 (2012): 7–20.

17. Henrik Jedig Jørgensen and Jon Rahbek-Clemmensen, *Keep it Cool! Four Scenarios for the Danish Armed Forces in Greenland 2030* (Copenhagen: Dansk Institut for Militær Studier, 2009), 19.

18. Jørgen Taagholt and Jens Claus Hansen, *Greenland: Security Perspectives* (Fairbanks: Arctic Research Consortium of the United States, 2001).

19. Rahbek-Clemmensen, "Denmark in the Arctic."

20. Taagholt and Hansen, *Greenland: Security Perspectives*, 14.

21. Rick Rozoff, "NATO's Arctic Military Alliance: Britain Spearheads 'Mini-NATO' in Arctic Ocean, Baltic Sea," *Global Research*, January 23, 2011, http://www.globalresearch.ca/nato-s-arctic-military-alliance.

22. Rahbek-Clemmensen, "Denmark in the Arctic," 14.

23. "Greenland and Denmark Submit Continental Shelf Claim," *IceNews*, June 23, 2012, http://www.icenews.is/index.php/2012/06/23/greenland-and-denmark-submit-continental-shelf-claim/#ixzz27mDb33a3.

24. Denmark, Greenland, and the Faroe Islands, *Kingdom of Denmark Strategy for the Arctic*, 16.

25. Adrian Humphreys, "New Proposal Would See Hans Island Split Equally between Canada and Denmark," *National Post*, April 11, 2012, http://news.nationalpost.com/2012/04/11/new-proposal-would-see-hans-island-split-equally-between-canada-and-denmark/.

26. Klaus Dodds, "Flag Waving and Finger Pointing: The Law of the Sea, the Arctic and the Political Geographies of the Outer Continental Shelf," *Political Geography* 29, no. 2 (2010): 63–73; "Gesture and Posture: Pointing the Finger and the Mapping of Outer Continental Shelves," *Polar Record* 46, no. 3 (2010): 282–284.

27. Nuttall, "Greenland: Emergence of an Inuit Homeland."

28. Nikolaj Petersen, "The Arctic as a New Arena for Danish Foreign Policy: The Ilulissat Initiative and Its Implications," in *Danish Foreign Policy Yearbook 2009*, ed. Nanna Hvidt and Hans Mouritzen (Copenhagen: Danish Institute for International Studies, 2009), 35–78.
29. USACOR, *The Future of the Arctic: A Key to Global Sustainability* (USA Club of Rome Report, 2012), http://www.usacor.org/news/sup2009/futureofthearctic.pdf.
30. Mark Nuttall, *Arctic Homeland: Kinship, Community and Development in Northwest Greenland* (Toronto: University of Toronto Press, 1992).
31. Mark Nuttall, "Living in a World of Movement: Human Resilience to Environmental Instability in Greenland," in *Anthropology and Climate Change: From Encounters to Actions*, ed. Susan A. Crate and Mark Nuttall (Walnut Creek, CA: Left Coast Press, 2009), 292–310. In January 2014 a report on Greenland's resource potential produced by the University of Greenland and the University of Copenhagen precipitated considerable debate in both Greenland and Denmark by warning that the development of mineral resources would not, in itself, provide the economic basis for independence. See the Committee for Greenland Mineral Resources for the Benefit of Greenland, *To the Benefit of Greenland* (Nuuk: University of Greenland; and Copenhagen: University of Copenhagen, 2014).
32. Fiona Harvey, "Europe Looks to Open up Greenland for Natural Resource Extraction," *The Guardian*, July 31, 2012, http://www.guardian.co.uk/environment/2012/jul/31/europe-greenland-natural-resources.

CHAPTER 10

SWEDEN AND ARCTIC POLICY

POSSIBILITIES FOR NEW WINE IN OLD BOTTLES?

E. Carina H. Keskitalo

INTRODUCTION

One prevailing conception of the Arctic as a political region today
is manifested in cooperation among the eight member states of the
Arctic Council (the United States, Russia, Canada, Denmark/Greenland,
Norway, Sweden, Finland, and Iceland). The council was established in
1996 in response to a Canadian initiative in the wake of the Cold War;
it works as consensus-based organization with no common budget.[1]
Among the eight member states, Sweden has often been seen as a laggard
in Arctic policy. It has only recently formulated an Arctic strategy, which
it made public in May 2011 when taking over the rotating chairmanship of the council. However, that Sweden has not traditionally defined
itself or its domestic areas as Arctic to any particular extent is hardly
surprising, given that it has no climatically Arctic areas or Arctic coastline (only climatically sub-Arctic areas, which are located in the northernmost parts of the country). Sweden was perhaps formally included
as an "Arctic state" when the Arctic Council was formed because it is

a Nordic state with some historical involvement in high Arctic exploration. The Arctic Council thereby changed the more traditional conception of the Arctic as related to five states—the littoral countries[2]—into an eight-state body that included Sweden, Finland, and Iceland. However, the creation of the council had limited direct impact on Swedish policy, either domestic or foreign.

Today, Sweden has been influenced in particular by the strong emerging interest in the Arctic on the part of the European Union. The impetus there is twofold: the promise of increased resource and transport access in the wake of climate change and the risk that the EU and its member countries face of being excluded from the recently rekindled talks among the five Arctic Ocean states "proper." Whereas Arctic cooperation in the wake of the Cold War was aimed mainly at normalizing tensions in the area by including regions and actors excluded from the security politics of the era, security concerns have recently become more pressing.[3]

This chapter discusses recent policy concerns in Sweden leading up to the formulation of a Swedish Arctic policy in May 2011 and compares official Swedish statements on the North with established Arctic Council and Cold War (military) discourses. The discussion here also situates Swedish policy statements within regionally relevant policy developed both outside and within the country, including that articulated in fora such as the Nordic Council, the EU Northern Dimension, Barents Euro-Arctic Council, and the Northern Sparsely Populated Areas cooperation. The theoretical framework informing the research draws mainly on earlier studies of the development of the Arctic as a political region, for instance, as this is manifested in the work of the Arctic Council, as well as the different types of Arctic discourses identified there.[4] The chapter asks two questions:

(1) How has a Swedish Arctic policy developed as reflected in recent official documents, reports and policies leading up to the release of the Swedish Arctic strategy in May 2011?

(2) What are the motives expressed for policy development, and to what extent do EU and Swedish descriptions of priorities for an Arctic issue area relate to different existing discourses of the Arctic (security, frontier, or other discourses)?

The chapter proceeds from an assumption that existing discourses, or ways of discussing the Arctic, have a strong impact on how Sweden is placed within the Arctic issue area.

DISCOURSES ON THE ARCTIC

Arctic discourse—the issues treated under the heading "Arctic"—has changed over time as regards its focal concerns and areas. This chapter proceeds from the assumption that development of an Arctic region can be conceived in terms of a region-building discourse.[5] Drawing upon work on imagined communities and nation-building,[6] region-building focuses on how units such as regions are constructed rather than given, that is, based on ways in which peoples and geographies are defined together and imagined as forming a unit.[7] Regions are thus politically created, and the ways in which they are defined may relate to making potential political gains through definition rather than as areas per se. In the Arctic, this partly imagined character has allowed different interpretations, discourses, and readings of the region. Historically the Arctic has largely been seen in terms of the high Arctic, or the unpopulated frozen center of the Arctic Ocean. In military security and scientific discourse, the Arctic has been mainly treated as an object for outside intervention. During the Cold War, interest focused on the importance of the Arctic for security and on the distance across the Arctic Ocean as being the shortest between the two superpowers, the United States of America and the USSR. The idea of a "circumpolar North," which includes a view of the Arctic Ocean as a waterway connecting the littoral states—and potentially an even wider range of countries—has been called "the most surprising geopolitical idea to emerge from the Second World War."[8]

The Arctic was a target for strategy rather than a subject in its own right with content or characteristics of its own. Developed as they were on the basis of this geopolitical strategizing, concepts of the circumpolar North were not very specific as to which areas should be included: for instance, the political geographer George T. Renner imagined a triangular "Washington-Chungking-Moscow alliance" centered on the North Pole.[9] The Arctic was also often seen as an object for outside intervention by large powers, for whom exploration could enhance national status, often combining geopolitical and scientific goals in the process.[10]

The East-West divide that characterized the Cold War drew not only the littoral states, who claim jurisdiction over Arctic waters, but also their allies into the political arena, broadening the sovereignty and security framework. Whereas the first expressions of a desire for such international cooperation were put forward by Canada in 1970 in the form of a five-state Arctic Basin Council—an initiative largely motivated by a sovereignty dispute with the United States over vessel traffic in what Canada saw as its internal waters[11]—the 1989 Canadian proposal for an Arctic Council by then prime minister Brian Mulroney was interpreted to include the eight countries that belong to the council today. This composition may have envisioned including all of the states that now cooperate under the Nordic Council and applying internationally the internal Canadian delineation of the Arctic as the area above 60 degrees north—a boundary that in Sweden would pass close to the capital, Stockholm.

However, a discourse on the Arctic that centered on a Canadian description of the region—albeit one to some extent embraced by other countries, notably Russia and Greenland—also carried historical baggage that may not be accurate as applied to the region today. As Scrivener noted, "In some ways, the whole Arctic Council idea could be seen as an external projection of the internal political processes related to indigenous peoples of the Canadian north."[12] That discourse applies a frontier logic whereby the Arctic is seen as an environmental and indigenous subsistence region of "untouched Northern environment and... Northern natives' traditional life-styles."[13] In such a description—both strongly expressed and strongly criticized by Canadian domestic authors —the Arctic has come to replace "the old North American preoccupation with the frontier."[14] In focusing on distinct features that can be seen as related to the nature pole of a nature-civilization dichotomy and high-lighting indigenous, subsistence, and non-market-based characteristics, this description omits important elements that feature prominently in northern life. Given the Canadian role in the development of the Arctic Council,[15] elements of frontier discourse have become widely used in descriptions of the Arctic, although those elements originate in accounts of very specific and limited areas.

In contrast to discourses on the Arctic emphasizing military secu-rity, science, and notions of a frontier, regimes have emerged in areas that have not traditionally seen themselves (or been seen) as Arctic. These describe Arctic areas as localities or in terms of other features (sometimes "northern" but then not connected to "Arctic"). Many such descriptions highlight prominent contemporary features of northern areas, such as local populations in which the majority do not neces-sarily describe themselves as indigenous, major industry, and integra-tion into the modern market economy. Such descriptions are often part of regional economic development paradigms and are notable in their strong divergence from Arctic discourse. The *Arctic Human Develop-ment Report* notes that in northern Sweden, Finland, and Norway, indige-nous people constitute about 5 percent of the population of the "Arctic" areas (as they are delineated in the report, which uses an administra-tive, region-based "Arctic" that is larger than the area defined with refer-ence to the Arctic Circle). However, together with Iceland, these areas of northern Norway, Sweden, and Finland account for 75 percent of the population of the Arctic outside Russia and one-fifth of the economy of the Arctic.[16] Settlement patterns over a longer time (the Old World as opposed to the frontier-developed New World), more extensive integra-tion among "indigenous" and "local" groups, and relatively strong infrastructure development under welfare-state regimes have resulted in situations where actors react with considerable reservation when described as "Arctic." For instance, one northern Norwegian author noted, "First, the whole of Finnmark [the northernmost county of Norway] is highly developed and modernised, not lagging behind the rest of the country in this respect."[17] Authors observe that people most often have blended identities, with the assumed distinction between local and indigenous—typical of frontier development and discourse—possibly posing problems: "It is not the categories in themselves which impose a violence, but the abstraction that takes place in the categorizations, which are not felt to include peoples' specific experiences."[18]

A conclusion from previous studies is that Arctic cooperation needs to tread carefully so as not to include terms that essentialize the area or even make it impossible to compare local descriptions with those expressed for region-building by omitting definitions of what areas region-building targets. This makes it relevant to review the interaction between—and degree of—military, frontier, and resistance discourses on "the Arctic" in cooperation and in foreign and domestic policy development related to the Arctic. In this way, one can best assess not only the relation to place-based rather than historical Arctic discourse features, but also the strategic external or internal roles ascribed to development. Such an assessment in turn constitutes a background for understanding the often externally driven focus in developing "Arctic" areas—one that Sweden has to some extent avoided by not having an "Arctic" focus on its own northern areas. Now, however, as a result of international development, Sweden is compelled to deal with Arctic discourse and has developed its first Arctic strategy, largely in response to developments at the EU level.

THE EU POLICY CONTEXT AND ITS APPLICATION TO SWEDEN

Oran Young has argued that following the change in focus on the Arctic at the end of the Cold War, the region has been going through a "second state change," in which it is becoming increasingly important as "biophysical changes, especially the melting of sea ice, is opening up a range of new opportunities in the Arctic in such forms as the exploitation of offshore oil and gas, the development of new shipping routes, the emergence of new fisheries and the growth of tourism."[19] Such a focus has been increasingly evident during the last few years not only in the large body of work on the new geopolitics in the Arctic but also in the EU and Swedish contexts.[20]

The most significant northern policy in the EU preceding this development was the Northern Dimension, originally a Finnish initiative to deal with Finnish-Russian issues following the Cold War.[21] Today the policy highlights cooperation between the EU and Russia. The most recent Northern Dimension Policy Framework Document was adopted in 2006 and focuses on northwest Russia, Kaliningrad, the Baltic and the Barents Seas, the Arctic, and sub-Arctic areas. The Northern Dimension thus encompasses a very wide range of interests and countries, including what Stålvant has called the "Low North, i.e....the capitals of Baltic Sea States south of the 60° parallel."[22] Departing significantly from what might be expected from a vantage point of Arctic discourses, the policy document notes that the Northern Dimension will, among other things, "promote cooperation between urban areas in the region to create a strong urban network and a well-functioning territorial structure facilitating the development of a globally competitive area."[23] Although Greenland has promoted an "Arctic Window" in the Northern Dimension, the initiative is not emphasized in the 2006 formulation of the policy.[24]

In 2008, the European Commission started developing a dedicated policy on the Arctic for the EU. This heightened EU interest in the Arctic was prompted to a large extent by the increased political importance of Arctic waters for transport and resource exploration (e.g., European Commission High Representative 2008, including a section on the Arctic with particular regard to concerns on Russian sovereignty assertion). In particular, as reflected in later documents, EU concerns were sparked by a separate meeting of the five Arctic littoral states in 2008, a forum that excluded explicit EU interests given that none but Denmark is a member of the EU. On November 20, 2008, the European Commission issued a communication on the Arctic that proposed three main policy objectives: "protecting and preserving the Arctic in unison with its population," "promoting sustainable use of resources," and "contributing to enhanced multilateral governance in the Arctic."[25] The document goes on to highlight the importance of a broad dialogue, one that does not exclude EU members. In a council resolution of October 9, 2008, the European Parliament "highlighted the importance of Arctic governance and called for a standalone EU Arctic policy urging the Commission to take a proactive role in the Arctic."[26] Criticizing present Arctic cooperation, the European Commission noted problems including "gaps in participation, implementation and geographic scope" and suggested that to "enhance input to the Arctic Council...[a]s a first step, the Commission will apply for permanent observer status in the Arctic Council."[27] It also proposed including discussions of Arctic issues in the Northern Dimension context, exploring possibilities for creating a European Arctic Information Centre, and linking with Arctic education networks.[28] These suggestions were welcomed in the council's conclusions on Arctic issues,[29] where the commission was asked to present a report on progress in main areas by the end of June 2011.

The commission noted both "frontier" and other conceptions of the Arctic. It recognized that the EU is "linked to the Arctic region" through historical, geographic, economic, and scientific factors. The communication defines the term "Arctic region" as covering "the area around the North Pole north of the Arctic Circle...[including] territories of the eight Arctic states."[30] Under the theme "Protecting and preserving the Arctic in unison with its population" were the sub-themes (1) environment and climate change, (2) support for indigenous peoples and local population, and (3) research, monitoring, and assessments. Under the second of these, it is noted, "hunting marine mammals has been crucial for the subsistence of Arctic populations since prehistoric times and the right to maintain their traditional livelihood is clearly recognized."[31] Proposals for action include the provision of possibilities for protection of indigenous lifestyles and support for Saami organizations and activities, including reindeer husbandry. Under the theme "Promotion of sustainable resource use," policy aims and proposals for action include efforts to facilitate "sustainable and environmentally friendly exploration, extraction and transportation of Arctic hydrocarbon resources" and "exploitation of Arctic fisheries resources at sustainable levels whilst respecting the rights of local coastal communities."[32]

The EU thus foresees increasing its input into the Arctic Council and Arctic issues, staking a claim for its role in the Arctic; here it is driven to some extent by a perceived risk that the coastal states may otherwise marginalize EU influence in what is identified as a geopolitically important area. Numerous other actors note similar strategic concerns, for instance, that the European Union "must prevent the emergence of a geopolitical 'great game' by minimising the risks of an increased conflict potential in the region and by furthering demilitarization and co-operation measures as much as possible."[33] A number of the issues that were discussed at the time are illustrated in figure 6. Thus, "[c]oncerning an EU Arctic Policy...Sweden will...be of great importance with its triple Presidency of the Nordic Council of Ministers in 2008, of the EU in autumn 2009, and of the Arctic Council from 2011–2013."[34]

THE COMING TOGETHER OF AN EU AND SWEDISH AGENDA

In May 2011, Sweden took over the chairmanship of the Arctic Council for a two-year period. This made the country a focal point for the EU's recently defined aims in the Arctic, which include actions that support the Arctic Council and thereby also non-coastal states' claims in the region. The European Commission's "Communication on the Arctic" prompted an assessment by and opinion of the Foreign Affairs Committee of the Swedish Parliament. The opinion notes the changing geostrategic dynamic of the Arctic and states that "like the Government, the Foreign Affairs Committee supports the efforts to form a coherent Arctic policy for the EU."[35] However, the opinion further points out that "[t]he Communication treats several policy areas; it is not comprehensive but *describes issues with regard to the Arctic that the Commission has come into contact with so far.*"[36] The committee thus distances itself from the descriptions in the commission document:

> The Government notes that the Communication, although referring throughout to "the Arctic," nevertheless primarily addresses situations which concern sea areas and that the Arctic land areas are given marginal treatment. For instance, the Communication says nothing about the development in area 1 industries such as agriculture and forestry, reindeer husbandry, mining and mineral exploration on land. The Communication could also have been more concrete with regard to environmental protection of land areas and the preservation of biological diversity.[37]

The committee's opinion further highlights the structure of both the economy and resource use in the land areas now highlighted as Arctic and the history of cooperation in Arctic issues at large. However, with regard to definition of the area, the document notes that "[i]t is, according to the Government, positive that the Commission has selected an ambitious and broad point of departure that accepts the definition of the Arctic as the area north of the Arctic Circle, which includes both land and sea areas where the eight Arctic states enjoy sovereignty or functional jurisdiction to different extents."[38] The committee thus accepted the definition of the Arctic in EU documents. This stance provides an established role for Sweden and resonates with the positions expressed by the Arctic Council but avoids including or referring to existing established definitions of northern cooperation that include larger and admin-

istratively defined sub-regions. An example is the Barents region cooperation, which includes the substantially larger area of the two northernmost Swedish counties involved in the cooperation. The committee
also noted, however, the global context of problems arising in the Arctic
and commented that the commission should have highlighted that the
reasons for deterioration of the Arctic environment lie outside the region
itself.

In December 2010, a motion was made for a European Parliament
resolution on a sustainable EU policy for the High North. Among other
things, the motion refers to the opinion of the Swedish Foreign Affairs
Committee. Its preamble, which persistently makes a case for EU inclusion in Arctic discourse, states, "Denmark, Finland and Sweden are
Arctic countries and both Finland and Sweden are partially located
within the Arctic Circle," and "the EU's only indigenous people, the
Saami people, live in the Arctic regions of Finland and Sweden as well
as Norway and Russia."[39] The strategic focus is very much stressed, with
discussion of the need to avoid a "scramble for the Arctic" and the need
to include both the Arctic Council as the cooperation body for the region
and the Northern Dimension "as a focal point for regional cooperation
in Northern Europe."[40]

Under the title "The EU and the Arctic," the motion addresses the
need to protect the fragile Arctic environment, the importance of peace
and stability in the region, and "the importance of interacting with
Arctic communities and supporting capacity-building programmes in
order to improve the quality of life of indigenous and local communities in the region and gain more understanding of the living conditions and cultures of these communities."[41] The document extends this
focus by underlining the importance of safety and security on the new
world transport routes, sustainable resource extraction, and sustainable
socioeconomic development and governance. In conclusion, the document "[r]equests the Commission to develop the existing Inter-Service
Group into a permanent inter-service structure to ensure a coherent,

coordinated and integrated policy approach across key policy areas relevant to the Arctic"[42] and to explore possibilities for the establishment of an EU Arctic Information Centre.

On January 20, 2011, the European Parliament passed a resolution on a sustainable EU policy for the High North. In line with EU concerns, the document stresses "the need for a united, coordinated EU policy on the Arctic region, in which both the EU's priorities and the potential challenges and a strategy are clearly defined."[43] The document urges "greater involvement of the Parliamentarians of the Arctic to underline the parliamentary dimension and be sure to include relevant non-Arctic players; furthermore [it] insists that continued high-level meetings of an inner exclusive core of States will merely undermine the status and role of the AC [Arctic Council] as a whole; [and it] wishes the AC to maintain its open and inclusive approach and thus to remain open to all stakeholders."[44] Because the European Commission was previously denied formal status as an observer in the Arctic Council, its desire for inclusion is reiterated. Among other things, the resolution requests that the EC consider a circumpolar joint multilateral research funding program and develop the permanent inter-service structure proposed in previous documents. The aim here would be "to ensure a coherent, coordinated and integrated policy approach across key policy areas relevant to the Arctic, such as the environment, energy, transport and fisheries." Accordingly, the document also recommends assigning co-leadership of this structure to the European External Action Service and Directorate-General for Maritime Affairs and Fisheries (DG MARE), thereby underscoring the EU's interest in the Arctic.[45]

ARCTIC POLICY DEVELOPMENT IN SWEDEN

Sweden has grappled with the new requirements placed on it by both the changes in security policy and the rather rapidly sharpened focus on Arctic issues in the EU. Developments in Sweden during the last decade have given rise to a number of different discourses. These have drawn to a large extent on security developments and a desire to understand Sweden's role in the changing security landscape, but they have also evoked existing Nordic priorities regarding economic development and, to some extent, Sweden's polar research history, which has focused on areas outside Sweden.

The recent nature of Arctic development as an issue of foreign policy can be traced in Swedish policy development. Whereas Sweden's foreign policy statement of 2010 does not specifically mention the Arctic,[46] the Opposition in the Swedish government included one page on the Arctic in a policy statement on international relations. Noting that climate change will result in sovereignty conflicts, the Opposition provided three aims: concluding an Arctic treaty, taking steps toward a moratorium on increased resource exploitation in order to limit extraction of natural resources in the area, and supporting arms control and confidence-building actions to limit "observed tendencies towards militarization."[47] Another exception to the silence on Arctic issues in Swedish politics can be seen in two parliamentary bills (Bill 2008/09:T388 and Bill 2008/09:T389), put forward by S. Bohlin and others. The first concerned an Arctic policy for shipping safety and suggested that, given the risks from future climate change, Sweden should support policies geared to improved cooperation on rescue services, including those for decontamination following oil spills. The second bill, on an Arctic policy for shipping, suggested improved harmonization of regulations to reduce pollution from shipping traversing the Arctic Ocean; here, among other things, the proposed legislation supports the Arctic Council's Arctic Marine Shipping Assessment.

In contrast to these specifically "Arctic" developments, Sweden's polar research history has largely been treated as a distinct policy area with little relation to political cooperation in the Arctic. In 2006, a special study of Swedish polar research was completed at the behest of the Swedish Research Council and its committee for research infrastructure.[48] The analysis sought to support future Swedish polar research on the premise that coordinated handling of infrastructure and logistics could improve the international standing and cost-efficiency of research work. The commission was thus based on an understanding of polar research as research focusing largely on the high Arctic and Antarctic. The report further defines such research as typically requiring infrastructure such as expeditions to extreme polar environments but also analyses of and information on the culture and politics of the polar areas. The report cites the history of exploratory polar research and the Swedish Polar Research Secretariat, which has operated in Sweden for some twenty years. It notes that none of the polar projects has involved research on the sub-Arctic areas in northern Sweden such as that conducted in the area around the research station at Abisko. The main area of social science taken up in the report is international politics, which includes international cooperation in the Arctic Council; however, this is discussed on only a few of the report's 180 pages.

In 2008–2010, Sweden's efforts to address developments in the Arctic manifested in three Swedish Defence Research Agency (FOI) reports on the Arctic, one commissioned by the Swedish Energy Agency and two by the Ministry of Foreign Affairs. The first, energy-focused, report describes the development of oil and gas energy issues in a warming Arctic.[49] The document does not focus on Sweden but rather treats issues as external to Sweden—discussing, for instance, Norway and Denmark in terms of an "Arctic Scandinavia"[50]—and considers the way in which "[t]he energy issue in the Arctic develops against the background of the region's increasing geostrategic importance."[51]

The second of the FOI reports was a pilot study commissioned by the Ministry of Foreign Affairs on the "developments in the wider Arctic area" (here defined as the area above 60 degrees north), whose "main purpose [was] to make an inventory of the factors and issues that Sweden will have to take into account in the coming years."[52] The report includes chapters on military strategy, energy, climate change, and shipping, as well as reviews of the interests of Russia, the United States, Norway, Denmark, Canada, and Iceland. As in the previous report, Sweden is not dealt with specifically, but rather issues are treated as external to but influencing Sweden. The study concludes that the region may see increased assertions of sovereignty, in particular by the littoral states, and that border disputes, jurisdictional issues, and strategic military concerns may increase in the area, making developments around the Kola Peninsula in particular important for Swedish security policy. The report notes that the ongoing change in these factors makes regional development difficult to analyze, as does "the elusive character of the Arctic."[53]

Granholm is the third FOI report on the Arctic, written at the request of the Ministry of Foreign Affairs. The study analyzes the development of Arctic policies in Denmark, Canada, and Iceland, noting, similarly to the previous report, that "[a] new Arctic is taking shape. Today it is not possible to say with certainty which role and relation to the rest of the world the region will achieve."[54] Concluding that the three countries are "highly dissimilar with large domestic differences that very clearly impact their lines of action with regard to the Arctic,"[55] the report states that "[t]he Canadian Arctic seems partly to play somewhat of a national mythological role for Canada; partly it is very thinly populated by Inuit, which affects the domestic political agenda for the minority government that rules federal Canada."[56] It summarizes that internal change in the three countries—such as the major impact of the global economic crisis, Canadian-U.S. foreign policy relations, and issues regarding the Northwest Passage—will affect the dynamic in the Arctic.

THE NORDIC CONTEXT OF SWEDISH POLICY DEVELOPMENT

Finally, another notable basis for Sweden's role in Arctic cooperation derives from its involvement in Nordic cooperation. In 2009, the Swedish Foreign Affairs Committee referred to the Nordic strategy for sustainable development as a way of coordinating the Nordic work on Arctic issues. This strategy takes a perspective decidedly different from that seen in the frontier-related discourse on the Arctic and focuses on general principles for cooperation in the Nordic area, among other things, the value of the Nordic welfare state as a tool for sustainable development. It recognizes the part the Nordic countries can play as role models for the transition toward low-fossil-fuel economies, for supporting a dynamic economy and full employment, and for high levels of education, good health, environmental quality, and social and territorial cohesion. The Arctic is mentioned in a few instances, including the Nordic countries' aim to support an understanding of the impacts of climate change in the Arctic, protection of the sea environment, local sustainability strategies at a municipal level, and general cooperation with fora that support sustainable development in northern regions, such as Baltic, Barents, Arctic, and Northern Dimension cooperation.[57]

In the Nordic context, some of the concerns over security policy and implications of warming in the Arctic were also addressed in a 2009 proposal for Nordic cooperation on foreign and security policy.[58] The proposal, drawn up by the former Barents region advocate and Norwegian Foreign Minister Thorvald Stoltenberg, concerns closer foreign and security cooperation and, among other things, suggests that the Nordic states cooperate in airspace and satellite surveillance, establishment of a Nordic system for monitoring and early warning of traffic in the marine environment, and a maritime response force. The document further suggests "Nordic cooperation on Arctic issues" be focused on "practical matters" such as "the environment, climate change, maritime safety and rescue services."[59] The Nordic Council also published a report titled "Common Concern for the Arctic," the outcome of a conference held under Swedish chairmanship in 2008 (followed in 2010 by a second conference under Danish chairmanship). In the report from the conference, which explored "how to best assist the different components of the EU to address Arctic issues more effectively and in a more coherent manner,"[60] mention was made in particular of the need to meet "challenges facing the Arctic region due to globalization and climate change."[61]

Another relevant forum for cooperation is the Barents Euro-Arctic Council, developed in response to a Norwegian initiative following the Cold War to normalize tensions between Norway, Sweden, and Finland and northwest Russia and organized on the national as well as county level. Sweden chaired the national cooperation level during the period 2009–2011, adopting in its work a development-oriented approach that "work[ed] towards a more eco-efficient economy in the Barents region" to "address the challenges of economic growth, sustainable use of natural resources, energy efficiency and climate change in an integrated way."[62] The document further noted that target areas and areas of cooperation include climate change, small and medium-size enterprises, renewable energy and energy efficiency cooperation, and transport infrastructure. At the county level, the two northernmost Swedish counties participate in the Barents cooperation (thereby defining a broader area than that targeted by Arctic Council or EU policy). In a document titled "Where Is Norrbotten and Sweden in the Barents Cooperation?" the County Administrative Board of Norrbotten highlighted both that the geopolitical importance of the Barents region will increase and that the Sixth Barents Programme (for 2009–2013) will set a high priority on economic and commercial cooperation.[63]

Sub-regional (county-level) development on northern issues also includes cooperation in the Northern Sparsely Populated Areas (NSPA) initiative, which held its first regional forum in 2009. The NSPA comprises fourteen regions in northern Norway, Sweden, and Finland that are "working together to raise awareness of the region in the EU institutions, influence EU policy and to provide a platform for best practice."[64] The NSPA political statement describes its membership region as a "strong, specific and promising region...an important part of the EU, most notably due to the large amount of natural resources, advanced research institutions and high performance process industries."[65] The document describes the NSPA as "a grouping of dynamic and modern regions with diversified economic profiles and with functional labour markets. Enterprises are highly competitive and at the forefront of developing green technology."[66]

SWEDISH ARCTIC POLICY

It is in the context of the range of different understandings of the Arctic just detailed that Sweden released the Swedish Strategy for the Arctic Region on May 12, 2011, as it took up the chairmanship of the Arctic Council. This policy—in the form of a strategy, but with relatively general aims—was developed relatively quickly, primarily during spring 2011, by a core group that included the new Swedish Senior Arctic Official (appointed in the second half of 2010). The document outlines Sweden's motivation for developing a strategy for the Arctic region, Sweden's historical role in the Arctic, its role in Arctic cooperation, and its three strategic priorities: climate and environment, economic development, and the human dimension. As motivation for development of a Swedish Arctic strategy, the document notes the importance of climate change in changing the conditions of life for the population in the Arctic as well as in sea transport, natural resource extraction, and security in the area. The document highlights that no uniform definition of the "Arctic" exists but that through their participation in the Arctic Council, the Arctic states have accepted the council's definition of it as including all areas above the Arctic Circle belonging to the eight Arctic states. The document describes at length the Swedish role in Arctic exploration in Spitzbergen and in security policy, one contribution to the latter being to strengthen the Nordic solidarity statement in April 2011 whereby any Nordic country will support a Nordic neighbor in case of emergency or attack. It also affirms Sweden's role in relation to economic activity, the environment, research, and culture in Arctic areas, with the last focus including Saami culture and languages. With regard to economic ties to the Arctic region, the strategy states,

Swedish companies carry out extensive activities in the Arctic. Exploration of ore and minerals is today high on the economic agenda around the world, which has led to significant industry investments in the Swedish mining industry. In the area one also finds projects for basic metals, iron and titanium. Forests, together with fisheries, constitute the most important renewable resources in the Arctic. Sweden's pulp, paper and mechanical wood-processing industries are among the world's leaders and these utilise forest resources from the Arctic areas. Hunting, fishing and reindeer husbandry constitute important industries for employment and local economy in Arctic Norway, Sweden, Finland and Russia. Swedish expertise in research and development in the Arctic environment is of a high standard and the country's cooperation and effective use of resources with industry is central. For instance, one can mention the internationally acknowledged Swedish research on construction in Arctic environments. The anticipated accelerating exploration of environmental resources in the Arctic is expected to increase the need for air, land and sea transport. Sweden has leading expertise on shipping under Arctic conditions and as a supplier of vehicle testing in the Arctic environment. The tourism industry is an important sector in Arctic Sweden and its potential for growth is considered substantial.[67]

The strategy thus highlights economic development and distances itself from the traditional frontier-related discourse on the Arctic. Furthermore, with regard to Sweden's aims in Arctic cooperation, the strategy supports the EU view that the Arctic should remain a low-tension area when it comes to security policy; the approach includes supporting the Arctic Council as the central multilateral forum for issues concerning the Arctic. The document also notes supporting Barents cooperation as the central forum for issues concerning the Barents region in particular. The strategy further states that synergies between EU cooperation programs, the Arctic Council, and Barents Euro-Arctic Council cooperation should be utilized and that Sweden will support a heightened focus on project work in the Nordic Council of Ministers with an Arctic orientation to complement that pursued by the Arctic Council. In addition, the strategy explicitly states that Swedish activities in the Arctic take as their starting point public international law and that a "vitalised Arctic Council could lead to a lesser need for the coastal states to pursue issues in the 'Arctic Five' format. It is important that Finland, Iceland and Sweden be able to participate in decision making where these countries have legitimate interests and that the standing of the Arctic Council is maintained."[68]

With regard to the three main priorities of the strategy, the first, "Climate and Environment," focuses on (among other things) Sweden acting to achieve significant global reductions of greenhouse gases, attention to Arctic impacts on global climate change negotiations, cooperation to support adaptation to climate change, and work on persistent organic pollutants, biological diversity, and environmental protection. The second priority, "Economic Development," reflects the background of economic ties to the Arctic region and includes priorities on sustainable exploration and cooperation in naval and air rescue, free trade, and developing competence for supporting Swedish commercial interests in the Arctic. Despite some of the large-scale economic interests this entails, the section emphasizes as priority that it is "[f]undamental to the people who live in the Arctic that there exist long-term optimism, possibilities for employment, communications and social care, that the social environment or natural environment for those persons who live in the region not be undermined, and that economic development be sustainable over the longer term."[69] An economic perspective on Arctic development is also reflected in an acknowledgment of the economic nature of reindeer husbandry: "Reindeer husbandry today, like all industries, faces different challenges that need to be addressed in order to subsist and provide an economic surplus."[70]

Finally, the third priority area, "Human Dimension," includes work on the Nordic Saami Convention as well as efforts to support indigenous identity, culture, and traditional industry; to increase communication between research and local communities; and to avoid negative effects of climate change and the increased use of Arctic resources. In addition, attention must be focused on "how local Arctic communities, in particular indigenous communities, may face the challenges presented by the changing Arctic climate."[71] Most of this third priority relates to the impacts climate change will have on the Saami population through reindeer husbandry—in Sweden, a livelihood practiced mainly by Saami and by Swedish or other groups only in specially designated areas—and to the effect on Saami culture and on language of instruments such as the UNESCO Convention on Immaterial Cultural Heritage. Although the section refers to some extent to international Arctic literature, noting that the population in "the Arctic areas of most countries have a somewhat lower life expectancy than the populations at large in the respective countries," it also notes that Sweden is an exception: "in the Nordic area it is nevertheless stressed that the external physical conditions play a limited role for health problems." With regard to social stress as a risk factor for small and sparse populations, the strategy observes that "as the degree of urbanization in [this part of] the Arctic is relatively high, this risk population is rather limited."[72]

CONCLUSION: THE ARCTIC FOR SWEDEN?

This chapter has highlighted the rapid policy developments regarding the Arctic in both the EU and in Sweden that have followed from concerns over the implications of climate change and especially the issue of the five-state declaration on the Arctic issued in 2008. It can be asserted that if the Arctic coastal states had for any reason wanted greater involvement in Arctic issues on the part of the EU and non-littoral states, issuing the declaration was, in hindsight, by far the most efficient way to go about this. Indeed, the declaration stirred sovereignty and resource concerns ranging far beyond any "Arctic" area and heightened pressure to avoid a five-state constellation. Strategic and resource-related interests have thus driven much of the development of the EU and official Swedish Arctic policy efforts.

In referring to the "Arctic" area, both EU and Swedish policy involve a variety of possible discourses. These include historical interests, with the EU in particular expressing some understandings that reflect the discourse of the Arctic as a frontier, which stand in marked contrast to its Northern Dimension priorities. The review of the broader context for policy development at the EU level and of the motivating factors cited in the Swedish documents thus evidences a continuation of an externally based resource- and security-motivated focus on the "Arctic." The delineation of the "Arctic" is also externally motivated by the Arctic Council and subsequent EU delineations (made to accord with those of the Arctic Council) rather than coinciding with county-level (administrative) borders, such as those applied in Barents and Northern Sparsely Populated Areas cooperation. The history of Arctic description and present policy development thus lend credence to region-building as an approach, given that they illustrate how descriptions of regions are used for different purposes.[73]

However, although they include or refer to some Arctic discourse features, official Swedish documents express a resistance to the less area-attuned focus presented in EU documents that were drawn up early in the process, that is, following the 2008 five-state meeting that prompted much of the EU's (and thereby also Sweden's) increased focus on the Arctic. A critique of the identification of Arctic issues on the EU level is provided in the statement of the Swedish Foreign Affairs Commission, which notes that in a previous document, the European Commission highlighted only issues it had so far "come into contact with." In Nordic Council work, which it refers to as relevant for coordinating work on Arctic issues, Sweden has adopted a focus highlighting broader development and welfare issues, one that is notably different from that seen in the frontier-related discourse on the Arctic.

Some of the emergent tendencies in how the "Arctic" is treated in this context thus promise a development whereby "Arctic" discourse at large may be brought more into the mainstream of regional development and distanced from the historical and mythical descriptions that have prevailed. By attracting greater economic interest as a result of the risks and consequences brought on by climate change—and thereby the interest of a broader community of states—the "Arctic" may thus move toward being normalized as a region, coming to be placed within Northern Dimension and other more general development frameworks.

However, at the same time, the increasing interest in the region will result in larger development conflicts between the different stakes in the sizable resources available there—and potential environmental as well as security conflicts. Although the region may move toward normalization in terms of being described within general regional development frameworks, a significant risk nevertheless remains that it will continue to be a focus for exploitation by parties external to it for geopolitical and economic gain. Whereas states previously benefited from using the "Arctic" as a blank canvas on which to project ideas, they now stand to benefit from economic development of the region if they can amass the geopolitical standing to capitalize on these. Development may thus still remain directed from outside rather than within what is in very general and varying terms defined as a "region." Given that the "Arctic region" has developed to such a high extent based on the aim of avoiding strategic conflict after the Cold War, the determination of low-politics issues for the Arctic Council, Barents Euro-Arctic Council, or Baltic Council may actually matter less to many of the national players than the fact that these developments offer insights into the national actors. As a result, the fluid and vacuous nature of "the Arctic" (including its geographical delineation) seen thus far in much of the development that is termed "Arctic" should perhaps not be a surprise.

Sweden has taken a stance in highlighting issues within the region, including descriptions that center on not only the traditional indigenous discourse but also local development for all people in the region. This conception resonates with sub-regional (Barents and NSPA) priorities as well as general Nordic ones. Sweden may have the chance to redefine what issues are seen as Arctic if it is able to continue to look beyond the established fora that address Arctic-level policies and interests.

Acknowledgment: The author is grateful for funding by the Mistra Arctic Futures program.

Figure 6. Arctic interests.

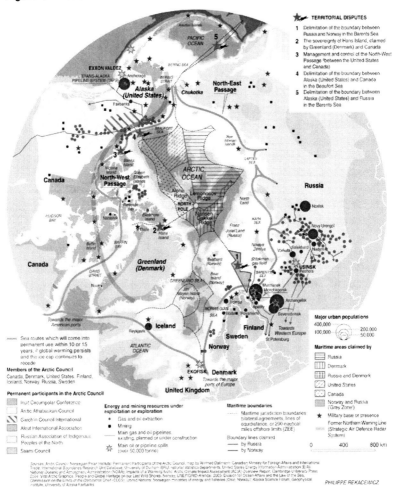

Source: Reproduced from R. Kefferpütz and D. Bocharev, *Expanding the EU's Institutional Capacities in the Arctic Region: Policy Briefing and Key Recommendations* (Brussels: Heinrich Böll Stiftung, EU Regional Office, 2008).

NOTES

1. E. C. H. Keskitalo, *Constructing "the Arctic": Discourses of International Region-Building* (Rovaniemi, Finland: Acta Universitatis Lapponiensis 47, 2002); and E. C. H. Keskitalo, *Negotiating the Arctic: The Construction of an International Region* (London and New York: Routledge, 2004).
2. Initially suggested in Canada as an "Arctic Basin Council." Cf. Keskitalo, *Negotiating the Arctic.*
3. Keskitalo, *Negotiating the Arctic.*
4. Keskitalo, *Constructing "the Arctic,"* and Keskitalo, *Negotiating the Arctic.*
5. Ibid.
6. B. Anderson, *Imagined Communities: Reflections on the Origin and Spread of Nationalism* (London and New York: Verso, 1996).
7. I. B. Neumann, *Russia and the Idea of Europe: A Study in Identity and International Relations* (London: Routledge, 1996).
8. A. K. Henrikson, "'Wings for Peace': Open Skies and Transpolar Civil Aviation," in *Vulnerable Arctic: Need for an Alternative Reorientation,* Research Report no. 47, ed. J. Käkönen (Tampere: Tampere Peace Research Institute, 1992), 107.
9. Ibid.
10. U. C. Knoepflmacher and G. B. Tennyson, *Nature and the Victorian Imagination* (Berkeley: University of California Press, 1977).
11. D. Pharand, "The Case for an Arctic Region Council and a Treaty Proposal," *Revue Générale de Droit* 23 (1992): 163–195; and Keskitalo, *Negotiating the Arctic.*
12. D. Scrivener, *Environmental Cooperation in the Arctic: From Strategy to Council,* paper submitted for publication to the Norwegian Atlantic Committee, Oslo, January 18, 1996, 13.
13. A. Y. Roginko, "Conflict between Environment and Development in the Soviet Arctic," in *Vulnerable Arctic: Need for an Alternative Reorientation,* Research Report no. 47, ed. J. Käkönen (Tampere: Tampere Peace Research Institute, 1992), 148.
14. K. Coates, "The Discovery of the North: Towards a Conceptual Framework for the Study of Northern/Remote Regions," *Northern Review* 12, no. 13 (1994): 21.
15. Keskitalo, *Negotiating the Arctic.*

16. AHDR [Arctic Human Development Report], *Arctic Human Development Report* (Akureyri, Iceland: Stefansson Arctic Institute, 2004).
17. E. Niemi, "Sami History and the Frontier Myth: A Perspective on Northern Sami Spatial and Rights History," in *Sami Culture in a New Era: The Norwegian Sami Experience*, ed. H. Gaski (Karasjok, Norway: Davvi Girji OS, 1997), 79.
18. B. Kramvig, "I kategorienes vold," in *Samer og nordmenn*, ed. H. Eidheim (Oslo: Cappelen Akademisk Forlag, 1999), 137.
19. O. Young, *The Pace of Change: Arctic State Changes: Implications for Governance* (Ottawa: Canadian Arctic Resources Committee, 2009), 10.
20. See, e.g., A. Crawford, A. Hanson, and D. Runnalls, *Arctic Sovereignty and Security in a Climate-Changing World* (Winnipeg: International Institute for Sustainable Development, 2008).
21. Keskitalo, *Negotiating the Arctic.*
22. C. E. Stålvant, "The Northern Dimension: A Policy in Need of an Institution?" BaltSeaNet Working Paper 1 (Gdansk/Berlin, 2001), 7.
23. European Commission, "Northern Dimension Policy Framework Document, 2006," http://ec.europa.eu/external_relations/north_dim/index_en.htm, 4.
24. Ibid.; cf. European Commission, "The Northern Dimension Policy, 2010," http://ec.europa.eu/external_relations/north_dim/index_en.htm.
25. European Commission, "Communication from the Commission to the European Parliament and the Council: The European Union and the Arctic Region. COM (2008) 763 Final" (Brussels: European Commission, 2008), 3.
26. Ibid., 10; and potentially including an Arctic Treaty, cf. T. Koivurova, E. J. Molenaar, and D. L. VanderZwaag, "Canada, the EU, and Arctic Ocean Governance: A Tangled and Shifting Seascape and Future Directions," *Journal of Transnational Law and Policy* 18, no. 2 (2009): 247–288.
27. European Commission, "Communication from the Commission to the European Parliament and the Council," 10–11.
28. Ibid., 11.
29. Council of the European Union, *Council Conclusions on Arctic Issues*, 2985th Foreign Affairs Council meeting, Brussels, December 8, 2009.
30. European Commission, "Communication from the Commission to the European Parliament and the Council," 2n.
31. Ibid., 4.
32. Ibid., 7.

33. R. Kefferpütz and D. Bocharev, *Expanding the EU's Institutional Capacities in the Arctic Region: Policy Briefing and Key Recommendations* (Brussels: Heinrich Böll Stiftung, EU Regional Office, 2008), 11.
34. Ibid.
35. Swedish Foreign Affairs Committee [Utrikesutskottet], Meddelande om EU och Arktis. Utrikesutskottets utlåtande 2009/10: UU4. Sveriges riksdag, Stockholm, 1.
36. Ibid., 5.
37. Ibid., 6.
38. Ibid.
39. European Parliament, "Motion for a European Parliament Resolution on a Sustainable EU Policy for the High North" (Brussels: European Parliament, 2010), point C.
40. Ibid., point II.53.
41. Ibid., point I.8.
42. Ibid., points III.56–58.
43. European Parliament, "European Parliament Resolution of 20 January 2011 on a Sustainable EU Policy for the High North" (2009/2214 (INI)) (Strasbourg: European Parliament, 2011), point 8.
44. Ibid.
45. Ibid., point 56.
46. Cf. D. Rudd, "Northern Europe's Arctic Defence Agenda," *Journal of Military and Strategic Studies* 12, no. 3 (2010): 45–71.
47. U. Ahlin et al., *En rödgrön politik för Sveriges relationer med världens länder*, policy statement (February 17, 2010), 5.
48. A. Karlqvist, *Svensk polarforskning: Ett utredningsuppdrag* (Stockholm: Vetenskapsrådet, 2006).
49. N. Granholm and I. Kiesow, *Olja och gas i ett nytt och förändrat Arktis: Energifrågans utveckling mot bakgrund av regionens strategiska dynamik* (Stockholm: Swedish Research Defence Agency [FOI], 2010).
50. Ibid., 65.
51. Ibid., 4.
52. N. Granholm, ed., *Arktis—Strategiska frågor i en region i förändring* (Stockholm: Swedish Defence Research Agency [FOI], 2008), 4.
53. Ibid.
54. N. Granholm, *Delar av ett nytt Arktis—Utvecklingar av dansk, kanadensisk, isländsk arktispolitik* (Stockholm: Swedish Defence Research Agency [FOI], 2009), 9.
55. Ibid., 62.

56. Ibid., 10.
57. Nordic Council of Ministers, *Hållbar utveckling—En ny kurs för Norden*, ANP Report 2009: 726 (Copenhagen: Nordic Council of Ministers, 2009).
58. T. Stoltenberg, *Nordic Cooperation on Foreign and Security Policy* (Oslo: Norwegian Government, 2009).
59. Ibid., 19.
60. H. Corell, "Chairman's Conclusions," in *Common Concern for the Arctic*, ed. Nordic Council of Ministers (Copenhagen: Nordic Council of Ministers, 2008), 15.
61. H. Asgrimsson and C. Husmark Pehrsson, "Introduction," in *Common Concern for the Arctic*, ed. Nordic Council of Ministers (Copenhagen: Nordic Council of Ministers, 2008), 11.
62. C. Bildt, "Working for a More Eco-Efficient Economy of the Barents Region," in *Swedish Chairmanship of the Barents Euro-Arctic Council, 2009–2011*, ed. Swedish Chair of the Barents Euro-Arctic Council (Kirkenes: International Barents Secretariat, 2009).
63. County Administrative Board of Norrbotten. "'Var finns Norrbotten och Sverige i Barentssamarbetet?'" Presentation för föreningen Norden, Luleå, May 6, 2008.
64. NSPA, "Welcome to the Northern Sparsely Populated Areas," http://www.nspa-network.eu/, para. 2.
65. NSPA, "The Northern Sparsely Populated Areas (NSPA) Political Statement Summary," January 28, 2010, http://www.nspa-network.eu/, 1.
66. Ibid.
67. Swedish Department of Foreign Affairs, "Sveriges strategi för den arktiska regionen" (Stockholm: Department of Foreign Affairs, 2011), http://www.sweden.gov.se/sb/d/1390/a/168312, 13.
68. Ibid., 17.
69. Ibid., 24.
70. Ibid., 31.
71. Ibid., 34.
72. Ibid., 35.
73. See Neumann, *Russia and the Idea of Europe*.

CHAPTER 11

FINLAND AS AN ARCTIC AND EUROPEAN STATE

FINLAND'S NORTHERN DIMENSION (POLICY)

Lassi Heininen

INTRODUCTION

Finland is geographically one of the world's northernmost countries. It is located in northern Europe and is an integral part of the Nordic region. It is also one of the eight Arctic states and has cultural, environmental, economic, political, and security interests in the region. According to official statements, "Finland has a primordial interest toward Arctic issues. Our geography and history make us an Arctic state."[1] This is emphasized in the country's Arctic strategy, which states, "As an Arctic country, Finland is a natural actor in the Arctic region."[2] Indeed, Finland has been active in, and even a forerunner of, recent international northern and Arctic initiatives, most notably the Arctic Environmental Protection Strategy (AEPS) and the European Union's Northern Dimension.[3] Despite this, Finland's circumpolar interests temporarily waned in the beginning of the 2000s.

Because of the significant and multifunctional change of the Arctic in the early twenty-first century, after the five coastal states of the Arctic Ocean held their first meeting in Ilulissat, Greenland, in May 2008, and after the first modern Arctic strategies were adopted, it could be argued that Finland "woke up" and started (again) to become interested in the Arctic region and issues. This renewed interest toward the Arctic was supported by the report on the Arctic of the Finnish Parliament in November 2009 and emphasized in Finland's Strategy for the Arctic Region, which was adopted in June 2010.

This chapter on Finland as a northern European country and Arctic nation examines its Northern Dimension policy and Arctic strategy. It begins with a brief introduction to Finland as a northern (European) and Nordic country, before moving to a discussion of the so-called de facto northern dimension (policy) of Finland. It then discusses Finland's deeper movement into Europe by way of its Northern Dimension initiative. Finally, the chapter considers Finland's Arctic strategy and provides analysis of Finland as an Arctic and (northern) European country. Finland adopted its first comprehensive strategy for the Arctic region in 2010, which clearly asserts Finland as an Arctic as well as (northern) European state. Based on the strategy, Finland provides strong support of international cooperation in Arctic issues and emphasizes the importance of stability based on international treaties. This is much in keeping with the long-term national interests of Finland.

FINLAND AS A NORTHERN AND NORDIC COUNTRY

Although Finland has a northern identity, the country is culturally and geopolitically located somewhere between East and West. Indeed, the Finns have long been influenced by a diversity of Eastern and Western cultures, and it is difficult to understand Finland without reference to this history.[4]

Following Finland's defeat in World War II, and particularly during the Cold War, Finland's foreign policy strongly emphasized the importance of a good relationship with the Soviet Union. In the post–Cold War period, this has been continued by good relations with Russia despite Finland's EU membership. The Friendship, Cooperation and Mutual Assistance (FCMA) agreement between Finland and the Soviet Union (in 1948) together with the Peace Treaty of Paris (in 1947) formed the basis for Finland's relations vis-à-vis the East (the so-called foreign policy of Paasikivi-Kekkonen). Although this was advantageous to Finland, for example by making a growing foreign trade with the Soviet Union possible, the policy was criticized in the West as Finland bowing to the Soviet Union and was negatively referred to as "Finlandization."[5]

The special relationship with the Soviet Union was not only positive for Finland's economy but also made it possible for Finland to have good relations with the West, including the United States. For example, it made it possible for Finland to maintain neutrality in foreign policy while being an active participant in international politics for peace and disarmament. It also allowed Finland to join in European economic integration efforts, such as the European Free Trade Area (EFTA) and later the European Union. During this period, Nordic cooperation—Finland joined the Nordic Council in 1955[6]—was important, given that it constituted the closest multilateral as well as Western international environment for Finland, an environment that concretely demonstrated Finland's position between the East and the West.[7]

Though the collapse of the Soviet Union and the end of the Cold War were a surprise, even a shock, to the Finnish political elite as well as a surprise to the majority of the Finnish people, these events helped Finland as a nation to become more open toward European integration.[8] Behind such feeling was, however, an acceptance by many that European integration was the only real option for Finland's future. Finland joined the European Community in 1995, and the irony is that Nordic cooperation, which after the end of the Cold War was initiated as an alternative to European integration, was, in the second half of the 1990s, seen by the political elite as something rather old-fashioned and no longer needed because of the possibility of being actively present in the (Western) European integration process.

As a result of, and following, these pivotal events, Finland's geopolitical and security-political positions have changed significantly. For example, although Finland is still militarily non-aligned and maintains its own independent army, it cooperates closely with NATO and its member states. One thing, however, did not change: the Finnish "Northern" identity and the Finns' natural inclination to be interested in and oriented toward the entire North, as the Finnish-Karelian national epic, *The Kalevala*, indicates.

FINLAND'S DE FACTO NORTHERN DIMENSION

An important part of this Finnish interest in the North is access to the Arctic Ocean. In the beginning of the nineteenth century, under Russian rule, some Finnish civil servants and politicians expressed a desire to the Russian emperor to have territory that extended to the coastline of the Barents Sea. In 1920, newly independent Finland and Soviet Russia signed a peace treaty that gave the Pechenga area (Petsamo in Finnish) to Finland, and with it a small part of the Arctic Ocean's coastline. The history of Pechenga, and the Petsamo Municipality, is a fascinating one spanning almost 200 years that saw a few examples of Finland's strong ambitions in Arctic affairs as well as a couple of sudden losses of interest by the Finnish political elite in the Arctic, which has often been seen as a marginalized periphery.[9]

In general, the North has been a rather delicate issue for Finland, in terms of both domestic policy, as indicated earlier, and foreign policy. After World War II, Finland issued a policy of neutrality and peace including a major bilateral foreign trade agreement, which was mostly trade by barter, with the Soviet Union. Correspondingly, there were the beginnings of Nordic cooperation and gradual integration with Western Europe. Even though Finland had been active in international northern and Arctic undertakings since the late 1980s, and successfully initiated the AEPS, it did not have a special northern or Arctic policy as part of its international, European, or Nordic (foreign) policy until the launch of the Finnish initiative on the European Union's Northern Dimension in 1997.

Taking into consideration Finland's foreign policy and its activities in the Nordic region and northern Europe more generally, one can interpret that Finland has, however, long had somewhat of a de facto northern dimension to its foreign policy.[10] Finland's policy of neutrality and peace entailed activities with regard to confidence-building measures concerning northern Europe and northern seas that extended to promoting Nordic cooperation through its membership in the North Calotte Council, which was established in 1967. The "northern dimension" of its foreign policy was further reflected in the Finnish initiative for international cooperation on environmental protection in the Arctic in 1989, following President Mikhail Gorbachev's speech in 1987,[11] that led to the AEPS, which was signed by ministers of the eight Arctic states in 1991 in Rovaniemi, Finland.

Finland is a founding member of the Barents Euro-Arctic Region (BEAR), which was established in 1993. It was based on a 1992 Norwegian initiative, and therefore it was not so easy for the Finnish political elite to accept. Behind such reluctance were Finland's special relations with the Soviet Union, as well as the fact that Finnish policy makers and business leaders were used to being given priority when it came to Russia and relations with the Russians. After the collapse of the Soviet Union and the end of the Cold War, there was a new geopolitical reality in (northern) Europe. By way of the European Union's Northern Dimension initiative, Finland felt it could get some compensation for its "lost privileges" in Russian relations.

THE FINNISH INITIATIVE ON A NORTHERN DIMENSION

The EU's Northern Dimension was initiated in 1997 by the Finnish government and developed further by the EU Commission.[12] The Northern Dimension policy placed northern, and partly also Arctic, issues on the political agenda of the European Union, and further, it led to the EU's Northern Dimension policy as stated by the European Council between 1997 and 1999. As an EU external policy, the Northern Dimension was approved and implemented by the first Action Plan in 2000 and the second one in 2003. The new "Policy Framework Document of the Northern Dimension," which was adopted in 2006, has emerged as a common policy of the EU, the Russian Federation, Iceland, and Norway for northern Europe.[13]

Originally, the Northern Dimension policy was primarily defined to be one of the external, foreign policies of the EU in northern Europe, particularly toward (northwest) Russia, but also including an Arctic aspect. Consequently, the main aims of the first Action Plan of the Northern Dimension were to increase stability and civic security, to enhance democratic reforms, and to create positive interdependence and sustainable development.[14] In this process, the partner countries and Greenland had an almost equal voice and were able to put forward initiatives, such as the "Arctic Window" within the Northern Dimension, which was initiated by the Home Rule government of Greenland in 1999. Although not always explicitly mentioned, the Arctic region, mostly meaning the European Arctic, has been an approach, or a cross-cutting issue, within the Northern Dimension policy.[15] Correspondingly, the Policy Framework Document of the EU's Northern Dimension is rhetorically a strong statement to promote dialogue and concrete cross-border cooperation and to strengthen stability and integration in the European part of the Arctic region.[16] All this is mostly according to long-term interests and aims of Finland and Finland's de facto northern dimension policy.

The main objective of the EU's Northern Dimension was to facilitate multilateral and/or bilateral cooperation between the Nordic countries and Russia across the national borders. Such cooperation needed to focus first on practical issues that would be in the fields of the so-called low politics and away from the political complexities of a legally binding international agreement. Among the fields of practical and functional cooperation are environmental protection (e.g., nuclear safety); economic development and cooperation (e.g., on energy); scientific and technology cooperation; social welfare, health, and well-being; and justice and home affairs (e.g., human trafficking). Perhaps the most relevant and important field here is environmental protection, particularly in the context of nuclear safety. It has been used as an example of a means to decrease military tension and increase confidence in international northern cooperation. In fact, it became the first field of cooperation for the newborn intergovernmental and multilateral Arctic cooperation between the eight Arctic states under the auspices of the AEPS.[17]

From the point of view of Finland, an initiative in the context of the European Union, which was made less than three years after Finland had joined the EU, was to make sure that the EU did not move only geographically toward the North and that Finland would be taken seriously as a European country among the established EU member states. Furthermore, with this initiative the Finnish government redefined Finland's relations with southern Europe and geopolitically remapped itself alongside Germany. Thus, Finland repositioned itself as a key player in Europe's Arctic issues. Membership in the EU with a focus on deeper political cooperation and integration was perceived by Finland as a security measure against any future threat from Russia, particularly in the absence of a NATO membership.

Thus, the Finnish initiative on the Northern Dimension as well as the concept behind it is according to the state interest of Finland, and that of the other Nordic countries, but it is also generally according to the post–Cold War state politics in north Europe.[18] In spite of this, it is not clear if the Northern Dimension has in the second decade of the twenty-first century the state interests of Finland as a high priority.

In some ways the Finnish initiative resembles the Norwegian initiative on the BEAR, because the two initiatives share many of the same premises and aims:[19] First, they can be interpreted as gateways for Norway and Finland to be associated with an integrated Europe and the European Union; although Norway is not an EU member state, it belongs to the European Economic Area. Furthermore, they can be interpreted as efforts to transform the geopolitics of these remote Nordic countries having an influence in the (European) North and by bringing northern, partly Arctic, regions and issues to the political agenda of the European Union. This might be relevant to remember and take into consideration during the next decade, when the European Union would like to become a real Arctic actor and develop its own Arctic strategy.[20]

Second, the Finnish and Norwegian initiatives can be taken as good examples of the so-called "stability" policy by, or the peace project of, the West—i.e., the Western countries and alliances in the 1990s.[21] In this policy the ultimate aim was to decrease the (military) tension of the Cold War, particularly in northern seas and the "military theaters" of the Cold War, such as the Barents Sea region.[22] Indeed, when the Northern Dimension became part of the political agenda of the EU, it was defined as "a part of the external and cross-border policies of the Union toward Russia."[23]

Behind this was the legacy of the Cold War with Russia as the main, though former, adversary of that period. Though the EU had several policies as a means to deal with Russia—such as the Partnership and Cooperation Agreement, TACIS, and the EU's Strategy on Russia, and later the four Common Spaces between the Union and the Russian Federation[24]— Russia was, and is still, seen as one of the biggest, if not the biggest, challenge to the EU.[25] Enhanced stability and peace in the post–Cold War period was therefore much needed when Russia was mostly seen as the "Other." Furthermore, one of the aims was to create a new kind of cooperative model for the divided north Europe region that would go beyond the "Iron Curtain" and be fruitful for further cooperation.[26] As a result of all these activities, in post–Cold War northern Europe, as well as throughout the Arctic region, there is much less military tension and more stability than during the Cold War period. Thus, the ultimate aim of both the EU's Northern Dimension and the BEAR to decrease military tension and increase stability and peace has been achieved. Furthermore, in the early twenty-first century, these regions, including one of the hottest military "theaters" of the Cold War, the Barents Sea region, are not overtly plagued by a war or armed conflict and are not even in potential danger of being so—as such they are among the most peaceful areas of the globe.[27]

Thirdly, cooperation through the Northern Dimension policy as well as the BEAR deals mostly with functional cooperation across national borders in certain priority fields and sectors, which are pragmatic. This is based on interests, agendas, and policies of the founding states, a process that prefers functional cooperation on areas of low politics and excludes traditional security and security policy. Although it has been said that the Northern Dimension of the EU is neither a regional initiative nor a regional policy, it is possible to interpret that it has elements of region-building, too. For example, according to the Policy Framework Document, the EU's Northern Dimension is for the promotion of dialogue and cooperation, economic integration, and sustainable development in north Europe on "areas of cooperation where a regional and sub-regional emphasis brings added value." Thus, the current Northern Dimension can also be interpreted to support the discourse of region-building (in the North) by state actors through, for example, an equal partnership of the EU, the Russian Federation, Iceland, and Norway, and the objective of visa-free travel between the EU and Russia. Further, the EU's Northern Dimension represents a state policy and initiative for the "new" north Europe of the post–Cold War without divisions and the Iron Curtain, where trans-boundary cooperation is not only possible but exciting and encouraged.

Fourth, both regional initiatives have attracted several non-state actors—research institutions, environmental movements, civil organizations, and sub-national governments—to become involved through bottom-up activities across national borders in various areas.[28] Here the "new" north Europe, or the western part of the Eurasian North, can be interpreted to be a microcosm, or workshop, for a study on relations of different international actors, transformations of political systems, and transition periods of the international system.

All in all, the aim of the EU's Northern Dimension defined by the Finnish government and Finnish policy makers was to bring Finland to and beside the tables of the EU, and also to its inner circles, where decisions are made. The presumption that this policy "empowers" Finland within the EU fold has met with some cynicism among the Finnish political elite. And actually, this was the main reason why Finland also joined the European Monetary Union (EMU) and the Euro Area—the decision was taken by the majority of the Parliament, and there was no referendum on the matter. Although the Northern Dimension is not always interpreted within Finland to be a success, the fact is that it became one of the external policies of the Union. From the point of view of Finland's foreign policy, this can, and maybe should, be interpreted as a big success.

In spite of the EU's Northern Dimension and the other successful initiatives such as the AEPS, Finland has neither shown great and continuous interest, at all times, toward the entire Arctic region nor had an (official) Arctic strategy or policy of its own before its first Arctic Strategy, adopted in 2010.[29]

FINLAND'S ARCTIC STRATEGY

The Finnish Ministry of Foreign Affairs began a process of developing Finland's Arctic agenda with the objective of creating a policy or strategy during the first decade of the twenty-first century. This was as a result of the significant and multifunctional change(s) in the Arctic, and after the five coastal states of the Arctic Ocean had their first meeting in Ilulissat in May 2008 and adopted their respective Arctic strategies or state policies, Finland realized that there is a new state of the Arctic and started to become interested again in Arctic issues. An ambassador for Arctic issues was named as Finland's "own northern envoy" in the summer of 2009. The Foreign Minister Alexander Stubb stated in a speech in Rovaniemi in September 2009 that "Finland needs a comprehensive and ambitious Arctic strategy of its own."[30] Previously, in July 2008, the Ministry of Foreign Affairs had prepared a confidential memorandum that served as a foundation for a national debate and policy statement on Arctic issues.[31]

The minister's speech sparked a growing interest in Arctic issues within Finland, particularly with regard to economic interests, in light of climate change. This emerging interest was especially evident among stakeholders in businesses and organizations involved in the pursuit of regional development, economics, and trade. This growing interest toward the Arctic was accelerated and supported by the report on "Finland and the Arctic Regions" issued by the Foreign Affairs Committee of the Finnish Parliament, as well as by a general discussion of Finland's activities in the Arctic at the Parliament in November 2009.[32] The first seminar of a Finnish research network on Northern Politics and Security Studies took place in September 2009 and the second one in Helsinki in February 2010 with representatives from the Ministry of Foreign Affairs.[33] A couple of days after the latter seminar, a working group representing all the ministries was appointed by the Prime Minister's Office in February 2010 "to prepare a report on Finland's policy review for the Arctic region."[34] By April 2010, the government had appointed an Advisory Board on Arctic Affairs to supervise follow-up work on the strategy and support, monitor, and harmonize Finland's activities in the Arctic.[35]

"Finland's Strategy for the Arctic Region" was adopted by the Finnish Cabinet Committee on the European Union (of the Government) in June 2010.[36] It is based on proposals made by the aforementioned working group of civil servants from different ministries (appointed by the Prime Minister's Office). The issue re-emerged on the agenda of the Foreign Policy Committee of the Finnish Parliament in autumn 2010, when the committee had its hearings and discussion on the strategy. The strategy defines Finland's objectives in the following substantial sectors: the environment, economic activities and know-how, transport and infrastructure, and indigenous peoples. These are followed by a list of the different levels of means with which to reach these Arctic policy goals. Additionally there is a chapter on the European Union and the Arctic Region. Finally, the strategy includes the principle conclusions and proposes further measures.[37]

At the very beginning, the strategy document states that Finland is one of the northernmost nations of the globe and that "as an Arctic country, Finland is a natural actor in the Arctic region."[38] The Arctic region is a stable and peaceful area, but, it adds, significant changes are taking place in the region, including climate change and increased transportation. As the global significance of the region grows, so does its geopolitical significance. Because of all this, a holistic evaluation on the current situation and circumstances is required, and it is briefly touched upon in the introduction to the strategy. All in all, the strategy has a specific focus on external relations. In addition to an introduction, the document consists of six substantial chapters, conclusions, and appendices. The first four chapters—"Fragile Arctic Nature," "Economic Activities and Know-How," "Transport and Infrastructure," and "Indigenous Peoples"—define Finland's political objectives in those important sectors. They are followed by a chapter on "Arctic Policy Tools," which includes policy activities at global and regional levels, bilateral cooperation, and funding. The next chapter, "The EU and the Arctic Region," deals with Finland's policy objectives on the European Union's activities in the Arctic. The final chapter presents conclusions and proposes further measures, and the document is rounded off by several informative and illustrative appendices, including maps.

According to the first section of the strategy, "Fragile Arctic Nature," Finland's policy objectives are described in the four substantial sections. "[T]he environmental perspective must be taken into account in all activities in the region, and climate change, pollution and biodiversity be given considerable attention."[39] Climate change is defined as one of the most serious challenges to the Arctic, and increased human activity in the region raises the risk of environmental pollution. Finland's main objectives here are threefold: first, to draw attention to the special features and risks facing the natural Arctic environment in international organizations; second, to give strong support for Arctic research, the development of regional climate models, and the monitoring of the environment as the basis for decision making; and third, to promote nuclear safety, particularly in the Kola Peninsula.[40] It is also said that Arctic research, regional climate models, and long-term monitoring of the environment should feed into decision-making processes, clearly indicating the importance of the interplay between science and politics.

Finland's objectives in "economic activities and know-how" are summarized by the slogan "Finnish know-how must be utilised and supported"[41] and are, first, to strengthen Finland's role as an international expert on Arctic issues; second, to make better use of Finnish technological expertise in winter shipping, transport, and shipbuilding; and third, to expand opportunities of Finnish companies to benefit from their Arctic expertise and know-how in the large and mega-large projects of the Barents region.

Finland's objectives in "Transport and Infrastructure" are, first, to improve business opportunities in the Arctic by developing transport, communication, logistical networks, and border crossings; second, to develop transport routes in the Barents region; and third, to harmonize international regulations concerning the safety of shipping and environmental protection in the Arctic region. Though the development of transport, communication, and logistic networks (in northern Finland and the Barents region) is emphasized, there is an urgent need to ensure safe navigation in northern seas, in terms of both the physical impact of climate change and growth in seagoing transport.

The fourth sector of the strategy, "Indigenous Peoples," will be realized by facilitating the participation of indigenous peoples in matters to do with their affairs, to safeguard the funding needed for efficient participation, and to strengthen the status of the Barents region's indigenous peoples in the work of the Arctic Council (AC) and the Barents Euro-Arctic Council (BEAC). Finland intends to continue backing the struggle of the Saami and other (northern) indigenous peoples. Absent, however, is a clear objective for Finland to ratify the ILO 169 Convention, which is long overdue and important for the Saami and their self-determination.

Correspondingly, Finland's Arctic policy tools include, first, to emphasize the AC as the primary cooperation forum on Arctic issues; second, to strengthen the BEAC vis-à-vis the EU as the voice of regional actors; third, to strengthen Finland's representation in the Russian North; and fourth, to use the neighboring area-cooperation funds to enable Finland's participation in multinational Arctic organizations. Several levels of international agreement and intergovernmental organization are mentioned, for instance, the United Nations Convention on the Law of the Sea (UNCLOS) and the International Maritime Organization (IMO) at the global level, and the AC, the BEAC, and the Nordic Council of Ministers at the regional level.

In declaring the Arctic Council as the main forum for Arctic affairs and policy and striving to promote international cooperation on Arctic issues at the global and regional level, as well as bilaterally, Finland is taking an important and timely step. Here it is imperative that the mandate of the council be renegotiated and broadened, as Finland has proposed, so that it can leave its current state of political "inability" behind. The question is, however, if there is enough political will among the eight Arctic states to do that and, further, whether they ready to engage with relevant non-state northern actors as well as non-Arctic states.

A special chapter on the European Union emphasizes the EU's recognition of "the importance of the Arctic Region"[42] and that the Union is accepted as a (global) Arctic player. Here, Finland—which could be seen to be promoting itself as an advocate of the EU in Arctic affairs—has the following three objectives: first, for the EU to take account of the special features of the Arctic in its various policy sectors and increase its contributions in the region. The EU's (emerging) Arctic policy should be developed further, in such a way as to give politics priority over economics. Second, the EU is to be approved as an observing member of the Arctic Council; and third, the EU's Northern Dimension is mentioned as a central tool for emerging Arctic policy in terms of external relations.

Finally, the conclusions of the strategy include a summary of the aforementioned objectives and proposals. They also present three general objectives for Finland's policy in the Arctic.[43] First, "Cooperation based on international treaties lays the foundation for Finland's activities in the Arctic region"; second, "Finland strives to increase international cooperation in Arctic issues at global and regional levels and in bilateral relations"; and third, "Finland considers it important that the EU develop its Arctic policy" and proposes to establish an EU Arctic Information Centre in Finland.

ANALYZING FINLAND'S ARCTIC STRATEGY AND POLICY[44]

When analyzing the strategy, there are a few relevant and interesting findings that describe Finland as an Arctic as well as (northern) European state: First, the strategy is comprehensive and ambitious and reflects great efforts in preparing and outlining Finland's first Arctic strategy, with the country clearly asserting itself as an Arctic state while referring to the European Union as "a global Arctic player." The document was prepared by a working group appointed by the Prime Minister's Office consisting of civil servants rather than a broader advisory board representing different stakeholders. A working group with broader representation and a mandate to follow up on the strategy was appointed two months later. However, the whole process was greatly accelerated by the Finnish Parliament and promoted through its Foreign Policy Committee's statement,[45] as mentioned earlier. Second, the four main sectors and related objectives are according to Finland's long-term traditional, national, political, and economic interests in the Arctic and generally in northern regions; they were also mentioned in the statement by the Parliament's Foreign Policy Committee. However, it is not entirely clear if they are in fact real priorities or priority area(s) or if they are mostly objectives. The Finnish strategy document emphasizes economic activities, as do most of the other Arctic states' strategies. It is business-oriented with a strong emphasis on economic activity, coupled with expertise and know-how, particularly the utilization of natural resources in the Arctic region. For example, it supports increasing marine traffic and transport and better infrastructure, and there is a perceived need to develop transport and other logistical networks in both the Barents region and north Finland. This is clearly indicated by a list of five transport networks and corridors of northern Finland, which are under discussion;[46] in reality only one or two of those might properly be implemented in the near future.[47] In contrast, some of the objectives, particularly those dealing with drilling for oil and gas in the Barents Sea, can be seen as hopeful expectations rather than realistic goals, although at least one Finnish company is involved in the Shtokman gas field project.[48] The same applied when the Snøhvit gas field in the Barents Sea was developed by the Norwegians; expectations among Finnish companies, particularly in north Finland, were high, but very little was gained by them from that project.

Thus, the strategy is business-oriented with a strong emphasis on economic activities, coupled with expertise, or know-how, particularly the utilization of natural resources, such as the oil and gas reserves of the Arctic region. To a certain extent, this is understandable, given that this is a national report that reflects strong Finnish national interests and expectations of stakeholders in both business and organizations engaged in the pursuit of regional development and economic interests. This is also in line with a strategic point of view, which emphasizes the importance of the High North's high strategic position and (global) energy security, and economically, thanks to its rich natural resources and potential for transportation (new global sea and air routes).

Third, the strategy reflects the desire to promote and strengthen Finland's position as an international expert on Arctic issues with know-how in the fields of winter shipping, sea transport, and shipbuilding technology, expertise in forest management, mining and metals industry, and cold-climate research. This sounds logical and sensible and might be the case in terms of some fields of research, but it is not necessarily the case when generally evaluating Finnish research in the context of international scientific cooperation.[49] Therefore, the proposal to launch a study program, with interdisciplinary and international cooperation on northern issues, is very welcome and needed.

Fourth, the strategy also emphasizes the special features of, and risks to, fragile Arctic ecosystems; importantly the term *fragile* has re-emerged, but of even greater importance is the protection of ecosystems. Climate change, pollution, and biodiversity receive considerable attention. A need for safe navigation in the Arctic Ocean is of great importance, both in terms of physical impacts of climate change and in terms of general increase in sea transports. Increasing sea transport is even defined as "the biggest threat to Arctic marine ecosystems,"[50] despite the fact that there are heavy impacts from long-range air and water pollution and mass-scale oil drilling. Furthermore, it says that Arctic research, regional climate models, and long-term monitoring of the state of the environment should feed into decision-making processes, clearly indicating the importance of the interplay between science and politics. Interestingly the uncertainty related to climate change is not emphasized (as a challenge), but nuclear safety in the Kola Peninsula is, though this problem has been under control for a few years now.

Although protecting Arctic ecosystems is prioritized, it seems somewhat short-sighted not to give greater emphasis to the promotion and export of Finnish know-how and expertise in environmental technology. Further, here the strategy has an inner contradiction. It states that "increased human activity in the region also raises the risk of environmental pollution,"[51] but then later in the text it states that "from the perspectives of Finnish—especially Northern Finnish—industry and employment, it is important that all types of economic activity increase both in large seaports and in land-based support areas of oil and gas fields in Norway and Russia."[52] Which of these is a priority? Is there a greater emphasis on more strict environmental protection, or is it mass-scale utilization of natural resources?

Fifth, likewise it shows a somewhat short-sighted view in a strategy like this with four broad priority areas to claim a focus "on external relations" and not adopt a holistic approach. For example, though somewhat abstract, it seems logical to give highest priority to protecting Arctic ecosystems, which are threatened or at risk from rapid climate change, for example by promoting and exporting Finnish know-how and expertise in environmental technology. Or, at the very least, one should identify more clearly linkages between the different sectors (i.e., the interactions of economic activities with both ecosystems and peoples) as is actually done later in the document when the "Arctic Window" of the Northern Dimension is introduced.[53] This would establish a more global perspective and invite an alternative interpretation as to why the Arctic region plays such an important role in world politics.

Sixth, the strategy includes objectives concerning indigenous peoples, particularly those of the Barents region such as the Saami, and their active participation in international cooperation. Absent, however, is a clear objective to ratify the ILO 169 Convention, which would be very timely and relevant for the Saami and their self-determination. Furthermore, Finland believes that UNCLOS is, and will be, a sufficient frame-work and tool to resolve Arctic issues and that there is no need for a new international, legally binding agreement or regime. Albeit political realism, this is a rather traditional and narrow state-oriented approach, when the real challenges are comprehensive and global, and request the attention and participation of a global community including a discourse on the global commons, coupled with a desire to engage in new ways of thinking.

Seventh, the strategy is perhaps at its best when emphasizing that the Arctic region is a stable and peaceful area ("High North—low tension") and that Finland supports "non-conflictual rules."[54] Further, in recog-nizing that significant changes are taking place, when for example, the global importance of the Arctic climate is obvious, consequently, the global significance of the region is increased. This is a clear statement in support of both the main discourse of the Arctic being a stable and peaceful region in spite of its challenges and a recent and emerging discourse on globalization.[55]

In declaring that the Arctic Council is now and should continue to be the main forum on Arctic affairs and policy, "Finland strives to increase international cooperation in the Arctic" at many levels and bilaterally.[56] This statement is both very important and timely. It is imperative that the mandate of the council be renegotiated and broadened so that it may move away from its current state, which is some sort of political "inability." Thus, there may be a good cause to organize a summit of the Arctic states, as Finland has proposed,[57] where challenges of the future, such as the interrelationship between the utilization of natural resources and the fragile environment, as well as the mandate of the AC and its further development will be discussed. In the meantime a more impor-tant and necessary prerequisite would be to have enough political will among the eight Arctic states to broaden the AC mandate and working methods to include discussion on the use of natural resources, security, and security policy.[58] Further, it is crucial that the Arctic states are ready for a deeper cooperation with all relevant non-state northern actors—such as indigenous peoples, academic institutions, and NGOs—and for them to be willing to enhance interactions with non-Arctic states interested in Arctic issues and thus allow the interested Asian and European states to become observers of the council, as well as with relevant intergovernmental organizations.

Finally, the strategy emphasizes the importance of the European Union's role in the Arctic region, referring to "the EU as a global Arctic player,"[59] and argues that the EU's Arctic policy should be further developed. This could be interpreted to mean that politics is a priority, trumping economics in the context of the union, though the reality in 2014 looks much the other way around. Consequently, Finland could be seen to be claiming itself an advocate for, or defender of, the EU in Arctic affairs. This sounds logical from Finland's point of view but may involve risks for Finland as an Arctic Council member and more generally in the context of multilateral Arctic cooperation. Behind this lies a divided opinion regarding the role of the EU as an Arctic actor among some Arctic states, particularly Canada, and northern indigenous peoples' organizations, particularly the Inuit Circumpolar Council (ICC), which is reflected in the somewhat hesitant responses to the EU's efforts.

All in all, Finland's Arctic strategy covers most of the features of a modern strategy document in adopting a holistic approach. It can also be seen as reflecting and responding to the recent significant and multifunctional environmental and geopolitical change(s) in the Arctic region and in its worldwide approach to the Arctic. It has neither clear priorities nor priority areas, though there is an apparent preference for economic activities including transport, infrastructure, and know-how and, in contrast, general objectives for international cooperation on Arctic issues based on international treaties.

CONCLUSION

In the early 1990s, Finland's geopolitical and security-political position fundamentally changed as a result of the collapse of the Soviet Union and the end of the Cold War. Finland keenly embraced the idea of political and economic (Western) European integration, though it is still militarily non-aligned and maintains its own independent army. One thing did not change, and that is the Finnish sense of a "northern" identity and some sort of "Arctic ambience."

The North has, however, been a rather delicate issue for Finland in terms of domestic policy and foreign policy. Finland is not a littoral state of the Arctic Ocean and has not shown great and continuous interest, at all times, toward the entire Arctic region. Nor did it have an (official) Arctic strategy or policy of its own as a part of its international, European, or Nordic (foreign) policy before the Arctic strategy of the 2010s. Finland is, maybe, more a Nordic and (northern) European country located geopolitically in the middle of northern Europe and neighboring Russia and having strong interests within the Baltic Sea region. Taking into consideration all this, its foreign policy, and its activities in the Nordic region and in northern Europe as a whole, Finland had some sort of a "de facto northern dimension" in its foreign policy. Relevant parts as well as results of this were Finland's two successful initiatives in the 1990s—first, the initiative for the Arctic Environmental Protection Strategy, which started the current intergovernmental cooperation in the Arctic and much promoted the foundation for the Arctic Council; and second, the Finnish initiative on a Northern Dimension of the European Union, which brought northern, and partly also Arctic, issues to the political agenda of the European Union and led to its Northern Dimension policy as one of the external foreign policies of the EU in north Europe.

Finally, based on the great efforts in preparing and outlining by the government and the Foreign Ministry, and promotion of the Parliament, Finland adopted its first strategy for the Arctic region in June 2010. It is comprehensive and ambitious and clearly asserts Finland as an Arctic as well as (northern) European state while referring to the European Union as "a global Arctic player." The Finnish strategy covers most features of a modern strategy adopting a holistic approach and responding to the recent significant and multifunctional (global) change in the Arctic region. It does not have clear priorities, though there is an apparent preference for economic activities. Finally, the strategy provides strong support of international cooperation in Arctic issues and emphasizes the importance of stability based on international treaties. This is much in keeping with the long-term national interests as well as the long-term foreign policy of Finland.

NOTES

1. Soili Mäkeläinen-Buhanist, *Finland's Approach to the Arctic: The Past and the Future*, Ministry for Foreign Affairs of Finland, Ottawa, Canada, May 27, 2010.

2. Prime Minister's Office, Finland, *Finland's Strategy for the Arctic Region* (Prime Minister's Office Publication, August 2010), 7.

3. Lassi Heininen, *Euroopan pohjoinen 1990-luvulla: Moniulotteisten ja ristiriitaisten intressien alue* (Rovaniemi, Finland: Acta Universitatis Lapponiensis 21—Arktisen keskuksen tiedotteita/Arctic Centre Reports 30, 1999).

4. Leif Salmén, "Rajamaa," *Helsingin Sanomat, Vierasykynä*, October 12, 1994, p. A2.

5. However, in the post–Cold War period, the term has been more deeply analyzed and partly re-evaluated to mean a wise policy by Finland and its political elite, also in the West.

6. For more information see, e.g., Håkan Branders, "Suomen liittyminen Pohjoismaiden neuvostoon," in *Suomi Pohjoismaana—Suomi 50 vuotta Pohjoismaiden neuvostossa*, ed. Larserik Häggman (Vaasa, Finland: Pohjola Norden, 2005), 8–16.

7. For more detailed information on Finland as a Nordic country, see *Suomi Pohjoismaana—Suomi 50 vuotta Pohjoismaiden neuvostossa*, ed. Larserik Häggman (Vaasa, Finland: Pohjola Norden, 2005).

8. Jyrki Käkönen, "Suomen ulkopolitiikan suuret traditiot ja tulevaisuuden valinnat." in *Uuden ulkopolitiikan haasteet: Kekkosen ajasta Koiviston kautta 2000-luvulle*, ed. Jouko Huru (Tampere, Finland: Rauhan- ja konfliktintutkimuslaitos, 1993), 23–48.

9. Heininen, *Euroopan pohjoinen 1990-luvulla*, 132–147; Maria Lähteenmäki, "Jäämeren valloitus—Naparetkeilijöitä ja skippareita Europan pohjoisilla rannoilla," in *Lappi—Maa, kansat, kulttuurit*, ed. Ilmo Massa and Hanna Snellman (Hämeenlinna, Finland: Suomalaisen Kirjallisuuden Seura, 2003), 64–83.

10. Heininen, *Euroopan pohjoinen 1990-luvulla*, 167–198; Lassi Heininen, "Ideas and Outcomes: Finding a Concrete Form for the Northern Dimension Initiative," in *The Northern Dimension: Fuel for the EU?*, ed. H. Ojanen (Kauhava, Finland: Ulkopoliittinen instituutti and Institut fur Europäis-

che Politik, Programme on the Northern Dimension of the CFSP, 2001), 20–53.

11. M. Gorbachev, "The Speech of President Mikhail Gorbachev on October 2, 1987 in Murmansk," *Pravda*, October 2, 1987.

12. The initiative was launched by the Finnish prime minister Paavo Lipponen in a speech delivered at an international conference in Rovaniemi, "Barents Region Today," on September 15, 1997. See Paavo Lipponen, "The European Union Needs a Policy for the Northern Dimension," in *Europe's Northern Dimension: The BEAR Meets the South*, ed. L. Heininen and R. Langlais (Rovaniemi, Finland: Publications of the Administrative Office of the University of Lapland, 1997), 39.

13. Heininen, "Ideas and Outcomes," 20–53.

14. The European Council, *Action Plan for Northern Dimension with External and Cross-Border Policies of the European Union 2000–2003*, Doc. no. 9401/00 NIS 78. Brussels, June 14, 2000.

15. For more information on the Finnish initiative and the chronology of the beginning of the Northern Dimension process, see Heininen, "Ideas and Outcomes."

16. *Policy Framework Document of the Northern Dimension of the European Union* (2006).

17. The Nordic-Russian bilateral cooperation on environmental protection, such as the Norwegian-Russian cooperation in 1992, had already started in the early 1990s.

18. Lassi Heininen, "The Barents Region in the State Interests and International Politics," *Barents Journal* 1, no. 7 (2009): 5–10.

19. Lassi Heininen, "Barents Euro-Arctic Region and Europe's Northern Dimension in State Interest—The 'BEAR' Meets the South," in *Arctic Geopolitics and Resource Futures*, ed. Mark Nuttall and Anita Dey Nuttall (Edmonton, Alberta: University of Alberta, forthcoming).

20. Commission of the European Communities, *Communication from the Commission to the European Parliament and the Council—The European Union and the Arctic Region*, Brussels, 20.11.2008 COM(2008) 763 final, 2008.

21. E.g., The European Council, *The Common Strategy of the European Union on Russia* (Cologne: The European Council, June 3 and 4, 1999); Lassi Heininen, "Building a Partnership—Russia as a Part of Europe," in *Northern Borders and Security—Dimensions for Regional Cooperation and Interdependence* (Turku, Finland: Turku School of Economics and Business Administration, 2002), 97–138.

22. Sverre Jervell, "10 Years of the Barents Cooperation," in *The Vision that Became Reality: The Regional Barents Cooperation 1993–2003*, ed. O. Pettersen (Kirkenes: The Barents Secretariat, 2002), 74–78; also Heininen, *Euroopan pohjoinen 1990-luvulla*, 236–239.

23. As a detail, one of the briefest definitions of the EU's Northern Dimension by a Finnish foreign affairs official is that "it is all about Russia!"

24. The four Common Spaces are Economic Cooperation; Freedom, Security, and Justice; External Security; and Research, Education, and Culture.

25. Heininen, "Building a Partnership," 97–138.

26. This was much supported, for example, by the European social-democratic parties, and social-democrats had the position of the then prime minister of Norway in 1992–1993 and of Finland in 1997.

27. E.g., Lassi Heininen, "Circumpolar International Relations and Cooperation," in *Globalization and the Circumpolar North*, ed. L. Heininen and C. Southcott (Fairbanks: University of Alaska Press, 2010), 265–304.

28. For example, the Baltic Forum for Non-Governmental Organizations is actively involved in the Northern Dimension.

29. An updated version of the strategy was adopted by the Finnish government in August 2013 (see *Finland's Strategy for the Arctic Region*, Prime Minister's Office Publications 16/2013).

30. Alexander Stubb, *A New Arctic Era and Finland's Arctic Policy*, keynote speech at the 20th Anniversary Seminar of the Arctic Centre, September 29, 2009 (mimeo).

31. Ulkoasiainministeriö, Itäosasto, Itä25/Jyrki Kallio, *Arktiset kysymyk-set—pohjustusta kansalliselle kannanmuodostukselle*, Muistio (Luonnos) [Memorandum (draft)], July 24, 2008.

32. Ulkoasiainvaliokunta, *Ulkoasiainvaliokunnan mietintö 12/2009 vp—Suomi ja arktiset alueet*, UaVM 12/2009 vp—K 3/2009, K 8/2009 vp, K 13/2009 vp.

33. Based on the presentations in the seminar, the book *Jäitä poltellessa: Suomi ja arktisen alueen tulevaisuus* (ed. Lassi Heininen and Teemu Palosaari, Rauhan- ja konfliktintutkimuskeskus TAPRI at University of Tampere) was published in May 2011.

34. Mäkeläinen-Buhanist, *Finland's Approach to the Arctic*; Prime Minister's Office, Finland, *Finland's Strategy for the Arctic Region*.

35. Valtioneuvoston viestintäyksikkö, *Tiedote* [Press release] 120/2010—[given at] 8.4.2010 13.36.

36. The strategy was first published in Finnish in June and in English in September 2010.

37. Prime Minister's Office, Finland, *Finland's Strategy for the Arctic Region.*
38. Ibid., 7.
39. Ibid., 13.
40. Ibid., 13–17.
41. Ibid., 18.
42. Ibid., 45.
43. Ibid., 52.
44. This section is based on my comparative study on Arctic strategies, including the Finnish strategy (see Lassi Heininen, *Arctic Strategies and Policies: Inventory and Comparative Study* (Akureyri, Iceland: The Northern Research Forum and the University of Lapland, 2011).
45. The statement received great interest and cross-party support in general discussions on Finland's interests at the Assembly of the Finnish Parliament in November 2009.
46. Prime Minister's Office, Finland, *Finland's Strategy for the Arctic Region,* 26 and 74.
47. This was seen already in October 2010, when mining company Northland Resources decided to transport iron ore mined in Pajala, just beside the Finnish border, to the port of Narvik in Norway instead of the port of Kemi, which is much closer.
48. The company, Steel Done Group, has signed a contract of 10 million euro with the Russians (HS 27.11.2008, A8).
49. The latest Finland's Strategy on Arctic Research was published in April 1999 (Kauppa- ja teollisuusministeriö, *Suomen arktisen tutkimuksen strategia,* Kauppa- ja teollisuusministeriön neuvottelukuntaraportteja, April 1999).
50. Prime Minister's Office, Finland, *Finland's Strategy for the Arctic Region,* 28.
51. Ibid., 15.
52. Ibid., 18.
53. The fragile natural environment, long distances, indigenous peoples, and the economic potential of the regions are tied together as the first requested element of the Northern Dimension's "Arctic Window."
54. E.g., Stubb, *A New Arctic Era and Finland's Arctic Policy.*
55. E.g., Lassi Heininen and C. Southcott, eds., *Globalization and the Circumpolar North* (Fairbanks: University of Alaska Press, 2010).
56. Prime Minister's Office, Finland, *Finland's Strategy for the Arctic Region,* 52.

57. Stubb, *A New Arctic Era and Finland's Arctic Policy*; Hannu Halinen, *Presentation in the Seminar of "Pohjoisen politiikan ja turvallisuuden tutkimuksen asiantuntijaverkosto,"* Tampere Peace Research Institute, Tampere, Finland, September 29, 2010 (personal notes).

58. Lassi Heininen and Lotta Numminen, "Suomi arktisena maana ja Euroopan unionin jäsenvaltiona: miten Arktista neuvostoa vahvistetaan," *Arcticfinland*, March 13, 2011, www.arcticfinland.fi.

59. Prime Minister's Office, Finland, *Finland's Strategy for the Arctic Region*, 45.

CHAPTER 12

ICELAND–A STATE WITHIN THE ARCTIC

Alyson J. K. Bailes and Margrét Cela

INTRODUCTION

When Iceland describes itself as the only state to lie entirely within the Arctic region (broadly defined!),[1] the political utility of the claim for asserting the country's legitimacy and right to a voice in Arctic affairs is obvious. Foreign observers may find it harder to grasp how Iceland's policy stance, in turn, is shaped by real and distinctive factors of location, long-term history, and economic and social structure. These features of the country's High Northern identity can be compared in importance only with the awareness of being a "small state"[2] in determining Iceland's concerns, norms, goals, and working methods in external affairs generally and on the emerging Arctic agenda in particular.

This chapter starts by offering some factual background to support these contentions. It continues with a brief account of the nation's post-independence history and international ties, then discusses how different dimensions of the current Arctic agenda and expected developments relate to Icelandic interests. Finally, it presents the Icelandic policy response, including the nation's preferred partners and its stance on relevant institutions and governance issues. The forward-looking conclusions speculate on the interplay between Iceland's domestic development and its evolving relations with the European Union and NATO.

Iceland was settled from the ninth century onward by emigrants from the other Nordic territories—mostly from western Norway—with an admixture of Celtic genes and cultural influence from Irish and Hebridean slaves. It was first established as a free commonwealth governed by a proto-parliamentary assembly (the Althingi—a name still carried by the Icelandic Parliament today) but fell under Norwegian control in 1262 after a period of anarchic civil conflict. Norway's rights passed to Denmark in 1380, and Denmark remained the sovereign power until Iceland claimed its full independence in 1944. Substantial gains of self-government were made in 1874, in 1904, and again in 1918 when a "Union" of Denmark and a separate Iceland was created but did not include the separate management of diplomatic and defense affairs. Thus, Iceland never had a significant political attachment to any other than a fellow Nordic state, even if the Danes at some points dreamed of selling it to Germany and Hanseatic and British merchants sometimes played a crucial part in its trade. The exception proving the rule was the twentieth-century role of the United States as the tutelary defense power for an independent Iceland that decided never to have military forces of its own. In de facto control from the end of World War II, the stationed U.S. forces' position was formalized with Iceland's entry into NATO in 1949 and the bilateral U.S.-Iceland Defence Agreement of 1951. The U.S. presence was, however, always opposed by many Icelanders, and after Washington chose to unilaterally end it in 2006, some would view it as a finite historical deviation.

Geographically, Iceland consists of a landmass of 103,000 square kilometers plus territorial waters (as defined for fisheries purposes) of 758,000 square kilometers. This makes it the second smallest Nordic state in physical terms, given that Denmark has 43,094 square kilometers, but the Danish population numbers 5.5 million to Iceland's 319,700.[3] With barely three persons per square kilometer, Iceland is in fact the fourth least populous sovereign state in the world (Greenland has just 0.026 people per square kilometers but is still part of the realm of Denmark). Less than 1 percent of the national territory is cultivable, and trees are sparse: grain, potatoes, and other root crops are sown afresh each year and must struggle with violent, salt-bearing winds.[4] Other foods like fruit (other than wild berries) and salad greens are produced in artificial conditions using low-cost geothermal power. The most productive branches of farming are sheep, horse, and cattle rearing, though the cattle—and smaller numbers of pigs and poultry—are kept indoors for part of the year.

Most famous of all is the dependence of the Icelandic economy and lifestyle on fish, the quintessential natural resource. Though the contribution of fisheries to the gross domestic product has halved since 1990 and the numbers employed have also reduced,[5] in 2008 marine products still accounted for 36.7 percent by value of all Icelandic exports, compared with just 1.4 percent for agricultural products. The largest category of exports in that year were manufactures (52.1 percent), but as much as 39 percent consisted of aluminum from foreign-owned factories processing imported ore with low-cost hydroelectric and geothermal energy.[6] To the extent that this energy can also be considered a primary natural resource, it is safe to say that the larger part of Iceland's exports and thus a dominant share of its national income relies on the gifts of nature.[7]

Together with substantial and growing profits from tourism, this adds up to an economic and occupational profile clearly fitting a High Northern rather than mainstream European model. It helps explain why the Icelanders, though not themselves defined as indigenous peoples, feel kinship with the Greenlanders as well as the Faroese and maintain a structured cooperation with those territories in the "West Nordic" framework (a grouping now gaining in political salience, discussed later).[8] It also illuminates Iceland's insistence on continuing commercial whaling, more now as a cultural tradition than profit-making venture. Some would say that Iceland's dalliance with international high finance in the early twenty-first century, when its overseas debts soared to around twelve times GDP, did not so much belie this "wild frontier" strand in the Icelandic identity as confirm its peculiarities: both in the reckless scale of the banking bubble and the chaos produced by its bursting in 2008.[9] The notion that Iceland must now draw in its horns and retrieve its close-to-nature roots has since become a popular theme both of the nationalist Right and radical Left.

POLITICAL AND STRATEGIC HISTORY SINCE 1944

Iceland gained full independence from Denmark in 1944, when Denmark was under German occupation during World War II and Iceland itself was occupied by Britain and the United States. That set its mark on Iceland's security policy, which from early days revolved around two major components: NATO membership on the one hand and the U.S.-run NATO base in Keflavik on the other.[10] In 1918 Iceland had declared everlasting neutrality, but its decision to become a founding member of NATO in 1949 abandoned this position to align Iceland with the West against the Eastern Bloc. Other signs of the new orientation were that Iceland joined the United Nations, permitted the United States to use the Keflavik base provisionally after World War II ended, and then made the arrangement permanent through the U.S.-Iceland bilateral defense agreement of 1951. The decision to join NATO was controversial at home, and Iceland insisted on acceptance of the following conditions before accession: (1) NATO could not use a base in Iceland in wartime without specific permission; (2) Iceland itself would never have an army;

(3) Iceland would not allow foreign forces on its territory in time of peace; and (4) all other NATO members must recognize these conditions.[11]

The outbreak of the Korean War in 1950 triggered the further Icelandic move to sign the 1951 defense agreement with the United States. Relations between the two states became very close—in Iceland it was called the "special" relationship. The United States was the first to recognize Iceland's independence in 1944, and geopolitically Iceland fell into an American zone of influence. During the Cold War, Iceland benefited from its strategic importance to gain economic as well as military support from Washington, in the form of Marshall Aid, trade and other forms of financial aid, or assistance, not to mention the jobs the U.S. military base provided for Icelanders.[12]

Being a non-military nation, Iceland has never had a Ministry of Defense but handles related matters through a defense department in the Ministry of Foreign Affairs, working with the Ministry of Justice and Prime Minister's Office. In this context it is revealing to note which political parties have controlled these three ministries over time, as shown in figure 7 (drawn from government and political-party sources).

The picture is one of long-term dominance by the Right-wing Independence Party (Sjálfstæðisflokkurinn, shown as *S*) and the liberal/centrist Progressive Party (Framsóknarflokkurinn, shown as *F*), moderated by a frequent presence—especially in the Foreign Ministry—of the Democrats (Alþýðuflokkurinn, shown as *A*) and the new Social Democratic Alliance (Samfylkingin, shown as *SF*, which absorbed Alþýðuflokkurinn in 2000).[13] Very unusually, in February 2009 a ruling coalition was formed by two left-of-center parties with the Left Green Party (shown as *VG*) joining the Social Democrats and obtaining the Ministry of Justice in spring 2010. Thus, for most of the Cold War period, the Right-wing strategy based on a close U.S. alliance ruled unchallenged in practice despite the unhappiness from parts of the population, leading to the sense that defense matters were monopolized by a small elite. "Security" was seen as essentially a military matter, both for ideological reasons and in the absence of other obvious threats aside from natural disasters. Iceland has not suffered internal conflict or major crime; is for the most part (80 percent) self-sufficient in energy; has no serious environmental problems; and can expect some benefits from climate change.[14] In practice, so long as Iceland benefited financially from the U.S. military base, the outsourcing of security and defense to the United States enjoyed at least passive acceptance. Only after the 2008 economic crash, as explained later, did the arrival of the radical Left in government lead to a more serious tussle over the balance of strategic policy.

As the Cold War neared its end, it became clear that Iceland was losing its strategic importance to the United States. As peace and stability grew in the High North, the United States started focusing on state and non-state threats in other regions in the world, and a new range of challenges, including non-military ones, entered the security agenda. The U.S. presence at Keflavik was cut back several times, considerably reducing its significance even before the final pullout of 2006.[15] Even so, Icelanders made several attempts to persuade the United States not to leave, and it has been hotly debated whether Iceland's support of the U.S.-led war on Iraq was in fact such an attempt.[16] When the base nevertheless closed, Icelanders were forced to take the matter of security and defense into their own hands. In the following years, Iceland made agreements on cooperation in security, defense, and search and rescue with Norway, Denmark, the United Kingdom, and Canada among others. An evolving vision of security and defense could be detected in a speech by the then Foreign Minister, Ingibjörg Sólrun Gísladóttir, in 2007 where she spoke of new security threats that defied borders and demanded greater international cooperation.[17] Gísladóttir's appointment of an independent risk assessment commission can be seen in the same light, and the commission's report in March 2009 duly noted a much extended range of "military, societal and global" security challenges now relevant for Iceland.[18]

In 2008, a new Defense Act established the Icelandic Defense Agency (IDA) under the Ministry of Foreign Affairs to manage the remaining NATO air defense installations at Keflavik and to handle NATO cooperation generally.[19] The IDA was always controversial because of its "military" overtones, and on January 1, 2011, it was closed down and its operations for the most part moved under the coast guard and the National Commissioner of the Icelandic Police within a new enlarged Ministry of the Interior. Policy relations with NATO remain under the Ministry of Foreign Affairs.

Iceland's external strategy has of course encompassed other strands, including participation in the European integration process and other international cooperation. Up until 2009, Iceland's European policy was one of partial integration through the European Free Trade Area (EFTA), succeeded by the European Economic Area (EEA), and adhesion to the Schengen Treaty. When EFTA was established in 1959, Iceland was not invited to be a founding member because of its fisheries dispute with Britain, but London reversed its position in 1965. For Iceland the main attractions of EFTA membership were that it would boost exports of fish and marine products, improve Iceland's competitive position on European markets, and possibly lead to a free trade agreement with the European Communities. Nevertheless, this was a very controversial decision, and there were severe protests outside the Althingi on the day it voted for membership.[20] Again, when Iceland chose to join the EEA in 1993, this was heavily disputed, not least because of arguments on the constitution and sovereignty.[21] Since that time, the EFTA pillar has shrunk in size because all other members except Liechtenstein and Norway have joined the EU. In July 2009, in the aftermath of the economic crash, Iceland applied for full membership of the EU: another controversial decision that was opposed from the start by some (mainly Left Green) MPs of the ruling coalition. A right-of-center coalition of the Independence and Progressive Parties, winning the May 2013 elections, has since put the application on hold.

Iceland has also been a member of the Schengen border control regime since 1996, even before it was formally brought within the EU treaties. Iceland and Norway were invited to participate to avoid severing the long-standing Nordic passport union with Denmark, Finland, and Sweden.[22] Through Schengen Iceland works closely with such EU agencies and programs as Europol, Eurojust, Cepol, Frontex, the External Borders Fund, the European Arrest Warrant, and the Dublin Agreement.

In 1998 it was decided that Iceland would for the first time run for a seat on the United Nations Security Council (UNSC). This was presented both as a chance to deepen practical cooperation with the rest of the world and a mark of Iceland's new would-be status as a strong and capable small state, not a weak micro-state.[23] To underline this, Iceland increased its contribution to development aid.[24] In 2000 the Icelandic Crisis Response unit was established, and in 2001 the first Icelandic civilian experts started operating in selected peace missions under the UN, EU, and NATO.[25] In autumn 2008, however, just after and partly because of the economic crash, Iceland lost out to Austria and Turkey in the UNSC elections.

In the North, Iceland has participated energetically in regional and sub-regional cooperation. It has been a member of the Nordic Council since 1952, Council of Baltic Sea States from 1992, Barents Euro-Arctic Council since 1993, and the Arctic Council from 1996.[26] From 2002 on, as noted in the first section, Iceland has also participated in West Nordic cooperation with Greenland and the Faroe Islands. The latest government taking office in May 2013 has called, in its policy platform, for an active and even "leading" Icelandic role in both the Arctic and West Nordic Councils.[27] Although the West Nordic alignment has a genuine historical and cultural base, it also serves Iceland's current purposes of self-differentiation from the larger Europe and highlights the current government's hopes of joining the other small participants in new oil and gas exploitation.

Given that NATO is still the cornerstone of Iceland's defense, it is interesting that all the major disputes Iceland has had in the past were with other Allied states: notably the cod "wars" (1952–1956, 1958–1961, 1972–1973, and 1975–1976) with the United Kingdom and the dispute over "Icesave" accounts with the United Kingdom and the Netherlands after London used anti-terrorism legislation to freeze Icelandic bank assets in 2008. A first agreement on Icesave was approved by Parliament in 2009 but blocked when the president of Iceland used his powers to call for a referendum, with a negative outcome.[28] In the aftermath the government made a new deal, somewhat reducing Iceland's payments, with the United Kingdom and the Netherlands, but on February 20, 2011, the president again refused to sign the legislation and provoked another referendum, again with a negative outcome.[29] This result was followed by a motion of no-confidence in the government, put forward by the leader of the Independence Party and narrowly defeated. In 2012 the EFTA court ruled that the Icelandic government was not after all responsible for Icesave reimbursements, and later that year commercial repayments began from the concerned banks' bankrupt estates.

This lingering and corrosive problem is just one aspect of the political crisis triggered in Iceland by the economic crash of 2008, which persists today. The largest banks were nationalized one after the other as the only way to avert formal bankruptcy and closure; the public felt angry and betrayed, not only by the so-called new "Viking raiders" (útrásarvíkingar) but also by the government that had failed to regulate and monitor the system. The biggest protests in the history of Iceland were held in front of the Althingi every Saturday, month after month, until the government resigned in February 2009 and elections were announced.

The resulting government of the Social Democratic Alliance and the Left Greens, as mentioned earlier, had to contend with considerable opposition not only from the displaced Right-wing parties but also from within its own ranks. Left Green leaders among other things renewed their questioning of NATO membership and proposed other anti-military and anti-nuclear initiatives.[30] The coalition's main policy changes, including Parliament's assent to the application for EU membership in 2009, all became targets for reversal when a more traditional right-of-center coalition regained power in May 2013; and one of the Left-wing coalition's highest aims—a revision of the Constitution—foundered even before the elections. Less clear (at the time of writing) is the fate of an initiative taken in early 2012 for a cross-party group of MPs to deliberate on a first-ever comprehensive security policy for Iceland.[31] Though the work could not be completed before the May 2013 elections, it is understood to have discovered some room for consensus notably on non-military aspects, and it remains to be seen if the new government may pick up and use the findings in some way.

In sum: any aspect of national policy invoking questions of "defense" and "security" has been contentious since creation of the modern Icelandic state and remains highly delicate today. However, regional and particularly Nordic cooperation has enjoyed broad support, and for similar reasons the Arctic agenda itself has not (yet) become a matter of dispute between parties. To the extent that the general public reflects on it at all, it is in a consensus mood of optimism, with some even arguing that growing strategic and commercial interest in the High North could be a factor pulling Iceland out of recession.

Arctic Prospects and Icelandic Interests

Territorial Claims

Below the peaceful and stable surface of the High North in past decades, there are underlying disputes that must be kept from surfacing and escalating. All five littoral states—Canada, Denmark (Greenland), Norway, the Russian Federation, and the United States of America—have made partly overlapping claims that would extend their ocean boundaries over areas where rich resources are suspected. The coastal states have full sovereignty for up to twelve nautical miles from shore and certain sovereign rights out to 200 miles, or even more, depending on the shape and sediments of the seabed.[32] Though not recognized as a coastal state in this sense, Iceland has nevertheless had some disputes over ocean boundaries. In 1981 Iceland and Norway agreed on a joint continental shelf zone near Jan Mayen, letting them share possible profits from hydrocarbon exploration, which has reached the stage of granting a first round of licenses.[33] In 1997 a dispute between Iceland and Denmark (Greenland) on continental shelf and fisheries boundaries was settled, and the same year Iceland, Denmark (Greenland), and Norway (Jan Mayen) reached a tri-point agreement.[34] Iceland claims continental shelf rights beyond 200 miles in the southern Síldarsmugan zone (literally "herring lair") but in 2006 agreed with Norway and Denmark (on behalf of the Faroe Islands) on a basic demarcation. Furthermore, under the Svalbard Treaty, Iceland enjoys rights to exploit natural resources, including fishing and continental shelf rights, within Svalbard's 200-nautical-mile jurisdiction.[35]

Military Aspects
Given that it has no tools, let alone intent, to impose such claims by force, Iceland can honestly claim to be the most opposed of all regional states to the "militarization" of the Arctic. Not only has it no armed forces—just a modest coast guard to patrol its fisheries—but its profile as a basing site has been reduced in recent years both by others' actions and the present government's wish. The departed U.S. forces have been replaced by paper guarantees of reinforcement in the revised U.S.-Iceland Defence Agreement. NATO force exercises are held just a few times a year, with a focus on air policing, including the annual or biennial "Northern Viking" deployment, which involves U.S. forces.[36] Although the air traffic radars at Keflavik remain linked to NATO's air defense system, their placing under Ministry of Interior operational control beginning in 2011 underscores Iceland's "civilian" approach.

For some time after the U.S. withdrawal, thinkers on the Right in Iceland cherished a lingering hope that the Arctic competition itself might reawaken U.S. interest in Iceland's strategic setting. But there has been no sign of that so far—it is Greenland that plays the key role in Washington's missile defense plans—and with shifts in the Icelandic public mood, it is now uncertain if the majority would want it. Rather, Iceland would prefer all players to keep military plans and actions to a minimum, not just to minimize its own exposure in any open fight but because of the sharp rise in accident and pollution risks that heavy military patrolling would bring. Dependency on fisheries has particularly sharpened Icelandic awareness of nuclear contamination risks, where concerns were especially high in the 1980s and early 1990s but are constantly reawoken, for instance by news of submarine accidents.[37] Iceland's best bet is thus to maintain the same regional security model that preserved peace and stability even in Cold War times, thanks to the physical separation of the largest U.S. and Russia forces and the interposition of structures for neighborly cooperation.[38] Although Iceland itself has not so far tabled proposals for arms control and restraint measures in the Arctic space, it would be among the first to embrace any such ideas that did surface.[39]

It may seem a contradiction that Iceland chose to co-host the first—and maybe last—special conference ever held by NATO on Arctic matters, at Reykjavik in January 2009.[40] Falling in the last days of the last Independence Party–led government, it reflected that party's traditional pro-NATO stance but also an effort to build more complex links with NATO to offset the U.S. withdrawal. More generally, Iceland saw and would still see a restrained and balanced collective NATO posture as better than leaving Arctic strategy to the individual judgment of its (sometimes over-nationalistic) members. At the 2009 event, accordingly, Icelandic speakers urged the alliance to work with Russia on using military assets primarily for multipurpose surveillance and data collection and cooperating in search and rescue. Whereas that approach drew wide support at the conference,[41] Icelandic suggestions to include similar conclusions in NATO's new Strategic Concept[42] fell flat because at least one nation[43] preferred not to see a binding alliance line developed on the subject.

Economic Aspects

Although state sovereignty defines the Arctic to a far greater degree than the Antarctic, it has been mitigated by the huge barren spaces involved and the harsh climate that has made them hard to penetrate and control, allowing old ways of life to survive. Intensive economic activity entered the region from outside in the age of whaling, only to retreat again when stocks were exhausted. Oil and gas exploration in the Norwegian and west Siberian zones has, however, been creeping steadily northward, and life in the occupied parts of the far North was showing many signs of exposure to globalization even before the forecasts of rapid ice melting gained currency.[44] The prospect of easier access for oil, gas, and mineral exploitation, long-distance transit shipping, and tourism has attracted a fast-growing interest from a widening range of states and non-state actors—apparently little deterred by the global recession. It is arguable that judgments taken in the business sphere, including by private business, and above all the calculations of financial and technical feasibility will do more to shape what actually happens in the Arctic than any exercise of top-down strategy or military power.

Iceland has long taken Arctic economics seriously and has been interested in exploiting its position not just by encouraging new investments and facilities on its land,[45] but by active commercial engagement. For instance, Icelandic companies are already profiting from oil exploration in Greenland by providing services such as flights.[46] Although such opportunities are welcome in thin times, the economic crash has also brutally underlined the risks facing the small Icelandic administration and companies that are not best known for professional planning and prudence. With the rising number of groups showing interest in the region, Icelandic actors, state and non-state, must get ready to compete with the best—or be left behind. To do so, a clear strategy is needed.

Icelandic companies have a good reputation in High Northern tourism and construction, as seen for instance in Greenland. Iceland is, further, in an ideal position to site any new facilities for monitoring sea and air traffic and for search and rescue in the North Atlantic gateway to the Arctic. It may or may not attract support and trans-shipment facilities for the new Arctic oil, gas, and shipping trade depending on what seabed areas are exploited and which shipping routes prove most economical.[47] There may be new opportunities to apply Iceland's large reserves of green energy in the process.[48] Different fish stocks are likely to appear in Icelandic territorial waters as the climate becomes warmer, though others currently fished by Icelandic vessels may also migrate farther north—and as noted earlier, the net outcome has massive relevance for Iceland's economy.[49] However, the very fact of Iceland's intense reliance on its natural resources gives it a compelling interest in ensuring that all new economic activities in the Arctic—oil and gas, shipping, tourism, and all aspects of marine harvesting—are properly regulated for the protection of the environment, safety, and civil security. Regulators will need to keep pace with and even ahead of private-sector thinking to defend the common interest in sustainable development against the risk of aggressive "plundering" by either large powers or large firms.

The scope for clashes of interest has already been illustrated by the movement of fish stocks. In 2010 Iceland disagreed with Norway and the EU over its right to harvest migrating stocks of mackerel, and the EU's protests were "welcomed" by the anti-EU school in Iceland as an example of how Brussels would usurp the island's natural resources for its own benefit if allowed.[50] Seen more objectively, however, the EU's and Iceland's current approaches to Arctic development are highly compatible and should allow close cooperation even if Iceland's entry bid evaporates. The policy guidelines on Arctic issues adopted by the EU Council of Ministers in 2009[51] start with environmental protection and advocate cooperative, prudent development within a framework of regulation. They do not speak of a sealing and whaling ban or a long-term fishing ban, as called for inter alia by the European Parliament, only a temporary fishing ban in new waters. Pro-EU Icelanders would in fact argue that Union membership offers the best protection available, both for Iceland's civil security and for its hopes of safely navigating the competitive new Arctic market.

Environmental Aspects

Even though climate change is now a familiar and, for most, incontestable prospect, its speed and local consequences are far less predictable. This uncertainty makes it hard to be prepared, not least for a small state with a more reactive than proactive security culture. Climate change may in fact have some positive impacts for Iceland, at least in the short run, on three main counts. First, as already noted, larger stocks of some fish including species new to this part of the northern North Atlantic may be found in Icelandic waters. The second category is agriculture: mild winters with less ice mean longer summers, and in the past two decades growing grain has become popular and profitable for Icelandic farmers. Forestry is also more productive with warmer summers. The third factor is the energy sector: the output of hydroelectric plants is very sensitive to climate and water level and in the short term can be boosted (so long as it is not swamped) by faster-melting glaciers.[52]

Long-term effects may not be as positive. Studies have shown that ocean acidification in the waters around Iceland is near twice the global average and is likely to become one of the most disturbing aspects of climate change for Iceland, along with changes in ocean currents.[53] New societal risks can also be expected, such as unfamiliar diseases and new infection carriers, heat waves, storms, floods, and drought. The more intense and complex society's patterns of economic activity become, the greater the risk of major disruption through pollution, disease, accidents, or financial/economic difficulties and the harder the challenge of ensuring true sustainability. For instance, though trout farming has boomed in recent years, research now shows the conditions for trout in Iceland worsening because of rising water temperatures.[54]

Environmental risks linked to the growth of shipping also deserve further comment.[55] In 2007 over 200 oil ships sailed from Murmansk in Russia: one in ten of them weighing 100,000 tons and one in five cruising near Iceland. Thus already in 2007, forty-seven oil ships from Murmansk heading to North America sailed past Iceland carrying 2.2 million tons of oil. Such transits have grown more numerous as a result both of oil/gas extraction in the Barents and White Seas and of the overall and still continuing rise in trans-Arctic shipping.[56] The oil disaster in the Gulf of Mexico in April 2010 has meanwhile underlined how offshore activity heightens environmental risks.[57] For Iceland, any such accident would be a triple blow: the immediate pollution, the longer-term effect on quality and marketability of Iceland's own critical marine resources, and perhaps also a human tragedy given that local rescue capacities are so limited. As things stand, Iceland lacks information on the sailing routes of gas tankers even when they transit fishing waters, lacks vessels large enough to tow the largest ships, and has very limited ability for oil cleansing.[58] All this helps explain the Icelandic government's relief and pleasure when a workshop of all eight Arctic Council states at Reykjavik in December 2010 reached agreement on the text of a legally binding mutual-assistance pact on Arctic search and rescue, duly adopted by ministers at the AC's 2011 Nuuk Ministerial.[59] A parallel agreement on mutual assistance with major offshore oil spills followed in May 2013.[60]

ICELAND'S POLICY RESPONSE

For much of the past decade, the Icelandic government focused largely on the economic side of High North development, measuring everything in terms of financial gain and loss. Official reports published between 2005 and 2007[61] shared a strong focus on the hope of new commercial bases in Iceland; for instance the 2007 report "Breaking the Ice" depicted Iceland as the ideal site for a trans-shipment port connecting different routes.[62] After the harsh lessons of the economic crash, a new attitude could be detected, not least in a Foreign Ministry report of 2009, which presented Iceland's interests in the region far more broadly, including international cooperation, security and defense, natural resources and conservation, transport, culture and human welfare, and science and monitoring.[63] The official Icelandic Arctic strategy that developed subsequently, as explained later, has maintained this broader, more values-driven than value-driven approach.

The High North today can be considered a regional sub-system characterized by cross-border interactions between states, indigenous peoples' organizations (IPOs), international governmental organizations (IGOs), international nongovernmental organizations (INGOs), subnational governments (autonomous territories, provinces), and transnational corporations. Typically for a small state finding itself in such a nexus—with much both to gain and to lose—Iceland sees its interest as avoiding primitive power-play between nations[64] and using the rule of law and institutions both to guide resource management and to resolve disputes.[65] Thus Icelandic politicians have emphasized the need for international cooperation to protect the fragile ecosystem of the Arctic.[66]

At the same time, Iceland tends to favor institutions that do not require heavy integration and substantial surrenders of sovereignty. The emphasis it places on the Arctic Council—a body that takes non-legally binding decisions for the most part—suggests this, while its strong opposition to separate meetings of the five "littoral states" reflects its preference for working in a large forum where small members have a nominally equal voice. For similar reasons, Iceland welcomes the growing interest in the region from larger multilateral institutions such as the EU, NATO, and UN agencies.[67] It hopes to avoid permanently "ganging up" with or opposing any particular player, instead aiming for businesslike relations with all Arctic states to maximize its chance of joining any profitable economic schemes.[68] However, Iceland works particularly closely with the other four states in the Nordic Council of Ministers, where Arctic issues have been included in a special cooperation program for the years 2012–2014.[69] The goals include research, development, the improvement of quality of life, culture promotion in the face of global-ization, and the preservation of Arctic nature, biological diversity, and sustainable resource use.

On March 28, 2011, a proposal on Iceland's new strategy for the High North was adopted by the Althingi.[70] Building on recommendations by the Foreign Minister, it listed twelve key principles that should guide the government's production of a detailed strategy document:

(1) Strengthen the Arctic Council.

(2) Secure Iceland's position as a coastal state. The claim will be based on legal, economic, ecological, and geographical argumentation. Priority will be given to working with institutions that support this claim.

(3) Increase the understanding that "the Arctic" for policy purposes includes both the area above the Arctic Circle and adjoining areas of the North Atlantic.

(4) Promote the UN Convention on the Law of the Sea as the tool to resolve overlapping claims.

(5) Strengthen cooperation with Greenland and the Faroese in order to increase the political leverage of all three states.

(6) Support the rights of indigenous peoples.

(7) Build on the institutional and legal framework of cooperation relevant to Iceland's interests in the High North.

(8) Fight against global warming caused by human activity and at the same time promote sustainability and local culture.

(9) Promote security in the broad sense and oppose any militarization of the region; increase cooperation in search and rescue.

(10) Promote business opportunities in the region.

(11) Increase Icelandic research and knowledge on the High North in cooperation with others.

(12) Increase domestic consultation and coordination on High North issues.

Most of these points reflect the logic of Icelandic interests and traditions of Icelandic policy as already analyzed, but some need further comment. First, the linkage of Iceland's vital interests with recognition as a coastal state relates to Iceland's resentment at being left out of the "inner" meetings of the five littoral powers and is meant to shift attention back to the need to work with and build the joint influence of all eight Arctic Council states.[71] The third point about defining the Arctic region also reflects Iceland's insistence on its Arctic identity, which is further served by its close cooperation and fostering of common economic interests with Greenland as well as the Faroe Islands. As explained earlier in this chapter, Icelandic support for the rights of indigenous peoples[72] and for shared traditions such as whaling runs in the same direction. Finally, Iceland is joining the common line of other Arctic states in promoting the UN Convention on the Law of the Sea (UNCLOS) as the right and only legal framework for resolving overlapping claims at sea, and in the process implicitly rejecting any need for a comprehensive "Arctic Treaty" on the lines of the Antarctic Treaty.

Also noteworthy is the last item in the policy manifesto about the need for improved internal coordination. Never an Icelandic strong point, this ought to be easier to achieve on a topic such as the Arctic, where party and sectoral interests concur, than on a full-spectrum security policy or (still less) external policy in general. In October 2013, indeed, the new right-of-center government showed its support for the existing policy line and for Parliament's advice by pledging to create a top-level ministerial coordination committee on Arctic affairs, chaired by the prime minister himself. However, the question remains of what resources can be mustered in the service of Iceland's ambitious plans, given that the Foreign Ministry retains a central role in Arctic-related work at home and abroad. As part of post-crash public expenditure cuts, in 2009 the Icelandic Foreign Service's budget was slashed by 26 percent, followed by 16.6 percent in 2010 and 9.2 percent in 2011. In 2010 it received only 2.12 percent of the total state budget, the lowest proportion among Nordic states.[73] There is thus still a question over how actively Iceland can pursue its Arctic interests, as distinct from encouraging others to see its location's advantages.

One relevant tool at Iceland's disposal that has proved important in the case of other small states is the activity of non-state experts especially in research, education, culture, and the media. Arctic research in Iceland has a long history especially at the University of Akureyri, which houses inter alia the Stefansson Arctic Institute and a Polar Law Institute and has lately received governmental support from Norway and France among others.[74] The University of Iceland in Reykjavik has relevant programs on resource management, engineering, health, and cultural studies and in 2013 created a Centre for Arctic Policy Studies to look especially at political and institutional topics.[75] Other research centers have internationally acknowledged expertise in fields like environmental analysis, shipping, and fisheries, and Iceland is consistently a net recipient from the EU and Nordic cooperative research funds where it participates.[76] Last but not least, Iceland's geographical position and its media visibility, including the activities of its president, make it a popular site for Arctic-related gatherings, as seen in October 2013 when nearly 2,000 attended the inaugural gathering of a multifunctional "Arctic Circle" in Reykjavik.

LOOKING AHEAD

Extrapolating Iceland's Arctic role to the future is particularly difficult because it depends on a whole Rubik's cube of partly independent variables. First, this small nation will clearly not shape, but must react and adapt to, the parameters of policy development set by others in the region. Second, it will do so while its entire territory is undergoing the imponderable impact of Arctic climate change. Third, of all the Arctic nations, Iceland has been thrown into the greatest economic, political, and even social and psychological uncertainty by the 2008 economic crash. It is hard to guess from week to week who will be setting the tone in Icelandic politics and what the key issues will be, let alone what policies will be applied and to what, if any, effect. It is fair to add, however, that the work done under both the last and current governments to get —at least—the broad principles of Arctic policy formally agreed through Parliament should limit the risk of more extreme policy swings.

Two staples of the Icelandic approach seem unlikely to change under any circumstances, exactly because they arise from the nation's smallness. First is the opposition to (and non-participation in) potential militarization. Because Iceland has no means to fight for its own claims and is not now a close satellite of any larger competitor, its logical strategy is to seek cooperation both with and between all the influential powers including Russia and China. Secondly, it must continue to oppose any persistent "inner group" activity by the littoral five, or indeed any smaller axis that forms among them—not necessarily because this would lead to bad policy outcomes but rather because Iceland's own hopes of pushing specific national interests would be lost.

It is easy to guess that a combination of both these aims will lead Iceland to continue supporting the Arctic Council as the central, coordinating forum for dialogue and policy making in the High North: even if Icelandic experts understand that some of the more important understandings reached in the council (e.g., on shipping) must seek a legally binding incarnation elsewhere. Like other actors who take this position, however, Iceland must consider whether the Arctic Council's primacy will be best served by a conservative approach to governance (as the indigenous peoples' representatives prefer) or by opening up to a wider range of actors and issues. In recent years the Icelanders have aligned themselves increasingly with the latter view, becoming one of the strongest advocates for reforms in the council's own structure as proposed by Finland[77] and succeeding in having an Icelander appointed as head of the council's new permanent secretariat when the decision to create it was made in 2012.[78] They also lobbied strongly for accepting the Asian powers (China, Japan, India, South Korea, and Singapore) that applied for Arctic Council observer status and were eventually admitted at the Kiruna Ministerial in May 2013: one Icelandic argument was that any powerful players left "outside the tent" might be tempted to create rival solutions undermining the council's authority. Iceland further believes that the EU's application for observer status—left in abeyance at Kiruna—should be granted, given the coincidence already noted between many concrete EU and Icelandic goals and the chances that an EU presence would tilt the scales further in favor of a multilateralist and law-based approach conducive to smaller players' interests.

Iceland's recent engagement in Arctic-related cooperation with China, including the visit of a Chinese ice-breaker in 2012 and other bilateral developments such as the signing of a free trade agreement that same year, have provoked some highly colored speculations about Iceland's becoming a Chinese strategic base or protégé in the High North.[79] More prosaically, intensifying contacts with China as well as Russia and Canada can be seen as serving a consistent Icelandic logic of reinsurance and diversification. China is one of the few potential players large enough to shake up the current High North power balance—especially to Russia's disadvantage—but at the same time is no enemy of Iceland and could be expected to favor multilateral solutions that lets it wield its power peacefully. Although actual—as against prospective—Chinese investments in the North Atlantic have so far been very modest,[80] Iceland must be aware that few other nations after 2008 have the capacity and nerve to fund really large commercial developments in the region.

Of course if Iceland should join the EU, it would become a more significant Arctic player simply by constituting the Union's furthest northern and western outpost. It could grow into a role as the EU's "Arctic expert," moderating the present influence over EU policies of Denmark, Finland,

Sweden, and (indirectly) Norway. Such a scenario is, however, even more of a long shot following the new government's decision in spring 2013 to put the Icelandic application on ice.[81] In the unlikely event of a "yes" vote in a future national referendum, questions might arise about Norway eventually joining too: but that country's dynamics are very different from Iceland's and its EU policy would only shift slowly, if at all. Another intriguing variable in the medium term is Greenland's possible decision to seek independence from Denmark, which—because Greenland rejects ✔ EU membership—would be more likely to bring U.S. influence farther eastward as the new republic's strategic protector. Iceland might well prefer in such a case to be safely under the EU's wing but would hope to maintain its good relations with Greenland across any new divide and to keep the West Nordic cooperation going.[82] Preserving the wider framework of Nordic cooperation, both for informal discussion and for potential joint initiatives, has become even more firmly entrenched since 2009 as a pillar of Icelandic Arctic policy.

On the evidence of the last decade, it would seem natural for sustainable exploration of Arctic resources to provide the final keystone in a long-term Icelandic strategy. Logically, if Iceland cannot escape the risks of pollution, accidents, natural disasters, and shifting fish stocks, the best chance of a positive cost-benefit balance lies in active engagement for profit in both offshore ventures and new on-shore construction. Here, however, is where the uncertainty of the domestic mood comes into play. During the last government's term from 2009 to 2013, the ecological Left was riding high in Iceland and did its best to block or slow down all new non-agricultural construction and new exploitation of natural energy sources.[83] The new right-of-center government now proposes actually to weaken the legal framework for environment protection and probably has majority support for at least exploring the country's sub-sea oil and gas potential; but it may still not have things all its own way in view of the unpromising prospects for necessary foreign investments.

Exactly what form Iceland's engagement in the new Arctic market-place will take thus still depends on too many factors to allow a safe guess, including the course of economic recovery, party fortunes, the role of individual politicians, and above all the volatile popular mood. The country's room for maneuver and ultimate role will be shaped perhaps even more by the largest variables of global development, regional geopolitics, and geo-economics. One irony is that the coming years seem likely to confront Icelanders, as a result, with some of the same life-altering choices that the older indigenous peoples of the region have been struggling with for some time. Whatever the issues are and what-ever shrewd or fateful moves it makes to handle them, Iceland will face the future as a quintessentially Arctic nation.

Figure 7. Party affiliations of the Prime Minister (PM), Minister of Foreign Affairs (MFA), and Minister of Justice (MJ).

	1944-47	1947-49	1949-50	1950-53	1953-56	1956-58	1958-59	1959-63	1963-70	1970-71	1971-74	1974-78	1978-79	1979-80	1980-83	1983-87	1987-88	1988-89	1989-91	1991-95	1995-99	1999-2003	2003-04	2004-06	2006-07	2007-09	2009-09	2009-
PM	S	A	S	F	S	F	A	S	S	S	F	S	F	A	S	F	S	F	F	S	S	S	S	F	S	S	SF	SF
MFA	S	S	S	F	A	A	A	A	A	F	F	A	A	F	S	F	A	A	A	F	F	F	S	F	SF	SF	SF	
MJ	A	S	S	S	S	F	A	S	S	S	F	F	F	A	S	F	A	F	B	S	S	S	S	S	S	S	X	VG

Source: Government Offices of Iceland, http://www.stjr.is/Rikisstjornartal/ nr/323; Independence Party, "History of the Party," http://www.xd.is/um-flokkinn/saga-flokksins/; Progressive Party, "Saga—I timans Rás" [History —in the flow of time]," http://www.framsokn.is/sagan-i-timans-ras/; Left Green Movement, "About the Movement," http://www.vg.is/um-flokkinn/; and Social Democratic Alliance, "About the Party," http://www.samfylkingin.is/ Flokkurinn.

NOTES

1. Iceland's territory lies between 63 and 67 degrees north and between 13 and 25 degrees west, just grazing the Arctic Circle with its northernmost extensions of the Melrakkaslétta peninsula and the island of Grimsey. Naturally Iceland prefers definitions of the Arctic that do not stop at the Arctic Circle but include further land areas with similar physical features and traditions.

2. The study of "small states" and the special challenges they face in the international community goes back to the late twentieth century; it has been pursued by many academics in northern Europe, above all in Iceland (see http://stofnanir.hi.is/ams, the website of the University of Iceland's Centre for Small State Studies). "Small" can be defined several ways: in practice it is rarely applied to states of more than 10 million inhabitants, but it also depends on *relative* size within a region.

3. Population data for 2010 from the Icelandic Statistical Office, www.statice.is. Ireland is comparable in size to Iceland with 70,273 square kilometers of land but has 4.2 million inhabitants.

4. The problem lies less in actual temperature, where the lowest mean for inhabited areas (on the north coast) is around −2 degrees Celsius. Summer temperatures reach the 20s, and climate change is manifest in the rapid retreat of Icelandic glaciers, plus extended growing and tourist seasons.

5. The contribution of fishing to GDP dropped from 9.6 percent to 4.8 percent between 1990 and 2008 and that of agriculture from 2.6 percent to 1.4 percent, while financial services and property transactions rose from 17.7 percent to 26.4 percent. All figures from www.statice.is.

6. Figures from www.statice.is.

7. Ministry for the Environment, *Iceland's Fifth National Communication on Climate Change, Under the United Nations Framework Convention on Climate Change*, http://unfccc.int/resource/docs/natc/isl_nc5_resubmit. pdf, 8.

8. See http://www.norden.org/en/nordic-council-of-ministers/council-of-ministers/ministers-for-co-operation-mr-sam/the-arctic-west-nordic-region-and-its-neighbours.

9. See, e.g., Roger Boyes, *Meltdown Iceland: How the Global Financial Crisis Bankrupted an Entire Country* (London: Bloomsbury, 2009), and Althingi,

Report of the Special Investigation Commission, April 12, 2010, English translation at http://sic.althingi.is/.

10. Michael T. Corgan, *Iceland and Its Alliances, Security for a Small State* (New York: Edwin Mellen Press, 2002), 2–3, 22–25.

11. In the 1980s, Iceland also formalized its rejection of any nuclear stationing or transit on its territory or in its territorial waters. On NATO entry, see Baldur Gudlaugsson and Páll Heidar Jonsson, *30. mars 1949. Innganga Íslands í Atlantshafsbandalagið og óeirðirnar á Austurvelli* [30 March 1949. Iceland's entry to NATO and the disturbances on Austurvöllur] (Reykjavik: Örn og Örlygur, 1976).

12. Gunnar Th. Bjarnason, *Óvænt áfall eða fyrirsjánleg tímamót, brottför bandaríkjahers frá Íslandi: aðdragandi og viðbrögð* [Bolt from the blue or foreseeable watershed? The US force withdrawal from Iceland: Antecedents and reactions] (Reykjavik: University of Iceland, 2008).

13. B stands for a small party splitting from the Independence Party in 1987 and X for a non-party appointee.

14. Alyson J. K. Bailes and Þröstur F. Gylfason, "Societal Security and Iceland," in *Stjórnmál og Stjórnsýsla*, vol. 1, 4th ed. (Reykjavik: Institute of Administration and Politics, 2008), http://stjornmalogstjornsysla.is/images/stories/eg2008v/alyson08.pdf.

15. Valur Ingimundarson, "Eftir 'bandarísku öldina': Samstarf Íslands við aðrar Evrópuþjóðir" [After the "American Age": Icelandic cooperation with other European nations], in *Ný staða Íslands í utanríkismálum: Tengsl við önnur Evrópulönd*, ed. Silja B. Ómarsdóttir (Reykjavik: University of Iceland, 2007), 153–163.

16. Bjarnason, *Óvænt áfall eða fyrirsjánleg tímamót*, 22.

17. Ingibjörg Sólrún Gísladóttir, "Breytt öryggisumhverfi—ný viðhorf í varnarmálum" [Changed security environment—new situation in defence], speech at the Association of Western Cooperation, November 27, 2007, http://www.utanrikisraduneyti.is/frettaefni/raedurISG/nr/4002.

18. Ministry of Foreign Affairs, *Risk Assessment for Iceland, Global, Civil and Military Aspects*, March 2009, http://www.utanrikisraduneyti.is/media/Skyrslur/Skyrsla_um_ahattumat_fyrir_Island_a.pdf.

19. Ministry of Foreign Affairs, *Varnarmálalög og Varnarmálastofnun Íslands* [The Defence Act and the Icelandic Defence Agency], 2008, http://www.utanrikisraduneyti.is/verkefni/althjoda-og-oryggissvid/varnar-og-oryggismal/varnarmalalog-og-vms/.

20. Baldur Thorhallsson and Hjalti Thór Vignisson, "The First Steps, Iceland's Policy on European Integration from the Foundation of the

Republic to 1972," in *Iceland and European Integration, On the Edge*, ed. Baldur Thorhallsson (London: Routledge, 2004), 28–30.

21. Baldur Thorhallsson and Hjalti Thór Vignisson, "A Controversial Step, Membership of the EEA," in Thorhallsson, *Iceland and European Integration, On the Edge*, 38–49.

22. Eirikur Bergmann, *Evrópusamruninn og Ísland* [European integration and Iceland] (Reykjavik: University of Iceland, 2003), 126.

23. Geir H. Haarde, "Iceland's Position in the International Community" [Staða Íslands í samfélagi þjóðanna], Speech at the University of Iceland, September 7, 2007, http://www.forsaetisraduneyti.is/radherra/raedurGHH/nr/2709.

24. Icelandic International Development Agency, *Stefna og verklag ÞSSÍ, stefnurit* [Policy and Operations of the Icelandic Development Aid Agency, policy report] (Reykjavik: ÞSSÍ, March 2004).

25. Alyson J. K. Bailes and Baldur Thorhallson, "Iceland and the European Security and Defence Policy," in *The Nordic Countries and the European Security and Defence Policy*, ed. Alyson J. K. Bailes, Gunilla Herolf, and Bengt Sundelius (Oxford: Oxford University Press, 2006), 328–348.

26. For the home pages of these bodies, see the bibliography.

27. The government's policy manifesto (in Icelandic) is at http://www.stjornarrad.is/Stefnuyfirlysing/.

28. Ólafur Ragnar Grimsson, *Declaration from the President of Iceland*, Bessastaðir, January 5, 2010, http://forseti.is/media/PDF/10_01_05_yfirlysing_med_skjaldarmerki.pdf.

29. Ólafur Ragnar Grimsson, *Declaration from the President of Iceland*, Bessastaðir, February 11, 2011, http://is/media/pdf/2011_02_20_icesave3_isl.pdf.

30. Left Green Movement, *Policy Declaration: Independent Foreign Policy, Social Internationalism*, http://www.vg.is/stefna/utanrikisstefna/.

31. "Utanríkisráðherra skipar nefnd til að vinna tillögur að þjóðaröryggisstefnu" [Foreign Minister creates committee to prepare proposals on national security policy], January 30, 2012, http://www.utanrikisraduneyti.is/frettir/nr/6925.

32. Michael Byers, *Who Owns the Arctic? Understanding Sovereignty Disputes in the North* (Vancouver: D&M Publishers Inc., 2009), 90–91.

33. This is what Iceland calls the "Dragon" (Dreki) field. It would only be profitable if large oil deposits were found.

34. Durham University, *Maritime Jurisdiction and Boundaries in the Arctic Region*, May 4, 2010, http://www.dur.ac.uk/resources/ibru/arctic.pdf.

35. Althingi, *Þingsályktun um stefnu Íslands í málefnum Norðurslóða*, document no. 1148 of the 139th session 2010–2011, http://www.althingi. is/altext/139/s/1148.html.

36. There are also more frequent, but discreet, visits by Danish and Norwegian warships in the framework of bilateral MOUs (memoranda of understanding). In the event of a serious air incursion, Norwegian and British warplanes would scramble to respond.

37. Lassi Heininen, "Globalization and Security in the Circumpolar North," in *Globalization and the Circumpolar North*, ed. Lassi Heininen and Chris Southcott (Fairbanks: University of Alaska Press, 2010), 1–24.

38. Barry S. Zellen, *Arctic Doom, Arctic Boom: The Geopolitics of Climate Change in the Arctic* (London: Praeger, 2009).

39. The present Foreign Minister, Össur Skarphedinsson, for instance, has personally advocated a nuclear-free zone in the region.

40. The chairman's conclusions from the event have not been published, but keynote speeches are reported at http://www.hq.nato.int/cps/en/natolive/ news_49745.htm?mode=news. See also Alyson J. K. Bailes, "Potential Roles of NATO and the EU in High Northern Security," in *Yearbook of Polar Law 2010* (Leiden: Martinus Nijhoff, 2010).

41. Even the larger Allies agreed that NATO's permanent posture in the High North should be keyed to "situational awareness," with rapid reinforcements kept over the horizon.

42. North Atlantic Treaty Organization, *Active Engagement, Modern Defence*, Strategic Concept adopted at the Lisbon Summit, November 19, 2010, http://www.nato.int/cps/en/natolive/news_68172.htm. See Jaap de Hoop Scheffer. Speech on security prospects in the High North, Reykjavik Summit, 2009, http://www.nato.int/docu/speech/2009/s090129a.html.

43. Believed to be Canada.

44. See Heininen, "Globalization and Security in the Circumpolar North."

45. Even the desirability of investment is, however, currently contentious between the ruling parties: whereas the Social Democrats favored an offer of tourist investment by the Chinese millionaire Huang Nubo in 2011, the Left Green Interior Minister rejected it apparently because of concerns about alienation of Iceland's patrimony and environmental risks. (Theories much debated abroad about China using such a foothold for strategic purposes played little part in the Icelandic discussion.)

46. Visir News Agency, "Íslendingar byrjaðir að græða á olíuleit við Grænland" [Icelanders begin to help with oil exploration at Greenland],

November 29, 2010, http://www.visir.is/islendingar-byrjadir-ad-graeda-a-oliuleit-vid-graenland/article/2010508222609.

47. It would now be generally agreed that Iceland cannot compete as a shipping hub for the near-term expansion of traffic through the Northern Sea Route over Russia but could come into its own later if a trans-polar route becomes viable or if developments in Greenland create significant new traffic from there to Europe.

48. Landsvirkjun, "The Market Development of Electricity and Future Visions of Landsvirkjun," in *Report from the Annual Meeting*, 2010, http://www.landsvirkjun.is/media/samradsfundir/arsfundur_LV_2010_hordur_arnarson.pdf.

49. Össur Skarphedinsson, "The High North and Iceland's Policy" [Norðurslóðir og stefna Íslands]. *Morgunblaðið*, January 18, 2011, http://www.utanrikisraduneyti.is/media/nordurlandaskrifstofa/OS-Moggi-18-jan-2011.PDF.

50. Samtök Fullveldissina, *Yfirgangur ESB og Norðmanna* [The behavior of the EU and of Norway], August 10, 2010, http://www.fullvalda.is/greinar/33-yfirgangur-esb-og-nordmanna.

51. Council of the European Union, "Council Conclusions on Arctic Issues," 2985th Foreign Affairs Council meeting, Brussels, December 8, 2009, http://www.consilium.europa.eu/uedocs/cms_Data/docs/pressdata/EN/foraff/111814.pdf.

52. Halldór Björnsson et al., "The Influence of Global Climate Change on Iceland" [Hnattrænar loftslagsbreytingar og áhrif þeirra á Íslandi], a report on Climate Change by the Scientific Committee (Ministry for the Environment, 2008), 52–63.

53. Ministry for the Environment, *Iceland's Fifth National Communication on Climate Change*, 9.

54. Björnsson et al., "Influence of Global Climate Change," 57.

55. Ministry for the Environment, *Iceland's Fifth National Communication on Climate Change*, 8.

56. Álfheiður Ingadóttir, *Risk Assessment for Oil Transportation through Icelandic Waters* [Áhættumat vegna siglinga olíuflutningaskipa í íslenskri efnahagslögsögu]. Discussions in the Parliament, Althingi (2009), http://www.althingi.is/skodalid.php?lthing=135&lidur=lid20080305T180103.

57. Valur Ingimundarson, *The Geopolitics of Arctic Natural Resources* (Brussels: Directorate-General for External Policies, European Parliament, 2010), http://www.tepsa.eu/download/Valur%20Ingimundarson.pdf, 4.

58. Baldursson, "Sustainable Development for the Residents of the High North," 19.
59. Össur Skarphedinsson, "Collective Governance of the High North" [Samvinnustjórn á norðurslóðum], *Fréttablaðið*, February 2, 2011, http://www.visir.is/samvinnustjorn--a-nordurslodum/article/20118089 29462.
60. For texts of the two agreements, see http://www.arctic-council.org/index. php/en/document-archive/category/20-main-documents-from-nuuk and http://www.state.gov/r/pa/prs/ps/2013/05/209406.htm, respectively.
61. The titles of the reports themselves convey the flavor: (in translation) "Working on the Sea," "Iceland on the Route," "Arctic Shipping and Iceland's Opportunities," "Breaking the Ice."
62. Valgerdur Sverrisdóttir, *Breaking the Ice*, report of the "Breaking the Ice" conference, Akureyri, March 27–28, 2007, http://www.utanrikisraduneyti. is/media/Utgafa/Breaking_The_Ice_Conference_Report.pdf, 5–7.
63. Ministry of Foreign Affairs, *Iceland and the High North*, 2009, http://www.utanrikisraduneyti.is/media/Skyrslur/Skyrslan_Island_a_nordurslodumm.pdf.
64. Althingi, *Þingsályktun um stefnu Íslands í málefnum Norðurslóða*.
65. Jean-Marc Rickli, "European Small States' Military Policies after the Cold War: From Territorial to Niche Strategies," *Cambridge Review of International Affairs* 21, no. 3 (September 2008): 307.
66. Skarphedinsson, "High North and Iceland's Policy."
67. Ministry of Foreign Affairs, *Iceland and the High North*.
68. Skarphedinsson, "High North and Iceland's Policy."
69. Nordic Council of Ministers, "Sustainable Development in the Arctic," *Nordic Council of Ministers' Arctic Co-operation Programme 2012–2014*, http://www.nordregio.se/Global/About%20Nordregio/Arktiskt%20samarbetsprogram/2012-14/Nordisk_Ministerr%c3%a5d_Program_for_arktis_2012-2014_ENGELSK.pdf.
70. Althingi, *Þingsályktun um stefnu Íslands í málefnum Norðurslóða*.
71. Skarphedinsson, "Collective Governance of the High North."
72. Skarphedinsson, "High North and Iceland's Policy."
73. Ministry of Foreign Affairs, *The Statistics of Icelandic Foreign Service Compared with Other Nordic States*, http://www.utanrikisraduneyti.is/raduneytid/samantekt/.
74. Details are at the university's website, www.unak.is.
75. Website at http://www.caps.hi.is/.

76. West Nordic cooperation is also intensifying in this field, as shown by the preparations to offer a joint West Nordic master's program at universities in Greenland, Iceland, the Faroes, and western Norway, from fall 2014, in governance and sustainable management for societies affected by Arctic warming.

77. See Heininen, chapter 11 in this volume.

78. See http://www.arctic-council.org/index.php/en/resources/news-and-press/news-archive/647-introduction-to-the-director-of-the-arctic-council-secretariat.

79. This idea is associated especially with President Ólafur Ragnar Grimsson, who expressed it in public comments in March 2010.

80. Sveinn Kjartan Einarsson, "China's Direct Investment in the 'West': Is There a Security Threat?" (MA thesis, University of Iceland, 2013), http://skemman.is/item/view/1946/14799;jsessionid=5CA8ACB66FF7B7324C4AA8D639972DB7.

81. Alyson J. K. Bailes and Baldur Thorhallsson, "Iceland and Europe: Drifting Further Apart?" Finnish Institute of International Affairs Briefing Paper 139, September 2013, http://www.fiia.fi/en/publication/360/iceland_and_europe/#.UlG2NyRO_w4.

82. Respective experiences with local oil/gas extraction could provide a new practical common bond between Greenlanders and Icelanders.

83. Cf. Byers, *Who Owns the Arctic?*

Part III

Shared Sovereignty and Global Security Interests

CHAPTER 13

THE ARCTIC AND THE
EUROPEAN UNION

Clive Archer

INTRODUCTION

During the last decade, a number of states, including Russia and the
United States, have developed Arctic strategies partly in response to
the growing environmental and resource importance of the region. The
Arctic has also seen increased security interest. More recently the European Union (EU) has developed and expressed its interest in the region.

In 2007, the European Commission's Integrated Maritime Strategy
referred to the Arctic, as did the High Representative and Commission policy paper on Climate Change and International Security, which
recommended an EU Arctic policy. After a European Parliament debate
on the subject, the Commission issued a communication on the EU and

the Arctic region at the end of 2008, and in December 2009 the Council of the European Union (hereafter "the Council") agreed to a conclusion on the Arctic issue. In June 2012, the Commission and the EU's High Representative for Foreign Affairs issued a joint communication on the EU and the Arctic region.

This chapter will examine concepts of sovereignty in the EU and the Arctic as the background to the EU's Arctic policy. It will look at the evolution of the current EU involvement in the region. The question is asked: why has the EU become involved with the Arctic? It will also examine what issues are now faced by this Arctic policy. The analysis will be undertaken using EU documents and material from interviews.

THE EUROPEAN UNION AND SOVEREIGNTY

When the European Union is considered in the context of Arctic sovereignty, not only does the nature of sovereignty have to be considered but so does that of the EU. This also has relevance for the involvement of the EU in the Arctic region. However, any consideration of the EU must take into account the different understandings of the nature of the EU and its various predecessors, the European Communities (EC), the European Economic Community (EEC), European Atomic Energy Community (Euratom), and the European Coal and Steel Community (ECSC). Broadly, the debate on understanding the EU is divided between those that place greater emphasis on European integration as a process driven by states for their own benefit and those that stress the manner in which European integration has transformed the nature of participating states.

State-Based Views

The former group tended to take a realist perspective of the organizations of European integration, where the EC and EU were perhaps seen as more sophisticated instruments of the member states for the furtherance of their policies, not too dissimilar to the North Atlantic Treaty

Organization (NATO) and the European Free Trade Association (EFTA) in their ends. A key proponent of this perspective is Alan Milward, who thought that

> the process of European integration, was...a part of that post-war rescue of the European nation-state, because the new political consensus on which this rescue was built required the process of integration, the surrender of limited areas of national sovereignty to the supranation.[1]

Whether a state used the framework of European integration for future policy depended on "the nature of national, domestic policy choices."[2] This view was later taken up by Andrew Moravcsik in his liberal intergovernmentalist framework that saw the activities of European integration as primarily being the outcome of bargains struck between states after governments had brought together and aggregated the interests of domestic interest groups within their state. Moravcsik thus saw the EU as "a successful intergovernmental regime designed to manage economic interdependence through negotiated policy co-ordination."[3] Such policy discussions were initiated with preferences being formulated at the national level, after which interstate bargaining took place, as did the decision as to which institutions—national ones, the EU, or some other international organization—should be used to advance the policy. Though the Commission of the EU could make an input into the policy-making process, it was more the "relative bargaining power of governments" rather than the supranational actors—such as the European Commission or European Parliament (EP)—that influenced policy outcomes.[4] For Moravcsik, the supranational institutions of the EU are seen as an efficient way used by member states to enforce basically intergovernmental agreements.

This view of the EU and European integration sees sovereignty being retained by the member states. They can join or leave the EU as they determine. They can agree to or reject new treaties. Once signed up to an agreement, they can expect high costs for not keeping to the rules of the club, but that is a way of making sure that all contracting parties keep their promises. The EU is thus seen as less of a threat to sovereignty and more as a means to keep the member states functioning cooperatively to a greater extent than if they were by themselves, within a still basically anarchical world system.

Liberal Institutionalist Perspectives

Ernst Haas's study of the ECSC saw its institutions—especially the High Authority, the forerunner of the EC's Commission—as being able to act independently of the member states. He saw political integration in Europe as

> the process whereby political actors in several distinct national settings are persuaded to shift their loyalties, expectations and political activities toward a new center, whose institutions possess or demand jurisdiction over the pre-existing national states.[5]

These new centers—the High Authority of the ECSC and then the European Commission of the EC and EU—thus seep away sovereignty from the member states and share it with them. The expansive logic of European integration is that progress is made in one policy area at the supranational level—above the sovereign states—only if the tasks handled are expanded, representing a spillover from one policy area to another.[6]

This expansive logic ran into trouble in the 1960s with the opposition by President Charles de Gaulle of France to ambitious Commission schemes; in the 1970s with "Eurosclerosis" slowing down the process of European integration; and with the opposition in Denmark and France to the Maastricht Treaty of 1992, and of France, the Netherlands, and Ireland to the European Constitution in 2004 and the Lisbon Treaty of 2007, all of which documents extended and deepened EU activities.

Nevertheless, the institutions of the EU have developed, and the balance between the European Parliament, Commission, and Council of Ministers has changed over the years. New areas of competence have been included, such as foreign and security policy and justice and home affairs, though the policy-making process for those has often been different from that required for the internal market policies of the EU. Pollack contended that, with institutional changes and an expansion of membership, it is more difficult for the member states to keep track of what the EU institutions are doing.[7] Others consider that institutions such as the EU tend to continue with a policy, sometimes despite its failure, because of the costs of the political—and financial—investments made in such policies.[8] It has been pointed out that, as the European integration process continues, national administrations and domestic policy making have become "Europeanized," which "implies converging policy content."[9]

This perspective on the EU tends to place its institutions on much more of a level with national governments than is the case with intergovernmentalism. Though some of the early hopes—or, in some cases, fears—of the EU becoming almost a federation have subsided, there is still the consideration that EU policy is something more than the sum of member states' wishes and that the member states themselves are increasingly having their own practices affected by being part of the integration. As noted, this leads to a more intricate view of sovereignty whereby its exercise can be shared by states and other institutions such as those of the EU.

Constructivists and Identity

A third approach to understanding the nature of the EU is to treat it as a construct, though "like no other in the international system."[10] Social constructivists have placed emphasis on the interrelationship between institutions and people, on how the former can constitute communities, shaping relations between people, and also on how the institutions themselves are human creations as "people make them."[11]

This plays on a key element of social constructivism, that of identity. Policy and institutions may be important, but European integration has to consider the question of a European identity. States, and individuals, can adopt a number of identities, though one may dominate over the others (for example Swede over European or Scandinavian). Birthe Hansen pointed out that "[m]ultiple identities flourish in all regions, but in Europe they have become institutionalized to a comparatively high degree, and it is in Europe that national identity has faced the greatest challenges."[12] Indeed, the strength or weakness of particular identities, among both decision makers and the wider population, can have an effect on the institutions used and on the policies undertaken by a state or by the EU.

With this view, sovereignty is also a construct, and precisely how it is constructed will depend partly on the identities of the peoples in Europe. Those identifying strongly with a sovereign state will strengthen the meaning of sovereignty for that state, whereas a strong identification with Europe by the peoples within that continent will chip away at the glue of national sovereignty and instead help to provide some of the elements of the exercise of sovereignty to the new institutions of Europe. Without a strong feeling of there being "Europeans" behind the EU institutions, they will have to rely more on the delegated powers of the member states and will be less able to claim credit for their own policies.

THE ARCTIC AND SOVEREIGNTY

If the existence of the European Union has caused a degree of puzzlement in the context of state sovereignty, the Arctic itself is not without questions when it comes to that topic. First, it is an area divided between seas and lands, and even the legal status of some Arctic waters (for example, and most notably, the Arctic Ocean and the seabed beneath it) is varied. Second, there have been disputes over sovereignty, some of which remain unresolved. Third, the issue of indigenous peoples and their rights, especially for those who move across state frontiers, throws up considerable challenges, as does the sparsely populated nature of vast tracts of land where the exercise of sovereignty has not always been easy.

These factors have meant that, at least in the past, sovereignty in the Arctic region has been something of a challenged concept, if somewhat less so than in the Antarctic. However, over time the situation has become clearer. First, the United Nations Convention on the Law of the Sea (UNCLOS) has helped clarify the distinctions between land and territorial sea and the contiguous zone (Part II), the exclusive economic zone (Part V), the continental shelf (Part VI), the high seas (Part VII), the Area (Part XI), and ice-covered areas (Article 234), as well as issues such as protection and preservation of the marine environment (Part XII), marine scientific research (Part XIII), and settlement of disputes (Part XV).[13]

Secondly, most of the territorial and maritime disputes within the Arctic have been solved by diplomacy and resort to international law. In particular, the long-standing disagreement between Russia and Norway about the division of the Barents Sea was ended with an agreement between the two states in 2010,[14] and the outer limits of the continental shelves of the Arctic littoral states is being decided by the Commission on the Limits of the Continental Shelf, established by Annex B of the UNCLOS.[15] Perhaps the most enduring legal dispute is over the nature of the waters around Svalbard.[16]

The special position of indigenous peoples in the Arctic has been recognized by the Arctic states. Norway, Sweden, and Finland have representation for the Saami people in the Saami Council;[17] Greenland and Nunavut in Canada are dominated by Arctic indigenous people and have a high degree of autonomy;[18] the Inuit Circumpolar Council (ICC) represents various indigenous groups from the United States, Canada, Russia, and Greenland;[19] and the Arctic Council (AC) has indigenous groups as "permanent participants."[20]

The vast areas within the Arctic region has often meant that the countries that claim them have sometimes found it difficult to exercise sovereignty. This was the nub of the dispute between Denmark and Norway over east Greenland, which was decided by the Permanent Court of International Justice in 1933, in Denmark's favor, and the Danish authorities in Greenland struggled to maintain oversight of that large island during World War II. The Cold War saw a more determined effort by the Arctic states to show presence in their Arctic territories, and since the end of the Cold War that effort has continued, with Canada making a particular point of patrolling Canadian Arctic land and maritime areas.

Indeed, during the Cold War, while the European Communities could be seen as challenging the traditional view of sovereignty in Europe—at least from a liberal institutionalist perspective—the Arctic seemed to represent more of a playground for power politics, realist views with sharp divisions between areas of undisputed sovereignty. The areas of dispute were mostly between Cold War allies and were quickly or peacefully settled (the "cod wars" between Iceland and the United Kingdom in the 1950s and 1970s being exceptions), whereas those between adversaries—such as the Barents Sea dispute between Norway and the Soviet Union—were "put on ice" for fear of causing more dangerous disputes. After the end of the Cold War, the Arctic area has become one of institutional diversity, cultivation of international law, greater recognition of the rights of indigenous peoples, and autonomy. Indeed, its current complexity in terms of sovereignty and a variety of forms of cooperation softens the contrast to the European Union compared with the previous sharper difference from the EC. Nevertheless, the Arctic has nothing like the EU, seen by some as a claimant to sovereignty.

There is also little within the Arctic region to demonstrate the emergence of an Arctic identity among the people who live and work there. The ICC provides the opportunity for indigenous peoples to meet together but, as yet, this has not led to the emergence of an identity that counters those of the states that have territory in the Arctic. The exception is that of Greenland, with its indigenous majority, where the links with Denmark are weakening over time. However, the obvious end point is a sovereign Greenlandic state; there is little to indicate the rise of Arctic institutions, backed by an Arctic identity, that will challenge the sovereignty of the Arctic states.

EUROPEAN UNION INVOLVEMENT IN THE ARCTIC[21]

The involvement of the EU in Arctic affairs has been largely determined by a series of external impetuses together with the involvement of some EU institutions plus a few key member state governments. It has advanced in fits and starts and is still at the stage whereby the EU is not a major Arctic player, though—because of its involvement in key policies such as the environment, energy, and shipping—the EU can expect to have a voice in certain aspects of the development of the Arctic, as seen in its interest in permanent observer status of the Arctic Council.

Summary of the EU's Involvement

Although Denmark, an EC and then EU member since 1973, has obvious interests in the Arctic through Greenland being part of the Danish Realm, Greenland was only part of the EC until 1985. Once Sweden and Finland became EU members in 1995, Arctic territory saw the EU flag. The Finnish initiative for a Northern Dimension (ND) of the EU brought greater attention to the region. However, this policy dealt primarily with the functional aspects of relations between Russia and members and candidate members in the Baltic Sea area and, to a lesser extent, the Barents region. It took some pressure from Denmark, representing Greenland, to create an Arctic Window to the ND in 2002.[22] Even that has been a fairly inactive part of the ND, which in itself is a low-key policy area.[23]

A major change came with the European Commission's 2007 Integrated Maritime Strategy paper, in which the Arctic Ocean was mentioned in the context of global warming. Furthermore, it promised a Commission paper on Arctic Ocean strategic issues for 2008.[24] In March 2008 the EU's High Representative and the Commission produced a policy paper on climate change and international security suggesting an EU Arctic policy. However, the question gained political momentum with a debate in the European Parliament in October 2008, leading to a resolution and to the subsequent Commission communication on the EU and the Arctic region in November 2008. The Council of the European Union in December 2009 issued a conclusion on the Arctic issue. The region was again debated in the European Parliament in March 2010 and once more in January 2011. Finally a joint communication was issued by the High Representative and the Commission in June 2012. This involvement will now be examined in greater detail.

The Preparation

The first mention of the Arctic in EU policy papers after the Arctic Window of the Northern Dimension had stuck on its hinges was in the Integrated Maritime Policy (IMP) in 2007. The Action Plan of the IMP promised not only a Commission report on the Arctic Ocean but also a "more detailed reflection on the European interests in the Arctic Ocean and the EU's role in this respect." The diversity of issues in the Arctic was seen as requiring an "integrated, cross-sectoral approach." Indeed, it reported that already stakeholders had responded on such areas "as environmental protection and biodiversity, energy, maritime transport, fisheries, arctic technology, tourism and security."[25] A small inter-service group was gathered together to prepare for the Commission paper on the Arctic.[26]

Meanwhile, another mention—this time somewhat alarmist—of the Arctic was found in the paper on climate change and international security jointly authored in March 2008 by the Commissioner for External Affairs, Benita Ferrero-Waldner, and the High Representative, Javier Solana. In this context, they mentioned that "more disputes over land and maritime borders and other territorial rights are likely." The need to "revisit existing rules of international law" was mentioned. The specter of "potential conflict over resources in Polar regions" was brandished. As regions previously inaccessible open up because of climate change, then "the scramble for resources will intensify."[27]

After this broaching of the issue of the Arctic, the European Parliament held a debate initiated by the Liberal ALDE group. The resulting resolution on Arctic governance, adopted on October 9, 2008, had as its prime reasons for concern the Russian flag incident of August 2007,[28] the UNCLOS, the effects in the Arctic of global warming, concerns about the environment, increased traffic and security issues, and the presence of three EU (Denmark, Finland, and Sweden) and two other European Economic Area states (Iceland and Norway) as members of the Arctic Council. The EP wanted special mention of the Arctic at the United Nations Climate Change Conference (COP15) in Copenhagen 2009; it outlined the basis for the Commission's communication on the Arctic; and it suggested observer status for the European Commission in the Arctic Council. It noted that the Arctic was never expected to be navigable or open for commercial exploitation and is therefore not governed by "specifically formulated multilateral norms and regulations."[29] An innovative aspect was the suggestion in the resolution for an international treaty to protect the Arctic, based on the Antarctic Treaty but taking into account differences between the two regions. This was to be at odds with the approach later taken by the European Commission and the Council, though, on the whole, the deliverable policy outcomes from the EP resolution were ones supportive of the Commission viewpoint.

As might be expected from an EP resolution, especially one from the more integrationist parties in the Parliament, it was not mostly concerned with the natural resources of the Arctic and the issue of the EU's access to them. Although it mentioned the presence of EU and European Economic Area (EEA) states in the region, it was scarcely one that tried to carve out EU territory in the Arctic. Indeed the resolution took a holistic and integrated view of the Arctic region and was particularly concerned by environmental questions and the position of indigenous peoples. However, it clearly signaled an institutional interest in Arctic affairs by at least one section of the EU.

THE COMMISSION COMMUNICATION AND AFTER

Since the EP's initial debate, the Arctic issue has become part of the EU's decision-making procedures with a Commission communication, a Council response, further EP discussion, and involvement of the High Representative of the Union for Foreign Affairs and Security Policy, Baroness Ashton.

The European Commission's 2008 Communication

The Commission's communication to the EP and the Council in November 2008 was on the subject of the EU and the Arctic. It set out EU interests there under three headings: protecting and preserving the Arctic in unison with its population; promoting sustainable use of resources; and contributing to enhanced Arctic multilateral governance.[30]

These three elements reflected the balance desired by the Commission and EU member states in their concerns for the Arctic—the environment and the indigenous peoples, access to resources, and the governance of the Arctic. Clearly the Commission wished to become engaged in certain policy aspects in the region. The Commission had in total forty-nine proposals for action under these three headings. Some had relevance for external relations—especially those with Russia—such as the Commission's support for an agreement on disaster response in the Barents Euro-Arctic Council (BEAC), long-term cooperation with Russia "facilitating the sustainable and environmentally friendly exploration, extraction and transportation of Arctic hydrocarbon resources," and avoiding "discriminatory practices...by any of the Arctic coastal states towards third countries' merchant ships."[31] Furthermore, there was to be a discussion with Northern Dimension partners about projects under the Northern Dimension Environmental Partnership to cover wider areas in the European Arctic.

On governance, the Commission paper noted the maritime disputes in the Arctic but mentioned that UNCLOS already provided an extensive and functioning legal framework that could provide the basis for settlement of disputes including those on delimitation. It noted that the May 2008 Ilulissat Declaration of the five Arctic coastal states— including Russia—committed these countries to using legal instruments to solve their disputes in the Arctic. The Commission wanted international negotiations and discussions on international marine protected areas to explore "the possibility of establishing new, multi-sector frameworks for integrated ecosystem management" and to enhance its input into the Arctic Council.[32] To that end, the Commission wished to apply for permanent observer status in the AC. However, it disagreed with the EP about the need for new legal instruments for the Arctic but rather aimed at the implementation of existing agreements.[33] The then maritime commissioner, Joe Borg, expressed the Commission viewpoint on this: "We believe an UNCLOS-based governance system could deliver security and stability, strict environmental management and the sustainable use of resources subject to open and equitable access—precisely the aims contained in our strategy."[34] It seems that just before the publication of the communication, the president of the Commission, José Manuel Barroso, had had his ear bent about the difficulties of the EP line on governance by the Norwegian prime minister, Jens Stoltenberg, and had indeed agreed with Mr. Stoltenberg in public.[35]

The Council Conclusions and After

The Council Conclusions on Arctic issues were adopted on December 8, 2009, and indicated that the Council agreed with the Commission that using existing instruments of governance for the Arctic was preferable to creating new legal institutions. The twenty-three points in the Council's conclusions included areas such as "climate, safeguarding the law of the

sea, environmentally hazardous chemicals, research, shipping, cooperation with indigenous peoples and cooperation with existing forums, such
as the Arctic Council."[36] An important objective was to assist closer EU
cooperation with the members of the AC and to support efforts by the
Commission (and Italy) to become permanent observers of the Arctic
Council.[37] This approach had already been rebuffed by Canada at the
April 2009 AC meeting, with the EU's consideration of a ban on sealskin
exports from Canada being the main reason.[38]

By the March 2010 EP debate on the Arctic, the whole issue had been
integrated into the EU's institutional structure, and Baroness Ashton, the
vice president of the Commission and High Representative of the Union
for Foreign Affairs and Security Policy, made a statement on the EU's
Arctic policy that stressed the environmental importance of the region.
In seeking fair treatment in transport and natural resources, while maintaining environmental safeguards, the role of the three EU members of
the AC was mentioned. On Arctic governance, the emphasis was again
on implementation of existing agreements and the importance of the
AC and of UNCLOS. The EP's proposal for an Arctic treaty drawing
on the experience of the Antarctic Treaty was rejected because of the
differences between the two areas.[39] A further EP debate and resolution
in January 2011 referred to the region by Norway's favored term, the
High North, and was a result of the Gahler report from the Committee
on Foreign Affairs.[40] The resolution was perhaps more concerned with
resources and transport routes than the 2008 resolution and shied away
from recommending a new Arctic treaty, instead preferring that existing
rules in the region be "developed, strengthened and implemented by all
parties concerned."[41] The Commission was tasked with reporting back
on developments by June 2011: the Arctic was well and truly on the EU's
agenda.

Meanwhile, the ministerial gathering of the Arctic Council, meeting
in Greenland's capital, Nuuk, in May 2011, spoke about the application of the European Commission, inter alia, for permanent observer

status in the AC.[42] In essence, the issue was postponed until 2013; it was handed over to a task force to make recommendations to the Senior Arctic Officials (SAOs) on how to implement this status based on the criteria for such membership that the SAOs had presented at the ministerial meeting. These were quite extensive and included what could be called an indigenous peoples' clause. This required successful candidates to show that they "respect the values, interests, culture and traditions of Arctic indigenous peoples and other Arctic inhabitants," something that presented the European Commission with a difficulty given the EU's treatment of sealskin imports since the early 1980s.[43] Although in March 2013 China and five other states were granted observer status in the AC, the Council decided not to progress with the EU's application until its members were agreed that "concerns of Council members" had been addressed by the EU.[44] This was in effect reference to the Canadian stand against the EU's position on sealskins.

The June 2012 joint communication "presents an elaborated synthesis of EU's contribution to the Arctic since 2008."[45] However, it is a modest document that scales back any notion of EU "benchmarks," "action plans," or objectives related to the Arctic. Extra spending is limited to greater resources for Arctic-related research.[46] The communication can be seen as the basis for the EU's application for permanent observer status of the AC, with an emphasis on the EU's role in research, environmental, sustainable development, and trade matters. One new area is that of satellite monitoring and surveillance.[47]

THE EU AND THE ARCTIC: WHY AN EU ARCTIC POLICY?

Why have the EU's various institutions interested themselves in the Arctic region? Answers to this can be found partly in factors external to the EU and partly within the EU itself. Some elements can be associated more with a realist vision of the Arctic, whereas others foresee a more cooperative future in the region. All have something to say about the image that the EU has of the Arctic.

The external factors relating to the importance of the Arctic became obvious from 2004 onward. The 2004 Arctic Climate Impact Assessment warned of climate changes within the Arctic region and their possible consequences elsewhere.[48] Given that the Arctic is a potentially resource-rich region, the shrinking and reduction of the extent of Arctic ice has meant greater accessibility in the exploitation of such resources, as pointed out in the paper on climate change and international security. The U.S. Geological Survey's 2008 report that 10 percent (or 240 billion barrels of oil and oil equivalents, BBOE) of the world's known conventional petroleum resources was in onshore fields in Canada, Alaska, and Russia and that "the total mean undiscovered conventional oil and gas resources of the Arctic are estimated to be approximately 90 billion barrels of oil, 1,669 trillion cubic feet of natural gas, and 44 billion barrels of natural gas liquids," in other words 412 BBOE.[49] This raised interest in the Arctic from an economic perspective and indicated that the member states of the EU might have a solid interest in the region that they could safeguard through the EU.

These reports affected expert opinion and gradually seeped into the public domain, but a more dramatic attraction of public attention to Arctic matters resulted from reports of a Russian flag being placed at the North Pole.[50] Though without legal implications, it attracted journalistic and academic comment and impinged on the minds of at least some of the decision makers. It seemed to indicate that a more traditional power struggle might be emerging through the melting ice of the Arctic. Some writers thus saw this move as a potential Russian "grab" of Arctic resources, involving issues of sovereignty and the use of military power.[51] This would have provided a less secure basis for an EU interest based on institutions, non-military issues, and cooperation.

Indeed, Russia had been developing its own Arctic strategy, which was issued in September 2008. It emphasized the importance of the

Arctic for the Russian economy and disclosed that special military forma-tions would be used to protect Russia's national interest in the region.[52] Other key states issued their Arctic strategies about the same time.[53] It appeared that the EU was being left behind when it came to carving a place in the ice, whereas the other Arctic states, especially the five littoral ones—Denmark/Greenland, Norway, Canada, Russia, and the United States—were increasingly marking their presence in the Arctic. It seemed that the inner clique of these Arctic coastal states, which had met at Ilulissat in May 2008, was making the running on Arctic matters. The only entrée that the EU had to this circle was the Danish govern-ment, which was there by virtue of representing Greenland in its external affairs. However, Greenland was on the verge of becoming more self-governing, even talking confidently about moving toward eventual inde-pendence.[54] This would leave the EU without even a foot in the door of the Arctic Five meetings. EU activity could thus be seen as being part of what some saw as the scramble for the Arctic.

This, however, would be a simplistic view. Although international events set the scene for EU involvement in Arctic affairs, internal factors determined the nature and speed of that response. After January 1, 2007, enlargement of the EU had ceased for the time being and the institutions of the EU could concentrate on the EU's relations with its surrounding neighborhood. If relations with the Mediterranean states and the east European countries were to gain some attention, then certainly some MEPs, and member state representatives, felt that the North should also be considered, especially after the Arctic Window of the ND had had such a meager response. The list of speakers in the two EP debates on the Arctic show MEPs from the Nordic states dominating, though by no means overwhelmingly.[55] EU members have interests in the Arctic —three of them have territory there, though Denmark's is not part of the EU—and can be expected to follow events there closely, the northern EU states particularly so. The Arctic is also interwoven into policy areas such as maritime policy, security, and trade and will not be absent in future discussions of those topics.

The formulation of an Arctic policy also shows the Commission and the EP competing and cooperating. The Commissioner for Maritime Affairs took the first step in 2007 by including references to the Arctic Ocean in the Integrated Maritime Strategy and promising a separate paper on the Arctic. This was matched by the more dramatic presentation by the Commissioner for External Affairs and the High Representative. Parliamentarians then took up the running and complemented Commission work (and think-tank input) on the subject. The northern EU members fed into the policy process, and there is some indication that Norway, an EEA state, had its say as well.

THE EU AND THE ARCTIC: QUESTIONS OF SOVEREIGNTY

The involvement of the EU in Arctic matters has grown significantly over the past seven years. This has partly been as a response to outside impetus but has also been a reflection of the interests of the member states—especially those from northern Europe—and of the functioning of the mechanisms of the EU itself. How does the story told in this chapter reflect on the EU's engagement with the sovereignty issue in the Arctic? Any response has to reflect the understandings of the nature of the EU as outlined at the start of this chapter.

A more realist, intergovernmentalist view of the EU's actions will point mainly to the questions of interests and power. The Arctic anyhow can be seen as an area where, in the Cold War period, power politics dominated. It was militarized and divided between NATO and the Soviet Union. There was scarcely any Arctic institution that stretched across the Cold War divide. The only presence that the EC had in the region was membership by Greenland as a part of the Danish Realm from 1973 to 1985, though this scarcely seemed to impinge on Brussels, and once the Greenlanders got home rule, they voted to leave the EC.

This view of the Arctic had already been complicated by disputes over fisheries in Arctic waters, which were often between NATO members such as the United Kingdom and Iceland, Denmark, and Norway (over waters around Jan Mayen), though a temporary solution to the Norwegian-Soviet dispute about the Barents Sea was quickly found for the fisheries side. However, such disputes can be seen in realist terms of states looking after their own interests in a fairly unregulated area.

A major change also came with Mr. Gorbachev's Murmansk speech in October 1987, in which he invited other Arctic states to cooperate in a range of activities, including transport, the environment, and research, as well as arms control.[56] Since then—and especially since the end of the Soviet Union—the Arctic has not been a center of military confrontation as before, though it has seen some increase in military presence. Furthermore, the extent of regulation has increased, though it is noticeable that the EU's Foreign Affairs Council—in which the states are represented—has called for implementation of existing measures in the Arctic rather than new instruments of governance and also sees the gradual formulation of a "policy on Arctic issues" to address *EU* interests and responsibilities "while recognising *Member States'* legitimate interests and rights in the Arctic."[57] The day of states' interests in the Arctic is certainly not past, and EU member states are just as concerned as others in protecting their interests in the region. The institutions of the EU can be seen as instruments to increase their relative bargaining power there, to use Moravcsik's term, but with not much of a shift of "loyalties, expectations and political activities" to Brussels in this area.

Although one accepts state interest and power considerations, the Arctic can also be seen in much more liberal institutionalist terms. Many aspects of offshore activity are covered by the UN Convention on the Law of the Sea, by which even the United States—a non-signatory—abides. The 1992 Paris Convention aims to regulate polluting activities in part of the marine Arctic area. Fisheries in some Arctic seas are covered by regional and bilateral agreements such as the 1980 North-East Atlantic Fisheries Convention, which established a commission (the NEAFC), and as the Norwegian-Russian Federation Fisheries Commission. Shipping is regulated not just by UNCLOS but also by such more specific agreements as the International Convention for the Prevention of Pollution from Ships (MARPOL), under the supervision of the International Maritime Organization (IMO), and with a wider range of agreements for shipping in the Arctic region.[58]

The European Union contributes to the cobweb of regulation and policy stretching across the Arctic region, including its seas.[59] For example, the EU's June 2008 Marine Strategy Framework Directive and the EU's Registration, Evaluation, Authorization of Chemicals (REACH) regulatory regime apply to EU Arctic lands. According to the EU, the exploitation of hydrocarbons in the Arctic should follow strict environmental standards, such as the Arctic Council's Offshore Oil and Gas Guidelines of 2009. The EU Council encourages member states in their capacity as flag, port, or coastal states to "promote and monitor the full implementation and further implementation of existing rules on navigation, maritime safety and security, vessel routing systems and environmental standards" in the Arctic.[60] All of the EU Arctic states and a number of non-Arctic EU members conduct Arctic research. During the International Polar Year (2007–2008), there was close cooperation within the EU's Polar Board, bringing together the work of Arctic observatories.[61]

This network stretches to other states. The EEA links EU states with Iceland and Norway, while Greenland has Overseas Countries and Territories (OCT) status with the EU. All three and Russia are involved in the EU's Northern Dimension initiative. The European Parliament's idea of the Commission opening international negotiations leading to the adoption of a treaty for the protection of the Arctic would have stressed the transnational problems of the region and entrenched the standing of the EU there. As it is, the EU remains on the outside when it comes to the five littoral Arctic states, the European Commission has no observer status in the Arctic Council, and the interests of its three Arctic members are more directed to the south of their countries than to the north. The various EU activities may help to blur the exercise of sovereignty within EU Arctic states, and by EU states' activities in maritime areas, they may bring into such regulatory regimes the other two EEA Arctic states, but they scarcely apply to Canada, the United States, and Russia and, in many cases, Greenland. Even the wider international regulations have their limits and are mostly enforceable at the national level.

The element of identity is also important here, and the start of this chapter dealt with the possible emergence of two identities: a European and an Arctic one. The European identity, at least as expressed through the EU integration process, is being increasingly challenged, both from increased nationalism within member states and by a failure to enhance a "European" voice on the world stage. Northern EU states—including the likes of Germany, the Netherlands, and the United Kingdom—might wonder whether the EU has particularly strong interests, let alone an identity to promote, in the case of membership of the Arctic Council. The Arctic region has seen certain identities emerging, not least among indigenous peoples but also among those who work and live in Arctic conditions, and these sometimes stretch across frontiers. In some cases the out-group, against which an identity is being constructed, is that of the EU with its action against sealing and whaling and its general igno- rance of the Arctic. Over the past five years, EU institutions have tried to combat this negative image by building up their knowledge of the Arctic and by interacting with the Norwegian government and with indige- nous peoples in forums such as the Conference of Parliamentarians of the Arctic Region. Their resolutions on the Arctic have become less demanding and more tentative and understanding.[62] This may reflect an image of the EU that is more self-knowing of its own limitations in the Arctic region, one that understands the potential of the institutional richness in the region but also accepts the power imbalance that works against the EU. The European Union will not be able to erase the lines of sovereignty in the Arctic—just as it has failed to do so within the EU itself —but, with its variety of institutions, agencies, regulations, and agreements and together with other institutions such as the Arctic Council, it may help to smooth the hard edges of state sovereignty in that region.

NOTES

1. Alan S. Milward assisted by George Brennan and Federico Romero, *The European Rescue of the Nation-State* (London: Routledge, 1992), 4.
2. Ibid., 438.
3. Andrew Moravcsik, "Preferences and Power in the European Community: A Liberal Intergovernmentalist Approach," in *Economic and Political Integration in Europe*, ed. Simon Bulmer and Andrew Scott (Oxford: Blackwell, 1994), 29.
4. Andrew Moravcsik, *The Choice for Europe: Social Purpose & State Power from Messina to Maastricht* (London: UCL Press, 1998), 482.
5. Ernst Haas, *The Uniting of Europe: Political, Social and Economic Forces, 1950–57* (Stanford, CA: Stanford University Press, 1958), 16.
6. Ernst Haas, "International Integration: The European and the Universal Process," *International Organization* 15, no. 3 (1961): 336–392.
7. Mark Pollack, "The Commission as an Agent," in *At the Heart of the Union: Studies of the European Commission*, ed. Neill Nugent (Basingstoke: Macmillan, 1997), 109–128.
8. Peter Hall and Rosemary Taylor, "Political Science and the Three New Institutionalisms," *Political Studies* 44, no. 5 (1996): 941.
9. Christoph Knill, *The Europeanisation of National Administrations: Patterns of Institutional Change and Persistence* (Cambridge: Cambridge University Press, 2001), 2.
10. Lauren McLaren, *Identity, Interests and Attitudes to European Integration* (London: Palgrave Macmillan, 2006), 1.
11. Alec Sweet Stone, Neil Fligstein, and Wayne Sandholz, "The Institutionalization of European Space," in *The Institutionalization of Europe*, ed. Alec Sweet Stone, Neil Fligstein, and Wayne Sandholz (Oxford: Oxford University Press, 2001), 9.
12. Birthe Hansen, "Multiple Identities of European States," in *Explaining European Integration*, ed. Anders Wivel (Copenhagen: Copenhagen Political Studies Press, 1998), 160–161.
13. Bo Johnson Theutenberg, *The Evolution of the Law of the Sea* (Dublin: Tycooly International Publishing Ltd., 1984). "The Area" refers to the international seabed area.
14. Jonas Gahr Støre and Sergey Lavrov, *Joint Statement on Maritime Delimitation and Cooperation in the Barents Sea and the Arctic Ocean,*

April 27, 2010 http://www.regjeringen.no/en/dep/ud/aktuelt/nyheter/2 010/fellesuttalelse_delelinjen.html?id=601983.

15. Theutenberg, *Evolution of the Law of the Sea*, 189–190.

16. Torbjørn Pedersen, *Conflict and Order in Svalbard Waters* (Tromsø: University of Tromsø, 2008). Svalbard itself is an interesting case study of sovereignty, whereby the 1920 Paris Treaty allocated sovereignty of the Arctic archipelago to Norway but also constrained its exercise in certain functional areas.

17. See Saami Council at http://www.saamicouncil.net.

18. For information about the government of Nunavut in Canada, see http://www.gov.nu.ca/en/, and for Greenland, see http://uk.nanoq.gl/.

19. See Inuit Circumpolar Conference at http://www.inuitcircumpolar.com.

20. These are Arctic indigenous representatives, of which there are six; see Arctic Council at http://www.arctic-council.org.

21. This section is based on Clive Archer, "An EU Arctic Policy," paper given at UACES Conference, Bruges, September 6–8, 2010.

22. Joe Borg, "The Arctic: A Matter of Concern to Us All," speech at the conference "Common Concern for the Arctic," Ilulissat, Greenland, September 9, 2008, http://europa.eu/rapid/press-release_SPEECH-08-4 15_en.htm?locale=en.

23. Clive Archer and Tobias Etzold, "The European Union and Kaliningrad: Taking the Low Road," *Geopolitics* 15, no. 2 (2010): 339–340.

24. Commission of the European Communities, *An Integrated Maritime Policy for the European Union*, COM(2007) 575 final, October 10, 2007 (Brussels: Commission of the European Communities, 2007), http://eur-lex.europa.eu/LexUriServ/LexUriServ.do?uri=COM:2007:0575:FIN:EN:PDF, 13.

25. Commission of the European Communities, *Commission Staff Working Document: Accompanying document to the Communication from the Commission to the European Parliament, the Council, the European Economic and Social Committee and the Committee of the Regions—An Integrated Maritime Policy for the European Union* (Brussels: Commission of the European Communities, October 10, 2007), http://eur-lex.europa.eu/LexUriServ/LexUriServ.do?uri=CELEX:52007SC1278:EN:HTML, 30.

26. The successor to this group remained active. See Adele Airoldi, *The European Union and the Arctic: Main Developments July 2008–July 2010* (Copenhagen: Nordic Council of Ministers, 2010), 27.

27. High Representative and the European Commission, *Climate Change and International Security Paper from the High Representative and the European*

Commission to the European Council, 2008, http://www.consilium.europa.
eu/ueDocs/cms_Data/docs/pressData/en/reports/99387.pdf.

28. This was when a Russian scientist and parliamentarian, Artur Chilingarov, planted a Russian flag at the North Pole. See BBC News, "Russia Plants Flag under North Pole," *BBC News*, August 2, 2007, http://news.bbc.co. uk/1/hi/world/europe/6927395.stm.

29. European Parliament, *Resolution of 9 October 2008 on Arctic Governance*, http://www.europarl.europa.eu/sides/getDoc.do?pubRef=-//EP//TEXT+ TA+P6-TA-2008-0474+0+DOC+XML+V0//EN&language=EN.

30. Commission of the European Communities, *The European Union and the Arctic Region: Communication from the Commission to the European Parliament and the Council*, Brussels COM 763 (2008) (Brussels: Commission of the European Communities, 2008), http://eur-lex.europa. eu/LexUriServ/LexUriServ.do?uri=COM:2008:0763:FIN:EN:PDF, 3.

31. Ibid., 7–8.

32. Ibid., 11.

33. Ibid., 10.

34. Joe Borg, "The European Union's Strategy of Sustainable Management for the Arctic," Tromsø, Norway, January 19, 2009, http://europa.eu/ rapid/press-release_SPEECH-09-9_en.htm?locale=en.

35. Economist Intelligence Unit, *Norway Country Report* (London: EIU, December 2008), 9.

36. Council of the European Union, *Council Conclusions on Arctic Issues*, 2985th Foreign Affairs Council meeting, Brussels, December 8, 2009. http://www.consilium.europa.eu/uedocs/cms_Data/docs/pressdata/EN/ foraff/111814.pdf, 2–5.

37. Council of the European Union, *Council Conclusions on Arctic Issues*, 4.

38. Leigh Phillips, "Arctic Council Rejects EU Observer Application," *EU Observer*, April 30, 2009. http://www.euobserver.com.

39. European Parliament, *EU Policy on Arctic Issues*, debate, March 10, 2010, http://www.europarl.europa.eu/sides/getDoc.do?pubRef=-//EP//TEXT+ CRE+20100310+ITEM-011+DOC+XML+V0//EN&language=EN.

40. European Parliament, *Report on a Sustainable Policy for the High North (2009/2214(INI)*, Committee on Foreign Affairs, Rapporteur: Michael Gahler (issued December 12, 2010), http://www.europarl.europa.eu/sides/ getDoc.do?pubRef=-//EP//NONSGML+REPORT+A7-2010-0377+0+DOC +PDF+V0//EN&language=EN. According to one source, Gahler had close connections with the Norwegians (interview of MEP, October 9, 2010).

41. European Parliament, *A Sustainable EU Policy for the High North*, January 20, 2011, http://www.europarl.europa.eu/sides/getDoc.do?pubRef=-//EP/ /TEXT+TA+P7-TA-2011-0024+0+DOC+XML+V0//EN.

42. Arctic Council, *Nuuk Declaration on the Occasion of the Seventh Ministerial Meeting of the Arctic Council*, Nuuk, Greenland, May 12, 2011, http:// library.arcticportal.org/1254/, 2.

43. Senior Arctic Officials, *Report to Ministers, Nuuk, Greenland, May 2011*, http://library.arcticportal.org/1251/, 50; Airoldi, *The European Union and the Arctic: Main Developments*, 34–36.

44. Arctic Council, *Observers*, 2013, http://arctic-council.org/index.php/en/ about-us/arctic-council/observers.

45. Steffen Weber, Cécile Pelaudeix, and Iulian Romanyshyn, "Commentary: EU's New Arctic Communication: Towards Understanding of a Greater Role," *Arctic Yearbook 2012*, http://www.arcticyearbook.com/ index.php/commentaries/31-eu-s-new-arctic-communication-towards-understanding-of-a-greater-role, 156–158.

46. The EU's 7th Framework Programme for Research (2007–2013) financed forty-six projects and scholarships directly related to the Arctic, at the cost of about €20 million a year. See Janos Herman, *EU Perspectives on the Arctic*, 2013, http://www.forskningsradet.no/servlet/Satellite?blobcol= urldata&blobheader=application%2Fpdf&blobheadername1=Content-Disposition%3A&blobheadervalue1=+attachment%3B+filename%3D%2 2HermanEUperspectivesontheArctic.pdf%22&blobkey=id&blobtable= MungoBlobs&blobwhere=1274487110964&ssbinary=true, slide 9.

47. European Commission, High Representative of the European Union for Foreign Affairs and Security Policy, *Joint Communication to the European Parliament and the Council: Developing a European Union Policy towards the Arctic Region: Progress since 2008 and the Next Steps*, http://ec.europa. eu/maritimeaffairs/policy/sea_basins/arctic_ocean/documents/join_201 2_19_en.pdf, 3 and 7.

48. ACIA, *Impacts of a Warming Arctic: Arctic Climate Impact Assessment* (Cambridge: Cambridge University Press, 2004), http://www.acia.uaf.edu.

49. Bird et al., *Circum-Arctic Resource Appraisal; Estimates of Undiscovered Oil and Gas North of the Arctic Circle: U.S. Geological Survey Fact Sheet 2008-3049*, http://pubs.usgs.gov/fs/2008/3049/, 1 and 4.

50. BBC News, "Russia Plants Flag under North Pole."

51. The most typical contribution in this vein was Scott Borgerson, "Arctic Meltdown: The Economic and Security Implications of Global Warming,"

Foreign Affairs, March/April 2008, http://www.foreignaffairs.org/20080
301faessay87206/scott-gborgerson/arctic-meltdown.html.

52. Security Council of the Russian Federation, *Foundations of State Policy of Russian Federation in the Arctic for the Period up to 2020 and Beyond*, September 18, 2008, http://www.scrf.gov.ru/documents/98.html.

53. Norwegian Institute for Defence Studies, *Arctic Strategy Documents*, http://www.geopoliticsnorth.org/index.php?option=com_content& view=article&id=84&Itemid=69.

54. Nanoq, *Self-Government Awakes International Interest*, 2009, http:// en.mipi.nanoq.gl/sitecore/content/Websites/uk,-d-,nanoq/Emner/News/ News_from_Government/2009/06/awakes_interest.aspx.

55. A count of the MEPs who spoke in the 2008 and 2010 debates shows that ten came from the Nordic states, six from Baltic states and Poland, seventeen from the United Kingdom and Germany, and ten from other states.

56. David Scrivener, *Gorbachev's Murmansk Speech: Soviet Initiative and Western Responses* (Oslo: Norwegian Atlantic Committee, 1989).

57. Council of the European Union, *Council Conclusions on Arctic Issues*. Emphasis added.

58. Timo Koivurova and Erik Molenaar, *International Governance and Regulation of the Marine Arctic: Overview and Gap Analysis* (Oslo: WWF International Arctic Programme, 2009), 16–25.

59. For a full account, see Adele Airoldi, *The European Union and the Arctic: Policies and Actions* (Copenhagen: Nordic Council of Ministers, 2008).

60. Council of the European Union, *Council Conclusions on Arctic Issues*, 2–4.

61. European Science Foundation, *Towards the Strengthening of European Coordination between Polar Environmental Observatories in the Arctic Region*, 2008, http://www.esf.org/fileadmin/Public_documents/ Publications/polar03_V09ppp.pdf.

62. Airoldi, *The European Union and the Arctic: Main Developments*, 21–24.

CHAPTER 14

THE UNITED NATIONS
ON ARCTIC ISSUES

W. Andy Knight

INTRODUCTION

On December 10 and 11, 2012, the United Nations General Assembly
devoted two days of plenary meetings of its sixty-seventh session to
the agenda item "Oceans and the Law of the Sea." This was part of
the General Assembly's commemoration of the thirtieth anniversary
of the opening for signature of the UN Convention on the Law of
the Sea (UNCLOS). It also marked the special role that former Maltese
Ambassador to the UN Arvid Pardo played in outlining the vision
for this international treaty, which now provides the legal framework
governing ocean space, contested territorial water/border claims, sovereignty rights over maritime and seabed resources, the protection of the
marine environment and ecology, and the conduct of activities related

to shipping, fishing, and other oceanic activities.[1] It is therefore timely that a chapter in this book, *International Relations and the Arctic*, be devoted to examining how the United Nations can address the international challenges arising from Arctic sovereignty issues in the face of climate change.

The UN system is, after all, a multilateral governance arrangement designed by sovereign states to address global issues of the kind of complexity and importance that individual states within the Arctic region may not be able to deal with adequately on their own. The UN is an intergovernmental body that governs issues that spill beyond national borders and even within states. The global organization encourages multilateral cooperation, coordination, and transnational interactions among states in an increasingly globalizing and changing world. Its primary goal was laid out explicitly by the founders of the organization in the preamble of the UN Charter: "to save succeeding generations from the scourge of war, which twice in our lifetime has brought untold sorrow to mankind." So conflict management, conflict mitigation, and conflict prevention are central to the UN's essential mandate.

Conflict in the Arctic, although exaggerated by some observers, is quite possible especially if global warming continues at the current rate and threatens to expose further the much-sought-after resources that lie beneath the once solidly frozen ice in the area around the North Pole. The rush by Arctic and non-Arctic states to exploit those resources could in the future quite conceivably lead to conflict, if not full-blown war. So, given the UN's primary mandate, it should not come as a surprise that the world body will be expected by its member states to forestall such conflicts and prevent any prospect of violence erupting over the scarce resources of the Arctic.

However, this global organization is about more than conflict management. The UN is a multipurpose body. So although the maintenance of international peace and security is its foremost aim, this universal organization is also concerned with principles of justice and international law; with developing friendly relations among its member states based on principles of equal rights and self-determination; with solving international problems of an economic, social, and humanitarian character; with encouraging respect for human rights and fundamental freedoms for all; and with harmonizing the actions of nation-states in achieving the previous goals.[2] Other equally high-minded goals were added to the UN's mandate over the years, such as facilitating the global spread of democracy and protecting the global commons. Clearly, the UN's broad mandate is relevant to many of the issues emerging in the Arctic today.

THE UN, GLOBAL GOVERNANCE, AND *MARE LIBERUM*

At its base, the UN should be viewed as a global governance institution operating within a society of sovereign states in an anarchical environment essentially held together, sometimes tenuously, by shared norms and values found within the UN Charter but also reflected in subsequent resolutions, conventions, declarations, protocols, and treaties crafted by UN member governments, occasionally with input from non-state actors.[3] These norms and values, combined with rules and soft and hard law,[4] result in a "normative order beyond the nation-states which mitigates and partly supersedes the structural conditions of international anarchy."[5] Such a pragmatic and constructivist vision of global governance is contrasted with the more utopian notion of world government that world federalists and some of the framers of the UN Charter had in mind when the organization was founded in 1945.

According to Robert Cox, international organizations such as the UN are actually by-products of particular historical junctures and specific sets of sociological, political, and economic circumstances. A historical structure, for Cox, is "a particular combination of thought patterns, material conditions and human institutions."[6] This configuration of elements reflects world order at a specific juncture. The UN system therefore represents, in part, one leg of the tripod of elements that constitute world order at any given moment. These three elements of course interact in the development or evolution of the structure of world order.

So for instance, the dominant ideas of the post–World War II world order were embedded within the UN, and those ideas became robust because they were supported materially by the most powerful members of the organization, namely, the United States, the United Kingdom, the USSR, China, and France. Thus, in understanding the place of the UN today, it is useful to unearth the ideological and philosophical matter that helped to bring it into being, as well as the ideas (and material support for those ideas) that undergird the organization. It is also imperative to understand how those dominant ideas are changing or how they are being replaced by other understandings as the world evolves. When the UN was established, the founders had no idea that global warming and climate change would become such a major issue. As one comes to understand the impacts and effects of global warming and climate change on the Arctic, certainly the UN governance structure should adjust in order to address adequately the issues that arise from this phenomenon.

At the present juncture, one of the dominant ideas supporting the need for international organization is the notion of evolving multilateral governance. The Commission on Global Governance defined governance as "the sum of the many ways individuals and institutions, public and private, manage their common affairs. It is a continuing process through which conflicting or diverse interests may be accommodated and cooperative action may be taken. It includes formal...as well as informal arrangements that people and institutions have agreed to or perceived to be in their interest."[7] This definition indicates that governance is more than an activity; it is a process that involves a plurality of actors operating at different levels (local, national, regional, transnational, and global), and it aims to use a variety of channels to settle sundry and potentially incompatible issues. Thus, the UN system is only one of many actors that play a role in the governance of the globe.

But the United Nations is a very important actor in global governance. It is the only universal body we have to date. It is the most comprehensive and inclusive multilateral organization the world has known so far. Founded in 1945, amid the smoldering ashes of World War II, the UN system was designed to replace the more limited-membership League of Nations. In an age of globalization, complex interdependence, multiple civil conflicts, global terrorism, the spread of HIV/AIDS and other infectious diseases, natural and man-made disasters, environmental disasters, climate change, collapsing of fish stocks, resource depletion, and proliferation of weapons of mass destruction (WMDs), the need for this universal governance body has become increasingly evident. As a former Canadian ambassador to the United Nations once said, if the United Nations did not exist, "we would have to invent it."[8]

One of the issues of pressing importance to the UN in the twenty-first century concerns the governance of the oceans. The UN inherited a principle of customary international law, *mare liberum*, which was first advocated by the Dutch jurist and philosopher Hugo Grotius in the early seventeenth century. At the heart of that principle is the notion that the sea, outside of national jurisdiction, should be regarded as international territory. That means that the ocean belongs to all nations and all nations are therefore free to use it for seafaring trade and other maritime activity. Prior to the advent of the UN, the rules governing the management of marine resources had their roots in the classical law of the sea, which gave sovereign states the authority to govern a three-mile territorial sea limit beyond their shores.[9] That three-mile limit was developed primarily for military and security reasons: at the time a cannon could fire up to three miles.[10] After the UN was founded, there was increasing pressure on the organization "to bring a wider area of the sea and its natural resources under coastal state jurisdiction."[11] Some states saw the opportunity to extend their sovereign jurisdiction seaward in order to exploit fish or natural resources that could be found outside the three-mile limit. The notion of economic zones that extend beyond the three-mile limit therefore began to replace the military/security rationale with respect to developing a maritime governance regime.

In 1958, the UN adopted four Conventions at the Conference on the Law of the Sea: (1) on the territorial sea, (2) on the continental shelf, (3) on the high seas, and (4) on fisheries.[12] The first UNCLOS did not reach an agreement on the width of the territorial sea, so most coastal states decided to use Iceland's declared territorial sea limit of twelve miles as the extension of their sovereign jurisdiction. Some Latin American states such as El Salvador, Chile, and Panama declared a 200-mile zone as an exclusive economic area and asserted the right of developing countries to adopt the principle behind *mare liberum* and to use UN General Assembly Resolution 2692 (XXV) as a rationale for utilizing the natural marine resources present in their "adjacent seas" for their economic development and advancement.[13] But the uncertainty that prevailed over the extent of the limits of national economic jurisdiction at sea led to the convening of the Third UN Conference on the Law of the Sea (UNCLOS III) in 1973. That conference addressed this issue as well as debated the potential for exploration and exploitation of resources (such as manganese, polymetallic nodules, oil, and gas) that can be found in the deep seabed.[14] Although this was largely a theoretical discussion in the 1970s, by the 1990s deep-sea mining had become a real possibility thanks to advancement in technology.

Back in 1967, the Maltese ambassador to the UN, Arvid Pardo, suggested that the UN General Assembly should declare that the seabed and the ocean floor were beyond the limits of any nation's jurisdiction and that the seabed should be considered "the common heritage of mankind" in the same way that the moon and other celestial bodies were pronounced as "the province of all mankind."[15] In 1970, the Pardo principle was incorporated into a UN General Assembly resolution—Resolution 2749 (XXV)—and this became one of the items for discussion at UNCLOS III.[16] By 1982, agreement was reached on the UN Convention on the Law of the Sea and on issues such as the territorial sea—

the width of which was limited to twelve nautical miles. This convention acknowledged coastal states' sovereignty over that territorial sea and the natural resources located within that zone. The convention also extended the continental shelf, introduced a 200-nautical-mile exclusive economic zone (EEZ), and laid out the rules to govern the exploration of oil and gas resources found within that zone. It should be pointed out that UNCLOS did not just grant jurisdictional rights to coastal states over the territorial sea, continental shelf extension, and the 200-mile EEZ; it also insisted that coastal states should be entrusted with certain duties and responsibilities to conserve resources within the EEZ, to avoid overexploitation of resources present therein, and to implement measures that would maintain or restore maximum sustainable yields in those seaward areas of jurisdiction. States were also obligated to preserve and protect the marine environment within that zone and to avoid or control pollution.[17]

The 1982 convention, inter alia, also laid out rules and regulations for any future seabed mining; provided rights to access to the deep-sea areas for landlocked states; delimited internal waters; granted right of archipelagic sea lane passage; outlined the right of navigation and freedom of transit; defined piracy on the high seas and laid out rules for dealing with this scourge; and established the International Seabed Authority (ISA) —headquartered in Kingston, Jamaica—and an International Tribunal (whose headquarters is located in Hamburg, Germany) to adjudicate disputes arising out of the interpretation and application of the convention.[18] After the conclusion of the Convention on the Law of the Sea, there was a series of technological developments that paved the way for further discussions about the exploitation of marine resources and mineral deposits on the deep-sea bed, which culminated in the drafting of a Supplementary Agreement to the Convention in 1994.[19]

Although the commercial possibilities of exploration and exploitation of the deep-sea bed became more real in the 1990s, there were ongoing concerns about the impact such economic development might have on the marine environment. Since the 1960s, the UN has been concerned about the tension between the conservation of natural resources and the exploitation of those resources for economic development purposes.[20] In 1972, the UN held the Conference on the Human Environment (UNCHE) in Stockholm, which adopted a declaration that clearly delineated a number of important precepts, including careful management and planning for safeguarding scarce natural resources; preservation and improvement, wherever practical, of the capacity of the earth to produce vital renewable resources; guarding against future exhaustion of non-renewable resources; and ensuring that resources on the seabed would be shared by all mankind. The aim of this conference was to situate issues of resource sovereignty within a sustainable development, conservation, and environmental context.[21]

An important principle adopted at the conference in Stockholm was Principle 21, which conferred on states "the responsibility to ensure that activities within their jurisdiction or control do not cause damage to the environment of other States or of areas beyond the limits of national jurisdiction." This principle is applicable to the Arctic coastal states. It is a principle that was echoed in the 1987 Brundtland Commission report, *Our Common Future.* That report provided a new intellectual framework for development that was based on sustainability: that is, "development that meets the needs of the present without compromising the ability of future generations to meet their own needs."[22] This report was welcomed by the UN General Assembly and the Conference on Environment and Development (UNCED) was convened by the General Assembly to address the serious issue of environmental degradation. The primary outcome of UNCED was the 1992 Rio Declaration on Environment and Development, which sought to strike a balance between protection of the environment and promotion of economic growth in developing countries. Other important outcomes of the 1992 Rio conference were the UN Framework Convention on Climate Change (UNFCCC)[23] and the Convention on Biological Diversity.[24] But the UNCED also produced Agenda 21—an international action program designed to protect the environment, and a new coordinating organ, the Commission on Sustainable Development.[25] In 2002, there was a follow-up World Summit on Sustainable Development in Johannesburg that evaluated the measures for sustainable development agreed upon in Rio and focused on issues of water, sanitation, energy, health care, agriculture, and biological diversity.[26] The World Summit was attended not only by state representatives but also by a variety of nongovernmental organizations (NGOs). The declaration that emerged from that meeting in Johannesburg in 2002 "reconfirmed collective responsibility for the living environment and the welfare of all people, both now and in the future." The summit also produced a concrete international action plan that outlined the steps needed to implement sustainable strategies for food production and food security, to change unsustainable consumption and production practices, to develop mechanisms for the protection and management of natural resources and sustainable fishing, and to introduce new private-public partnerships that would help with ecosystem management.[27]

Oran Young, specialist in the Arctic and global environmental governance, remarked at the end of the last century, "The demand for governance in world affairs has never been greater."[28] Certainly, the challenges of the twenty-first century are of such that the needs and demands of humanity cannot be met solely by states acting on their own. This explains, in large part, the continued appeal of, growth in, and dependence on multilateral organizations to deal with a variety of issues requiring governance. Clearly the UN has been involved in governance issues of interest to the Arctic.[29] One of the concerns of this chapter is the question of what kind of governance structure is needed to address evolving Arctic issues. I argue here that the foundation for that governance structure can be found in the UN, particularly within UNCLOS and its Supplementary Agreement; in declarations such as the Declaration on Permanent Sovereignty over Natural Resources and the Stockholm and Rio Declarations; and in various commissioned reports, such as *Our Common Future*; but also in the work the principal organs of the UN system—particularly the Security Council, the General Assembly, and the Economic and Social Council (ECOSOC), some specialized agencies like the UN Development Programme (UNDP) and UN Environmental Programme (UNEP), and the International Court of Justice (ICJ). But as one understands more about how global warming and climate change is affecting the Arctic region, it is important to consider the possibility that other institutions of governance, besides those in the UN system, may be needed to address evolving Arctic issues adequately.

THE ARCTIC AND ITS INTERNATIONAL CHALLENGES

One way to think of the Arctic is as a large body of water surrounded by land. According to the Arctic Monitoring and Assessment Programme's definition of the Arctic, this region is 33 million square kilometers—larger than Africa or Asia. The marine boundary of the Arctic is eight times the size of the Mediterranean Sea. The Arctic Ocean basin is surrounded by five countries: Canada, the United States, Russia, Norway, and Denmark/Greenland. But the region is sparsely populated (around 4 million people). It should be noted that whereas the territories of Finland, Iceland, and Sweden do not abut the Arctic Ocean, those countries' territories nevertheless extend to or beyond the Arctic Circle, so they are technically considered to be Arctic states. The Arctic is essentially "a region of vast natural resources and a clean environment compared with most areas of the world. But it is also the end point for contaminants transported by atmosphere, ocean and rivers. Some of these become highly concentrated as they move up in the simple arctic food chain. This can cause impacts on animals that are well adjusted to the natural conditions but not to these new factors."[30]

Global Warming and Climate Change

There is no question that global warming is bringing with it major changes to the Arctic region. Some observers have noted that "the melting of sea ice and Greenland glaciers is increasing faster than scientists predicted."[31] On a visit to the Arctic in 2009, UN Secretary General Ban Ki-Moon expressed alarm at the rapid pace of change occurring there. He noted that those changes in the Arctic were also accelerating global warming, as thawing permafrost releases methane—a greenhouse gas that is twenty times more powerful than carbon dioxide. Indeed, at the current rate, the Arctic could be completely ice-free by 2030.[32] This could mean that the Northwest Passage could become open for navigation purposes for the first time in history.[33] This would also mean a significant increase in shipping and offshore mineral exploration in this region. Such activity will definitely have an impact on the Arctic ecosystems, and that impact could be quite negative.[34] For instance, it is predicted by some scientists that polar bears could become extinct and seals will be endangered. "Because seals use the ice as a breeding habitat, they are having difficulty reproducing due to a reduction in sea ice."[35] The survival of reindeer and caribou will also be in question because their migratory patterns are disrupted by the melting ice. Some fish and vegetation in the Arctic region will not survive the climate change because they will not be able to adapt fast enough to the warmer weather, and some birds will have to migrate because of loss of habitats and food sources.[36]

Furthermore, as pointed out in the UN Security Council during the 2011 thematic debate on the "Maintenance of International Peace and Security: The Impact of Climate Change," the adverse effects of climate change could actually aggravate existing threats to international peace and security. During that debate, held at UN headquarters in New York on July 20, 2011, Ban Ki-Moon pointed out that in fact climate change is itself a threat to international peace and security. Rising sea levels brought about by the thawing of sea ice in the Arctic could become an existential threat to small island developing states (SIDS), some of which could literally disappear off the face of the map. If that happens, forced migration could result in increasing social and political tensions and the possibility of violent conflict.[37] So climate change and global warming must be considered a global security issue that must be taken up by the United Nations system, including the UN Security Council. The UN system is well placed to help address some of the problems that could occur as a result of global warming and climate change in the Arctic.[38]

Impact on Indigenous Peoples' Health and Way of Life

Climate change and global warming are clearly having serious consequences for the people who live in the Arctic.[39] Indigenous peoples in the Arctic include Aleuts, who live primarily in coastal southwest Alaska; Inuit, who live on the coast and inland from northwestern Alaska east to Greenland; Athabascans, who live mainly inland in eastern Alaska, the central Yukon, and the Northwest Territories of Canada; and Dene, Saami, and native groups who live in northern Russia. Many of these indigenous people who have lived for generations hunting, fishing, herding, and gathering will find it increasing difficult to sustain their way of life as the sea ice melts in the Arctic and both terrestrial and marine wildlife are reduced or become extinct.[40] Arctic communities could also face serious health complications when wastes and contaminants that were frozen in ice over many years are released as the temperature warms up. Indeed, as some observers put it, what happens to the Arctic and its human population should be of concern to people living in other parts of the globe because the response of the area and its people to climate change will serve as an indicator for what could occur in other regions on this planet.[41]

The Arctic, in a sense, is like the canary in the mine shaft. Further, local populations in the Arctic region will suffer major dislocation and change in their traditional subsistence way of life not only as a result of the melting permafrost and damage to buildings and infrastructure but also because of the increase in economic activity that will come from mining, oil and gas exploration, and increased shipping and industrial fishing activity. Thus the challenges in the Arctic are not just environmental in nature. They also include legal, economic, and social adjustments in an area that few paid much attention to in the past. These challenges have been on the UN system's agenda for some time, and the organization is thus well placed to address them. See, for example, "The Declaration on the Rights of Indigenous Peoples," which was adopted by the UN General Assembly on September 13, 2007, by a majority of UN member states.[42]

Contested Sovereignty Claims and Legal Challenges

As a result of the increased economic activity in the Arctic, this region can become a contested area because of unresolved maritime boundary disputes. For example, each coastal state in the Arctic can claim sovereign rights over resources in the water column and the seabed up to 200 nautical miles from its coasts. Portions of the seabed outside of that 200-nautical-mile limit can also be claimed by states that can prove there is a "natural prolongation" of their territory that extends beyond that 200-nautical-mile limit. However, surprisingly, there are not yet as many contentious disputes between the Arctic states as one might think. The last major juridical dispute was between Norway and Denmark over Eirik Raudes Land (Eastern Greenland). This dispute went to the Permanent Court of Justice (PCIJ) in 1933, and that judicial body ruled in favor of Denmark.[43]

One possible source of contention could involve Norway. "The Norwegian continental shelf extends about 800 nautical miles north of Svalbard, and along with Russia, the United States, Canada, Denmark, Sweden, Finland, and Iceland, Norway is expected to stake its claim as the resources in the Arctic become more available."[44] It disagrees with Iceland and Russia about the exploitation of the resources around the Svalbard archipelago in the Arctic Ocean north of Norway, and it claims sovereignty over those islands. Both Canada and Denmark claimed sovereignty over the tiny uninhabited Hans Island—which is about 1.3 square kilometers in total and lies between Canada's Ellesmere Island and Greenland. But in 2012 both countries discussed a new proposal that indicates the dispute could be settled amicably by splitting jurisdiction over the island.[45] Similarly, in 2010, Norway and Russia ended a bitter forty-year dispute over the Barents Sea, with the signing of a treaty by then Russian president Dmitry Medvedev and the Norwegian prime minister, Jens Stoltenberg.[46]

Canada's maritime boundary with the United States in the Beaufort Sea off the coast of the Yukon and Alaska is in dispute. As well, there is perennial disagreement over the status of the waters that lie between the Canadian islands in the North—that is, the Northwest Passage. According to one Arctic observer, Martin Frost,

> The Canadian government claims that some of the waters of the Northwest Passage, particularly those in the Canadian Arctic Archipelago, are internal to Canada, giving Canada the right to bar transit through these waters. Most maritime nations, including the United States and the nations of the European Union, consider them to be an international strait, where foreign vessels have the right of "transit passage." In such a régime, Canada would have the right to enact fishing and environmental regulation, and fiscal and smuggling laws, as well as laws intended for the safety of shipping, but not the right to close the passage.[47]

To prove a point, in 1985 the U.S. Coast Guard icebreaker *Polar Sea* passed through from the Northwest Passage without getting permission from Canada.[48] Although eventually the United States submitted to inspection by the Canadian Coast Guard, the event became a diplomatic incident, with the United States maintaining that it was not legally required to ask Canada for permission to sail through the Passage. The Canadian government quickly issued a declaration, in 1986, that reaffirmed Canada's rights to the waters, but the United States refused to recognize the Canadian government's claim. Two years later, both governments signed an agreement on "Arctic Cooperation" that resolved the issue without solving the sovereignty question. They both agreed that under the law of the sea, ships engaged in transit passage are not permitted to engage in research. Since U.S. Coast Guard vessels are engaged in different forms of research, this means that the United States is required to request permission from the government of Canada in order to pass through the Northwest Passage.

In 2005, another incident involving the United States sparked outrage in Canada. U.S. nuclear submarines are alleged to have traveled unannounced through Canadian Arctic waters.[49] News of this incident arose after the U.S. Navy released photographs of the USS *Charlotte* surfaced at the North Pole. This sparked outrage in Canada and forced the incoming prime minister, Stephen Harper, to declare that the Canadian government had every intention of enforcing its sovereignty in Canadian Arctic waters. A year later, Canada's Joint Task Force North issued a formal declaration, which stated that the Canadian military would refer to the region no longer as the Northwest Passage but as Canadian Internal Waters. The declaration came after the successful completion of Operation Nunalivut (Inuktitut for "the land is ours")—which was an expedition into the region by five military patrols to demonstrate Canada's capability of enforcing its sovereignty in the Arctic. After the Nunalivut exercise in 2012, Canadian Defence Minister Peter MacKay asserted that Operation Nunalivut "continues to exemplify the Government of Canada's commitment to exercise security and sovereignty in the North and ensure the Canadian Forces are well-trained to meet the challenges of the Arctic." He went on to say that "the Canadian Forces are a critical factor in our government's vision for that region, and with operations like Nunalivut, we help ensure they have what they need to carry out a full range of tasks effectively in the North."[50] Canadian scientists are now joining Canadian soldiers on the front lines of this battle to establish Canadian sovereignty over the Passage. The fact remains, however, that this part of the Arctic continues to be a source of contention among Arctic coastal states.

Contested sovereignty claims can be resolved by the states involved in the dispute, and as the examples of Norway-Russia and Canada-Denmark seem to show, there is a definite preference by Arctic states to resolve territorial disputes bilaterally rather than through the multilateral channels of the UN system. But some of these claims are so complex that there will probably be the need for the ICJ or the International Tribunal to become involved. Indeed such complex disputes may very well require the UN's attention. Again, because of its primary mandate to settle international disputes and avoid outright violence, the UN is well placed to address this issue of contested sovereignty claims. If Arctic states are unable to settle their boundary and resource disputes bilaterally, then they may have to settle for third-party intervention and mediation. Under Part XV of the UN Convention on the Law of the Sea, those states can also take up their dispute with the ICJ, with the International Tribunal for the Law of the Sea, or to ad hoc arbitration, as per Annex VII of UNCLOS.[51]

Economic Development and its Consequences in the Arctic
Climate change and the melting of the sea ice, permafrost, and glaciers in the North have sparked major interest in bringing economic development to the Arctic: mineral exploration and exploitation; increased shipping through the Canadian Northwest Passage and the Northern Sea Route in the Russian Arctic; increased fishing as fish stocks move north with the warming temperatures; overfishing; marine debris from discarded nets; dramatic increases in tourism and cruise vessels; non-benign scientific research and bioprospecting.

Oil and Gas Exploration
There is now sufficient evidence to suggest that the Arctic may hold the world's largest remaining untapped gas reserves and undeveloped oil reserves. Much of these reserves lie offshore in the Arctic's shallow and biologically productive shelf seas and beneath the frozen Arctic Ocean. A 2008 U.S. Geological Survey estimated that there may be 90 billion barrels of undiscovered, technically recoverable oil (and 44 billion barrels of natural gas liquids) in areas north of the Arctic Circle.[52] Once the sea ice continues to melt at the current rate, minerals such as oil and gas in the Arctic will become increasingly accessible. Also, the breakup of the permafrost will mean that transportation of oil and gas could become much easier. According to the oil industry, the Arctic is the final frontier for petroleum development.[53] But the acceleration of oil

and gas exploration and exploitation in the Arctic has become a major cause for concern. Whereas oil and gas finds have the potential to bring rapid economic growth and activity to this part of the globe, the greatest threat to the pristine Arctic marine environment is the possibility of a major oil spill. According to the World Wide Fund for Nature (WWF), the increased economic and development activity in the Arctic could destroy sensitive habitat, fragment migration routes, cause major soil erosion, pollute freshwater, and do significant damage to benthic organisms (such as corals) and to sea-floor habitats from subsea infrastructure, like pipelines from offshore installations.[54]

Environmental groups are rightly concerned about the prospects of a major oil spill in the Arctic similar to the *Exxon Valdez* incident in 1989. That particular oil spill has shown that the deleterious effects of oil spills on marine organisms and ecosystems can last for decades.[55] It is for that reason that many environmental groups decried the sale of oil and gas leases in the Chukchi Sea. Despite assurances from Shell that it will be able to deal expeditiously with any oil spill in this area, most environmentalists found it difficult to accept the decision by the U.S. Bureau of Safety and Environmental Enforcement (BSEE) to approve Shell's Chukchi Sea oil spill response plan, particularly knowing that the U.S. Geological Survey predicts that two-thirds of the world's polar bears could be wiped out in the event of an oil spill in the Arctic.

The concerns environmentalists have expressed with respect to possible oil spills in the Arctic and the negative impact those spills can have on the fragile ecosystems of that area have been voiced as well at the UN. One catalyst for urgent UN consideration of this problem was the disastrous BP oil spill in the Gulf of Mexico in April 2010. This incident gave greater urgency to the fifth Global Oceans Conference that took place at the UN Educational, Scientific, and Cultural Organization (UNESCO) meeting in Paris May 3–7, 2010. This meeting brought together delegates from eighty countries to discuss ways of preserving marine biodiversity and improving the "governance of the oceans" in the face of similar-type disasters. It would be foolhardy to think that somehow the Arctic will be spared from such catastrophes. Indeed, given the instability of temperatures and the changes in climate in the North, and given that some of the oil installations could in fact be placed on shifting sea ice, the chances are higher that there will be oil spills in the Arctic.

As one report puts it, "In the Arctic, dangerous conditions could include gale force winds, extreme fog, prolonged periods of darkness, shifting sea ice and sub-zero temperatures." That report goes on to state that when "multiple risk factors combine, accidents are even more likely to occur."[56] A good example of this is the spate of recent spills on the North Slope as a result of aging oil infrastructure at Prudhoe Bay. Increases in oil exploration and production could also result in oil spills from offshore platforms, from associated pipelines, and from storage tanks and shipping activities in the Arctic.

Increased frequency of ships through the region also elevates the potential risk of oil spills beyond the oil and gas industry. It is because of these potential risks that the eight Arctic states signed the Search and Rescue Agreement in May 2011, which legally binds them to address the issue of unforeseen emergencies arising from oil spill, pollution, and other environmental damage caused by increased shipping in Arctic waters.[57]

Clearly, the many lessons that have been learned through debates and discussions in various UN bodies can be used to inform policy makers from the Arctic states about the potential dangers and negative effects of unregulated exploration and exploitation of that very fragile area. This is one contribution that the UN system can make with respect to this emerging Arctic issue.

But there are other major issues that must be addressed as well. First, the technology that could keep oil rigs ice-free is not yet developed. Second, it is possible that melting ice in the Arctic could make Arctic waters more hazardous (with roads, houses, and infrastructure becoming increasingly unstable, with an increase in the number of icebergs, and with multi-year ice drifting into shipping lanes). And third, drilling in the Arctic could be both expensive and dangerous.

Fisheries

One other area of particular concern is the state of fisheries in the Arctic, as global warming takes hold and as commercial fishers see the possibilities of maximizing their catch. Some species of fish are already altering their location by moving farther north in search of colder water and food. But not all species of fish will survive the warming temperature in the Arctic. Climate change and the changes in thermohaline circulation in that region will alter the speed and patterns of ocean currents, and this may in turn have an impact on fish stocks. According to a recent Intergovernmental Panel on Climate Change (IPCC) study, "Arctic fisheries are among the most productive in the world. Changes in the velocity and direction of ocean currents affect the availability of nutrients and the disposition of larval and juvenile organisms, thereby influencing recruitment, growth and mortality."[58] Some species of fish are likely to survive and even thrive under the new conditions. But others will not be able to survive. As fish cross national jurisdictions to spawn, to search for food, or simply to try to survive, bilateral and multilateral arrangements with respect to fisheries management and conservation will most likely need to be revised to ensure sustainability of the fishing industry and avoid fishing disputes in the Arctic. Sustainable fisheries have been an agenda item at the UN since the 1980s. The organization has been discussing this issue over the years since then.

On March 28, 2012, the UN General Assembly adopted Resolution A/res/66/68, which reaffirmed all its previous resolutions on sustainable fisheries. It made reference to the "1995 Agreement for the Implementation of the Provisions of the United Nations Convention on the Law of the Sea of 10 December 1982 relating to the Conservation and Management of Straddling Fish Stocks and Highly Migratory Fish Stocks ('the

Agreement')" and noted that not only was the ratification and accession by states to the agreement on the rise; states and sub-regional and
regional fisheries management organizations and arrangements were
also beginning "to take measures, as appropriate, towards the implementation of the provisions of the Agreement."[59] What is clear from
that resolution is that various bodies within the UN system have been
addressing many issues related to fisheries in the Arctic and elsewhere.

One such body is the Food and Agriculture Organization (FAO) and
its Committee on Fisheries, which adopted, on March 12, 2005, the Rome
Declaration on Illegal, Unreported and Unregulated Fishing. The General
Assembly also recognized the important contribution of the FAO's Code
of Conduct for Responsible Fisheries. That "Code," as well as other
related instruments (such as its international plans of action), laid out
principles and global standards of behavior for responsible practices for
the conservation of fisheries resources and the management and development of fisheries. At the heart of that GA resolution is an understanding that sustainable fisheries can make a significant contribution to
food security, income, wealth, and poverty alleviation for present and for
future generations. Thus the UN, through these normative positions, and
with the assistance of some of its agencies, can contribute to an important issue that affects the people of the Arctic, namely, fisheries and their
management and conservation. The Arctic will need a multilateral fisheries agreement if it is to stymie conflicts over this marine resource and
develop an economically viable and sustainable fishing industry in that
region. The UN system (particularly with help from UN organs such as
the FAO, the IPCC, ECOSOC, and the International Maritime Organization, or IMO) can assist with the drafting and development of such an
agreement.

CONCLUSION

The central purpose of this chapter was to understand how the United Nations might contribute to addressing the challenges that are emerging in the Arctic. The challenges are many, and they include global warming and climate change; dislocation and change in the traditional subsistence way of life for the indigenous people of the region; contested sovereignty claims and legal challenges over land and marine boundaries; and economic development and its impact on the fragile Arctic ecosystem. The Arctic region is becoming increasingly important for military, commercial, and environmental reasons, and this raises questions about the type of governance system that ought to be put in place to address these challenges, particularly if the individual Arctic states are unable to deal with them acting on their own.

As pointed out earlier, the UN is a particular type of governance institution. It is a multilateral, universal governance body. Through its charter, principles, norms, values, and agencies, the UN is able to assist with the governance of the Arctic, as well as other regions. Indeed, the UN system, with its multiple agencies, has influenced the workings and principles of subsequent multilateral and plurilateral organizations—including regional forums such as the Arctic Council. Chapter VIII of the UN Charter provides the organization with the mandate to work with various regional arrangements in maintaining peace and security and in improving the lot of people in those regions. So, for example, the UN can work with the Arctic Council to establish rules and cooperative instruments that would aid in the protection of the Arctic environment. Different parts of the UN system are capable of dealing with the major geopolitical issues that are still unresolved across the Arctic basin, whether they be issues of access and rights of transit and passage in disputed waters, claims of seaward ownership within the Arctic oceanic basin, boundary disputes, or land claims. After all, the primary mandate of the UN is to prevent the scourge of war by being both proactive and reactive.

The multipurpose character of the UN system allows it to address the multiple issues that have emerged within the Arctic. Those issues range from security threats, human rights violations, and environmental degradation to unchecked capitalism. The UN Security Council has already taken up the agenda item of climate change and global warming in the Arctic as a possible existential security threat to small island developing states and as a residual destabilizing force that could lead to social and political tensions. The world body also has a range of instruments, specialized agencies, and affiliated bodies that can deal with protecting the rights of indigenous peoples (declarations, resolutions, treaties), disputes (ICJ or the International Tribunal), environmental issues (UNEP, IPCC), fisheries (IMO, FAO), and other economic issues (ECOSOC, World Food Program [WFP], UNDP, International Development Association [IDA], International Bank for Reconstruction and Development or the World Bank [IBRD], International Monetary Fund [IMF], and World Trade Organization [WTO]). Indeed, the UN has had economic development as a priority item since the days of decolonization, in the 1960s and 1970s, when a large number of poverty-stricken, newly independent states entered the world body from the developing world. The UN was forced to adapt reflexively and to create a new specialized agency —the UN Development Programme—to address the issue of accelerated economic development. The UNDP worked on this issue in tandem with ECOSOC and the General Assembly and also with affiliated bodies to the UN such as the IDA, the World Bank and the International Monetary Fund, and the General Agreement on Tariffs and Trade (GATT, now the WTO). So the UN is well placed to tackle economic development issues arising out of the Arctic.

But at the UN there has also been a concern that unchecked economic development could be disastrous for the fragile Arctic environment. Extensive shipping activity in Arctic waters could cause environmental and ecosystem damage if there are oil spills, disturbance of wildlife movement, operational and accidental pollution, the introduction of alien species, habitat fragmentation, and noise.

Although there is no overarching international legal regime to regulate activities in the Arctic, the 1982 United Nations Convention on the Law of the Sea provides a legal framework for addressing many of the issues discussed here. In particular, UNCLOS has established a legal regime governing ocean space, sovereign rights over ocean resources, the protection of the maritime environment, and the conduct of shipping, fisheries, tourism, research, and other activities in the Arctic. But UNCLOS cannot operate in a vacuum. Its principles, norms, rules, and institutions must be supported in the Arctic region. And this is where the Arctic Council comes in. The Arctic Council was created by the eight states of the Arctic region (the five coastal states, plus Finland, Iceland, and Sweden). This council has become a plurilateral forum for discussing the multiple issues in the Arctic referred to in this chapter. According to the Ilulissat Declaration of the five Arctic states, UNCLOS, the IMO, and the Arctic Council collaborate to form the core of the regime that governs the Arctic.

This plurilateral arrangement is important because some states have not yet ratified UNCLOS. The United States is one of those states. Although the United States has recognized UNCLOS as a codification of customary international law, thirty years after the treaty was adopted in Montego Bay, Jamaica, by 162 states and the European Union, the United States still has not signed or ratified it. However, recent developments indicate that this could soon change. At the time of writing, two U.S. security officials were calling on the U.S. Senate to ratify UNCLOS. The former defense secretary, Leon Panetta, and the current chairman of the Joint Chiefs of Staff, General Martin Dempsey, both agreed that endorsing the treaty is very important for dealing with issues such as U.S.-China relations over the South China Sea. The chairman of the U.S. Foreign Relations Committee, John Kerry (who is now the U.S. Secretary of State), is optimistic that UNCLOS could soon be ratified by the U.S. Senate. The then U.S. Secretary of State, Hillary Clinton, put it bluntly thus: "Whatever arguments may have existed for delaying US accession no longer exist and truly cannot even be taken with a straight face." She pointed out that by not ratifying the treaty, the United States stands to lose out on exploitation of untapped oil and gas deposits that are buried beneath the offshore seabed in the Arctic, and it could lose ground to Arctic countries such as Russia, Norway, and Canada in staking claims to the Arctic Ocean as melting ice in that region exposes the vast mineral riches that lie there. Certainly, failure to ratify the treaty could lead to the United States losing "credibility in reining in China's maritime ambitions in the South China Sea."[60]

The combination of multilateral and plurilateral governance arrangements in the Arctic is a reminder of the limitations of the United Nations system. The UN is a multilateral organization designed by states to carry out the wishes of states. Although it is universal in its membership and goals, there are times when particular instruments of this organization are unable to function in the way they were intended. When that happens, the work of governance must still go on. In the case of the Arctic, that governance can be shared between the Arctic Council (a regional forum) and the UN system (the global governance body).

NOTES

1. See UN General Assembly Resolution 66/231 (December 24, 2011).

2. United Nations, *The Charter of the United Nations* (New York: Department of Public Information, 2012), chapter 1, article 1.

3. Michael Barnett and Martha Finnemore, "Political Approaches," in *The Oxford Handbook on the United Nations*, ed. Thomas G. Weiss and Sam Daws (Oxford: Oxford University Press, 2007), 47.

4. Kenneth W. Abbott and Duncan Snidal, "Hard and Soft Law in International Governance," *International Organization* 54, no. 3 (Summer 2000): 421–456.

5. Volker Rittberger, Bernhard Zangl, and Andreas Kruck, eds., *International Organization*, 2nd ed. (London: Palgrave Macmillan, 2012), 274.

6. Robert W. Cox, "Social Forces, States and World Order: Beyond International Relations Theory," *Millennium: Journal of International Studies* 10, no. 2 (1986): 219.

7. Commission on Global Governance, *Our Global Neighbourhood* (Oxford: Oxford University Press, 2005), 4.

8. Paul Heinbecker, "The UN: If It Didn't Exist, We Would Have to Invent It," http://www.heinbecker.ca/Writing/The_UN_If_It_Didnt_Exist.pdf.

9. Robin R. Churchill and Alan V. Lowe, *The Law of the Sea*, 3rd ed. (Manchester: Manchester University Press, 1999), 78.

10. For a fuller discussion see H. S. K. Kent, "The Historical Origins of the Three-Mile Limit," *American Journal of International Law* 48, no. 4 (October 1954): 537–553.

11. Nico Schrijver, "Natural Resource Management and Sustainable Development," in *The Oxford Handbook on the United Nations*, ed. Thomas G. Weiss and Sam Daws (Oxford: Oxford University Press, 2007), 598.

12. UN Convention on the Law of the Sea, UN Document A/CONF.13, Geneva Conference Report (1958).

13. See Karen Hjertonsson, *The New Law of the Sea: Influence of the Latin American States on Recent Developments of the Law of the Sea* (Leiden, the Netherlands: Martinus Nijhoff, 2004). Also see the preamble of UN General Assembly Resolution 2692 (XXV), December 11, 1970.

14. United Nations, "Convention on the Law of the Sea of 10 December 1982: Overview and Full Text," http://www.un.org/Depts/los/convention_agreements/convention_overview_convention.htm.

15. UN Document A/C.1/PV.1515, and United Nations, *Yearbook of the United Nations* (New York: UN, 1967).

16. UN General Assembly Resolution 2749 (XXV): "Declaration of Principles Governing the Sea-Bed and the Ocean Floor, and the Subsoil Thereof, Beyond the Limits of National Jurisdiction," December 12, 1970.

17. See United Nations, "Convention on the Law of the Sea," especially part XII, dealing with "Protection of the Marine Environment."

18. The International Tribunal for the Law of the Sea, http://www.itlos.org/index.php?id=15&L=0.

19. The Supplementary Agreement to UNCLOS basically laid out the manner in which seabed resources would be administered by the International Sea Bed Authority. See Center for Oceans Law and Policy, University of Virginia School of Law, *UNCLOS 1982 Commentary—Supplementary Documents* (Leiden, the Netherlands: Martinus Nijhoff, 2012), xi.

20. See, for instance, UN General Assembly 1831 (XVII) on "Economic Development and the Conservation of Nature" (1962).

21. See UNEP, "Declaration of the United Nations Conference on Human Environment," June 16, 1972, http://www.unep.org/Documents.Multilingual/Default.asp?documentid=97andarticleid=1503.

22. World Commission on Environment and Development, *Our Common Future* (Oxford: Oxford University Press, 1987), 8.

23. United Nations Framework Convention on Climate Change, http://unfccc.int/2860.php.

24. See the convention at http://www.cbd.int/convention/.

25. United Nations, *Report of the United Nations Conference on Environment and Development*, vol. 1, *Resolutions Adopted by the Conference* (UN document A/CONF.151/26, 1993).

26. See excellent discussion of this meeting in Michael G. Schechter, *United Nations Global Conferences* (London: Routledge, 2005).

27. For a copy of the declaration, see http://www.joburg.org.za/pdfs/johannesburgdeclaration.pdf.

28. Oran R. Young, *Governance in World Affairs* (New York: Cornell University Press, 1999), 1.

29. References to the United Nations General Assembly's involvement in discussions and debates about Arctic governance can be found cited throughout the following document—Timo Koivurova and Erik J. Molenaar, *International Governance and Regulation of the Marine Arctic: Three Reports Prepared for the WWF International Arctic Programme* (Oslo, February 8, 2010).

30. Olav Orheim, "Protecting the Environment of the Arctic Ecosystem," UN Open-Ended Informal Consultative Process on Oceans and the Law of the Sea, 4th meeting, June 2–6, 2003, http://www.un.org/Depts/los/consultative_process/documents/no3_npi2.pdf.

31. Louise Angélique de La Fayette, "Oceans Governance in the Arctic," *International Journal of Marine and Coastal Law* 23 (2008): 531; and Charles H. Greene, Andrew J. Pershing, Thomas M. Cronin, and Nicole Ceci, "Arctic Climate Change and Its Impact on the Ecology of the North Atlantic," *Ecology* 89, no. 11 (supplement 2008): S24–S38.

32. Ban Ki-Moon, "The Arctic," United Nations Environmental Programme, http://www.unep.org/Documents.Multilingual/Default.asp?DocumentID=596&ArticleID=6316&l=en.

33. Louise Angélique de La Fayette, "Oceans Governance in the Arctic," *International Journal of Marine and Coastal Law* 23, no. 3 (2008): 534.

34. See Vera Alexander, "Arctic Marine Ecosystems," in *Global Warming and Biological Diversity*, ed. Robert L. Peters and Thomas E. Lovejoy (New Haven, CT: Yale University Press, 1992), 221–229.

35. De La Fayette, "Oceans Governance in the Arctic," 535.

36. Ibid., 535–536.

37. International Institute for Sustainable Development, "UN Security Council Debates Security Impacts of Climate Change," July 20, 2011, http://climate-l.iisd.org/news/un-security-council-debates-security-impacts-of-climate-change/.

38. See Stephanie Cousins, "UN Security Council: Playing a Role in the International Climate Change Regime," *Global Change, Peace and Security* 25, no. 2 (2013): 191–210.

39. See Subhanker Banerjee, ed., *Arctic Voices: Resistance at the Tipping Point* (New York: Seven Stories Press, 2012).

40. See David L. Peterson and Daryll R. Johnson, eds., *Human Ecology and Climate Change: People and Resources in the Far North* (Washington, DC: Taylor and Francis, 1995), ACIA, *Arctic Climate Impact Assessment* (Cambridge: Cambridge University Press, 2005).

41. Peterson and Johnson, *Human Ecology and Climate Change*, xvi.

42. United Nations, General Assembly, A/66/142, March 30, 2012.

43. See "Legal Status of Eastern Greenland," Permanent Court of International Justice, 22nd session, judgment no. 20 (September 5, 1993).

44. Jorunn Gran, "Law and Order in the Arctic," Center for International Climate and Environmental Research—Oslo (CICERO), http://www.cicero.uio.no/fulltext/index_e.aspx?id=4271.

45. Adrian Humphreys, "New Proposal Will See Hans Island Split Evenly between Canada and Denmark," *National Post*, April 11, 2012, http://news.nationalpost.com/2012/04/11/new-proposal-would-see-hans-island-split-equally-between-canada-and-denmark/.

46. Luke Harding, "Russia and Norway Resolve Arctic Border Dispute," *Guardian*, September 15, 2010, http://www.guardian.co.uk/world/2010/sep/15/russia-norway-arctic-border-dispute.

47. See Frost's Meditations, http://www.martinfrost.ws/htmlfiles/oct2007/northwest_passage.html. Also see CBC News Canada, "Battle for the Arctic Heats Up," February 27, 2009, http://www.cbc.ca/news/canada/story/2009/02/27/f-arctic-sovereignty.html.

48. CBC News, "The Arctic Grail," August 8, 2008, http://www.cbc.ca/news/background/northwest-passage/.

49. "US Sub May Have Toured Canadian Arctic Zone," *National Post*, December 19, 2005, http://www.canada.com/nationalpost/story.html?id=fb21432a-1d28-415e-b323-ceb22d477732&k=69493.

50. "Canadian Forces Winds up High Arctic Exercise," *Ottawa Citizen*, April 27, 2012, http://blogs.ottawacitizen.com/2012/04/27/canadian-forces-winds-up-high-arctic-exercise/.

51. It is important to point out here that the Ilulissat Declaration of 2008 by the five Arctic coastal states, in fact, acknowledges the Law of the Sea as the governing legal framework for the Arctic Ocean.

52. U.S. Geological Survey, "90 Billion Barrels of Oil and 1.670 Trillion Cubic Feet of Natural Gas Assessed in the Arctic," July 23, 2008, http://www.usgs.gov/newsroom/article.asp?ID=1980&from=rss_home.

53. See Chris Arsenault, "Melting Arctic Heats up Resource Scramble," *Al Jazeera*, September 20, 2012, http://www.aljazeera.com/indepth/features/2012/09/2012916133717451622.html.

54. WWF Global, "Arctic Oil and Gas," http://wwf.panda.org/what_we_do/where_we_work/arctic/what_we_do/oil_gas/.

55. "Exxon Valdez Oil Spill Impacts Lasting Far Longer Than Expected, Scientists Say," *Science Daily*, December 23, 2003, http://www.sciencedaily.com/releases/2003/12/031219073313.htm.

56. PEW Environmental Group, "Exploration & Development Risks," *Oceans North U.S.: U.S. Arctic Program*, http://oceansnorth.org/exploration-development-risks.

57. CBC News, "Arctic Council Leaders Sign Rescue Treaty," May 12, 2011, http://www.cbc.ca/news/canada/north/story/2011/05/12/arctic-council-greenland.html.

58. Intergovernmental Panel on Climate Change (IPCC), *Third Assessment Report: Climate Change 2001 (TAR)*, http://www.ipcc.ch/publications_ and_data/publications_and_data_reports.shtml.
59. United Nations, General Assembly, A/Res/66/68 (March 28, 2012), http://daccess-dds-ny.un.org/doc/UNDOC/GEN/N11/462/90/PDF/N1146 290.pdf?OpenElement.
60. Mark Landler, "Law of the Sea Treaty Is Found on Capitol Hill, Again," *New York Times*, May 23, 2012.

CHAPTER 15

THE FUTURE OF THE ARCTIC COUNCIL

NAVIGATING BETWEEN SOVEREIGNTY AND SECURITY

Timo Koivurova and Piotr Graczyk

INTRODUCTION

Intergovernmental cooperation between the eight Arctic states has continued for over twenty years. The Arctic Council (AC), preceded by the 1991 Arctic Environmental Protection Strategy (AEPS), was established in 1996 and ever since has been the prime forum for circumpolar cooperation on a wide range of Arctic issues.[1] In recent years, however, climate change consequences, including new possibilities to exploit natural resources and increase shipping activities, as well as certain Arctic states' actions,[2] have triggered discussions on Arctic governance, but also concerns about security and sovereignty prospects above the Arctic Circle, placing them high on the international (geo)politics agenda. At the same time, states and political entities from outside the region want to become involved in decision-making processes, indicating that the Arctic Council is in the center of debate on whom, and in what manner, should govern an area undergoing profound transformation.

The Arctic institutional framework, involving both legal and political arrangements with the 1982 UN Convention on the Law of the Sea (UNCLOS) and the Arctic Council as its anchors, is affected by state sovereignty and jurisdiction.[3] The central question is how to adapt existing regional governance structure to improve its ability to deal with new phenomena occurring in the Arctic.[4] Whereas one may argue that institutionalized regional cooperation on soft issues plays a prevailing role in providing stability and security,[5] there are also many voices raising issues of hard security concerns in the Arctic, including jurisdictional and sovereignty disputes,[6] militarization of the region,[7] and emergence of the new geopolitics.[8] Still, an open question remains about which discourse track will prevail and what remedies the Arctic countries will seek.[9]

This chapter examines whether the Arctic Council is likely to retain its current role as the predominant forum where a wide range of Arctic issues is considered and debated, thereby contributing to enhancing regional stability. It discusses the role of the AC in regional security and sovereignty discourses, even though military-related issues are explicitly excluded from its mandate and more controversial issues are implicitly banned from its agenda. The chapter identifies the main challenges to the council's position that could diminish its role in the midst of pressures to address issues related to traditional security and stronger and more exclusive multilateral options to govern the region, as well as what means could be devised to overcome them. These tasks will be dealt with in three stages. First, it is important to highlight the context in which Arctic-wide intergovernmental cooperation was established, how it evolved into its current form, and what impact the AC has had on the region. To understand more clearly what changed (or not), it is important to examine the core area of the Council, the policy and assessment work done in the working groups, many of which have continued from the beginning of the AEPS to the present day, and how these developments contributed to regional stability and security.

Our argument is that before 2007–2008 none of the fundaments of circumpolar cooperation changed within the Arctic Council. What did change was the image of the Arctic, which in turn has gradually effected a change in the AC. Hence, the second section will trace the way the actors in the Arctic Council have perceived the Arctic as a place for governance, especially because of the Arctic Climate Impact Assessment (ACIA) conducted under the auspices of the Arctic Council. We argue that the ACIA did not trigger full-scale policy developments but only those within its own confines. It was the renewed debate over jurisdictional issues sparked by the Russian flag planted on the seabed beneath the North Pole and the almost simultaneous discovery of the vast reduction in sea ice that enabled the media narrative of a "scramble for resources"[10]—drawing a picture of states competing over who gets to occupy most of the Arctic's safe and supposedly plentiful resources —which affected the Arctic policy developments, ultimately challenging also the Arctic Council. These policy developments will be studied in the third section, after which the fourth and final part of this chapter will consider- whether the Arctic Council can retain its place as the predominant Arctic intergovernmental forum or whether it will be gradually bypassed by other forms of governance that can potentially address issues related to traditional security and sovereignty concerns, which seem unlikely to be taken up within the Arctic Council in the foreseeable future.

SETTING THE STAGE

Before proceeding to further analysis, it is important to clarify how we frame the concepts of security and sovereignty because this will have far-reaching consequences for thinking about the role of the Arctic Council in the emerging international environment in the Arctic. First, there is a need to determine the nature of contemporary security and sovereignty challenges in the Arctic and whether they provide the basis for a possible new security regime in the region. Second, it is important to identify the theoretical preconditions for the creation of such an institution. Accordingly, this section relates briefly the current form and position of the Arctic Council to adopt an understanding of security and sovereignty.

A framing of these concepts will implicate supposed options for the creation of new institutions or strengthening existing ones, depending on what one understands as security in the region. The nature of contemporary challenges in the Arctic has changed significantly from high militarization and geostrategic concerns to, among others, environmental, economic, social, and human security issues. At the same time all threats in these areas are interconnected[11] and stem primarily from effects of climate change, globalization, and the internationalization of the Arctic. Over the last twenty years, civil areas of cooperation have been predominant, but it is important to bear in mind that in special Arctic conditions, military and civil spheres are highly interdependent.

Some authors, however, argue that "securitizing Arctic politics draws attention to the potential for conflict in the Arctic in contrast to opportunities for promoting cooperation in meeting emerging needs for governance."[12] The argument that security may not be the most pertinent framing to comprehend regional challenges was raised at the dawn of Arctic cooperation. It was assumed that inherent difficulties in negotiations or cooperation on security issues, especially when old enemies were only getting to know new circumstances and collaboration prospects, were still imposing.[13] As noted by Franklyn Griffiths, "a security concept appropriate to the region will have early policy relevance only if it is generated in a process that produces consensus on the problem and the implications for collective action," thus "creation and use of integrated security conception of Arctic security is decidedly unpromising."[14] Furthermore, it was also pointed out that preferably the word "*security*" should not even be mentioned in crafting regional cooperation because it could direct it onto a "wrong track (...) as having a strong nationalistic and militaristic burden."[15]

At this juncture it is useful to revisit theoretical considerations on regime formation, especially in the security realm. Given that the basic function of international regimes (principles, norms, rules, and decision-making procedures) is "to coordinate state behavior to achieve desired outcomes in particular issue-areas,"[16], there is a need to identify common interests and those issue areas in which cooperation is plausible. They are well established within the existing cooperation structures, in which the Arctic Council plays a central role, and include a wide range of issues such as environmental protection, sustainable development, or maritime safety to mention a few. Nevertheless, it is essential to recognize emerging patterns of behavior that may potentially influence the collaborative approach. These are to be found in "national policy debates and in the international interplay between otherwise separate debates."[17] Such a conduct, evincing reckoning of interests, tends to lead to the creation of regimes, which in turn reinforce patterned behavior.[18]

However, regimes in the security sphere are weak because pure power motivations preclude them.[19] Conditions for forming a security regime include the willingness of great powers involved (it must be in their interest) to act in a more regulated environment and conviction of the actors that "others share the value they place on mutual security and cooperation."[20] It might be said that a common ground for creation of a security regime in the Arctic could possibly be found. But is there really a need for that? How relevant is such an arrangement in the region where well-developed multilateral cooperation unfolds on the most pertinent environmental, sustainable development, and shipping safety concerns? Jurisdictional issues are managed successfully by the Arctic Ocean coastal states, which have made a concerted effort to stabilize the situation by agreeing on the legal framework applying in the region. And finally, probably the most preeminent problem is whether there exist common threats to countries' specific interests in the Arctic or diverse threats to their common interests.

Although military security was excluded from the agenda of the Arctic Council (Declaration on the Establishment of the Arctic Council 1996), primarily because of strong resistance from the United States,[21] a concept of security in wider understanding has not been completely ruled out in its work. Environmental and human security—even if not explicitly framed—are dealt with in the council.[22] Moreover, the body may be seen as an institutional arrangement regulating the interplay of inside and outside entities to protect the integrity of the region where Arctic and non-Arctic actors pursue their own interests.[23]

There are still certain realms in which its activity may contribute to improvement of security in a wide sense. They include, for instance, hegemonic discourse on development,[24] regional identity, harmonization of national interests, and the decision-shaping component in Arctic governance and its interplay with a broader set of institutions.[25]

The leading role of the AC is stated in Arctic states' policies and strategies towards the region. Some non-Arctic actors are also formulating official positions on the Arctic and seek actively to hold an observer status at the council. A challenging area in this regard is a question of security and pursuit of national interests in the region by Arctic and non-Arctic states, which are not always harmonized. Nonetheless, it is fair to say that together with a well-developed and inclusive international cooperation on civil issues that enhances common interests and understanding, there are better prospects for regional security.[26]

To a large extent it is also closely linked with the question of sovereignty, understood here as the sum of the various types of jurisdiction possessed by the state within its territorial boundaries, subject only to certain limitations imposed by international law.[27] In addition, this definition includes forms of jurisdiction that a state may exercise over maritime and submarine areas beyond its boundaries (exclusive economic zone and continental shelf). Given the importance of this institution for the state, one may say that it is inextricably linked with the security issue, given that the threat to sovereignty is automatically a challenge to the very essence of national security in traditional terms. Issues of sovereignty and security are therefore interrelated, unfolding an additional dependent variable in the form of stability.

In this context, the Arctic Council should be viewed in connection with the entire regional governance framework encompassing a wide range of regional and global agreements and institutions with competence in the Arctic.[28] Furthermore, it may be seen as the political pillar of the international architecture in the Arctic, along with UNCLOS as its legal cornerstone, which can be perceived as a good platform to handle disputes and dissonance among engaged parties.[29] Even if the United States is not a party to UNCLOS (also a reason why the Ilulissat Declaration speaks of "law of the sea"), it has repeatedly confirmed that it accepts most provisions of UNCLOS as codifying customary international law.[30]

As noted by Griffiths, "good government is at once a precondition and a consequence of security."[31] Hence, the argument stemming from these considerations is that the Arctic Council and UNCLOS provide the framework for dealing with regional sovereignty and security issues and thus contribute to strengthening Arctic stability. As long as there are no major disputes either among the Arctic states or between Arctic and non-Arctic actors (or they are well managed elsewhere), these two institutions will play a central role. These initial assumptions and observations may prove useful in better understanding how the AC practically affects the security environment in the Arctic.

FROM THE AEPS TO THE ARCTIC COUNCIL

Before the negotiations for the AEPS commenced in 1989, inspired by Secretary-General Gorbachev's speech in Murmansk in 1987, the Arctic was not perceived as a place for intergovernmental cooperation. Instead it was dominated by military-strategic calculations between the United States and the USSR and their allies. The geographical distance between the two superpowers was closest over the North Pole, which made the Arctic one of the main theaters of Cold War rivalry.[32] Traditional security concerns dominated the region to the extent that no real chance existed to create Arctic-wide multilateral cooperation (the only modest exception to this is the Agreement on the Conservation of Polar Bears[33] that the five Arctic Ocean littoral states concluded in 1973).

Under the circumstances, the Finnish government, encouraged by Gorbachev's words and aware of the significant change in its powerful neighbor's policy, demonstrated a good sense of the situation by calling the other seven Arctic states in 1989 to launch joint actions to address environmental issues in the region. It was critical to provide a concrete response to the Soviet proposals by offering some form of institutionalization of cooperation in the region, even at the cost of concessions in terms of its range. The idea behind the Finnish Initiative was to establish a platform for collaboration—especially with the USSR—on topics important to all eight Arctic countries that would not be difficult to accept for political reasons.[34] Still, the possibility of a spillover effect on the other areas of cooperation in the future was not excluded. After consultations with the other Arctic countries, it turned out that the least controversial field would be transnational environmental problems affecting the Arctic.[35] As the Finnish ambassador Esko Rajakoski—lead of the negotiation process—later commented, at this early stage of discussion inclusion of any additional elements with political connotations touching upon differences or disputes between the states would have destined the entire initiative to failure.[36]

To some extent, it can be argued that the Finns did not attach particular importance to the theme of cooperation but rather sought ground for launching nonbelligerent interstate connections. Development of peaceful relations and opportunity to discuss common problems on a regular basis with a hitherto antagonistic neighbor in a highly militarized and strategically relevant region did have significant consequences for regional security and stability, regardless of the subject of joint endeavors. Thus, scientific cooperation on less-controversial environmental and sustainable development issues provided a mechanism to initiate and maintain an ongoing dialogue that allowed the cooperation to deepen over time.[37]

Moreover, Finland also sought legitimacy of its Arctic identity as a country that does not have access to the coast of the Arctic Ocean, although a substantial part of its territory lies within the Arctic Circle. In Finland's national interest, therefore, was widening the circle of countries traditionally considered to be the five Arctic coastal states with an additional three circumpolar nations –Sweden, Iceland, and Finland.[38] The concept of the "Arctic Eight" (A8) as a new regional identity was laid down as the basis of the draft proposed by Finland.[39] This enabled emergence of the Arctic as a new international region in political terms.[40] The concept may also be regarded as one of the main factors decisive for the success of the entire Finnish project because it helped to create a sense of responsibility for the region among the northern countries.[41] It seemed to be especially important for the Nordic countries, which sought to use this opportunity to reduce tensions and military presence in the region. Nevertheless, not all actors considered this grouping as an appropriate one and strenuous efforts were made to limit this initiative to the five littoral states.[42] After Finland succeeded in persuading the Arctic states to follow its initiative, this question was put aside. In the current circumstances, the concept has met with renewed interest.[43]

Whereas traditionally understood security concerns could be seen as the main incentives for launching environmental cooperation in the Arctic, state sovereignty issues were immanent aspects of the negotiations toward the AEPS and throughout the Rovaniemi Process.[44] According to Monica Tennberg, "the rule of sovereignty [within the AEPS and the Arctic Council] does collapse into practices of power,"[45] which means that states were actually more focused on preserving their interests and securing existing power relations than solving certain problems both inside and outside individual Arctic states.[46] Nevertheless, the Finnish Initiative succeeded in bringing together all the "Arctic Eight" nations to protect the Arctic environment despite the context being highly influenced by security and sovereignty interests.

TRANSITION FROM THE AEPS TO THE ARCTIC COUNCIL— WHAT CHANGED IN THE END?

The AEPS was adopted by the eight Arctic states (the five Nordic states, the United States, Canada, and the Soviet Union/the Russian Federation[47]) in 1991 in Rovaniemi, Finland, without any clear definition of what spatial scope would be used for defining the Arctic in this cooperative endeavor. The countries that were invited to take part in this cooperative effort were states that had areas of territorial sovereignty above the Arctic Circle.[48] Yet the Arctic Circle has not been used as the definition of the southernmost boundary of the Arctic, since all the Arctic states and the working groups have defined "the Arctic" for their own purposes.

The Arctic Council was established in 1996, and the AEPS was merged into this new high-level circumpolar forum over the next two years without any significant changes. The four initial working groups of the AEPS cooperation—Conservation of Arctic Flora and Fauna (CAFF), the Protection of the Arctic Marine Environment (PAME), Emergency Prevention, Preparedness and Response (EPPR), and the Arctic Monitoring and Assessment Programme (AMAP)—were integrated as part of the Arctic Council. A new working group, the Sustainable Development Working Group (SDWG), was established when the Arctic Council was adopted, and in general the mandate of the council was defined in broad terms to include all common issues facing the Arctic.[49] At first sight, there seemed to be a clear departure from the AEPS, which focused on environmental protection. Yet the AEPS also worked on sustainable development issues via its Task Force on Sustainable Development and Utilisation (TFSDU), which had on its agenda more high-level and controversial sustainable development issues that the SDWG eventually came to deal with.[50] Overall, there was no real change in the mandate of the AEPS and the council, given that both dealt with environmental protection and sustainable development issues.

Institutional forms have also not changed much during the transition. The AEPS had Senior Arctic Affairs Officials (SAAOs) to coordinate its work. Normally, they were high-level civil servants from the foreign and environmental offices. SAAOs also prepared the ministerial meetings of the AEPS, which took place in Nuuk, Greenland, in 1993; Inuvik, Canada, in 1996; and the final one in Alta, Norway, in 1997. Very much the same architecture has been retained in the council, although its organizational structure and procedures have been clarified with rules of procedure.[51] Yet, it is still the Senior Arctic Officials (SAOs), with only a slightly changed name, who coordinate the work in the AC. SAOs prepare the ministerial meetings in the same way SAAOs did in the AEPS, and ministerial meetings take place after the end of a country's chair period. These have been in Iqaluit (Canada, 1996–1998), Barrow (United States, 1998–2000), Inari (Finland, 2000–2002), Reykjavik (Iceland, 2002–2004), Salekhard (Russia, 2004–2006), Tromsø (Norway, 2006–2009), Nuuk (Denmark, 2009–2011), and Kiruna (Sweden, 2011–2013). All member states have served one term as a chair, with Canada resuming the chair in 2013.

The secretariat services for the Arctic Council have been provided by the chair state, although a change was introduced when the three consecutive Scandinavian chairs (Norway, Denmark, and Sweden) agreed to establish the secretariat in Tromsø, Norway, until 2012 and also decided that ministerial meetings are to be organized during the spring rather than autumn.[52] In the ministerial meeting in Nuuk in May 2011, it was agreed to commence preparations for establishing a permanent secretariat in Tromsø. The Host Country Agreement with Norway was signed in January 2013, and the Arctic Council Secretariat became operational in June 2013. As the first director of the secretariat, the AC appointed Magnus Johannesson from Iceland, the former chair of PAME.

The only clear change that took place when moving from the AEPS to the Arctic Council was an improvement in the status of membership accorded to the region's indigenous peoples, or more specifically, their organizations that represent either one people living in many Arctic states or many indigenous peoples living in one state.[53] In the AEPS, the indigenous peoples' organizations were observers together with nongovernmental and intergovernmental organizations and non-Arctic states. This was changed with the Ottawa Declaration by giving Arctic indigenous peoples' organizations a unique status in an intergovern-mental forum: they are now permanent participants whom the members need to fully consult before consensual decision making.[54]

There is no clear change in the way the members of the Arctic Council have committed to the cooperation; that commitment, however, has been low in terms of the scale of Arctic cooperation since the beginning of the AEPS, and it continues to be the situation with the council today. This is manifested in how the funding is organized, what kind of legal instruments are used in the cooperation, and how controversial and high-level questions can be discussed and decided. Funding has, from the beginning, been *ad hoc* in the sense that no permanent contributions are required from the eight Arctic states or other participants. There have been discussions of a project-support instrument, which is a plan for pooling resources from various actors to help realize some of the projects adopted by the Arctic Council, especially those designed to function in Russia.[55] No serious discussion has taken place to date over changing the funding system from the present *ad hoc* system to a stable permanent funding mechanism. Another factor signaling the low level of commit-ment to Arctic cooperation is the way the AEPS and the Arctic Council were established. The Rovaniemi Declaration and Ottawa Declaration, establishing respectively the AEPS and the Arctic Council, were only signed by representatives of the A8 and thus created not by an international treaty but by declaratory documents, effectively and deliberately keeping the cooperation at a level of soft-law arrangement. According to Evan Bloom, the U.S. Department of State representative in the negotiations on and the meetings of the Arctic Council, these types of cooperative forms were an objective for the United States, given the enhanced flexibility they provide.[56]

Finally, controversial and high-level issues, such as fisheries, have not been taken up on the forum. This was obvious in the AEPS, which focused on coordinating the countries' action in the field of environmental protection, but the Declaration on the Establishment of the Arctic Council at least laid the basis for taking action on all common issues facing the Arctic. The declaration was also promising in describing the council as a high-level intergovernmental forum, which could have signaled an institution that would also tackle more controversial issues other than military security. Yet the council has remained a body that produces, via its working groups, technical recommendations and guidelines and scientific assessments. It has not become a regulatory body, although the recent scientific assessments have been accompanied by policy recommendations. Legally binding agreements have also been developed under the auspices of the AC, which represents the closest the council has come to the realm of regulation. No serious effort has been made, however, to go beyond non-binding technical guidance or fairly abstract policy recommendations. Without any legal status, the council seems likely to continue as this kind of body, its primary focus being to sponsor scientific assessments and to function as a platform for environmental protection and sustainable development discussions between the established Arctic actors.

Nevertheless, the Arctic Council is the only intergovernmental body covering the whole area of the Arctic. Together with the initial stage of the AEPS, the AC contributed significantly to the deepening of interaction and confidence building in the post–Cold War Arctic, becoming an example of a successful project to enhance regional stability and creating an innovative and sustainable model of cooperation.[57] A practically open mandate (albeit limited in individual cases to the lack of consent to engage in certain areas, or a consensus to postpone them) allows for the initiating of projects relevant to current developments on the most pertinent issues emerging in the region. Unconstrained exchange of views between representatives of governments and indigenous peoples' organizations contributes to faster and more appropriate actions to solve common problems. Although lacking the ability to make legally binding decisions, the Arctic Council has proved to be quite successful in resolving certain issues by promoting them in the relevant institutions that have such powers. Most countries in the Arctic seem to believe that the essential and unique mission of the AC is basically to deal with problems of the Arctic at a high political level.[58] According to the most-shared view between the member countries, it should act as a decision-shaping rather than decision-making body.[59] Nevertheless, the importance of this institution is revealed primarily through its ability to generate knowledge and encourage innovation in approaches to the issues arising from the predictions about the consequences of climate change in the Arctic. This is done primarily by providing guidance, best practices and expertise to other international fora where decisions can be made.

Here the question emerges whether these developments and the work of AC projects have indirectly contributed to stability and thus security in the region. If yes, in what manner has it happened? Although one may argue that it is inadequate to perceive the Arctic Council as a security-relevant institution, there are certain insights that can be derived from the AC's role in enhancing regional stability. First and foremost, the projects and assessments create a common understanding of issues and thus limit the possibility of different views on the fundamentals and facts. Interaction and joint ventures mitigate the potential for conflicts and disputes on new and unexpected questions that may emerge. This in turn results in an increased predictability, which is essential for maintaining peaceful and effective cooperation. Second, the council enhances stability by its very existence and by providing the "first choice" channel for discussions on the Arctic issues within its mandate. This is further strengthened by a rather rigid calendar of meetings and activities as well as continued dialogue. Third, the council plays a crucial role in alleviating misunderstandings both among Arctic countries and between them and non-Arctic actors by providing the forum and services for discussion, information exchange and jointly generated knowledge. It proved to be particularly important, though not always successful, in communicating to the world, especially after the heated and media-driven debate following the flag planting by a Russian expedition, that there is peaceful and well-established cooperation going on in the region. Hence, it contributes to mitigating the perception of the Arctic as a place for potential conflict and disputes over access to natural resources.

One last observation, in contrast to the other three, concerns the role of the council in sovereignty discussions. As noted by Tennberg, shortly after the establishment of the Arctic Council, the Canadian government in its Report of the House of Commons Standing Committee on Foreign Affairs and International Trade stated that even though "on the question of sovereignty the AC cannot help to resolve long-standing disputes between members," it is expected that "over time such disputes are likely to become less important as regional cooperation replaces national sovereignty as priority for the Arctic states."[60] Nowadays, however, some Arctic states attach at least as much attention to sovereignty issues as to cooperation efforts. It is not to say that disputes on sovereignty questions will prevail among the Arctic countries. Today, it becomes more and more apparent that they would rather include sovereignty issues on the regional cooperation agenda (also outside the Arctic Council, as shown in the Ilulissat Declaration) to harmonize their actions and protect common interests against outside actors. This also illustrates how international circumstances in the Arctic have shifted.

Overall, it can be concluded that even though there was indeed a rapid conversion from the AEPS to the Arctic Council cooperation, the fundamentals of cooperation have remained very much the same. The Arctic Council has become broader in its organizational structure, in particular by the recent establishment of the standing secretariat, but the basics of cooperation have not been changed. It can be seen from the foregoing, however, that the council may be perceived as an important factor in regional security and stability and it has potential for further developments in this respect. Yet, because the main workload in the council has been carried out in the working groups, especially via those that have functioned from the beginning of the AEPS cooperation, it is pertinent to study whether a new set of priorities have developed for Arctic cooperation.

Changing perception of the Arctic Influencing the Priorities of Working Groups

There seems to be a clear about-face in the way the Arctic Council's working groups function largely as a result of changes in how the Arctic is understood and perceived as a region. Negotiations that led to the adoption of the AEPS constructed the Arctic as one integrated region for international policy purposes. The AEPS was very much built on the idea of protecting vulnerable Arctic ecosystems from human-induced pollution, originating both in the region and, perhaps more importantly, outside it. This is an intensely conservationist document, albeit taking into account the cultural values of the region's indigenous peoples in protecting these ecosystems. This is apparent from the first two objectives of the AEPS:

(1) To protect the Arctic ecosystem including humans;

(2) To provide for the protection, enhancement, and restoration of environmental quality and the sustainable utilization of natural

resources, including their use by local populations and indigenous peoples in the Arctic.[61]

The AEPS was an ambitious instrument of international environmental protection, given the final promise of its objectives, which was to do no less than "[to] identify, reduce, and, as a final goal, eliminate pollution."[62] It was built on the traditional image of the Arctic as a "frozen desert", which is well captured in the opening passage of the AEPS:

> The Arctic is highly sensitive to pollution and much of its human population and culture is directly dependent on the health of the region's ecosystems. Limited sunlight, ice cover that inhibits energy penetration, low mean and extreme temperatures, low species diversity and biological productivity and long-lived organisms with high lipid levels all contribute to the sensitivity of the Arctic ecosystem and cause it to be easily damaged. This vulnerability of the Arctic to pollution requires that action be taken now, or degradation may become irreversible.[63]

The image is one of ecosystems that are inherently vulnerable because of the cold and hostile environment, requiring stronger action for ensuring environmental protection. From the beginning, the AMAP working group was tasked with studying the function of these vulnerable remote ecosystems, whose function had not been studied enough, as well as pollution problems that threatened them. There is no sign here of a region that was undergoing a broad and intense transformation.

It was not the founding of the Arctic Council that changed the image of the "frozen desert" to one of the "Arctic in Dynamic Change" but rather the process that produced the Arctic Climate Impact Assessment (ACIA). It is important to remind oneself that during the 1990s, climate change efforts were focused on mitigating—even stopping—climate change from taking place. The policy discourse and the general media did not yet seriously think of adaptation to climate change consequences but how to prevent this phenomenon from occurring (in much the same way as the international community was able to take affirmative action to reduce chlorofluorocarbons [CFCs] and, in the long run, to control and erase the problem of ozone depletion). This priority in the climate regime was about to change dramatically, and, arguably, one of the main reasons for this perceptual change was the ACIA conducted under the auspices of the Arctic Council. ACIA, as a scientific assessment, was not only an objective undertaking but also involved choices that needed to be made throughout the process, thus making it an act of producing knowledge.[64]

As has been shown by Nilsson, the planning process for ACIA was multifaceted and also involved organizations other than the Arctic Council.[65] The work carried out in the International Arctic Science Committee (IASC)—a nongovernmental circumpolar scientific body— was instrumental in ensuring that ACIA took place. Another important factor was the willingness of the United States as chair of the Arctic Council (1998–2000) to push for such an assessment and to fund it. These were the times of the Clinton administration—when the United States was one of the key players in negotiating the Kyoto Protocol to the United Nations Framework Convention on Climate Change (UNFCCC)[66]—which partly explains the important role the United States was willing to play in its making. After a couple of seminars on the topic during the U.S. chair period, it was decided to launch ACIA with CAFF, AMAP, IASC and indigenous representatives sitting as members on the steering committee.

The ACIA was the first ever regional climate change assessment (it also considered the effects of ozone depletion in the Arctic), and it focused very much on the consequences of climate change for the region and its indigenous peoples. Even though the 2001 Intergovernmental Panel on Climate Change (IPCC) synthesis report also mentioned the Arctic in passing (IPCC 2001), it was the ACIA that established the Arctic as the early warning place of global climate change, a region where this phenomenon had already caused very concrete problems for ecosystems and human communities, and a place that was likely to warm twice as fast compared to the rest of the world.

The ACIA dramatically changed the way people perceive the Arctic as a region. Instead of the "frozen desert" image that had influenced the work of the AEPS, it became almost the opposite, a region undergoing a fundamental and dramatic transformation process. Some of the key findings of the ACIA synthesis report identify decisive aspects of such a pronounced shift:[67]

(1) The Arctic climate is now warming rapidly and much larger changes are projected;

(2) Arctic vegetation zones are very likely to shift, causing wide-ranging impacts;

(3) Animal species' diversity, ranges, and distribution will change;

(4) Many coastal communities and facilities face increasing exposure to storms;

(5) Reduced sea ice is very likely to increase marine transport and access to resources;

(6) Thawing ground will disrupt transportation, buildings, and other infrastructure;

(7) Indigenous communities are facing major economic and cultural impacts; and

(8) Multiple influences interact to cause increased impacts to people and ecosystems.

The ACIA began to influence the perceptions of the Arctic among the Arctic Council actors even before the synthesis report was released in 2004. As early as the 2002 Inari ministerial meeting, it was emphasized that the Arctic ministers noted with concern "the ongoing significant warming of most of the Arctic, and recognize that the impacts of global climate change with increased possibilities of extreme weather events will have large consequences in the Arctic, and that the Arctic can act as an early warning of global climate changes."[68] This development culminated in the release of the synthesis report before the 2004 Reykjavik ministerial, which in turn led to policy recommendations in the Reykjavik Declaration and the acknowledgment of "the need to further organize the work of the Arctic Council and its subsidiary bodies based on the findings of the ACIA and direct the SAOs to report on the progress made at the 2006 Ministerial Meeting."[69]

Presentation of the ACIA conclusions at the ministerial meeting in Reykjavik attracted considerable media attention. For the first time on such a scale, the output of the Arctic Council program met with similar interest.[70] Not without significance was the fact that the Arctic countries made special efforts for the study to have the widest possible impact. It also demonstrated how influential the ACIA results were in shaping the perception and understanding of climate issues of decision makers from these countries.[71]

It is also important to realize that the climate change issue, perceived as far-reaching by all involved parties, elevated the Arctic Council's position in the eyes of policy makers.[72] This was possible because of the dramatic impression of the shift occurring in the region conveyed by the ACIA, and thus the increased awareness of the Arctic Council and its programs among the Arctic inhabitants. To a large extent, the climate change issue proved to be crucial in paving the way to expanding the council's agenda[73] and enhancing its status.

Extensive studies, such as the ACIA, generated new activities designed to further explore issues raised. In this regard, the ACIA went even further given that it changed the priorities for most of the working groups, directing them to take the ACIA conclusions into account in their activities and conduct scientific assessments on the consequences of climate change in the region.[74] These "second-generation" assessments examine in more detail some of the consequences to the Arctic environment and the growing interests of the business community in making use of the Arctic, and they also contain policy recommendations.

The 2004 Arctic Marine Strategic Plan prepared by the PAME working group established the Arctic Marine Shipping Assessment (AMSA) as a major priority. This inclusive and high-profile assessment mapped out the current (as of 2004) shipping volumes in various parts of the Arctic marine regions and made projections for 2020 and 2050, given the opening of sea ice and economic globalization. AMSA findings and policy recommendations were released at the April 2009 ministerial meeting that ended the Norwegian chairmanship period.[75] Another major AMAP assessment concluded in 2007 evaluated the volume and consequences of increasing oil and gas activities in light of climate change and economic globalization.[76] The Arctic Biodiversity Assessment—completed by CAFF in 2013—aimed to evaluate the changes in Arctic biodiversity caused by increasing economic activities, climate change, and ultra-violet radiation.[77] The third generation of assessments, such as the Adaptation Actions for a Changing Arctic (AACA) is currently under way. The AACA project aims at evaluating the overall patterns of change in the Arctic and attempts to determine how the existing work of the Arctic Council can contribute to and inform adaptation processes within the Arctic states.

By carrying out these projects, the Arctic Council has established itself as the most significant contributor to knowledge about the Arctic, its environment, natural processes, degree of contamination, and above all the impact of climate change on northern regions and its implications.

Often the scale of these research programs would preclude them from being run by individual countries or indigenous organizations because it would require considerable financial resources and overcoming many problems, including political ones.[78] The most recent assessments addressed possible challenges and prospects resulting from exploitation of natural resources and increased activity in Arctic Ocean, thus extending the interest of the Arctic Council on emerging human activities and related concerns. At the same time, the influence of these assessments implies the council is able to affect discourses on the most pending and politically relevant issues. These instances suggest that the council establishes its position on the issues potentially related to security considerations.

Furthermore, knowledge and recommendations contained in Arctic Council reports have had an impact on the development of national Arctic policies by the member-states. In some cases, for instance the AMSA report recommendations, states incorporate them into their domestic rules of conduct in the region. In other matters they agree to transfer certain issues to the other, more appropriate forums capable of decision making. A good illustration of such an action is the recommendation from the council to push for a mandatory Polar Code within the International Maritime Organization.[79]

THE POLICY DEVELOPMENTS

Even if the ACIA did change the way the Arctic was perceived—at least within the confines of the Arctic Council—it did not yet effect any major policy developments. It was enough, however, to increase the interest of non-Arctic actors in involvement in the Arctic Council as observers. Spain started to participate as an *ad hoc* observer in 2005, to be eventually admitted as observer at the ministerial meeting in Salekhard in 2006.[80] In subsequent years, new outside actors such as China, Italy, the European Union, Republic of Korea, Japan, Singapore, and India applied for observer status. Decision on admittance was postponed twice—at the ministerial meetings in Tromsø in 2009 and in Nuuk in 2011—to be ultimately made during the 2013 Kiruna ministerial meeting concluding the Swedish chairmanship. However, although the EU's application was "received affirmatively" by the Arctic states, they deferred the final decision on implementation until resolution of issues between the European Commission and the AC members.[81]

Although drawing the attention of the outside world to the situation in the Arctic was one of the ACIA report publication objectives, this interest has focused on the economic opportunities associated with an ice-free Arctic rather than on counteracting the effects of climate change. It can be regarded as quite ironic that the study that was created to identify threats to wildlife and people of the Arctic and to assist in their prevention could potentially contribute to the creation of additional challenges and causes for concern.[82]

Nevertheless, it may be argued that only the two events that took place almost simultaneously triggered the serious policy actions by the Arctic actors. First, in August 2007, the Russian private research expedition "Arktika 2007," collecting evidence to support the revised (the first one was in 2001) planned submission to the Commission on the Limits of the Continental Shelf (CLCS) planted a national flag on the sub-sea Lomonosov Ridge at the North Pole, provoking diplomatic consternation among the Arctic Ocean coastal states. Second, a vast drop in Arctic sea ice coverage was detected in September 2007, reported widely as one of the clearest signals of climate change proceeding in general and in particular in the Arctic. These developments enabled the world media to describe the unfolding reality in the Arctic as one of a scramble for resources among Arctic Ocean coastal states, possibly leading to military conflicts.

Even if this was an erroneous description of what was taking place in the region (as most experts agree that continental shelf entitlements have been pursued on the basis of the Law of the Sea [United States] and UNCLOS [other Arctic coastal states]), the media has perpetuated this narrative to this day, given that it certainly has an appeal to wider readership. According to this narrative, climate change is opening the formerly ice-locked Arctic—a region that contains plentiful hydrocarbons and short-distance navigational highways for all the commercial fleets of the world to use. It was this narrative that also triggered the serious policy developments from both Arctic Council actors and others.

The main reason for organizing the meeting of Arctic coastal states in Ilulissat, Greenland, in May 2008 was to tell the rest of the world and the media that what is going on in the region is not a scramble for resources but rather an orderly development on the basis of the Law of the Sea. The core of the Ilulissat Declaration is an affirmation that the five coastal states will pursue continental shelf entitlements in accordance with international law. Yet it so clearly changed the discourse of Arctic governance that it had the effect of further provoking reactions from actors interested in Arctic governance. Coastal states perceived that the Arctic Ocean (defining the relevant Arctic) is at a threshold of significant changes from climate change and melting sea ice, and thus, "[b]y virtue of their sovereignty, sovereign rights and jurisdiction in large areas of the Arctic Ocean the five coastal states are in a unique position to address these possibilities and challenges."[83] They also presented themselves as protecting the environment and indigenous and other local inhabitants in the Arctic Ocean in the following way:

> Climate change and the melting of ice have a potential impact on vulnerable ecosystems, the livelihoods of local inhabitants and indigenous communities...The Arctic Ocean is a unique ecosystem, which the five coastal states have a stewardship role in protecting. Experience has shown how shipping disasters and subsequent pollution of the marine environment may cause irreversible disturbance of the ecological balance and major harm to the livelihoods of local inhabitants and indigenous communities.[84]

The Arctic Ocean coastal states perceived that there is "no need to develop a new comprehensive international legal regime to govern the Arctic Ocean" because

> [n]otably, the law of the sea provides for important rights and obligations concerning the delineation of the outer limits of the continental shelf, the protection of the marine environment, including ice-covered areas, freedom of navigation, marine scientific research, and other uses of the sea. We remain committed to this legal framework and to the orderly settlement of any possible overlapping claims. This framework provides a solid foundation for responsible management by the five coastal States and other

users of this Ocean through national implementation and application of relevant provisions.[85]

Even though Denmark insisted in the 2007 Narvik SAO meeting prior to the Ilulissat gathering that the coastal state cooperation would not compete with the council, the meeting caused friction among the Arctic Council members.[86] Iceland was the most concerned of the three states (the others are Finland and Sweden) not invited to Ilulissat. It expressed its concern in Narvik and also in the August 2008 Conference of the Arctic Parliamentarians.[87] The Ilulissat Declaration may be perceived as a narrowing of the group of legitimate Arctic actors to the five littoral states of the Arctic Ocean and as outlining an agenda for cooperation between them over high-level ocean policy issues, potentially challenging the Arctic Council, with its eight members, broad circumpolar focus, and soft work on environmental protection and sustainable development. To the surprise of many, a second[88] meeting of the coastal states was organized in Chelsea, Canada, in March 2010.

The coastal states' meetings prompted a "legalization" of policy stances of other actors interested in Arctic affairs. The European Parliament reacted to the "A5 meeting" by arguing that the Antarctic Treaty and its Madrid Protocol should be used as a source of inspiration when negotiating a comprehensive Arctic treaty.[89] WWF's Global Arctic Programme, the most active observer in the Arctic Council, has called for an Arctic Convention, which could bring at least the possibility of retaining sustainability in the Arctic with concomitant possibilities to engage in various new economic activities.[90] The most vocal party, however, was the strongest of the indigenous organizations—also a permanent participant in the Arctic Council—the Inuit Circumpolar Council (ICC). Its position comes as no surprise when one reads the previously cited parts of the Ilulissat Declaration.

As is readily clear, the coastal states defined themselves as sovereigns with stewardship over the "livelihoods of local inhabitants and indigenous communities." This was a difficult issue for the Inuit, because they were not given any active role in the meeting and were, in effect, seen as under the stewardship—together with the region's ecosystem—of the coastal states. Hence, soon after the Greenland meeting, November 6–7, 2008, the ICC and Inuit leaders issued their "Inuit Leaders' Statement on Arctic Sovereignty," in which they noted that the Ilulissat Declaration did not go far enough in affirming the rights Inuit have gained through international law, land claims, and self-government processes. They further noted the

> meaningful and direct role that indigenous peoples have at the Arctic Council, while at the same time expressing concern that the Council leaves many issues considered sensitive by member states off the table, including security, sovereignty, national legislation relating to marine mammal protection, and commercial fishing.[91]

This statement was then further refined for the Arctic Council ministerial meeting at the end of April 2009, when the ICC issued the Circumpolar Inuit Declaration on Sovereignty in the Arctic.

The basic legal architecture of the Inuit declaration relies on the self-determination of indigenous peoples. For the Inuit, the Arctic and the world at large do not consist only of sovereign states and their territories but have grown to be a very complex governance system, where authority and power is exercised on various levels and with various mandates and legal or non-legal bases. This is undoubtedly the case. For a long time, one has not been able to speak only of "government," but increasingly has referred to forms of authority bypassing the nation-states as forms of "governance" or "international governance." In a similar vein, indigenous peoples have various levels of governance of their own, ranging in the case of Inuit from their international organization, the ICC, to national ICC offices and down to indigenous governance arrangements under domestic law. Different parts of the Inuit declaration emphasize the various governance forms where the Inuit act in these legally relevant positions, from the international level to the domestic and down to the sub-unit level. With their sovereignty declaration, the

Inuit set out to find a way to reconcile their self-determination rights as a people and state sovereignty, as well as international policy-making.

CAN THE ARCTIC COUNCIL STILL NAVIGATE BETWEEN SOVEREIGN AND SECURITY?

As noted in the first section of this chapter, it would be a mistake to think that the Arctic Council could be easily turned into a treaty-based body with regulatory powers. Arctic-wide intergovernmental coopera-tion has followed a similar format since 1991. This is not to say that no evolution has occurred in Arctic cooperation. As the preceding analysis shows, within the limits of the Arctic Council structure, the working groups have started to function on the basis of a new perception of the "Arctic in Change." Along with the AEPS before it, the Arctic Council has contributed significantly to strengthening regional stability and thus security. Drawing on these observations, it can be said that the days are over when the council could be celebrated as the symbol of the emer-gence of the Arctic as an international political region[92] because nowa-days it is much more. There is a new dynamic in the region; various states and entities such as the EU are redrawing their Arctic policies and framing new governance possibilities. This discourse has finally reached the halls of power, having been a topic of scholarly concern for many years, then being taken on by nongovernmental organizations and finally entering the policy-making agendas by states. Have these devel-opments had an effect on the way the Arctic Council functions?

There are clear signs that the Arctic Council is stepping up its efforts to retain the status of a predominant intergovernmental forum dealing with Arctic affairs. By issuing the AMSA report—a study and policy docu-ment rather than a scientific assessment[93]—at the ministerial meeting in Tromsø in April 2009, the council has established its role as a key actor in shaping regional marine shipping governance. That is particularly mean-ingful when taking into consideration that almost all economic activities considered as posing potential for conflicts in the region depend on marine transport.[94] Although the assessment is kept within the mandate of the council, and as such it does not deal with military- and naval-related issues, there are certain ramifications for marine navigation rights and infrastructure with respect to security.[95] Creation of a regional search and rescue (SAR) instrument was also called for in AMSA recommendations, which was a driver to complete this first ever legally binding agreement negotiated under the auspices of the Arctic Council. The SAR agreement, however, may be seen as going much further in terms of security, given that it requires close cooperation and use of military capabilities as well as exchange of best practices and joint exercises, and thus supporting confidence building and stability.[96] As Lawson Brigham, the chair of the AMSA, put it,

> AMSA is a message from the Arctic states [AC] to the world that contains an environmental security framework and strategy to address the many complex challenges of protecting Arctic people and the environment in an era of expanding use in the Arctic Ocean.[97]

As in many cases, hard security concerns spring from soft security issues, and the Arctic Council may play a critical role in alleviating them at the earliest possible stage.

At the same meeting, the Arctic states adopted a more cautious approach toward observers. It was not necessarily a bad thing, as it is better to have well-considered rules in place before admitting new actors and increasing the role of the group. However, at the next ministerial meeting in Nuuk, Greenland, in May 2011, the Arctic states also decided to postpone decisions on the issue but published criteria for admitting observers and description of their role in the forum.[98] It may be said that by this act the council has also defined its place in the regional discourse on sovereignty issues. As stated in the criteria, applications for observer status will be considered by taking into account, inter alia, the extent to which candidates:

-recognize Arctic States' sovereignty, sovereign rights, and jurisdiction in the Arctic:

-recognize that an extensive legal framework applies to the Arctic
Ocean including, notably, the Law of the Sea, and that this framework provides a solid foundation for responsible management of
this ocean.[99]

Still, it remains unclear how the recognition of Arctic states' sovereignty
will be assessed by the member-states given that they do not fully agree
on certain issues among themselves. Furthermore, it has not been determined yet whether sovereignty questions related to non-Arctic actors
will be debated at AC meetings. To a certain extent, inclusion of sovereignty issues (even if associated only with outside entities) in the Arctic
Council agenda may be perceived as an attempt to bridge the gap that has
opened between the Arctic Five and the Arctic Eight in political terms.[100]
It is fair to say that increased activity of the five littoral states of the
Arctic Ocean has been caused by outside rather than regional factors,
primarily media, experts, and the EU-driven debate on an Arctic treaty
or some other form of a legally binding basis for Arctic governance.
What makes this point even more relevant is the nature of sovereignty
issues in the Arctic, which may indicate that most likely they are to be
dealt with bilaterally among the Arctic states. The Arctic Five formula
(Arctic Ocean Meetings) has been, therefore, refurbished to address challenges for sovereignty rising from the south.[101] Inclusion of the key principles of the Ilulissat Declaration into the Arctic Council documents may
suggest that Arctic states have chosen to move these discussions into
the council's forum. Thus, the body can be perceived as an actor in mitigating regional sovereignty issues, at least those emerging from outside
the region.

The policy profile of the council has been strengthened by the
recently established practice of having deputy ministers meet bienni-
ally to complement ministerial meetings. Moreover, if one compares

who participates in the latter ones, there is clear change in this respect. Formerly, not all countries even sent their ministers to the biennial ministerial meetings, but the 2011 ministerial meeting in Nuuk for the first time ever was attended by the U.S. Secretary of State, Hillary Clinton. The Nuuk ministerial was an important culmination of many processes that strengthened the Arctic Council. Preparations for establishing a permanent secretariat in Tromsø commenced, and discussions on both financial issues and the criteria and role of observers advanced to some extent. The Arctic Council could also celebrate the making of a first legally binding treaty on search and rescue that was adopted as part of the Nuuk ministerial meeting. Moreover, the ministers commenced in Nuuk another project that led to an international agreement on oil pollution preparedness and response, signed in May 2013 in Kiruna. All the attention that has spotlighted the lack of governance in the Arctic has clearly played a role in effecting discernible changes in the structure and functioning of the Arctic Council.

The question emerges as to whether the Arctic Council can still navigate between sovereignty and security in governing the Arctic and retain its role as the predominant forum of Arctic discussions. With decreasing presence of sea ice and an increasing amount of commercial activities, it seems difficult to communicate the "Arctic message" in such a way that this is just a region, that needs more solid scientific research and environmental and sustainable development measures.

This is not so much a question of what is the correct interpretation as to what is unfolding in the Arctic. It seems that the civil servants and experts of Arctic affairs have tried to convey that there is no scramble for resources or threats of military security in the Arctic. Yet it is the perceived reality that seems to dominate the Arctic narrative much more than what the experts and civil servants try to say. Media keep telling of possible military threats arising in the Arctic because of a scramble for resources, even if most experts agree that no such narrative is viable to capture what is taking place in the region. And it is the perceived reality spread by the media that keeps feeding the southern constituencies and policy makers. Therefore, there is yet another important role for the Arctic Council to include these actors as observers and to inform them about the situation. In this connection it may serve as a platform for building common understanding with outside entities and thus alleviate their perception of the media-driven picture.

Yet one can hope that the managerial soft-law reality of the Arctic Council can with certain improvements such as the ones that took place in Nuuk in May 2011 survive as the main platform of governance discussions in the Arctic. This presupposes that the major actors foresee no possibility for serious disagreements or sovereignty threats in the fast-changing socio-ecological reality of the Arctic and that the council indeed keeps consolidating its governance efforts. It is in this latter case that the Arctic Council can continue to serve as the main platform for Arctic intergovernmental cooperation and feed important scientific assessment information on various levels of governance conducting Arctic governance.

CONCLUSIONS

High politics issues have been present since the very inception of (and even long before) current environmental cooperation in the Arctic and to a large extent laid the fundamentals for this endeavor. Behind the timely idea of conservation of the environment, they were meant to mitigate controversial and security-related issues by providing regular consultations and discussions on common issues, enhancing mutual confidence and understanding and preparing the ground for deeper and more far-reaching collaboration that could spill over to other areas.

The AEPS, and to a lesser extent the Arctic Council, emerged in a highly securitized international environment. Although security and sovereignty issues have been constantly present in Arctic international politics, it has been possible to preserve and develop multilateral collaboration, and thus contribute to regional stability. It took over twenty years to evolve, but today it may be argued that the level of interaction among the Arctic states, primarily within the AC but as revealed in other efforts such as the Ilulissat Declaration, would need real and lethal threats to be undermined.

Although the AEPS and the Arctic Council were not created as institutions focused strictly on security, they have nonetheless played an important role in building and ensuring regional stability and security (at least in minimizing the likelihood of conflicts). In recent years, however, a number of challenges have emerged that could undermine this. Scientific findings on the dramatic effects of climate change in the Arctic altered the profile of the Arctic Council and its working groups, revealing a need to reflect upon how to adapt substantially to the rapid change. Recent developments in international relations in the Arctic will also require appropriate adjustments within the council. However, it is only one of the pillars of regional governance architecture. In our view, the Arctic Council is in the right position to retain its current role and even strengthen it in the years to come given a new impetus in its regulatory abilities. What acts in favor of the council is its already established and recognized status as the main circumpolar forum for cooperation and the mere logic of international relations, which is especially clear when it comes to principles that inform sovereignty and security issues.

Although there is little likelihood of the emergence of new structures that would marginalize the Arctic Council, it cannot be completely ruled out. Even though the Arctic states invested considerable effort to strengthen it both institutionally and substantially, there still exist issues that preferably are dealt with elsewhere. The Arctic Five formula seems to be held in reserve and ready to resume operation or take action if necessary, as evinced by the April 2013 meeting in Washington, DC on possible accord on fisheries in the high Arctic Ocean. The "Arctic Circle" initiative of the Icelandic president Ólafur Ragnar Grímsson stirred concerns about whether it is to offer outside, especially Asian, actors yet another pathway to political discussions about the Arctic, almost on the eve of the Kiruna ministerial meeting, where decisions on observers were to be made. Hence the AC must retain flexibility and adaptability to new global circumstances because the international system does not tolerate a vacuum, which always, sooner or later, will be filled. The question emerges whether the current profile of the Arctic Council—based on cooperation of the Arctic states with indigenous peoples' organizations on environmental and sustainable development issues—corresponds to the current situation in the Far North and its international implications. From the viewpoint of the Arctic states' interests, it seems important to seek common understanding and to strengthen regional cooperation instruments, among which the council plays a central role. The interests of outside actors also seem to compel the member-states of the council to assign a definitive role that it has to play in the region. The important strides made by the Arctic states to re-devise the Arctic Council and equip it with all the necessary tools seem to shrink the specter of weakening or marginalization of this forum. Therefore, the other forms of cooperation will rather complement the preeminent political direction set within the council.

The Arctic Council has demonstrated an ability to adapt to changing natural conditions. Currently, it also needs to continue adjusting to new international circumstances. Could this be done even more ably? There are good reasons to answer positively, but this task might prove to be far more difficult than redirecting the focus of the working groups. To a large extent, the answer will depend on the Arctic states and the track they choose to follow. At the same time, it must be done in a very careful and sustainable manner to ensure that the council will not lose its unique bottom-up character allowing for the special position of indigenous peoples' organizations as permanent participants for the benefit of high politics. The Arctic includes not only the Arctic Ocean but also vast inhabited territories of the eight Arctic states. Drawing these views together, one might argue that any attempt to dismantle the key elements of the existing Arctic international architecture could have an adverse effect and cause an erosion of the cooperation and stability level reached in the region.

Notes

1. Timo Koivurova and David VanderZwaag, "The Arctic Council at 10 Years: Retrospect and Prospects," *University of British Columbia Law Review* 40, no. 1 (2007): 121–194.
2. Cf. Scott G. Borgerson, "Arctic Meltdown: The Economic and Security Implications of Global Warming." *Foreign Affairs* 2 (March/April 2008).
3. Alf Håkon Hoel, "The High North Legal-Political Regime," in *Security Prospects in the High North: Geostrategic Thaw or Freeze?* NDC Forum Paper 7, ed. Sven G. Holtsmark and Brooke A. Smith-Wilson (Rome: NATO Defense College, 2009), 81–101.
4. Cf. Olav Schram Stokke and Geir Hønneland, eds., *International Cooperation and Arctic Governance: Regime Effectiveness and Northern Region-Building* (London and New York: Routledge, 2007); Timo Koivurova, E. Carina H. Keskitalo, and Nigel Bankes, eds., *Climate Governance in the Arctic* (Np: Springer, 2009).
5. Dmitri Trenin and Pavel K. Baev, *The Arctic: A View from Moscow* (Washington, DC: Carnegie Endowment for International Peace, 2010); Kristian Åtland, "Security Implications of Climate Change in the Arctic," *FFI-rapport* 2010/01097 (Oslo: The Norwegian Defence Research Establishment [FFI], 2010); Sven G. Holtsmark and Brooke A. Smith-Wilson, eds., *Security Prospects in the High North: Geostrategic Thaw or Freeze?* NDC Forum Paper 7 (Rome: NATO Defense College, 2009); David Scrivener, *Environmental Cooperation in the Arctic: From Strategy to Council*, Security Policy Library No. 1/1996 (Oslo: The Norwegian Atlantic Committee, 1996).
6. E.g., Michael Byers, *Who Owns the Arctic? Understanding Sovereignty Disputes in the North* (Vancouver: Douglas & McIntyre, 2010); Shelagh D. Grant, *Polar Imperative: A History of Arctic Sovereignty in North America* (Vancouver: Douglas & McIntyre, 2010).
7. E.g., R. Huebert, *United States Arctic Policy: The Reluctant Arctic Power*, SPP Briefing Papers: Focus on the United States 2, no. 2 (Calgary: School of Public Policy, University of Calgary, 2009), http://www.policyschool.ucalgary.ca/sites/default/files/research/sppbriefing-huebertonline.pdf.
8. E.g., Barry Scott Zellen, *Arctic Doom, Arctic Boom: The Geopolitics of Climate Change in the Arctic* (Santa Barbara, CA: Praeger, 2009).

9. Cf. Oran R. Young, "Arctic State Changes: Implications for Governance," paper prepared for 2030 North, A National Planning Conference, Ottawa, June 1–4, 2009.

10. E.g., J. Graff, "Fight for the Top of the World," *Time*, October 1, 2007, www.time.com/time/world/article/0,8599,1663445,00.html.

11. Cf. Barry Buzan, Ole Wæver, and Jaap De Wilde, *Security: A New Framework for Analysis* (Boulder, CO: Lynne Rienner Publishers, 1997).

12. Oran R. Young, "Foreword—Arctic Futures: The Politics of Transformation," in *Arctic Security in an Age of Climate Change*, ed. James Kraska (Cambridge: Cambridge University Press, 2011), xxvi.

13. Franklyn Griffiths, "Epilogue: Civility in the Arctic," in *Arctic Alternatives: Civility or Militarism in the Circumpolar North*, ed. Franklyn Griffiths (Toronto: Science for Peace/Samuel Stevens, 1992), 299.

14. Ibid.

15. Cf. Monica Tennberg, *Arctic Environmental Cooperation: A Study in Governmentality* (Aldershot: Ashgate, 2000), 90–91.

16. Stephen D. Krasner, ed., *International Regimes* (Ithaca, NY, and London: Cornell University Press, 1983).

17. Franklyn Griffiths, "Arctic Security: The Indirect Approach," in *Arctic Security in an Age of Climate Change*, ed. James Kraska (Cambridge: Cambridge University Press, 2011), 4.

18. Krasner, *International Regimes*.

19. Ibid., 8.

20. Robert Jervis, "Security Regimes," in *International Regimes*, ed. Stephen D. Krasner (Ithaca, NY, and London: Cornell University Press, 1983), 176.

21. Scrivener, *Environmental Cooperation in the Arctic*, 22.

22. Cf. Alyson J. K. Bailes, "Options for Closer Cooperation in the High North: What Is Needed?" in *Security Prospects in the High North: Geostrategic Thaw or Freeze?* NDC Forum Paper 7, ed. Sven G. Holtsmark and Brooke A. Smith-Windsor (Rome: NATO Defense College, 2009), 45.

23. Cf. Oran R. Young and Arkady I. Cherkasov, "International Co-operation in the Arctic: Opportunities and Constraints," in *Arctic Alternatives: Civility or Militarism in the Circumpolar North*, ed. Franklyn Griffiths (Toronto: Science for Peace/Samuel Stevens, 1992), 9.

24. Tennberg, *Arctic Environmental Cooperation*.

25. Stokke and Hønneland, *International Cooperation and Arctic Governance*.

26. Cf. Griffiths, "Arctic Security," 4.

27. Donat Pharand, "Sovereignty in the Arctic: The International Legal Context," in *Sovereignty and Security in the Arctic*, ed. Edgar Dosman (London and New York: Routledge, 1989), 145.
28. Cf. Alf Håkon Hoel, "Do We Need a New Legal Regime for the Arctic Ocean?" *International Journal of Marine and Coastal Law* 24, no. 2 (2009): 443–456; "High North Legal-Political Regime."
29. Cf. Njord Wegge, "The Political Order in the Arctic: Power Structures, Regimes and Influence." *Polar Record* 47, no. 241 (2010): 173.
30. Administration of Ronald Reagan, "Statement by the President on United States Ocean Policy." 19 WEEKLY COMP. PRES. DOC. 383 (March 10, 1983). 22 I. L. M. 461, 464 (1983).
31. Griffiths, "Arctic Security," 4.
32. Edgar Dosman, ed., *Sovereignty and Security in the Arctic* (London and New York: Routledge, 1989); K. Möttölä, The Arctic Challenge: Nordic and Canadian Approaches to Security and Cooperation in an Emerging International Region (Boulder, CO: Westview, 1988).
33. Polar Bear Agreement 1973, The 1973 Agreement on the Conservation of Polar Bears. The agreement is reproduced in 13 I.L.M. 13 (1974).
34. Esko Rajakoski, "Multilateral Cooperation to Protect the Arctic Environment: The Finnish Initiative," in *The Arctic: Choices for Peace and Security, Proceedings of a Public Inquiry*, ed. Thomas R. Berger et al. (West Vancouver and Seattle: Gordon Soules Book Publishers Ltd., 1989), 56; cf. Oran R. Young, *Creating Regimes: Arctic Accords and International Governance* (Ithaca, NY: Cornell University Press, 1998), 170.
35. Huebert, *United States Arctic Policy*, 10.
36. T. Berger et al., "Question Session," in *The Arctic: Choices for Peace and Security. Proceedings of a Public Inquiry*, ed. Thomas R. Berger et al. (West Vancouver and Seattle: Gordon Soules Book Publishers Ltd., 1989), 79.
37. Cf. H. R. Nilson, *Arctic Environmental Protection Strategy: Process and Organization, 1991–1997*, Rapportserie no. 103 (Oslo: Norwegian Polar Institute, 1997), 4.
38. Cf. E. C. H. Keskitalo, *Negotiating the Arctic: The Construction of an International Region* (New York and London: Routledge, 2004), 59–61.
39. Young, *Creating Regimes*, 57.
40. Ibid., 36, 170; cf. Keskitalo, *Negotiating the Arctic*, 34–39.
41. Young, *Creating Regimes*, 59, 63.
42. Young, "Foreword—Arctic Futures," xxiii.
43. Ibid.
44. Cf. Tennberg, *Arctic Environmental Cooperation*, 13–14.

45. Ibid., 131.
46. Ibid.
47. The Soviet Union was still the signatory to the AEPS that was signed on June 14, 1991.
48. Iceland also has areas of territorial sovereignty above the Arctic Circle, as its territorial sea extends above the circle. For an analysis of the various definitions, see T. Koivurova, *Environmental Impact Assessment in the Arctic: A Study of International Legal Norms* (Farnham, UK: Ashgate, 2002), 25–28.
49. Ottawa Declaration on the Establishment of the Arctic Council, 35 I.L.M. 1385–1390 (1996), para. 1, http://www.arctic-council.org/index.php/en/document-archive/category/4-founding-documents. The first footnote of the Ottawa Declaration (Arctic Council Declaration) provides that "The Arctic Council should not deal with matters related to military security."
50. C. Keskitalo, "Constructing 'the Arctic,'" *Acta Universitatis Lapponiensis* 47, University of Lapland, Rovaniemi (2002): 113–158.
51. "Rules of Procedure," The Arctic Council Rules of Procedure as adopted by the Arctic Council at the First Arctic Council Ministerial Meeting, Iqaluit, Canada, September 17–18, 1998, http://arctic-council.org/filearchive/official%20rules%20and%20procedures.pdf.
52. "Common Objectives," Common Objectives and Priorities for the Norwegian, Danish, and Swedish Chairmanships of the Arctic Council (2006–2012), 2006.
53. Ottawa Declaration, para. 2.
54. Ibid.
55. "Final Report," Svolvaer, Norway, SAO meeting, April 23–24, 2008, para. 12.2, http://www.arctic-council.org/index.php/en/document-archive/category/43-sao-meeting-svolvaer-april-2008.
56. E. Bloom, "The Establishment of the Arctic Council," *American Journal of International Law* 93 (1999): 721.
57. Lassi Heininen, "Circumpolar International Relations and Cooperation," in *Globalization and the Circumpolar North*, ed. Lassi Heininen and Chris Southcott (Fairbanks: University of Alaska Press, 2010), 279–280.
58. Anton Vasiliev, "Russian Policy in the Arctic and the Arctic Council," Final Report on Northern Research Forum Plenary Session "The Future of Northern Co-Operation" and Special Roundtable Discussion "The Arctic Council and Multilateral Cooperation: Reports and Articles," 5th NRF Open Assembly "Seeking Balance in a Changing North," Anchorage, Alaska, September 24–27, 2008.

59. Jonas Gahr Støre, *Welcoming Remarks at the Sixth Ministerial Meeting of the Arctic Council*, Tromsø, Norway, April 29, 2009.

60. Monica Tennberg, *Arctic Environmental Cooperation: A Study in Governmentality* (Aldershot: Ashgate, 2000), 128.

61. Arctic Environmental Protection Strategy (AEPS), 1991, 2.1. (i, ii). The AEPS is reproduced in 30 International Legal Materials (I.L.M.) 1624 (1991), http://www.arctic-council.org/index.php/en/document-archive/category/4-founding-documents.

62. Ibid., 2 (1v).

63. Ibid., 1 ("Introduction").

64. Nilsson argued in her conclusions, "In the scientific assessment, the regional perspective was partly lost in the global-local dichotomy. However, in the overview document, the pan-Arctic region is given a much stronger emphasis and also given a symbolic role as the "a canary in the mine" warning system for what could be in store globally. As this framing is not as prominent in the scientific report, the immediate drivers appear to be the team that was responsible for the production of the overview and their wish to be policy relevant within the context of the global climate negotiations." A. E. Nilsson, *A Changing Arctic Climate: Science and Policy in the Arctic Climate Impact Assessment*, Linköping Studies in Arts and Science no. 386 (Linköping: Linköping University Electronic Press, 2007), 204.

65. Ibid., 98–110.

66. United Nations Framework Convention on Climate Change (UNFCCC). The text is reproduced in 31 I.L.M. 849 (1992), http://unfccc.int/resource/docs/convkp/conveng.pdf.

67. ACIA, *Arctic Climate Impact Assessment Policy Document*, Fourth Arctic Council Ministerial Meeting, Reykjavik, November 24, 2004, http://www.acia.uaf.edu/PDFs/ACIA_Policy_Document.pdf.

68. Inari Declaration on the Occasion of the Third Ministerial Meeting of the Arctic Council, 2002, para. 8, http://arctic-council.org/filearchive/The%20signed%20Inari%20Declaration.pdf.

69. Reykjavik Declaration on the Occasion of the Fourth Ministerial Meeting of the Arctic Council, 2004, "Climate Change in the Arctic," http://www.arctic-council.org/index.php/en/document-archive/category/32-4th-ministerial-meeting-in-reykjavik-iceland-2004.

70. Alf Håkon Hoel, "Climate Change," in *International Cooperation and Arctic Governance: Regime Effectiveness and Northern Region-Building*, ed.

Olav Schram Stokke and Geir Hønneland (London and New York: Rout-ledge, 2007), 126, 135.

71. Ibid., 127–128, 131.
72. Ibid., 130.
73. Ibid.
74. ACIA, *Arctic Climate Impact Assessment Policy Document*; cf. Hoel, "Cli-mate Change," 126.
75. See AMSA, Arctic Marine Shipping Assessment 2009 Report, 2009, and related documents at http://pame.is/about-amsa.
76. "Oil and Gas Assessment Overview Report," AMAP, May 1, 2008, http://www.amap.no/oga/.
77. See http://arcticportal.org/en/caff/aba.
78. Elana Wilson and Indra Øverland, "Indigenous Issues," in *International Cooperation and Arctic Governance: Regime Effectiveness and Northern Region-Building*, ed. Olav Schram Stokke and Geir Hønneland (London and New York: Routledge, 2007), 44.
79. Tromsø Declaration on the Occasion of the Sixth Ministerial Meeting of the Arctic Council, 2009, http://www.arctic-council.org/index.php/en/document-archive/category/15-6th-ministerial-meeting-in-tromso-norway.
80. Piotr Graczyk, "Observers in the Arctic Council—Evolution and Prospects," *Yearbook of Polar Law* 3 (2011): 606.
81. Kiruna Declaration on the Occasion of the Eighth Ministerial Meeting of the Arctic Council, 2013, http://www.arctic-council.org/index.php/en/document-archive/category/425-main-documents-from-kiruna-ministerial-meeting.
82. Young, " oungc State Changes," 10.
83. Ilulissat Declaration, Arctic Ocean Conference, Ilulissat, Greenland, 2008, http://www.oceanlaw.org/downloads/arctic/Ilulissat_Declaration.pdf.
84. Ibid.
85. Ibid.
86. "Final Report," Narvik, Norway, SAO meeting November 28–29, 2007, http://www.arctic-council.org/index.php/en/document-archive/category/48-sao-meeting-2007-2-in-narvik-norway-november-2007.
87. Conference Report 2008, 36, http://www.arcticparl.org/files/files%20from%208th%20conference/Conference_Report_Fairbanks_final.pdf.
88. Before the meeting in Ilulissat, a rather informal meeting on the level of senior officers from the ministries of foreign affairs of the five coastal

states took place in Oslo, Norway, in October 2007. Conclusions from this meeting were, in large part, included in the Ilulissat Declaration.

89. European Parliament resolution, October 9, 2008, on Arctic governance, http://www.europarl.europa.eu/sides/getDoc.do?pubRef=-//EP//TEXT+ TA+P6-TA-2008-0474+0+DOC+XML+V0//EN.

90. T. Saksina, Presentation at the Arctic Frontiers Conference, Tromsø, Norway, January 20, 2009, http://archive.arcticfrontiers.com/index.php? option=com_docman&task=cat_view&gid=82&Itemid=418 (presentation can be viewed via webcam); Timo Koivurova, "Alternatives for an Arctic Treaty—Evaluation and a New Proposal," *Review of European Community & International Environmental Law—RECIEL* 17, no. 1, Special International Polar Year Issue (2008): 22–24.

91. Inuit Leaders Statement 2008.

92. Oran R. Young, *The Structure of Arctic Cooperation: Solving Problems/ Seizing Opportunities* (2000), 15, http://www.arcticparl.org/_res/site/File/ images/conf4_sac.pdf.

93. Lawson Brigham, "The Challenges and Security Issues of Arctic Marine Transport," in *Arctic Security in an Age of Climate Change*, ed. James Kraska (Cambridge: Cambridge University Press, 2011), 21.

94. Ibid., 20.

95. Ibid., 21.

96. Griffiths, "Arctic Security," 6.

97. Ibid.

98. SAO, *Senior Arctic Officials Report to Ministers*, Nuuk, Greenland, May 2011, 50–51.

99. Ibid., 50.

100. Young, "Foreword—Arctic Futures," xxiv.

101. Cf. ibid.

CHAPTER 16

INTERNATIONAL LAW
AND THE ARCTIC

HOW TERRITORIALITY, HUMAN RIGHTS, AND
THE ENVIRONMENT CAN SHAPE SOVEREIGNTY

Betsy Baker

In the early twenty-first century, thawing permafrost and melting sea ice in the Arctic are reshaping geophysical and biological barriers, and geopolitical barriers are changing in response. Concepts of sovereignty in public international law also need to adapt, to reflect new ways of managing uses and sharing jurisdiction. International law is capable of shifting from fixed notions of sovereignty and territorial integrity to acknowledging and acting on specific ways in which states are connected, not separated, by shared environmental systems and shared circumpolar indigenous rights. International law has moved slowly in this direction over the last century, but its traditional realm of bounded territorial integrity has remained impervious to certain incursions of human rights and environmental protection.

I propose that public international law can make "A Case for Shared Sovereignty," the question that animates this section of the book.[1] I argue that international law can best provide practical solutions for the Arctic by weaving three of its strands—boundaries, environment, and human rights—more closely and in new ways to admit a shared sovereignty that respects existing international law even while building on it to meet new challenges.[2] I demonstrate how the UN Convention on the Law of the Sea, recognized by all Arctic states as a key instrument of international law, contains the seeds of shared sovereignty and weaves elements of environmental law, if not human rights, into the fabric of traditional notions of bounded international law.

I characterize the first strand of public international law, that of boundaries and borders, as one where states still relate to each other in terms of state sovereignty, territorial integrity, shared borders, and maritime boundaries. I consider the second strand to be international environmental law (IEL), which best addresses problems such as oil spills, habitat loss, ocean warming, and acidification by coordination across maritime and terrestrial boundaries, given that marine life and shipping pass through the maritime zones of all five Arctic coastal states. The third strand is the international law of human rights and indigenous rights. Indigenous peoples have organized across national boundaries, around the pole and around the globe, declaring the shared rights of all indigenous peoples, regardless of nationality or location.

Elements of the first strand—boundaries, borders, and territorial integrity—have defined the limits of international law since its inception. As long as nation-states have existed, public international law has served primarily to guide relations between them, to regulate how they assert sovereignty, ensure national security, resolve competing territorial interests, and exercise jurisdiction over and manage resources. In the twentieth century, the interests of individuals, and of the environment, began to breach the rigid boundaries of traditional international law. Individuals obtained international fora in which to call their states to account publicly, and the international community began to assert the need to breach territorial integrity for certain limited purposes such as monitoring a state's treatment of individuals.[3] International environmental law established the duty of states not to allow uses in their territories to harm the territory of others.[4] These defining achievements of human rights and international environmental law helped create new categories and spheres of protection that expanded, but still meet resistance from, the traditionally bounded approach to international law.

To propose how the international law of environmental protection and of indigenous rights can be better integrated with traditional public international law in the Arctic,[5] I begin with a snapshot of Arctic law and policy from 2008, the year after the first greatest decline in summer sea ice extent since such measurements began.[6] I then identify key principles and institutions in all three strands, offering a chronology of developments in environmental law and, to a lesser extent, human rights law that are most relevant to the Arctic. Throughout, I draw on the Law of the Sea Convention and its role in these developments. What follows is not a compendium of all institutions and actors relevant to the Arctic but a sketch of developments in international law that can be applied to changing conditions there.[7]

A Snapshot: The Law of the Sea and Arctic Law and Policy in 2008

The 2008 Ilulissat Declaration of the five Arctic coastal states, arguably this century's most frequently cited declaration on international law in the Arctic, keeps the third strand of indigenous rights safely separate from the first two.[8] The declaration, the product of a meeting about the Arctic Ocean, does not mention human rights. It simply begins by noting the potential effects of climate change on "vulnerable ecosystems, the livelihoods of local inhabitants and indigenous communities, and the potential exploitation of natural resources."[9] The declaration, which is not binding international law, then states

> that an extensive international legal framework applies to the Arctic Ocean...[t]he law of the sea provides for important rights and obligations concerning the delineation of the outer limits of the continental shelf, the protection of the marine environment, including ice-covered areas, freedom of navigation, marine scientific research, and other uses of the sea. We remain committed to this legal framework and to the orderly settlement of any possible overlapping claims.[10]

Here, the first strand of territorial integrity is in full evidence, from shelf limits to state navigational rights to overlapping claims; the second strand of environmental protection is mentioned as marginally related. This juxtaposition reflects a major accomplishment of the 1982 UN Convention on the Law of the Sea (UNCLOS), even though the declaration does not reference it directly but uses the more general phrase "law of the sea."[11] UNCLOS, which entered into force in 1994, was groundbreaking in introducing the exclusive economic zone (EEZ) and tying coastal state jurisdiction over different maritime zones to graduated degrees of sovereign rights and obligations, including environmental protection. The Ilulissat Declaration acknowledges the distinction between the coastal states' "sovereignty, sovereign rights and jurisdiction in large areas of the Arctic Ocean," by virtue of which "the five coastal states are in a unique position to address these possibilities and challenges." The five conclude from this claimed unique position and the existence of "the law of the sea" that "[w]e...see no need to develop a comprehensive international legal regime to govern the Arctic Ocean."

Others disagreed. Indigenous peoples of the North and the three remaining Arctic states of Finland, Iceland, and Sweden objected to being excluded from the Ilulissat meeting and from what they saw as unnecessary assertion of the power of the "Arctic Five."[12] Whereas these responses differed as to the adequacy of the international legal regime, early calls for a new and comprehensive treaty for the Arctic or an Antarctic Treaty–style agreement[13] have generally given way to recognition that any new international instruments in the region should be limited to filling gaps that "the law of the sea" and other existing international laws do not cover.[14] Most calls for new agreements are limited to matters of environmental protection, sometimes with a nod to indigenous rights. The Inuit Circumpolar Council (ICC) issued its own Circumpolar Inuit Declaration on Sovereignty in the Arctic in 2009 and, in 2011, a Circumpolar Inuit Declaration on Resource Development Principles in Inuit Nunaat. The ICC declarations have no force as international law but they do reference specific binding international agreements by name and draw on certain principles of international law, developing them further. It is to these and other principles of international law relevant to the Arctic that I now turn.

STRAND ONE—THE INTERNATIONAL LAW OF BOUNDARIES AND BORDERS

Space limitations dictate that this brief survey of Arctic-relevant international law principles and institutions skip several centuries to pick up in 1945, with the charter of the United Nations. By its terms, members shall refrain "from the threat or use of force against the territorial integrity or political independence of any state," Article 2(4), even as nothing in the charter "shall authorize the United Nations to intervene in matters which are essentially within the domestic jurisdiction of any state," Article 2(7). Other core principles—state sovereignty, self-determination of peoples, and the equality of nation-states—are either mentioned in the charter or undergird the structure of international organizations that grew from postwar belief in the power of collective state action to create the conditions for a peaceful, prosperous world. Human rights are central to the UN Charter,[15] but 1945 was too early for the environment to be addressed in the document.

In 1945, states had long possessed universally recognized international legal personality. Intergovernmental organizations (IGOs), however, had to seek it—and finally gained it—by judicial determination in 1949 and by subsequent practice;[16] nongovernmental organizations (NGOs) are still working toward it.[17] The Arctic Council, which is neither state organization, IGO, nor NGO, does not enjoy legal personality.[18] The Ottawa Declaration of the eight Arctic states established the council in 1996 as a "high-level forum" for international cooperation on sustainable development, environmental protection, and other common interests, excluding military security. The Arctic Council is sui generis in international law, comprising members—the eight Arctic states—and Permanent Participants, whose status is also unique in international law and who represent different indigenous peoples of the North.[19] Members decide by consensus only after "full consultation" with Permanent Participants. Observer status, borrowed from classic international law, is also an unusual hybrid of IGOs, NGOs, and non-Arctic states, raising political and procedural questions about how to choose among the additional states and other groups clamoring to "observe."[20]

The Arctic Council, characterized by some as a "soft-law body," nonetheless loosely braids the three international law strands of territory, environment, and indigenous rights.[21] It cannot address classic first-strand (military security) issues but often combines second- (environment) and third-strand (indigenous rights) concerns in its studies on health, shipping, human development, and environment writ large. The only two legally binding agreements negotiated under the auspices of the Arctic Council, Search and Rescue (SAR) in the Arctic (2011) and Marine Oil Pollution Preparedness and Response in the Arctic (2013), stay largely within the traditional boundaries of the first strand of international law and are instruments not of the council itself but of its state members.[22] Under Article 3.3 of the Arctic SAR agreement, for example, each state shall "promote the establishment, operation and maintenance of an adequate and effective search and rescue capability within its area," which is territorially defined, even as all states pledge to exchange information and coordinate joint training sessions and other operational details.

The peaceful and secure relations that have emerged in the post–Cold War Arctic are due in large part to the indispensable territorial certainty that derives from the first strand of international law. The 2010 resolution of a long-standing maritime boundary disagreement between Norway and the Russian Federation[23] by agreed delimitation is a recent example of the cooperative diplomatic culture that prevails among the Arctic states in the twenty-first century and is founded on international law. As the Norwegian Arctic strategy states, "The principal purpose of a delimitation line is to determine which state has jurisdiction over an area for specific purposes. Agreement on a delimitation line will thus make it possible to establish the predictable framework that is necessary for economic and other actors, and also for cross-border cooperation schemes in the petroleum sector."[24] Despite misinformed media reports finding conflict where there is none, the ongoing process under Article 76 of the Law of the Sea Convention, whereby Arctic Ocean coastal states submit information about their extended continental shelves to the Commission on the Limits of the Continental Shelf, is peaceful and cooperative and rests firmly on structures of traditional international law.[25]

The 1982 UN Convention on the Law of the Sea is both a product of first-strand international law and groundbreaking in weaving second-strand environmental concerns into the traditional fabric of state sovereignty and jurisdiction over maritime zones.[26] It applies to all seas, Arctic or otherwise, and establishes successive maritime zones in which coastal state sovereignty diminishes as the zones move seaward: from the full sovereign rights of internal waters and the territorial sea (and archipelagic waters, for archipelagic states), to more limited rights in the EEZ and continental shelf, and, finally, to the areas beyond national jurisdiction—the High Seas and "The Area"[27]—where all states, coastal and non-coastal, share rights and responsibilities.[28] In territorial waters, coastal states may impose their own legislation and exercise jurisdiction over foreign vessels, and provisions on innocent passage (Article 19, and transit passage in international straits, Article 39) require full regard for the "the sovereignty, territorial integrity or political independence of States." By contrast, in its 200-nautical-mile EEZ, a coastal state's "legislative and enforcement jurisdiction over foreign vessels is substantially curtailed" and it may impose only international, not domestic, pollution standards.[29] As for its continental shelf, a coastal state does not enjoy full sovereign rights over it, only the sovereign right to "explore and exploit" the natural resources there (Article 77).

How the convention differentiates between sovereignty and jurisdiction is instructive for making a case for shared sovereignty in the Arctic. For example, under Article 56 a coastal state has "(a) sovereign rights for the purpose of exploring and exploiting, conserving and managing the natural resources, whether living or non-living," of the water column, seabed, and its subsoil, and "for the economic exploitation and exploration of the [EEZ], such as the production of energy from the water, currents and winds." But it has "(b) jurisdiction...with regard to:...marine scientific research [and] the protection and preservation of the marine environment." In exercising both its sovereign rights and its jurisdiction, the coastal state "shall have due regard to the rights and duties of other States." The distinction between sovereignty and jurisdiction is standard in international law but, combined with the convention's system of progressively diminishing coastal state sovereignty over maritime zones as one moves seaward, suggests a model for allowing entities other than states to share sovereignty in certain limited areas and ways. This shared sovereignty could exist within each state for limited functional purposes, for example between indigenous peoples and the state for resource management as a matter of domestic law. Externally it could take place under international law, between states.

The convention does not expressly allow for the possibility of internally shared sovereignty as a matter of international law.[30] Domestically, even on the narrow question of co-management, the internal relations between national governments and indigenous peoples is as unique to each Arctic state as it is complex and evolving within each national system.[31] However, in appropriate settings, the limited coastal state sovereign right to explore, exploit, manage, and conserve resources in its EEZ might be complemented by the (international) right of indigenous peoples to free and informed consent "prior to the approval of any project affecting their lands or territories and other resources" recognized in Article 32(2) of the UN Declaration of the Rights of Indigenous Peoples (UNDRIP).[32] That right would have to be incorporated appropriately into the domestic law of the state in question. The case for internally shared sovereignty would be even stronger if the indigenous peoples in question have developed means of managing and conserving resources potentially affected by exploitation that are supplementary to (or, indeed, more protective than) domestic law management of the resource in question. One such possible example is the 1988 Inuvialuit–Inupiat Polar Bear Management Agreement in the Southern Beaufort Sea.[33] The agreement addresses any concerns that it could conflict with overlapping federal or international regimes by specifying that the Inuit signatories act "solely as representatives of the local traditional user group of the polar bear resource in furthering the consultation, management, and information exchange goals of the International Agreement on the Conservation of Polar Bears."[34] The non-state entities acknowledge their agreement's interplay with an international treaty, the domain of states.

In the latter case of possible shared sovereignty between states, when a coastal state has limited sovereign rights—to explore, exploit, conserve, and manage the natural resources of its EEZ—what happens to the balance of its sovereign rights? Do they simply disappear? Did they ever exist, since the EEZ was one of the convention's great innovations and previously unknown in international law? Or should they exist in another entity, or in "the international community"? Is there an argument for "peoples" under international law whose members live in more than one domestic legal system, as with the Inuit and the Saami in the

Arctic, to constitute a unique part of this "international community"? The convention acknowledges that the "international community" has an interest in cases where the treaty "does not attribute rights or jurisdiction to the coastal State or to other States" in the EEZ and a conflict arises between the coastal state and other states (Article 59). Several factors are to be considered in resolving the conflict, including "the respective importance of the interests involved to the parties as well as to the international community as a whole." The interest of the international community might also provide a basis for acknowledging sovereignty that is shared among states for certain limited purposes, beyond those already agreed in the work of the International Seabed Authority, which oversees activity in the Area. Each of these questions, pertinent for negotiation of the treaty,[35] deserves yet further research to begin to weave second- and third-strand international law into the first strand of boundaries and borders.

UNCLOS limits states' sovereign rights not only spatially (e.g., in the continental shelf and the EEZ) but also functionally.[36] The convention's Part XII, which is devoted to "protection and preservation of the marine environment," imposes that obligation on all States Party. It acknowledges states' sovereign rights to exploit their natural resources yet restricts them by requiring exploitation to occur "pursuant to their environmental policies and in accordance with their duty to protect and preserve the marine environment" (Article 193). Sovereign states thus may treat the environment not however they like but in accord with their obligations under the convention (and customary law).

Under Part XII, the International Maritime Organization (IMO) is considered a "competent international organization" to establish rules for pollution from vessels, dumping, the atmosphere, and other sources. Several IMO treaties relevant to the Arctic predated the Law of the Sea Convention, including the 1972 Convention on the Prevention of Marine Pollution by Dumping of Wastes and Other Matter (which invokes the precautionary approach in a 1996 protocol); the International Convention for the Prevention of Pollution from Ships (1973), as modified by the Protocol of 1978, known as MARPOL;[37] the 1990 International Convention on Oil Pollution Preparedness, Response and Co-operation, and its 2000 Protocol on Preparedness, Response and Co-operation to Pollution Incidents by Hazardous and Noxious Substances.[38] A non-pollution-focused IMO convention, on Safety of Life at Sea (SOLAS) in 1974, was also of this era, though rooted in predecessor agreements in the early twentieth century, and continues to play an important role in the Arctic.[39]

Other Arctic-relevant IMO outputs include non-binding voluntary guidelines for construction of ships operating in the Arctic; a similar Polar Code for north and south that is moving slowly toward becoming mandatory;[40] regulations on journeys to remote areas;[41] and ice navigator training requirements.[42] Other more general but potentially applicable IMO tools include designation of Particularly Sensitive Sea Areas, vessel routing schemes, and discussion in the Marine Environment Protection Committee (MEPC) of measures to reduce black carbon emissions.[43]

The IMO is a classic first-strand institution, established in 1948 as a specialized agency in the UN system and known since 1982 as the IMO. As its multiple and widely subscribed oil pollution treaties attest, long before the MEPC was established in 1985, the IMO was dealing with aspects of environmental protection.[44] This comports with the understanding that the first phase of international environmental law was primarily marine focused, driven by catastrophic events such as oil spills that led countries to turn to existing first-strand organizations such as the IMO for initial collective responses.[45]

STRAND TWO—INTERNATIONAL ENVIRONMENTAL LAW

International environmental law, the second strand of public international law for purposes of this chapter, emerged from existing first-strand institutions while also creating new institutions of its own. When considering where international cooperation, if not international law, has jelled in the Arctic, environmental protection comes to the fore. The Arctic Council's predecessor, the 1991 Arctic Environment Protection Strategy (AEPS), was an agreement of the eight Arctic states to cooperate on a range of environmental matters, including persistent organic pollutants, Arctic monitoring and assessment, preserving the marine environment in keeping with the Law of the Sea Convention,[46] and conserving Arctic flora and fauna, among others. The AEPS led to the landmark 2004 Arctic Climate Impact Assessment (ACIA), a project of the Arctic Council and the International Arctic Science Committee (IASC).[47]

The AEPS was established as a non-binding strategy at an important time in the development of the second (environmental) strand of international law, as traced through four major UN conferences on environment. The 1972 UN Conference on the Human Environment established the UN Environmental Programme (UNEP) as a subsidiary organ of the General Assembly and introduced "future generations" into mainstream discourse. In 1987, "Our Common Future," a report by the UN World Commission on Environment and Development, did the same for sustainable development.[48] Just four years later, the AEPS began concrete steps to improve sustainability in the Arctic.[49] This was well before the 1992 Rio de Janeiro UN Conference on Environment and Development (UNCED) produced Agenda 21, a global plan to balance development and poverty reduction with environmental protection. Agenda 21's failure to mention the Arctic[50] led the Inuit Circumpolar Conference, later known as the Inuit Circumpolar Council, to suggest studying whether and how Arctic states referenced the Arctic in their national sustainable development strategies for implementing Agenda 21.[51] Ten years later, the Johannesburg World Summit on Sustainable Development and Plan of Implementation established quantifiable targets to better implement Agenda 21, calling for broader participation and inclusiveness of those affected by decisions in the decision-making process.[52] The summit only partly realized the vision that the ICC had expressed for greater inclusion of Arctic and indigenous concerns in that summit's outcome.[53]

Beyond these soft-law instruments, many multilateral environmental agreements (MEAs) emerged in the same thirty-year time span, some at the same conferences; UNCED, for example, produced both the Convention on Biological Diversity and the Framework Convention on Climate Change. MEAs moved beyond the reciprocal advantages that motivated most bilateral treaties to help create non-reciprocal regulatory regimes for matters of larger international concern.[54] Many MEAs are based in part on a principle that developed from traditional, first-strand notions of territorial integrity, namely that one state cannot allow transboundary environmental harm in another.[55] The 1992 UNCED Rio Declaration rephrased this principle to reflect the essential transboundary nature of the environment, combining it with another touchstone of first-strand international law, state sovereign rights to resources in their territory:

> States have, in accordance with the Charter of the United Nations and the principles of international law, the sovereign right to exploit their own resources pursuant to their own environmental and developmental policies, and the responsibility to ensure that activities within their jurisdiction or control do not cause damage to the environment of other States or of areas beyond the limits of national jurisdiction.[56]

Several MEAs and accompanying institutions from this era are central to addressing challenges facing the Arctic. Finland's Arctic Strategy states, "The agreements, programmes and organisations central to Arctic environmental issues include the UNFCCC, the IPCC, the Vienna Convention for the Protection of the Ozone Layer, the UNEP, the UNECE Convention on Long-Range Transboundary Air Pollution, the Convention on EIA in a Transboundary Context (Espoo Convention), [and] the CBD."[57] Other multilateral agreements can be added to this list of Arctic-critical treaties, including UNCLOS, MARPOL, and SOLAS discussed previously, all of which are rooted in first-strand international law, some addressing concerns broader than the environment.

The lack of effective MEA implementation that has plagued international environmental law globally[58] also affects the Arctic. As with any conventional international law, effectiveness depends largely on national implementation of treaty obligations. National legal systems do not generally have a separate set of laws for their Arctic regions, which are subject to the same laws that apply elsewhere in each jurisdiction.[59] Notable exceptions do not exempt the Arctic from other national laws but rather add additional protections as with, for example, Canada's Arctic Waters Pollution Prevention Act. By imposing special requirements for ships passing through its internal and territorial waters and EEZ, the act directly implicates rules established under the LOS Convention.[60]

The relationship between national legislation and international treaty obligations is critical to addressing current challenges in the Arctic and offers opportunities for creative use of existing international norms to strengthen national interests there. As a 2011 Aspen Institute study states, the "sovereignty of Arctic governments...affords the strongest foundation and greatest opportunity for international cooperation and shared responsibility for sustainably protecting the Arctic marine environment."[61] When multiple sovereigns act within their own national boundaries to require adherence to treaty obligations, the collective effects external to those borders also amount to a form of shared external sovereignty, complementary to the practical shared and self-limiting sovereignty that arises when states sign a treaty.[62] Within each national territory, sovereign strength can be seen as dependent not only on military security but also on environmental and human security, to the extent the domestic law of each nation-state values environmental protection and attributes some limited sovereignty to indigenous peoples resident there.[63] Although a long way from acknowledging shared sovereignty with Arctic indigenous peoples, some traditional state-based bodies have recognized the need to enhance or preserve conditions for indigenous residents or (more commonly) for relating environmental protection to national security, as seen for example in the Russian Arctic policy,[64] the Arctic Road Map of the U.S. Navy and the U.S. Coast Guard Arctic Strategy,[65] and a report titled "Nordic Cooperation on Foreign and Security Policy."[66]

How can international law best strengthen sustainable protection of the Arctic marine environment and thereby national sovereignty? With the goal of improving implementation, one approach would be examining whether values and principles of international environmental law contained in MEAs can be distilled for national application in Arctic-specific settings.[67] The non-binding 2009 Arctic Offshore Oil and Gas Guidelines (AOOGG)—produced by the Arctic Council's working group Protection of the Arctic Marine Environment (PAME) and endorsed by the Arctic Council ministers—take steps in this direction, if not intentionally. The AOOGG did not systematically survey MEA principles but rather identified four driving principles for the guidelines that also happen to have their roots in international environmental law: the Precautionary Approach and Polluter Pays, which the AOOGG ties respectively to Rio Declaration Principles 15 and 16; Continuous Improvement; and Sustainable Development. The guidelines specify that Sustainable Development has multiple components, including

(1) the duty to cooperate on a regional basis for protection and preservation of the marine environment;

(2) broad public participation in decision making; and

(3) integration of environmental and social concerns into all development processes.

Other Sustainable Development components under the guidelines amount to a compendium of contemporary second- and third-strand international law values and even some first-strand elements.[68] For example, the AOOGG's language on indigenous concerns regarding offshore development parallels Article 32 of UNDRIP but stops short of that declaration's requirement that broad public participation requires free prior and informed consent (PIC) by indigenous communities to resource development.[69] This language appearing in the AOOGG is a step in the right direction even if the PIC provisions are not yet included, as even industry is recognizing that prior informed consent promises to be an effective way to improve predictability in project outcomes.[70] PIC can allow states and Arctic indigenous peoples to "share sovereignty" in a way that builds on existing traditional and environmental strands of international law in the Arctic to strengthen, not weaken, state sovereignty, as explored later.

Strand Three of International Law—Human Rights and Indigenous Rights[71]

I began this brief survey of first-strand public international law with the UN Charter. It speaks broadly of fundamental human rights,[72] overlaying them on traditional structures (sovereign nation-states) and principles (territorial integrity) of first-strand international law. Over the intervening six decades, the substance and meaning of those rights have been fleshed out in hundreds of agreements and thousands of individual provisions, some of which serve as touchstones for indigenous rights in the Arctic. The ICC Circumpolar Inuit Declaration on Sovereignty in the Arctic, for example, states that Inuit are a single people and enjoy the rights of all peoples recognized in "the Charter of the United Nations; the International Covenant on Economic, Social and Cultural Rights; the International Covenant on Civil and Political Rights; the Vienna Declaration and Programme of Action; the Human Rights Council; the Arctic Council; and the Organization of American States" (Article 1.3). The ICC declaration also asserts for Inuit the more specialized rights of indigenous peoples recognized "in and by international legal and political instruments and bodies, such as the recommendations of the UN

Permanent Forum on Indigenous Issues, the UN Expert Mechanism on the Rights of Indigenous Peoples, [and] the 2007 [UNDRIP]."

If these human rights norms emerged from the same sources as international law's first strand of boundaries and territories, if not from that strand itself, why do the two strands not weave more easily together? Human rights norms are largely individual-based, not state-based, yet the state has the duty to promote and protect them. When traditional first-strand institutions were faced with enforcing human rights, they had to do so using existing categories of protection. The entire development of international human rights law can be viewed as an ongoing effort to expand those categories and establish its own independent subfield within public international law.[73] The UN Permanent Forum on Indigenous Issues (PFII) is a body that has grown out of first-strand institutions, in this case the UN Economic and Social Council, to which it is an advisory body. The PFII combines elements of second- and third-strand international law, providing recommendations on "development, culture, environment, education, health and human rights of indigenous peoples."[74]

Such developments have led to expressions of the "inherent sovereignty" of indigenous peoples. For example, the Alta Outcome Document, issued in preparation for the 2014 World Conference on Indigenous Peoples, states,

> *Pursuant* to the universal application of the right of self determination for all Peoples, recommends that the UN recognize Indigenous Peoples and Nations based on our original free existence, inherent sovereignty and the right of self determination in international law. We call for, at a minimum, permanent observer status within the UN system enabling our direct participation through our own governments and parliaments. Our own governments include *inter alia* our traditional councils and authorities.[75]

This statement does not call for a status identical to states; it requests an observer status to the body in which the world's states convene to discuss common concerns. It does, however, call for acknowledgment of indigenous sovereign entities and engagement with indigenous governments.

Self-determination of peoples has also developed from first-strand international law. Now a leading principle of human rights law, it appeared as one of the purposes of the United Nations in Article 1 of the charter: "To develop friendly relations among nations based on respect for the principle of equal rights and self-determination of peoples." Self-determination has expanded over the years to become a critical issue for indigenous peoples in the Arctic, advancing farthest in Greenland. The preamble to a 2009 domestic law, the Act on Greenland Self-Government, recognizes "the people of Greenland" as "a people pursuant to international law with the right of self-determination." It also provides that any decision "regarding Greenland's independence shall be taken by the people of Greenland." Greenland's former premier Kuupik Kleist saw the partnership with Denmark as being "developed upon principles laid out in" UNDRIP and the Greenland-Denmark relationship as "operationalizing" rights affirmed there.[76] Greenland's emergence from Danish colonization to its current self-governing status is one example of how a concept found in traditional international law expanded through the interplay among international human rights norms, national legislation, and institutions of traditional international law.[77]

Greenland's story is also an example of progress toward external self-determination on the international plane, which international law distinguishes, albeit ambiguously, from internal self-determination ("e.g., territorial and non-territorial self-governance"[78]). Discussions around implementation of land claims agreements in Canada[79] and federal-tribal co-management in the United States[80] relate to internal self-determination and might be considered manifestations of shared sovereignty.

One can read the ICC's sovereignty declaration as raising the possibility of shared sovereignty without using the term per se. Noting that "[s]overeignty is a contested concept," it seeks "creative" approaches to sovereignty by using developments in national[81] and international law regarding self-determination of peoples and representation in international matters.[82] The ICC declaration is not an instrument of international law, but it contains many references to international law institutions covering all three strands of territory, environment, and human rights.

The ICC declaration connects indigenous rights not only with environment but also with a broad range of cultural and political rights and the effective enforcement of treaties:

> 1.5 Our rights as an indigenous people include the following rights recognized in the United Nations Declaration on the Rights of Indigenous Peoples [UNDRIP], all of which are relevant to sovereignty and sovereign rights in the Arctic: the right to self-determination, to freely determine our political status and to freely pursue our economic, social and cultural, including linguistic, development [Art. 3]; the right to internal autonomy or self-government [Art. 4]; the right to recognition, observance and enforcement of treaties, agreements and other constructive arrangements concluded with states [Art. 37];...; the right to own, use, develop and control our lands, territories and resources and the right to ensure that no project affecting our lands, territories or resources will proceed without our free and informed consent [Art. 25–32]; the right to peace and security [Art. 7]; and the right to conservation and protection of our environment [Art. 29].

The 2011 Aspen Institute report makes a critical point: "Arctic Indigenous Peoples are not merely another group of stakeholders with an interest in the region; they are rights-holders under a number of formal international and domestic mechanisms."[83] It identifies the range of international laws and mechanisms that apply to the Arctic, beginning with classic human rights instruments such as the Universal Declaration of Human Rights (UDHR); the International Covenant on Civil and Political Rights (ICCPR) and case law under its Article 27; the 1992 UN Declaration on the Rights of Persons Belonging to National or Ethnic,

Linguistic and Religious Minorities; and the work of the Inter-American Commission on Human Rights (IACHR).[84] Alfredsson highlighted the emerging category of "Solidarity Rights" including "the right to development and the right to peace."[85] A newer set of indigenous rights institutions, which are not Arctic-specific, includes the 1989 ILO Convention Concerning Indigenous and Tribal Peoples in Independent Countries (ILO Convention No. 169). Beyond the UN PFII described before, two relevant bodies of the UN Human Rights Council are the Special Rapporteur and the Expert Mechanism on the Rights of Indigenous Peoples.[86]

All of these indigenous rights institutions emerged from classic international law, as the human rights strand became better established. ILO Convention No. 169[87] explicitly recognizes these changes in its preamble: "Considering that the developments which have taken place in international law since 1957, as well as developments in the situation of indigenous and tribal peoples in all regions of the world, have made it appropriate to adopt new international standards on the subject with a view to removing the assimilationist orientation of the earlier standards." Still, indigenous rights institutions must operate within a first-strand world of state sovereignty and territorial integrity. By its terms, nothing in UNDRIP shall be "construed as authorizing or encouraging any action which would dismember or impair, totally or in part, the territorial integrity or political unity of sovereign and independent States" (Article 46). This can be viewed as either the resistance of first-strand institutions to full acceptance of indigenous rights or as a springboard for proposing how the two strands might be woven together into something that resembles shared sovereignty. Historically, Article 46 is an explicit product of state resistance, being added to UNDRIP only after it became clear that the General Assembly would not accept the declaration without such language asserting the bedrock principles of strand-one international law: sovereignty and territorial integrity.[88]

Until Arctic states recognize and experience in practice that increased protections for indigenous rights strengthen state sovereignty and territorial integrity rather than weakening it, they will deprive themselves of solid foundation for stable and predictable cooperation in the North. There is some progress in this area but more is needed.[89] The draft Nordic Saami Convention offers a way to accept the importance of national boundaries and territorial integrity without viewing them as a threat to indigenous rights. Article 1 states as a convention objective, "to confirm and strengthen such rights for the Sami people as to allow the Saami people to safeguard and develop their language, culture, livelihoods and way of life with the least possible interference by national borders" (Article 1). The convention contains no reference to territorial integrity of states,[90] yet the preamble refers constructively to the existence of national boundaries when the Saami Parliaments declare they "hold the vision that the national boundaries of the states shall not obstruct the community of the Saami people and Saami individuals."[91]

Indeed. National boundaries need not obstruct; they can construct. The natural movement of environmental phenomena and the intentional cross-border bonds of indigenous peoples are facts that traditional public international law has learned to recognize in developing the two newer strands of international environmental law and indigenous rights law. In this chapter, I have attempted a modest introduction to how these strands emerged from traditional international law. I have also tried to demonstrate how the two newer strands can strengthen traditional approaches to public international law in the Arctic: states can be more open to understanding increased environmental protections and greater indigenous rights as ways to solidify state sovereignty and shore up territorial integrity. States that use international law to protect a changing environment and to promote human health, prosperity, and engagement in political processes will be stronger individually and as Arctic neighbors.

NOTES

1. It does *not* adopt Krasner's understanding of "Shared Sovereignty," i.e., a solution for "failed, failing, and postconflict countries." Stephen D. Krasner, "The Case for Shared Sovereignty," *Journal of Democracy* 16, no. 1 (January 2005): 70.

2. Patricia Birnie, Alan Boyle, and Catherine Redgwell, *International Law & the Environment* (New York: Oxford University Press, 2009), 3-5, 106, 271, emphasized that neither human rights nor environmental law are separate from but rather part of international law.

3. The imperviousness of classic international law to human rights remained after creation of the UN Committee on Human Rights in 1966 (see *International Covenant on Civil and Political Rights*, December 19, 1966, S. Exec. Doc. E, 95-2 (1978), 999 U.N.T.S. 171) and still remains, though diminished after years of practice by institutions such as the Human Rights Council and the European Court of Human Rights. More controversial is the emerging doctrine of Responsibility to Protect. See generally Anne Peters, "The Security Council's Responsibility to Protect," *International Organisations Law Review* 8, no. 1 (2011).

4. See *Trail Smelter Arbitration (U.S. v. Can.)*, 3 R.I.A.A. 1905 (1938) and 3 R.I.A.A. 1938 (1941).

5. The Canadian Council of International Law Fall 2010 Annual Meeting offers an example of how separate the three strands remain. Concurrent sessions required choosing between panels on indigenous rights *or* natural resource development *or* traditional security and boundary concerns. An indigenous rights scholar commented on this to the closing plenary, to little reaction. Just two of the five sessions are detailed here to make the point, but all sessions separated the strands. Session I: "International Arctic Shipping" *or* "International Investor-State Arbitration over Natural Resources" *or* "Savoir traditionnel Inuit et le partage des bénéfices en vertu de la convention sur la diversité biologique." Session II: "International Law and the Emerging Arctic Security Environment" *or* "Offshore Drilling & Exploration: Environmental and Regulatory Risks" *or* "Climate Change and the Arctic: What Role For Human Rights?" See http://www.ccil-ccdi.ca/storage/2010-program-english%20final.pdf. More recently, the inaugural meeting of the Icelandic "Arctic Circle" exhibited the same

stove-piping of these subject matters; see the program available at http://www.arcticcircle.org/#program.

6. See "NSIDC Scientist Discusses Sea Ice at AGU Nye Lecture," *National Snow and Ice Data Center Notes* 62 (Winter 2008): 2; and Stroeve et al., "The Arctic's Rapidly Shrinking Sea Ice Cover: A Research Synthesis," *Climatic Change* (forthcoming), http://www.springerlink.com/content/c4m01048200k08w3/.

7. For more complete overviews of international law relevant to the Arctic, see, e.g., Michael Byers, *International Law and the Arctic* (Cambridge: Cambridge University Press, 2013); J. Ashley Roach, "International Law and the Arctic: A Guide to Understanding the Issues," *Southwestern Journal of International Law* 15 (2009): 301–326; and Davor Vidas, ed., *Protecting the Polar Marine Environment: Law and Policy for Pollution Prevention*(New York: Cambridge University Press, 2000).

8. Canada, Greenland (Denmark), Norway, Russia, and the United States. *The Ilulissat Declaration*, May 28, 2008, 48 I.L.M. 362.

9. Ibid.

10. Ibid.

11. This phrase can be read to encompass both customary law of the sea and the LOS Convention; the United States is the only Arctic coastal state not party. See UN Convention on the Law of the Sea, December 10, 1982, 1833 U.N.T.S. 397.

12. *A Circumpolar Inuit Declaration on Sovereignty in the Arctic*, Article 4.1. See also http://www.cbc.ca/news/canada/north/story/2008/05/20/arctic-meeting.html.

13. See, e.g., Melissa A. Verhaag, "It Is Not Too Late: The Need for a Comprehensive International Treaty to Protect the Arctic Environment," *Georgetown International Environmental Law Review* 15 (2003): 557; and Donald Rothwell, "The Arctic in International Affairs: Time for a New Regime?," *Brown Journal of World Affairs* 15 (Fall/Winter 2008): 250.

14. See Rosemary Rayfuse, "Melting Moments: The Future of Polar Oceans Governance in a Warming World," *Review of European Community & International Environmental Law* 16 (2007): 196–216; Timo Koivurova and Erik J. Molenaar, *International Governance and Regulation of the Marine Arctic: Overview and Gap Analysis* (Oslo: WWF International Arctic Programme, 2009), 35–43; and *The Shared Future: A Report of the Aspen Institute Commission on Arctic Climate Change* (Washington, DC: The Aspen Institute, 2011), part I, 4.

15. See, e.g., Preamble, and Articles 1, 13, 55, 62, 68, and 76.

16. See *Reparation for Injuries Suffered in the Service of the United Nations*, 1949 I.C.J. 174, 1949 WL 3 (I.C.J.), April 11, 1949, and, e.g., Philippe Gautier, "The Reparation for Injuries Case Revisited: The Personality of the European Union," *Max Planck Yearbook of United Nations Law* 4 (2000): 332.

17. On IGOs, see, e.g., *Legal Consequences for States of the Continued Presence of South Africa in Namibia (South West Africa)*, 1971 I.C.J. 16, 1971 WL 8 (I.C.J.), June 21, 1971; on NGOs, see Steve Charnowitz, "Nongovernmental Organizations and International Law," *American Journal of International Law* 100 (April 2006): 356.

18. See, e.g., Evan Bloom, "Establishment of the Arctic Council," *American Journal of International Law* 93 (July 1999): 712–722.

19. Indigenous participation is key to the Barents Euro-Arctic Council, but it takes a different form. Oran R. Young, *Creating Regimes: Arctic Accords and International Governance* (Ithaca, NY, and London: Cornell University Press, 1998), chapter 5.

20. Timo Koivurova, Erik Molenaar, and David VanderZwaag, "Canada, the EU, and Arctic Ocean Governance: A Tangled and Shifting Seascape and Future Directions," *Journal of Transnational Law and Policy* 18 (Spring 2009): 273. The 2011 Ministerial Meeting of the Arctic Council in 2011 addressed this question by adopting the so-called Nuuk Observer Rules, which set out criteria for admitting new observers, subsequently applied at the 2013 Ministerial Meeting in Kiruna, Sweden.

21. Timo Koivurova, "Environmental Protection in the Arctic and Antarctica," in *Polar Law Textbook*, ed. Natalia Loukacheva (Copenhagen: Nordic Council of Ministers, 2010), 29.

22. *Agreement on Cooperation on Aeronautical and Maritime Search and Rescue in the Arctic*, April 21, 2011, Nuuk, Greenland; and *Agreement on Marine Oil Pollution Preparedness and Response in the Arctic*, May 15, 2013, Kiruna, Sweden.

23. Thilo Neumann, "Norway and Russia Agree on Maritime Boundary in the Barents Sea and the Arctic Ocean," *American Society of International Law Insights* 14 (November 9, 2010): 1–4.

24. Norwegian Ministry of Foreign Affairs, *The Norwegian Government's High North Strategy*, 2006, www.regjeringen.no/upload/UD/Vedlegg/strategien.pdf, 16–17.

25. See, e.g., Betsy Baker, "Law, Science and the Continental Shelf: The Russian Federation and the Promise of Arctic Cooperation," *American University International Law Review* 25 (2010): 251–281.

26. The preamble recognizes the need for, "with due regard for the sovereignty of all States, a legal order for the seas and oceans which will...promote the peaceful uses of the seas and oceans, the equitable and efficient utilization of their resources, the conservation of their living resources, and the study, protection and preservation of the marine environment."

27. Article 1.1.1: "'Area' means the seabed and ocean floor and subsoil thereof, beyond the limits of national jurisdiction"; Article 136: "The Area and its resources are the common heritage of mankind."

28. David VanderZwaag, "Law of the Sea and Governance of Shipping in the Arctic and Antarctic," in *Polar Law Textbook*, ed. Natalia Loukacheva (Copenhagen: Nordic Council of Ministers, 2010), 50–64, surveys LOS Convention issues in an Arctic context; e.g., Article 234 (ice-covered waters); is the Arctic Ocean a semi-enclosed sea; maritime boundary disputes and continental shelf submissions; debates over the Northwest Passage and the Northern Sea Route as international straits vs. internal waters; the status of Svalbard.

29. Ibid., 50.

30. International law differentiates "an overseas territory entitled to decolonisation" (Greenland) and "indigenous and minority groups who live within the metropolitan boundaries of States." Gudmundur Alfredsson, "Human Rights and Indigenous Rights," in *Polar Law Textbook*, ed. Natalia Loukacheva (Copenhagen: Nordic Council of Ministers, 2010), 161.

31. Chanda Meek, "Comparing Marine Mammal Co-Management Regimes in Alaska: Three Aspects of Institutional Performance" (PhD diss., University of Alaska Fairbanks, 2009), http://www.uaf.edu/rap/rap-resources/alumni-dissertations-and-/, offers an example of shared management authority in the United States; for Canada see Helen Fast et al., "Integrated Management Planning in Canada's Western Arctic: An Adaptive Consultation Process," in *Breaking Ice: Renewable Resource and Ocean Management in the Canadian North*, ed. Fikret Birkes et al. (Calgary: University of Calgary Press, 2005), 95.

32. *Declaration on the Rights of Indigenous Peoples*, G.A. Res. 61/295, U.N. Doc. A/RES/61/295 (September 13, 2007).

33. *Inuvialuit–Inupiat Polar Bear Management Agreement in the Southern Beaufort Sea*, http://pbsg.npolar.no/en/agreements/USA-Canada.html.

34. Ibid., Article V(c).

35. See John R. Stevenson and Bernard H. Oxman, "The Preparations for the Law of the Sea Conference," *American Journal of International Law* 68

(January 1974): 18, noting issues in the UN Seabed Committee's work 1970–1974 and economic-zone-related proposals, e.g., "to establish an intermediate zone of mixed coastal and international authority."

36. W. Riphagen, "Some Reflections on Functional Sovereignty," *Netherlands Yearbook of International Law* 7 (1975): 121–165.

37. MARPOL, "Annexes I (oil) and II (noxious liquid substances) are mandatory for all parties to the Convention while the others Annexes III (harmful substances in packaged form), IV (sewage), V (garbage) and VI (air emissions) are optional." VanderZwaag, "Law of the Sea and Governance of Shipping," 58.

38. VanderZwaag, "Law of the Sea and Governance of Shipping," 55–64, surveys these agreements in an Arctic context. See also Erik Molenaar, "International Regulation of Arctic Marine Shipping—Recent Developments and Options for Multilateral Reform Outside IMO," *Arctic Frontiers*, January 2011.

39. See, e.g., SOLAS 74 Regulation V/5 Meteorological Services and Warnings, Regulation V/6 Ice Patrol Service and Appendix "Rules for the Management, Operation and Financing of the North Atlantic Ice Patrol."

40. VanderZwaag, "Law of the Sea and Governance of Shipping," 60.

41. IMO Assembly Resolution A.999(25).

42. Section B-V/g (new) of the Standards of Training, Certification and Watchkeeping Code: Guidance regarding training of Masters and officers for ships operating in Polar waters, entry into force expected 1 January 2012.

43. See, e.g., "Work Plan for the Reduction of Black Carbon Emissions from International Shipping," submitted by Norway, Marine Environment Protection Committee, MEPC 62/4/10, 62nd session, Agenda item 4, May 6, 2011.

44. E.g., in 1969 the IMO, still known as the Inter-Governmental Maritime Consultative Organization, joined the FAO, UNESCO, and WMO to establish a Joint Group of Experts on the scientific aspects of marine pollution. A/C.2/L.1083/Rev. 1, December 4, 1969, Twenty-Fourth Session, Second Committee, Reports of the ECOSOC.

45. See, e.g., Koivurova, "Environmental Protection in the Arctic and Antarctica," 24–25.

46. AEPS, para. 7.i), the states agree to "[a]pply the principles concerning the protection and preservation of the Marine Environment as reflected in the 1982 [UNCLOS and in] accordance with the continuing development

of international environmental law, to further strengthen rules in order to protect the Arctic."

47. ACIA Secretariat, Arctic Council, Arctic Climate Impact Assessment (2005), available at http://www.acia.uaf.edu/pages/scientific.html. See Young, *Creating Regimes*, 35–41 passim, on development of the AEPS.

48. World Commission on Environment and Development (WCED), "Our Common Future," 1987, defined sustainable development: "development which meets the needs of the present without compromising the ability of future generations to meet their own needs" (43).

49. AEPS projects include the Arctic Monitoring and Assessment Programme; the Working Groups on the Conservation of Arctic Flora and Fauna; Emergency Prevention, Preparedness and Response; and the Protection of the Arctic Marine Environment. See http://www.carc. org/index.php?option=com_content&view=article&id=155%3Atoward-sustainable-development-in-the-circumpolar-north&catid=51%3Aother-publications&Itemid=200.

50. *An Inuit Vision for the WSSD*, Inuit Circumpolar Conference General Assembly, August 2002, Kuujjuaq, Quebec, reported in the *Environment Times*, http://www.grida.no/publications/et/at/page/2556.aspx

51. See http://www.inuitcircumpolar.com/index.php?ID=160&Lang=En.

52. *Plan of Implementation of the World Summit on Sustainable Development, Annex*, World Summit on Sustainable Development, August 26–September 4, 2002, at 7, U.N. Doc. A/CONF.199/20 (January 8, 2003), 22 and 42.

53. See *An Inuit Vision for the WSSD*, http://www.grida.no/publications/et/at/page/2556.aspx.

54. Alexandre Kiss and Dinah Shelton, *A Guide to International Environmental Law* (Boston: Martinus Nijhoff Publishers, 2007), 5–8.

55. *Trail Smelter Arbitration (United States v Canada Arbitral Tribunal)*, 1941, 3 U.N. Rep. Int'l Arb. Awards (1941), 1965: "under the principles of international law...no State has the right to use or permit the use of its territory in such a manner as to cause injury by fumes in or to the territory of another or the properties or persons therein, when the case is of serious consequence and the injury is established by clear and convincing evidence."

56. *UNCED Rio Declaration*, Principle 2.

57. Finland, Prime Minister's Office, Finland's Strategy for the Arctic, July 5, 2010, p. 20, 3.2. See *United Nations Conference on Environment and Development: Framework Convention on Climate Change*, 31 I.L.M. 851, May 9, 1992; *Vienna Convention for the Protection of the Ozone Layer*, U.N.

Doc. UNEP/IG.53/Rev.1, at 11 (1985), reprinted in 26 I.L.M. 1529 (1987); *Convention on Long-Range Transboundary Air Pollution*, November 13, 1979, T.I.A.S. No. 10541, reprinted in 18 I.L.M. 1442 (1979); *Convention on Environmental Impact Assessment in a Transboundary Context*, February 25, 1991, 1989 U.N.T.S. 310 (entered into force September 10, 1997); and *Convention on Biological Diversity of the United Nations Conference on the Environment and Development*, opened for signature June 5, 1992, U.N. Doc. DPI/1307, reprinted in 31 I.L.M. 818.

58. See, e.g., Peter H. Sand, ed., *The Effectiveness of International Environmental Agreements* (Cambridge: Grotius Publications, 1992), for an early effort to measure such effectiveness.

59. This national law dynamic is of "utmost importance" to grasping how international environmental law works in the Arctic. Koivurova, "Environmental Protection in the Arctic and Antarctica," 29.

60. Arctic Waters Pollution Prevention Act, R.S., c. 2 (1st Supp.), s. 1. See also UNCLOS, Article 234 on ice-covered waters, which is one basis for the AWPPA; and, on Russia's Northern Sea Route legislation, Erik Franckx, "The Legal Regime of Navigation in the Russian Arctic," *Journal of Transnational Law and Policy* 18 (Spring 2009): 327–342.

61. *Shared Future*, part I.

62. Kiss and Shelton, *Guide to International Environmental Law*, 11.

63. See, e.g., Dalee Sambo Dorough, "Inuit of Alaska: Current Issues," in *Polar Law Textbook*, ed. Natalia Loukacheva (Copenhagen: Nordic Council of Ministers, 2010), 215.

64. *Russian Federation, The Fundamentals of State Policy of the Russian Federation in the Arctic in the Period Up to 2020 and Beyond*—Osnovy Gosudarstvennoi Politiki Rossiiskoi Federatsii v A, section 7.f and 8.a on improving conditions for indigenous peoples.

65. The U.S. Arctic Navy Roadmap, 2009, refers in only two sentences to the need for outreach to indigenous peoples (18–19) but contains an entire section on environmental assessment and prediction (19–21). The U.S. Coast Guard Strategy, 2013, observes for example, "The unique and valuable relationship established with tribal entities builds mutual trust and improves mission readiness" (31).

66. Thorvald Stoltenberg, "Nordic Cooperation on Foreign and Security Policy," proposals presented to the extraordinary meeting of Nordic foreign ministers, Oslo, Norway, February 9, 2009, does not address indigenous issues but see, e.g., p. 13 on "new challenges that are arising in

relation to management of the environment" and p. 20 urging cooperation on the Arctic environment (http://www.regjeringen.no/nb/dep/ud.html).

67. Such an analysis exceeds the scope of this chapter. For surveys of Arctic-relevant treaties see, e.g., Linda Nowlan, *Arctic Legal Regime for Environmental Protection* (Cambridge: International Union for Conservation of Nature and Natural Resources, 2001); Rayfuse, "Melting Moments"; Koivurova and Molenaar, *International Governance and Regulation of the Marine Arctic*, 85; and PAME, *The Arctic Ocean Review Project, Final Report (Phase II 2011–2013), Kiruna, May 2013* (Akureyri, Protection of the Arctic Marine Environment (PAME) Secretariat, 2013), www.aor.is.

68. AOOGG, 1.3: "In permitting offshore oil and gas activities, Arctic governments should be mindful of their commitment to sustainable development, including, inter alia, protection of biological diversity; the duty not to transfer, directly or indirectly, damage or hazards from one area of the marine environment to another...; promotion of the use of best available technology/techniques and best environmental practices...; the duty to cooperate...; the need to maintain hydrocarbon production rates in keeping with sound conservation practices as a means of minimizing environmental impacts; development which meets the needs of the present without compromising the ability to meet the needs of the future; integration of environmental and social concerns...; and broad public participation."

69. Where UNDRIP says "shall," the guidelines use "should"; the guidelines replace the declaration's phrase "in order to obtain their free and informed consent prior to the approval of" any project with "in order to understand and integrate their needs and concerns with" any project. The inclusion of even this watered-down version of UNDRIP Article 32 in the AOOGG, which was negotiated between all eight Arctic states, can be considered an acknowledgment of the importance of the declaration, notwithstanding that the PIC provisions are removed.

70. "[I]n the long-term, the benefits for oil and gas companies of obtaining community agreement based on FPIC principles, and thereby both supporting their social license to operate and reducing legal and reputational risks, are likely to outweigh the substantial challenges of securing consent." Amy K. Lehr and Gare A. Smith, *Implementing a Corporate Free, Prior, and Informed Consent Policy: Benefits and Challenges* (Foley Hoag eBook, May 2010), http://www.foleyhoag.com/NewsCenter/Publications/eBooks/Implementing_Informed_Consent_Policy.aspx?ref=1, 8.

71. Alfredsson, "Human Rights and Indigenous Rights," 147ff, surveys these in an Arctic context; see also *Shared Future*, 28ff.

72. See UN Charter Preamble, Articles 1.3, 13, 55, 62, and 68.

73. But see note 2.

74. Finland's Arctic Strategy, p. 37.

75. *Alta Outcome Document*, Global Indigenous Preparatory Conference for the United Nations High Level Plenary Meeting of the General Assembly to be known as the World Conference on Indigenous Peoples, Alta, Norway, June 10–12, 2013, Theme 2, para. 10, p. 5.

76. K. Kleist, Statement, 2nd Session of the Expert Mechanism on the Rights of Indigenous Peoples, Geneva, August 10–14, 2009, Geneva, August 11, 2009, quoted in *Making the Declaration Work: The United Nations Declaration on the Rights of Indigenous Peoples*, ed. C. Charters and R. Stavenhagen (Copenhagen 2009, Document No. 127, IWGIA), 248–251.

77. For an introduction to this complex history, see Mininnguaq Kleist, "The Status of the Greenlandic Inuit," in *The Right to National Self-Determination—The Faroe Islands and Greenland*, ed. Sjúrdur Skaale (Boston: Martinus Nijhoff, 2004), 95–122.

78. Alfredsson, "Human Rights and Indigenous Rights," 133, 161.

79. See, e.g., Barry Scott Zellen, *Breaking the Ice: From Land Claims to Tribal Sovereignty in the Arctic* (Lanham, MD: Lexington Books, 2008).

80. See, e.g., Marren Sanders, "Ecosystem Co-Management Agreements: A Study of Nation Building or a Lesson in Erosion of Tribal Sovereignty?" *Buffalo Environmental Law Journal* 15 (2007–2008): 97–176; and Greta Swanson, Kathryn Mengerink, and Jordan Diamond, "Understanding the Government-to-Government Framework for Agency Activities that Affect Resources in the U.S. Arctic," *Environmental Law Reporter* 43, no. 10 (October 2013): 10872ff.

81. *A Circumpolar Inuit Declaration on Sovereignty in the Arctic*: "Sovereignties overlap and are frequently divided within federations in creative ways to recognize the right of peoples. For Inuit living within the states of Russia, Canada, the USA and Denmark/Greenland, issues of sovereignty and sovereign rights must be examined and assessed in the context of our long history of struggle to gain recognition and respect as an Arctic indigenous people having the right to exercise self-determination over our lives, territories, cultures and languages" (Article 2.1).

82. Ibid., Article 2.4.

83. *Shared Future*, 28.

84. Ibid., 28n3; "The American Declaration of the Rights and Duties of Man...., [OAS Res. XXX (1948),...(May 2001) at 16, Preamble]; "the Inter-American Court and the Inter-American Commission on Human Rights have held that, although originally adopted as a declaration and not as a legally binding treaty, the American Declaration is today a source of international obligations for the OAS member States." Inter-Am. Court H.R., Advisory Opinion OC-10/89, paragraphs 35, 45 (1989); and UNDRIP, Article 8.2(a)–(b).

85. Alfredsson, "Human Rights and Indigenous Rights," 156.

86. Ibid., 158.

87. *Convention Concerning Indigenous and Tribal Peoples in Independent Countries*, 169 I.L.O. 1989, entered into force September 5, 1991.

88. Mattias Åhrén, "Some Provisions That Are Notably Absent from the Saami Convention," *Gáldu Cála—Journal of Indigenous Peoples Rights* 3 (2007): 35n94, says the working group negotiating UNDRIP could not agree whether to "include an explicit reference to territorial integrity... The chairperson-rapporteur...decided not to [and] presented [it] to the UN Human Rights Council [where it was adopted]. However,...in the UN General Assembly, it became evident that it would be extremely difficult, if not impossible...to pass a Declaration without an explicit reference to territorial integrity. Hence, Article 46 was modified as described, and the General Assembly subsequently adopted [UNDRIP]."

89. For example, the Nunavut Land Claims Agreement recognizes "Canada's sovereignty over the waters of the arctic archipelago is supported by Inuit use and occupancy," Article 15.1.1.(c); Inuit have the right to harvest from landfast ice "in a manner consistent with Canada's sovereignty, sovereign rights and jurisdiction, and with Canada's international obligations" (Articles 15–16).

90. Åhrén, "Some Provisions," 35.

91. Text of the Declaration in English, in Mattias Åhrén, Martin Scheinin, and John B. Henriksen, "The Nordic Sami Convention: International Human Rights, Self-Determination and Other Central Provisions," *Gáldu Cála—Journal of Indigenous Peoples Rights* 3 (2007): 98.

CHAPTER 17

ARCTIC OIL, INUIT RESOURCE GOVERNANCE, AND THE ARCTIC COUNCIL

Jessica M. Shadian

Indigenous peoples would like to engage in active dialogue with all governments here, so we can jointly address any remaining obstacles to recognizing the rights of indigenous peoples...This rights-based approach is the same approach indigenous peoples would apply to corporate accountability. We call on mining corporations to respect the rights of indigenous peoples. We call for tripartite approaches between governments, corporations and indigenous peoples, as discussed during a workshop on Indigenous Peoples, Human Rights and Extractive Industries, organized

under the auspices of the office of the UN High Commissioner on
Human Rights.
—Concluding Remarks by Indigenous Peoples at the Multi-
Stakeholders Dialogue at the World Summit on Sustainable
Development, January–June 2002

The role and meaning of the Arctic and who has the legitimacy to decide
cannot be abstracted from the larger processes of ongoing global political change. In recent years, the international political field has grown
to include a wide variety of non-state actors, from scientists and consultants to indigenous collectivities and private companies. Alongside these
changes, global politics has taken a turn toward governance frameworks,
which often include stakeholder participation.[1] The incorporation of
non-state political actors into the processes of governance has challenged the traditional theoretical assumptions about the state and state
sovereignty. Under traditional international law, the principle of territorial integrity gives the state the sovereign authority to control resource
development. In recent decades, however, the introduction of new international policies, legal doctrines, and legal norms has provided a formal
means for non-state actors to participate in the processes of global politics.

In the Arctic, recent debates about who owns the Arctic and who
decides have become symbolic of these changes. Arctic governance
has become an amalgamation of traditional state politics and non-state
stakeholders with the power to help decide the course of development.
Yet, even further, Arctic governance includes indigenous groups who
sit at the decision-making table on the only circumpolar Arctic political regime. They also co-manage if not outright own Arctic land and
resources.

The Arctic's indigenous peoples point out that they are not merely
stakeholders and that they have a much greater formal authority to
decide the future course of Arctic resource development than the host of
non-Arctic states and other stakeholders. The Inuit Circumpolar Council

(ICC) has often made it clear that Inuit are "rights holders" when it comes to Arctic governance and resource development.[2] The debates over who owns the Arctic, nevertheless, often seek solutions that try to squeeze the politics of the Arctic into the Westphalian political framework in which only states govern.

Arctic indigenous governance arrangements consist of a myriad of local indigenous models, from public governments to indigenous corporations and co-management resource management regimes. These institutions and governance arrangements are played out in tandem with traditional state sovereignty by the eight Arctic states that function under the rules of international law. To highlight this point, in 2009 the ICC—a transnational organization that represents approximately 160,000 Inuit living throughout Alaska, Canada, Russia, and Greenland—released a declaration on Inuit sovereignty. In the declaration the ICC states,

> The conduct of international relations in the Arctic and the resolution of international disputes in the Arctic are not the sole preserve of Arctic states or other states; they are also within the purview of the Arctic's indigenous peoples. The development of international institutions in the Arctic, such as multi-level governance systems and indigenous peoples' organizations, must transcend Arctic states' agendas on sovereignty and sovereign rights and the traditional monopoly claimed by states in the area of foreign affairs.[3]

What Inuit sovereignty actually means in terms of Arctic governance and practice, however, is not so readily understood. Although not inhabiting their own sovereign states, the Arctic's indigenous peoples have, in many cases, the rights to receive royalties from and in some instances maintain outright ownership over considerable portions of the Arctic's land and marine resources. This complex reality brings into question the efficacy of traditional international relations theory—which assumes that the state is the sole creator and enforcer of policy and that non-state actors are merely epistemic communities at best[4]—when it comes to the larger international discussions over the future of Arctic governance. As the international community debates over what is best for the Arctic and how it should be governed, too often the realities of indigenous governance and, further, what one might learn from these experiences goes unacknowledged. What types of frameworks and policies should be adopted as melting ice is vastly transforming the physical and political realities of the Arctic? Who owns the Arctic and who should decide?

This chapter takes a normative approach to these questions to explore what and how one might learn from existing indigenous governance arrangements in the Arctic and how they may contribute to the larger debates over Arctic governance and who decides. It begins with a brief exploration of the existing literature on co-management. It specifically focuses on what some legal scholars call post-Westphalian resource management as well as the ongoing discussions about co-management as it pertains to the Arctic. This chapter then turns to the Alaska Eskimo Whaling Commission (AEWC) as a case study and possible starting point for governing newly emerging resource issues in the Arctic, particularly in terms of the current governance discussions regarding Arctic offshore oil and gas development. Lastly, this chapter will offer preliminary reflections as to how a postsovereign resource management approach could contribute to the broader theoretical debates concerning who owns the Arctic, who decides, and the role of the Arctic Council (AC) within these debates.

POSTSOVEREIGN RESOURCE MANAGEMENT

The AC has, in recent years, begun to create legally binding policies for dealing with expanded interest in the Arctic's resources (both renewable and non-renewable). Arctic resource extraction and development has local, regional, and global implications. Environmental pollution, animal migration patterns, and fish, for example, have limited if any regard for political boundaries. At the same time, the political, social, and economic ramifications of local Arctic resource development are directly tied to the global economy and the global market value of these resources. Arctic resource management, thus, requires models that accommodate the multiple scales and types of governance that are concurrently at play.

The complex reality of resource management such as that in the Arctic is actually quite common to many ecosystems and political regions around the world. Taking note of this, a group of legal experts have written about ways to reconceptualize the traditional practices of environmental regulation and natural resource management to meet the changing nature of resource rights, ownership, and use. Rather than traditional top-down regulatory models, these authors[5] focus on the need to take into account the various scales and levels of governance that are implicated in regional resource development. Bradley Karkkainen called this approach postsovereign governance.[6]

According to Karkkainen, the traditional model of environmental protection that materialized in the 1960s "assumes that an expert decision maker—the regulatory agency [which was] an arm of the state —would identify the most important environmental problems, gather sufficient expert information to specify effective solutions, express those solution[s] as a series of specific legally binding commands, and finally enforce those commands by employing the coercive sanctioning power of the state."[7] Postsovereign governance, instead, is locally or regionally based (or both), integrative, collaborative, adaptive, and polyarchic governance arrangements that often aim to deal with entire ecosystems.[8] It is also based on the principle that all post-management systems are dynamic and therefore continuously evolve to adapt to new scientific findings, improved information, changing conditions, and reflection of previous management efforts.[9] Postsovereign governance also requires integrated management plans, which address the multiple resources composing the ecosystem being managed. It recognizes that the competences of varying actors are multilayered among mission-specific agencies and are dispersed over various tiers of government.

Postsovereign resource management also aims to deal with the fact that often resource management is controlled equally by states and various non-state actors including private companies. Non-state actors in general under postsovereign governance regimes are, therefore, not considered merely stakeholders or consultants, epistemic communities or lobbyists to the sovereign authority (e.g., a federal or city government). The state, as such, must often engage "in an open-ended effort at collaborative problem-solving" with non-state actors in order to use their expertise and resources.[10] This includes the recognition that the necessary knowledge and science are often based in the local community as well as the scientific community, NGOs, and other organizations. Essentially, postsovereign resource management acknowledges and accounts for the fact that very often resources, land, economic decision making, power, knowledge, and expertise are owned and controlled by multiple types of non-state actors and, as such, governance cannot be considered a state-based (whether federal or local) effort;[11] the sovereign acting alone does not have the power or competence to make the final policy decisions and legally binding laws. Postsovereign governance, instead, views resource management as an ongoing collaborative "hybrid public-private"[12] process where states and non-state actors (whether local community members, private businesses, the scientific community, or NGOs) work side by side as "co-participants, co-authors, and co-executors of policy." Because the state relies on information from and cooperation with non-state actors, they collaborate roughly as formal equals although certainly often of unequal capacity and resources. "Conventional distinctions between state and non-state, sovereign and subject, and command and compliance become blurred."[13]

The challenge is to successfully create an evolving rather than static regime, which can fill gaps in knowledge that emerge over time, generate top-quality research, and put into place an adequate monitoring process that can incorporate the latest research. Where a regional collaborative approach is able to accommodate these challenges, redundancy is minimized as research and baseline information are assembled as a single collaborative effort and made available to all parties involved. To accompany this, an adequate means for all parties to participate on equal grounds must exist. Funding and human resources can inhibit the ability for all parties to participate equally, and very often local community organizations and local governments have far less money and human resources than private companies and federal agencies.

When it comes to the Arctic, existing practices of co-management have much to contribute to these academic discussions. The Arctic Human Development Report (AHDR), for instance, discusses co-management in the Arctic by first distinguishing between devolution and co-management. According to the authors, "Devolution refers to the transfer of power to more local and regional jurisdictions and governments," whereas co-management "typically involves a sharing of power between the state and resource-user communities."[14]

Examples of devolution include the Alaska Native Claims Settlement Act (ANCSA) and the Nunavut Land Claims Agreement. Co-management pertains specifically to resource use and is a regime in which stakeholders share power in managing specific resources. In the North American context, co-management commonly refers to a "shared decision-making process, formal or informal, between a government authority and a user group for managing a species of fish and wildlife, or other resources."[15] Co-management systems include a system of rights and obligations, rules that outline all shareholders responsibilities and collective decision making.[16]

Much like Karkkainen's framework of postsovereign resource management, co-management, as practiced in the Arctic, offers a space for knowledge sharing between users and scientists; acts as a balance of power between users and government officials;[17] provides a means for continual cooperation in research and education; and recognizes cultural and linguistic differences as they influence effective understanding.[18] Co-management, as such, is not merely about consultation with indigenous communities after a project has been determined but includes local community involvement from a project's inception.

Unlike the land claims agreements in Alaska and Canada, which helped create Inuit co-management resource regimes, Greenland Self Rule, according to Frank Sejersen, has been a process of state building rather than devolution. The Greenlandic government is the central authority, and there is little discussion about co-management.[19] Instead citizens participate in resource management through citizen groups such as the Association of Fishermen and Hunters in Greenland (KNAPK) or the Greenland Employers' Association (GA), which represent their constituents and lobby the central government to enact policies in their favor. When it comes specifically to extractive industries, local communities are involved through processes of stakeholder dialogues (where citizen groups speak on behalf of community members) or consultation processes, where the companies involved in a project visit the communities that will be affected. These visits are often viewed as "explanations" *to* rather than consultations *with* local community members. Community frustrations with consultation processes include feelings that the information provided is too technical, it fails to address the questions that are of importance to the community members, there is not enough time to learn about the project before the consultation, and community members are not well enough informed beforehand for the meeting.[20] In September 2011, Ilisimatusarfik/University of Greenland and the University of Nordland, Bodø, Norway, co-hosted the first Greenlandic stakeholder dialogue in Nuuk on oil and gas development. A panel on stakeholder and consultation processes that included Greenlandic stakeholder groups such as KNAPK and GA concluded that "new ways of thinking were necessary in order to engage Greenlandic citizens and help them cope and benefit with a rapid pace of change."[21] Two years later, in October 2013, the Greenlandic government overturned its zero tolerance policy on uranium mining. In an op-ed following the decision, Sara Olsvig, a member of the Danish and Greenlandic Parliaments, wrote,

> As elected officials it is our responsibility and our duty to make sure that we legislate in a way that is open, fair and transparent. I also see it as our responsibility to strive for the highest degree of democracy in our decision-making. When it comes to the zero-tolerance policy on uranium mining and the proposal of the government of Greenland to lift the ban, the democratic process is being held to an absolute minimum. The government has made no effort to include the public of Greenland in the decision-making process.[22]

Postsovereign resource management avoids these problems in that the communities affected are part of the project's planning from the outset.

THE GLOBAL POLITICS OF LOCAL ARCTIC RESOURCE MANAGEMENT

Inuit co-management practices have been in place in Inuit areas of the North American Arctic since the early 1970s. They were born from the Inuit land claims processes in Alaska and Canada.[23] Although the land claims processes themselves are local governance arrangements and the co-management regimes that were created are to deal with particular resources on Inuit-inhabited lands, they are also arrangements frequently made in collaboration with the federal governments and largely controlled by indigenous corporations, relying directly on the forces of the global economy. Inuit corporations, for instance, such as Makivik in Quebec or the Ukpeagvik Inupiat Corporation[24] in Alaska, each earn over US$300 million in annual revenues. The Kuukpik Corporation in Alaska earns close to US$5 million per year,[25] and the Arctic Slope Regional Corporation's earned revenues exceeded US$2.3 billion in 2010.[26] Inuit development and exportation of hydrocarbons and other resources (such as diamonds) and shipping or flying them to markets around the world (with Inuit shipping, airline, and other transportation companies) make Inuit and Inuit-controlled resources a necessary and significant component of any resource management plan and therefore central to the larger debates over who governs the Arctic and who should decide.

Inuit political leaders and organizations such as the ICC make similar arguments. For many Inuit communities, resource development is viewed as a means to improve standards of living and gain further economic autonomy. The May 2011 ICC Circumpolar Inuit Declaration on Resource Development Principles in Inuit Nunaat states that

> responsible non-renewable resource development can also make an important and durable contribution to the well-being of current and future generations of Inuit. Managed under Inuit Nunaat governance structures, non-renewable resource develop-ment can contribute to Inuit economic and social development through both private sector channels (employment, incomes, businesses) and public sector channels (revenues from publicly owned lands, tax revenues, infrastructure)...Inuit welcome the opportunity to work in full partnership with resource developers, governments and local communities in the sustainable devel-opment of resources of Inuit Nunaat, including related policy-making, to the long-lasting benefit of Inuit and with respect for baseline environmental and social responsibilities.[27]

The ICC declaration complements the underlying ideas of postsovereign resource management. The declaration calls on the use of the best avail-able science and Inuit knowledge and notes that through varying chan-nels such as land rights settlement legislation, land claims agreements and treaties, self-government arrangements, and intergovernmental and constitutional provisions, the "Inuit have acquired critical means and levels of control over the governance of Inuit Nunaat. Many of these mechanisms provide for direct Inuit participation in specialized resource management bodies, including planning, project review, and regulatory bodies."[28] The declaration also directly connects global and Arctic poli-tics to local Inuit resource development and management. The declaration states that "[p]rivate sector resource developers, and governments and public bodies charged with the public management of resource development, must all conduct themselves in concert with the UN Declaration on the rights of indigenous peoples. Respect for the UN Declaration should be open and transparent, and be subject to independent and impartial review."[29]

INUIT RESOURCE MANAGEMENT MODELS: WHAT CAN WE LEARN FROM THEM?

Inuit co-management operates in vastly different ways depending on the region. Yet one example that seems most relevant for the current discussion and might possibly serve as a framework for other areas of Arctic resource management is the Alaska Eskimo Whaling Commission, which was set up by the Inupiat of northern Alaska to conserve bowhead stocks and control and regulate all aspects of the bowhead harvest. The reason for choosing the AEWC as an example is based on the simple fact that it creatively bridges local Inuit governance structures to global policy making, thereby offering an Arctic-specific case for postsovereign resource management in practice.

A History of Arctic Whaling

The Inupiat have subsistence hunted bowhead whales since they have lived in Alaska (essentially for several thousand years). They used the entire whale. The skin, blubber, flesh, and internal organs were eaten. Baleen and bones were used for buildings, furniture, and other smaller items, and oil provided heat and light.[30] Beginning in the early sixteenth century, subsistence whale hunting in the Arctic was transformed into commercial whaling for the global market with the arrival of the Basque. Since this time, whale populations have been threatened to the point of near extinction before making a partial recovery. The Basque whaled in the Strait of Belle Isle between Labrador and Newfoundland. They would extract the whale oil and fat for export to Europe to satisfy the energy market and for industrial production. The fat was used for lamps, soap, and candles, to cure leather, and to grease machinery in factories.[31]

In 1613 the British company Muscovy set out to break the Basque monopoly by hunting whales off the coast of Spitsbergen. The British successfully ousted the Basque as well as the Dutch whalers there. In response the Dutch set up the Noordsche Compagnie (North Company), which whaled off the coast of Greenland. The Noordsche Compagnie, however, found new competition from the British as well as the Danish and other Dutch companies. Consequently, a truce was called between Holland, England, and Denmark, making the Arctic waters a commercial free zone for all—the idea was justified by the notion of *terra nullius* for the seas—*mare nullius*.[32]

By the 1780s, the Greenlandic bowhead whale stocks were nearly extinct, and by the mid-1800s, commercial whaling had made its way to Alaska. It began in 1826 when Captain Frederick W. Beechey of the British Royal Navy brought back reports of whales in Arctic waters. Twenty years later, in 1848, Captain Thomas Roys led a whaling procession of more than 200 whaling ships to Alaska. Over the next seven decades, American, French, German, Hawaiian, and Australian whaling companies carried out 2,700 annual whaling cruises and killed over 20,000 bowhead whales.[33] By the mid-nineteenth century, bowhead whales in the Northwest and Arctic Alaskan waters were hunted to the point that commercial companies turned to Canada in search of new hunting grounds.[34] Throughout this period, the Inupiat in Alaska and Inuit in Canada began to trade whales for European goods and soon sought cash incomes to supplement their once all subsistence lifestyles. At this time they also began to work for the whaling companies on the boats, as guides, hunters, or other manual labor. Dependency on non-subsistence commodities expanded and many Inuit became dependent on foreign companies and eventually on the Alaskan and Canadian federal governments. Yet, throughout its entirety, subsistence whaling remained a central and critical piece of Inupiat and Inuit livelihoods.

In the 1920s and 1930s, new factory-ship technologies renewed whaling off the coast of Alaska. By this time, however, the possibility of commercial whaling several species into complete extinction generated global attention, and in 1946 the first International Whaling Agreement was signed. The International Convention for the Regulation of Whaling was established in order to conserve whale populations. The convention consisted of fifteen original signatories, all of which were whaling nations. Under the convention, the International Whaling Commission (IWC) was created. The purpose of the IWC was to provide for the conservation, development, and optimum utilization of whale resources. It was agreed that all regulations would be based on scientific findings and that funding would be made available to ensure scientific studies would continuously be carried out. Although whaling continued to play a significant role in the cultural and economic life of the Alaskan Inupiat, they were not invited to take part in the making of the IWC or its accompanying scientific research.

Since the founding of the IWC, the number of signatories has grown to eighty-nine, and the vast majority of new signatories are non-whaling countries. Beginning in the 1970s, the UN Stockholm meeting on the environment took place and, with the emergence of an international environmental movement, the atmosphere within the IWC began to change. Rather than conservation—which was the basis for the creation of the IWC—the majority of non-whaling countries began to seek a total ban. This included a ban on what many IWC members saw as the negative impacts of increased subsistence whaling. The IWC, at the time, did not have a formal definition of terms relating to indigenous subsistence whaling. In the 1946 International Convention for the Regulation of Whaling, the term *aborigine* was used in that it stated, "It is forbidden to take or kill gray or right whales, except when the meat and products of such whales are to be used exclusively for local consumption by the aborigines." By the late 1970s, the IWC scientific committee began to raise questions regarding the management of aboriginal subsistence hunts of Alaskan bowhead whales.[35] According to their studies, the number of aboriginal catches had increased markedly, as had the number of struck whales that were lost.[36] In light of these factors, at the 1977 IWC convention, the committee voted to delete the right whale part of the aboriginal exemption clause, which, in effect, put a ban on all subsistence hunting of bowhead whales.[37]

Immediately following the IWC meeting, Inupiat subsistence whalers in Alaska organized to create the AEWC, which would work to overturn the ban on their traditional subsistence hunt of the bowhead whale, disseminate information on the nutritional and cultural significance of bowhead whales for Inupiat subsistence whalers, and promote research on bowhead whales.[38] Contrary to the findings of the IWC scientific committee, Inupiat elders found that the bowhead whale stock was healthy and had been steadily growing since commercial whaling had decreased beginning in the early twentieth century.[39] The newly formed AEWC lobbied the U.S. government, and after negotiations with the U.S. National Marine Fisheries Service (NMFS) as well as legal proceedings, the AEWC was able to convince the U.S. government to call for a special IWC meeting.

The meeting took place the same year. At that time, several resolutions were passed, including a resolution to reinstate a "modest take of bowhead whales" to the United States to "satisfy [the] subsistence and cultural needs" of the Inupiat subsistence whalers.[40] It was also decided that an ad hoc technical committee working group would be created to examine the issues surrounding aboriginal subsistence whaling, and a special panel meeting of experts on aboriginal subsistence whaling would form and meet in 1979 (the final report was published in 1982).[41] At the 1980 convention, the United States presented an interim report, and in the lead-up to the 1982 IWC convention, the technical committee released its report. The report formally defined aboriginal subsistence whaling as "whaling for purposes of local aboriginal consumption carried out by or on behalf of aboriginal, indigenous, or native peoples who share strong community, familial, social, and cultural ties related to a continuing traditional dependence on whaling and on the use of whales."[42] The technical committee further determined that the "definition of subsistence whaling does not prevent the use of modern technology, and there is good reason to recommend improvement in the weapons, powder and bombs currently employed to further reduce the struck but lost rate."[43]

The IWC concluded its discussions on aboriginal subsistence whaling with a proposal to create a dual system of management involving the United States. The IWC would determine catch rates based on U.S. documentation of the needs of Inupiat subsistence whalers. It was recommended that the United States would develop a management plan to determine catch limits and reporting and data requirements, allow for a reduction in the struck and lost rate, and implement an appropriate research program.[44] At the 1982 IWC convention, a resolution was adopted to institute an aboriginal subsistence whaling regime in order to achieve the objectives of the published (1982) report. The resolution recognized that "full participation and cooperation of the affected aboriginal peoples are essential for effective whale management."[45] That same year the IWC also voted in favor of a moratorium on all commercial whaling.[46] Under the allotted quotas, whaling under scientific auspices was also still allowed, as was indigenous subsistence whaling,[47] although the quota was, and remains, subject to continued renewal.

In response to the moratorium, Canada withdrew from the IWC, arguing that the moratorium was inconsistent with IWC measures allowing the harvesting of stocks at safe levels. Iceland and Norway also eventually withdrew from the IWC. Norway continues to hunt commercially. Countries against the commercial moratorium also argued that the IWC was only focusing on one type of whale while neglecting other serious threats to global whale populations, such as ship strikes (collisions with ships), as well as the more general impacts of climate change.[48] These debates go on today and continue to inhibit the ability of the IWC to regulate commercial whaling effectively.

A History of the AEWC

Going back to the late 1960s, the Alaska native land claims were brought to an apex with the discovery of the largest petroleum deposit in North America to date on the North Slope. The native land claims were finally resolved in 1972 with the passage of the Alaska Native Claim Settlements Act. ANCSA was followed by the creation of local governments. In order to accommodate the rights and control over resources awarded to indigenous groups through ANCSA, a corporate structure was established to handle the accompanying financial transfers. In total, ANCSA created 12 regional corporations and 200 village corporations. The corporations received title to surface and subsurface lands, and 70 percent of the revenue from natural resources had to be redistributed equally among the 12 regional corporations. For the most part, the Alaska indigenous corporations were created out of the American corporate model.

Following the passage of ANCSA, the Inupiat of the North Slope filed a petition for a first-class borough, and that same year the North Slope Borough was created. The North Slope Borough is a public borough that is majority Inupiat. In Barrow, the Ukpeagvik Inupiat Corporation (UIC —the Barrow Village Corporation) was also created. ANCSA, however, did not create specific land use management structures, which has since become a source of major criticism regarding the U.S. land claims agreement model.

To rectify these shortcomings and address the problems this produced, many of the local native communities and boroughs eventually created their own unique resource management bodies. The AEWC is one example. The AEWC is a collaboration between eleven Inupiat subsistence whaling associations from St. Lawrence Island in the Bering Sea to Kaktovik in the Beaufort Sea.[49] The AEWC came into being as a consequence of the shifting direction of the IWC from the conservation of bowhead whales to eliminating all bowhead whaling. Yet it was also established as an outcome of a growing concern regarding the increase of oil exploration and development in Alaska.[50]

The aim of the AEWC is to protect the bowhead whale and to ensure the future of the subsistence hunt by representing the hunters in their negotiations with the NMFS, Alaska Region, and its parent organization, the National Oceanic and Atmospheric Administration (NOAA), as well as the IWC at the international level.[51] The AEWC consists of both voting and non-voting members. Voting members include whaling captains, and non-voting members are members of the crew. The AEWC is directed by a board of commissioners who are responsible for the management of the commission's affairs. Since its origins, the AEWC has helped initiate some of the most advanced research on the status of the bowhead stock, including a program where subsistence whalers attach satellite tags for scientists to follow whale migration patterns.[52]

Once it was established, one of the first items of the AEWC was to draw attention to what the members regarded as the inadequacies of the U.S. government bowhead consensus carried out off of the coast of Barrow.[53] Soon enough, the AEWC concluded that they actually had two specific issues to contend with (rather than merely a general whaling problem): an overall lack of data concerning the population of the bowhead whale and the divergent views between the Inupiat subsistence hunters and the scientists who traveled to the north to carry out the surveys.[54]

By 1980, the AEWC had established its own management plan and a Science Advisory Committee (SAC). Due to its immediate expansion, in 1982 it was re-designated as the North Slope Borough Science Advisory Committee.[55] At that time, the AEWC was able to convince NMFS to hand over the responsibility of consensus findings to the North Slope Borough's Department of Wildlife Management.[56] The AEWC also entered into a cooperative agreement with NOAA. NOAA is the primary body in the United States in charge of the management and enforcement for all programs dealing with bowhead whales and is the U.S. representation in the IWC. The cooperative agreement between the AEWC and NOAA was set up to protect the bowhead whale and Inupiat culture, promote scientific investigation of bowhead whales, and support the Marine Protection Act, the Whaling Convention, and the Endangered Species Act as it relates to aboriginal whaling. The AEWC more broadly felt that impartial oversight on proposed research and impartial reviews of government and industrial analyses of plans affecting its activities was needed.[57]

The AEWC/NOAA agreement also sought to carry out further scientific research in response to growing petroleum exploration and development. To complement this scientific work, in 1986, the AEWC created an Open Water Season Conflict Avoidance Agreement (CAA) to manage offshore oil and gas impacts. The CAA is a regional management tool based on sound science, which is informed directly from the observations by Inupiat subsistence hunters.[58] CAA is an ecosystem-based management tool, and in conjunction with CAA, the AEWC has created an insurance agreement that provides logistical support to subsistence hunters and compensation should an oil spill occur. NMFS relies on the CAA, as does the Bureau of Ocean Energy Management, Regulation and Enforcement, in order to meet requirements for its permits.[59] The CAA provides equipment and procedures for communications between subsistence whalers and industry participants, avoidance guidelines, measures to be taken in the case of an emergency, and dispute resolution.[60]

Whereas the IWC has become mired in a political rivalry over commercial whaling, affecting the commission's scientific purpose, the AEWC in collaboration with NOAA has created a scientific process for documenting subsistence hunting for the IWC and to deal with offshore oil and gas development in the North Slope. The AEWC has also undertaken a project to combine nineteenth-century whaling tools with modern technology to make the process more humane. Whereas early on NOAA personnel monitored the whale hunts and the AEWC assisted personnel with the monitoring, the AEWC and the individual whaling captains now work directly with scientists from the North Slope

Borough's Department of Wildlife Management to collect specimens from landed whales.[61]

The AEWC/NOAA agreement has also led to joint enforcement, inspection, and conflict resolution. In addition, through local revenues generated from taxes on oil industry infrastructure on the North Slope, the North Slope Borough has in the past been able to hold biannual conferences on bowhead whales through the SAC. This group provides advice on an as-needed basis when the North Slope Borough and the AEWC have a science question that requires expert knowledge. Funded by NOAA and the North Slope Borough, the AEWC has also become a representative at the IWC meetings and therefore a source of negotiating power when it comes to subsistence whaling quotas. In this way the AEWC, a local Alaskan organization, works directly with and is able to represent its constituents at the meetings of an international organization.[62]

Although the continuing politics of the IWC bring into question its future capacity to regulate commercial whaling at the international level, the particular management processes of the AEWC, which bridges local resource use and international collaboration with the IWC, as well as the AEWC's existing collaboration with Alaska's offshore oil and gas industry are worthy of analysis when it comes to the current discussions concerning the management of offshore oil and gas exploration at the broader Arctic level.

THE POLITICS OF ARCTIC OIL AND GAS

In April 2010, the largest oil spill in history occurred off the Gulf Coast of Mexico in the United States. The spill put an immediate damper on the growing excitement surrounding the potential oil and gas discoveries in a melting Arctic.[63] Certain environmental groups[64] and pundits including certain EU parliamentarians called for a total moratorium on all Arctic oil and gas projects. According to these advocates, the oil spill was a tragic reminder not only that a major offshore oil spill is possible but moreover that systematic prevention and response measures are either lacking entirely or confined to domestic policy where they do exist. Transferring these possibilities to the Arctic, if an oil spill occurred, the ability to respond sufficiently would be exponentially more challenging.[65]

These debates over regulating offshore oil and gas development in the Arctic are, however, part of a long-standing discussion within the region itself. They reach back prior to the *Exxon Valdez* spill to at least the 1970s, when an Alaskan Inupiat, Eben Hopson, founded the ICC to address the need to regulate possible offshore oil and gas development in Alaskan and the Canadian Beaufort Sea. At the first ICC meeting in 1976, Hopson, speaking on the reasons he was setting out to create a Pan-Arctic Inuit organization, stated, "We hope that our Inuit Circumpolar Conference will initiate dialogue between the five Arctic coastal nations necessary to lead to formal agreements for safe and responsible Arctic oil and gas development."[66]

Since that time, the debates over offshore oil and gas development have shifted from possibility to reality. Existing projects include thirteen awarded leases off the coast of Greenland, which began in August 2010. Likewise, Shell has spent over US$3.4 billion in investments for developing offshore projects in the Chukchi and Beaufort Seas. Arctic oil and gas drilling has been underway off the coasts of Labrador in Canada for over a decade. In September 2010, Russia and Norway resolved a thirty-year border dispute in the Russian Barents Sea, an area where a wealth of offshore resources are said to exist and will lead to new development projects.[67] Russia, in its Arctic Strategy, has also made it public that its future economy lies in Arctic oil and gas exploration.[68] This is coupled by Norway's already operational Arctic Snøhvit field near its northern town of Hammerfest.

Norway's history is particularly tied to its offshore oil and gas production. Leading up to the 1900s it was one of the poorest countries in

Europe. Oil and gas were first discovered in 1979, and since then hydro-carbon development has grown to represent half of its exports and 30 percent of its annual state revenues.[69] Norway has also become the world's sixth-largest oil exporter and has the second-largest sovereign wealth fund in the world after Abu Dhabi, according to the Sovereign Wealth Fund (SWF) Institute.[70] As southern oil and gas fields dry up, the Norwegian government is turning to its Arctic waters for securing future domestic revenues.

Accompanying these developments, in 2000, the U.S. Geological Survey (USGS) released an assessment of the potential for undiscovered and—in the event of an ice-free sea—technically recoverable oil and gas resources. This was followed by a joint Geological Survey by Denmark and Greenland (GEUS) and another USGS assessment in 2007 of potential Arctic oil—this time in the East Greenland Rift Basins Province. The 2007 USGS Circum-Arctic Resource Appraisal was the "the first systematic and comprehensive analysis of the undiscovered petroleum resources of the Circum-Arctic in the public domain." According to the USGS director Mark Myers, uncovering the potential for resource exploitation in the Arctic—an area that he points out as also being environmentally sensi-tive—maintaining technological risk and geological uncertainty will be "critical to our understanding of future energy supplies to the United States and the world."[71] Taking note of Norway's economic successes, in June 2009, Greenlanders voted for a change from Greenland Home Rule to Self Rule. One of the major aspects of the shift was that the new government would have outright ownership over its surface and subsurface minerals. The expected revenues generated from mineral and oil and gas developments are intended to be used toward paying off the yearly block grant Greenland receives from the Danish government and thereby helping pave the way for formal secession from Denmark. Greenland has chosen to adopt many of Norway's own offshore oil and gas policies and regulations (which includes discussion of creating its own sovereign wealth fund)], and in 2011 Greenland and Norway signed a memorandum of understanding to cooperate on oil and gas development.[72]

The greatest challenge facing future policies to govern Arctic oil and gas is how to create a governance structure that can connect the global geopolitical reality of oil and gas development as well as accompanying international environmental and other international policies to local communities and local government structures where the development is taking place. If not possessing outright ownership over the resources themselves, as is the case in certain circumstances, indigenous peoples in the North American Arctic, for instance, very often have rights to their resources and are co-managers in its development. Rather than the argument over who owns the Arctic (and therefore its petroleum resources), a much more central question is how to govern the Arctic (including offshore oil and gas) where policy must connect the local, the domestic, regional, and international levels of politics.

BRIDGING LOCAL RESOURCES TO THE GLOBAL POLITICS OF OIL AND GAS: A ROLE FOR THE ARCTIC COUNCIL?

In 2002, the Arctic Council set out to "develop a strategic plan for the protection of the Arctic marine environment under the leadership of [the Protection of the Arctic Marine Environment Working Group] PAME." One aspect of the Arctic Council's plan was to promote pilot projects that would demonstrate the use of an ecosystem approach to management.[73] The Arctic marine environment, it was decided, required integrated ecosystem-based management in order to be protected. The project's progress report defines an adequate pilot project as one that takes into consideration multiple scales, includes a long-term perspective, recognizes that humans are an integral part of ecosystems, takes an adaptive management perspective, and has a concern for sustaining production and consumption potential for goods and services.[74] The Arctic Council Sustainable Development Working Group (SDWG) and PAME then created a Best Practices in Ecosystems Based Oceans Management (Bepomar) project. The project was initiated by Norway in 2006 and adopted by the senior Arctic officials (SAOs) meeting in April 2007. According to the report, "Many Arctic communities and settlements are based on the sustainable use of natural resources, and see themselves as integrated parts of these ecosystems."[75] The report goes on to state that the importance of non-renewable resources is growing, and offshore petroleum developments are expanding to new areas of the Arctic.[76] The purpose of the Bepomar project, therefore, was to present the concepts and practices the Arctic countries have developed in order to apply an ecosystem-based approach to oceans management for the Arctic.[77]

When it comes to the governance aspects of ecosystem management, the report concludes that "rule-based relationships between countries in oceans affairs, based on applicable international law and agreements, have to be promoted." Likewise, "cooperation in science and exchange of relevant information within and between countries is important for understanding the cumulative impacts to the marine environment...various forms of scientific, traditional, and management knowledge need to be integrated to improve ecosystem based management." The report's conclusions call for a multisector approach and "contributing to common understandings of challenges and thereby an increased trust between authorities with different sector responsibilities/interests." Stakeholder and Arctic resident participation, the report concludes, can be achieved through public participation that enables stakeholders and members of the public who lack the capacity to prepare for and attend meetings "to make their voices heard in a meaningful fashion."[78]

As a follow-up, in May 2011 the Arctic Council's SAOs tasked the ministers with creating an ecosystem-based management expert group to report to the SAOs. The purpose of the group is to develop a common understanding of ecosystem-based management and to consider ecosystem-based management principles for marine and terrestrial areas. They also recommended that the expert group develop Arctic-specific guidelines for applying the ecosystem approach to all relevant areas of work in the Arctic Council.[79]

The task for the Arctic Council now becomes putting into practice these recommendations and creating adequate processes of Arctic resource management that accommodate the needs and existing governance institutions of the Arctic's communities as well as related legal instruments and other federal and regional policies. The earlier Bepomar Arctic Council Report made it clear that indigenous peoples should be involved in all aspects of resource management, from identifying problems to the evaluation stage.[80] At the same time, the report concedes that many indigenous communities and peoples are sparsely populated and that many companies have more employees than the total population of many indigenous communities. The report also points to the fact that many small communities are overworked and lack the resources and capacity to address the issues they see as priorities.[81]

It is here that one can turn to the AEWC as a tangible example of how Inupiat whalers consistently work to acquire and maintain the capacity to represent themselves formally in local, state, and international whaling discussions as well as local oil and gas development issues. The AEWC includes, from the outset, local involvement in sharing the responsibilities over resource development. The local Inupiat subsistence captains, through the AEWC, are responsible for local management of the bowhead whales. The AEWC works in collaboration with NOAA and the U.S. delegation to the IWC to have quotas set by the IWC. The standards for setting the quotas are based on the health of the bowhead stock (this research is done by the North Slope Borough Department of Wildlife Management in collaboration with consulting scientists and whalers) and documented subsistence need for bowhead whales.[82] The Department of Wildlife Management also leads the census of bowhead whales. The censuses are visual and acoustic methods that were developed based on hunters' knowledge of where to find the whales (which is often under the ice).[83] The AEWC also cooperates directly with the oil and gas industry and the U.S. federal government to help manage offshore oil- and gas-related activities in the Beaufort and Chukchi Seas through the conflict avoidance agreements.

Because financial capacity is a chief concern for many local communities, the AEWC has a means to access funding relating to the management of subsistence whaling from the North Slope Borough tax base, which includes North Slope oil development and related infrastructure. The AEWC also receives federal funding through NOAA and occasional grants and donations from private sources.[84] In terms of science, the AEWC collaborates on research projects through work with the Department of Wildlife Management and other state and federal entities (for example, NMFS and the National Science Foundation, or NSF). The North Slope Borough additionally funds the Arctic Science Advisory Committee, which, in the past, has funded biannual conferences on bowhead whales.[85]

Finally, the AEWC provides a means for sharing best practices through its collaboration with the North Slope Borough Department of Wildlife Management (which often receives research grants from NMFS) and federal agencies, namely NOAA, as well as the IWC.[86] Through the conflict avoidance agreements, the AEWC also shares best practices with operators carrying out hydrocarbon activities in the region. Having to live within a quota at the outset aside, thus far the AEWC has successfully lobbied to ensure the Inupiat hunters are able to continue to participate in subsistence whaling. Perhaps most significantly, the AEWC provides one example of how to successfully bring local and national governments, non-state actors, and international legal instruments under a single resource management regime.

When it comes to managing Arctic offshore oil and gas development, the Arctic Council could turn to the AEWC as an example framework for putting into practice the recommendations of the Bepomar project. At the outset, however, the Arctic Council needs to write the rules for

Arctic offshore oil and gas development. This includes passing further binding laws to establish certain guidelines that all Arctic states, companies, and local communities where offshore oil and gas development will take place must adhere to. With a set of rules in place, the Arctic Council could then become the coordinating organization for creating and managing new offshore oil and gas regimes. An Arctic offshore oil and gas regime, for instance, would be regulated and administered by the local communities involved and state agencies and adhere to bilateral, regional, and international regulations. Once potential oil and gas projects are identified, the Arctic Council could be the host political body for bringing the relevant players together to establish the basis and priorities for the expected management regime before development even begins (exploratory or otherwise). The Arctic Council could also establish, as part of its guidelines for development, a revenue-sharing scheme that would allow indigenous and non-indigenous communities lacking resources and capacity to participate to become full partners in the management regime. Often this would require taking the discussions to the communities themselves.

Given that the rules for development include adhering to "applicable international law," the Arctic Council, like the AEWC, can also serve as the official bridge between local and regional bodies and international institutions. The Arctic Council already often collaborates with, lobbies to, or contributes through its scientific work to international organizations: the Arctic Council's 1998 AMAP report "Arctic Pollution Issues," for instance, was used in the negotiations leading to the Stockholm Convention on Persistent Organic Pollutants (POPs). The Arctic Council also supports the work of the International Maritime Organization (IMO) in creating its Polar Code for Arctic shipping and has lobbied the UN Climate Change Conference (COP15) to curb black carbon.[87] The Arctic Council could continue to strengthen its ties to the international community by working with legal bodies from the IMO to the UN Permanent Forum on indigenous issues (see specifically Articles 27 and 32 of the UN Declaration on the Rights of Indigenous Peoples)[88] to ensure that international organizations are representing the interests of the Arctic Council's members (and constituents). One means for achieving this would be to work toward obtaining observer status on varying international bodies.

The Arctic Council could also bring together international and local organizations to coordinate and manage research carried out in relation to new and existing management regimes (and in certain cases the Arctic Council could link together projects of overlapping interests). The scientific results would contribute to the Arctic Council's efforts to create legally binding policies, which can be used to lobby international institutions to make new policies that favor the Arctic Council's interests. Much like the AEWC, which calls for impartial oversight on proposed research and impartial reviews of government and industrial analyses of plans affecting its activities, the Arctic Council, through its experiences with leading major research projects, could act as a sound nonpartisan venue for carrying out impartial research and reviews.

The Arctic Council also has the critical capacity, through the indigenous permanent participants, to be sure that local communities are involved and that traditional indigenous knowledge (often referred to as TEK) is taken seriously and brought together in a complimentary manner with "Western" science. Indigenous and other local communities, in this fashion, would be co-authors in determining and writing up the problems and research questions to be addressed at the outset. Indigenous permanent participants would also be the official link to local indigenous communities and therefore manage all local aspects of new resource management regimes. Scientific research, like stakeholder dialogues, could be funded through an established revenue-sharing program that would include, at the least, state funding and the funding from companies operating in the Arctic. According to the IR scholar Stephen Krasner, arguably one of the most cited authorities on regime theory, by creating shared sovereignty arrangements where institutions would share authority with external and internal actors, possibilities for improving agreements that would not otherwise be available can come into being.[89]

ARCTIC GOVERNANCE REVISITED

One of the major lessons learned from the oil spill in the Gulf of Mexico was the lack of a co-managed system such as described here. If a structure had been put in place where the fishing industry and the oil and gas industry had a joint plan for oil spill preparedness and response, the ensuing confusion and devastation could have been minimized. Monetary resources could have been generated through revenue sharing by the oil and gas industry as well as from the federal government. The money could have been allocated to the fishing industry and other local coastal companies and communities for attaining the proper equipment and training to respond immediately to an emergency. Rather than leaving BP in charge of the clean-up and waiting for the U.S. government to write up its own response plan, those who live near and work on the water where the spill occurred could have taken immediate action. A co-management regime for the Gulf of Mexico not only would have created a clear predetermined channel between the proper federal authorities in charge, local authorities, private industry, and community members, but the plan itself would have been co-authored by various levels of government and non-state actors from its origins. And, given that scientists have found that the effects of the Gulf spill have reached the Arctic in terms of wildlife migration patterns, clearly international environmental policies should have already been put into place.

Beyond the focus on traditional sovereignty issues and particularly the media's focus on dividing up the physical borders of the Arctic seabed, one could foresee a conflict arising from an instance where defined and delineated borders have little meaning. Rather than a conflict over who owns the seabed, one could imagine a conflict emerging from an oil spill beginning in Greenland and making its way to Canada without any formal joint mechanisms in place to address the spill. Who would oversee compensation when an oil spill on one side of a state border (e.g., Greenland/Denmark) destroys the local economy (e.g., St. John's, Newfoundland) of a community in the bordering country?

The Arctic Council Agreement on Cooperation in Aeronautical and Maritime Search and Rescue in the Arctic (SAR) and Cooperation on Marine Oil Pollution, Preparedness, and Response in the Arctic are positive starts. Concrete disaster plans, however, need to be determined in advance (SAR, for instance, is an agreement to cooperate rather than specific steps to deal with a disaster). As a first step in this direction, in October 2011, delegates from the Arctic Council met in Whitehorse, Canada, for a conference on Arctic search and rescue cooperation. According to Steve Waddell, a spokesperson for the Canadian Forces,

> What we want to do is bring [the Arctic states] all together, talk about how about how they do it in their own areas, but more importantly how can they collaborate, bring those resources to bear, in areas that are a little more challenging to get to, that we might need an international response.[90]

Efforts to deal with a possible oil spill or other disaster, however, need to go beyond state cooperation. Successful policy requires a regime that takes into account and includes those who fish and live off of the same waters and inhabit its shores. An effective Arctic search and rescue plan would be co-authored and designed with the help of local communities, and resources would be allocated to these same communities to carry out rescue efforts. If a disaster should ensue, those living closest to the disaster should be equipped as first responders.

The roadmap detailing the future course of Arctic governance is far from complete. Yet what can be discerned is that although the Arctic states and their physical territorial boundaries remain (if they are not in fact expanding), these same boundaries are shared with new layers of political authority acting below, above, and across state boundaries. The

Arctic Council has the potential to evolve into a globally unique regional political regime that bridges local, state, regional, transnational, and international institutions to address the growing global geopolitics of the Arctic. Karkkainen argued that it is time to rethink global governance agreements and global institutions altogether. Global governance agreements and institutions would be better served if they supported regional governance processes that situate governance at the appropriate eco-regional scale. These regional scales could then be nested within a larger set of global institutions that can monitor the various regional governance arrangements as well as provide technical assistance, among other things.[91] Global governance, in this context, would become arenas for supporting adaptive ecosystem management at ecologically appropriate scales (post-Westphalian resource management) rather than the commanders of top-down fixed rules and standard approaches (i.e., treaty making).[92] Learning how to strengthen the operational mechanisms of such policy initiatives is where political bodies such as the AEWC become relevant examples for how and where effective governance is possible and where it needs to be improved. Moreover, the AEWC serves as an effective foundation for moving the debate from who owns the Arctic to how to govern in a post-state-centered political world.[93]

NOTES

1. Bradley Karkkainen, "Marine Ecosystem Management & A 'Post-Sovereign' Transboundary Governance," *San Diego International Law Journal* 6 (2004): 113–120.
2. Patricia Cochran, "Arctic Council: Meeting of Ministers of Foreign Affairs, Tromsø, Norway: Introductory Remarks: Chair, Inuit Circumpolar Council," April 29, 2009.
3. ICC, *A Circumpolar Inuit Declaration on Sovereignty in the Arctic*, April 2009, https://www.itk.ca/sites/default/files/Declaration_12x18_Vice-Chairs_Signed.pdf.
4. For example, see Oran Young, *Creating Regimes: Arctic Accords and International Governance* (Ithaca, NY: Cornell University Press, 1993).
5. Karkkainen, "Marine Ecosystem Management"; Harriet Bulkeley, "Reconfiguring Environmental Governance: Towards a Politics of Scales and Networks," *Political Geography* 24 (2005): 875–902; Ruth Meinzen-Dick and Rajendra Pradhan, "Legal Pluralism and Dynamic Property Rights," Capri Working Paper 22 (Washington, DC: International Food Policy Research Institute, 2002).
6. Karkkainen, "Marine Ecosystem Management."
7. Ibid., 120.
8. Ibid.
9. Ibid., 122.
10. Ibid., 123.
11. Ibid.
12. Bradley Karkkainen, "Collaborative Ecosystem Governance: Scale, Complexity, and Dynamism." *Virginia Environmental Law Journal* 189, no. 21 (2002): 3.
13. Karkkainen, "Marine Ecosystem Management," 124.
14. *Arctic Human Development Report* (Akureyri: Stefansson Arctic Institute, 2004), 129.
15. Ibid., 131.
16. Ibid.
17. Ibid.
18. Ibid.
19. Frank Sejersen, "Local Knowledge in Greenland: Arctic Perspectives and Contextual Differences," in *Cultivating Arctic Landscapes: Knowing and*

Managing Animals in the Circumpolar North, ed. David G. Anderson and Mark Nuttall (Oxford: Berghahn, 2004), 33–56.

20. For example, see "2011 Arctic Dialogue Greenland Conference and Workshop Nuuk, Greenland, September 24–26, 2011 Meeting Summary," Ilisimatusarfik, University of Greenland, December 2011, http://www.hcahome.com/.
21. Ibid.
22. Sara Olsvig, "Greenland's Decision-Making on Uranium: Towards a Democratic Failure," *Arctic Journal*, October 18, 2013, http://arcticjournal.com/opinion/greenlands-decision-making-uranium-towards-democratic-failure.
23. ANSCA was the first Inuit land claim agreement and was signed in 1971. This was followed by the James Bay and Northern Quebec Agreement (JBNQA) passed in 1975; the Inuvialuit Final Agreement, Northwest Territories in 1984; the Nunavut Agreement in 1993 (put into effect in 1999); the Inuit agreement in Labrador in 2005; and finally, in Nunavik, a series of agreements were reached with the federal government in 2007.
24. *Inupiat* is the term for the Alaskan Inuit.
25. *Arctic Human Development Report*, 133.
26. http://www.asrc.com/Pages/We%20are%20ASRC.aspx.
27. ICC, *Circumpolar Inuit Declaration on Resource Development Principles in Inuit Nunaat*, May 2011.
28. Ibid.
29. Ibid.
30. Daniel Francis, "Whaling," in *The Canadian Encyclopedia* (Historica Foundation, 2011), http://www.thecanadianencyclopedia.com/en/article/whaling/.
31. Jonathan Greenberg, "The Arctic in World Environmental History," *Vanderbilt Journal of Transnational Law* 42 (2009): 1307–1392.
32. Ibid.
33. John Bockstoce and John Burns, "Commercial Whaling in the North Pacific Sector." *The Bowhead Whale Special Publication Number 2* (1993): 563–577.
34. Alaska History and Cultural Studies Curriculum Project, "Northwest and Arctic 1732–1871 Age of Arctic Exploration and Whaling," 2004–2011, http://www.akhistorycourse.org/articles/article.php?artID=64.
35. R. Gambell, "International Management of Whales and Whaling: An Historical Review of the Regulation of Commercial and Aboriginal Subsistence Whaling," *Arctic* 46, no. 2 (1993): 102.

36. Ibid.
37. IWC (International Whaling Commission) Secretariat, Background information for the Commission's aboriginal subsistence whaling working group (ASWWG), Metropole Hotel, Brighton, 1981.
38. Gambell, "International Management of Whales and Whaling," 102.
39. William Aron, "The International Whaling Commission: A Case of Malignant Neglect," *IIFET Proceedings*, 2000.
40. Gambell, "International Management of Whales and Whaling," 102.
41. IWC Secretariat.
42. Ibid., 3.
43. Ibid., 4.
44. Gambell, "International Management of Whales and Whaling," 103; IWC Secretariat, 3.
45. Gambell, "International Management of Whales and Whaling," 104.
46. Aron, "International Whaling Commission."
47. See C. Hedley, "IWC 54: Analysis of Selected Issues: Aboriginal Subsistence Whaling," Reporter 15, 2002, http://www.oceanlaw.net/people/profiles/hedley/pubs/ifb/2002-reporter-15.htm.
48. Earl Comstock, "Testimony of Earl Comstock Counsel for the Alaska Eskimo Whaling Commission before the Subcommittee on International Organizations, Human Rights and Oversight and the Subcommittee on Asia, the Pacific and the Global Environment," in *US Leadership in the International Whaling Commission and H.R. 2455, the International Whale Conservation and Protection Act of 2009 Joint Hearing Before the Subcommittee on International Organizations, Human Rights and Oversight and the Subcommittee on Asia, the Pacific and the Global Environment of the Committee on Foreign Affairs of the House of Representatives One Hundred Eleventh Congress Second Session*, Serial No. 111–95, May 6, 2010.
49. Aron, "International Whaling Commission."
50. J. J. Kelley and A. Brower, Sr., "The NARL and Its Transition to the Local Community in Fifty More Years Below Zero," in *Tributes and Meditations for the Naval Arctic Research Laboratory's First Half Century at Barrow, Alaska*, ed. D. W. Norton (Calgary and Fairbanks: Arctic Institute of North America, 2001), 262.
51. Mathias Albert, David Jacobson, and Yosef Lapid, eds., *Identities, Borders, Orders: Rethinking International Relations Theory* (Minneapolis: University of Minnesota Press, 2001), 267.
52. Comstock, "Testimony of Earl Comstock."
53. Albert, Jacobson, and Lapid, *Identities, Borders, Orders*, 267.

54. Ibid.
55. Kelly and Brower, "The NARL and Its Transition to the Local Community," 262.
56. Albert, Jacobson, and Lapid, *Identities, Borders, Orders*, 268.
57. Kelley and Brower, "The NARL and Its Transition to the Local Community," 262.
58. H. Brower, Alaska Eskimo Whaling Commission presentation to the White House Ocean Policy Task Force, Anchorage, 2009, http://www.whitehouse.gov/assets/formsubmissions/54/7b0421829d8a4c1e8508d876aa40f61b.pdf.
59. Ibid.
60. AEWC (Alaska Eskimo Whaling Commission), 2012 Open Water Season Programmatic Conflict Avoidance Agreement, March 2012, www.nmfs.noaa.gov/pr/pdfs/permits/bp_openwater_caa2012.pdf.
61. Glenn Sheehan, founding executive director of the Barrow Arctic Science Consortium (BASC), personal communication, April 6, 2012.
62. Garch Nettheim, Gary D. Meyers, and Donna Craig, *Indigenous Peoples and Governance Structures: A Comparative Analysis of Land and Resource Management Rights* (Toronto: Aboriginal Studies Press, 2002).
63. E.g., Michael McCarthy, "Oil Exploration under Arctic Ice Could Cause 'Uncontrollable' Natural Disaster," *The Independent*, September 6, 2011.
64. E.g., U.S. Arctic Program: Pew Environment Group, "Oil Spill Prevention and Response in the U.S. Arctic Ocean: Unexamined Risks, Unacceptable Consequences," PEW Environment Group, November 2010, http://www.pewtrusts.org/uploadedFiles/wwwpewtrustsorg/Reports/Protecting_ocean_life/PEW-1010_ARTIC_Report.pdf.
65. Frances Beinecke, "Obama Administration Allows More Offshore Drilling without More Safeguards for Arctic and Gulf," *Natural Resource Defense Council Staff Blog*, November 9, 2011, http://switchboard.nrdc.org/blogs/fbeinecke/obama_administration_allows_mo.html.
66. Eben Hopson, "Letter to the Hon. Jimmy Carter, Americana Hotel, 801 Seventh Avenue, New York, New York. From Eben Hopson," July 12, 1976, http://www.ebenhopson.com/papers/1976/DemoConfab.html.
67. Luke Harding, "Russia and Norway Resolve Arctic Border Dispute: Treaty Allows for New Oil and Gas Exploration and Settles 40-Year Row over Barents Sea," *The Guardian*, 22, September 16, 2010.
68. http://www.rg.ru/2009/03/30/arktika-osnovy-dok.html.
69. Economy Watch, "Norway Economic Statistics and Indicators," http://www.economywatch.com/economic-statistics/country/Norway/.

70. SFW Institute, "Norway Government Pension Fund Global," http://www. swfinstitute.org/swfs/norway-government-pension-fund-global/.
71. USGS, "USGS Releases New Oil and Gas Assessment of Northeastern Greenland," August 28, 2007, http://www.usgs.gov/newsroom/article_ pf.asp?ID=1750.
72. "Norwegian Petroleum Directorate Signs Agreement with Greenland," *Offshore Energy Today.Com*, January 16, 2011, http://www. offshoreenergytoday.com/norwegian-petroleum-directorate-signs-agreement-with-greenland/.
73. Arctic Council, *PAME Progress Report on the Ecosystem Approach to Arctic Marine Assessment and Management 2006–2008*, 2006, 1.
74. Ibid., 2.
75. Alf Håkon Hoel, ed., "Observed Best Practices in Ecosystem-Based Oceans Management in the Arctic Countries," *Norsk Polarinstitutt*, April 2009, http://www.sdwg.org/content.php?doc=75, 111.
76. Ibid.
77. Ibid.
78. Ibid., 112.
79. Arctic Council, "Senior Arctic Officials (SAO) Report to Ministers," Nuuk, Greenland, May 2011, 7.
80. Hoel, "Observed Best Practices," 15.
81. Ibid.
82. Jessica Lefevre, AEWC Legal Counsel, personal communication, June 6, 2012.
83. Ibid.
84. Sheehan, personal communication, April 6, 2012.
85. Ibid.
86. Lefevre, personal communication, June 6, 2012.
87. U.S. Department of State Bureau of Oceans and International Environmental and Scientific Affairs, "Strategy to Reduce Black Carbon Emissions Affecting the Arctic," fact sheet, United Nations: UN Climate Change Negotiations, 2009, http://cop15.state.gov/pressroom/133771. htm.
88. UN Declaration on the Rights of Indigenous Peoples, 2007.
89. Stephen D. Krasner, "The Case for Shared Sovereignty," *Journal of Democracy* 16, no. 1 (January 2005): 1.
90. CBC News, "Arctic Nations Talk Search and Rescue Meeting in White-horse This Week to Build on Agreement Signed in May," October 7, 2011.
91. Karkkainen, "Marine Ecosystem Management," 141.

92. Ibid.
93. A version of this paper has been published in *Polar Record*. See Jessica Shadian, "Of Whales and Oil: Inuit Resource Governance and the Arctic Council," *Polar Record*, July 2013.

CHAPTER 18

A WORK IN PROGRESS

THE UNITED KINGDOM AND THE ARCTIC REGION

Klaus Dodds

The United Kingdom has long been connected to the Arctic region—
exploratory, exploitative, and trading activities helped to assemble this
relationship and cultivate, and at times captivate, public enthusiasm.
Public and private life in Victorian Britain was littered with multifarious
examples of "Arctic fever," including public art, panoramas, museum
exhibitions, tableaux vivants, exhibitions, books, public lectures, journal
articles, board games, and illustrated magazines.[1] Millions of pounds
were invested in British-sponsored Arctic exploration, discovery, and
resource exploitation. Lives were lost and, most famously, Sir John
Franklin's mysterious disappearance in the Canadian Arctic in the 1850s
captivated and thrilled generations.[2] Recent exhibitions, such as one
hosted in 2009–2010 by the National Maritime Museum in London on
the search for the Northwest Passage, offer a timely reminder of Britain's
historic interest in the Arctic, stretching over 500 years if one starts the
exploratory encounter with people such as John Cabot.

At the beginning of the twentieth century, however, this northern connection (one might even term it a form of enchantment) faded somewhat as both public and government interest in the Antarctic and Southern Ocean grew, in part at the expense of the Arctic, as the living resource potential of the northerly latitudes diminished and Britain acquired new imperial heroes in the shape of Antarctic explorers such as Robert Falcon Scott and Ernest Shackleton.[3] One key factor in the shift southward was the role of sponsoring organizations such as the Royal Geographical Society (RGS) and leading patrons including Sir Clements Markham (1830–1916) in promoting a different geographical vision for British exploration and science. The Antarctic and surrounding ocean was, in the aftermath of World War I, subject to intense scientific and geopolitical targeting.[4]

In the last ten years, however, U.K. policy and scholarly communities have arguably become re-enchanted with the Arctic region. This intensification of interest has shifted from hard security concerns during the Cold War to something that is far more diverse, encompassing energy, climate change, shipping, scientific research, governance, and the like. Contemporary U.K. interest in the Arctic is indisputably multidimensional and, increasingly, involves a more diverse set of stakeholders in the wake of widespread acceptance within scientific and policy-orientated communities that the Arctic is becoming more accessible and, in the process, is undergoing a profound state-change.

This idea of state-change involves two interrelated elements. The first vector in this transformation involves the environmental qualities of the Arctic region.[5] The scientific concern with the thinning of perennial sea ice in the Arctic Ocean is held to be illustrative of the transition from a view of this northerly region as a "frozen desert" to something more akin to a "polar Mediterranean."[6] This transformation is not straightforward, however. The United Kingdom stood accused of transforming parts of the European Arctic. In the 1980s and 1990s, for example, successive U.K. governments came under pressure from the Norwegian governments to close the Sellafield nuclear processing facility in northern England because it was blamed for discharging radioactive materials via sea currents toward the entire Norwegian coastline including the Arctic portion. Although decommissioning work continues, concern has focused away from radioactive materials and "acid rain" toward the fate of sea ice. The distribution and thickness patterns are varied, and some parts of the Arctic Ocean are potentially more accessible than others, such as the maritime region to the north of Russia (specifically, the Northern Sea Route). This has, as a consequence, brought to the fore challenges of making sense of scientific data and likely future trends such as warming, melting, and environmental baselines more generally.[7] The second vector, which is strongly related to the first one, involves a step-change in present and future activity in the Arctic, especially in the area of resource exploitation, governance, and risk management. The management of these areas is controversial as Arctic states, northern communities, multinational corporations, extraterritorial states, and organizations intermingle with one another, working within and beyond local, national, regional, and global jurisdictions and frameworks. Although some analysts have argued that the Arctic region is facing unprecedented levels of exposure to "outside" pressures and influences, this runs the risk of under-acknowledging the degree to which the Arctic has been for hundreds of years connected to flows of people, trade, ideas, technologies, and objects.

What is indisputable is that the Arctic region is generating a great deal of public attention. One area of sustained interest is the role of extraterritorial parties in the Arctic region (e.g., those parties not defined as "Arctic states" or "northern communities" depending on political/geographical scale). Such a concern brings to the fore not only how one might define the Arctic but also how extraterritoriality is conceived in the first place. In the case of the former, there has been a tradition of defining the circumpolar North with reference to latitude, such as 66 degrees North, which is a cartographic abstraction marking the southernmost point where polar day and polar night occur in the Northern

Hemisphere. Other possible criteria such as the 10 degrees Celsius isotherm, the treeline, and continuous permafrost all fail to capture adequately the ways that people, wildlife, and weather cross boundaries and lines imposed on maps. In the Canadian context, for example, the "North" is often said to start at 60 degrees North, whereas cities such as Edmonton are often thought of as "northern" cities enduring far colder climates than towns in northern Norway.[8]

Mindful of such geographical complexity, it has often been assumed that a term such as the sub-Arctic refers to regions—both land and maritime—lying between the 55th and 65th parallels. This matters because it would "grant" the U.K. sub-Arctic status. As the website of the Foreign and Commonwealth Office (FCO) pertaining to the Arctic notes, "Today, as the Arctic's closest neighbour, the UK continues to engage actively in and with the Arctic in a multitude of ways."[9] This notion of "closest" is highly pertinent in contemporary discussions of Arctic geopolitics and security. Defining the Arctic region has never been politically innocent, and contemporary mappings are proving no different. For countries such as the United Kingdom and regional bodies including the European Union, their involvement in the region is through a series of stretched relationships with Arctic-based states and organizations and/or functional complicity via international and regional legal regimes, including fishing quotas and rights of innocent/transit passage.[10] So the absence of a recognizably Arctic coastline or landmass is no barrier to such interest, and for much of modern European history it never has been. In the present era, attention is turning again to how extraterritorial parties become, once more, implicated in Arctic-based development, science and technology, economic organization, resource exploitation, environmental monitoring, and diplomacy. But, as this chapter reflects on, such definitions also empower close neighbors such as the United Kingdom to reimagine themselves as nations with Arctic-based interests.

In this short chapter, I devote my attention to auditing contemporary U.K. interests in the Arctic region following some brief reflection on Cold War legacies and interests. The latter is important because the United Kingdom's geographical position as a nation proximate to the North Sea and North Atlantic Ocean placed it on the proverbial "front line" of Cold War militarized posturing against the Soviet Union.[11] Notwithstanding the formal ending of the Cold War, some legacies remain such as military training, geographical depictions such as "Northern Flank," and alliance-building with close allies including Norway and the Netherlands in the Norwegian Arctic.[12] Thereafter, this chapter addresses three key vectors of contemporary U.K. interest—science/environment, military, and energy. Other areas such as shipping and insurance have merited attention from organizations such as Lloyd's Register, a marine classification society and independent risk assessment service.[13] Finally, some assessment is offered about the possible development of a U.K. Arctic strategy, which might be released by the U.K. government in 2013–2014. Such a strategy, if it is made publicly accessible, will in part audit such Arctic interests but at the same time reinforce the United Kingdom's commitment to support existing intergovernmental governance, such as the Arctic Council, and maintain and strengthen bilateral relations with allies such as Norway and Canada. The U.K.-Norwegian relationship, especially in the energy sector, is particularly noteworthy.

UNITED KINGDOM, THE COLD WAR, AND THE ARCTIC

The United Kingdom's interests and connections with the Arctic region were, for the purposes of the Cold War, largely shaped by membership of NATO (formed in 1949). During this period, the main preoccupation lay with countering the Soviet Union's naval forces based in the Arctic (primarily the Northern Fleet operating from ports on the Kola Peninsula) and their transiting through the North Atlantic and beyond. In the military planning discourse of the era, this region was described as the Northern Flank, with due emphasis to not only stop Norway becoming a Soviet satellite state but also monitor the so-called Greenland-Iceland-United Kingdom (GIUK) Gap to ensure that Soviet naval forces, especially submarines, were detected before they had a chance to strike against NATO forces. The decision of Denmark, Iceland, and Norway to join NATO imposed a substantial burden on U.K. and U.S. armed forces to prepare and expand plans to defend maritime lines of communication, as well as strategically located islands, including Greenland, Iceland, the Faroes, and Svalbard.

In 1952, NATO established Supreme Atlantic Command (Atlantic) and this signaled greater emphasis devoted to naval planning in the North Atlantic and Arctic theaters. In the same year, U.K. forces joined North American and Nordic counterparts in the first regional exercise called Operation Mainbrace, operating in Danish and Norwegian waters. In the one scenario, NATO forces were instructed to protect an escorted convoy that departed from Scotland heading to Norway with emergency assistance in the event of war with the Soviet Union. This established a pattern of regular Arctic military training for U.K. forces (especially well developed with Dutch and Norwegian counterparts) and routinized surveillance activities of the North Atlantic/Arctic by naval forces and, more controversially, fishing vessels operating in the Norwegian Sea.

For the next forty years, U.K. engagement with the Arctic region was driven primarily by so-called hard security concerns. Military engagement was driven by a series of anticipatory logics, which sought to prepare for an unwelcome future in the present. In the 1950s and 1960s, it was assumed that a Soviet attack would come primarily from long-range bombers, and what was critical was establishing early warning posts in the North American Arctic, Greenland, and Iceland for the purpose of detecting military interventions. In the 1970s and 1980s, fears of a possible Soviet assault by submarine fleets placed further emphasis on patrolling and monitoring the icy waters of the North Atlantic Ocean and Norwegian Sea. Cold War geopolitics in the Arctic was volumetric in character—the United States and allies were as determined to monitor the horizon as they were to collate vital oceanographic information about ocean depths and atmospheres.[14] U.S. and U.K. naval submarines in particular were vital agents in this collection of geographical data on sea ice, underwater geology, and oceanic currents. For those who enjoy James Bond films, *The Spy Who Loved Me* (1977) captures this enduring feature of British maritime strategy as a nuclear-powered submarine goes missing somewhere in the Barents Sea region. The Soviets are initially suspected, but later it becomes clear that an evil genius is behind the fiendish plot to extort and terrorize an entire population.

The decision by the then Soviet leader Mikhail Gorbachev to propose East-West cooperation in Murmansk in October 1987 was widely judged to have been instrumental in facilitating a shift in the Cold War geopolitics of the Arctic.[15] His references to scientific cooperation, political dialogue, and environmental protection marked a shift away from the prevailing militarizing discourses and practices associated with the region. Within a decade, the Arctic states and associated actors such as indigenous peoples' organizations managed to secure the creation of the Arctic Council (in 1996), which signaled a move toward greater cooperation and overall improvement in interstate relations in the Arctic region. Within that general political climate, the establishment of the International Arctic Scientific Committee (IASC, in 1990), the implementation of an Arctic Environmental Protection Strategy (AEPS, 1991), and the creation of the Barents Euro-Arctic Council (BEAC, 1993) all helped to shift Arctic geopolitics away from its overwhelming focus on military preparation and preparedness.

From a U.K. perspective, this general trend enabled extraterritorial parties to recalibrate their interest and involvement in the Arctic region. As state observers to the Arctic Council and BEAC alongside U.K. scientific involvement in the IASC, the United Kingdom has further embedded itself in Arctic affairs. In the post–Cold War era, the United Kingdom continues to monitor the North Atlantic and Arctic regions, but whereas there was once an interest in Soviet attack submarines, now the focus is more on transboundary pollutants, sea ice thinning, resource potential, and migratory species movement between the northerly latitudes and the United Kingdom. U.K. scientists and political figures may look north, but they do so with a very different kind of interest from that of their Cold War counterparts.

CONTEMPORARY U.K. INTERESTS IN THE ARCTIC REGION

The current U.K. government (elected in May 2010), when addressing the Arctic region, highlights seven core interests, namely, the protection of the Arctic ecosystem, the consolidation of cooperation among Arctic states and other interested parties through fora such as the Arctic Council, the monitoring of climate change impacts on the Arctic environment and societies, the role of the Arctic as a source of resources, the opening up of the Arctic to increased shipping, the sustainable management of fisheries, and finally the scientific study of the region by U.K. scientists and their funding bodies.[16] Although this short chapter cannot assess in detail those seven core interests, their very existence gives an indication of current and future-orientated U.K. government thinking on the Arctic region.[17]

Although it is important to delve a little further into this list of key British interests, it is also necessary to acknowledge how military/strategic/security-related concerns interweave with those aforementioned topics. For example, U.K. interest in the Arctic's resource base is intimately tied to debates on energy security and the recognized need to enjoy a close working relationship with Norway in particular because of its status as a major gas supplier to the United Kingdom.[18] This national self-interest is, however, juxtaposed with other kinds of observations regarding U.K. legal and political connections to the Arctic. As the FCO reminds readers on its website pertaining to the Arctic, "The UK is party to, and at the forefront of discussions in, numerous conventions relating to the Arctic. We have a clear and legitimate interest in the continued well-being of the Arctic marine and terrestrial environment, and the sustainable development of the region's resources."[19]

In terms of government departments, the primary actors in Whitehall[20] are the FCO, the Ministry of Defence (MOD), the Department of Energy and Climate Change (DECC), the Department of Business, Industry and Skills (BIS), and the Department of Environment, Food, Resources and Agriculture (DEFRA). DECC and BIS would be expected to take the lead on issues such as the regulation of energy exploration and exploitation. FCO would address bilateral relations with Arctic states and multinational governance. MOD would focus on defense and strategic matters either on a bilateral or a NATO/multilateral basis. DEFRA would consider, for example, issues such as illegal, unregulated, and unreported fishing. The FCO has established a so-called Arctic network under the remit of the Polar Regions Section to encourage information sharing and coordination with regard to U.K. policy development.[21]

Before considering some of the key areas of contemporary U.K. Arctic interest, it is also worth noting that Arctic-based policy discussion has to cope with a number of constraints at the present—public-sector cuts in spending, limited political attention from government ministers, resourcing (especially when the United Kingdom is committed to supporting British Antarctic Survey and a military presence on the Falkland Islands in the South Atlantic), and other commitments laid out in successive reviews. *A Strong Britain in an Age of Uncertainty: The National Security Strategy, Securing Britain in an Age of Uncertainty: The Strategic Defence and Security Review*, and the spending review have highlighted some profound changes to Britain's defense capabilities, with particular implications for maritime power projection, exemplified by the scrapping of the Harrier force and the withdrawal from service of HMS *Ark Royal*. What this means for the Arctic region, for example, is that it is not judged to be an area of high threat level to the United Kingdom. However, given stated interest in the strategic implications posed by climate change and energy security, the Arctic has caught the interest of the MOD. It is now widely believed that in 2013, the MOD will be developing and possibly releasing an updated Arctic strategy following earlier incarnations in 2007–2008.[22]

So what needs to be borne in mind is that the United Kingdom's involvement in the Arctic is evolving and there is evidence of different kinds of government-led activities—auditing, strategizing, risk assessment, monitoring, studying, and assessing. The purpose of this is to assist U.K. government planning in terms of engaging with the Arctic both present and future. For example, the kind of auditing process being carried out within government departments and beyond (e.g., House of Commons committees, public media, academic workshops, think-tank reports) is designed in large part to contribute to a debate about how far the United Kingdom should invest, participate, and potentially benefit from Arctic matters.

INTERNATIONAL ARCTIC COOPERATION

The United Kingdom is a state observer to the Arctic Council. Created in 1996, the Arctic Council is widely acknowledged to be the foremost intergovernmental forum addressing Arctic cooperation and collaboration.[23] With its eight member states and six permanent participants composed of indigenous peoples' organizations, it is an important forum for ensuring that those addressing questions of sustainable development, environmental management, and the like are aware of the interests and wishes of those who live in the Arctic region. Fundamentally, those who have been granted observer status, including the United Kingdom, explicitly accept that the governance of the Arctic is, in very large part, defined by the sovereign interests of those eight states (Canada, Denmark, Finland, Iceland, Norway, Russia, Sweden, and the United States) and complemented by international agreements and treaties. The United Nations Convention on the Law of the Sea (UNCLOS), alongside customary international law, is highly relevant when discussing the governance of the Arctic Ocean. In May 2008, the five Arctic Ocean coastal states reaffirmed their commitment (via the Ilulissat Declaration) to the legal framework established by the international Law of the Sea (not UNCLOS because the United States is not a party to it), and they committed themselves to resolving any differences of opinion via that body of law.[24]

The Arctic Council does not address military/security issues and has, in recent times, concentrated on developing mandatory commitments in areas such as search and rescue (as realized during the Ministerial Meeting of the Arctic Council in May 2011). Under the chairmanship of Sweden (2011–2013), hopes have been expressed that a similar approach might be adopted for oil spill management. If so, then the Arctic Council is arguably moving into a different phase of concerted action among the eight member states, while at the same time deliberating on whether to expand the number of state observers. The U.K. government is committed to retaining its position as an observer and is supportive of others joining the Arctic Council as observers, including ad hoc observers such as China and the European Union. The U.K. government has not played any role, as an observer, in the development of search and rescue and oil spill managing planning. Indeed, as the Arctic Council member states potentially enhance its mandatory qualities, there is a danger that U.K. and other observers will find themselves marginalized in favor of more intense cooperation among the Arctic eight and not just the five Arctic Ocean coastal states.

The United Kingdom's commitment to the Arctic Council and its foundational principles/practices is vital in terms of maintaining support from established allies such as Canada and Norway. Endorsing the council's vision of Arctic cooperation, moreover, facilitates the possibility of the United Kingdom playing a brokerage role with observers such as the European Union, which are eager to develop further Arctic policies and strategies. In the recent past, a British MEP, Diana Wallis, was one of the most vocal contributors regarding EU Arctic interest.[25]

Despite some public unease among the Arctic states about growing EU involvement, the United Kingdom and other observers such as Germany and Netherlands have worked with the EU Parliament and Commission to reposition EU Arctic policy away from discussions about an "Arctic Treaty" and toward how the EU might contribute to better understanding Arctic ecosystems, to promoting sustainable development, and to respecting Arctic governance within Arctic states and beyond.

ARCTIC ENERGY

The United Kingdom has publicly noted its interest in advocating a well-managed process of mineral exploration and extraction. There are two fundamental reasons for such a stance. First, Arctic oil and gas, especially sources in the Norwegian Arctic sector, are likely to continue to be highly important in supplying the U.K. domestic energy demand. Second, U.K.-located companies including BP and Cairn Energy are major players in Arctic energy exploration and exploitation with particular focus on newer energy frontiers such as offshore Greenland.[26] If the Arctic, as is widely believed in the aftermath of a much-cited 2008 U.S. Geological Survey report,[27] does contain substantial unproven reserves in oil and gas, then there is likely to be not only sustained interest in U.K. companies bidding for future licenses from Arctic states but also a desire by U.K. governments to carefully watch market opportunities for further oil and gas supplies in the context of dwindling reserves in the North Sea.

Two Arctic states are particularly important in the context of energy relations—Norway and Russia. In the case of the former, Norway is a major contributor to the U.K. domestic energy mix. As the world's second-largest gas exporter, the United Kingdom is a major market and increasingly so for European customers more generally. Norwegian oil and gas strategy suggests that further investment in the Norwegian and Barents Seas is to be expected, and the Norwegians (through Statoil) will be working closely with Russian partners (e.g., GAZPROM) to help further exploit and develop the Barents Sea region. Russia needs European investment in technology and expertise, and the Norwegians have over forty years of energy-related experience working in the North Sea and the Norwegian Sea. Looking to offshore Arctic resources is also critical to Norway's future revenue streams. The current Norwegian government predicts that oil and gas production will decline around 2020 unless new areas are developed in the High North.

Britain's relationship with Russia is strained, and this is due to a number of reasons, one of which is a fractious commercial relationship between BP and its Russian partners, TNK-BP. The Deepwater Horizon disaster in April 2010 also hurt BP's public credibility and led to growing concern about what damage might have been done if Deepwater Horizon had been operating in the Arctic rather than the warmer waters of the Gulf of Mexico. Notwithstanding the reputational damage, in January 2011, BP signed a joint venture agreement with the Russian energy firm Rosneft for exploiting oil and gas resources on the Russian Arctic continental shelf around the southern part of the Kara Sea. But the deal was undermined by a dispute between BP and its joint venture partners TNK-BP. Since the collapse of the deal in 2011, BP has sought to downplay expectation that it was deeply interested in Russian Arctic energy exploration. But there is a widespread belief that BP is eager to work alongside ExxonMobil and Statoil in developing one of the world's largest opportunities in terms of oil and gas deposits. The shale gas revolution in North America, however, has brought into sharper focus the development and production costs likely to be encountered in the Russian Arctic region.

The United Kingdom has every incentive to ensure that relations with Russia remain workable even if cordiality is not always possible at present.[28] In the case of Norway, a close ally, the relationship is more straightforward and strategic in terms of gas supplies to the United Kingdom (supplying some 40 percent of U.K. current gas demand). Further exploitation is not uncontroversial, however. In their January 2012 U.K. Arctic Principles statement, the World Wide Fund for Nature

(WWF) and associated partners such as Greenpeace called on the U.K. government to refuse to authorize or undertake any new drilling for oil and gas in the offshore Arctic until "gaps" were addressed in three areas —knowledge of Arctic ecosystems and their response to intensifying oil and gas exploration, technological capacity to handle spills and "blow outs" in Arctic waters, and finally the securing of a legally binding international instrument addressing Arctic oil and gas operating standards.[29]

ARCTIC SCIENCE

The United Kingdom has, through its past history of exploration and discovery, been interested in the scientific study of the Arctic.[30] What is particularly noteworthy, however, is in the last decade the profile for Arctic scientific research has grown in the wake of established interest in the Antarctic as manifested in the activities of the British Antarctic Survey (BAS) based in Cambridge. One profound difference, which serves as a reminder that science and politics are never divorced from one another, is that BAS's scientific work remains concentrated in British Antarctic Territory. With substantial territorial, resource, and strategic interests at play in the southwest Atlantic and Antarctic, successive British governments have in the last sixty years committed the United Kingdom to funding and supporting BAS. Funding support increased in the aftermath of the 1982 Falklands/Malvinas conflict when it became clear that the then Conservative government recognized that Argentina was an active and indeed threatening counter-claimant both north and south of the Antarctic Treaty zone of application. Under the terms of the 1959 Antarctic Treaty, claimants and non-claimants alike are expected to put their sovereignty differences to one side in order to concentrate on peaceful coexistence. The terms and conditions imposed by the treaty have suited the United Kingdom in the main because it allowed them to concentrate resources into science without having to worry, on the face of it, about the activities of two counter-claimants, Argentina and Chile.

Building capacity and credibility in Arctic science has thus been a strategic priority for the United Kingdom. It is recognized that the United Kingdom's capacity to influence, more generally, in fora such as the Arctic Council will be enhanced if it is widely considered to be undertaking high-quality research in areas that matter to Arctic states and Northern inhabitants.[31] U.K. involvement in the fourth International Polar Year (2007–2009) amounted to funding of four major projects in the Arctic worth nearly £5 million. In the period between 2011 and 2015, the Natural Environment Research Council (NERC) will invest £15 million in a five-year Arctic research program designed "to improve our capability to predict changes in the Arctic, particularly over timescales of months to decades, including regional impacts and the potential for feedbacks on the global Earth system."[32] Nine projects are currently being funded, focusing on understanding rapid change in Arctic ecosystems, bio-geochemical processes such as methane release, modeling Arctic climate change, ocean warming, and hazards research. Another organization worth noting in terms of scientific output is the U.K. Met Office's Hadley Centre, which contributes research on climate modeling.

NERC, as the main funder of U.K. Arctic science, has through its Arctic Research Programme worked with government departments such as the FCO and the DECC to provide reports on Arctic science and climate change/energy issues respectively.[33] U.K. scientists also assert their collective presence through international scientific conferences and networking and via contributions to Arctic Council–sponsored scientific assessments. Some good examples include U.K. participation in the IASC, which brings together international science associations working in the Arctic. It provides, most notably, independent scientific advice to the Arctic Council through the activities of its five working groups—Terrestrial, Cyrosphere, Marine, Atmosphere, and Social and Human. The U.K. representative on the IASC Council is the current science coordinator of the NERC Arctic Office.

Thus, the decision to create a so-called Arctic Office in May 2009, hosted at BAS headquarters in Cambridge, was highly significant in the aftermath of the International Polar Year. Funded by NERC, it is intended to facilitate research collaboration and assist U.K. polar scientists in accessing either logistical infrastructure or facilities based in the Arctic, namely the NERC Arctic station located at Ny-Ålesund in Svalbard. Established in 1991, the station operates during the spring and summer seasons (April to September) and focuses on polar ecology and life sciences field projects. Up to forty scientists can be housed at the station, and its very presence is taken to be indicative of the United Kingdom's commitment to conduct polar research in the Arctic region. The launch of the Arctic Office was also designed to help manage a recently signed memorandum of understanding between Britain and Canada regarding the sharing of polar logistics, including ships, aircraft, and station facilities in both the Canadian Arctic and the Antarctic Peninsula.

ARCTIC STRATEGY

In January 2009, the then Minister for International Defence and Security, Baroness Ann Taylor, outlined in a joint NATO/Icelandic government conference some U.K. interests in the Arctic. She noted,

> Today, in having this discussion we are explicitly acknowledging that the changing Arctic climate has serious implications for us all...The UK government is evaluating the challenges and opportunities of a melting Arctic. The UK MOD has developed its first Arctic strategy and this was endorsed by the Defence Board in December 2008...It's clear to us that security in the Arctic is not foremost a military concern. We are not returning to the Cold War. But security cannot be divorced from economic activity, environmental interests and political considerations. If ever that was the case, it is certainly not the case now.[34]

This "Arctic strategy" has not been publicly released, but it is known that defense planners in the MOD carried out a desk-top analysis of geopolitical risk and concluded that attention needed to be focused on soft-security issues that were of cross-cutting interest in terms of government departments. No one within the MOD expects the Arctic region to become a scene of discord, but MOD officials will frequently note in private and public that the United Kingdom is a sub-Arctic state especially if one takes into account the 200-nautical-mile exclusive economic zone around the Shetland Islands. The United Kingdom is, widely considered within the U.K. defense community, an Arctic neighbor.

Although recognizing that Cold War tension is not likely to reemerge in the short to medium term, the then Defence Secretary Liam Fox was particularly animated on the subject of the United Kingdom retaining a strategic interest on the "Northern Flank." In 2010, a Northern Group of Defence Ministers[35] was established for the explicit purpose of encouraging regional defense cooperation. In a meeting of defense ministers of the Nordic and Baltic States in January 2011, he proclaimed, "The deepening of our bilateral and multilateral relationships with partners in the Nordic region is well worth exploring. We would like to create a broader framework that makes it easier for both NATO and non-NATO members to have a closer relationship with the region."[36] Deepening bilateral and multilateral relations has, thus, been undertaken with an explicit sense that Britain should be attentive to its northern neighbors, especially NATO allies such as Norway and non-NATO countries including Finland and Sweden.

Between January and March 2012, the United Kingdom and Norway signed two agreements with one another. In January, a Bilateral and Global Partnership was established that committed both countries to strengthening cooperation and interoperability in order to maximize capabilities of the United Kingdom and Norway within a NATO context. In March, a memorandum of understanding (MOU) was declared on the subject of enhancement of bilateral defense cooperation with due emphasis given to situational awareness and strategic surveillance in the High North. However, these agreements with Norway come at a time of substantial defense reductions to U.K. forces and capabilities (as witnessed by the Strategic Defence and Security Review, or SDSR), so it remains to be seen whether the United Kingdom has the resources to pursue more than joint training exercises such as Norwegian-led Exercise Cold Response.[37] The changing state of the Arctic Ocean has not gone unnoticed by U.K. defense planners, even if the Arctic per se is not explicitly mentioned in the SDSR.[38] So participation in military exercises such as Cold Response is valued by both the British and Norwegian militaries alike—the United Kingdom gets to test its capabilities in Arctic-like conditions and Norway reinforces a close relationship with a military ally. In 2013, as noted earlier, one might well see the release of a specific Arctic strategy by the MOD following speculation that the MOD Defence Board's meeting on December 18, 2008, actually endorsed the United Kingdom's first Arctic strategy.[39]

CONCLUSION

In 2006, the House of Lords (Parliament) recognized that the U.K. government did not possess a coherent Arctic strategy. Despite a second House of Lords debate on the "Arctic ice cap" in December 2010, concern was expressed again that this remained the case. In the intervening period, there is growing evidence that is changing, as witnessed in part by the release of reports, media reporting, and the public workings of the House of Commons Environmental Audit Committee. In 2012, the Environmental Audit Committee heard from a number of stakeholders concerning U.K. interests in the Arctic. Henry Bellingham, the Foreign Office Minister responsible for the Arctic, noted in July 2012 that the U.K. government was much preoccupied with better understanding a region that is a "close neighbour" to the United Kingdom.[40] The minister reaffirmed U.K. interest in issues such as climate change, sustainable development, energy, fishing, and shipping and their implications for the Arctic region. The Environment Audit Committee released a report on "Protecting the Arctic" in September 2012,[41] and this will clearly contribute to an ongoing U.K. dialogue about future interest and investment.

Looking ahead, it is highly likely that the United Kingdom's Arctic interests will not diminish in the future. There is much evidence to suggest that U.K. government departments are busy auditing, strategizing, assessing, and monitoring the Arctic region in multiple sites including the United Kingdom and beyond, as well as the NERC research station in Svalbard. Within Whitehall, there remains a debate about whether the United Kingdom should officially develop and indeed publicly release an Arctic strategy. On the one hand, advocates have contended that such a document would highlight and prioritize Arctic interests and help in maintaining political attention at the ministerial level. On the other hand, there is some concern that such a strategy might unsettle Arctic states in suggesting that the United Kingdom could become more forceful in pursuing interests in fields such as energy, fishing, and shipping. As an observer to the Arctic Council and the Barents Euro-Arctic Council, the United Kingdom is in a position to work with European and other states and organizations to represent wider interest in the Arctic while recognizing that care needs to be taken when it comes to jurisdictional matters, indigenous self-determination, and environmental concerns relating to intensifying oil and gas exploitation.

Coda

In October 2013, the United Kingdom published an Arctic Policy Framework, which avoids the word *strategy* and downplays the military/defensive relationships that the United Kingdom has with key NATO partners such as Norway and Canada. For further details, see K. Dodds and D. Depledge, "'No "Strategy" Please, We're British': The UK and the Arctic Policy Framework," *RUSI Journal* 160 (forthcoming 2014).

Notes

1. For a detailed review, see R. David, *The Arctic in the British Imagination 1818–1914* (Manchester: Manchester University Press, 2001).
2. See, for example, F. Spufford, *I May Be Some Time: Ice and the English Imagination* (London: Faber and Faber, 1997).
3. M. Jones, "From Noble Example to Potty Pioneer: Rethinking Scott of the Antarctic c. 1945–2011," *Polar Journal* 2 (2011): 191–206.
4. P. Roberts, *The European Arctic* (London: Palgrave Macmillan, 2011).
5. For one assessment, P. Berkman and O. Young, "Governance and Environmental Change in the Arctic Ocean," *Science* 324, no. 5925 (April 17, 2009): 339–340, http://www.sciencemag.org/content/324/5925/339.summary.
6. For a critique of this particular place-based metaphor, see K. Dodds, "A Polar Mediterranean: Accessibility, Resources and Sovereignty in the Arctic Ocean," *Global Policy* 1 (2011): 303–311.
7. Arctic Climate Impact Assessment, *Arctic Climate Impact Assessment: Scientific Report* (Cambridge: Cambridge University Press, 2005); Arctic Monitoring and Assessment Programme, "Snow, Water, Ice and Permafrost in the Arctic (SWIPA)," 2011, http://amap.no/swipa/.
8. J. McCannon, *The Arctic: A Global History* (London: Reaktion Books, 2012).
9. Foreign and Commonwealth Office [FCO], "The Arctic," 2012, http://www.fco.gov.uk/en/global-issues/polar-regions/uk-engagement-arctic/.
10. T. Koivurova, "Limits and Possibilities of the Arctic Council in a Rapidly Changing Scene of Arctic Governance," *Polar Record* 46 (2010): 146–156.
11. See, for example, C. Archer, *Northern Waters: Resources and Strategic Issues* (New York: Barnes and Noble, 1996).
12. D. Depledge and K. Dodds, "The UK and the Arctic: The Strategic Gap," *RUSI Journal* 156 (2011): 72–79; D. Depledge and K. Dodds, "Testing the Northern Flank: UK-Norwegian Relations and the Arctic," *RUSI Journal* 158 (2012): 72–78.
13. Lloyd's Register *Insight Magazine: Arctic Challenge: Maintaining the Balance*, no. 4 (March 2012), http://www.lr.org/Images/Insight%20issue%204%20Mar%202012_tcm155-236296.pdf.

14. K. Dodds, "The Arctic: From Frozen Desert to Open Polar Sea?" in *Maritime Strategy and Global Order*, ed. D. Moran and J. Russell (Washington, DC: Georgetown University Press, forthcoming 2014).

15. K. Åtland, "Mikhail Gorbachev, the Murmansk Initiative, and the Desecuritization of Inter-State Relations in the Arctic," *Cooperation and Conflict* 43 (2008): 289–311.

16. FCO, "The Arctic."

17. Duncan Depledge, based at Royal Holloway, University of London, and the Royal United Services Institute (RUSI), is completing a doctoral-length study on U.K. Arctic interests.

18. On U.K. energy dilemmas, see M. Bradshaw, "Global Energy Dilemmas: A Geographical Perspective," *Geographical Journal* 176 (2010): 275–290.

19. FCO, "The Arctic."

20. Whitehall is the short-hand term used to describe the area of central London where the main government departments such as the Foreign and Commonwealth Office and the Ministry of Defence are located.

21. An interesting development was the hosting of a meeting of U.K. Arctic stakeholders and reported on in "Report of the Conference held at the Scottish Association for Marine Sciences," March 10–12, 2008. See also Depledge and Dodds, "UK and the Arctic."

22. Depledge and Dodds, "Testing the Northern Flank."

23. For a tenth-anniversary review, T. Koivurova and D. VanderZwaag, "The Arctic Council at 10 Years: Retrospect and Prospects," *University of British Columbia Law Review* 40, no. 1 (2007): 121–194.

24. For an initial view, see P. Berkman and O. Young, "Governance and Environmental Change in the Arctic Ocean." *Science* 324, no. 5925 (April 17, 2009): 339–340, http://www.sciencemag.org/content/324/5925/339. summary.

25. Diana Wallis was a member of the European Parliament between 1999 and 2012.

26. M. Nuttall, "Imaging and Governing the Greenlandic Resource Frontier," *Polar Journal* 2, no. 1 (2012): 113–124.

27. USGS, "Circum-Arctic Resource Appraisal: Estimates of Undiscovered Oil and Gas North of the Arctic Circle," http://pubs.usgs.gov/fs/2008/3049/.

28. For a review of energy prospects, C. Emmerson, "Russia's Arctic Opening," *Foreign Policy*, March 30, 2011, http://www.foreignpolicy.com/articles/2011/03/30/russias_arctic_opening.

29. WWF, "UK Arctic Principles: Principles to Inform a Policy Statement on UK Interests in the Arctic," January 2012.

30. Depledge and Dodds, "UK and the Arctic."
31. FCO, "UK Government Arctic Policy," 2009, http://www. oceanstewardship.com/IOSF%202009/Presentations_2009/RMills_2009. pdf.
32. NERC, "Arctic Research Programme," 2012, http://www.nerc.ac.uk/ research/programmes/arctic/index.asp?cookieConsent=A.
33. NERC, *NERC Arctic Research Programme for the UK: Communication, Engagement & Knowledge Exchange A Strategy 2010–2016* (Swindon: NERC, 2010).
34. Cited in Depledge and Dodds, "UK and the Arctic," 72.
35. The Northern Group of Defence Ministers was established in November 2010, and the membership of the group includes those with direct access to the North Sea, the Baltic, and the Norwegian Sea.
36. Cited in Depledge and Dodds, "Testing the Northern Flank."
37. Exercise Cold Response (EX CR) was established in 2006 and is directed by Norway working with NATO allies including the United Kingdom. EX CR has been held in northern Norway in 2006, 2007, 2009, 2010, and 2012 (and in 2012 in northern Sweden). In 2012, over 16,000 armed forces personnel from fourteen different countries participated. Canada, France, the United Kingdom, the United States, Sweden, and the Netherlands supplied the largest contingents. See also Depledge and Dodds, "Testing the Northern Flank."
38. U.K. forces in the Arctic region are likely to remain modest and tied in part to military exercises hosted by allies such as Canada and Norway. U.K. Atlantic Patrol Task (North) is primarily focused on the Caribbean rather than the North Atlantic in large part because of the presence of overseas U.K. territories in the region.
39. The official minutes pertaining to the "summary of conclusions" of the MOD Defence Board on December 18, 2008, make no reference to Arctic strategy. http://www.mod.uk/NR/rdonlyres/F432C229-CDBB-4296-AC5 A-06C6BD6BA5AB/0/20081218_dbsummary.pdf (page now archived).
40. House of Commons, Evidence presented to the Environment Audit Committee "Protecting the Arctic," 2012, http://www.parliament.uk/ business/committees/committees-a-z/commons-select/environmental-audit-committee/news/announcement-of-report-publication1/.
41. http://www.parliament.uk/business/committees/committees-a-z/ commons-select/environmental-audit-committee/news/announcement-of-report-publication1/.

CHAPTER 19

EMERGING INTERESTS OF NON-ARCTIC COUNTRIES IN THE ARCTIC

CHINA, JAPAN, SOUTH KOREA, AND INDIA

Nong Hong and Anita Dey Nuttall

INTRODUCTION

The new geopolitical realities of the Arctic today are a significant departure from the great power politics that existed in the region during the Cold War era. The supremacy of military presence and security interests of the two superpowers during that time is now replaced by multiple political interests of the eight Arctic states, although dominated mainly by the military and security interests and naval capacity of Russia, Canada, the United States, Norway, and Denmark. Through the Ilulissat Declaration in 2008, these five Arctic coastal states (the Arctic Five) have asserted a predominant role in addressing both territorial issues and emerging issues related to resource development in the Arctic region.[1] Recent moves to resolve boundary disputes by the Arctic Five demonstrate their view of the Arctic as a regional rather than an international territory by preferring to settle disagreements and contested issues bilaterally instead of through international tribunals.

But the exclusivity of the region is countered by the activities of major powers from outside the region, such as the United Kingdom, France, Germany, China, Japan, and India, which take a special interest in many aspects of the Arctic that focus on scientific research, shipping, and resource development. The estimated oil and gas reserves in the continental shelves of the northern seas and visions of new trans-Arctic sea routes are also attracting the attention of transnational corporations that are increasingly becoming interested in the potential commercial value of Arctic energy resources.[2]

This chapter explores the growing interests of a select group of non-Arctic states—China, Japan, South Korea, and India—in the Arctic and examines the nature of their interests and motivations in wanting to maintain both their involvement and a presence in the region in light of their recent admission to the Arctic Council as observer states. The interests of these states range from participating in Arctic governance affairs and accessing potential resources to exploiting shipping opportunities and undertaking polar research.

SEEKING PARTICIPATION IN THE ARCTIC COUNCIL

The Arctic Council is a high-level intergovernmental forum that addresses issues faced by the governments of the eight Arctic states relating to environment preservation, sustainable development, and the cultures and well-being of Arctic peoples. Promoting "cooperation, coordination and interaction amongst Arctic states," the Arctic Council does not deal with security issues and has no binding effect on the parties. However, it is unique as a forum for states in that it allows six indigenous peoples' organizations permanent participant status, giving them full consultation rights in the council's negotiations and decision-making processes.[3]

Observer status at the Arctic Council is open to non-Arctic states, intergovernmental and interparliamentary organizations, and NGOs. States that enjoy "permanent" observer status receive automatic invitations to attend Arctic Council meetings. The participation of the permanent observer states is seen by the council as "a valuable feature through their provision of scientific and other expertise, information and financial resources."[4]

The composition of the observer states until recently had been predominantly European and had included France, Germany, the Netherlands, Poland, Spain, and the United Kingdom. The changing geopolitical realities in the region as a result of climate change that enable accessibility to potential Arctic resources have broadened the international focus on the Arctic to include more geographically distant countries such as China, Japan, South Korea, and India. These four Asian countries have viewed seeking observer status in the Arctic Council as an important step toward formalizing their involvement in determining the course of the future of the Arctic region, which they perceive will have an impact on their economic interests and global environmental concerns.

In May 2013, China, India, Italy, Japan, South Korea, and Singapore were granted observer status at the eighth ministerial meeting of the Arctic Council in Kiruna, Norway,[5] increasing the membership of this group to twelve states. As the Norwegian Foreign Minister Espen Barth Eide stated, "There is no such thing as a free lunch. By becoming an observer you're also signing up to the principles embodied by this organization."[6] These non-Arctic states have been working hard to make that happen, though some analysts still question the new criteria for permanent observer status on the Arctic Council.[7]

As a maritime state, Japan has long shown interest in the developments in the Arctic region, including its participation as an observer at the Ottawa conference in 1996 that launched the establishment of the Arctic Council from the Arctic Environmental Protection Strategy (AEPS) framework. The government of Japan expressed interest in gaining greater access to discussions and negotiations on the Arctic. It had submitted its application to the Arctic Council for observer status in 2009. An official at the Japanese Foreign Ministry's Ocean Division remarked, "If Japan is admitted as an observer of the council, we'll have the advantage of being able to collect information on matters of concern to each country related to the utilization of the Arctic Circle."[8] At the meeting between the Swedish chairmanship of the Arctic Council and observers/ad hoc observers in Stockholm in November 2012, the parliamentary senior vice-minister for Foreign Affairs of Japan, Shuji Kira, reaffirmed Japan's intent on cooperation with the Arctic states and reiterated that "once granted the observer status, Japan will be ready to further contribute to the Arctic Council by sharing its expertise built upon its years of research and observation of the Arctic, enjoying more stable status than ad-hoc one."[9] Japan could benefit greatly from the opening of the Northwest Passage because it would establish a route circumventing the Suez Canal and shorten transit times between Asia and Europe by 40 percent.[10]

With a growing reputation of having an edge in shipbuilding and engineering, South Korea sees the thawing Arctic as an opportunity to have a stake on "future sea routes to ensure stable energy supplies and liven up its shipbuilding, logistics and trading industries."[11] In August and September 2012, South Korea's then president Lee Myung-bak's visit to Greenland and Norway reflected the country's anticipation of economic opportunities in the Arctic, placing emphasis on the importance of "forg[ing] a future-oriented partnership aimed at tackling climate change and environment-friendly development and preservation of the Arctic."[12] South Korea viewed an economic cooperation agreement signed with Norway as gaining support from this Arctic state to back Seoul's bid for permanent observer status. "Being an observer of the Arctic Council will help us enter the discussion among the Arctic nations over preservation and development of the area. That will also help our government brainstorm policies on development of marine transportation," a ministry official told *The Korea Times*.[13]

India's association with the Arctic was anchored at the time of British India when Britain and its overseas dominions became signatories to the Svalbard Treaty of 1920. By virtue of history and colonial relations, India became a "stakeholder" in the Arctic, but it was not until 2007 that India made its first official expression of interest in the region with the launch of an Arctic research program in Svalbard. For India,

> [t]he Arctic cannot be at the margins of India's mental map and New Delhi must find its way to the center of the evolving Arctic order and issues which will challenge and define the High North politics in the 21st Century: oil and gas to ensure energy security, marine living and non-living wealth for resource security, new shipping routes shaping global trade patterns, great power competition and above all climate change, global warming and its consequences that will result in melting of sea ice and permafrost and impact on people and ecosystems even in the tropics.[14]

However, political thinking in India regarding its involvement in the Arctic and engagement with the Arctic Council has ranged from critiquing the exclusiveness of the council and voicing a preference for treating the Arctic as a global commons subject to an international legal regime along the lines of the Antarctic Treaty, to calling for serious consideration in becoming an observer state within the Arctic Council.[15]

Initially the argument against membership in the Arctic Council suggested that "India should consider carefully whether it should pursue its reported application to join the Arctic Council as a permanent observer...it should be noted that a condition for being granted this status is acceptance of the sovereign rights of the Arctic Council members over the Arctic Ocean. India should instead press for the Antarctic Treaty template."[16] This thinking was, however, superseded by an acknowledgment that it would, in fact, serve India better if it applied for observer status in the Arctic Council. Arguing for observer status, Sakhuja pointed to the need for India to forge strong relationships with the Arctic Council members and increase cooperation with Nordic countries by establishing bilateral dialogues and discussions to understand the evolving developments in the Arctic region. He called for India to have an "Arctic Strategy" that not only promotes the idea of a nuclear-free Arctic but would also include undertaking Arctic resource assessment and exploitation studies; sending regular expeditions to the Arctic and consolidating scientific research; and developing technological capability to exploit Arctic living and non-living resources.[17]

In October 2012, a senior Ministry of External Affairs (MEA) official told *The Indian Express*, a major national newspaper, that "India will apply for being a permanent observer in the Arctic Council...We have to make a case for India's application, pointing out that we meet all the seven conditions for being a permanent observer."[18] Supporting this statement, Shailesh Nayak, secretary of the Union Ministry of Earth Sciences, told national media, "We are seeking an observer status in the Arctic Council as we want to undertake scientific studies from Antarctica to the Arctic. We receive inputs on North Atlantic temperature from our station (*Himadri*) to study the ocean currents."[19]

Connected to India's position on wanting observer status is, no doubt, the political calculation India made when noting China's efforts at gaining permanent observer status at the Arctic Council. India's historic rivalry with China—which saw two wars fought between them, as well as their competing geostrategic ambitions centering on the Siachen Glacier in the eastern Karakoram range of the Himalaya mountains (the Hindu Kush-Himalayan and Tibetan plateau region is often regarded as the "Third Pole")—brings another geopolitical dimension to the nature of the interests expressed by these two large Asian countries in the polar regions, particularly the developments taking place in the Arctic.

Compared to the other three Asian states that expressed interest in developments in the Arctic, it is China's northward gaze that continues to receive the most attention in political, media, and academic circles. Much of this arises from the perceived concern over the impact a vast, resource-hungry economy such as China's will have on the Arctic, where new maritime routes for trade could potentially be charted and resources such as hydrocarbons and minerals could become economically viable for exploitation.

Since 2007, China has participated as an ad hoc observer at Arctic Council meetings, which allowed it to gain a better understanding of the council's work. It had also officially expressed its intentions to become a permanent observer to the Arctic Council since 2008. Although no official policy by China has yet been articulated for the Arctic, different voices are heard in China's academic circles on how China should approach Arctic governance. Guo Peiqing, a law professor from China's Ocean University, held that China has great strategic interest in the Arctic, but rather than adopting a "neutral" position as an outsider, it should push for the internationalization of the region instead.[20] In connection with this point of view, some other scholars see Guo's proposal of internationalizing the Arctic as posing a risk of damaging China's image in the international community, given that taking such a stance would not conform to its consistent position supporting a principle of "non-interference."

Although Hu Zhengyue, the Chinese assistant Minister of Foreign Affairs, has said, "China does not have an Arctic strategy," China does appear to have a clear agenda regarding the Arctic.[21] In his speech at Svalbard, Hu acknowledged that the Arctic is mainly a regional issue but said that it is also an inter-regional issue because of climate change and international shipping. Unsurprisingly, China would like to see the Arctic states recognize the interests of non-Arctic states.[22]

A statement by Ambassador Lan Lijun at a meeting between the Swedish chairmanship of the Arctic Council and observers in November

2012 reaffirmed China's view on the importance of involving non-Arctic states at the Arctic Council:

> Arctic issues are trans-regional, such as climate change and international shipping, which involve the interests of non-Arctic states. Arctic states and non-Arctic states share common interests in addressing trans-regional issues and should further their communication and cooperation.[23]

The statement also recognized that the "participation of observers in the work of the Council is based on the recognition of Arctic States' sovereignty, sovereign rights and jurisdiction in the Arctic as well as their decision-making power in the Council."

INTERESTS IN SHIPPING

China, Japan, and South Korea in particular see the melting Arctic Ocean as a unique opportunity for international trade and potential access to resources. In September 2012, China's icebreaker *Xue Long* (*Snow Dragon*) made history by becoming the first vessel from China to cross the Arctic Ocean. The eighty-five-day voyage (the vessel crossed from the Pacific to the Atlantic and carried out oceanographic research) was a reminder of Beijing's interests in increasing its presence in the Arctic. The Shanghai-based Polar Research Institute of China said in a statement that the *Snow Dragon* gained "first-hand information about navigation in Arctic sea lanes as well as the oceanic environment, and carried out useful exploration and practice for our nation's ships that use Arctic passages in the future."[24]

China has been ranked as the world's third-largest trading country and fourth most important maritime state on the basis of the size of its merchant fleet and its 6.77 percent contribution to the world's total tonnage.[25] China (excluding Hong Kong and Taiwan) experienced a 12.7 percent growth rate of merchandise exports in 2010.[26] Because China's economy is reliant on foreign trade—46 percent of its GDP is thought to be shipping dependent—there are substantial commercial implications if shipping routes are shortened during the summer months each year.[27] For instance, the voyage from Shanghai to Hamburg via the Northern Sea Route—which runs along the north coast of Russia from the Bering Strait in the east to Novaya Zemlya in the west—is 6,400 kilometers shorter than the route via the Strait of Malacca and the Suez Canal.[28] The shortest route for maritime transport between Europe and Asia may then transit via the Barents Sea, reducing substantially the maritime distance between Western Europe and Asia by over 7,400 kilometers, providing strategic alternatives to countries such as China, and potentially making it a key player because of its shipping industry and current dependence on foreign energy.[29]

Any events that affect international shipping will have a measure-able effect on the Chinese economy and its dependence on it; and the changing physical landscape of the Arctic region will certainly have a major impact on China's economic future.

China is 4,000 nautical miles closer to the European Union and to the east coast of North America when sailing across the Arctic Ocean, and currently there are no vessel size restrictions and other regulations, unlike in the Suez or Panama Canals. There are at present no fees for Arctic routes. In addition, the smaller ecological footprint of reduced fuel costs per ton-mile might also be an added incentive for the development of an Arctic route. Arctic shipping could be another aspect of the new green wave that is sweeping the shipping industry, as more attention is being paid to the environmental impact of shipping, including fuel effi-ciency and emission reduction of commercial shipping.[30]

Li Zhenfu, an associate professor at Dalian Maritime University, and a team of specialists have assessed China's advantages and disadvan-tages when the Arctic sea routes open up. "Whoever has control over the Arctic route will control the new passage of world economics and inter-national strategies," wrote Li, referring to the shortened shipping routes between East Asia and Europe or North America and to the abundant oil, gas, mineral, and fishery resources presumed to be in the Arctic.[31]

Commenting on the successful test voyages from South Korea to the Netherlands via the Northeast Passage by two German commercial vessels in the summer of 2009, Chen Xulong of the China Institute of International Studies wrote that "the opening of the Arctic route will advance the development of China's north-east region and eastern coastal area...It is of importance to East Asian cooperation as well."[32]

The ship design technology currently exists for vessels to operate year-round in the Arctic. It simply needs to make economic sense. It appears that China has not engaged in the development of ice technology, which tends to be dominated by the Nordic countries, and the focus in recent years has been the development of the Russian gas field in the Barents Sea.[33] Yet the technology is commercially readily available, and technology transfer agreements could be developed between ship design and engineering firms and China. This approach has been used in South Korean shipyards for new vessel construction destined for the ice-breaking tankers used in the Russian Arctic gas fields. It is likely that China will soon come up to speed on this technology.

On November 22, 2010, the Sovcomflot Group (SCF), a Russian maritime company specializing in shipping petroleum and liquid natural gas (LNG), and the China National Petroleum Corporation (CNPC) signed a strategic long-term cooperation agreement. The parties agreed to develop a partnership in the sphere of seaborne energy solutions, with the SCF fleet serving the continually growing Chinese imports of hydrocarbons. Taking into account the significant experience gained by SCF in developing the transportation of hydrocarbons in Arctic seas, SCF and CNPC agreed upon the format for coordination in using the transportation potential of the Northern Sea Route along Russia's Arctic coast, both for delivering transit shipments of hydrocarbons and for the transportation of oil and gas from Russia's developing Arctic offshore fields to China. A new fleet of tankers designed to operate in ice as well as additional heavy-duty icebreakers will be built to that end. In an article that appeared in the *Financial Times* of London in January 2008, Robert Wade of the London School of Economics wrote about China's special interest in Iceland:

> Tiny Iceland suddenly takes on new geo-economic significance. It sits at the mouth of the Arctic Ocean, ideally located for transhipment of cargoes to or from giant container ships travelling between Iceland and a transhipment port in the Bering Sea. It has at least three plausible deep fjord sites. China maintains the biggest of all the embassies in Reykjavik and it welcomed the president of Iceland with all the pomp normally reserved for the head of a major state on his visit in 2007. [China] has been very helpful as Iceland seeks election to the United Nations Security Council in 2008.[34]

South Korea, by contrast, is interested in the economic benefit of Arctic shipping, given that it hosts the largest shipbuilding yards in the world. Samsung Heavy Industries has developed a double-acting vessel that has the same open sea characteristics as other ships in its class combined with the breaking capacity of an icebreaker. Whereas the bow is shaped for regular sailing, the stern is designed for ice-breaking, with the ship turned around when there is heavy ice and the stern used as the bow. South Korean industry (and, incidentally, its subsidiaries in Finland) thus has a vested economic interest in the development of a trans-Arctic shipping route and industry.[35] South Korea's Samsung Heavy Industries is looking into filling the technological gap to make it possible to deliver Arctic natural gas across the Pacific. Construction is underway on two 70,000-tonne ships and two more 125,000-tonne ships, and there are rumors that another five are on order.[36]

With the same interests in shipping as its neighbor China, Japan also calls for joining hands with the United States and other Arctic states in ongoing multilateral efforts to create a new shipping regime in the Arctic Ocean. Japan believes that as a result of receding sea ice, caused by global warming, the Arctic is expected to open up for global shipping in the future. This will present strategic options for Japan's industry in light of shorter shipping routes from Japan to Europe via the Arctic Ocean. Yoichi Fujiwara, a spokesman for the Japanese Embassy in Ottawa, said, "We are interested in environmental programs, and transportation or passage through the Arctic area, and development of resources in the Arctic Circle."[37]

From Japan's perspective, ships traveling from Yokohama to Rotterdam cover 21,000 kilometers. The Arctic route could reduce that distance to 13,000 kilometers and the travel time to twenty-five days. According to Japan's Transport Ministry, the northern route could cut total one-way shipping costs by 40 percent, including sailing fees, personnel expenses, and fuel. As Borgerson pointed out,

> Japan, which is vitally dependent on the Strait of Malacca for the overwhelming majority of its energy supplies, would be a natural investor in such a project since it has an interest in limiting the risk of a disruption in its oil supply.[38]

Like most nations, India is a full member of the International Maritime Organization (IMO) and is following closely the developments as regards a new polar shipping code currently being developed by the IMO. India may, however, see the opening up of the Arctic with the potential for shorter shipping routes and impact on world shipping from a slightly different lens. The impact of an emerging polar sea route could potentially take away shipping for four months a year from the Indian Ocean region, where Indian ports draw an increasing amount of global mercantile traffic. Given the high volume of traffic in the Indian Ocean, India is placing the highest priority on the development of its maritime sector based on its location. For example, in January 2011, India's Minister of Shipping, G. K. Vasan, launched India's ten-year Maritime Agenda (2010–2020), which called for an investment of about $36 billion (165,000 crores rupees) in the sector. Among the goals of India's long-term maritime agenda are to create a port capacity of around 3,200 million tons to handle an anticipated traffic of about 2,500 million tons by 2020;

to put India's ports on par with the best international ports in terms of performance and capacity; to increase India's share in global shipbuilding to 5 percent from the present 1 percent; and to increase the percentage of Indian seafarers in the global shipping industry from between 6 and 7 percent to at least 9 percent by 2015.[39] Gadihoke pointed out,

> Given such endeavours, the Arctic melt, with its potential to divert the shipping traffic away from the Indian peninsula, will need to get factored into India's long term maritime development plan. This is owing to the fact that the container volumes and shipping loads, handled by India's present and future ports, which are astride the main east-west sea transportation lanes in the Indian Ocean Region, may decrease for four months a year.[40]

For China, Japan, South Korea, India, and other non-Arctic states, one fundamental question is their position on the legal status of the Northwest Passage and the Northern Sea Route. Sooner or later, they have to adopt a clear position on whether these two passages enjoy the status of international waters for navigation, as the United States and the European Union hold, or whether they are internal waters, as Canada and Russia insist on. Alexeeva and Lasserre pointed out that non-Arctic states such as China have far more to gain by cooperating with Arctic states. For example, should China take the position of the United States and the EU, it will weaken its own argument that Qiongzhou Strait, between Hainan and Continental China, lies in China's internal waters.[41] It is worth noting, however, that Qiongzhou Strait has rarely, if ever, been a question for debate, whereas the Northwest Passage and the Northern Sea Route have been at the core of academic debate.

INTERESTS IN RESOURCE DEVELOPMENT

The U.S. Geological Survey estimates that the Arctic contains up to 30 percent of the world's undiscovered gas and 13 percent of the world's undiscovered oil. Successful development of these reserves would help to alleviate the pressure on the global oil and gas markets and potentially enhance energy security as a result.[42]

The melting of Arctic sea ice in combination with developments elsewhere concerning future energy security have led to some commentators and analysts constructing scenarios of different futures for the region that range from low-level friction to potential conflict between Arctic states, which leads to the legal question of who owns the energy resources in those parts of the Arctic that do not fall under national jurisdiction.[43]

The United Nations Convention on the Law of the Sea (UNCLOS) contains provisions regarding the delineation of the outer limits of continental shelves and maritime boundaries. It obliges states to submit their boundary claims to the UN Commission on the Limits of the Continental Shelf (CLCS) within ten years of ratifying UNCLOS.[44] Russia, the United States, Canada, Denmark, and Norway have all claimed a twelve-nautical-mile territorial sea and a 200-nautical-mile exclusive economic zone (EEZ) in the Arctic Ocean. Like the EEZ, the continental shelf automatically extends out to 200 nautical miles, save for the need for a boundary with a neighboring state. Within the extended continental shelf, a state has sovereign rights on and under the seabed, including hydrocarbons (e.g., oil, gas, and gas hydrates), minerals, and the like. In the Arctic Ocean, it is thought that 88 percent of the seabed is subject to coastal state control if all the claims are accepted as presented.

Article 136 of UNCLOS provides that the "Area" beyond national jurisdiction and its resources are the common heritage of mankind and declares, "No State shall claim or exercise sovereignty or sovereign rights over any part of the Area or its resources. All rights in the resources of the Area are vested in mankind as a whole, on whose behalf the International Seabed Authority shall act."[45] The non-Arctic states have interests in the exploration and exploitation of the natural resources in the seabed beyond the jurisdiction of any Arctic states in this region. However, the general conduct of states in relation to the Area shall be in accordance with the provisions of UNCLOS, the principles embodied in the Charter of the United Nations, and other rules of international law in the interests of maintaining peace and security and promoting international cooperation. Outside the EEZ (200 nautical miles) the waters in the Arctic Ocean are considered to be the High Seas under Part XI of the Law of the Sea Convention. To this purpose, these non-Arctic states, with no sovereignty claims and coasts, see their interests only as access to resources in the Area. Before the CLCS comes out with any recommendation to the Arctic states who have submitted applications, it is too early to define what the boundary between national jurisdiction and the Area will be.

The forecast by the International Energy Outlook 2011 published by the U.S. Energy Information Administration suggests that the world energy consumption will grow by 53 percent from 2008 to 2035. It points to Asia's rapidly growing economies, which will be the primary drivers of increasing global energy demand. China and India are emerging as major importers of oil. By 2035, China's and India's combined energy use are projected to account for 31 percent of total world energy consumption.[46] Chinese companies, some with close government ties, are investing heavily across the Arctic. In Canada, Chinese firms have acquired interests in two oil companies that could afford them access to Arctic drilling. India has also managed to reach the Arctic for its resources. A consortium led by the public-sector unit Oil and Natural Gas Corporation (ONGC) has recently acquired a 15 percent stake, worth US $3.4 billion, in the South Tambeyskoye LNG project on the northeastern part of the Yamal Peninsula, being developed by Russia's largest independent natural gas producer, Novatek. ONGC has also acquired stakes in oil and gas fields in Sakhalin in Russia's Far East.

INTERESTS IN POLAR RESEARCH

China is taking a much more active role in intensifying research in both the Arctic and Antarctic and maintains an active polar research program. China opened its first Arctic scientific research station, Huang He Zhan (Yellow River Station), at Ny-Ålesund in Svalbard in 2004. Furthermore, with the world's largest non-nuclear research icebreaker, *Xue Long*, China has embarked on four Arctic research expeditions in recent years into Arctic waters. Chinese research scientists from the fourth research expedition traveled to the North Pole via the vessel's helicopter on August 20, 2010.[47] Such activities are part of China's larger polar scientific research effort, which has seen a total of twenty-six expeditions in the Arctic and Antarctic since 1984. Viewing itself as a "near Arctic state," China perceives the environmental changes and economic development happening in the Arctic to have "a significant impact on [its] climate, ecological environment, agricultural production as well as social and economic development."[48]

Affiliated with the State Oceanic Administration, the Chinese Arctic and Antarctic Administration (CAA) is the national competent authority that organizes, coordinates, and supervises Chinese Arctic and Antarctic expeditions. The functions of CAA cover the following areas: (1) drawing up the development strategies, principles, and policies of Chinese Arctic and Antarctic expeditions, framing the expedition plan, and formulating the corresponding laws, regulations, and rules concerning polar activities; (2) organizing the examination and verification of major projects on infrastructure and large-scale material equipment for Chinese polar expeditions and being responsible for the implementation supervision and acceptance check of the projects; (3) establishing major polar scientific research projects, formulating the implementation plan and supervising the practice, and managing the data, samples, files, and scientific results of polar expeditions; (4) organizing and participating in international affairs and the organizations involved in polar research.

The Polar Research Institute of China (PRIC) was founded in 1989 and coordinates national polar research. PRIC is the domestic base and provides logistics for Chinese National Arctic/Antarctic Research Expeditions (CHINARE); it is also in charge of running and managing the M/V *Xue Long* and the Great Wall and Zhongshan Antarctic stations.

China has taken steps to augment Arctic scientific cooperation and governmental dialogue with Norway and relevant cooperation with Canada and United States. Although it has enjoyed Arctic scientific cooperation with Russia, there has not yet been any formal governmental dialogue between the two countries. Norway has welcomed China's increased involvement in polar research. The Norwegian Minister of Research and Higher Education Tora Aasland, who attended the signing ceremony in Shanghai of an agreement on cooperation on polar research, said, "Chinese polar researchers are among the best in the world, and we are happy that China is now investing increased efforts in polar research."[49]

In Japan, scientists have been involved in Arctic research since the 1950s, but it was not until 1990 that Arctic research became institutionalized under the aegis of the Arctic Environment Research Center (AERC). AERC was established within the National Institute of Polar Research (NIPR) in June 1990 and reorganized in April 2004. The center aims to cooperate with researchers at universities and other research institutes as a central aspect of the organization of Japanese Arctic and Antarctic research. The center is responsible for the management and the administration of the Japanese research station at Ny-Ålesund, is in charge of the collection of Arctic information and data, and publishes the Arctic Research Directory.[50] Other institutions engaged in Arctic research in Japan include the Japan Agency for Marine-Earth Science and Technology (JAMSTEC), the Japan Aerospace Exploration Agency (JAXA), and universities such as Hokkaido University, Tokyo University of Marine Science, and Kitami Institute of Technology. Japan's Arctic research focuses on understanding the mechanism of warming amplification in the Arctic, understanding the Arctic system for global climate and future change, evaluation of the effects of Arctic change on weather in Japan, marine ecosystems and fisheries, prediction of sea ice distribution, and effects upon Arctic sea routes.[51]

Japan also established the International Arctic Research Center (IARC) in 1999. Based in Alaska, the research institute is focused on integrating and coordinating study of climate change in the Arctic. The primary partners in IARC are Japan and the United States. Participants include organizations from Canada, China, Denmark, Germany, Japan, Norway, Russia, the United Kingdom, and the United States. In a statement at an Arctic Council meeting of deputy ministers in Stockholm in May 2012, the Japanese delegation outlined that it has taken two major steps to promote Arctic environmental research:

> First, the Japanese Ministry of Education, Culture, Sports, Science and Technology (MEXT) launched a new interdisciplinary Arctic science project to clarify and evaluate the global influence of the Arctic, entitled the "Green Network of Excellence (GRENE)" project. The GRENE project will be conducted for five years, focusing on four strategic topics regarding the Arctic environment. Second, the Japan Consortium for Arctic Environmental Research (JCAR) was initiated, with the participation of approximately 300 researchers. JCAR was established in order to strengthen research capability and collaboration among relevant researchers, and it will address long-term Arctic environmental research planning, human resource development, and community outreach inside and outside Japan.[52]

South Korea's polar research history began in 1987 with the Polar Research Center of Ocean Research Institute, which was set up as part of an Antarctic station construction program. Since then, it has expanded from a polar research laboratory to a polar research institute, a subsidiary research unit of the Korea Ocean Research Institute. The Korea Polar Research Institute is now an international polar institute operating the King Sejong Station in Antarctica and the Dasan Station in the Arctic.

South Korea actively participates in several relevant international orga-nizations, such as the Antarctic Treaty Consultative Parties (ATCP), the Scientific Committee on Antarctic Research (SCAR), and the Interna-tional Arctic Science Committee (IASC), and became recognized inter-nationally by publishing research achievements in prominent interna-tional journals. Since 2002, South Korea has run the Arctic research station Dasan at Ny-Ålesund, conducting research on climate and marine species ecology.

India's involvement and interest in the Arctic evolved from its long-term engagement in the Antarctic, where it has been sending annual scientific expeditions since 1981 and maintains two year-round research stations (Maitri and Bharti). Since then India has developed a long-term national polar research program that included research in the Arctic beginning in 2007. More than seventy institutions including universities and research institutes participate and contribute to India's polar research programs. The National Centre for Antarctic and Ocean Research (NCAOR) in Goa, an autonomous institution under the Ministry of Earth Sciences, is the designated agency for polar research in India. Coinciding with the Fourth International Polar Year (IPY), 2007–2008, India's national Arctic research program was launched in August 2007, and India became the eleventh country to establish a full-fledged research station, Himadri, in Svalbard. NCAOR is charged with the planning, coordination, promotion, and implementation of India's polar research programs in order to ensure that India maintains an influen-tial presence in both Antarctica and the Arctic and upholds its strategic interests in the polar regions. The changing climate of the Arctic region has a special significance for India because of the potential impact it could have on "Indian monsoons...which forms the backbone of [the] Indian economy."[53] India's Arctic research program thus has a focus on climate change in the region; its major objectives were outlined in 2009 during a session of Question Hour of the Lok Sabha (Lower House), the Parliament of India, as follows:

(1) To study the hypothesized tele-connections between the Arctic climate and the Indian monsoon by analyzing the sediment and ice core records from the Arctic glaciers and the Arctic Ocean;

(2) To characterize sea ice in the Arctic using satellite data to estimate the effect of global warming in the northern polar region;

(3) To research the dynamics and mass budget of Arctic glaciers to focus on the effect of glaciers on sea-level change and on the fresh input into fjords and embayments;

(4) To carry out a comprehensive assessment of the flora and fauna of the Arctic vis-à-vis their response to anthropogenic activities. In addition, it is proposed to undertake a comparative study of the life forms from both the polar regions in terms of environment.[54]

So far India has undertaken several expeditions to the Arctic and has commissioned a dedicated vessel to support research in both polar regions.[55] The Ministry of Earth Sciences has also signed a memorandum of understanding (MOU) with the Norwegian Polar Institute in Tromsø, indicating that both parties consider that the "potential for enhancing collaborative polar research between India and Norway is immense... Such collaborative research, the scientists of the two countries believe, will yield new insights into the effects of climate change...Geology, glaciology and bacteriology were identified as the key areas for future collaboration in polar science[and] for joint exploration and investigations."[56] Relations between India and Iceland are also strong, with Iceland supportive of India's bid for observer status at the Arctic Council. In November 2012, a four-member delegation from the Icelandic Parliament (which included the Speaker) visited India to discuss strengthening political relations and economic cooperation (as well as inaugurating the new Icelandic consulate general in Chennai). During the visit, the Speaker of the Lok Sabha expressed gratitude for Iceland's position in relation to India's efforts to achieve observer status.[57]

CONCLUSION

The gradual disappearance of Arctic sea ice raises serious sovereignty and security issues, some of which are increasingly evident in evolving relationships between the eight Arctic states and observer states such as China, Japan, South Korea, and India. In the same token, there is a strong and practical need to strengthen international cooperation on Arctic matters. The interrelations among the Arctic states involve sovereignty issues, jurisdiction claims, resource competition, and military capacity expansion, while non-Arctic interests in the region draw into the picture new elements of access through international shipping, seabed resources exploitation, environmental concern, scientific research, and so on. The involvement of a growing group of observer states will likely have a significant impact on the nature of Arctic governance and the effectiveness of the Arctic Council.

Some of the most critical Arctic issues are national, but many of them are regional or transregional concerning environmental impacts of climate change, shipping, and resource development, which require a more comprehensive understanding of the causes and influences of natural variability and human-induced environmental changes in the Arctic. The areas of international Arctic cooperation are continuously expanding, creating enormous potential as well as significant challenges. Arctic cooperation began in the early 1990s with a focus on environmental protection and scientific research but quickly expanded to encompass sustainable development. Cooperation between Arctic and non-Arctic states has continued to develop on a number of levels, either bilaterally or within the existing frameworks of regional fora and international organizations, on scientific research, environmental protection, and sustainable development.

Recognizing and respecting each other's rights constitutes the legal basis for cooperation between Arctic and non-Arctic states. In accordance with UNCLOS and other relevant international legal frameworks, Arctic states have sovereign rights and jurisdiction in their respective areas in the Arctic region, though non-Arctic states also enjoy rights of scientific research and navigation. To strengthen a partnership of cooperation, Arctic states and observer states have to work on the basis of recognizing and respecting each other's rights under international law.

Second, mutual understanding and trust provide the political guarantee for cooperation between Arctic and non-Arctic states. Arctic states, with a larger stake in Arctic-related issues, argue that they should play a more important role in Arctic affairs than non-Arctic countries. In the meantime, given the transregional implications of certain Arctic issues, non-Arctic states that fall under such influence also argue that they have legitimate interests in Arctic-related issues. With their interests intertwined, the recent inclusion of a further six new states as observers in the Arctic Council is evidence of the recognition of non-Arctic states' stakes in the region.

Third, joint research endeavors addressing transregional issues represent the major field of cooperation between Arctic and non-Arctic states. Enhanced cooperation in scientific research will enable Arctic and non-Arctic states to view transregional issues from a wider perspective, send a more comprehensive message to the international scientific community, and facilitate the settlement of relevant issues. This model of cooperation has already yielded sound results in addressing such issues as climate change and Arctic shipping.

Arctic and non-Arctic states have different rights, interests, and specific concerns with regard to Arctic-related issues. However, peace, stability, and sustainable development in the Arctic serve the common interests of both, and mutually beneficial cooperative partnerships that promote and enhance these interests will surely be the most appropriate way forward in a region of growing global importance.

NOTES

1. Brooks B. Yeager, "The Ilulissat Declaration: Background and Implications for Arctic Governance," Arctic Governance Project, November 5, 2008, http://arcticgovernance.custompublish.com/the-ilulissat-declaration-background-and-implications-for-arctic-governance.4626039-137746. html.
2. J. Robinson, "The Power of Petroleum," *Newsweek*, November 4, 2007, 21.
3. http://www.arctic-council.org/.
4. "Observer Recommendation by Arctic Council Deputy Ministers," Deputy Ministers' Meeting, Stockholm, May 15, 2012, http://www. arctic-council.org/index.php/en/about/documents/category/118-deputy-ministers-meeting-stockholm-15-may-2012.
5. CBC News, "Arctic Council Grants China, Japan Observer Status," May 15, 2013, http://www.cbc.ca/news/canada/north/arctic-council-grants-china-japan-observer-status-1.1375121.
6. Ibid.
7. Guo Peiqing, "Analysis of New Criteria for Permanent Observer Status on the Arctic Council and the Role of Non-Arctic States to Arctic," *KMI International Journal of Maritime Affairs and Fisheries* 4, no. 2 (2012): 21.
8. Ibid.
9. Meeting between the Swedish Chairmanship of the Arctic Council and Observers/Ad Hoc Observers Stockholm, Sweden, November 6, 2012, Statement by Parliamentary Senior Vice-Minister for Foreign Affairs of Japan Mr. Shuji Kira, http://www.mofa.go.jp/announce/svm/pdfs/statement121108.pdf.
10. Mia Bennett, "Japan Applies for Arctic Council Observer Status," *Foreign Policy Association*, April 20, 2009, http://arctic.foreignpolicyblogs.com/2 009/04/20/japan-applies-for-arctic-council-observer-status/.
11. Shin Hyon-hee, "S. Korea Seeks Bigger Role in Arctic," *Korea Herald*, May 15, 2012, http://www.asianewsnet.net/home/news.php?id=30743.
12. An Myungok,"President Lee Steps into the Arctic Circle for South Koreas Arctic Initiative," *Korea Net*, September 17, 2012, http://www.korea.net/NewsFocus/Policies/view?articleId=102568.
13. Kim Se-jeong, "Korea Wants to Join in Arctic Projects," *Korea Times*, August 24, 2009,http://www.koreatimes.co.kr/www/news/special/2009/04/176_29902.html.

14. Vijay Sakhuja, "The Arctic Council: Is There a Case for India," Indian Council of World Affairs Policy Brief, New Delhi, January 12, 2010, 5, http://www.icwa.in/pdfs/policy%20briefs%20dr.pdf.
15. S. Chaturvedi, "Geopolitical Transformations: 'Rising' Asia and the Future of the Arctic Council," in *The Arctic Council: Its Place in the Future of Arctic Governance and the Future of the Arctic Council,* ed. T. Axworthy, T. Koivurova, and W. Hasanat (Toronto: Munk-Gordon Arctic Security Program, 2012), 233, http://gordonfoundation.ca/publication/530.
16. Shyam Saran, "India's Stake in Arctic Cold War," *Hindu,* February 1, 2012, http://www.thehindu.com/opinion/op-ed/article2848280.ece.
17. Sakhuja, "Is There a Case for India," 4.
18. Devirupa Mitra, "Taking Cue from China, India Eyeing Arctic Region," *Indian Express,* October 2, 2012, http://newindianexpress.com/nation/article1282303.ece.
19. Kalyan Ray, "Resource-Hungry India Seeks a Seat at the Arctic Table," *Deccan Herald,* January 15, 2012, http://www.deccanherald.com/content/219579/resource-hungry-india-seeks-seat.html%20%20.
20. Guo Peiqing et al., eds., 北极航道的国际问题研究 [A study of the international issues of the Arctic route] (Beijing: Ocean Press, 2009), 323–326.
21. X. Ning, "Di qui weilai de suo yin: waijiaobubuzhangzhu li tan 'beijiyjanjiuzhi lv'" [A microcosm of the world's future—Assistant Minister of Foreign Affairs talks about "High North Study Tour"], *Shijie Bolan* 349, no. 19 (2009): 58.
22. Ibid.
23. Jóhanna Vagadal Joensen, "A New Chinese Arctic Policy? An Analysis of China's Policies towards the Arctic in the Post-Cold War Period," thesis, Aarhus University, 2013, http://www.academia.edu/4675427/A_New_Chinese_Arctic_Policy_An_Analysis_of_Chinas_Policies_towards_the_Arctic_in_the_Post-Cold_War_Period.
24. "China's Snow Dragon Icebreaker Makes 85-Day Voyage to Become Country's First Vessel to Cross Arctic Ocean," *National Post,* September 28, 2012, http://news.nationalpost.com/2012/09/28/chinas-snow-dragon-icebreaker-makes-85-day-voyage-to-become-countrys-first-vessel-to-cross-arctic-ocean/.
25. U.S.-China Business Council Report, November 2005.
26. UNCTAD, Review of Maritime Transport, 2010. See the table on p. 145.
27. Linda J. Jakobson, "China Prepares for an Ice-Free Arctic," *SIPRI Insights on Peace and Security* 2010, no. 2 (March 2010): 5.
28. Guo et al., 北极航道的国际问题研究, 323–326.

29. "Shipping across the Arctic Ocean: A Feasible Option in 2030–2050 as a Result of Global Warming," Research and Innovation, Position Paper, April 2010, 4–20.
30. Joseph Spears, "China and the Arctic: The Awakening Snow Dragon," *China Brief* 9, no. 6 (March 18, 2009), http://www. jamestown.org/programs/chinabrief/single/?tx_ttnews[tt_news]=34725 &tx_ttnews[backPid]=25&cHash=1c22119d7c.
31. Jakobson, "China Prepares for an Ice-Free Arctic," 5.
32. Chen Xulong, quoted in Z. Zhou, "北极通航引发'深海'暗战" [The opening of Arctic shipping triggers an unclear battle in the "deep" sea], *Liaoning Ribao*, October 15, 2009.
33. Spears, "China and the Arctic."
34. Robert Wade, "A Warmer Arctic Needs Shipping Rules," *Financial Times of London*, January 16, 2008, http://www.ft.com/cms/s/0/0adece78-c3d8 -11dc-b083-0000779fd2ac.html#axzz2HUgjGNtf.
35. Heather Exner-Pirot, "What Route for Arctic Shipping?" March 25, 2011, http://eyeonthearctic.rcinet.ca/en/blog/136-heather-exner-pirot/7 93-what-route-for-arctic-shipping.
36. Lauren Krugel, "Chinese Interest in Arctic Riches Heating Up: Calgary Political Scientist (Arctic-Natural-Gas)," Canadian Press, February 25, 2008, http://www.david-kilgour.com/2008/Feb_27_2008_09.htm.
37. Bryn Weese, "Japan Latest Non-Arctic Country to Claim Stake in North Pole," *Toronto Sun*, September 3, 2010, http://www.torontosun.com/news/ canada/2010/09/03/15241971.html.
38. Scott G. Borgerson, "Arctic Meltdown: The Economic and Security Implications of Global Warming," *Foreign Affair* 87, no. 2 (2008): 63–77.
39. "Maritime Agenda 2010–2020 Launched" (Press Information Bureau, Government of India, January 13, 2011), http://pib.nic.in/newsite/erelease. aspx?relid=69044.
40. Neil Gadihoke, "Arctic Melt: The Outlook for India," *Maritime Affairs: Journal of the National Maritime Foundation of India* 8, no. 1 (2012): 1–12.
41. Olga Alexeeva and Frédéric Lasserre, "China and the Arctic," *Arctic Yearbook 2012*: 86.
42. Peter F. Johnston, "Arctic Energy Resources and Global Energy Security," *Journal of Military and Strategic Studies* 12, no. 2 (Winter 2010): 3.
43. See Barry S. Zellen, "Viewpoint: Cold Front Rising—As Climate Change Thins Polar Ice, A New Race for Arctic Resources Begins," *Strategic Insights*, February 2008.

44. Vsevolod Gunitskiy, "On Thin Ice: Water Rights and Resource Disputes in the Arctic Ocean," *Journal of International Affairs* 61, no. 2 (Spring/Summer 2008): 261–262.

45. UNCLOS, Part XI, section 2, http://www.un.org/depts/los/convention_agreements/texts/unclos/part11-2.htm.

46. U.S. Energy Information Administration, "China and India Account for Half of Global Energy Growth through 2035," September 19, 2011, http://www.eia.gov/todayinenergy/detail.cfm?id=3130.

47. Joseph Spears, "The Snow Dragon Moves into the Arctic Ocean Basin," *China Brief* 11, no. 2 (January 28, 2011), http://www.jamestown.org/programs/chinabrief/single/?tx_ttnews%5Btt_news%5D=37429&cHash=a076c446d9.

48. Joensen, "A New Chinese Arctic Policy?"

49. Mari Solerød, Norwegian Research Council, 2010, http://www.norway.cn/News_and_events/Education-and-research/Research/Norway-and-China-strengthen-polar-research-cooperation/.

50. http://www-arctic.nipr.ac.jp/.

51. Kazuyuki Shiraishi, "Japanese National Activity in the Arctic Science," Presentation at the Forum of Arctic Research Operators (FARO) Meeting at the Arctic Science Summit Week, Montreal, April 21, 2012, http://faro-arctic.org/fileadmin/Resources/DMU/GEM/faro/2012_Kazuyuki_Shiraishi_s_presentation.pdf.

52. Japan's written statement by the Delegation of Japan at the Second Meeting of Deputy Ministers of the Arctic Council, Stockholm, Sweden, May 15, 2012, http://www.arctic-council.org/index.php/en/about/documents/category/118-deputy-ministers-meeting-stockholm-1 5-may-2012.

53. Shailesh Nayak, "Polar Research in India," *Indian Journal of Marine Sciences* 37, no. 4 (December 2008): 352–357.

54. http://dod.nic.in/Parliament/Lok_Sabha/2nd_15_2009/unstarred/LU259 1_2_15_2009.pdf.

55. Sakhuja, "Is There a Case for India," 1–5.

56. R. Ramachandran, "India, Norway for Joint Polar Research," *Hindu*, February 7, 2011, http://www.thehindu.com/news/national/article116 2914.ece.

57. Office of the Speaker Lok Sabha, "Parliamentary Delegation from Iceland Calls on Lok Sabha Speaker," Press Release, November 20, 2012, http://speakerloksabha.nic.in/pressrelease/PressreleaseDetails.asp?PressId=1 119&button=Edit.

CHAPTER 20

SOVEREIGNTY, SECURITY, AND INTERNATIONAL COOPERATION

SIGNIFICANCE OF THE ANTARCTIC EXPERIENCE FOR THE ARCTIC

Anita Dey Nuttall

> The Antarctic Treaty is a unique example of international coop-
> eration. Its main focus is to ensure that Antarctica is used for
> peaceful purposes only.
> —United Nations Secretary-General Ban Ki-Moon on the fiftieth
> anniversary of the Antarctic Treaty

INTRODUCTION

The last continent to be discovered, explored, surveyed, and mapped,
Antarctica is regarded as belonging to no nation. Yet seven signatory
states[1] of the Antarctic Treaty of 1959 claim territory there. Within their
domestic jurisdictions, these claimant states treat their territorial claims
in Antarctica as part of their overall national territory, even though the

governance of Antarctica stipulated by the treaty neither recognizes nor denies such claims. An international legal agreement that is perceived as "a unique example of international cooperation" among fifty signatory states, the Antarctic Treaty attempts to balance issues of contested sovereignty, safeguarding security, and advancing scientific research in Antarctica for the benefit of all of mankind.

In recent years, considerable discussion has centered on whether the environmental, social, economic, and political changes occurring in the Arctic require an international response in the form of a specific treaty for the Arctic Ocean or a much more comprehensive treaty that covers a greater part or all of the Arctic.[2] Whether one or the other is realistic, Antarctica often figures prominently in considerations of Arctic governance regimes.[3] Understanding the Antarctic experience is instructive for the Arctic, particularly for debates on sovereignty, security, and international cooperation. However, this chapter does not examine or analyze the Antarctic Treaty as a model for Arctic governance. There is a germane literature that focuses on the legal and regulatory dimensions of this. My concern is to emphasize the significance of the politics that led to the culmination of the Antarctic Treaty and, in particular, the pragmatism shown by the original signatories in accommodating change and representing multiple state interests.

The membership of the Antarctic Treaty, once viewed as an "exclusive club of rich and powerful states,"[4] eventually became more inclusive of both developed and developing countries, claimants and nonclaimant states. Common interests in the pursuit of scientific research and environmental protection, as well as conflicting positions on the banning of mining activities and the varying views on the application of the common heritage of mankind principle in the Antarctic, have presented opportunities, challenges, and pressures with the Antarctic Treaty and its various legal instruments. I argue that when one compares the Antarctic to the Arctic, the focus should be less on the contrasts in the historical, geopolitical, and social bases between the two polar regions and more on the political rationality espoused in the universal princi-ples of peace, cooperation, and reciprocity that guided the establishment of the Antarctic Treaty in 1959 and has enabled its continuation to the present day. Integral in supporting those principles was the pursuit of science, which acted as a compass in navigating the complex political landscape of Antarctica.

All the Arctic states, barring Iceland, are signatories of the Antarctic Treaty. Five of these Arctic states[5] are Consultative Parties (those who have voting rights). Furthermore, all of the Arctic Council observer states (except Singapore) are also Antarctic Treaty Consultative Parties (ATCPs). The collective and long-term association of particularly the Arctic Council observer states with Antarctica and its governance, the perspectives and experiences they bring from their involvement there, and the positions they hold need to be contemplated and considered in the context of the growing global interest in Arctic governance issues.[6] Furthermore, in many respects, the significance of the political dynamics of the Antarctic Treaty provides a useful context for understanding the underlying interests of emerging economies in the polar regions.

Should a political treaty in the Arctic (in whatever form) be pondered, then a historical overview of the context in which the principles of peace, cooperation, and reciprocity were developed and applied to Antarc-tica is useful for expanding understanding of the direction Arctic poli-tics could take in the face of pressures that emanate external to the region. Also, given that many of the Arctic and non-Arctic states have a historical connection with Antarctica's discovery and exploration and, in some cases, more recent involvement in scientific research there, noting the strategic behavior of these states in the development of politics in Antarctica and the choices they made unilaterally or in concert with other states could offer a glimpse into how they might drive and influ-ence the politics and governance of the Arctic in the future.

ECONOMIC MOTIVES AND THE ISSUE OF ANTARCTIC CLAIMS

Antarctica was the last continent to be discovered and the last to be explored geographically. Very little of its coastline had been delineated by the middle of the nineteenth century, and its interior remained unexplored for almost another century. The search for *terra australis incognita* or "the unknown southern land," which imaginative geographers had endowed with vast resources, was a product of both geographical and scientific curiosity. Interest in this unknown continent originated in Europe when the increasing power and influence of ambitious maritime nations were augmented by the acquisition of new territories and new resources; exploration became a key policy instrument. The discovery and exploration of Antarctica was the beginning of a process that often resulted in laying claim to parts of the continent. It was a product of European expansion in commerce in which the search for empire and resources led to the dispatch of national expeditions to the south. Three European powers—France, England, and, later, Russia—were at the fore in the discovery of Antarctica. Their role in such an endeavor was a reflection of their political predominance. The beginning of the eighteenth century had seen England and France emerge as major maritime nations. England had replaced Spain as the dominant imperial power, and France replaced Holland as England's principal commercial rival. The prospect of colonial gains in the as yet undiscovered southern continent played some part in their maritime and colonial strategies.[7] Russia's search for the southern continent was influenced by its lack of harbors, ports, and bases along the trade routes of the Indian Ocean and the South and Central Pacific, which were dominated by the French and the British. Russia therefore looked along the perimeter of the Antarctic seas for the "possibilities of establishing future sea-communications or places for the repair of ships."[8] Britain, France, and Russia were already engaged in the pursuit for the northern trade routes of the northwest and northeast passages to Cathay and were seeking trade in the unexplored high latitudes of the Southern Hemisphere.

It cannot be overstated that economic motives played an important role in sustaining political interest in the Antarctic, especially when southern waters were perceived by the United States and several European countries to be lucrative with the start of the whaling industry. Whaling had become the chief economic impetus for the exploration of Antarctica in the early twentieth century, resulting in the first of the claims to territorial sovereignty. It was also the catalyst that launched the first long-term organized scientific program in Antarctica. The use of science to support protection of an economic enterprise such as the whaling industry was a significant development that took place in this context.

Up until the eve of World War II, five countries that claimed territory in the Antarctic (Britain, New Zealand, Australia, France, and Norway) had mutually recognized each other's claims. The claims were based on acts of discovery and had been dominated by Europe (the claims of New Zealand and Australia were made by Britain on their behalf). But after 1939, serious stress was placed on these claims, for the first time, with the revival of political interests of Chile and Argentina in the Antarctic and the interests of countries such as Germany, Japan, the United States, and the Soviet Union in Antarctica's resource potential.

The evolution of political interests in the Antarctic is one of many cases confirming that governments consider their interests and choose their policies on international questions in light of the attitudes of other states and the competition for power that exists among them. Even at the time of the discovery and early exploration of the Antarctic, political rivalry between Britain and France, as well as between the United States and Britain, prompted the dispatch of expeditions for economic gains or scientific objectives. This was a period that witnessed British supremacy in Antarctica. Previously the strongest power in world politics, possessing an enormous empire, Britain saw its position begin to change at the outbreak of World War II, when the emerging importance of the United States in international politics brought about changes in the way political claims in Antarctica were perceived. During World War II, not only were British claims challenged by Argentina and Chile, but a war-damaged Britain suffered serious economic setbacks and the loss of colonies from which it never recovered. In a self-appointed role of defender of the Western Hemisphere, the United States stimulated pan-American thinking by bringing about the more active participation of Chile and Argentina in Antarctic politics. Antarctica assumed a geopolitical and even strategic position in international affairs, which both the American and European states sought to control.

The geostrategic relevance of Antarctica was dominant during World War II, when the general question of sovereignty was most sensitive and the desire to defend national territories zealously was especially strong. The protection and consolidation of these claims led to national Antarctic operations, which later provided the conditions for the establishment of permanent national Antarctic science programs. The long-term experience of these countries in the conduct of science in the polar regions enabled them to remain at the forefront of developments in Antarctic science and to determine the future of the continent.

THE ANTARCTIC TREATY OF 1959 AND SCIENCE AS A CURRENCY OF INVOLVEMENT

Although the post–World War II period came to be dominated by the Cold War, the 1950s particularly were marked by a surge of internationalism, which was especially evident in the realm of science. The Pugwash Conferences beginning in 1957 emphasized the supranational character of science and created opportunities for international cooperation.[9] It was against this background that the International Geophysical Year (IGY), a worldwide program of research in various scientific disciplines that ran from July 1957 to December 1958, was able to exploit the desire for international cooperation in science among sixty-six countries. In Antarctica, it marked the beginning of a new era.[10]

The IGY transformed national activities in the Antarctic from primarily political to primarily scientific operations and initiated the concept of a unified international program for science. It set in motion a process of organized and concerted scientific investigation in Antarctica. The huge costs of undertaking Antarctic science required strong political support. The presence of such central powers as the United Kingdom, the United States of America, and later the Soviet Union, each to some degree politically at variance with the other, paved the way for permanent activity.

Arising from the multinational effort of the IGY, in 1959 the twelve nations[11] that had participated in Antarctic research signed the Antarctic Treaty. Since then, thirty-eight other nations have joined the treaty, full membership of which is limited to states that demonstrate "substantial scientific interest" in the continent. Seventeen of these countries have become consultative parties of the treaty, and this gives them decision-making powers. Diverse countries, developed and developing, claimant and non-claimant—nations with often opposing ideologies, interests, and aspirations—work together under the treaty with a common goal: using Antarctica to make substantial contributions to scientific knowledge resulting from international cooperation in scientific investigation.[12]

When the IGY was concluded, the Antarctic Treaty provided the political framework to continue scientific research. Although the treaty does not stipulate permanent national activity, the original parties to the treaty each gave shape to their political, economic, and scientific interests in Antarctica by establishing a permanent presence on the continent through the conduct of long-term national Antarctic programs.

The importance of the IGY in Antarctica not only lay in the extent of its contribution to knowledge about the continent; it also mitigated in some measure the politicization of Antarctica—territorial rivalry had turned it into an area highly vulnerable to potential conflict. In the midst of the political tensions, the twelve nations recognized that rational conduct and cooperation were possible at the scientific level; the IGY established a situation where there was a preeminence of science over sovereignty in Antarctica, with the governments concerned reaching a "gentlemen's agreement" to dissolve sovereignty claims during the period of the IGY. It was agreed that all scientific activities in the Antarctic were not to be considered as having any legal or political value. The pursuit of science became and continues to be the main currency of credibility in Antarctica's political setting.

The Antarctic Treaty achieved four main objectives in response to the prevailing perceptions of Antarctica. First, in response to the Cold War, the treaty was a step toward an arms-control agreement between the United States and the Soviet Union. Article I established that Antarctica "be used for peaceful purposes only. There shall be prohibited, inter alia, any measures of a military nature, such as the establishment of military bases and fortifications, the carrying out of military manoeuvers as well as the testing of any type of weapons." Additionally, Article V prohibited "nuclear explosions in Antarctica and the disposal there of radioactive waste." To help enforce its arms-control provisions, Article VII of the treaty established a mechanism for enforcing compliance through on-site inspection. In some ways the treaty heralded other arms-control negotiations between the then superpowers.

Second, in response to the success of the IGY in terms of the research output, the expansion of scientific research, the perceived benefits of international cooperation, and the potential for further research on a continuing basis and within an international framework, the treaty established scientific activity as the only legitimate national activity in Antarctica. The preamble of the treaty acknowledges the substantial contributions to scientific knowledge resulting from the scientific investigations in Antarctica, and Article II established "freedom of scientific investigation in Antarctica and cooperation toward that end."

Third, it was not part of the treaty's brief to attempt to achieve a permanent settlement of territorial claims, but scientific cooperation of course had not disposed of the issue. The only option for the treaty was to adopt an approach that would maintain the status quo. The treaty established that nothing in it would be interpreted as "renunciation, diminution, recognition, or non-recognition of any nation's rights, claim, or basis of claim to sovereignty in Antarctica." What the treaty achieved was an agreement that overrode the disagreement on territorial claims. By neither denying nor recognizing claims to Antarctic territory, the treaty in a way protected them and so in some measure removed from the claimant countries the political and legal necessity of demonstrating permanent occupation. Nevertheless, the claimant countries have continued to remain active on the continent and in fact established the practice of sending annual scientific research expeditions.

Fourth, the treaty set the scene for future patterns of activity in Antarctica. Whereas the "claims of sovereignty" of seven of the IGY countries and the "historic association" of the other five gave them a permanent place in Antarctica, for those countries not part of that history, the treaty provided new terms for establishing their permanent interests in Antarctica. Acceding countries needed to fulfill a set of conditions in order to acquire powers equal to those of the original signatories. For new members to gain decision-making power or consultative status, Article IX requires them to "demonstrate [their] interest in Antarctica by conducting substantial scientific research activity there, such as the establishment of a scientific station or the despatch of a scientific expedition." Acceding countries needed to demonstrate continuing interest in the region if they were to maintain consultative status. This obligation did not apply to the treaty's original signatories. The standard practice for countries interested in long-term involvement in Antarctica was to establish stations and dispatch expeditions and then develop the appropriate infrastructure.

Although the political and legal contexts of Antarctica sketched out here have evolved substantially and their relevance to the Arctic today may appear distant, the power rivalry, dominant state interests, changing political alliances, economic motives, competition for resources, and protection of state jurisdictions continue to remain key drivers of national interests in both polar regions. The founding of the Antarctic Treaty sought to address some of these challenges, albeit at a time when the political milieu was significantly different from that of today. But the relevance of the Antarctic Treaty to Arctic affairs lies in the use of science as a political currency, its receptiveness to managing diverse sets of national interests that persist regardless of the temporal and spatial contexts, and its ability to anticipate disputes or debates from unknown variables.

BROADENING THE MEMBERSHIP OF THE ANTARCTIC TREATY

Having reached a tentative decision to maintain the status quo on territorial claims, the original treaty members very quickly turned their attention to the issue next closest to ownership: the management of Antarctic resources. The first meetings of the ATCPs assigned priority to the preservation and conservation of Antarctic living resources. Agreement on the recommendations of a "code of conduct" finally led to the adoption of the Agreed Measures for the Conservation of the Antarctic Fauna and Flora (1964), the Convention for the Conservation of Seals (1972), the Convention for the Conservation of Marine Living Resources (1982), the Convention for the Regulation of Antarctic Mineral Resource Activities (opened for signature in 1988 but not ratified), and the Environmental Protocol (1991). These instruments complement the treaty, and together they form the Antarctic Treaty System (ATS). As noted by Duyck, "the most enriching lesson that Arctic states could draw from Antarctic governance relates to the more proactive approach adopted by the states party to the ATS in relation to the regulation of economic activities prior to their development."[13]

Such developments have taken place as a result of the changing international political, economic, and technological environment. First, an expanding international community of former colonies achieved state-hood, joining the ranks of nation-states and assuming concomitant responsibility in the United Nations. The wider international community not only began to express interest in the resource-base of the Antarctic but also opposed territorial claims in Antarctica. Second, the development in the advanced countries of technology for harnessing resources pushed back the frontiers of resource exploitation beyond national boundaries, prompting negotiations to establish legal regimes for exploitation in such areas as the oceans and the deep-sea bed, which were not under sovereign jurisdiction.

After the treaty came into force in 1961, a new international order emerged as a result of the transformation of the international community as it moved from the imperial era into the postcolonial era. European states that had built empires in the Americas, Asia, and Africa had justified their overseas programs with theories of proximity, discovery, and occupation, which were later applied by claimant states to Antarctica. But the emergence of newly independent states, sensitive to economic and political control by the major powers, represented a new political force. Many of these states challenged the doctrines used to build the empires from which they eventually wrested independence, strongly influencing the evolution of international law. Evolution in legal doctrines brought about by political change has been reinforced by new economic and social conditions. Newly independent states at the time acquired a role without precedent in history on the international scene. Developing nations not only increased the membership of the UN but also fostered new concepts with which to challenge traditional doctrines.

In the 1960s and 1970s, international attention was focused on finding resources in areas not under the jurisdiction of any state. In particular, the oil crisis in the 1970s—the result of rising prices dictated by Middle East politics—diverted attention to unexploited parts of the world as potential sources of supply. One of the important concepts to evolve from the demise of colonial empires is the New International Economic Order (NIEO). As equal members of the international community, developing nations wanted the right to participate fully in international decision-making processes.[14] Their interests extended to participating in discussions on international issues such as resource management, peace and security, disarmament, international trade and finance, environmental issues, and decolonization. Antarctica became a legitimate area of concern for developing nations; since 1961, seven such nations (Brazil, China, Ecuador, India, Peru, the Republic of South Korea, and Uruguay) have become Consultative Parties to the Antarctic Treaty. Other signatories to the treaty are Papua New Guinea, Cuba, North Korea, Colombia, Guatemala, Venezuela, Malaysia, and Pakistan, thus reflecting the potential interests of a wider group of developing countries.

The technological advances of many developed countries have enabled them to exploit natural assets off their own coasts, and their growing fishing industries began to exploit marine resources, marking the beginning of a struggle to dominate the oceans of the world. Advanced techniques in the mining industry resulted in the extraction of minerals from progressively greater depths under the sea, well outside any existing legal restrictions. This naturally prompted a reaction from countries not technologically capable of such exploitation. Developing countries, especially in Latin America, took the line that the resources in adjacent seas must be safeguarded. The concept of "broad zones" was proposed by the Latin American states to allow the coastal states to control the exploitation of resources in a wide belt around their coasts. During the 1950s, several Latin American states actually established broad zones; the figure of 200 nautical miles, first mentioned in the Santiago Declaration of 1952, has become the standard. Proposals were presented at such international fora as the first and second UN Conferences on the Law of the Sea (UNCLOS) in Geneva in 1958 and 1960. Shortly after the first Conference on the Law of the Sea, Latin American states established exclusive zones for fishing, and the practice soon spread to Afro-Asian countries. Growing international political awareness since the mid-1970s of Antarctica's resource potential and of its role in environmental processes led the original twelve Antarctic Treaty members to begin negotiations on the marine resources of the Antarctic in order to ensure the establishment of their own resource arrangements. In 1977, they called for "a definitive regime for the Conservation of Antarctic Marine Living Resources."

The 1980s witnessed an even greater international visibility of Antarctica, a trend reflecting the "impact of changing political and legal attitudes that was related to the democratization of international relations, and the application of the common heritage of mankind principle, and the concern to safeguard the last great wilderness on earth."[15] As in the whaling era, resource issues once again appeared on the scene but this time on a much wider scale; they included the interests of a greater number of countries involved in Antarctica and focused not only on whales but on such other resources as fish, krill, minerals, and indeed Antarctic ecology as a whole. Diverse views on the sovereignty issue now extended to other areas—for example, the equitable distribution of resources, sharing of benefits between the developed and the developing countries, and most recently the decision to ban mineral activities indefinitely.

A major catalyst for such developments was the start in 1982 of ATCP negotiations for a minerals regime. This attracted the attention of the UN, particularly in relation to the conclusions reached by UNCLOS III the same year. According to this, "the sea bed and ocean floor, beyond the limits of national jurisdiction, as well as the resources of the area, are common heritage of mankind." With the development of the notion of a common heritage, developing states could put forth an argument that, because it is part of the common heritage of mankind, Antarctica is already, or should become, *res communis*. These changing political and legal attitudes manifested themselves in the debates on the region that the United Nations conducted with regularity from 1983 to 2005. With the granting of consultative status to countries such as India (1983),

China (1985), and South Korea (1989)—and more recently with Malaysia (2011) and Pakistan (2012) becoming signatories of the Antarctic Treaty —attempts to apply the principle of the common heritage of mankind to Antarctica or regularly placing the "Question of Antarctica" in UN debates have tempered. It was a pragmatic decision on the part of the treaty powers to include among others India, China, and South Korea in the decision-making apparatus of the Antarctic Treaty. In doing so, the treaty powers had reduced the external opposition that came primarily from developing countries to the continuance of the treaty. Their admission was seen as a way of maintaining the stability of the Antarctic Treaty System within the context of international politics.

The Convention for the Regulation of Antarctic Mineral Resource Activities (CRAMRA) did not come into force, a result of pressures from environmental groups and a general worldwide environmental campaign. However, an important element of CRAMRA was that it took into account the changing international order that had brought about a new interest group among the ATCPs. Never before in any of the conventions negotiated by the consultative parties was there a special role or privilege for developing countries. Articles 29(3)(b) of CRAMRA provided for "adequate and equitable representation of developing country members of the Commission, having regard to the overall balance between developed and developing country members of the Commission, including at least three developing country members of the Commission."[16] Moreover, with regard to decision making in the Regulatory Committee, it was agreed that the two-thirds majority should include at least one developing country (Article 32).[17] It has been pointed out by Chaturvedi that "in the absence of India and the other three developing nations (Brazil, China and Uruguay), as ATCPs, it is difficult to imagine what worthwhile consideration or accommodation of interests of the developing nations would have occurred in the proposed Convention."[18]

PROTECTING THE FRAGILE ANTARCTIC ENVIRONMENT

The Antarctic experiment provides a useful reference for provision of regulatory frameworks in case of the resumption of activities that could have an impact on Antarctica's fragile environment. During the close of the 1980s and the start of the 1990s, there were concerns about environmental practices in Antarctica and the potential for further damage arising from the exploitation of mineral resources, which resulted in the demise of CRAMRA and led the treaty nations to recognize the need for enhanced stewardship of Antarctica. In the environmental arena, no single topic has engendered such diverse opinions as a discussion of environmental disturbances in Antarctica. On the one hand, there is a view that, in the overall context of the immensity of the continent, the number of humans and the limited activities produce near-field perturbations that are negligible. On the other hand, there are those who view any intrusion as a negative influence that ultimately affects and degrades what they perceive to be the last pristine region on earth. At a time of increasing global and environmental awareness, Antarctica generated intense interest in both the use and future regulation of this truly multinational continent.

In 1991, following a series of negotiations, an international consensus for stewardship and protection of the Antarctic environment emerged in the form of the Protocol on Environmental Protection, which prohibited mineral activities for a period of fifty years. The Environmental Protocol, which is an instrument of the Antarctic Treaty, took as its point of departure the principle that the Antarctic must be regarded as a protected area, a natural reserve, to be utilized only for peaceful purposes, for science, and for its unique aesthetic value as a wilderness.

Most of the countries that acceded to the treaty particularly in the 1980s sought membership with the sole objective of achieving consultative status. This is reflected in the sequence of events that took place in these countries soon after their accession to the treaty. In keeping with its requirements to achieve consultative status, the countries followed the pattern of first acceding to the treaty, second sending expeditions to the continent, and third establishing a scientific presence through the erection of a refuge hut, weather station, a summer field station, or a year-round scientific station. The mix of such different types of a "scientific station" reflected the room available to stretch what "substantial scientific research interest" comprised. It is clearly no coincidence that the greatest increase in national operations in the Antarctic occurred during the 1980s, the period dominated by the minerals development issue. The high cost of research and the need for major infrastructure to support long-term scientific research activity in Antarctica demonstrated a state's willingness to invest in continued involvement in the continent. The breakdown of CRAMRA and its replacement by negotiations on the Protocol for Environmental Protection interestingly seemed to coincide with a receding urgency to establish national presence there. The adverse environmental effects as a result of stations crowded into the few easily accessible coastal areas of Antarctica and of mutual interference among the different research programs or logistics activities, however, are major concerns.

Although the political factor continues to be essential in the development of national Antarctic science programs, particularly because of the large sums of public funding required for their operation, there has been a shift from the political importance of having a presence in Antarctica to defend territorial claims, or the non-recognition of such claims, to the political importance of ensuring that the quality of science in Antarctica is at a sufficiently high level to enable countries to remain at the forefront of Antarctic decision making.

The influence of politics on science in Antarctica intensified as a result of environmental pressures. A significant change in the function of science there is that, rather than being used to support political ends like permanent occupation, it is now being used as a tool for the protection of the environment and indeed to bring about measures for the conservation of resources. As a result, the definition of political interests in the

Antarctic changed. The political influence a state wields over Antarctic affairs is no longer derived simply from its territorial claims in Antarctica but must now be combined with the conduct of high-quality scientific research and with technology that is environmentally sound, and this has meant that "international cooperation rather than unrestrained international competition"[19] remains the hallmark of Antarctic politics and science.

CALL FOR AN ARCTIC TREATY?

In contrast to the experience of Antarctica, where an international treaty provides the mechanism for its governance, there is no comprehensive treaty or international agreement for the entire Arctic region. In recent years, a number of scholars, commentators, and policy makers have considered this to be problematic for Arctic governance and have called for an Arctic Treaty.[20] In doing so, they have often invoked the spirit of the Antarctic Treaty as offering a model for addressing Arctic issues, particularly those relating to contested sovereignty, governance and resource management, and peace and security. Opponents to this idea have drawn attention to the contrasts between both polar regions and have put forward compelling arguments for why a treaty like the Antarctic Treaty would not be relevant for the Arctic. Indeed, many question the need for an international agreement covering the Arctic at all. Implicit in this discussion is of course an assumption that the Antarctic Treaty is in itself an effective instrument of international governance that has worked well for over fifty years protecting Antarctica from becoming a stage for military confrontation or resource exploitation and environmental ruin. It could be argued that we do not know how well the Antarctic Treaty really works. It has not yet been challenged in a serious manner, for example by competing state interests arising from the prospect of commercially viable resource development activities in the region. That said, the principles upon which the Antarctic Treaty was established continue to be upheld by all its signatories, claimant and non-claimant states, and they probably provide a solid foundation to make the ATS robust enough to meet the challenges or disputes that may arise in Antarctica in the future. In their assessment of Antarctic security in the twenty-first century, Hemmings, Rothwell, and Scott pointed out that "at the level of the individual state, their Antarctic security interests exist in a context of other global security interests and relationships with other states outside the ATS."[21] And inherent among the signatory states' calculation and interpretation of their security interests in the Antarctic is the "basic commitment to Antarctic regime security."[22]

The need for an Antarctic Treaty–style agreement in the Arctic has been perceived to be minimal given that territorial demarcation of the eight Arctic states is defined and governed by the individual state's domestic laws. National jurisdictions over territories in the Arctic region are not internationally unrecognized or challenged. The maritime boundaries of these states too have been delineated according to the laws of the sea manifested in UNCLOS.[23] But given the transregional consequences of environmental changes in the Arctic, there is growing interest from diverse sources and an emerging economic involvement of non-Arctic states in the region, which have the potential to put significant pressure on the eight Arctic states with implications for sovereignty over resources, rights, and regulations. Like Antarctica, the Arctic has attracted considerable interest from countries interested in establishing long-term scientific research programs there.[24] Twenty-one countries are members of the International Arctic Science Committee (IASC), which indicates that substantial resources directed to Arctic science is not just limited to the eight Arctic states and that international interest in the region is being defined and consolidated through the pursuit of science. As I have argued in this chapter, international cooperation in science in the Antarctic has been a defining characteristic of national activities on the continent. The Antarctic experience with science seems more fitting in providing a model for the Arctic than its governance regime:

> In the next 50 years, the Arctic will experience massive phys-
> ical and social changes, which will make it critical to ensure
> that scientific knowledge is incorporated into decision-making
> processes and that the interaction among science, law, and policy
> is strengthened...In Antarctica, science has given rise to practices
> in areas such as environmental assessment and data management
> that allow a common approach to regional monitoring, reporting,
> and verification. Development of similar standardized data collec-
> tion, management, and analysis procedures among the Arctic
> nations will be needed to integrate, interpret, and feed this infor-
> mation into policy-making processes in the future.[25]

The dominant force in addressing the issues of sovereignty, security, and
international cooperation in the southern continent has been the pursuit
of science. Science performs a political task of advancing the national
interests of the Antarctic Treaty Consultative Parties in a geopolitical
landscape.

The Arctic Council, an intergovernmental "forum where a wide range
of Arctic issues are considered and debated,"[26] has often been critiqued
as being "a soft law regime," and some argue that in the Arctic "there
has never been any intention to create legally binding obligations for the
Arctic states."[27] Furthermore, the Ilulissat Declaration in 2008 of the five
Arctic coastal states has been interpreted as an "effort to block an Arctic
treaty, a defense of the institutional status quo in the region."[28]

Recent activities of the Arctic Council—including the signing of the
Arctic Search and Rescue Agreement in May 2011—suggest that developments in international cooperation in the Arctic are directed toward
considering some form of a comprehensive legal instrument that is
specific to the Arctic. As Timo Koivurova observed, "Although the Arctic
Council is not a treaty-based organization, it seems to have gradually
institutionalized itself to the extent that it can act as a foundation for
permanent cooperation between various regional stakeholders. Moreover, the Council has been able to combine its scientific work with

soft and hard law mechanisms, a mixture that functions creatively in responding to multi-faceted challenges posed by climate change to the region."[29]

Whereas there has been some doubt about the relevance of the Antarctic Treaty to Arctic issues, of late there appears to be a resurgence of the idea of an Arctic Treaty. At the 10th Conference of Parliamentarians of the Arctic Region in Akureyri September 5–7, 2012, one of the recommendations made in the conference statement on Arctic governance and the Arctic Council was to "[i]nitiate discussions toward developing the Arctic Council into a formal international organization by adopting an exclusive treaty among the eight Arctic states to give themselves more binding powers."[30] This is likely to play out in the context of rethinking the very nature of the Arctic Council and whether it undergoes a transformation from that of a "forum" to a "governance" body.[31]

The majority of the states involved in the Arctic Council have long-term and active involvement in Antarctica. New observer states such as China, India, Japan, and South Korea are also countries that, taken together, have been involved in Antarctica over the last three decades; and, in some cases, as with the United Kingdom, France, Germany, and Japan, they have been historically involved in the history of Antarctica's discovery and exploration. What might their expectations be, and how do their experiences of participating in the governance of Antarctica have an impact upon the views and positions they take or will take on Arctic governance issues?[32] Any negotiations for a future Arctic Treaty will need to balance the protection of the national interests of the eight Arctic states and at the same time accommodate the influence and expectations that non-Arctic observer states of the Arctic Council will bring to bear on debates over issues of sovereignty, security, and international cooperation in the Arctic region. Finally, should there be an Arctic Treaty negotiated in the future, what would be the place of science in it that would benefit a majority and not just a minority of mankind?

NOTES

1. The United Kingdom, Argentina, Chile, Norway, France, Australia, and New Zealand.
2. Oran R. Young, "If an Arctic Ocean Treaty Is Not the Solution, What Is the Alternative?" *Polar Record* 47, no. 243 (2011): 327–334.
3. Timo Koivurova, "Environmental Protection in the Arctic and Antarctic: Can the Polar Regimes Learn from Each Other?" *International Journal of Legal Information* 33, no. 2 (2005): 204–218.
4. Davor Vidas, "The Antarctic Treaty System in the International Community: An Overview," in *Governing the Antarctic: The Effectiveness and Legitimacy of the Antarctic Treaty System*, ed. Olav Schram Stokke and Davor Vidas (Cambridge and New York: Cambridge University Press, 1996), 55.
5. Norway, the United States of America, Russia, Finland, and Sweden.
6. See Anne-Marie Brady, *The Emerging Politics of Antarctica* (London: Routledge, 2012), for an analysis of country case studies for India, China, South Korea, and France.
7. L. P. Kirwan, *The White Road: A Survey of Polar Exploration* (London: Hollis and Carter, 1959), 44.
8. Ibid., 109.
9. John Heap, "Cooperation in the Antarctic: A Quarter of a Century's Experience," in *Antarctic Resources Policy*, ed. F. O. Vicuna (Cambridge: Cambridge University Press, 1983), 105.
10. See D. Olsen Belanger, "The International Geophysical Year in Antarctica: Uncommon Collaborations, Unprecedented Results," *Journal of Government Information* 30 (2004): 482–489.
11. Argentina, Australia, Belgium, Chile, France, Japan, New Zealand, Norway, South Africa, the former Soviet Union, United Kingdom, and the United States of America.
12. See Gillian D. Triggs, *The Antarctic Treaty Regime* (Cambridge: Cambridge University Press, 1987).
13. Sebastien Duyck, "Drawing Lessons for Arctic Governance from the Antarctic Treaty System," in *The Yearbook of Polar Law*, vol. 3, ed. Gudmundur Alfredsson, Timo Koivurova, and Kamrul Hossain (Leiden: Brill Editions, 2011), 683–713.

14. Anthony Parsons, *Antarctica: The Next Decade* (Cambridge: Cambridge University Press, 1987), 110.

15. Peter J. Beck, "A New Polar Factor in International Relations," *World Today* 45, no. 4 (1989): 65.

16. Peter J. Beck, "Convention on the Regulation of Antarctic Mineral Resource Activities: A Major Addition to the Antarctic Treaty System," *Polar Record* 25, no. 152 (1989): 19–32.

17. "Final Report of the Fourth Special Antarctic Treaty Consultative Meeting on Antarctic Mineral Resources," Antarctic Treaty Special Consultative Meeting on Antarctic Mineral Resources, Ministry of Foreign Affairs, Wellington, New Zealand, June 2, 1988, 41.

18. Sanjay Chaturvedi, *Dawning of Antarctica: A Geopolitical Analysis* (New Delhi: Segment Books, 1990), 177.

19. A. D. Hemmings, Donald R. Rothwell, and Karen N. Scott, "Antarctic Security in a Global Context," in *Antarctic Security in the Twenty-First Century*, ed. A. D. Hemmings, Donald R. Rothwell, and Karen N. Scott (London: Routledge, 2012), 336.

20. Molly Watson, "An Arctic Treaty: A Solution to the International Dispute over the Polar Region," *Ocean & Coastal Law Journal* 14, no. 2 (2009): 307–334.

21. Hemmings et al., "Antarctic Security in a Global Context," 333.

22. Ibid.

23. See Donald R. Rothwell, "The Law of the Sea and the Antarctic Treaty System: Rougher Seas Ahead for the Southern Ocean?" in *The Antarctic: Past, Present and Future*, Antarctic CRC Research Report #28, ed. J. Jabour-Green and M. Haward (Hobart: Antarctic CRC, 2002), 113–125.

24. See chapter 19 by Hong and Dey Nuttall in this volume.

25. Francesca Cava, David Monsma, and Oran R. Young, "Workshop on Arctic Governance: Drawing Lessons from the Antarctic Experience," in *Science Diplomacy: Antarctica, Science and the Governance of International Spaces*, ed. Paul Arthur Berkman, Michael A. Lang, David W. H. Walton, and Oran R. Young (Washington, DC: Smithsonian Institution Scholarly Press, 2011), 296.

26. See chapter 15 by Koivurova and Graczyk in this volume.

27. Donald R. Rothwell, "The Arctic in International Affairs: Time for a New Regime?" ANU College of Law Research Paper No. 08-37, December 10, 2008, http://ssrn.com/abstract=1314546.

28. Brooks B. Yeager, "The Ilulissat Declaration: Background and Implications for Arctic Governance," prepared for the Aspen Dialogue

and Commission on Arctic Climate Change, November 5, 2008, http://arcticgovernance.custompublish.com/the-ilulissat-declaration-background-and-implications-for-arctic-governance.4626039-137746.html.

29. Timo Koivurova, "New Ways to Respond to Climate Change in the Arctic," *Insights: American Society of International Law* 16, no. 33 (October 23, 2012): 3, http://www.asil.org/insights/volume/16/issue/33/new-ways-respond-climate-change-arctic.

30. The 10th Conference of Parliamentarians of the Arctic Region, Akureyri, September 5–7, 2012, www.uarctic.org/Conference_statement,_final_draft_K20O5.pdf.file.

31. See chapter 15 by Koivurova and Graczyk in this volume.

32. See chapter 18 by Dodds and chapter 19 by Hong and Dey Nuttall in this volume.

Conclusion

Arctic Politics
Moving Forward

Robert W. Murray

In 2013, the Russian Deputy Prime Minister Dmitry Rogozin told the Russian newspaper *Pravda*, "An active development of the Arctic shelf will inevitably lead to a conflict of interests between countries. Addressing these conflicts may go beyond diplomatic means. It is likely that Russian oil and gas production facilities become targets of hidden sabotage by competitor countries."[1] It is statements like these by politicians from various Arctic states and interested non-Arctic states that have led to widespread international attention in the Arctic region in recent years.

The reasoning behind intense scrutiny of circumpolar politics is varied, and this volume clearly demonstrates the multifaceted nature of Arctic affairs for scholars, states, and organizations that are all watching an evolving political and security environment in the region. Variables such as militarism, environmentalism, human development, and resource extraction all play into the complexities of Arctic policies and how best to approach the study of the politics of the Arctic. Although interpretations about exactly which variables rank higher than others in determining precisely why there has been increased interest, the inescapable reality facing the world today is that the Arctic region is the next great frontier of international relations.

This volume has provided three elements in the understanding of Arctic affairs. The first section is focused on theories of international politics that impact the lenses through which circumpolar politics are studied. The section presents four distinctly different, yet equally important, theoretical perspectives that have relevance in helping observers place themselves and their own ideological preferences when debating or discussing Arctic politics.

The realist perspective is grounded very much in the thinking proposed by Rogozin, in seeing the Arctic as a forum for competition, self-interest, and military buildup. Regardless of whether a state employs an offensive or defensive realist strategy, the ultimate argument according to realism is that states are interested in the Arctic solely out of self-interest calculations about what matters most to their security and ability to enhance their role on the world stage.

Opposing the strictly realist view is the liberal argument, which emphasizes the role of international institutions and cooperation as the primary means through which states pursue Arctic interests. The liberal perspective is grounded in conceptions of peace, diplomacy, and rights, all of which have emerged in Arctic discourse through the various organizations involved in, or dedicated to, Arctic politics.

Between these two seemingly antithetical perspectives is the international society, or English School, approach to studying world politics. Rather than dismissing either the realist or liberal theoretical assumptions, the English School attempts to bridge the gap between the two and seeks to forge a middle way of comprehending how and why states are approaching Arctic affairs. Self-interest and security may play into the equation, according to an international society perspective, but so do efforts at promoting peace and law through institutions.

The final theoretical contribution in the first section provides a critical theoretical approach to why the Arctic matters as much as it does. Sovereignty, according to the ecological viewpoint, is less about security and far more about the ecological consequences of how states perceive their own interests in the North. As such, the argument is made that the Arctic is actually a postsovereign space that requires a very different understanding than realism, liberalism, or the English School is capable of providing.

In all, the purpose of these theoretical chapters is not to delve specifically into the Arctic policies of individual states or institutions but rather to help readers contemplate diverse issues of Arctic politics against the backdrop of the theories in international relations. The varying theoretical commitments of each author throughout the remainder of the volume also become more comprehensible when discussing individual or institutional strategies in the High North. For instance, Huebert's realist interpretation of Canada's Arctic policies stands in stark contrast to Knight's liberal arguments for the role of the UN in influencing state action.

After having explored some of the theoretical and philosophical elements of international political thought in the first section, the volume turns to the policies of individual states in their pursuit of Arctic interests. Because this project is an effort to highlight the international relations of the Arctic, the book looks at how Arctic states and interested non-Arctic states have gone about setting their northern agenda and how and why those agendas are pursued. If the theory chapters in section 1 provide the reader with the building blocks to understand international relations, section 2 puts those ideas into practice.

One thing that is abundantly clear from the perspectives provided on state behavior is that states articulate their Arctic interests for different reasons, but all are cognizant and, in some cases, concerned about the behaviors of neighboring or competing states. Cultural, political, historical, anthropological, economic, security, and geographical factors are all aspects of why states have such an intense interest in the Arctic region and why they appear so willing in recent years to commit national resources to attaining their goals. Great power Arctic states, such as the United States and Russia, are able to pursue their interests in very different ways compared to the less powerful Arctic states, Canada, Denmark, Iceland, Norway, Sweden, and Finland. The same is true for interested non-Arctic states as well, seeing that China, India, and the United Kingdom have a greater likelihood of extending their spheres of influence in the Arctic than smaller states with Arctic interests.

Comparing and contrasting the approaches of each Arctic and select non-Arctic states demonstrates the multifaceted nature of circumpolar affairs. Canada's combination of militarization and development has been welcomed by some, though strongly criticized by others, and little true progress has been made toward Canada's stated Arctic goals to this point. The United States to date has been mostly disinterested with the Arctic beyond its strategic necessity in aerial and naval defense. This has changed significantly in recent years with the promise of resources and potential competition, exacerbated by Russian posturing. Russia's claims are being reinforced by strong political rhetoric and military building and deployment. Norway, Finland, and Sweden are all committing national resources to bolstering their claims in the High North. These efforts from all three states include increased military spending, institutional binding, and diplomatic negotiating. In many senses, these states are reacting to what they perceive as a Russian threat and aggressive behavior by great powers in the region. Denmark is forging its own path aside from the Scandinavian states but still very much urging development, particularly in the context of Greenland, while simultaneously increasing its military capabilities. Iceland's approach to the High North is distinctive, given that it has no military resources to speak of and is traditionally totally dependent on alliances to pursue its interests. As such, Iceland's northern strategy is almost entirely economic in nature.

Those non-Arctic states such as China, India, and the United Kingdom pose a unique challenge to circumpolar affairs. Unlike Arctic states, territoriality is not the key issue for these states; rather, their concern is purely self-interest and perceptions of both national security and global power shifts. If the resource base under the polar ice caps is as prosperous as some believe, no great power wants to be left out of the hunt. China's determination to augment oil tanker capabilities—and having already successfully navigated the Arctic seaways—speaks to just how important the region is. The fact that these three states, along with nine others, now have observer status in the Arctic Council highlights how the Arctic has influenced foreign and defense policies of states without Arctic borders.

Section 3 provides a further dynamic of international relations that affect Arctic affairs: institutions and organizations. The global governance architecture has played a prominent role in the global political landscape in attempting to coordinate, pacify, and shape the relations between states. There are various types of international institutions that are differentiated by size, scope, geographical focus, or issues that are covered. In areas ranging from security to economics and trade to issue management, institutions have become effective forums through which states can pursue their interests and pool resources and expertise while mitigating the possibility of war. These institutions are also the bodies through which legitimate international decision-making and legal frameworks are developed, enacted, and enforced.

Arctic politics have benefited greatly from the role of institutions to date, but these institutions and the norms and values upon which they are founded face tests moving into the future. The United Nations and the Arctic Council are working diligently to ensure competing claims are addressed and settled through amicable and legally codified means, though it seems some states remain unsatisfied with the processes and decisions to date. The indigenous governance variable adds a particularly interesting aspect to debates over legitimate governance and sovereignty in the Arctic, given that certain indigenous groups have their own unique structures and modes of self-governance that fall well outside of state or international organizational frameworks. Further, the role of the European Union comprising both Arctic states and non-Arctic states lends another layer of complexity as it becomes increasingly interested in contributing more actively to circumpolar issues.

Taken as a whole, the three sections serve to highlight the complexities and opportunities facing the Arctic region now and in the future. As Mark Nuttall has noted, "In the post-Cold War world [the Arctic] is seen as a natural scientific laboratory, understood as a homeland for indigenous peoples, a place of sovereignty conflicts, an emerging hydrocarbon province with which the world is coming to think of as one of the last major frontiers for oil and gas, and a region of dramatic environmental change."[2] The years of the Cold War saw the Arctic as a space for military competition but not for territorial or legal claims per se. Instead, the Arctic was a key geostrategic space for both the Soviet Union and the United States for naval and aerial superiority. The race for the Arctic is a race for the Arctic itself, and not simply as an area to traverse.

As states are able to access the Arctic more freely and widely, interest in the region will undoubtedly continue to grow. The circumpolar North, with all its opportunities and challenges, represents one of the final frontiers on the planet. There remains plenty of mystery surrounding just how high the levels of natural resources are and how greater shipping access will alter the geopolitical landscape. If the events of the last twenty years are any indication, the Arctic will continue to be at the forefront of international political discussion and debate and will play a pivotal role in geostrategic calculations of states and institutions well into the future.

Notes

1. Andrei Mikhailov, "World's Strongest Powers Get Ready to Fight for Arctic Riches," *Pravda*, July 1, 2013, http://english.pravda.ru/world/europe/01-07-2013/124989-arctic-0/.
2. Mark Nuttall, "Afterword: the North and Global Gaze," in *In Canada's and Europe's Northern Dimensions*, ed. Anita Dey Nuttall and Mark Nuttall (Oulu, Finland: University of Oulu Press, 2009), 95.

BIBLIOGRAPHY

"2011 Arctic Dialogue Greenland Conference and Workshop Nuuk, Greenland, September 24–26, 2011 Meeting Summary." Ilisimatusarfik, University of Greenland, December 2011. http://www.hcahome.com/.

Abbott, Kenneth W., and Duncan Snidal. "Hard and Soft Law in International Governance." *International Organization* 54, no. 3 (Summer 2000): 421–456.

Abele, Frances. "Northern Development: Past, Present and Future." In *Northern Exposure: Peoples, Powers and Prospects for Canada's North*, edited by Frances Abele, Thomas Courchene, Leslie Seidle, and France St-Hilaire, 20–21. Ottawa: Institute for Research on Public Policy, 2009.

Abele, Frances, and Thierry Rodon. "Inuit Diplomacy and the Global ERA: The Strengths of Multilateral Internationalism." *International Journal* 13, no. 3 (2007): 45–63.

Administration of Ronald Reagan. "Statement by the President on United States Ocean Policy." 19 WEEKLY COMP. PRES. DOC. 383 (March 10, 1983). 22 I. L. M. 461, 464 (1983).

AEWC (Alaska Eskimo Whaling Commission). 2012 Open Water Season Programmatic Conflict Avoidance Agreement. March 2012. www.nmfs.noaa.gov/pr/pdfs/permits/bp_ openwater_caa2012.pdf.

Agamben, Giorgio. *Homo Sacer: Sovereign Power and Bare Life*. Stanford, CA: Stanford University Press, 1998.

Agreement on Cooperation on Aeronautical and Maritime Search and Rescue in the Arctic, August 18, 2011. http://www.ifrc.org/docs/idrl/N813EN.pdf.

AHDR (Arctic Human Development Report). Arctic Human Development Report. Akureyri, Iceland: Stefansson Arctic Institute, 2004.

Ahlin, Urban, Lena Hjelm Wallén, Hans Linde, Ulla Hoffmann, Per Gahrton, Peter Rådberg. *En rödgrön politik för Sveriges relationer med världens länder.* Policy statement, February 17, 2010.

Åhrén, Mattias. "Some Provisions That Are Notably Absent from the Saami Convention." *Gáldu Cála—Journal of Indigenous Peoples Rights* 3 (2007): 34–35.

Åhrén, Mattias, Martin Scheinin, and John B. Henriksen. "The Nordic Sami Convention: International Human Rights, Self-Determination and Other Central Provisions." *Gáldu Cála—Journal of Indigenous Peoples Rights* 3 (2007): 1–108.

Airoldi, Adele. *The European Union and the Arctic: Main Developments July 2008–July 2010.* Copenhagen: Nordic Council of Ministers, 2010.

———. *The European Union and the Arctic: Policies and Actions.* Copenhagen: Nordic Council of Ministers, 2008.

Alaska History and Cultural Studies Curriculum Project. "Northwest and Arctic: 1732–1871 Age of Arctic Exploration and Whaling." 2004–2011. http://www.akhistorycourse.org/articles/article.php?artID=64.

Albert, Mathias, David Jacobson, and Yosef Lapid, eds. *Identities, Borders, Orders: Rethinking International Relations Theory.* Minneapolis: University of Minnesota Press, 2001.

Alexander, Vera. "Arctic Marine Ecosystems." In *Global Warming and Biological Diversity,* edited by Robert L. Peters and Thomas E. Lovejoy, 221–229. New Haven, CT: Yale University Press, 1992.

Alexeeva, Olga, and Frédéric Lasserre. "China and the Arctic." *Arctic Yearbook 2012*: 80–90.

Alfredsson, Gudmundur. "Human Rights and Indigenous Rights." In *Polar Law Textbook,* edited by Natalia Loukacheva, 147–170. Copenhagen: Nordic Council of Ministers, 2010.

Alta Outcome Document. Global Indigenous Preparatory Conference for the United Nations High Level Plenary Meeting of the General Assembly to be known as the World Conference on Indigenous Peoples, Alta, Norway, June 10–12, 2013.

Althingi. *Þingsályktun um stefnu Íslands í málefnum Norðurslóða* [Parliament's conclusions on Iceland's Arctic policy]. Document no. 1148 of the 139th session 2010–2011. http://www.althingi.is/altext/139/s/1148.html.

———. *Report of the Special Investigation Commission*, April 12, 2010. http://sic.althingi.is/.

———. "Results from the Voting on a Motion of Non-Confidence." http://.althingi.is/dba-bin/nafnak.pl?btim=2011-04-13+21:12:12&etim=2011-04-13+21:59:04&timi=21:12-21:59.

AMSA. *Arctic Marine Shipping Assessment 2009 Report.* 2009.

An Myungok. "President Lee Steps into the Arctic Circle for South Koreas Arctic Initiative." *Korea Net*, September 17, 2012. http://www.korea.net/NewsFocus/Policies/view?articleId=102568.

Anaya, James. *Report of the Special Rapporteur on the Situation of the Human Rights and Fundamental Freedoms of Indigenous People.* Advanced version, January 2011. http://www2.ohchr.org/english/issues/indigenous/rapporteur/.

Anderson, Benedict. *Imagined Communities: Reflections on the Origin and Spread of Nationalism.* London and New York: Verso, 1996.

Antrim, Caitlin. "The New Maritime Arctic: Geopolitics and the Russian Arctic in the 21st Century." *Russia in Global Affairs*, October 15, 2010. http://eng.globalaffairs.ru/number/The-New-Maritime-Arctic-15000.

Archer, Clive. *Northern Waters: Resources and Strategic Issues.* New York: Barnes and Noble, 1996.

———. "An EU Arctic Policy." Paper given at UACES Conference, Bruges, September 6–8, 2010.

Archer, Clive, and Tobias Etzold. "The European Union and Kaliningrad: Taking the Low Road." *Geopolitics* 15, no. 2 (2010): 329–344.

Arctic Climate Impact Assessment (ACIA). *Arctic Climate Impact Assessment: Scientific Report.* Cambridge: Cambridge University Press, 2005.

———. *Arctic Climate Impact Assessment Policy Document.* Fourth Arctic Council Ministerial Meeting, Reykjavik, November 24, 2004. http://www.acia.uaf.edu/PDFs/ACIA_Policy_Document.pdf.

———. *Impacts of a Warming Arctic: ACIA Overview Report.* Cambridge: Cambridge University Press, 2004. http://amap.no/acia/.

Arctic Council. *Agreement on Cooperation on Aeronautical and Maritime Search and Rescue in the Arctic.* Tromsø, Norway: Arctic Council, 2011. http://www.arctic-council.org/index.php/en/about/documents/category/20-main-documents-from-nuuk?download=73:arctic-search-and-rescue-agreement-english.

———. *Nuuk Declaration on the Occasion of the Seventh Ministerial Meeting of the Arctic Council.* Nuuk, Greenland, May 12, 2011. http://library.arcticportal.org/1254/.

———. *Observers.* 2013. http://www.arctic-council.org/index.php/en/about-us/arctic-council/observers.

———. *PAME Progress Report on the Ecosystem Approach to Arctic Marine Assessment and Management 2006–2008.* 2006.

———. "Senior Arctic Officials (SAO) Report to Ministers." Nuuk, Greenland, May 2011.

Arctic Council and PAME. *Arctic Marine Shipping Assessment (AMSA) Report.* 2009. http://www.pame.is/amsa-2009-report.

Arctic Council Panel. "To Establish an International Arctic Council: A Framework Report." *Northern Perspectives* 19, no. 2 (Summer 1991). http://carc.org/pubs/v19no2/2.htm.

Arctic Environmental Protection Strategy—Declaration of the Protection of the Arctic Environment, June 14, 1991. http://www.arctic-council.org/index.php/en/document-archive/category/4-founding-documents.pdf.

Arctic Human Development Report. Akureyri: Stefansson Arctic Institute, 2004.

Arctic Monitoring and Assessment Programme. "Snow, Water, Ice and Permafrost in the Arctic (SWIPA)." 2011. http://amap.no/swipa/.

Arctic Ocean Conference. *The Ilulissat Declaration.* Ilulissat, Greenland: Arctic Ocean Conference, 2008. http://www.oceanlaw.org/downloads/arctic/Ilulissat_Declaration.pdf.

Arendt, Hannah. *The Human Condition*. Chicago: University of Chicago Press, 1958.

Aron, William. "The International Whaling Commission: A Case of Malignant Neglect." *IIFET Proceedings*, 2000.

Arsenault, Chris. "Melting Arctic Heats up Resource Scramble." *Al Jazeera*, September 20, 2012. http://www.aljazeera.com/indepth/features/201 2/09/2012916133717451622.html.

Art, Robert, and Robert Jervis. "Anarchy and Its Consequences." In *International Politics: Enduring Concepts and Contemporary Issues*, 1–6. New York: Pearson Education, 2007.

Asgrimsson, Halldór, and Cristina Husmark Pehrsson. "Introduction." In *Common Concern for the Arctic*, edited by Nordic Council of Ministers, 11–12. Copenhagen: Nordic Council of Ministers, 2008.

Åtland, Kristian. "Mikhail Gorbachev, the Murmansk Initiative, and the Desecuritization of Interstate Relations in the Arctic." *Cooperation and Conflict* 43, no. 3 (2008): 289–311.

———. "Security Implications of Climate Change in the Arctic." FFI-rapport 2010/01097. Oslo: The Norwegian Defence Research Establishment (FFI), 2010.

Auburn, Frances M. "International Law and Sea-Ice Jurisdiction in the Arctic Ocean." *International and Comparative Law Quarterly* 22 (1973): 552–557.

Avant, Deborah D., Martha Finnemore, and Susan K. Sell, eds. *Who Governs the Globe?* Cambridge: Cambridge University Press, 2010.

Bailes, Alyson J. K. "Options for Closer Cooperation in the High North: What Is Needed?" In *Security Prospects in the High North: Geostrategic Thaw or Freeze?* NDC Forum Paper 7, edited by Sven G. Holtsmark and Brooke A. Smith-Windsor, 28–57. Rome: NATO Defense College, 2009.

———. "Potential Roles of NATO and the EU in High Northern Security." In *Yearbook of Polar Law 2010*. Leiden: Martinus Nijhoff, 2010.

Bailes, Alyson J. K., and Baldur Thorhallsson. "Iceland and Europe: Drifting Further Apart?" Finnish Institute of International Affairs

Briefing Paper 139, September 2013, http://www.fiia.fi/en/publication/360/iceland_and_europe/#.UlG2NyRO_w4.

———. "Iceland and the European Security and Defence Policy." In *The Nordic Countries and the European Security and Defence Policy*, edited by Alyson J. K. Bailes, Gunilla Herolf, and Bengt Sundelius, 328–348. Oxford: Oxford University Press, 2006.

Bailes, Alyson J. K., and Þröstur F. Gylfason. "Societal Security and Iceland." In *Stjórnmál og Stjórnsýsla*, vol. 1, 4th ed. Reykjavik: Institute of Administration and Politics, 2008. http://stjornmalogstjornsysla.is/images/stories/eg2008v/alyson08.pdf.

Baker, Betsy. "Law, Science and the Continental Shelf: The Russian Federation and the Promise of Arctic Cooperation." *American University International Law Review* 25 (2010): 251–281.

Baldursson, Ragnar. "Sustainable Development for the Residents of the High North, Opportunities Related to the Opening of New Sailing-Routes in the Arctic Ocean." In *Ideas about Heavy Industry in the Vestfjords.* Fjordungssambandid, 2008. http://www.fjordungssamband.is/fv/upload/files/malthing_um_storidnad/ragnarbaldursson.pdf.

Ball, John. "Soviet Work in the Arctic." *Geographical Journal* 81, no. 6 (1933): 532–535.

Banerjee, Subhanker, ed. *Arctic Voices: Resistance at the Tipping Point.* New York: Seven Stories Press, 2012.

Barents Euro-Arctic Region. *The Kirkenes Declaration from the Conference of Foreign Ministers on Co-operation in the Barents Euro-Arctic Region.* Kirkenes, January 11, 1993.

Barkin, J. Samuel. "The Evolution and the Constitution of Sovereignty and the Emergence of Human Rights Norms." *Millennium: Journal of International Studies* 27, no. 2 (1998): 229–252.

Barkin, J. Samuel, and Bruce Cronin. "The State and the Nation: Changing Norms and the Rules of Sovereignty in International Relations." *International Organization* 48, no. 1 (1994): 107–130.

Barnett, Michael, and Martha Finnemore. "Political Approaches." In *The Oxford Handbook on the United Nations*, edited by Thomas G. Weiss and Sam Daws, 41–57. Oxford: Oxford University Press, 2007.

Barry, Andrew. "The Anti-Political Economy." *Economy and Society* 31, no. 2 (2002): 268–284.

Barsegov, Yury Georgievich, et al. *The Arctic: Russia's Interests and International Conditions of Their Realization* [Arktika: Interesy Rossii i mezhdunarodnye usloviya ih realizatsii]. Moscow: Nauka, 2002.

Bartelson, Jens. *A Genealogy of Sovereignty*. Cambridge: Cambridge University Press, 1995.

"Basics of the State Policy of the Russian Federation in the Arctic for the Period until 2020 and for a Further Perspective." Moscow; adopted September 18, 2008, promulgated March 30, 2009. Published in *Rossiyskaya Gazeta*. http://www.scrf.gov.ru/documents/98.html.

BBC News. "Russia Plants Flag under North Pole." *BBC News*, August 2, 2007. http://news.bbc.co.uk/1/hi/world/europe/6927395.stm.

Beazley, Charles Raymond. "The Russian Expansion Towards Asia and the Arctic in the Middle Ages (to 1500)." *American Historical Review* 13, no. 4 (1908): 731–741.

Beck, Peter J. "Convention on the Regulation of Antarctic Mineral Resource Activities: A Major Addition to the Antarctic Treaty System." *Polar Record* 25, no. 152 (1989): 19–32.

———. "A New Polar Factor in International Relations." *World Today* 45, no. 4 (1989): 65–68.

Beinecke, Frances. "Obama Administration Allows More Offshore Drilling without More Safeguards for Arctic and Gulf." *Natural Resource Defense Council Staff Blog*, November 9, 2011. http://switchboard.nrdc.org/blogs/fbeinecke/obama_administration_allows_mo.html.

Belanger, D. Olson. "The International Geophysical Year in Antarctica: Uncommon Collaborations, Unprecedented Results." *Journal of Government Information* 30 (2004): 482–489.

Bellamy, Alex. *The Responsibility to Protect*. Cambridge: Polity Press, 2009.

Bellinger, John. "Treaty on Ice." *The New York Times*, June 23, 2008. http://www.nytimes.com/2008/06/23/opinion/23bellinger.html.

Benjaminson, Eric. "Letter from Eric Benjaminson (Minister-Counselor for Economic, Energy, and Environment Affairs, Embassy of the United States of America in Canada) to Robert Turner (Manager for Navigation Safety and Radiocommunications, Transport Canada)," March 19, 2010. http://www.state.gov/documents/organization/179286.pdf.

Bennett, Mia. "Japan Applies for Arctic Council Observer Status." *Foreign Policy Association*, April 20, 2009. http://foreignpolicyblogs.com/2009/04/20/japan-applies-for-arctic-council-observer-status/.

Berger, Thomas, Joseph F. Merritt, Esko Rajakoski, Mary Simon, and E. R. Weick. "Question Session." In *The Arctic: Choices for Peace and Security. Proceedings of a Public Inquiry*, edited by Thomas R. Berger et al., 79. West Vancouver and Seattle: Gordon Soules Book Publishers Ltd., 1989.

Berger, Thomas. *Northern Frontier/Northern Homeland: The Report of the Mackenzie Valley Inquiry* 1. Ottawa: Department of Supply and Services, 1977.

Bergh, Kristofer. *The Arctic Policies of Canada and the United States: Domestic Motives and International Context (SIPRI Insights on Peace and Security, no. 2012/1)*. Solna, Sweden: Stockholm International Peace Research Institute, 2012.

Bergmann, Eirikur. *Evrópusamruninn og Ísland* [European integration and Iceland]. Reykjavik: University of Iceland, 2003.

Berkman, Paul, and Oran Young. "Governance and Environmental Change in the Arctic Ocean." *Science* 324, no. 5925 (April 17, 2009): 339–340. http://www.sciencemag.org/content/324/5925/339.summary.

Biersteker, Thomas, and Cynthia Weber. "The Social Construction of Sovereignty." In *State Sovereignty as Social Construct*, edited by Thomas Biersteker and Cynthia Weber, 1–21. Cambridge: Cambridge University Press, 1996.

Bildt, Carl. "Working for a More Eco-Efficient Economy of the Barents Region." In *Swedish Chairmanship of the Barents Euro-Arctic Council,*

2009–2011, edited by Swedish Chair of the Barents Euro-Arctic Council. Kirkenes: International Barents Secretariat, 2009.

Bill 2008/09:T388. Sinikka Bohlin, Helene Petersson, and Peter Jonsson. "Motion till riksdagen: Arktisk policy för sjösäkerhet." October 1, 2008.

Bill 2008/09:T389. Sinikka Bohlin, Helene Petersson, and Peter Jonsson. "Motion till riksdagen: Arktisk policy för sjöfart." October 2, 2008.

Bird, Kenneth J., Ronald R. Charpentier, Donald L. Gautier, David W. Houseknecht, Timothy R. Klett, Janet K. Pitman, Thomas E. Moore, Christopher J. Schenk, Marilyn E. Tennyson, and Craig J. Wandrey. *Circum-Arctic Resource Appraisal; Estimates of Undiscovered Oil and Gas North of the Arctic Circle: U.S. Geological Survey Fact Sheet 2008-3049.* http://pubs.usgs.gov/fs/2008/3049/.

Birnie, Patricia, Alan Boyle, and Catherine Redgwell. *International Law & the Environment.* New York: Oxford University Press, 2009.

Bjarnason, Gunnar Th. *Óvænt áfall eða fyrirsjánleg tímamót, brottför bandaríkjahers frá Íslandi: aðdragandi og viðbrögð [Bolt from the Blue or Foreseeable Watershed? The US Force Withdrawal from Iceland: Antecedents and Reactions].* Reykjavik: University of Iceland, 2008.

Björnsson, Halldór, et al. "The Influence of Global Climate Change on Iceland" [Hnattrænar loftslagsbreytingar og áhrif þeirra á Íslandi]. A report on Climate Change by the Scientific Committee. Ministry for the Environment, 2008.

Bjørst, Lill Rastad. "Arktiske diskurser og klimaforandringer i Grønland: Fire (post)humanistiske klimastudier." PhD thesis, University of Copenhagen, 2011.

Bloom, Evan T. "Establishment of the Arctic Council." *American Journal of International Law* 93, no. 3 (July 1999): 712–722.

Blunden, Margaret. "Geopolitics and the Northern Sea Route." *International Affairs* 88, no. 1 (2012): 115–129.

Bockstoce, John, and John Burns. "Commercial Whaling in the North Pacific Sector." *The Bowhead Whale Special Publication Number 2* (1993): 563–577.

Bodin, Jean. *Six Books of the Commonwealth.* Edited and translated by M. J. Tooley. 1576; repr., New York: MacMillan Company, 1955.

Bolkhovitinov, Nikolai Nikolaevich. "The Sale of Alaska: Documents, Letters, Memoirs" [Prodazha Alyaski: dokumenty, pis'ma, vospominaniya]. *The USA—Economics, politics, ideology* [SSHA—Ekonomika, politika, ideologiya] 3 (1990): 47–55.

Borg, Joe. "The Arctic: A Matter of Concern to Us All." Speech at the Conference "Common Concern for the Arctic," Ilulissat, Greenland, September 9, 2008. http://europa.eu/rapid/press-release_SPEECH-0 8-415_en.htm?locale=en.

———. "The European Union's Strategy of Sustainable Management for the Arctic." Tromsø, Norway, January 19, 2009. http://europa.eu/rapid/press-release_SPEECH-09-9_en.htm?locale=en.

Borgerson, Scott G. "Arctic Meltdown: The Economic and Security Implications of Global Warming." *Foreign Affairs* 87, no. 2 (2008): 63–77. http://www.foreignaffairs.org/20080301faessay87206/scott-gborgerson/arctic-meltdown.html.

Boyes, Roger. *Meltdown Iceland: How the Global Financial Crisis Bankrupted an Entire Country.* London: Bloomsbury, 2009.

Bradshaw, Michael. "Global Energy Dilemmas: A Geographical Perspective." *Geographical Journal* 176 (2010): 275–290.

Brady, Anne-Marie. *The Emerging Politics of Antarctica.* London: Routledge, 2012.

Branders, Håkan. "Suomen liittyminen Pohjoismaiden neuvostoon." In *Suomi Pohjoismaana—Suomi 50 vuotta Pohjoismaiden neuvostossa,* edited by Larserik Häggman, 8–16. Vaasa, Finland: Pohjola Norden, 2005.

Breitfuss, Leonid Lyudvigovich. *Siberian Sea Route to the Far East* [Morskoi sibirskii put' na Dal'nii Vostok]. St. Petersburg: Izdatel'stvo Sudokhodnogo Obshchestva, 1904.

Brigham, Lawson. "The Challenges and Security Issues of Arctic Marine Transport." In *Arctic Security in an Age of Climate Change,* edited by James Kraska, 20–32. Cambridge: Cambridge University Press, 2011.

Brodie, Bernard. *Strategy in the Missile Age.* Santa Monica, CA: Rand Corporation, 1959.

Brosnan, Ian G., Thomas M. Leschine, and Edward L. Miles. "Cooperation or Conflict in a Changing Arctic?" *Ocean Development & International Law* 42, nos. 1–2 (2011): 173–210.

Brower, Harry. Alaska Eskimo Whaling Commission presentation to the White House Ocean Policy Task Force. Anchorage, 2009. http://www.whitehouse.gov/assets/formsubmissions/54/7b0421829d8a4c1e8508d876aa40f61b.pdf.

Brown, Chris. "World Society and the English School: An 'International Society' Perspective on World Society." *European Journal of International Relations* 7, no. 4 (2001): 423–441.

Bukovansky, Mlada. *Legitimacy and Power Politics: The American and French Revolutions in International Political Culture.* Princeton: Princeton University Press, 2002.

Bulkeley, Harriet. "Reconfiguring Environmental Governance: Towards a Politics of Scales and Networks." *Political Geography* 24 (2005): 875–902.

Bull, Hedley. *The Anarchical Society: A Study of Order in World Politics.* New York: Columbia University Press, 1995.

———. "The Grotian Conception of International Society." In *Diplomatic Investigations: Essays in the Theory of International Relations*, edited by Herbert Butterfield and Martin Wight, 51–73. Cambridge, MA: Harvard University Press, 1966.

Bush, George W. *National Security Presidential Directive and Homeland Security Presidential Directive: Arctic Region Policy (NSPD-66 and HSPD-25).* Washington, DC: The White House, 2009. http://www.fas.org/irp/offdocs/nspd/nspd-66.htm.

———. *The President's News Conference with Prime Minister Stephen Harper of Canada and President Felipe de Jesus Calderon Hinojosa of Mexico in Montebello, Canada*, August 21, 2007. http://www.presidency.ucsb.edu/ws/index.php?pid=75725.

Buzan, Barry. "Canada and the Law of the Sea." *Ocean Development & International Law* 11, nos. 3–4 (1982): 149–180.

———. *From International to World Society? English School Theory and the Social Structure of Globalisation.* Cambridge: Cambridge University Press, 2004.

———. "International Political Economy and Globalization." In *International Society and Its Critics*, edited by Alex J. Bellamy, 115–34. New York: Oxford University Press, 2005.

Buzan, Barry, Ole Wzan,, and Jaap De Wilde. *Security: A New Framework for Analysis.* Boulder, CO: Lynne Rienner Publishers, 1997.

Byers, Michael. *International Law and the Arctic.* Cambridge: Cambridge University Press, 2013.

———. *Who Owns the Arctic? Understanding Sovereignty Disputes in the North.* Vancouver: Douglas & McIntyre, 2010.

Callon, Michel, ed. *The Laws of the Markets.* Oxford: Blackwell, 1998.

Canada. DEW System and Mid-Canada Line. In Canada, Documents on Canadian External Relations. Vol. 19, 1953, edited by Donald Barry. Ottawa: Supply and Services Canada, 1991.

Canada, Canada's Northern Strategy. "Achievements under Canada's Northern Strategy, 2007–2011," January 1, 2012. http://www.northernstrategy.gc.ca/cns/au-eng.asp.

———. "Exercising Our Arctic Sovereignty," August 15, 2012. http://www.northernstrategy.gc.ca/sov/index-eng.asp.

Canada, Department of National Defence. *Canada's International Policy Statement: A Role of Pride and Influence in the World—Defence.* Ottawa: Department of National Defence, 2005.

Canada, Foreign Affairs and International Trade Canada. *Dismantling of Nuclear Submarines*, January 11, 2011. http://www.international.gc.ca/gpp-ppm/nuclear_submarines-sousmarins_nucleaires.aspx?lang=eng.

Canadian Arctic Resource Committee (CARC). *Northern Perspectives* 30, no. 1 (Winter 2006): 1–24. http://www.carc.org/pubs/v30no1/CARC_Northrn_Perspctves_Winter_2006.pdf.

"Canadian Forces Winds up High Arctic Exercise." *Ottawa Citizen*, April 27, 2012. http://blogs.ottawacitizen.com/2012/04/27/canadian-forces-winds-up-high-arctic-exercise/.

CanWest Media. "Russians Plant Flag on North Pole Seabed." *Regina Leader-Post*, August 3, 2007. http://www.canada.com/reginaleaderpost/story.html?id=55f5b74e-3728-4245-97ed-f6713c3f1 bb8&k=40585.

Caporaso, James. "Changes in the Westphalian Order: Territory, Public Authority, and Sovereignty." *International Studies Review* 2, no. 2 (2000): 1–28.

Carr, E. H. *The Twenty Years' Crisis*. New York: Palgrave Macmillan, 2001.

Carter, Lee. "Canada in Arctic Show of Strength." BBC News, August 16, 2009. http://news.bbc.co.uk/2/hi/8204531.stm.

Cava, Francesca, David Monsma, and Oran R. Young. "Workshop on Arctic Governance: Drawing Lessons from the Antarctic Experience." In *Science Diplomacy: Antarctica, Science and the Governance of International Spaces*, edited by Paul Arthur Berkman, Michael A. Lang, David W. H. Walton, and Oran R. Young, 296. Washington, DC: Smithsonian Institution Scholarly Press, 2011.

CBC News. "Arctic Council Grants China, Japan Observer Status." May 15, 2013. http://www.cbc.ca/news/canada/north/arctic-council-grants-china-japan-observer-status-1.1375121.

———. "Arctic Council Leaders Sign Rescue Treaty." May 12, 2011. http://www.cbc.ca/news/canada/north/story/2011/05/12/arctic-council-greenland.html.

———. "The Arctic Grail." August 8, 2008. http://www.cbc.ca/archives/categories/economy-business/transport/breaking-the-ice-canada-and-the-northwest-passage/the-arctic-grail.html.

———. "Arctic Nations Talk Search and Rescue Meeting in Whitehorse This Week to Build on Agreement Signed in May." October 7, 2011.

———. "Arctic Naval Facility Downgrade due to High Cost, Says DND," May 27, 2012. http://www.cbc.ca/news/canada/north/story/2012/03/27/north-nanisivik-high-cost.html.

———. "Arctic of Strategic Importance to Canada: PM," August 19, 2009. http://www.cbc.ca/news/canada/story/2009/08/19/harper-nanook-arctic-north-sovereignty414.html.

———. "Health Minister Leona Aglukkaq to Chair Arctic Council," August 23, 2012. http://www.cbc.ca/news/politics/story/2012/08/23/pol-arctic-council-leona-aglukkaq-chair.html.

CBC News Canada. "Battle for the Arctic Heats Up." February 27, 2009. http://www.cbc.ca/news/canada/story/2009/02/27/f-arctic-sovereignty.html.

CBC News North. "Arctic Ice Could Vanish in 10 Years, Scientists Warn," August 13, 2012. http://www.cbc.ca/news/canada/north/story/2012/08/13/arctic-ice-melting-faster.html.

Center for Oceans Law and Policy, University of Virginia School of Law. *UNCLOS 1982 Commentary—Supplementary Documents.* Leiden, the Netherlands: Martinus Nijhoff Publishers, 2012.

Charnowitz, Steve. "Nongovernmental Organizations and International Law." *American Journal of International Law* 100 (April 2006): 348–372.

Chaturvedi, Sanjay. "Geopolitical Transformations: 'Rising' Asia and the Future of the Arctic Council." In *The Arctic Council: Its Place in the Future of Arctic Governance and the Future of the Arctic Council,* edited by T. Axworthy, T. Koivurova, and W. Hasanat, 225–260. Toronto: Munk-Gordon Arctic Security Program, 2012. http://gordonfoundation.ca/publication/530.

———. *Dawning of Antarctica: A Geopolitical Analysis.* New Delhi: Segment Books, 1990.

Chayes, Abram, and Antonia Handler Chayes. *The New Sovereignty: Compliance with International Regulatory Agreements.* Cambridge, MA: Harvard University Press, 1995.

"China's Snow Dragon Icebreaker Makes 85-Day Voyage to Become Country's First Vessel to Cross Arctic Ocean." *National Post,* September 28, 2012. http://news.nationalpost.com/2012/09/28/chinas-snow-dragon-icebreaker-makes-85-day-voyage-to-become-countrys-first-vessel-to-cross-arctic-ocean/.

Christley, Jim. *US Nuclear Submarines: The Fast Attack.* London: Osprey, 2007.

Churchill, Robin R., and Alan V. Lowe. *The Law of the Sea.* 3rd ed. Manchester: Manchester University Press, 1999.

Clarkson, Stephen, and Stepan Wood. "Canada's External Constitution and Its Democratic Deficit." In *The Globalized Rule of Law*, edited by Oonagh E. Fitzgerald, 97–124. Toronto: Irwin Law, 2006.

Clinton, Hillary R. "Interview on CTV's *Power Play with Tom Clark*," March 29, 2010. http://www.state.gov/secretary/rm/2010/03/139207.htm.

Coates, Ken. "The Discovery of the North: Towards a Conceptual Framework for the Study of Northern/Remote Regions." *Northern Review* 12, no. 13 (1994): 15–43.

Coates, Ken, and W. R. Morrison. *The Alaska Highway in World War II: The American Army of Occupation in Canada's Northwest.* Norman: University of Oklahoma Press; Toronto: University of Toronto Press, 1992.

Coates, Ken, Whitney Lackenbauer, William Morrison, and Greg Poelzer. *Arctic Front: Defending Canada's Interests in the Far North.* Toronto: Thomas Allen, 2008.

Cochran, Patricia. "Arctic Council: Meeting of Ministers of Foreign Affairs, Tromsø, Norway: Introductory Remarks: Chair, Inuit Circumpolar Council." April 29, 2009.

Cohen, Hymen Ezra. *Recent Theories of Sovereignty.* Chicago: University of Chicago Press, 1937.

Cohen, Jean. "Whose Sovereignty? Empire versus International Law." *Ethics & International Affairs* 18, no. 3 (2004): 1–24.

Comiso, Josefino C., Claire L. Parkinson, Robert Gersten, and Larry Stock. "Accelerated Decline in the Arctic Sea Ice Cover." *Geophysical Research Letters* 35 (2008): 1–6.

Commission of the European Communities. *Commission Staff Working Document: Accompanying Document to the Communication from the Commission to the European Parliament, the Council, the European*

Economic and Social Committee and the Committee of the Regions —An Integrated Maritime Policy for the European Union. Brussels: Commission of the European Communities, October 10, 2007. http:// eur-lex.europa.eu/LexUriServ/LexUriServ.do?uri=CELEX:52007SC1 278:EN:HTML.

———. *Communication from the Commission to the European Parliament and the Council—The European Union and the Arctic Region.* Brussels, 20.11.2008 COM(2008) 763 final, 2008.

———. *The European Union and the Arctic Region: Communication from the Commission to the European Parliament and the Council.* Brussels COM 763 (2008). Brussels: Commission of the European Communities, 2008. http://eur-lex.europa.eu/LexUriServ/LexUriServ.do?uri=COM:2 008:0763:FIN:EN:PDF.

———. *An Integrated Maritime Policy for the European Union,* COM(2007) 575 final, October 10, 2007. Brussels: Commission of the European Communities, 2007. http://eur-lex.europa.eu/LexUriServ/LexUriServ. do?uri=COM:2007:0575:FIN:EN:PDF.

Commission on Global Governance. *Our Global Neighbourhood.* Oxford: Oxford University Press, 2005.

"Common Objectives." Common objectives and priorities for the Norwegian, Danish, and Swedish chairmanships of the Arctic Council (2006–2012). 2006.

Comstock, Earl. "Testimony of Earl Comstock Counsel for the Alaska Eskimo Whaling Commission before the Subcommittee on International Organizations, Human Rights and Oversight and the Subcommittee on Asia, the Pacific and the Global Environment." In *US Leadership in the International Whaling Commission and H.R. 2455, the International Whale Conservation and Protection Act of 2009 Joint Hearing Before the Subcommittee on International Organizations, Human Rights and Oversight and the Subcommittee on Asia, the Pacific and the Global Environment of the Committee on Foreign Affairs of the House of Representatives One Hundred Eleventh Congress Second Session,* Serial No. 111–95, May 6, 2010.

"Concept of Sustainable Development of Indigenous Small-Numbered Peoples of the North, Siberia and the Far East of the Russian

Federation." Moscow: adopted February 4, 2009. http://www.kamchatka.gov.ru/oiv_doc/2023/6461.doc.

Copeland, Dale. *The Origins of Major War*. Ithaca, NY: Cornell University Press, 2000.

Corell, Hans. "Chairman's Conclusions." In *Common Concern for the Arctic*, edited by Nordic Council of Ministers, 15–32. Copenhagen: Nordic Council of Ministers, 2008.

Corgan, Michael T. *Iceland and Its Alliances, Security for a Small State*. New York: Edwin Mellen Press, 2002.

Council of the European Union. "Council Conclusions on Arctic Issues." 2985th Foreign Affairs Council meeting. Brussels, December 8, 2009. http://www.consilium.europa.eu/uedocs/cms_Data/docs/pressdata/EN/foraff/111814.pdf.

Council of Federation. *Opinion on the Draft Federal Law No. 608695-5 "On Amendments to Some Legislative Acts of the Russian Federation Regarding State Regulation of Merchant Shipping in the Waters of the Northern Sea Route."* October 28, 2012. http://severcom.ru/activity/section5/doc340.html.

County Administrative Board of Norrbotten. "'Var finns Norrbotten och Sverige i Barentssamarbetet?'" Presentation för föreningen Norden, Luleå, May 6, 2008.

Cousins, Stephanie. "UN Security Council: Playing a Role in the International Climate Change Regime." *Global Change, Peace and Security* 25, no. 2 (2013): 191–210.

Cox, Robert W. "Social Forces, States and World Order: Beyond International Relations Theory." *Millennium: Journal of International Studies* 10, no. 2 (1986): 219.

Crawford, Alec, Arthur Hanson, and David Runnalls. *Arctic Sovereignty and Security in a Climate-Changing World*. Winnipeg: International Institute for Sustainable Development, 2008.

Cronin, Bruce. *Institutions for the Common Good: International Protection Regimes in International Society*. Cambridge: Cambridge University Press, 2003.

CTV.ca. "Harper Pledges Larger Arctic Presence." December 22, 2005. http://www.ctv.ca/servlet/ArticleNews/story/CTVNews/20051222/harper_north051222/20051222?s_name=election2006.

Cutler, Claire. "Critical Reflections on the Westphalian Assumptions of International Law and Organization: A Crisis of Legitimacy." *Review of International Studies* 27 (2001): 133–150.

David, Robert. *The Arctic in the British Imagination 1818–1914.* Manchester: Manchester University Press, 2001.

de La Fayette, Louise Angélique. "Oceans Governance in the Arctic." *International Journal of Marine and Coastal Law* 23, no. 3 (2008): 531–566.

Dege, Wihelm. *The Last German Arctic Weather Station of World War II.* Translated by William Barr. Calgary: University of Calgary Press, 2004.

Deleuze, Gilles, and Félix Guattari. *A Thousand Plateaus: Capitalism and Schizophrenia.* Minneapolis: University of Minnesota Press, 1987.

Denmark, Greenland, and the Faroe Islands. *Kingdom of Denmark Strategy for the Arctic 2011–2020.* Copenhagen: Ministry of Foreign Affairs; Nuuk: Department of Foreign Affairs; and Tóshavn: Ministry of Foreign Affairs, 2011.

Department of Foreign Affairs and International Trade. "The Arctic Council: Objectives, Structures and Program Priorities," May 1995.

———. *Statement on Canada's Arctic Foreign Policy: Exercising Sovereignty and Promoting Canada's Northern Strategy,* August 2012. http://www.international.gc.ca/arctic-arctique/arctic_policy-canada-politique_arctique.aspx?lang=eng.

Depledge, Duncan and Klaus Dodds. "Testing the Northern Flank: UK-Norwegian Relations and the Arctic." *RUSI Journal* 158 (2012): 72–78.

———. "The UK and the Arctic: The Strategic Gap." *RUSI Journal* 156 (2011): 72–79.

Derrida, Jacques. *Force de loi.* Paris: Galilée, 1994.

Die Grünen. *The Programme of the German Green Party.* London: Heretic, 1983.

Dmitriev, Aleksandr Alekseevich, and Vladimir Timofeevich Sokolov. *Chronology of the Main Events in the History of AASRI, Arctic and Antarctic in the XXth and the Beginning of the XXIst Century* [Khronologiya vazhneishikh sobytii v istorii AANII, Arktiki i Antarktiki v XX i nachale XXI veka]. St. Petersburg: AANII, 2010.

Dmitriev, Michail. "Russia-2020: Challenges to Long-Term Development" [Rossiya-2020: Dolgosrochnye vyzovy razvitiya]. A public lecture delivered December 21, 2007. http://www.polit.ru/article/2007/12/21/dmitriev.

Dodds, Klaus. "The Arctic: From Frozen Desert to Open Polar Sea?" In *Maritime Strategy and Global Order*, edited by D. Moran and J. Russell. Washington, DC: Georgetown University Press, forthcoming 2014.

———. "Flag Waving and Finger Pointing: The Law of the Sea, the Arctic and the Political Geographies of the Outer Continental Shelf." *Political Geography* 29, no. 2 (2010): 63–73.

———. "Gesture and Posture: Pointing the Finger and the Mapping of Outer Continental Shelves." *Polar Record* 46, no. 3 (2010): 282–284.

———. "A Polar Mediterranean: Accessibility, Resources and Sovereignty in the Arctic Ocean." *Global Policy* 1 (2011): 303–311.

Dodds, Klaus, and Duncan Depledge. "'No "Strategy" Please, We're British': The UK and the Arctic Policy Framework." *RUSI Journal* 160 (forthcoming 2014).

Dodds, Klaus, and Valur Ingimundarson. "Territorial Nationalism and Arctic Geopolitics: Iceland as an Arctic Coastal State." *The Polar Journal* 2, no. 1 (2012): 21–37.

Dorough, Dalee Sambo. "Inuit of Alaska: Current Issues." In *Polar Law Textbook*, edited by Natalia Loukacheva, 199–219. Copenhagen: Nordic Council of Ministers, 2010.

Dosman, Edgar. "The Northern Sovereignty Crisis 1968–70." In *The Arctic in Question*, edited by Edgar Dosman, 33–62. Toronto: Oxford University Press, 1976.

Dosman, Edgar, ed. *Sovereignty and Security in the Arctic.* London and New York: Routledge, 1989.

Downie, David, and Terry Fenge, eds. *Northern Lights against POPs: Combatting Toxic Threats in the Arctic.* Montreal and Kingston: McGill-Queen's University Press, 2003.

Doyle, Michael. *Ways of War and Peace.* New York: W. W. Norton, 1997.

Dryzek, John. *Deliberative Global Politics: Discourse and Democracy in a Divided World.* Cambridge: Polity Press, 2006.

———. *Rational Ecology: Environment and Political Economy.* Oxford: Basil Blackwell, 1987.

———. "Transnational Democracy." *Journal of Political Philosophy* 7, no. 1 (1999): 30–51.

Dunne, Tim, and Brian Schmidt. "Realism." In *The Globalization of World Politics,* edited by John Baylis, Steve Smith, and Patricia Owens, 161–183. Oxford: Oxford University Press, 2005.

Durham University. *Maritime Jurisdiction and Boundaries in the Arctic Region.* May 4, 2010. http://www.dur.ac.uk/resources/ibru/arctic.pdf.

Duyck, Sebastien. "Drawing Lessons for Arctic Governance from the Antarctic Treaty System." In *The Yearbook of Polar Law,* vol. 3, edited by Gudmundur Alfredsson, Timo Koivurova, and Kamrul Hossain, 683–713. Leiden: Brill Editions, 2011.

Eayrs, James. In Defence of Canada—Peacemaking and Deterrence. Toronto: University of Toronto Press, 1972.

Eckersley, Robyn. *The Green State: Rethinking Democracy and Sovereignty.* Cambridge, MA: MIT Press, 2004.

Economist Intelligence Unit. *Norway Country Report.* London: EIU, December 2008.

Economy Watch. "Norway Economic Statistics and Indicators." http://www.economywatch.com/economic-statistics/country/Norway/.

Einarsson, Sveinn Kjartan. "China's Direct Investment in the 'West': Is There a Security Threat?" MA thesis, University of Iceland, 2013. http://skemman.is/item/view/1946/14799;jsessionid=5CA8ACB66FF7B7324C4AA8D639972DB7.

Ekspertutvalg for nordområdene. *Mot nord!: Utfordringer og muligheter i nordområdene: ekspertutvalg for nordområdene nedsatt av regjeringen*

3. mars 2003: Avgitt til Utenriksdepartementet 8. desember 2003, Norges offentlige utredninger; NOU 2003:32. Oslo: Statens forvaltningstjeneste, Informasjonsforvaltning, 2003.

Elkins, David. *Beyond Sovereignty: Territory and Political Economy in the Twenty-First Century.* Toronto: University of Toronto Press, 1995.

Elliot-Meisel, Elizabeth. "Still Unresolved after Fifty Years: The Northwest Passage in Canadian-American Relations, 1946–1998." *American Review of Canadian Studies* 29 (1999): 407–430.

Embassy of the United States of America in Canada. *Diplomatic Note no. 625, August 18, 2010.* http://www.state.gov/documents/organization/179287.pdf.

Embassy of the United States, Ottawa–Canada. "Podcast Transcript: Evan Bloom, Director, Office of Ocean and Polar Affairs, Department of State," July 21, 2010. http://canada.usembassy.gov/2010-podcasts.html.

Emmerson, Charles. "Russia's Arctic Opening." *Foreign Policy*, March 30, 2011. http://www.foreignpolicy.com/articles/2011/03/30/russias_arctic_opening.

Eriksen, Knut Einar, and Helge Øystein Pharo. *Kald krig og internasjonalisering, 1949–1965.* Vol. 5 of *Norsk utenrikspolitikks historie.* Oslo: Universitetsforlaget, 1997.

European Commission. "Communication from the Commission to the European Parliament and the Council: The European Union and the Arctic Region. COM (2008) 763 Final." Brussels: European Commission, 2008.

———. "The Northern Dimension Policy, 2010." http://ec.europa.eu/external_relations/north_dim/index_en.htm.

———. "Northern Dimension Policy Framework Document, 2006.". http://ec.europa.eu/external_relations/north_dim/index_en.htm.

European Commission (High Representative). "Climate Change and International Security." Paper from the High Representative and the European Commission to the European Council, S113/08. March 14, 2008. Brussels: European Commission.

European Commission, High Representative of the European Union for Foreign Affairs and Security Policy. *Joint Communication to the European Parliament and the Council: Developing a European Union Policy towards the Arctic Region: Progress since 2008 and the Next Steps.* http://ec.europa.eu/maritimeaffairs/policy/sea_basins/arctic_ocean/documents/join_2012_19_en.pdf.

The European Council. *Action Plan for Northern Dimension with External and Cross-Border Policies of the European Union 2000–2003.* Doc. no. 9401/00 NIS 78. Brussels, June 14, 2000.

———. *The Common Strategy of the European Union on Russia.* Cologne: The European Council, June 3 and 4, 1999.

European Parliament. *EU Policy on Arctic Issues.* Debate, March 10, 2010. http://www.europarl.europa.eu/sides/getDoc.do?pubRef=-//EP//TEXT+CRE+20100310+ITEM-011+DOC+XML+V0//EN&language=EN.

———. "European Parliament Resolution of 20 January 2011 on a Sustainable EU Policy for the High North" (2009/2214 (INI)). Strasbourg: European Parliament, 2011.

———. "Motion for a European Parliament Resolution on a Sustainable EU Policy for the High North, 2010." Brussels: European Parliament, 2010.

———. *Report on a Sustainable EU Policy for the High North (2009/2214(INI).* Committee on Foreign Affairs, Rapporteur: Michael Gahler (issued December 12, 2010). http://www.europarl.europa.eu/sides/getDoc.do?pubRef=-//EP//NONSGML+REPORT+A7-2010-0377+0+DOC+PDF+V0//EN&language=EN.

———. *Resolution of 9 October 2008 on Arctic Governance.* http://www.europarl.europa.eu/sides/getDoc.do?pubRef=-//EP//TEXT+TA+P6-TA-2008-0474+0+DOC+XML+V0//EN&language=EN.

———. *A Sustainable EU Policy for the High North.* January 20, 2011. http://www.europarl.europa.eu/sides/getDoc.do?pubRef=-//EP//TEXT+TA+P7-TA-2011-0024+0+DOC+XML+V0//EN.

European Science Foundation. *Towards the Strengthening of European Coordination between Polar Environmental Observatories in the*

Arctic Region. 2008. http://www.esf.org/fileadmin/Public_documents/ Publications/polar03_V09ppp.pdf.

Exner-Pirot, Heather. "What Route for Arctic Shipping?" March 25, 2011. http://eyeonthearctic.rcinet.ca/en/blog/136-heather-exner-pirot/793 -what-route-for-arctic-shipping.

"Exxon Valdez Oil Spill Impacts Lasting Far Longer Than Expected, Scientists Say." *Science Daily*, December 23, 2003. http://www. sciencedaily.com/releases/2003/12/031219073313.htm.

Eyre, Kenneth. "Forty Years of Defence Activity in the Canadian North, 1947–87." *Arctic* 40, no. 4 (1987): 292–299.

Fast, Helen, et al. "Integrated Management Planning in Canada's Western Arctic: An Adaptive Consultation Process." In *Breaking Ice: Renewable Resource and Ocean Management in the Canadian North*, edited by Fikret Birkes et al., 95ff . Calgary: University of Calgary Press, 2005.

Fedorov, Aleksei Fedorovich, and Sergei Alekseevich Kovalev. "Is Norway in Compliance with Svalbard Treaty Obligations of 1920?" [Soblyudaet li Norvegia dogovornye obyazatel'stva 1920 g. o Shiptsbergene?]. *Fish Industry* [Rybnoe hozyaistvo] 5 (2006): 12–15.

"Final Report." Narvik, Norway, SAO meeting, November 28–29, 2007. http://www.arctic-council.org/index.php/en/document-archive/ category/48-sao-meeting-2007-2-in-narvik-norway-november-2007.

"Final Report." Svolvaer, Norway, SAO meeting, April 23–24, 2008. http:// www.arctic-council.org/index.php/en/document-archive/category/4 3-sao-meeting-svolvaer-april-2008.

"Final Report of the Fourth Special Antarctic Treaty Consultative Meeting on Antarctic Mineral Resources." Antarctic Treaty Special Consultative Meeting on Antarctic Mineral Resources, Ministry of Foreign Affairs, Wellington, New Zealand, June 2, 1988.

Finnemore, Martha. *National Interests in International Society*. Ithaca, NY: Cornell University Press, 1996.

Fitzgerald, Oonagh. "Question of Legitimacy in the Interplay between Domestic and International Law." In *The Globalized Rule of Law*, edited by Oonagh E. Fitzgerald, 135–149. Toronto: Irwin Law, 2006.

Ford, James. "Dangerous Climate Change and the Importance of Adaptation for the Arctic's Inuit Population." *Environmental Research Letters* 4, no. 2 (2009): 1–10.

Foreign and Commonwealth Office. "The Arctic." 2012. http://www.fco.gov.uk/en/global-issues/polar-regions/uk-engagement-arctic/.

———. "UK Government Arctic Policy." 2009. http://www.oceanstewardship.com/IOSF%202009/Presentations_2009/RMills_2009.pdf.

Fowler, Michael, and Julie Bunck. *Law, Power, and the Sovereign State: The Evolution and Application of the Concept of Sovereignty*. University Park: Pennsylvania State University Press, 1995.

Fox, Gregory. "New Approaches to International Human Rights: The Sovereign State Revisited." In *State Sovereignty: Change and Persistence in International Relations*, edited by Sohail H. Hashmi, 105–130. University Park: Pennsylvania State University Press, 1997.

Francis, Daniel. "Whaling." In *The Canadian Encyclopedia*. Historica Foundation, 2011. http://www.thecanadianencyclopedia.com/en/article/whaling/.

Franckx, Erik. "The Legal Regime of Navigation in the Russian Arctic." *Journal of Transnational Law and Policy* 18 (Spring 2009): 327–342.

Freedman, Lawrence. *The Evolution of Nuclear Strategy*. 3rd ed. New York: Palgrave Macmillan, 2003.

Frolov, Vyacheslav Vasil'evich. "Studies of the Soviet Arctic at the Present Stage" [Issledovaniya Sovetskoi Arktiki na sovremennom etape]. In *Problems of the Arctic* [Problemy Arktiki], 5–18. Leningrad: Morskoi Transport, 1957.

Fukuyama, Francis. *The End of History and the Last Man*. New York: Free Press, 1992.

Gadihoke, Neil. "Arctic Melt: The Outlook for India." *Maritime Affairs: Journal of the National Maritime Foundation of India* 8, no. 1 (2012): 1–12.

Gambell, Ray. "International Management of Whales and Whaling: An Historical Review of the Regulation of Commercial and Aboriginal Subsistence Whaling." *Arctic* 46, no. 2 (1993): 97–107.

GAO, United States Government's Accountability Office. "Russian Nuclear Submarines: U.S. Participation in the Arctic Military Environmental Cooperation Program Need Better Justification." *Report to Congress* GAO-04-924 (September 2004). http://www.gao.gov/assets/250/243985.pdf.

Gautier, Philippe. "The Reparation for Injuries Case Revisited: The Personality of the European Union." *Max Planck Yearbook of United Nations Law* 4 (2000): 331–361.

Gel'man, Vladimir. "Russia in Institutional Trap" [Rossiya v institutsional'noi lovushke]. *Pro et Contra* 14, nos. 4–5 (2010): 23–37.

Gillies, Rob. "Clinton Rebukes Canada on Arctic Meeting." *Associated Press*, March 29, 2010. http://www.msnbc.msn.com/id/36085624/ns/world_news-americas/t/clinton-rebukes-canada-arctic-meeting/#.UCbKC0TR6jc.

Gísladóttir, Ingibjörg Sólrún. "Breytt öryggisumhverfi—ný viðhorf í varnarmálum" [Changed security environment—new situation in defence]. Speech at the Association of Western Cooperation, November 27, 2007. http://www.utanrikisraduneyti.is/frettaefni/raedurISG/nr/4002.

Global Research: Centre for Research on Globalization. "Arctic War Games: Canada, Denmark Team up for Military Exercise," March 23, 2010. http://www.globalresearch.ca/index.php?context=va&aid=18287.

Goodin, Robert. *Green Political Theory.* Cambridge: Polity Press, 1992.

Gorbachev, Mikhail. "The Speech of President Mikhail Gorbachev on October 2, 1987 in Murmansk." *Pravda*, October 2, 1987.

———.*Mikhail Gorbachev's Speech in Murmansk at the Ceremonial Meeting on the Occasion of the Presentation of the Order of Lenin and the Gold*

Star to the City of Murmansk, October 1, 1987. http://teacherweb.com/FL/CypressBayHS/JJolley/Gorbachev_speech.pdf.

———. "Speech of Comrade Gorbachev M.S." [Rech' tovarishcha Gorbacheva M.S.]. *Pravda* 275, no. 25262 (October 2, 1987).

Government of Norway. *Nye byggesteiner i nord: Neste trinn i Regjeringens nordområdestrategi.* Oslo: Government of Norway, 2009.

Government of Norway and Ministry of Foreign Affairs. *Regjeringens nordområdestrategi.* Oslo: Government of Norway and Ministry of Foreign Affairs, 2006.

Graczyk, Piotr. "Observers in the Arctic Council—Evolution and Prospects." *Yearbook of Polar Law* 3 (2011): 575–633.

Graff, James. "Fight for the Top of the World." *Time*, October 1, 2007. www.time.com/time/world/article/0,8599,1663445,00.html.

Gran, Jorunn. "Law and Order in the Arctic." Center for International Climate and Environmental Research—Oslo (CICERO). http://www.cicero.uio.no/fulltext/index_e.aspx?id=4271.

Granberg, Aleksandr Grigor'evich, and Vsevolod Il'ich Peresypkin, eds. *Problems of the Northern Sea Route* [Problemy Severnogo Morskogo Puti]. Moscow: Nauka, 2006.

Granholm, Niklas. *Delar av ett nytt Arktis—Utvecklingar av dansk, kanadensisk, isländsk arktispolitik.* Stockholm: Swedish Defence Research Agency (FOI), 2009.

———., ed. *Arktis—Strategiska frågor i en region i förändring.* Stockholm: Swedish Defence Research Agency (FOI), 2008.

Granholm, Niklas., and Ingolf Kiesow. *Olja och gas i ett nytt och förändrat Arktis: Energifrågans utveckling mot bakgrund av regionens strategiska dynamik.* Stockholm: Swedish Defence Research Agency (FOI), 2010.

Grant, Shelagh D. *Polar Imperative: A History of Arctic Sovereignty in North America.* Vancouver: Douglas & McIntyre, 2010.

Greenberg, Jonathan. "The Arctic in World Environmental History." *Vanderbilt Journal of Transnational Law* 42 (2009): 1307–1392.

Greene, Charles H., Andrew J. Pershing, Thomas M. Cronin, and Nicole Ceci. "Arctic Climate Change and Its Impact on the Ecology of the North Atlantic." *Ecology* 89, no. 11 (supplement 2008): S24–S38.

Griffiths, Franklyn. "Arctic Security: The Indirect Approach." In *Arctic Security in an Age of Climate Change*, edited by James Kraska, 3–19. Cambridge: Cambridge University Press, 2011.

———. "Epilogue: Civility in the Arctic." In *Arctic Alternatives: Civility or Militarism in the Circumpolar North*, edited by Franklyn Griffiths, 280–309. Toronto: Science for Peace/Samuel Stevens, 1992.

———. "The Shipping News: Canada's Arctic Sovereignty Not on Thinning Ice." *International Journal* 58, no. 2 (2003): 257–282.

Griffiths, Franklyn, ed. *Politics of the Northwest Passage*. Kingston and Montreal: McGill-Queen's University Press, 1987.

Griffiths, Franklyn, Rob Huebert, and Whitney Lackenbauer. *Canada and the Changing Arctic: Sovereignty, Security and Stewardship*. London, ON: Wilfrid Laurier Press, 2011.

Grimsson, Ólafur Ragnar. *Declaration from the President of Iceland*. Bessastaðir, January 5, 2010. http://forseti.is/media/PDF/10_01_05_yfirlysing_med_skjaldarmerki.pdf.

———. *Declaration from the President of Iceland*. Bessastaðir, February 11, 2011. http://is/media/pdf/2011_02_20_icesave3_isl.pdf.

Gudlaugsson, Baldur, and Páll Heidar Jonsson. *30. mars 1949. Innganga Íslands í Atlantshafsbandalagið og óeirðirnar á Austurvelli* [*30 March 1949. Iceland's Entry to NATO and the Disturbances on Austurvöllur*]. Reykjavik: Örn og Örlygur, 1976.

Guehenno, Jean-Marie. *The End of the Nation-State*. Translated by Victoria Elliot. Minneapolis: University of Minnesota Press, 1995.

Gunitskiy, Vsevolod. "On Thin Ice: Water Rights and Resource Disputes in the Arctic Ocean." *Journal of International Affairs* 61, no. 2 (Spring/Summer 2008): 261–262.

Guo Peiqing. "Analysis of New Criteria for Permanent Observer Status on the Arctic Council and the Role of Non-Arctic States to Arctic."

KMI International Journal of Maritime Affairs and Fisheries 4, no. 2 (2012): 21.

Guo Peiqing et al., eds. 北极航道的国际问题研究 [A study of the international issues of the Arctic route]. Beijing: Ocean Press, 2009.

Gurowitz, Amy. "International Law, Politics, and Migrant Rights." In Reus-Smit, *Politics of International Law*, 131–150.

Haarde, Geir H. "Iceland's Position in the International Community" [Staða Íslands í samfélagi þjóðanna]. Speech at the University of Iceland, September 7, 2007. http://www. forsaetisraduneyti.is/radherra/raedurGHH/nr/2709.

Haas, Ernst. "International Integration: The European and the Universal Process." *International Organization* 15, no. 3 (1961): 336–392.

———. *The Uniting of Europe: Political, Social and Economic Forces, 1950–57*. Stanford, CA: Stanford University Press, 1958.

Haglund, David G., and Tudor Onea. "Victory without Triumph: Theodore Roosevelt, Honour, and the Alaska Panhandle Boundary Dispute." *Diplomacy & Statecraft* 19, no. 1 (2008): 20–41.

Hainsworth, Susan. "Sovereignty, Economic Integration, and the World Trade Organization." *Osgoode Hall Law Journal* 33, no. 3 (1995): 583–622.

Halinen, Hannu. *Presentation in the Seminar of "Pohjoisen politiikan ja turvallisuuden tutkimuksen asiantuntijaverkosto."* Tampere Peace Research Institute, Tampere, Finland, September 29, 2010 (personal notes).

Hall, Peter, and Rosemary Taylor. "Political Science and the Three New Institutionalisms." *Political Studies* 44, no. 5 (1996): 936–957.

Hannaford, Nigel. "The Russians—and Everyone Else—in Canada's Arctic." *C2C: Canada's Journal of Ideas*, June 22, 2009. http://c2cjournal. ca/2009/06/the-russians-and-everyone-else-in-canadas-arctic/.

Hansen, Birthe. "Multiple Identities of European States." In *Explaining European Integration*, edited by Anders Wivel, 147–165. Copenhagen: Copenhagen Political Studies Press, 1998.

Harding, Luke. "Russia and Norway Resolve Arctic Border Dispute: Treaty Allows for New Oil and Gas Exploration and Settles 40-Year Row over Barents Sea." *The Guardian*, September 15, 2010. http://www.guardian. co.uk/world/2010/sep/15/russia-norway-arctic-border-dispute.

Hay, Colin. "Environmental Security and State Legitimacy." In O'Connor, *Is Capitalism Sustainable?*, 65–79.

———. *Why We Hate Politics.* Cambridge: Polity Press, 2007.

Hayman, P. A., and John Williams. "Westphalian Sovereignty: Rights, Intervention, Meaning and Context." *Global Society* 20, no. 4 (October 2006): 521–541.

Heap, John. "Cooperation in the Antarctic: A Quarter of a Century's Experience." In *Antarctic Resources Policy*, edited by F. O. Vicuna, 105. Cambridge: Cambridge University Press, 1983.

Hedley, Charles. "IWC 54: Analysis of Selected Issues: Aboriginal Subsistence Whaling." Reporter 15. 2002. http://www.oceanlaw.net/ people/profiles/hedley/pubs/ifb/2002-reporter-15.htm.

Hehir, Aidan. *Humanitarian Intervention after Kosovo: Iraq, Darfur and the Record of Global Civil Society.* Houndmills, UK: Palgrave Macmillan, 2008.

Heinbecker, Paul. "The UN: If It Didn't Exist, We Would Have to Invent It." http://www.heinbecker.ca/Writing/The_UN_If_It_Didnt_Exist.pdf.

Heininen, Lassi. *Arctic Strategies and Policies: Inventory and Comparative Study.* Akureyri, Iceland: The Northern Research Forum and the University of Lapland, 2011. http://www.nrf.is/images/stories/ Hveragerdi/Arctic_strategies_6th_final.pdf.

———. "Barents Euro-Arctic Region and Europe's Northern Dimension in State Interest—The 'BEAR' Meets the South." In *Arctic Geopolitics and Resource Futures*, edited by Mark Nuttall and Anita Dey Nuttall. Edmonton, Alberta: University of Alberta, forthcoming.

———. "The Barents Region in the State Interests and International Politics." *Barents Journal* 1, no. 7 (2009): 5–10.

———. "Building a Partnership—Russia as a Part of Europe." In *Northern Borders and Security—Dimensions for Regional Cooperation and Inter-*

dependence, edited by Lassi Heininen, 97–138. Turku, Finland: Turku School of Economics and Business Administration, 2002.

———. "Circumpolar International Relations and Cooperation." In *Globalization and the Circumpolar North,* edited by Lassi Heininen and Chris Southcott, 265–305. Fairbanks: University of Alaska Press, 2010.

———. *Euroopan pohjoinen 1990-luvulla: Moniulotteisten ja ristiriitaisten intressien alue.* Rovaniemi, Finland: Acta Universitatis Lapponiensis 21—Arktisen keskuksen tiedotteita/Arctic Centre Reports 30, 1999.

———. "Globalization and Security in the Circumpolar North." In *Globalization and the Circumpolar North,* edited by Lassi Heininen and Chris Southcott, 1–24. Fairbanks: University of Alaska Press, 2010.

———. "Ideas and Outcomes: Finding a Concrete Form for the Northern Dimension Initiative." In *The Northern Dimension: Fuel for the EU?,* edited by Hanna Ojanen, 20–53. Kauhava, Finland: Ulkopoliittinen instituutti and Institut fur Europäische Politik, Programme on the Northern Dimension of the CFSP, 2001.

Heininen, Lassi, Aleksandr Sergunin, and Gleb Yarovoy. "New Russian Arctic Doctrine: From Idealism to Realism?" July 15, 2013. http://valdaiclub.com/russia_and_the_world/60220.html.

Heininen, Lassi, and Chris Southcott, eds. *Globalization and the Circumpolar North.* Fairbanks: University of Alaska Press, 2010.

Heininen, Lassi, and Lotta Numminen. "Suomi arktisena maana ja Euroopan unionin jäsenvaltiona: miten Arktista neuvostoa vahvistetaan." *Arcticfinland,* March 13, 2011. www.arcticfinland.fi.

Hemmings, Alan D., Donald R. Rothwell, and Karen N. Scott. "Antarctic Security in a Global Context." In *Antarctic Security in the Twenty-First Century,* edited by A. D. Hemmings, Donald R. Rothwell, and Karen N. Scott, 328–336. London: Routledge, 2012.

Henriksen, Anders, and Jens Ringsmose. "What Did Denmark Gain? Iraq, Afghanistan and the Relationship with Washington." In *Danish Foreign Policy Yearbook 2012,* edited by Nanna Hvidt and Hans Mouritzen, 157–181. Copenhagen: Danish Institute for International Studies, 2012.

Henriksen, John B. "The Continuous Process of Recognition and Implementation of the Saami People's Right to Self-Determination." *Cambridge Review of International Affairs* 21, no. 1 (2008): 27–40.

Henriksen, Tore, and Geir Ulfstein. "Maritime Delimitation in the Arctic:
The Barents Sea Treaty." *Ocean Development & International Law* 42,
nos. 1–2 (2011): 1–21.

Henrikson, Alan K. "'Wings for Peace': Open Skies and Transpolar Civil
Aviation." In *Vulnerable Arctic: Need for an Alternative Reorientation*,
Research Report no. 47, edited by Jyrki Käkönen. Tampere: Tampere
Peace Research Institute, 1992.

Herd, Alexander. "A Practical Project: Canada, the United States, and the
Construction of the Dew Line." In *Canadian Arctic Sovereignty and
Security: Historical Perspectives, Calgary Papers in Military and Strategic Studies*, Occasional Paper no. 4, edited by Whitney Lackenbauer,
171–200. Calgary: Centre for Military and Strategic Studies, 2011.

Herman, Janos. *EU Perspectives on the Arctic*, 2013. http://
www.forskningsradet.no/servlet/Satellite?blobcol=urldata&
blobheader=application%2Fpdf&blobheadername1=Content-
Disposition%3A&blobheadervalue1=+attachment%3B+filename
%3D%22HermanEUperspectivesontheArctic.pdf%22&blobkey=id&
blobtable=MungoBlobs&blobwhere=1274487110964&ssbinary=true.

High Representative and the European Commission. *Climate Change
and International Security Paper from the High Representative and
the European Commission to the European Council*. 2008. http://www.
consilium.europa.eu/ueDocs/cms_Data/docs/pressData/en/reports/
99387.pdf.

Hinsley, F rancis Harry. *Sovereignty*. Cambridge: Cambridge University
Press, 1986.

Hjertonsson, Karen. *The New Law of the Sea: Influence of the Latin American States on Recent Developments of the Law of the Sea*. Leiden, the
Netherlands: Martinus Nijhoff, 2004.

Hobbes, Thomas. *Leviathan*. Edited by Edwin Curley. 1668; repr., Indianapolis: Hackett Publishing Company, 1994.

Hoel, Alf Håkon. "Climate Change." In *International Cooperation and Arctic Governance: Regime Effectiveness and Northern Region-Building*, edited by Olav Schram Stokke and Geir Hønneland, 112–137. London and New York: Routledge, 2007.

———. "Do We Need a New Legal Regime for the Arctic Ocean?" *International Journal of Marine and Coastal Law* 24, no. 2 (2009): 443–456.

———. "The High North Legal-Political Regime." In *Security Prospects in the High North: Geostrategic Thaw or Freeze?* NDC Forum Paper 7, edited by Sven G. Holtsmark and Brooke A. Smith-Wilson, 81–101. Rome: NATO Defense College, 2009.

Hoel, Alf Håkon, ed. "Observed Best Practices in Ecosystem-Based Oceans Management in the Arctic Countries." *Norsk Polarinstitutt*, April 2009. http://www.sdwg.org/content.php?doc=75.

Holbrook, Jon. "Humanitarian Intervention and the Recasting of International Law." In *Rethinking Human Rights*, edited by David Chandler, 136–156. Houndmills, UK: Palgrave Macmillan, 2002.

Holtsmark, Sven G., and Brooke A. Smith-Wilson, eds. *Security Prospects in the High North: Geostrategic Thaw or Freeze?* NDC Forum Paper 7. Rome: NATO Defense College, 2009.

Hønneland, Geir. *Barentsbrytninger: norsk nordområdepolitikk etter den kalde krigen.* Kristiansand: Høyskoleforlaget, 2005.

———. *Coercive and Discursive Compliance Mechanisms in the Management of Natural Resources: A Case Study from the Barents Sea Fisheries.* Dordrecht and Boston, MA: Springer, 2000.

———. "Compliance in the Fishery Protection Zone around Svalbard." *Ocean Development and International Law* 29 (1998): 339–360.

———. "East–West Collaboration in the European North." *International Journal* 65 (2010): 837–850.

———. *Kvotekamp og kyststatssolidaritet: norsk-russisk fiskeriforvaltning gjennom 30 år.* Bergen: Fagbokforlaget, 2006.

Hønneland, Geir, and Lars Rowe. *Fra svarte skyer til helleristninger: norsk-russisk miljøvernsamarbeid gjennom 20 år.* Trondheim: Tapir Akademisk Forlag, 2008.

———. *Nordområdene—hva nå?* Trondheim: Tapir Akademisk Forlag, 2010.

———. "Western vs. Post-Soviet Medicine: Fighting Tuberculosis and HIV/AIDS in North-West Russia and the Baltic States." *Journal of Communist Studies and Transition Politics* 21 (2005): 395–415.

Hønneland, Geir, and Leif Christian Jensen. *Den nye nordområdepolitikken.* Bergen: Fagbokforlaget, 2008.

Hopson, Eben. "Letter to the Hon. Jimmy Carter, Americana Hotel, 801 Seventh Avenue, New York, New York. From Eben Hopson." July 12, 1976. http://www.ebenhopson.com/papers/1976/DemoConfab.html.

House of Commons. Evidence presented to the Environment Audit Committee "Protecting the Arctic." 2012. http://www. parliament.uk/business/committees/committees-a-z/commons-select/ environmental-audit-committee/news/announcement-of-report-publication1/.

Howard, Michael. *War and the Liberal Conscience.* New York: Columbia University Press, 2008.

Howard, Roger. *The Arctic Gold Rush: The New Race for Tomorrow's Natural Resources.* London: Continuum, 2009.

Huebert, Rob. *United States Arctic Policy: The Reluctant Arctic Power.* SPP Briefing Papers: Focus on the United States 2, no. 2. Calgary: School of Public Policy, University of Calgary, 2009. http://www.policyschool. ucalgary.ca/sites/default/files/research/sppbriefing-huebertonline. pdf.

———. "New Directions in Circumpolar Cooperation: Canada, the Arctic Environmental Protection Strategy and the Arctic Council." *Canadian Foreign Policy* 5, no. 2 (Winter 1998): 37–57.

———. "Polar Vision or Tunnel Vision: The Making of Canadian Arctic Waters Policy." *Marine Policy* 19, no. 4 (July 1995): 343–364.

———. "Renaissance in Canadian Arctic Security?" *Canadian Military Journal* 6, no. 4 (2005–2006): 17–29.

Huebert, Rob, Heather Exner-Pirot, Adam Lajeunese, and Jay Gulledge. *Climate Change and International Security: The Arctic as a Bellwether.*

Washington, DC: Center for Climate and Energy Solutions, 2012. http://www.c2es.org/publications/climate-change-international-arctic-security.

Humphreys, Adrian. "New Proposal Would See Hans Island Split Equally between Canada and Denmark." *National Post*, April 11, 2012. http://news.nationalpost.com/2012/04/11/new-proposal-would-see-hans-island-split-equally-between-canada-and-denmark/.

Hurd, Ian. "Legitimacy and Authority in International Politics." *International Organization* 53, no. 2 (1999): 379–408.

Ibbitson, John. "Dispute over Hans Island Nears Resolution: Now for the Beaufort Sea." *Globe and Mail*, January 26, 2011. http://www.theglobeandmail.com/news/politics/dispute-over-hans-island-nears-resolution-now-for-the-beaufort-sea/article563692/.

ICC. *A Circumpolar Inuit Declaration on Resource Development Principles in Inuit Nunaat*. May 2011.

———. *A Circumpolar Inuit Declaration on Sovereignty in the Arctic*. April 2009. https://www.itk.ca/sites/default/files/Declaration_12x18_Vice-Chairs_Signed.pdf.

Icelandic International Development Agency. *Stefna og verklag ÞSSÍ, stefnurit* [Policy and Operations of the Icelandic Development Aid Agency, policy report]. Reykjavik: ÞSSÍ, March 2004.

Icelandic Statistical Office. *Population Data for 2010*. www.statice.is.

Ignatieff, Michael. "How Syria Divided the World." *New York Review of Books*, July 11, 2012, http://www.nybooks.com/blogs/nyrblog/2012/jul/11/syria-proxy-war-russia-china/.

Ikenberry, G. John. "The Future of the Liberal World Order." *Foreign Affairs* 90, no. 3 (2011): 56–68.

———. "Liberal Internationalism 3.0: America and the Dilemmas of Liberal World Order." *Perspectives on Politics* 7, no. 1 (2009): 71–87.

Ilulissat Declaration. Arctic Ocean Conference, Ilulissat, Greenland, May 27–29, 2008. http://www.oceanlaw.org/downloads/arctic/Ilulissat_Declaration.pdf.

Ingimundarson, Valur. "Eftir 'bandarísku öldina': Samstarf Íslands við aðrar Evrópuþjóðir" ["After the 'American Age': Icelandic Cooperation with Other European Nations"]. In *Ný staða Íslands í utanríkismálum: Tengsl við önnur Evrópulönd*, edited by Silja B. Ómarsdóttir, 153–163. Reykjavik: University of Iceland, 2007.

———. *The Geopolitics of Arctic Natural Resources*. Brussels: Directorate-General for External Policies, European Parliament, 2010. http://www. tepsa.eu/download/Valur%20Ingimundarson.pdf.

Intergovernmental Panel on Climate Change (IPCC). *Climate Change 2007: Synthesis Report*. Geneva: Intergovernmental Panel on Climate Change, 2007.

———. *Third Assessment Report: Climate Change 2001 (TAR)*. http://www. ipcc.ch/publications_and_data/publications_and_data_reports.shtml.

International Commission on Intervention and State Sovereignty. *The Responsibility to Protect*. Ottawa: International Development Research Centre, 2001.

International Institute for Sustainable Development. "UN Security Council Debates Security Impacts of Climate Change." July 20, 2011. http://climate-l.iisd.org/news/un-security-council-debates-security-impacts-of-climate-change/.

Inuit Circumpolar Council. *A Circumpolar Inuit Declaration on Sovereignty in the Arctic*. Tromsø, Norway: Inuit Circumpolar Council, 2009. http:// inuitcircumpolar.com/section.php?ID=25&Lang=En&Nav=Section.

IWC (International Whaling Commission) Secretariat. Background information for the Commission's aboriginal subsistence whaling working group (ASWWG). Metropole Hotel, Brighton, 1981.

Jackson, Robert. "Pluralism in International Political Theory." *Review of International Studies* 18, no. 3 (1992): 271–281.

———. *Sovereignty: Evolution of an Idea*. Malden, MA: Polity, 2007.

Jakobson, Linda J. "CHINA: Potential Benefits of Arctic Melting." *University World News*, May 2010. http://www.universityworldnews. com/article.php?story=20100528190101228.

———. "China Prepares for an Ice-Free Arctic." *SIPRI Insights on Peace and Security* 2010, no. 2 (March 2010): 5. http://books.sipri.org/files/insight/SIPRIInsight1002.pdf.

Japan's written statement by the Delegation of Japan at the Second Meeting of Deputy Ministers of the Arctic Council. Stockholm, Sweden, May 15, 2012. http://www.arctic-council.org/index.php/en/about/documents/category/118-deputy-ministers-meeting-stockholm-15-may-2012.

Jensen, Leif Christian, and Geir Hønneland. "Framing the High North: Public Discourses in Norway after 2000." *Acta Borealia* 28 (2011): 37–54.

Jensen, Øystein. "Towards Setting the Outer Limits of the Continental Shelf in the Arctic: On the Norwegian Submission and Recommendations of the Commission." In *Law, Technology and Science for Oceans in Globalisation: IUU Fishing, Oil Pollution, Bioprospecting, Outer Continental Shelf*, edited by Davor Vidas, 519–538. Leiden, the Netherlands, and Boston, MA: Martinus Nijhoff, 2010.

Jervell, Sverre. "10 Years of the Barents Cooperation." In *The Vision that Became Reality: The Regional Barents Cooperation 1993–2003*, edited by O. Pettersen, 74–78. Kirkenes: The Barents Secretariat, 2002.

Jervis, Robert. "Security Regimes." In *International Regimes*, edited by Stephen D. Krasner, 173–194. Ithaca, NY, and London: Cornell University Press, 1983.

Jockel, Joseph. *No Boundaries Upstairs: Canada, the United States, and the Origins of North American Air Defence, 1945–1958*. Vancouver: University of British Columbia Press, 1987.

Joensen, Jóhanna Vagadal. "A New Chinese Arctic Policy? An Analysis of China's Policies towards the Arctic in the Post-Cold War Period." Thesis, Aarhus University, 2013. http://www.academia.edu/4675427/A_New_Chinese_Arctic_Policy_An_Analysis_of_Chinas_Policies_towards_the_Arctic_in_the_Post-Cold_War_Period.

Johnston, Peter F. "Arctic Energy Resources and Global Energy Security." *Journal of Military and Strategic Studies* 12, no. 2 (Winter 2010): 1–20.

Jones, Max. "From Noble Example to Potty Pioneer: Rethinking Scott of the Antarctic c. 1945–2011." *The Polar Journal* 2 (2011): 191–206.

Jørgensen, Henrik Jedig, and Jon Rahbek-Clemmensen. *Keep It Cool! Four Scenarios for the Danish Armed Forces in Greenland 2030*. Copenhagen: Dansk Institut for Militær Studier, 2009.

Käkönen, Jyrki. "Suomen ulkopolitiikan suuret traditiot ja tulevaisuuden valinnat." In *Uuden ulkopolitiikan haasteet: Kekkosen ajasta Koiviston kautta 2000-luvulle*, edited by Jouko Huru, 23–48. Tampere, Finland: Rauhan-ja konfliktintutkimuslaitos, 1993.

Kanevsky, Zinoviy Mikhailovich. *The Whole Life Is Expedition (Life and Work of R. L. Samoylovich)* [Vsya zhizn'—expeditsiya (Zhizn' i deyatel'nost' R. L. Samoylovicha)]. Moscow: Mysl', 1982.

Kant, Immanuel. *Perpetual Peace*. New York: Columbia University Press, 1939.

Karkkainen, Bradley. "Collaborative Ecosystem Governance: Scale, Complexity, and Dynamism." *Virginia Environmental Law Journal* 189, no. 21 (2002): 3.

———. "Marine Ecosystem Management & A 'Post-Sovereign' Transboundary Governance." *San Diego International Law Journal* 6, no. 120 (2004): 113.

Karlqvist, Anders. *Svensk polarforskning: Ett utredningsuppdrag*. Stockholm: Vetenskapsrådet, 2006.

Kauppa- ja teollisuusministeriö. *Suomen arktisen tutkimuksen strategia*. Kauppa- ja teollisuusministeriön neuvottelukuntaraportteja, April 1999.

Kazuyuki Shiraishi. "Japanese National Activity in the Arctic Science." Presentation at the Forum of Arctic Research Operators (FARO) Meeting at the Arctic Science Summit Week, Montreal, April 21, 2012. http://faro-arctic.org/fileadmin/Resources/DMU/GEM/faro/201 2_Kazuyuki_Shiraishi_s_presentation.pdf.

Keene, Edward. *Beyond the Anarchical Society: Grotius, Colonialism and Order in World Politics*. Cambridge: Cambridge University Press, 2002.

Kefferpütz, Roderick and Danila Bochkarev. *Expanding the EU's Institutional Capacities in the Arctic Region: Policy Briefing and Key Recommendations.* Brussels: Heinrich Böll Stiftung, EU Regional Office, 2008.

Kelley, John J., and Harry Brower Sr. "The NARL and Its Transition to the Local Community in Fifty More Years below Zero." In *Tributes and Meditations for the Naval Arctic Research Laboratory's First Half Century at Barrow, Alaska,* edited by D. W. Norton, 259–264. Calgary and Fairbanks: Arctic Institute of North America, 2001.

Kent, H. S. K. "The Historical Origins of the Three-Mile Limit." *American Journal of International Law* 48, no. 4 (October 1954): 537–553.

Keohane, Robert. "Hobbes's Dilemma and Institutional Change in World Politics: Sovereignty in International Society." In *Whose World Order? Uneven Globalization and the End of the Cold War,* edited by Hans-Henrik Holm and Georg Sorensen, 165–186. Boulder, CO: Westview Press, 1995.

Keohane, Robert O. *After Hegemony: Cooperation and Discord in the World Political Economy.* Princeton: Princeton University Press, 1984.

———. "International Institutions: Two Approaches." *International Studies Quarterly* 32, no. 4 (1988): 379–396.

———. "Constructing 'the Arctic.'" *Acta Universitatis Lapponiensis* 47, University of Lapland, Rovaniemi (2002): 113–158.

Keskitalo, E. C. H. *Constructing "the Arctic": Discourses of International Region-Building.* Rovaniemi, Finland: Acta Universitatis Lapponiensis 47, 2002.

———. *Negotiating the Arctic: The Construction of an International Region.* London and New York: Routledge, 2004.

Khramchikhin, Aleksandr Anatol'evich. "Politico-Military Situation in the Arctic and Scenario of Possible Conflicts" [Voenno-politicheskaya situatsiya v Arktike I stsenarii vizmozhnyh confliktov]. *Arctic and North* [Arktika i Sever] 2 (2011): 1–15. http://narfu.ru/upload/iblock/7f9/grjopufvqlvzveqamx.pdf.

Ki-Moon, Ban. "The Arctic." United Nations Environmental Programme. http://www.unep.org/Documents.Multilingual/Default.asp?DocumentID=596&ArticleID=6316&l=en.

Kim Se-jeong. "Korea Wants to Join in Arctic Projects." *Korea Times*, August 24, 2008. http://www.koreatimes.co.kr/www/news/special/2009/04/176_29902.html.

King, Preston. *The Ideology of Order: A Comparative Analysis of Jean Bodin and Thomas Hobbes.* New York: George Allen & Unwin, 1974.

Kirton, John, and Don Munton. "Protecting the Canadian Arctic: The Manhattan Voyages, 1969–1970." In *Canadian Foreign Policy: Selected Cases*, edited by John Kirton and Don Munton. Toronto: Prentice-Hall, 1992.

Kirwan, Laurence. *The White Road: A Survey of Polar Exploration.* London: Hollis and Carter, 1959.

Kiss, Alexandre, and Dinah Shelton. *A Guide to International Environmental Law.* Boston: Martinus Nijhoff Publishers, 2007.

Kjærgaard, Thorkild. "Den Amerikanske livline." *Weekendavisen*, April 20, 2012, 12–13.

Kleist, Mininnguaq. "The Status of the Greenlandic Inuit." In *The Right to National Self-Determination—The Faroe Islands and Greenland*, edited by Sjúrdur Skaale, 95–122. Boston: Martinus Nijhoff, 2004.

Knill, Christoph. *The Europeanisation of National Administrations: Patterns of Institutional Change and Persistence.* Cambridge: Cambridge University Press, 2001.

Knoepflmacher, Ulrich C., and G. B. Tennyson. *Nature and the Victorian Imagination.* Berkeley: University of California Press, 1977.

Koivurova, Timo. "Limits and Possibilities of the Arctic Council in a Rapidly Changing Scene of Arctic Governance." *Polar Record* 46 (2010): 146–156.

Koivurova, Timo, and David VanderZwaag. "The Arctic Council at 10 Years: Retrospect and Prospects." *University of British Columbia Law Review* 40, no. 1 (2007): 121–194.

Koivurova, Timo. "Alternatives for an Arctic Treaty—Evaluation and a New Proposal." *Review of European Community & International Environmental Law—RECIEL* 17, no. 1, Special International Polar Year Issue (2008): 14–26.

———. *Environmental Impact Assessment in the Arctic: A Study of International Legal Norms.* Farnham, UK: Ashgate, 2002.

———. "Environmental Protection in the Arctic and Antarctic: Can the Polar Regimes Learn from Each Other?" *International Journal of Legal Information* 33, no. 2 (2005): 204–218.

———. "Environmental Protection in the Arctic and Antarctica." In *Polar Law Textbook*, edited by Natalia Loukacheva, 23–43. Copenhagen: Nordic Council of Ministers, 2010.

———. "Limits and Possibilities of the Arctic Council in a Rapidly Changing Scene of Arctic Governance." *Polar Record* 46 (2010): 146–156.

———. "New Ways to Respond to Climate Change in the Arctic." *Insights: American Society of International Law* 16, no. 33 (October 23, 2012): 3. http://www.asil.org/insights/volume/16/issue/33/new-ways-respond-climate-change-arctic.

———. "The Regime of the Espoo Convention in the Arctic: Towards a Strategic Environmental Assessment Procedure." In *Arctic Governance*, Juridica Lapponica 29, edited by Timo Koivurova, Tanja Joona, and Reija Shnoro, 61–87. Rovaniemi: Sevenprint, 2004.

Koivurova, Timo, and David VanderZwaag. "The Arctic Council at 10 Years: Retrospect and Prospects." *University of British Columbia Law Review* 40, no. 1 (2007): 121–194.

Koivurova, Timo, E. Carina H. Keskitalo, and Nigel Bankes, eds. *Climate Governance in the Arctic.* Np: Springer, 2009.

Koivurova, Timo, and Erik Molenaar. *International Governance and Regulation of the Marine Arctic: Overview and Gap Analysis.* Oslo: WWF International Arctic Programme, 2009.

Koivurova, Timo, and Erik J. Molenaar. *International Governance and Regulation of the Marine Arctic: Three Reports Prepared for the WWF International Arctic Programme.* Oslo, February 8, 2010.

Koivurova, Timo, Erik Molenaar, and David VanderZwaag. "Canada, the EU, and Arctic Ocean Governance: A Tangled and Shifting Seascape and Future Directions." *Journal of Transnational Law and Policy* 18, no. 2 (Spring 2009): 247–288.

Koivurova, Timo, and Leena Heinamaki. "The Participation of Indigenous Peoples in International Normmaking in the Arctic." *Polar Record* 42, no. 221 (2006): 101–109.

Kolodkin, Anatoliy, and Sergei Glandin. "The Russian Flag on the North Pole." *International Affairs* 53, no. 6 (2007): 6–16.

Konyshev, Valeriy Nikolaevich, and Aleksander Anatol'evich Sergunin. "Arctic on the Crossroads of the Geopolitical Interests" [Arktika na perekrest'e geopoliticheskih interesov]. *World Economy and International Relations* [Mirovaya ekonomika in mezhdunarodnye otnosheniya] 9 (2010): 43–53.

———. *The Arctic in International Politics: Cooperation or Competition?* [Arktika v mejdunarodnoi politike: Sotrudnichestvo ili sopernichestvo?] Moscow: RISI, 2011.

———. "National Interests of Russia in the Arctic: Myths and Realities" [Nacional'nye intersy Rossii v Arktike: Mify i real'nost']. *Russia's Priorities* [Prioritety Rossii] 29 (2011): 2–11.

Kramvig, Britt. "I kategorienes vold." In *Samer og nordmenn*, edited by H. Eidheim. Oslo: Cappelen Akademisk Forlag, 1999.

Kraska, James. "Arctic Strategy and Military Security." In *Changes in the Arctic Environment and the Law of the Sea*, edited by Myron H. Nordquist, John N. Moore, and Tomas H. Heidar, 251–281. Leiden, the Netherlands: Martinus Nijhof, 2010.

———. "The New Arctic Geography and U.S. Strategy." In *Arctic Security in an Age of Climate Change*, edited by James Kraska, 244–266. Cambridge: Cambridge University Press, 2012.

———. "Northern Exposures." *American Interest*, Summer (May/June 2010): 61–68.

Krasner, Stephen. "The Accomplishments of International Political Economy." In *International Theory: Positivism and Beyond*, edited by Steve

Smith, Ken Booth, and Marysia Zalewski, 108–127. Cambridge: Cambridge University Press, 1996.

———. "Problematic Sovereignty." In *Problematic Sovereignty*, edited by Stephen Krasner, 1–23. New York: Columbia University Press, 2001.

———. *Sovereignty: Organized Hypocrisy.* Princeton: Princeton University Press, 1999.

Krasner, Stephen D. "The Case for Shared Sovereignty." *Journal of Democracy* 16, no. 1 (January 2005): 69–83.

Krasner, Stephen D., ed. *International Regimes.* Ithaca, NY: Cornell University Press, 1983.

Krugel, Lauren. "Chinese Interest in Arctic Riches Heating Up: Calgary Political Scientist (Arctic-Natural-Gas)." *Canadian Press*, February 25, 2008. www.david-kilgour.com/2008/Feb_27_2008_09.htm.

Kuehls, Thom. *Beyond Sovereign Territory: The Space of Ecopolitics.* Minneapolis: University of Minnesota Press, 1996.

Kuijpers, Antoon, Niels Abrahamsen, Gerd Hoffmann, Veit Hühnerbach, Peter Konradi, Helmar Kunzendorf, Naja Mikkelsen, Jörn Thiede, Wilhelm Weinrebe, shipboard scientific party of RV *Poseidon*, and surveyors of the Royal Danish Administration for Navigation and Hydrography. "Climate Change and the Viking-Age Fjord Environment of the Eastern Settlement, South Greenland." *Geology of Greenland Survey Bulletin* 183 (1999): 61–67. http://geus.dk/publications/review-greenland-98/gsb183p61-67.pdf.

Kvalvik, Ingrid. "Assessing the Delimitation Negotiations between Norway and the Soviet Union/Russia." *Acta Borealia* 21, no. 1 (2004): 55–78.

Lackenbauer, Whitney. "Canada's Northern Defenders: Aboriginal Peoples in the Canadian Rangers, 1947–2005." In *Aboriginal Peoples and the Canadian Military: Historical Perspectives*, edited by P. W. Lackenbauer and Craig Mantle, 171–208. Kingston: CDA Press, 2007.

———. "The Canadian Rangers: A Postmodern Militia That Works." *Canadian Military Journal* 6, no. 4 (2005–2006): 49–60.

———. "From Polar Race to Polar Saga: An Integrated Strategy for Canada and the Circumpolar World." In Griffiths, Huebert, and Lackenbauer, *Canada and the Changing Arctic*, 118–145.

———. "Mirror Images? Canada, Russia, and the Circumpolar World." *International Journal* 65, no. 4 (2010): 879–897.

Lähteenmäki, Maria. "Jäämeren valloitus—Naparetkeilijöitä ja skippareita Europan pohjoisilla rannoilla." In *Lappi—Maa, kansat, kulttuurit*, edited by Ilmo Massa and Hanna Snellman, 64–83. Hämeenlinna, Finland: Suomalaisen Kirjallisuuden Seura, 2003.

Lake, David. "Rightful Rules: Authority, Order and the Foundations of Global Governance." *International Studies Quarterly* 54 (2010): 587–613.

Landler, Mark. "Law of the Sea Treaty Is Found on Capitol Hill, Again." *New York Times*, May 23, 2012.

Landsvirkjun. "The Market Development of Electricity and Future Visions of Landsvirkjun." In *Report from the Annual Meeting*, 2010. http://www.landsvirkjun.is/media/samradsfundir/arsfundur_LV_2010_hordur_arnarson.pdf.

Lapidoth, Ruth. "Sovereignty in Transition." *Journal of International Affairs* 45, no. 2 (1992): 325–346.

Lasserre, Frédéric. "China and the Arctic: Threat or Cooperation Potential for Canada?" *China Papers* no. 11, Canadian International Council, June 2010. http://www.opencanada.org/wp-content/uploads/2011/05/China-and-the-Arctic-Frederic-Lasserre.pdf.

Latour, Bruno. *Politics of Nature: How to Bring Science into Democracy.* Cambridge, MA: Harvard University Press, 2004.

———. *Reassembling the Social: An Introduction to Actor-Network Theory.* Oxford: Oxford University Press, 2005.

Left Green Movement. *Policy Declaration: Independent Foreign Policy, Social Internationalism.* http://www.vg.is/stefna/utanrikisstefna/.

"Legal Status of Eastern Greenland." Permanent Court of International Justice, 22nd session, judgment no. 20, September 5, 1993.

Lehr, Amy K., and Gare A. Smith. *Implementing a Corporate Free, Prior, and Informed Consent Policy: Benefits and Challenges.* Foley Hoag eBook, May 2010. http://www.foleyhoag.com/NewsCenter/Publications/eBooks/Implementing_Informed_Consent_Policy.aspx?ref=1.

Linklater, Andrew, and Hidemi Suganami. *The English School of International Relations: A Contemporary Reassessment.* Cambridge: Cambridge University Press, 2006.

Lipponen, Paavo. "The European Union Needs a Policy for the Northern Dimension." In *Europe's Northern Dimension: The BEAR Meets the South*, edited by L. Heininen and R. Langlais, 39. Rovaniemi, Finland: Publications of the Administrative Office of the University of Lapland, 1997.

Litfin, Karen, ed. *The Greening of Sovereignty.* Cambridge, MA: MIT Press, 1998.

Loukacheva, Natalia, ed. *Polar Law Textbook.* Copenhagen: Nordic Council of Ministers, 2010.

Lukin, Yury Fedorovich. *The Great Redivision of the Arctic* [Velikii peredel Arktiki]. Arkhangelsk: Northern (Arctic) Federal University, 2010.

Mackrael, Kim. "Canada, Denmark Closer to Settling Border Dispute." *Globe and Mail*, November 29, 2012. http://www.theglobeandmail.com/news/national/canada-denmark-closer-to-settling-border-dispute/article5831571/.

Madar, Daniel. "Fate, Will, and Forecasting." *International Journal* 62 (Spring 2007): 279–290.

Mäkeläinen-Buhanist, Soili. *Finland's Approach to the Arctic: The Past and the Future.* Ministry for Foreign Affairs of Finland, Ottawa, Canada, May 27, 2010.

Mandelbaum, Michael. *The Ideas that Conquered the World: Peace, Democracy, and Free Markets in the Twentieth Century.* New York: Public Affairs, 2002.

Marsden, Michael. "Arctic Contrasts: Canada and Russia in the Far North." *International Journal* 14, no. 1 (1959): 33–41.

McCannon, John. *The Arctic: A Global History.* London: Reaktion Books, 2012.

McCarthy, Michael. "Oil Exploration under Arctic Ice Could Cause 'Uncontrollable' Natural Disaster." *The Independent*, September 6, 2011.

McLaren, Alfred S. *Unknown Waters: A First-Hand Account of the Historic Under-Ice Survey of the Siberian Continental Shelf by USS Queenfish (SSN-651).* Tuscaloosa: University of Alabama Press, 2008.

McLaren, Lauren. *Identity, Interests and Attitudes to European Integration.* London: Palgrave Macmillan, 2006.

Meadowcroft, James. "From the Welfare State to the Ecostate." In *The Global Ecological Crisis and the Nation-State*, edited by John Barry and Robyn Eckersley, 3–24. Cambridge, MA: MIT Press, 2005.

Mearsheimer, John. "The False Promise of International Institutions." *International Security* 19, no. 3 (Winter 1994–1995): 5–49.

———. "Structural Realism." In *International Relations Theories: Discipline and Diversity*, 1st ed., edited by Tim Dunne, Milja Kurki, and Steve Smith, 71–88. Oxford: Oxford University Press, 2007.

———. *The Tragedy of Great Power Politics.* New York: W. W. Norton & Company, 2001.

Medvedev, Dmitry. "Russia Forward!" September 10, 2009. http://www.kremlin.ru/news/5413.

Meek, Chanda. "Comparing Marine Mammal Co-Management Regimes in Alaska: Three Aspects of Institutional Performance." PhD diss., University of Alaska Fairbanks, 2009. http://www.uaf.edu/rap/rap-resources/alumni-dissertations-and-/.

Meinzen-Dick, Ruth, and Rajendra Pradhan. "Legal Pluralism and Dynamic Property Rights." Capri Working Paper 22. Washington, DC: International Food Policy Research Institute, 2002. http://www.capri.cgiar.org/pdf/CAPRIWP22.pdf.

Melville, Andrey Yur'evich. "A Liberal Foreign Policy Alternative for Russia?" [Liberal'naya vneshnepoliticheskaya al'ternative dlya Rossii?]. In *Foreign Policy and Security of the Modern Russia, 1991– 2002* [Vneshnyaya politika i bezopasnost' sovremennoi Rossii, 1991–

2002], edited by Tat'yana Alekseevna Shakleina, 330–339. Moscow: ROSSPEN, 2002.

Mendelsohn, Barak. "Sovereignty under Attack: The International Society Meets the Al Qaeda Network." *Review of International Studies* 21 (2005): 45–68.

Merchant, Carolyn. *The Death of Nature: Women, Ecology and the Scientific Revolution.* San Francisco: Harper & Row, 1980.

Miller, David H. "Political Rights in the Arctic." *Foreign Affairs* 4, no. 1 (1925): 47–60.

Milner, Marc. *Canada's Navy: The First Century.* Toronto: University of Toronto Press, 2010.

Milov, Vladimir. "Russian Economy in Limbo." July 13, 2010. http://russia-2020.org/ru/2010/07/13/russian-economy-in-limbo.

Milward, Alan S., assisted by George Brennan and Federico Romero. *The European Rescue of the Nation-State.* London: Routledge, 1992.

Ministry of Economic Development and Trade of the Russian Federation. "Conceptual Foundations of Long-Term Socio-Economic Development of Russian Federation" [Kontseptsiya Dolgosrochnogo Soysial'no-Economicheskogo Razvitiya Rossiiskoi Federatsii]. Moscow, 2007. http://www.economy.gov.ru/minec/activity/sections/strategicplanning/concept/doc1185283411781.

Ministry for the Environment. *Iceland's Fifth National Communication on Climate Change, Under the United Nations Framework Convention on Climate Change.* http://unfccc.int/resource/docs/natc/isl_nc5_resubmit.pdf.

Ministry of the Environment. *Overenskomst mellom Kongeriket Norges Regjering og Unionen av Sovjetiske Sosialistiske Republikkers Regjering om samarbeid på miljøvernområdet.* Oslo: Ministry of the Environment, January 15, 1988.

Ministry of Fisheries. *Protokoll for den 39. sesjon i Den blandete norsk-russiske fiskerikommisjon.* Oslo: Ministry of Fisheries, 2010.

———. *Supplement til protokoll for den 21. sesjon i Den blandede norsk-russiske fiskerikommisjon.* Oslo: Ministry of Fisheries, 1993.

Ministry of Foreign Affairs. "Avtale mellom Norge og Sovjetunionen om en midlertidig praktisk ordning for fisket i et tilstøtende område i Barentshavet med tilhørende protokoll og erklæring." In *Overenskomster med fremmede stater*, 436. Oslo: Ministry of Foreign Affairs, 1978.

———. "Avtale mellom Regjeringen i Unionen av Sovjetiske Sosialistiske Republikker og Regjeringen i Kongeriket Norge om samarbeid innen fiskerinæringen." In *Overenskomster med fremmede stater*, 546–549. Oslo: Ministry of Foreign Affairs, 1975.

———. *Iceland and the High North.* 2009. http://www.utanrikisraduneyti. is/media/Skyrslur/Skyrslan_Island_a_nordurslodumm.pdf.

———. *Plan of Action for the Implementation of Report No. 34 (1993–94) to the Storting on Nuclear Activities and Chemical Weapons in Areas Adjacent to Our Northern Borders.* Oslo: Ministry of Foreign Affairs, 1995.

———. *Risk Assessment for Iceland, Global, Civil and Military Aspects.* March 2009. http://www.utanrikisraduneyti.is/media/Skyrslur/Skyrsla_um_ ahattumat_fyrir_Island_a.pdf.

———. "Treaty between Norway and the Russian Federation Concerning Maritime Delimitation and Cooperation in the Barents Sea and the Arctic Ocean." Temporarily available at www.regjeringen.no/up-load/UD/Vedlegg/Folkerett/avtale_engelsk.pdf.

———. *The Statistics of Icelandic Foreign Service Compared with Other Nordic States.* http://www.utanrikisraduneyti.is/raduneytid/samantekt/.

———. *St.meld. nr. 15 (2008–2009) Interesser, ansvar og muligheter: Hovedlinjer in norsk utenrikspolitikk.* Oslo: Ministry of Foreign Affairs, 2009.

———. *St.meld. nr. 30 (2004–2005) Muligheter og utfordringer i nord.* Oslo: Ministry of Foreign Affairs, 2005.

———. *Varnarmálalög og Varnarmálastofnun Íslands* [The Defence Act and the Icelandic Defence Agency]. 2008. http://www. utanrikisraduneyti.is/verkefni/althjoda-og-oryggissvid/varnar-og-oryggismal/varnarmalalog-og-vms/.

Ministry of Foreign Affairs of Denmark and the Home Rule Government of Greenland. *Arktis i en brydningstid: Forslag til strategi for aktiviteter i det arktiske område.* May 2008. www.hum.dk.

Ministry of Foreign Affairs and International Trade. *Statement on Canada's Arctic Foreign Policy,* last modified June 3, 2013. http://www. international.gc.ca/polar-polaire/canada_arctic_foreign_policy_booklet-la_politique_etrangere_du_canada_pour_arctique_livret. aspx?lang=eng.

Mitra, Devirupa. "Taking Cue from China, India Eyeing Arctic Region." *Indian Express,* October 2, 2012. http://newindianexpress.com/nation/article1282303.ece.

Mol, Arthur. "Ecological Modernisation and Institutional Reflexivity: Environmental Reform in the Late Modern Age." *Environmental Politics* 5, no. 2 (1996): 302–323.

Molenaar, Erik. "International Regulation of Arctic Marine Shipping— Recent Developments and Options for Multilateral Reform Outside IMO." *Arctic Frontiers,* January 2011.

Monin, Sergei. "Routes of Lend-Lease" [Marshruty lend-liza]. *Обозреватель-Observer* 6 (2010): 50–57.

Moore, John N. "The UNCLOS Negotiations on Ice-Covered Areas." In *Changes in the Arctic Environment and the Law of the Sea,* edited by Myron H. Nordquist, John N. Moore, and Tomas H. Heidar, 17–26. Leiden, the Netherlands: Martinus Nijhof, 2010.

Moravcsik, Andrew. *The Choice for Europe: Social Purpose & State Power from Messina to Maastricht.* London: UCL Press, 1998.

———. "Preferences and Power in the European Community: A Liberal Intergovernmentalist Approach." In *Economic and Political Integration in Europe,* edited by Simon Bulmer and Andrew Scott, 29–80. Oxford: Blackwell, 1994.

Morgenthau, Hans. *Politics Among Nations.* New York: McGraw-Hill, 2006.

Morrison, William. *Showing the Flag: The Mounted Police and Canadian Sovereignty in the North: 1894–1925.* Vancouver: University of British Columbia Press, 1985.

Möttöla, Karl., ed. *The Arctic Challenge: Nordic and Canadian Approaches to Security and Cooperation in an Emerging International Region.* Boulder, CO: Westview, 1988.

Mouffe, Chantal. *On the Political.* London: Routledge, 2005.

Murashko, Olga. "Why Did the Important Events in the Indigenous Peoples' Life Take Place in the Atmosphere of Alienation?" http://www.raipon.info/en/component/content/article/8-news/35-why-did-the-important-events-in-the-indigenous-peoples-life-take-place-in-the-atmosphere-of-alienation.html.

Murphy, Craig. *International Institutions and Industrial Change.* New York: Polity Press, 1994.

Murray, Robert. "Arctic Politics in the Emerging Multipolar System: Challenges and Consequences." *The Polar Journal* 2, no. 1 (2012): 7–20.

Nanoq. *Self-Government Awakes International Interest.* 2009. http://en.mipi.nanoq.gl/sitecore/content/Websites/uk,-d-,nanoq/Emner/News/News_from_Government/2009/06/awakes_interest.aspx.

National Defence and the Canadian Forces. *Backgrounder: The Canadian Forces in the North*, February 28, 2012. http://www.forces.gc.ca/en/news/article.page?doc=canadian-forces-northern-area/hnlhlxi9.

Natural Resources Canada. "Canada's Arctic Continental Shelf: Research under Ocean and Ice." May 18, 2010. http://publications.gc.ca/collections/collection_2010/nrcan/M34-4-9-2010-eng.pdf.

Nayak, Shailesh. "Polar Research in India." *Indian Journal of Marine Sciences* 37, no. 4 (December 2008): 352–357.

NEFCO. *Updating of Environmental "Hot Spots" List in the Russian Part of the Barents Region: Proposal for Environmentally Sound Investment Projects.* Oslo: AMAP Secretariat, 2003. http://www.amap.no/documents/doc/updating-of-environmental-hot-spots-list-in-the-russian-part-ofank-the-barents-region/838.

NERC. *NERC Arctic Research Programme for the UK: Communication, Engagement & Knowledge Exchange A Strategy 2010–2016.* Swindon: NERC, 2010.

Nettheim, Garch, Gary D. Meyers, and Donna Craig. *Indigenous Peoples and Governance Structures: A Comparative Analysis of Land and Resource Management Rights.* Toronto: Aboriginal Studies Press, 2002.

Neumann, Iver B. *Russia and the Idea of Europe: A Study in Identity and International Relations.* London: Routledge, 1996.

Neumann, Thilo. "Norway and Russia Agree on Maritime Boundary in the Barents Sea and the Arctic Ocean." *American Society of International Law Insights* 14 (November 9, 2010): 1–4.

Niemi, Einar. "Sami History and the Frontier Myth: A Perspective on Northern Sami Spatial and Rights History." In *Sami Culture in a New Era: The Norwegian Sami Experience,* edited by H. Gaski. Karasjok, Norway: Davvi Girji OS, 1997.

Nilson, Haken. R. *Arctic Environmental Protection Strategy: Process and Organization, 1991–1997.* Rapportserie no. 103. Oslo: Norwegian Polar Institute, 1997.

Nilsson, Annika E. *A Changing Arctic Climate: Science and Policy in the Arctic Climate Impact Assessment.* Linköping Studies in Arts and Science no. 386. Linköping: Linköping University Electronic Press, 2007.

Ning, Xi. "Di qui weilai de suo yin: waijiaobubuzhangzhu li tan 'beijiyjanjiuzhi lv'" [A microcosm of the world's future—Assistant Minister of Foreign Affairs talks about "High North Study Tour"]. *Shijie Bolan* 349, no. 19 (2009): 58.

Nordic Council of Ministers. *Common Concern for the Arctic.* Conference report ANP 2008: 750. Copenhagen: Nordic Council of Ministers, 2008.

———. *Hållbar utveckling—En ny kurs för Norden.* Report ANP 2009: 726. Copenhagen: Nordic Council of Ministers, 2009.

———. "Sustainable Development in the Arctic." *The Nordic Council of Ministers´ Arctic Cooperation Programme 2009–2011.* 2009. http://www.nordregio.se/Global/About%20Nordregio/Arktiskt%20

samarbetsprogram/2012-14/Nordisk_Ministerr%c3%a5d_Program_
for_arktis_2012-2014_ENGELSK.pdf.

Nordlinger, Eric. *Isolationism Reconfigured.* Princeton: Princeton University Press, 1995.

North Atlantic Treaty Organization. *Active Engagement, Modern Defence.* Strategic Concept adopted at the Lisbon Summit, November 19, 2010. http://www.nato.int/cps/en/natolive/news_68172.htm.

Norwegian Institute for Defence Studies. *Arctic Strategy Documents.* http://www.geopoliticsnorth.org/index.php?option=com_content&view=article&id=84&Itemid=69.

"Norwegian Petroleum Directorate Signs Agreement with Greenland." *Offshore Energy Today.Com*, January 16, 2011. http://www.offshoreenergytoday.com/norwegian-petroleum-directorate-signs-agreement-with-greenland/.

Nowlan, Linda. *Arctic Legal Regime for Environmental Protection.* Cambridge: International Union for Conservation of Nature and Natural Resources, 2001.

"NSIDC Scientist Discusses Sea Ice at AGU Nye Lecture." *National Snow and Ice Data Center Notes* 62 (Winter 2008): 2.

NSPA. "The Northern Sparsely Populated Areas (NSPA) Political Statement Summary." January 28, 2010. http://www.nspa-network.eu/.

———. "Welcome to the Northern Sparsely Populated Areas." http://www.nspa-network.eu/.

Nuttall, Mark. *Arctic Homeland: Kinship, Community and Development in Northwest Greenland.* Toronto: University of Toronto Press, 1992.

———. "Greenland: Emergence of an Inuit Homeland." In *Polar Peoples: Self-Determination and Development*, edited by Minority Rights Group, 1–28. London: Minority Rights Group, 1994.

———. "Imagining and Governing the Greenlandic Resource Frontier." *The Polar Journal* 2, no. 1 (2012): 113–124.

———. "Living in a World of Movement: Human Resilience to Environmental Instability in Greenland." In *Anthropology and Climate*

Change: From Encounters to Actions, edited by Susan A. Crate and Mark Nuttall, 292–310. Walnut Creek, CA: Left Coast Press, 2009.

O'Connor, Martin, ed. *Is Capitalism Sustainable? Political Economy and the Politics of Ecology.* New York: Guilford Press, 1994.

O'Rourke, Ronald. *Navy SSBN(X) Ballistic Missile Submarine Program: Background and the Issues for Congress.* Congressional Research Service 7-5700, May 3, 2010.

Obama, Barack. *National Security Strategy for the Arctic Region.* Washington, DC: The White House, 2013. http://www.whitehouse. gov/sites/default/files/docs/nat_arctic_strategy.pdf.

"Observer Recommendation by Arctic Council Deputy Ministers." Deputy Ministers' Meeting, Stockholm, May 15, 2012. http://www.arctic-council.org/index.php/en/deputy-ministers-meeting-2012/487-final-report-from-the-deputy-ministers-meeting.

Office of the Speaker Lok Sabha. "Parliamentary Delegation from Iceland calls on Lok Sabha Speaker." Press Release, November 20, 2012. http:// speakerloksabha.nic.in/pressrelease/PressreleaseDetails.asp?PressId= 1119&button=Edit.

Ojanen, Hanna, ed. *The Northern Dimension: Fuel for the EU?* Helsinki: UPI, 2001.

Olsvig, Sara. "Greenland's Decision-Making on Uranium: Towards a Democratic Failure." *Arctic Journal,* October 18, 2013. http:// arcticjournal.com/opinion/greenlands-decision-making-uranium-towards-democratic-failure.

Onuf, Nicholas. *The Republican Legacy in International Thought.* Cambridge: Cambridge University Press, 1998.

———. "Sovereignty: Outline of a Conceptual History." *Alternatives* 16 (1991): 425–446.

Oreshenkov, Aleksandr. "The Arctic's Square of Possibilities" [Arkticheskii kvadrat vozmojnostei]. *Russia in Global Affairs* [Rossiya v global'noi politike] 6 (2010): 194–202. http://www. globalaffairs.ru/number/Arkticheskii-kvadrat-vozmozhnostei-15069.

―――. "The Norwegian Assault to the North-East: Dedicated to the Memory of A. Kvitsinsky" [Norvejskii natisk na severo-vostok: Pamyati Yu. A. Kvicinskogo posvyaschaetsya]. *Representative Power—XXI Century* [Predstavitel'naya vlast'—XXI vek] 1 (2011): 26–29.

Orheim, Olav. "Protecting the Environment of the Arctic Ecosystem." UN Open-Ended Informal Consultative Process on Oceans and the Law of the Sea, 4th meeting, June 2–6, 2003. http://www.un.org/Depts/los/consultative_process/documents/no3_npi2.pdf.

Oye, Kenneth, ed. *Cooperation Under Anarchy.* Princeton: Princeton University Press, 1986.

Paehlke, Robert, and Douglas Torgerson, eds. *Managing Leviathan: Environmental Politics and the Administrative State.* 2nd ed. Peterborough, ON: Broadview Press, 2005.

PAME. *The Arctic Ocean Review Project, Final Report (Phase II 2011–2013), Kiruna, May 2013.* Akureyri, Protection of the Arctic Marine Environment (PAME) Secretariat, 2013. www.aor.is.

Paperny, Anna. "Ottawa Investing $10 Million in Arctic Surveillance." *Globe and Mail,* June 18, 2012. http://m.theglobeandmail.com/news/politics/ottawa-investing-10-million-in-arctic-surveillance/article4104646/?service=mobile.

Parsons, Anthony. *Antarctica: The Next Decade.* Cambridge: Cambridge University Press, 1987.

Paterson, Matthew. "Global Environmental Governance." In *International Society and Its Critics,* edited by Alex J. Bellamy, 163–177. New York: Oxford University Press, 2005.

―――. "Green Theory." In *Theories of International Relations,* 4th ed., edited by Scott Burchill et al., 89–115. London: Palgrave Macmillan, 2009.

Pauly, Louis. "Good Governance and Bad Policy: The Perils of International Organizational Overextension." *Review of International Political Economy* 6, no. 4 (1999): 401–424.

Pearson, Lester. *Words and Occasions.* Toronto: University of Toronto Press, 1970.

Pedersen, Torbjørn. *Conflict and Order in Svalbard Waters*. Tromsø: University of Tromsø, 2008.

———. "The Constrained Politics of the Svalbard Offshore Area." *Marine Policy* 32 (2008): 913–919.

———. "Denmark's Policies Toward the Svalbard Area." *Ocean Development & International Law* 40, no. 4 (2009): 319–332.

———. "International Law and Politics in U.S. Policymaking: The United States and the Svalbard Dispute." *Ocean Development and International Law* 42 (2011): 120–135.

———. "Norway's Rule on Svalbard: Tightening the Grip on the Arctic Islands." *Polar Record* 45 (2009): 147–152.

Peters, Anne. "The Security Council's Responsibility to Protect." *International Organisations Law Review* 8, no. 1 (2011).

Petersen, Nikolaj. "The Arctic as a New Arena for Danish Foreign Policy: The Ilulissat Initiative and Its Implications." In *Danish Foreign Policy Yearbook 2009*, edited by Nanna Hvidt and Hans Mouritzen, 35–78. Copenhagen: Danish Institute for International Studies, 2009.

Peterson, David L., and Daryll R. Johnson, eds. *Human Ecology and Climate Change: People and Resources in the Far North*. Washington, DC: Taylor and Francis, 1995.

PEW Environmental Group. "Exploration & Development Risks." *Oceans North U.S.: U.S. Arctic Program*. http://oceansnorth.org/exploration-development-risks.

———. "Oil Spill Prevention and Response in the U.S. Arctic Ocean: Unexamined Risks, Unacceptable Consequences." PEW Environment Group, November 2010. http://www.pewtrusts.org/uploadedFiles/wwwpewtrustsorg/Reports/Protecting_ocean_life/PEW-1010_ARTIC_Report.pdf.

Pharand, Donat. "The Case for an Arctic Region Council and a Treaty Proposal." *Revue Générale de Droit* 23 (1992): 163–195.

———. "Arctic Waters and the Northwest Passage: A Final Revisit." *Ocean Development and International Law* 38, nos. 1–2 (2007): 3–69.

———. *Canada's Arctic Waters in International Law*. Cambridge: Cambridge University, 1988.

———. "Sovereignty in the Arctic: The International Legal Context." In *Sovereignty and Security in the Arctic*, edited by Edgar Dosman, 145–158. London and New York: Routledge, 1989.

Phillips, Leigh. "Arctic Council Rejects EU's Observer Application." *EU Observer*, April 30, 2009. http://euobserver.com/environment/28043.

Philpott, Daniel. *Revolutions in Sovereignty: How Ideas Shaped Modern International Relations*. Princeton: Princeton University Press, 2001.

Pika, Aleksandr Ivanovich, and Bruce Grant, eds. *Neotraditionalism in the Russian North: Indigenous Peoples and the Legacy of Perestroika*, Circumpolar Research Series 6. Edmonton: Canadian Circumpolar Institute; Seattle: University of Washington Press, 1999.

Plumwood, Val. *Feminism and the Mastery of Nature*. London: Routledge, 1993.

Plyais, Yakov. "The Evolution of the Foreign Policy of the New Russia" [Evolutsiya vneshnei politiki novoi Rossii]. *Обозреватель— Observer* 5 (1996). http://www.rau.su/observer/N05_96/5_05.HTM.

Pollack, Mark. "The Commission as an Agent." In *At the Heart of the Union: Studies of the European Commission*, edited by Neill Nugent, 109–128. Basingstoke: Macmillan, 1997.

Polmar, Norman, and Jurrien Noot. *Submarines of the Russian and Soviet Navies, 1718–1990*. Annapolis, MD: Naval Institute Press, 1991.

Portsel, Aleksandr Konstantinovich. "Spitsbergen, or Svalbard? Problems of Russia's Presence on the Archipelago in the XX–Early XXI Centuries" [Shpitsbergen ili Sval'bard? Problemy prisutstviya Rossii na arhipelage v XX–nachale XXI vekov]. *Bulletin of the Murmansk State Technical University* [Vestnik Murmanskogo gosudarstvennogo tehnicheskogo universiteta] 13, no. 2 (2010): 261–264.

Prime Minister's Office. *The Faroe Islands: A Nation in the Arctic*. Tórshavn: The Prime Minister's Office/The Foreign Service, 2013.

Prime Minister's Office, Finland. *Finland's Strategy for the Arctic Region*. Prime Minister's Office Publication, August 2010.

Radyuhin, Vladimir. "Russia Sets Up Arctic Forces." *Hindu*, July 1, 2011.

Rahbek-Clemmensen, Jon. "Denmark in the Arctic." *Atlantisch Perspectief* 3 (2011): 9–14.

Rajakoski, Esko. "Multilateral Cooperation to Protect the Arctic Environment: The Finnish Initiative." In *The Arctic: Choices for Peace and Security*, edited by Thomas R. Berger, 53–60. Vancouver: Gordon Soules, 1989.

Ramachandran, Rahul. "India, Norway for Joint Polar Research." *Hindu*, February 7, 2011. http://www.thehindu.com/news/national/article1 162914.ece.

Ray, Kalyan. "Resource-Hungry India Seeks a Seat at the Arctic Table." *Deccan Herald*, January 15, 2012. http://www.deccanherald.com/content/219579/resource-hungry-india-seeks-seat.html%20%20.

Rayfuse, Rosemary. "Melting Moments: The Future of Polar Oceans Governance in a Warming World." *Review of European Community & International Environmental Law* 16 (2007): 196–216.

———. "Protecting Marine Biodiversity in Polar Areas Beyond National Jurisdiction." *Review of European Community & International Environmental Law* 17 (2008): 3–13.

"Resolution of the 6th Congress of the Indigenous Peoples of the North, Siberia and Far East of the Russian Federation." Moscow: adopted April 24, 2009. http://www.indigenousportal.com/News/RESOLUTION-OF-THE-6TH-CONGRESS-OF-THE-INDIGENOUS-PEOPLES-OF-THE-NORTH-SIBERIA-FAR-EAST-OF-RUSSIA.html.

Reus-Smit, Christian. "The Constructivist Challenge after September 11." In *International Society and Its Critics*, edited by Alex J. Bellamy, 81–94. New York: Oxford University Press, 2005.

———. *The Moral Purpose of the State: Culture, Social Identity, and Institutional Rationality in International Relations*. Princeton: Princeton University Press, 1999.

Reus-Smit, Christian, ed. *The Politics of International Law*. Cambridge: Cambridge University Press, 2004.

Riabova, Larisa. "Community Viability and Well-Being in the Circumpolar North." In *Globalization and the Circumpolar North*, edited by Lassi Heininen and Chris Southcott, 119–147. Fairbanks: University of Alaska Press, 2010.

Rickli, Jean-Marc. "European Small States' Military Policies after the Cold War: From Territorial to Niche Strategies." *Cambridge Review of International Affairs* 21, no. 3 (September 2008): 307–325.

Riddell-Dixon, Elizabeth. "Canada and Arctic Politics: The Continental Shelf Extension." *Ocean Development & International Law* 39 (2008): 343–359.

Riphagen, Willem. "Some Reflections on Functional Sovereignty." *Netherlands Yearbook of International Law* 7 (1975): 121–165.

Rittberger, Volker, Bernhard Zangl, and Andreas Kruck, eds. *International Organization*. 2nd ed. London: Palgrave Macmillan, 2012.

Roach, J. Ashley. "International Law and the Arctic: A Guide to Understanding the Issues." *Southwestern Journal of International Law* 15 (2009): 301–326.

Roberts, Peder. *The European Arctic.* London: Palgrave Macmillan, 2011.

Roginko, Alexei Y. "Conflict between Environment and Development in the Soviet Arctic." In *Vulnerable Arctic: Need for an Alternative Reorientation*, Research Report no. 47, edited by J. Käkönen. Tampere: Tampere Peace Research Institute, 1992.

Rose, Gideon. "Neoclassical Realism and Theories of Foreign Policy." *World Politics* 51, no. 1 (1998): 144–172.

Rosenau, James. *Along the Domestic-Foreign Frontier: Exploring Governance in a Turbulent World.* Cambridge: Cambridge University Press, 1997.

Rothwell, Donald R. "The Arctic in International Affairs: Time for a New Regime?" ANU College of Law Research Paper No. 08-37, December 10, 2008. http://ssrn.com/abstract=1314546.

———. "The Arctic in International Affairs: Time for a New Regime?" *Brown Journal of World Affairs* 15 (Fall/Winter 2008): 241–256.

———. "The Law of the Sea and the Antarctic Treaty System: Rougher Seas Ahead for the Southern Ocean?" In *The Antarctic: Past, Present and Future*, Antarctic CRC Research Report #28, edited by J. Jabour-Green and M. Haward, 113–125. Hobart: Antarctic CRC, 2002.

———. *The Polar Regions and the Development of International Law.* New York: Cambridge University Press, 1996.

Roucek, Joseph S. "The Geopolitics of the Arctic." *American Journal of Economics and Sociology* 42, no. 4 (1983): 463–471.

Rudd, David. "Northern Europe's Arctic Defence Agenda." *Journal of Military and Strategic Studies* 12, no. 3 (2010): 45–71.

"Rules of Procedure." The Arctic Council Rules of Procedure as adopted by the Arctic Council at the First Arctic Council Ministerial Meeting, Iqaluit, Canada, September 17–18, 1998. http://arctic-council.org/filearchive/official%20rules%20and%20procedures.pdf.

Russett, Bruce. "Liberalism." In *International Relations Theories: Discipline and Diversity*, 2nd ed., edited by Tim Dunne, Milja Kurki, and Steve Smith, 94–113. Oxford: Oxford University Press, 2010.

Sakhuja, Vijay. "The Arctic Council: Is There a Case for India." Indian Council of World Affairs Policy Brief, New Delhi, January 12, 2010. http://www.icwa.in/pdfs/policy%20briefs%20dr.pdf.

Saksina, Tatiana. "New Governance for the Arctic: Is a New Framework Convention the Solution." Presentation at the Arctic Frontiers Conference, Tromsø, Norway, January 20, 2009. http://archive.arcticfrontiers.com/index.php?option=com_docman&task=cat_view&gid=82&Itemid=418.

Sale, Kirkpatrick. *Human Scale.* San Francisco: W. H. Freeman, 1980.

Sale, Richard, and Eugene Potapov. *The Scramble for the Arctic: Ownership, Exploitation, and Conflict in the Far North.* London: Francis Lincoln, 2010.

Salmén, Leif. "Rajamaa." *Helsingin Sanomat, Vieraskynä*, October 12, 1994, p. A2.

Samtök Fullveldissina. *Yfirgangur ESB og Norðmanna* [The behavior of the EU and of Norway]. August 10, 2010. http://www.fullvalda.is/greinar/33-yfirgangur-esb-og-nordmanna.

Sand, Peter H., ed. *The Effectiveness of International Environmental Agreements.* Cambridge: Grotius Publications, 1992.

Sanders, Marren. "Ecosystem Co-Management Agreements: A Study of Nation Building or a Lesson in Erosion of Tribal Sovereignty?" *Buffalo Environmental Law Journal* 15 (2007–2008): 97–176.

Sands, Philippe. *Lawless World.* London: Penguin Books, 2006.

SAO. Senior Arctic Officials Report to Ministers. Nuuk, Greenland, May 2011.

Saran, Shyam. "India's Stake in Arctic Cold War." *Hindu*, February 1, 2012. http://www.thehindu.com/opinion/op-ed/article2848280.ece.

Savel'eva, Svetlana Borisovna, and Anton Nikolaevich Savel'ev. "Spatial Reorientation of the National Interests of Russia" [Prostranstvennaya pereorientatsiya natsional'nyh interesov Rossii]. *Vestnik MGTU* 13, no. 1 (2010): 73–76.

Schechter, Michael G. *United Nations Global Conferences.* London: Routledge, 2005.

Scheffer, Jaap de Hoop. Speech on security prospects in the High North. Reykjavik Summit, 2009. http://www.nato.int/docu/speech/2009/s090129a.html.

Schmidt, Brian. "The Primacy of National Security." In *Foreign Policy: Theories, Actors, Cases*, edited by Steve Smith, Amelia Hadfield, and Tim Dunne, 155–170. Oxford: Oxford University Press, 2008.

Schrijver, Nico. "Natural Resource Management and Sustainable Development." In *The Oxford Handbook on the United Nations*, edited by Thomas G. Weiss and Sam Daws, 592–610. Oxford: Oxford University Press, 2007.

Scrivener, David. *Environmental Cooperation in the Arctic: From Strategy to Council.* Paper submitted for publication to the Norwegian Atlantic Committee, Oslo, January 18, 1996.

———. Environmental Cooperation in the Arctic: From Strategy to Council. Security Policy Library No. 1/1996. Oslo: The Norwegian Atlantic Committee, 1996.

———. *Gorbachev's Murmansk Speech: Soviet Initiative and Western Responses.* Oslo: Norwegian Atlantic Committee, 1989.

Security Council of the Russian Federation. Foundations of State Policy of Russian Federation in the Arctic for the Period up to 2020 and Beyond. September 18, 2008. http://www.scrf.gov.ru/documents/98.html.

Sejersen, Frank. "Local Knowledge in Greenland: Arctic Perspectives and Contextual Differences." In *Cultivating Arctic Landscapes: Knowing and Managing Animals in the Circumpolar North,* edited by David G. Anderson and Mark Nuttall, 33–56. Oxford: Berghahn, 2004.

Senior Arctic Officials. *Report to Ministers, Nuuk, Greenland, May 2011.* http://library.arcticportal.org/1251/.

SFW Institute. "Norway Government Pension Fund Global." http://www. swfinstitute.org/swfs/norway-government-pension-fund-global/.

The Shared Future: A Report of the Aspen Institute Commission on Arctic Climate Change. Washington, DC: The Aspen Institute, 2011.

Shin Hyon-hee. "S. Korea Seeks Bigger Role in Arctic." *Korea Herald,* May 15, 2012. http://www.asianewsnet.net/home/news.php?id=30743.

"Shipping across the Arctic Ocean: A Feasible Option in 2030–2050 as a Result of Global Warming." Research and Innovation, Position Paper, April 2010, 4–20.

Skarphedinsson, Össur. "Collective Governance of the High North" [Samvinnustjórn á norðurslóðum]. *Fréttablaðið,* February 2, 2011. http://www.visir.is/samvinnustjorn--a-nordurslodum/article/2011808929462.

———. "The High North and Iceland's Policy" [Norðurslóðir og stefna Íslands]. *Morgunblaðið,* January 18, 2011. http://www. utanrikisraduneyti.is/media/nordurlandaskrifstofa/OS-Moggi-18-jan-2011.PDF.

Slaughter, Anne-Marie. "Judicial Globalization." *Virginia Journal of International Law* 40 (1999–2000): 1103–1124.

Smith, Mick. "Against Ecological Sovereignty: Agamben, Politics, and Globalisation." *Environmental Politics* 18, no. 1 (2009): 99–116.

Smolka, Harry P. "Soviet Strategy in the Arctic." *Foreign Affairs* 16, no. 2 (1938): 272–278.

Solerød, Mari. Norwegian Research Council, 2010. http://www.norway.cn/News_and_events/Education-and-research/Research/Norway-and-China-strengthen-polar-research-cooperation/.

Sosnin, Vassiliy Ivanocich. "The Arctic—A Complex Knot of Interstate Contradictions" [Arktika—Slozhnyi uzel mezhgosudarstvennyh protivorechii]. *Military Thought* [Voennaya Mysl'] 7 (2010): 3–9.

Southcott, Chris. "History of Globalization in the Circumpolar World." In *Globalization and the Circumpolar North*, edited by Lassi Heininen and Chris Southcott, 23–56. Fairbanks: University of Alaska Press, 2010.

"Soviet Work in the Arctic, 1938." *Polar Record* 3, no. 17 (1939): 13–14.

"Soviet Work in the Arctic, 1939." *Polar Record* 3, no. 18 (1939): 106–107.

Spears, Joseph. "China and the Arctic: The Awakening Snow Dragon." *China Brief* 9, no. 6 (March 18, 2009). http://www.jamestown.org/programs/chinabrief/single/?tx_ttnews[tt_news]=34725&tx_ttnews[backPid]=25&cHash=1c22119d7c.

———. "The Snow Dragon Moves into the Arctic Ocean Basin." *China Brief* 11, no. 2 (January 28, 2011). http://www.jamestown.org/programs/chinabrief/single/?tx_ttnews%5Btt_news%5D=37429&cHash=a076c446d9.

Spielman, Brian. "An Evaluation of Russia's Impending Claim for Continental Shelf Expansion: Why Rule 5 Will Shelve Russia's Submission." *Emory International Law Review* 23, no. 1 (2009): 309–349. http://www.law.emory.edu/fileadmin/journals/eilr/23/23.1/Spielman.pdf.

Spufford, Francis. *I May Be Some Time: Ice and the English Imagination.* London: Faber and Faber, 1997.

Stålvant, Carl-Einar. "The Northern Dimension: A Policy in Need of an Institution?" BaltSeaNet Working Paper 1. Gdansk/Berlin, 2001.

Stein, Arthur A. "Neoliberal Institutionalism." In *The Oxford Handbook of International Relations*, edited by Christian Reus-Smit and Duncan Snidal, 201–221. Oxford: Oxford University Press, 2008.

Steinberg, Philip E. "Free Sea." In *Sovereignty, Spatiality, and Carl Schmitt: Geographies of the Nomos*, edited by Stephen Legg, 268–275. London: Routledge, 2011.

———. *The Social Construction of the Ocean*. Cambridge: Cambridge University Press, 2001.

———. "Sovereignty, Territory, and the Mapping of Mobility: A View from the Outside." *Annals of the Association of American Geographers* 99 (2009): 467–495.

Stevenson, John R., and Bernard H. Oxman. "The Preparations for the Law of the Sea Conference." *American Journal of International Law* 68 (January 1974): 1–32.

Stimson. "Evolution of Arctic Territorial Claims and Agreements: A Timeline (1903–Present)." April 15, 2013. http://www.stimson.org/infographics/evolution-of-arctic-territorial-claims-and-agreements-a-timeline-1903-present/.

Stokke, Olav Schram, and Geir Hønneland. *International Cooperation and Arctic Governance: Regime Effectiveness and Northern Region Building*. London and New York: Routledge, 2007.

Stokke, Olav Schram, and Ola Tunander. *The Barents Region: Cooperation in Arctic Europe*. London and Thousand Oaks, CA: Sage, 1994.

Stoltenberg, Thorvald. *Nordic Cooperation on Foreign and Security Policy*. Oslo: Norwegian Government, 2009.

———. "Nordic Cooperation on Foreign and Security Policy." Proposals presented to the extraordinary meeting of Nordic foreign ministers, Oslo, Norway, February 9, 2009.

Støre, Jonas Gahr. *Welcoming Remarks at the Sixth Ministerial Meeting of the Arctic Council*. Tromsø, Norway, April 29, 2009.

Strange, Susan. *The Retreat of the State: The Diffusion of Power in the World Economy*. Cambridge: Cambridge University Press, 1996.

———. "Wake up, Krasner! The World Has Changed." *Review of International Political Economy* 1 (1994): 209–219.

"Strategy for the Development of the Arctic Zone of the Russian Federation and National Security Protection for the Period up to 2020." Moscow; adopted February 20, 2013. http://government.ru/news/432.

Stroeve, Julienne C., Mark C. Serreze, Marika M. Holland, Jennifer E. Kay, James Malanik, and Andrew P. Barrett. "The Arctic's Rapidly Shrinking Sea Ice Cover: A Research Synthesis." *Climatic Change.* http://www.springerlink.com/content/c4m01048200k08w3/.

Struck, Doug. "Russia's Deep-Sea Flag-Planting at North Pole Strikes a Chill in Canada." *The Washington Post*, August 7, 2007. http://www.washingtonpost.com/wp-dyn/content/article/2007/08/06/AR2007080601369.html.

Stubb, Alexander. *A New Arctic Era and Finland's Arctic Policy.* Keynote speech at the 20th Anniversary Seminar of the Arctic Centre, September 29, 2009. (mimeo)

Suprun, Mikhail Nikolaevich. *The Arctic in the Strategy of World Powers during the Second World War* [Arktika v strategii mirovyh derzhav v gody Vtoroi mirivoi voiny]. http://arcticwar.pomorsu.ru/sea/nc3/research/souprun.html.

Sutherland, Robert J. "The Strategic Significance of the Canadian Arctic." In *The Arctic Frontier*, edited by Ronald St. John Macdonald, 256–278. Toronto: University of Toronto Press, 1966.

Sverrisdóttir, Valgerdur. *Breaking the Ice.* Report of the "Breaking the Ice" conference, Akureyri, March 27–28, 2007. http://www.utanrikisraduneyti.is/media/Utgafa/Breaking_The_Ice_Conference_Report.pdf.

Swanson, Greta, Kathryn Mengerink, and Jordan Diamond. "Understanding the Government-to-Government Framework for Agency Activities that Affect Resources in the U.S. Arctic." *Environmental Law Reporter* 43, no. 10 (October 2013): 10872ff.

Swedish Chair of the Barents Euro-Arctic Council. "Swedish Chairmanship of the Barents Euro Arctic Council 2009–2011." http://www.regeringen.se/content/1/c6/12/33/24/ce36ee04.pdf.

Swedish Department of Foreign Affairs. "Sveriges strategi för den arktiska regionen." Stockholm: Department of Foreign Affairs, 2011. http://www.sweden.gov.se/sb/d/1390/a/168312.

Swedish Foreign Affairs Committee [Utrikesutskottet]. Meddelande om EU och Arktis. Utrikesutskottets utlåtande 2009/10: UU4. Sveriges riksdag, Stockholm.

Sweet Stone, Alec, Neil Fligstein, and Wayne Sandholz. "The Institutionalization of European Space." In The Institutionalization of Europe, edited by Alec Sweet Stone, Neil Fligstein, and Wayne Sandholz, 1–28. Oxford: Oxford University Press, 2001.

Taagholt, Jørgen, and Jens Claus Hansen. Greenland: Security Perspectives. Fairbanks: Arctic Research Consortium of the United States, 2001.

Taracouzio, Timothy A. Soviets in the Arctic: An Historical, Economic and Political Study of the Soviet Advance into the Arctic. New York: Macmillan, 1938.

Tennberg, Monica. Arctic Environmental Cooperation: A Study in Governmentality. Aldershot: Ashgate, 2000.

Theutenberg, Bo Johnson. The Evolution of the Law of the Sea. Dublin: Tycooly International Publishing Ltd., 1984.

Thomson, Janice, and Stephen Krasner. "Global Transactions and the Consolidation of Sovereignty." In Global Changes and Theoretical Challenges, edited by Ernst Czempiel and James Rosenau, 195–219. Lexington, MA: Lexington Books, 1989.

Thorhallsson, Baldur, and Hjalti Thór Vignisson. "A Controversial Step, Membership of the EEA." In Iceland and European Integration, On the Edge, edited by Baldur Thorhallsson, 38–49. London: Routledge, 2004.

———. "The First Steps, Iceland's Policy on European Integration from the Foundation of the Republic to 1972." In Iceland and European Integration, On the Edge, edited by Baldur Thorhallsson, 22–37. London: Routledge, 2004.

Tilly, Charles. "War Making and State Making as Organized Crime." In Bringing the State Back In, edited by Peter Evans, Dietrich

Rueschemeyer, and Theda Skocpol, 169–191. Cambridge: Cambridge University Press, 1985.

Timoshenko, Al'bina Ivanovna. "Soviet Initiatives in the Arctic in 1920s (The Strategic Continuity Revisited)" [Sovetskie initsiativy v Arktike v 1920-e gg (K voprosu o strategicheskoi preemstvennosti)]. *Humanitarian Sciences in Siberia* [Gumanitarnye nauki v Sibiri] 2 (2010): 48–52.

Trainer, F. E. *Abandon Affluence!* London: Zed, 1985.

Trenin, Dmitri, and Pavel K. Baev. *The Arctic: A View from Moscow* [Arktika: Vzglyad iz Moskvy]. Washington, DC: Carnegie Endowment for International Peace, 2010.

Trenin, Dmitry. "Perspectives of Russian Foreign Policy" [Vneshnepoliticheskie perspektivy Rossii]. *Pro et Contra* 15, nos. 1–2 (2011): 101–116.

Treshnikov, Aleksey Fedorovich. "The Order of Lenin's Arctic and Antarctic Science and Research Institute Celebrates the 50th Anniversary" [Ordena Lenina Arkticheskomu i Antarkticheskomu Nauchno-Issledovatel'skomu Institutu—50 Let]. *Problems of Arctic and Antarctic* [Problemy Arktiki I Antarktiki] 36–37 (1970): 5–16.

Triggs, Gillian D. *The Antarctic Treaty Regime.* Cambridge: Cambridge University Press, 1987.

Tsyganok, Anatoly Dmitrievich. "Russian Confrontation in the Arctic: Will Russia Be Able to Defend the North?" [Rossiiskoe protivostoyanie v Arktike: Smozhet li Rossiya otstoyat' Sever]. *Bulletin of Analytics* [Vestnik analitiki] 1 (2010): 83–89.

U.S. Department of Defense. *Maritime Claims Reference Manual (DOD 2005.1-M).* Washington, DC: United States Department of Defense, 2005. http://www.jag.navy.mil/organization/documents/mcrm/MCRM.pdf.

U.S. Department of Homeland Security, U.S. Coast Guard. *Arctic Strategy.* 2013. http://www.uscg.mil/seniorleadership/DOCS/CG_Arctic_Strategy.pdf.

U.S. Department of the Navy. "Strategic Objectives for the U.S. Navy in the Arctic Region." Memorandum for Distribution, 5000/Ser. N00/10063,

May 21, 2010. http://greenfleet.dodlive.mil/files/2010/09/US-Navy-Arctic-Strategic-Objectives-21-May-2010.pdf.

U.S. Department of State Bureau of Oceans and International Environmental and Scientific Affairs. "Strategy to Reduce Black Carbon Emissions Affecting the Arctic." Fact sheet. United Nations: UN Climate Change Negotiations, 2009. http://cop15.state.gov/pressroom/133771.htm.

U.S. Department of State (Office of Oceans Affairs, Bureau of Oceans and International Environmental and Scientific Affairs). *Limits in the Seas: National Claims to Maritime Jurisdictions (No. 36, 8th revision)*. Washington, DC: United States Department of State, 2000. http://www.state.gov/documents/organization/61543.pdf.

U.S. Energy Information Administration. "China and India Account for Half of Global Energy Growth through 2035." September 19, 2011. http://www.eia.gov/todayinenergy/detail.cfm?id=3130.

U.S. Geological Survey. "90 Billion Barrels of Oil and 1.670 Trillion Cubic Feet of Natural Gas Assessed in the Arctic." July 23, 2008. http://www.usgs.gov/newsroom/article.asp?ID=1980&from=rss_home.

U.S. Senate Foreign Relations Committee. *United Nations Convention on the Law of the Sea: 103-39*, last modified June 28, 2012, http://www.foreign.senate.gov/treaties/details/103-39.

"US Sub May Have Toured Canadian Arctic Zone." *National Post*, December 19, 2005. http://www.canada.com/nationalpost/story.html?id=fb21432a-1d28-415e-b323-ceb22d477732&k=69493.

U.S.-China Business Council Report, November 2005.

Ulfstein, Geir. *The Svalbard Treaty: From Terra Nullius to Norwegian Sovereignty*. Oslo: Scandinavian University Press, 1995.

Ulkoasiainministeriö, Itäosasto, Itä25/Jyrki Kallio, *Arktiset kysymykset—pohjustusta kansalliselle kannanmuodostukselle*. Muistio (Luonnos) [Memorandum (draft)], July 24, 2008.

Ulkoasiainvaliokunta. *Ulkoasiainvaliokunnan mietintö 12/2009 vp—Suomi ja arktiset alueet*. UaVM 12/2009 vp—K 3/2009, K 8/2009 vp, K 13/2009 vp).

UNCTAD. Review of Maritime Transport, 2010.

UNEP. "Declaration of the United Nations Conference on Human Environment." June 16, 1972. http://www.unep.org/Documents. Multilingual/Default.asp?documentid=97&articleid=1503.

United Nations. *Agreement for the Implementation of Part XI of the United Nations Convention on the Law of the Sea of 10 December 1982 (UNGA 48/263).* New York: United Nations, 1994. http://www.un.org/Depts/los/convention_agreements/texts/unclos/closindxAgree.htm.

———. *The Charter of the United Nations.* New York: Department of Public Information, 2012.

———. "Convention on the Law of the Sea of 10 December 1982: Overview and Full Text." http://www.un.org/Depts/los/convention_agreements/convention_overview_convention.htm.

———. *Report of the United Nations Conference on Environment and Development*, vol. 1, *Resolutions Adopted by the Conference.* UN document A/CONF.151/26, 1993.

———. *The United Nations Convention on the Law of the Sea of 10 December 1982 (A/Conf.62/122).* New York: United Nations, 1982. http://www.un.org/Depts/los/convention_agreements/texts/unclos/unclos_e.pdf.

———. *Yearbook of the United Nations.* New York: UN, 1967.

USACOR. *The Future of the Arctic: A Key to Global Sustainability.* USA Club of Rome Report, 2012, http://www.usacor.org/news/sup2009/futureofthearctic.pdf.

USGS. "USGS Releases New Oil and Gas Assessment of Northeastern Greenland." August 28, 2007. http://www.usgs.gov/newsroom/article_pf.asp?ID=1750.

Valtioneuvoston viestintäyksikkö, *Tiedote* [Press release] 120/2010–[given at] 8.4.2010 13.36.

Van Eert, Gib. "What Is Reception Law?" In *The Globalized Rule of Law*, edited by Oonagh E. Fitzgerald, 88. Toronto: Irwin Law, 2006.

VanderZwaag, David. "Law of the Sea and Governance of Shipping in the Arctic and Antarctic." In *Polar Law Textbook*, edited by Natalia Loukacheva, 45–64. Copenhagen: Nordic Council of Ministers, 2010.

Vasiliev, Anton. "Russian Policy in the Arctic and the Arctic Council. Final Report on Northern Research Forum Plenary Session 'The Future of Northern Co-operation' and Special Roundtable Discussion 'The Arctic Council and Multilateral Cooperation': Report and Articles.p 5th NRF Open Assembly "Seeking Balance in a Changing North," Anchorage, Alaska, September 24–27, 2008. http://www.nrf.is/images/ stories/pdf/anchorage_2008/reports/5th_nrf_report_1st_plenry_and_ special_roundtable_arctic_council_final.pdf.

Vasilyeva, Nataliya. "Putin Doesn't See War over Resources in the Arctic." *The Star*, September 23, 2010. http://www.vcstar.com/news/2010/sep/ 23/putin-doesnt-see-war-over-resources-in-the/.

Verhaag, Melissa A. "It Is Not Too Late: The Need for a Comprehensive International Treaty to Protect the Arctic Environment." *Georgetown International Environmental Law Review* 15 (2003): 555–579.

Vidas, Davor. "The Antarctic Treaty System in the International Community: An Overview." In *Governing the Antarctic: The Effectiveness and Legitimacy of the Antarctic Treaty System*, edited by Olav Schram Stokke and Davor Vidas, 55. Cambridge and New York: Cambridge University Press, 1996.

Vidas, Davor, ed. *Protecting the Polar Marine Environment: Law and Policy for Pollution Prevention.* New York: Cambridge University Press, 2000.

Visir News Agency. "Íslendingar byrjaðir að græða á olíuleit við Grænland" [Icelanders begin to help with oil exploration at Greenland]. November 29, 2010. http://www.visir.is/islendingar-byrjadir-ad-graeda-a-oliuleit-vid-graenland/article/2010508222609.

Vize, Vladimir Yul'evich. *The Northern Sea Route* [Severnyi Morskoi Put']. Moscow and Leningrad: Izdatel'stvo Glavsevmorputi, 1940.

Voronov, Konstantin Valentinovich. "The Arctic Horizons of Russia's Strategy: Current Dynamics" [Arkticheskie gorizonty strategii Rossii: Sovremennaya dinamika]. *World Economy and International Relations* [Mirovaya ekonomika in mezhdunarodnye otnosheniya] 9 (2010): 54–65.

Vylegzhanin, Aleksandr N., and V. K. Zilanov. *Spitsbergen: Legal Regime of Adjacent Marine Areas*. Utrecht: Eleven International Publishing, 2007.

Wade, Robert. "A Warmer Arctic Needs Shipping Rules." *Financial Times of London*, January 16, 2008. http://www.ft.com/cms/s/0/0adece78-c3 d8-11dc-b083-0000779fd2ac.html#axzz2HUgjGNtf.

Walker, R. B. J. *Inside/Outside: International Relations as Political Theory*. Cambridge: Cambridge University Press, 1993.

Waltz, Kenneth. "Foreword: Thoughts about Assaying Theories." In *Progress in International Relations Theory*, edited by Colin Elman and Miriam Fendius Elman, vii–xii. Cambridge, MA: MIT Press, 2003.

———. *Man, the State and War*. New York: Columbia University Press, 1959.

———. *Theory of International Politics*. New York: McGraw-Hill, 1979.

Water.ca. *The Water Chronicles: Special Feature: Northern Sovereignty*, September 17, 2007. http://www.water.ca/listenaod.asp?artid=227.

Watson, Molly. "An Arctic Treaty: A Solution to the International Dispute over the Polar Region." *Ocean & Coastal Law Journal* 14, no. 2 (2009): 307–334.

Weber, Cynthia. *Simulating Sovereignty: Intervention, the State and Symbolic Exchange*. Cambridge: Cambridge University Press, 1995.

Weber, Max. "Politics as a Vocation." In *From Max Weber: Essays in Sociology*, edited by H. H. Gerth and C. Wright Mills, 77–128. New York: Oxford University Press, 1946.

———. "Politics as a Vocation." Lecture at Munich University, 1919, http://anthropos-lab.net/wp/wp-content/uploads/2011/12/Weber-Politics-as-a-Vocation.pdf.

Weber, Steffen, Cécile Pelaudeix, and Iulian Romanyshyn. "Commentary: EU's New Arctic Communication: Towards Understanding of a Greater Role." *Arctic Yearbook 2012*: 156–158. http://www.arcticyearbook.com/index.php/commentaries/31-eu-s-new-arctic-communication-towards-understanding-of-a-greater-role.

Webster, Clifford J. "The Economic Development of the Soviet Arctic and Sub-Arctic." *Slavonic and East European Review* 29, no. 72 (1950): 177–211.

Weese, Bryn. "Japan Latest Non-Arctic Country to Claim Stake in North Pole." *Toronto Sun*, September 3, 2010. http://www.torontosun.com/news/canada/2010/09/03/15241971.html.

Wegge, Njord. "The Political Order in the Arctic: Power Structures, Regimes and Influence." *Polar Record* 47, no. 241 (2010): 165–176.

Weinert, Matthew S. *Democratic Sovereignty: Authority, State and Legitimacy in a Globalizing World.* London: University College of London Press, 2006.

———. "Reframing the Pluralist-Solidarist Debate." *Millennium: Journal of International Studies* 40 (2011): 21–41.

Wendt, Alexander. *Social Theory of International Politics.* Cambridge: Cambridge University Press, 1999.

West, Robin. "The Power of Petroleum." *Newsweek*, November 4, 2007, 21.

Wight, Martin. *International Theory: The Three Traditions.* New York: Holmes & Meier, 1992.

Williams, John. "Pluralism, Solidarism, and the Emergence of World Society in English School Theory." *International Relations* 19, no. 1 (2005): 19–38.

Wilson, Elana, and Indra Øverland. "Indigenous Issues." In *International Cooperation and Arctic Governance: Regime Effectiveness and Northern Region-Building*, edited by Olav Schram Stokke and Geir Hønneland, 27–49. London and New York: Routledge, 2007.

Wohlforth, William. "Realism." In *The Oxford Handbook of International Relations*, edited by Christian Reus-Smit and Duncan Snidal, 131–149. Oxford: Oxford University Press, 2008.

———. "Realism and Foreign Policy." In *Foreign Policy: Theories, Actors, Cases*, edited by Steve Smith, Amelia Hadfield, and Tim Dunne, 31–48. Oxford: Oxford University Press, 2008.

World Commission on Environment and Development. *Our Common Future*. Oxford: Oxford University Press, 1987.

Wright, David. *The Panda Bear Readies to Meet the Polar Bear: China and Canada's Arctic Sovereignty Challenge*. Calgary: Canadian Defence and Foreign Affairs Institute, March 2011. http://www.cdfai.org/PDF/The%20Panda%20Bear%20Readies%20to%20Meet%20the%20Polar%20Bear.pdf.

WWF. "UK Arctic Principles: Principles to Inform a Policy Statement on UK Interests in the Arctic." January 2012.

WWF Global. "Arctic Oil and Gas." http://wwf.panda.org/what_we_do/where_we_work/arctic/what_we_do/oil_gas/.

Yalowitz, Kenneth, James Collins, and Ross Virginia. *Arctic Climate Change and Security Policy Conference: Final Report and Findings*. Washington, DC: Carnegie Endowment for International Peace, 2008.

Yarovoy, Gleb. "Russia's Arctic—A Call for the New Arctic Thinking." *Baltic Rim Economies* 4 (2011). http://www.tse.fi/FI/yksikot/erillislaitokset/pei/Documents/BRE2011/BREArctic%2030.11.2011.pdf.

Yeager, Brooks B. "The Ilulissat Declaration: Background and Implications for Arctic Governance." Prepared for the Aspen Dialogue and Commission on Arctic Climate Change, November 5, 2008. http://arcticgovernance.custompublish.com/the-ilulissat-declaration-background-and-implications-for-arctic-governance.4626039-13774 6.html.

Young, Oran R.. *Creating Regimes: Arctic Accords and International Governance*. Ithaca, NY: Cornell University Press, 1993.

———. *Creating Regimes: Arctic Accords and International Governance*. Ithaca, NY: Cornell University Press, 1998.

———. *Governance in World Affairs*. Cornell, NY: Cornell University Press, 1999.

———. *The Structure of Arctic Cooperation: Solving Problems/Seizing Opportunities*. 2000. http://www.arcticparl.org/files/images/conf4_sac.pdf.

———. "Whither the Arctic? Conflict or Cooperation in the Circumpolar North." *Polar Record* 45 (2009): 73–82.

———. *The Pace of Change: Arctic State Changes: Implications for Governance.* Ottawa: Canadian Arctic Resources Committee, 2009.

———. "Arctic Ocean Governance: Status and Prospects." Presentation at the Arctic Frontiers conference, January 21, 2009. Presentation can be viewed via webcam. http://leo.infotek.no/uit4/Viewer/Viewers/Viewer320BR.aspx?mode=Default&peid=01f5346e-8e05-45 d1-9fd4-41dcfdf621e6&pid=cb0c95aa-c9c6-48b9-8e96-2b577bb01150 &playerType=WM7.

———. "Arctic State Changes: Implications for Governance." Paper prepared for 2030 North, A National Planning Conference, Ottawa, June 1–4, 2009.

———. "Foreword—Arctic Futures: The Politics of Transformation." In *Arctic Security in an Age of Climate Change*, edited by James Kraska, xxi–xxvii. Cambridge: Cambridge University Press, 2011.

———. "If an Arctic Ocean Treaty Is Not the Solution, What Is the Alternative?" *Polar Record* 47, no. 243 (2011): 327–334.

Young, Oran. R., and Arkady I. Cherkasov. "International Cooperation in the Arctic: Opportunities and Constraints." In *Arctic Alternatives: Civility or Militarism in the Circumpolar North*, edited by Franklyn Griffiths, 9–25. Toronto: Science for Peace/Samuel Stevens, 1992.

Zaitsev, Nikolai. "The Battlefield Is Arctic" [Pole boya—Arktika]. *North* [Sever] 5–6 (1996): 98–104.

Zellen, Barry S. *Arctic Doom, Arctic Boom: The Geopolitics of Climate Change in the Arctic.* London: Praeger, 2009.

———. "Viewpoint: Cold Front Rising—As Climate Change Thins Polar Ice, A New Race for Arctic Resources Begins." *Strategic Insights*, February 2008.

———. Breaking the Ice: From Land Claims to Tribal Sovereignty in the Arctic. Lanham, MD: Lexington Books, 2008.

Zenzinov, Vladimir. "The Soviet Arctic." *Russian Review* 3, no. 2 (1944): 65–73.

Zhirnov, Evgenii. "Cold War in the Arctic" [Holodnaya voina v Arktike]. *Kommersant Vlast'* 46, no. 397 (November 21, 2000). http://www.kommersant.ru/doc/18022.

Zhou, Z. "北极通航引发'深海'暗战" [The opening of Arctic shipping triggers an unclear battle in the "deep" sea]. *Liaoning Ribao*, October 15, 2009.

Zisk, Kimberly M. "Soviet Academic Theories on International Conflict and Negotiation: A Research Note." *Journal of Conflict Resolution* 34, no. 4 (1990): 678–693.

Zubarevich, Natalia. "Regions and Cities in Russia: Scenarios-2020" [Regiony i goroda Rossii: Scenarii-2020]. *Pro et Contra* 15, nos. 1–2 (2011): 57–71. http://carnegieendowment.org/files/ProetContra_51_57-71_all.pdf.

———. "Social-Economic Development of Russian Regions by 2020" [Sotsial'no-ekonomicheskoe razvitie regionov Rossii k 2020 godu]. http://russia-2020.org/ru/2010/08/23/soc-ec-development-of-rus-regions.

INDEX

About the Contributors

Clive Archer is an Emeritus Professor and Jean Monnet Ad Personam Professor in the Department of Politics and Philosophy, Manchester Metropolitan University, U.K.

Alyson J. K. Bailes is Visiting Professor at the University of Iceland, Reykyavik.

Betsy Baker is Associate Professor and Senior Fellow for Oceans and Energy at Institute for Energy and the Environment, Vermont Law School, U.S.A.

Margrét Cela is Project Manager at the Centre for Arctic Policy Studies, University of Iceland.

Guy-Serge Côté is a part-time professor at the School of Political Studies, University of Ottawa, Canada.

Anita Dey Nuttall is Associate Director of the Canadian Circumpolar Institute, University of Alberta, Canada.

Piotr Graczyk is Research Fellow at the Department of Sociology, Political Science and Community Planning, University of Tromsø, Norway.

Klaus Dodds is Professor of Geopolitics in the Department of Geography, Royal Holloway, University of London, U.K.

E. Carina H. Keskitalo is Professor of Political Science in the Department of Geography and Economic History, Umeå University, Sweden.

Lassi Heininen is Professor of Arctic Politics in the Faculty of Social Sciences, University of Lapland, Finland.

Nong Hong is Research Fellow at the China Institute, University of Alberta, Canada; Deputy Director, Research Center for Oceans Law & Policy, National Institute for South China Sea Studies, China.

Geir Hønneland is Research Director/Research Professor at the Fridtjof Nansen Institute, Norway.

Rob Huebert is Associate Professor in the Department of Political Science, and Centre for Military and Strategic Studies, University of Calgary, Canada.

Tom Keating is Professor in the Department of Political Science, University of Alberta, Canada.

W. Andy Knight is Professor and Director of the Institute of International Relations, The University of the West Indies, Trinidad.

Timo Koivurova is Research Professor, Director of the Northern Institute for Environmental and Minority Law, Arctic Centre/University of Lapland, Finland.

Robert W. Murray is Vice President of Research at the Frontier Centre for Public Policy and an adjunct professor of political science at the University of Alberta.

Mark Nuttall is Professor and Henry Marshall Tory Chair in the Department of Anthropology, University of Alberta, Canada; Professor of Climate and Society at Ilisimatusarfik/University of Greenland and Greenland Climate Research Centre, Greenland.

Matthew Paterson is Professor in the School of Political Studies, University of Ottawa, Canada

Jessica M. Shadian is Associated Researcher at the Arctic Centre, University of Lapland, Finland.

Philip E. Steinberg is Professor of Political Geography and Director of the International Boundaries Research Unit in the Department of Geography, University of Durham, U.K.

Matthew Weinert is Associate Professor in the Department of Political Science and International Relations, University of Delaware, U.S.A.

Gleb Yarovoy is Associate Professor in the Department of Political Science and International Relations, Petrozavodsk University, Russia.

CPSIA information can be obtained at www.ICGtesting.com
Printed in the USA
BVOW03*0308260215

389347BV00003B/8/P